1 MONTH OF
FREE
READING

at

www.ForgottenBooks.com

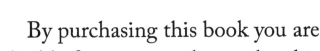

By purchasing this book you are
eligible for one month membership to
ForgottenBooks.com, giving you
unlimited access to our entire
collection of over 1,000,000 titles via
our web site and mobile apps.

To claim your free month visit:

www.forgottenbooks.com/free922819

ISBN 978-0-260-02164-9
PIBN 10922819

INVESTIGATION

RE

EPARTMENT OF MARINE AND FISHERIES

BEFORE THE

HON. MR. JUSTICE CASSELS

PART I

OTTAWA
PRINTED BY S. E. DAWSON, PRINTER TO THE KING'S MOST
EXCELLENT MAJESTY
1908

INVESTIGATION RE DEPARTMENT OF MARINE AND FISHERIES

BEFORE THE

HONOURABLE MR. JUSTICE CASSELS

AT

OTTAWA, MAY 2, 1908,

12 NOON

Dr. Charles Morse,   Nelson R. Butcher,
Deputy Registrar Exchequer Court.   *Official Reporter.*

Geo. H. Watson, K.C., and J. L. Perron, K.C., appear as counsel assisting in the investigation.

Hon. Mr. Cassels.—I think at the opening I will state what I consider the scope of this commission.

I wish to state my view as to the scope of the investigation imposed upon me by the commission dated 6th April, 1908.

My duties are defined by the commission. I cannot enlarge its scope, and on the other hand within its scope I feel it my duty to have a thorough investigation.

The report of the Civil Service Committee referred to in the commission states as follows:

'There would also seem to be a lack of conscience in connection with the enormous expenditures which are deemed necessary, the word 'discount' never appears. It is tacitly assumed there is no such thing; but the whole commercial world knows otherwise. If one gets any benefit from trade with the government except the trader then it must be clear that in these great purchases made for the government without discount, its officers must be assisting the trader to get better prices from the government than he can get anywhere else; for everywhere else he has to give a discount. In other words some of the government officers are serving two masters and apparently succeeding with both—Scripture not withstanding.'

The construction placed on this charge is shown by a reference to the order in council attached to the commission. It reads as follows:

'The minister further observes that it is assumed by that statement (referring to the statement previously quoted) that commissions are received improperly or enhanced prices paid through dishonesty on the part of the officials of the Department of Marine and Fisheries. But unfortunately the report does not mention any names which would enable him to take definite action concerning the officials. It is, however, in the interest of the Department of Marine and Fisheries and of the country that immediate steps should be taken in order to determine what officials (if any) deserve condemnation and to give to all an opportunity to meet the charges implied.'

3262—1

The charge is of a grave and serious nature. Every official of the Marine and Fisheries Department is under a cloud of suspicion.

As I understand the object of the commission is to afford each official of the department the opportunity to free himself from the charge if the facts justify it, or if the facts sustain the truth of the charges as to any official then it should be so found and the guilty official reported.

A difficulty presents itself in determining what period of time should be covered by the investigation.

The Civil Service Committee are not explicit as to the years embraced in their sweeping charge.

I have read through their report as also the evidence and notes, and as far as I can gather, the charges are mainly confined to the fiscal years 1904-5, 1905-6 and 1906-7.

I think an investigation into the alleged wrongdoings for these three years will suffice for the present. If during the progress of the investigation it be shown that an investigation into years more remote, or to a subsequent period of 1907 be necessary, it can be taken up.

Next is the question as to the scope of the inquiry.

What should be inquired into?

It is obvious:—

(1) That all contracts entered into for or on behalf of the crown by any official of the Department of Marine and Fisheries during the fiscal years 1904-5, 1905-6, 1906-7, either for work to be performed on the property of the Dominion, or for supplies purchased for or on behalf of the Dominion, must be investigated.

(2) That the prices paid must be ascertained.

(3) That the current market rates for wages or goods at the time of such contracts or purchases should be ascertained, also the prices governing such purchases for large quantities, and the discounts (if any) usually allowed.

If it appears that a larger amount has been contracted to be paid in any particular case or cases, then it becomes necessary to inquire into the reasons for such overpayment, and the official making such overpayment should have the opportunity afforded him of exculpating himself, if possible.

I have set out in a general way only my views as to the scope of the inquiry. I have only indicated certain heads of inquiry.

The task imposed is an onerous one, and must necessarily occupy a great deal of time.

The government have selected Mr. Watson, K.C., as counsel, and the many years I have known him satisfies me that his work will be well done.

Associated with Mr. Watson is Mr. Perron, K.C. I have not had the pleasure of the same personal relations with him as with Mr. Watson, but I am satisfied that he will assist his senior in every way in bringing out the evidence.

The investigation is a judicial one and open to all.

I propose, as far as possible, to hold the sittings in such places and rooms as will enable the facts to be ascertained with the least inconvenience to the business of the department.

In conclusion, I wish it to be clearly understood that the work of the Excehquer Court has the first claim upon my time, and if the investigation is delayed on this account, it cannot be avoided, so far as I am concerned.

Those are the views I entertain with regard to what is to be done. It is manifest it must be a pretty long and serious investigation.

Mr. WATSON.—My lord, I am quite sure that your lordship understands that we appreciate to the fullest extent the public importance of this inquiry, and the responsibility which we have been asked to assume, and which we have undertaken, in accepting the position of counsel in the conduct of the investigation.

I know, my lord, that this applies equally to my learned friend, Mr. Perron, who is associated with me.

The confidence which your lordship has expressed, in relying upon our assistance, is quite indispensable to a thorough inquiry and to a proper report.

We shall present all the evidence that is available from any source that may bear upon the subject of the inquiry.

We are pleased, too, that the proceedings will be conducted in open court, and with the dignity and accuracy which attaches to a judicial forum.

Speaking as counsel, we are confident that the executive of the commission, under your direction, will be deemed wholly for the public welfare.

Might I add that we desire and expect the co-operation and help of everyone who has information that may be considered material.

Hon. Senator CHOQUETTE.—May it please your lordship, I just ask permission to appear on behalf of Mr. Gregory, the agent of the department in Quebec.

Hon. Mr. CASSELS.—You see, Senator, there is no charge whatever made against Mr. Gregory. I will try to define as clearly as possible what I consider is the scope of the investigation. If, during the investigation, it appears that any particular officer must come forward and shield himself, then it is time enough for him to appear, and then every officer of the department may have the best assistance he can procure. I think what we want is to do everything possible to free these gentlemen from the suspicion they are under, but until the time arrives at which somebody is charged, or called upon to exculpate himself, counsel need not appear.

Hon. Senator CHOQUETTE.—I think Mr. Gregory, may it please your lordship, is in a special position. Immediately after the report he was suspended. Perhaps they thought he was one in whom there was lack of conscience, I do not know, but after the report it was said in the House that he was suspended. Mr. Gregory is anxious to clear himself at once. He is an old man, over 75 years of age, and as your lordship will easily understand a matter of this kind will worry an old gentleman. He asks me to state to your lordship that as he is accused indirectly by his suspension, he is quite willing and anxious to have his *enquete* begin at once.

Hon. Mr. CASSELS.—I know nothing about that. If, on behalf of Mr. Gregory, you choose to bring forward a statement showing he has made over payments, and is, *prima facia,* guilty, but desires to clear himself at the earliest possible moment, that is another thing. He may never come under my province. I know nothing of him officially. At present there is no accusation against him so far as this inquiry is concerned.

I would like it to be understood that every officer will have the fullest opportunity, if occasion arises, of clearing himself, and every official of the Marine Department, who feels that without specific charges being brought up, their honour or reputation is stained in any way, will have a perfect right to come forward and clear themselves under oath.

Hon. Senator CHOQUETTE.—I am very glad to hear that statement. It is because Mr. Gregory has been suspended that there is a kind of indirect accusation. I have nothing more to say now. I am pleased that the court hears him declare he is glad to have his *enquete* at once, is ready for it, and he denies everything that has been said against him so far.

Hon. Mr. CASSELS.—Now, Mr. Watson, what do you propose to do?

Mr. WATSON.—We will be very pleased indeed, as counsel, to receive any communications from my learned friend, that may assist, when the time arrives, when it is deemed necessary to answer, if it becomes necessary.

Hon. Mr. CASSELS.—I think anyone who has any information to give that will be of assistance should communicate the facts. The object is to get the facts in the shortest way, but thoroughly.

Mr. WATSON.—We will appreciate it very much, and it will assist us in the performance of our duty.

Of course it is difficult in the commencement to fix upon and to establish a system which we think very necessary in order to expedite the matter. We have not had much opportunity so far of personal investigation as counsel ; but I think we are able to give your lordship some particulars and information which may be taken as a starting point or basis for further investigation and consideration.

We find, my lord, that the Department of Marine and Fisheries has very many branches.

Referring to the marine branch by itself we find that there are in all 27 branches in that department.

For your lordship's information and assistance, I am pleased to be able to hand to you a memorandum showing these branches, and what they consist of.

(Marked Exhibit No. 1.; General Sub-Divisions of the Marine Branch.)

1. The construction of lighthouses and fog-alarms.
2. The maintenance of lights, gas buoys and other buoys.
3. The lighthouse board, which decides the necessity for aids to navigation.
4. Hydrographic surveys.
5. Tidal surveys.
6. The ship channel, St. Lawrence river, and Sorel works.
7. Meteorological and magnetic service.
8. Investigation into wrecks.
9. Board of steamboat inspection.
10. Cattle shipments inspection.
11. Wireless telegraph service.
12. Signal service.
13. Life-saving service.
14. Marine hospitals.
15. Submarine signalling.
16. Shipping under the Merchants' Shipping Act.
17. Legislation and administration of laws relating to the Department of Marine and Fisheries.
18. Humane service in connection with seamen.
19. Subsidizing wrecking plants.
20. Winter communication between P. E. I. and mainland.
21. Removal of obstructions to navigation.
22. Examination of masters and mates.
23. Naval militia and pilotage.
24. Government of ports and proclaiming harbours in the Dominion.
25. Control of government wharves.
26. Dominion steamers, marine and fisheries.
27. Hudson Bay navigation.

Your lordship will see it is very extended and important in that department.
Then taking the Fisheries Branch, there are six departments or branches:
Fishing bounty branch.
Fish breeding establishments.
Fisheries protection service.
Fisheries museum.
Oyster culture, E. Kemp, expert.
Fisheries matters generally.
Now, my lord, a word with regard to the scope of the commission.

We have thought it proper to inquire, and at this stage to report to your lordship the list of officers in the department who negotiate or recommend expenditures in connection with the Marine and Fisheries Department. I have a copy of that, my lord, which I will be glad to hand in for the information of your lordship.

(Marked Exhibit No. 2. List of officers who negotiate or recommend expenditure.)

It may be found that in some cases the duties or functions have been extended, necessarily perhaps, by reason of occupation or engagement, or matters of that kind, but generally speaking, these are the officials who negotiate or recommend expenditures. In addition to the deputy minister, who is of course at the head of the department, directly under the minister, and therefore in charge of all the officials, and of the performance of the departmental work, we find first the chief engineer, Colonel Anderson, and the assistant chief engineer, Mr. B. H. Fraser, in charge of construction of lighthouses and fog alarms, chartering steamers for ice-breaking in Thunder Bay, and removal of wrecks.

Next we find the commisioner of lights, Mr. J. F. Fraser, purchase of gas buoys, &c., and submarine signals.

We find Mr. C. Doutre, in charge of wireless telegraphy, and establishment of wireless telegraph stations.

Next Mr. W. W. Stumbles, in charge of the contracts and purchasing of supplies for lighthouses, &c.

Mr. Stewart is the chief hydrographer, in charge of all hydrographic surveys.

Commander Spain, in charge of Dominion steamers, fisheries protection steamers, investigations into wrecks, &c.

Dr. W. B. Dawson, in charge of the tidal survey branch.

Mr. F. H. Cunningham, in charge of fish culture, in charge of fish hatcheries, &c.

Mr. Regis Roy in charge of the stationery branch.

Mr. F. W. Cowis, in charge of the River St. Lawrence ship channel dredging operations, &c.

Speaking in a general way, my lord, these are the officers of the department, as I understand, who have imposed upon them the duty and obligation of introducing matters of expenditure, and making their recommendations, which pass on directly to the deputy minister, and which are considered and confirmed or declined by him.

Hon. Mr. CASSELS.—That is Colonel Gourdeau, the Deputy Minister?

Mr. WATSON.—Yes, my lord.

We have also to-day obtained, and are now ready to produce to your lordship the contracts which I am particularly anxious should be before your lordship from the earliest possible stage, for the purpose of inspection and examination, as your lordship has referred particularly to them in the remarks that have been made. We therefore produce all the contracts which are in writing, and which have been executed in the department, affecting the expenditure of money, and in addition, my lord, we have a record, as far as it is made in the department, and our observation leads us to the conclusion that the record is a reasonably accurate one, of all expenditures that occur under verbal orders. We find that small amounts are necessarily expended from time to time without calling for a written contract. A record is made of this, and we have that. It will not be convenient, perhaps, to have these marked at the present time. I am rather now producing them to indicate to your lordship the work that we are undertaking, and the efforts that we are making, in the introduction of the matter, to show what we conceive to be the work that is before us.

Hon. Mr. CASSELS.—Have you made a statement of the moneys voted for this department during the three years to ascertain whether it corresponds in any way with the expenditure?

Mr. WATSON.—Not for the purpose of testing the correspondence, but I am glad to say that I am able to give your lordship now an estimate of the appropriations that have been made.

Hon. Mr. CASSELS.—That is what I mean.

Mr. WATSON.—And the average expenditure. I think your lordship will find that attached to the first document I handed in (referring to Exhibit No. 1).

Hon. Mr. CASSELS.—Yes, I see it.

Mr. WATSON.—Taking the second page, your lordship will see the average annual expenditure is about $760,000.

The services under this branch comprise:—

Construction of lighthouse towers and dwellings, construction of fog-alarm buildings, construction of fish-hatcheries, &c., removal of obstructions to navigation, ice-breaking, Thunder bay.

Then under the head of 'Commissioner of Lights branch,' the annual expenditure is about $1,300,000, besides $300,000 for light keepers' salaries, and then follows upon that some details which your lordship will find, indicating the sources of expenditure, and the application of it.

Then next, under Commander Spain, we find in regard to Dominion steamers, investigations into wrecks, fisheries protection cruisers, St. Lawrence pilotage and lightships, an annual expenditure of about $900,000; and in addition to that the annual expenditure and maintenance of Dominion steamers about $600,000; the annual expenditure for fisheries fleet $250,000.

The importance of the department is best illustrated and shown by the amounts which are shown to be necessarily involved in the expenditures for the purposes of the department.

Then the wireless telegraphy under Mr. Doutre, the annual expenditure in that service is about $130,000. Then steamboat inspection under Mr. Adams, an annual expenditure of about $47,000.

Examination of masters and mates, Capt. Demers in charge, an annual expenditure of about $13,000.

Marine hospitals and care of sick seamen, Dr. Godin in charge, an annual expenditure of about $50,000.

Meteorological and magnetic service under Mr. Stupart, an annual expenditure of about $115,000.

Life-saving service, under Captain McElhinney, an annual expenditure of about $30,000.

St. Lawrence ship channel, under Mr. Cowie, engineer in charge, an annual expenditure of about $1,113,000.

Fish-hatcheries, under Mr. Cunningham as superintendent, an annual expenditure of about $240,000.

Fishing bounty branch, under Mr. Kent, expenditure estimated at about $160,000.

I think that covers the point your lordship indicated.

Although I had not the opportunity of any prior direction, we were fortunate enough to have this in hand in answer to your inquiry. Other information and details we are in the course of obtaining, and we hope to be able to present the fullest kind of a statement of all matters of a financial character, that are the subject of the enquiry, and referred to in the commission.

I will also be able to hand to your lordship a full list in writing of the contracts classified. As they are here, in bulk, it would be difficult to proceed with an inquiry and investigation, and of course it occurs to your lordship, as it has to us, that it will be necessary to have a classification in regard to the several departments. We have that about completed, so that when your lordship desires to commence an investigation as to those contracts, we will have them classified for each department, and supplied to each individual officer in charge of the department.

We are endeavouring in that way to establish a system which we hope may assist the court, save time, and otherwise facilitate.

Then, as reference is made in the commision which your lordship has handed to us as counsel, to the report heretofore made by certain gentlemen, acting as civil service commissioners, we have asked one or two of those commissioners if they would be good enough to attend here this morning, with the hope and expectation that we may obtain from them information which is indicated in their report, bearing directly upon the charges of want of integrity and dishonesty on the part of officials, and that being so, my lord, we have asked Mr. Fyshe and Mr. Bazin to be here, and I understand they are here.

I would be very glad if Mr. Fyshe would be kind enough to come forward, my lord.

THOMAS FYSHE, sworn. Examined by Mr. Watson:—

WITNESS.—I am somewhat deaf.

Q. You were acting as one of the commissioners appointed in connection with the civil service?—A. Yes.

Q. And in that capacity I understand that you obtained information that bears upon the subject of the present commission and inquiry before his lordship ? You made investigations and obtained information bearing upon the subject of the commission that has been issued to his lordship?—A. Yes.

Q. And in that way directly affecting the question of the conscience or lack of conscience of some of the officials, and directed to acts or conduct of dishonesty on their part?—A. I do not quite understand that question.

Q. Do you not?—A. No.

Q. I may perhaps make it more clear to you by reference to a paragraph of your report, if you will permit me, where you say in the report, ' There would also seem to be a lack of conscience ?'—A. Yes.

Q. In connection with the enormous expenditures which are deemed necessary the word ' discount ' never appears; it is tacitly assumed there is no such thing. The whole commercial world knows otherwise. No one gets any benefit from trade with the government except the trader. Then it must be clear that in these great purchases made for the government without discount, its officers must be assisting the trader to get better prices from the government than he can get anywhere else; for everywhere else he has to give a discount. In other words some of the government officers are serving two masters and apparently succeeding with both, Scripture notwithstanding. —A. Yes.

Q. I understand that is dictated by you?—A. Yes, written by me.

Q. The matters, as I understand, before his lordship for inquiry, relate particularly to two parts of this paragaph; first, the reference to the ' lack of conscience '?—A. Yes.

Q. And next, in other words, some of the government officers are serving two masters and apparently succeeding with both '?—A. Yes.

Q. Will you be kind enough to mention now one of the officers that you regard in that position?—A. I am not called upon to do so.

Q. I was very much in hopes, Mr. Fyshe, that you would be inclined, and that you would desire to give information that might assist his lordship in the execution of the commission?—A. I do not think the commission covered work of that kind.

Q. Your commission did not cover work of that kind?—A. No, I think not.

Q. At the same time we find that this is contained in your report?—A. Yes, but it has reference to the department as a whole. We were appointed to investigate the condition of the civil service, and in pursuance of that we were justified, and in fact called upon, to take account of anything that affected the efficiency of the civil service as a service, but we were certainly not appointed as public detectives or prosecutors.

Q. Then did you pursue an investigation for the purpose of ascertaining whether or not there was dishonesty on the part of any officer?—A. We could not possibly examine into the efficiency of the civil service without taking into account whether there was every indication that they were honest and straightforward and alive to their duty; all the considerations which we could not ignore, or which nobody could ignore, if looking into the service.

Q. Then doing so, did you obtain information upon that point affecting the honesty or dishonesty of an official?—A. All the information we received and on which

we based our judgment, and is given in our report, is shown in the report, and in the
appendices to it.

Q. Well, I find that that is expressed, so far as the appendices are concerned
particularly as well, in a general way, without reference to names in many instances,
or for the most part?—A. Well, it is one thing to find out what the department as a
whole is doing, and a totally different thing to find out what particular members are
doing the most or least mischief.

Q. Quite so, but what we are concerned in investigating now is the question of
the dishonesty or lack of conscience on the part of any official?—A. Yes.

Q. Then are you able to give us information which you obtained as to any act of
dishonesty of any official?—A. You want evidence, don't you?

Q. Evidence, if you please, or statements?—A. We were merely appointed to
examine into the efficiency of the civil service. In doing so we could only take up
one department at a time. We made special inquiry into the Marine and Fisheries
Department, but in doing our work we could not ascertain the amount of blame or
praise, or the credit or discredit to be awarded to every particular member of the
department. As a matter of fact, it would require a great deal of inside knowledge
and inside experience extending perhaps over months or years to find out exactly what
the value or non-value of each particular member of the department was.

Q. We know that you expended considerable time in that personal investigation?
—A. Yes.

Q. In the department?—A. Yes.

Q. And no doubt during that investigation certain facts came to your knowledge?
—A. Yes.

Q. Now, then, as applying to particular officials?—A. Yes.

Q. And I would like to ask you to make a statement?—A. You will find it all in
our report.

Q. I have a copy of the report here?—A. Yes.

Q. And I suppose there is not anyone that is more familiar, or perhaps as familiar
with it as you are?—A. Perhaps not.

Q. Will you be good enough, then, to point to me, in the report, information and
facts bearing upon this question of honesty or dishonesty?—A. Do you not think, sir,
that——

Q. I am desiring your assistance, as much as I can get of it?—A. I know, but
don't you think it is asking a little too much of us, after we have devoted so much
time to our investigation, with very great care, and taken extracts all along as we
went, putting them all down in chronological order, so that they could be consulted—

Hon. Mr. CASSELS.—You might ask him to particularize.

The WITNESS.—And with great care prepared our report; and don't you think it
is asking a little too much of us, before another commission, before a court, to go and
trace a connection between our general remarks and every particular item which we
discovered? Don't you think you are asking too much of us?

By Mr. Watson:

Q. I trust I may not be asking too much. I do not want for a moment to tres-
pass upon your good nature and patience?—A. I understand this commission is
appointed to go further into some questions than we did.

Q. Now, then, perhaps we may make ourselves quite direct. The head of the
department, under the minister, is of course the deputy, Colonel Gourdeau?—A. Yes.

Q. Did you obtain, in the course of your investigation and inquiry, facts or
information which bear upon any dishonesty on his part, applying it directly to the
deputy minister?—A. I do not think it is proper to ask me that question. We have
given our report. We have stated that that report is based upon data arrived at by
us from going over the different files of the department, all of which we extracted
verbatim and have had reprinted. It is open to this board, or to any one who wants

further information, or who wants confirmation of anything that we have said, to consult those extracts, or consult any other data to be found in the department, and see whether or not our judgment is correct.

Q. Now, you have a fund of information?—A. It is all detailed there.

Q. Beyond that of his lordship, the commissioner, or of us as counsel, or anyone else, by reason of the time that you have expended, you have that fund of information?—A. Yes. We have shown, however, how we obtained it.

Q. That was obtained, as I understand, by personal investigation?—A. By personal investigation.

Q. The evidence is not of record in regard to the chief part of it?—A. The evidence is all on record.

Q. Evidence has been taken, but in the personal inquiry that you made with Mr. Bazin in the department, of which you have made a record, taking extracts from correspondence and the like, the evidence was not given under oath in regard to those matters, I believe?—A. Which evidence?

Q. These extracts that you have here are not the result of evidence given before you?—A. Certainly not. They are extracts from the written letters of the department.

Q. It is just that, then. You therefore are in a more advantageous position than we are, or can possibly be, without very great expenditure of time, and it is not of record in evidence, and therefore I ask you what fact, if any, was ascertained by you, that bears upon the question of dishonesty of the deputy minister?—A. You will find it all among those extracts.

Q. You have a copy there. Will you be good enough to refer me to that—upon what you rely in making the report?—A. What particular statement do you wish evidence of?

Hon. Mr. CASSELS.—Mr. Fyshe, I would like to ask you a question. Have you any information whatever upon which this charge is based, that does not appear in that book?

(The witness being deaf, Mr. Watson repeats the question as follows):

Mr. WATSON.—Have you any information upon which the charge is based against officials, that does not appear in this report?—A. Nothing but hearsay.

Q. Nothing but hearsay. And did you act upon that in making the charge?—A. We have not acted on any hearsay, and our statements are not based upon any hearsay.

Q. I should assume not, of course. Then you have no information, as I understand, beyond what appears in this report, and in this volume containing the extracts from correspondence?—A. I would not like to say that. It would be impossible for a man to go all through the records of his memory to find whether he has any information or not, not printed there—that would be an impossibility.

Q. That might necessitate considering the matter, of course?—A. Not only that; you might consider it for months and not be able to recall to your mind things that some other thing might bring up to your notice and which you had forgotten all about.

Q. Then will you be kind enough to look at the report and assist me if you can? I am asking you if you will be kind enough to assist me by referring to any part of your report that you deem affects the question of the integrity or dishonesty of the deputy minister?—A. The report and the evidence, it seems to me, must be taken as a whole.

Q. Will you refer to any specific matter, if you please?—A. Well, it is not for me to do that; it is for this court to do it.

Q. Will you assist in doing so?—A. If you call my attention to anything that you want further information about I shall try and give it, but it is for you to point out what is wanted.

Q. Then I want the particular part of the report that reflects upon the deputy minister?—A. You will have to take the whole report for that, and all the evidence and all the extracts. You are asking an improper thing from me, excuse me for saying so.

Q. I hope not?—A. Because you are asking me now, as a member of a civil service commission, appointed for a special purpose, and we have carried out that purpose to the best of our ability—you are asking me to go further than that (and my colleagues, I presume, you are asking the same way) not only to report upon the civil service, but to state specially and further what particular individuals in our opinion should not be in the service.

Q. Oh, no, I am not asking you in that way?—A. It is the same thing.

Q. I have before me, and his lordship has before him, a list of the chief officers or officials of the department?—A. Yes.

Q. I ask if you will give me a specific item?—A. That is too general a question altogether. Take any particular sentence or statement in that report, or in any of the excerpts, and ask me for further information, if you think it necessary, and I will try and give it, but to go beyond the record, beyond that report, and condescend to the individualization of special parties whom I consider guilty, and the meaning conveyed by the paragraph you have referred to—I do not think it would be proper to ask that.

Q. Are there officials in that department whom you consider guilty?—A. Yes.

Q. Then, will you give me the name of one?—A. No.

Q. Your conclusion that some officials are guilty is of course based upon facts and information which you obtained?—A. On the evidence that we have had taken from the files of the correspondence and printed in that report.

Q. Now, will you assist his lordship and assist us as counsel?—A. Is it not open to you to take the same trouble we took, in fact very much less trouble, because you have only got to read what we collated with great difficulty and with great trouble without the assistance of anybody. We were left entirely to our own resources. There was nothing put in our way. We got no assistance. We went into the department. We took our data as we could get it, and formed our own conclusions, and we have shown you on what our report was based. There is not one word in that report that we can alter or withdraw.

Q. Quite so.

Hon. Mr. CASSELS.—Ask him if he realizes the gravity of his charge against the whole body?

Mr. WATSON.—His lordship asks that I should ask you whether you realize the gravity of the charge which has been made against the class of officials?—A. Most emphatically I realize it—most emphatically.

Q. I understand you take the full responsibility?—A. I take the full responsibility, and my confrère does also.

Q. And that being so, I have no doubt that you are quite prepared to point to the fact or information upon which you reach your conclusion?—A. That is all in our report.

Mr. WATSON.—Perhaps if your lordship is going to rise for luncheon, this would be the proper time.

Adjournment from 1 p.m. until 2.15 p.m.

Mr. Watson resuming:

Q. Is Colonel Gourdeau, the deputy minister, one of the parties to whom you have referred as guilty?—A. As what?

Q. As guilty?—A. It is not for me to say.

Q. I am asking, from the information and facts which you obtained, is he one of the parties under the charge of guilty?—A. I do not see how you can make any statement that I should make in answer to that question a matter of evidence.

Q. Do I understand that you wish to decline to answer the question?—A. I am not called upon to answer it. I do not think I am called upon to answer it.

Q. And therefore you decline?—A. Yes.

Q. You won't answer. Do you consider the circumstances that Colonel Gourdeau now lies under an imputation?—A. His position in that respect is no worse to-day than it has been for years, and the same applies to any other officer of the department who may or may not be suspected of impropriety. Anything that we have done has not altered the situation one iota.

Q. Then do you suspect him of impropriety or misconduct?—A. I do not think it matters to anybody what we suspect. I do not think that would be evidence.

Q. Do you charge him with such?—A. We charge nobody with anything.

Q. You have throughout in many places in your report made a reference to him? —A. Yes, which was necessary.

Q. Now, I have before me an extract from your report of all references made to the deputy minister?—A. Yes.

Q. You are familiar with these—fairly so?—A. Well, my memory is not as good as it might be, but I presume I am, more or less.

Q. Can you yourself now point to any reference in your report which reflects upon his honesty or integrity?—A. All I have to say——

Q. Well, can you do so?—A. I must answer it in my own way.

Q. If you please?—A. All I can say in regard to that is, that our report must be taken as a whole, and we decline to divide it up and distinguish the merits or demerits of individuals in the department.

Q. Then I will be under the necessity, I think, of referring to your report and the portions of it which mention his name?—A. Yes.

Q. Will you look first at page 33. I find the first reference there to him?—A. Yes.

Q. A reference to correspondence?—A. Yes.

Q. In connection with what is there referred to, did you find any information which led you to the conclusion that he was guilty?—A. Of what?

Q. Misconduct or dishonesty?—A. What passage do you refer to?

Q. Page 33?—A. What part? What line?

Q. He is referred to in the last paragraph there?—A. When answers are prepared to the letters that are presented for signature to the deputy minister he assumes to know all about them, but which is practically impossible. In not a few cases letters are written, signed by the deputy, notwithstanding that they may be in conflict with previous correspondence or instructions on the same subject, and therefore calculated to bring reproach and discredit upon the department. I say this is a fact.

Q. Then do you intend there to reflect upon his honesty?—A. I intend to reflect upon the bad management of the department.

Q. I am not asking about that. I am asking about matters that affect the integrity or honesty?—A. I cannot say that has any special reference to honesty.

Q. Then we will pass that. Then the next reference is at page 36. That just refers to his appointment. There is manifestly nothing there. Then page 75 is the next place where I find any reference to him. There is a reference there in the latter part of that page to correspondence between the deputy and Mr. Gregory?—A. Yes.

Q. Is there anything there that you intended should reflect upon his honesty or integrity?—A. I may say generally and specially we did not intend anything about anything we did except to get at the naked fact. Any of those extracts were taken out for that purpose and for no other. We intended to take no improper or biased meaning out of anything. We may have taken a great many extracts that were not particularly necessary, but it was all done with the single view of getting a clear idea of how the management was carried on. That is all I have to say about it.

Q. Then, is there anything there that reflects or is intended to reflect upon his honesty?—A. I don't know. It is for you to say. You can form as correct a judgement of it as I can.

Q. But do you rely upon anything there in connection with his honesty or dishonesty?—A. I rely as to my judgment, and as to statements in the report, on the whole of the information we gathered. It is impossible for me, and it would be impossible for anybody to take one item out of perhaps a thousand and say that particular item induced me to have a certain opinion as to a certain fact. I cannot say that in this case.

Q. Then, do I understand from you that putting all these matters together you concluded that they reflected upon his honesty or integrity?—A. I have never attempted, and I do not believe my colleague, Mr. Bazin, has attempted to ascertain just how much or how little any particular official of the department was or was not guilty.

Q. Then, referring again to page 34, 'There would also seem to be a lack of conscience'?—A. Yes.

Q. Did you find anything that made that applicable to the deputy minister?—A. Well——

Q. Can you answer that, yes or no?—A. I do not think I am called upon to say yes or no to that question.

Q. I am asking you if you can do so?—A. Well, I won't do so.

Q. You won't do so. Do you not think that you may be under some obligation to do so?—A. No.

Q. Either to the public or to the individual?—A. Neither.

Q. Neither one. Then will you look at the last sentence of that paragraph?—A. Yes.

Q. 'In other words, some of the government's officers are serving two masters, and apparently succeeding with both, Scripture notwithstanding'?—A. Yes, that is emphatically true.

Q. That is emphatically true?

Hon. Mr. CASSELS.—Ask him first what Scripture he relies on?

Mr. WATSON.—His lordship would like to know the particular passage in the Scripture that you rely upon?—A. It is so long since I was taught my Scripture, I am afraid I have forgotten it.

Q. You had it in mind, no doubt, when you penned that sentence?—A. Yes, I had.

Hon. Mr. CASSELS.—Something about serving God and Mammon, he may have had in his mind.

Mr. WATSON.—Then, did you intend that observation that you wrote there to apply to the deputy minister?—A. I had no special member of the department in my mind. I treated the department as a whole.

Q. Then, did you have in mind, when you penned that line, the conduct of any particular officer of the department . Yes or no, if you can ?—A. I had in mind in a very decided way, that is, I had very fresh in my mind the cumulative evidence covering the whole department.

Q. Against whom? What individual?—A. Against the department.

Q. But what individual?—A. It is not our business to make any special reference to individuals.

Q. Did you know at that time what individual was referred to?—A. There was no special individual referred to.

Q. Then, did you intend by that to identify any particular individual?—A. I did not intend any identification at all, but it was distinct enough for our purpose. It meant the department.

Q. What was your purpose?—A. My purpose was to give a clear idea of the kind of management that characterized the department.

Q. But this sentence is specific and refers to government officers?—Yes.

Q. In the department?—A. Yes.

Q. Now, to what government officer or officers does that refer?—A. We were never commissioned to make inquiry as to the individual doings of different members of the department. We were commissioned to investigate the condition of the civil service as a whole, and we have done so, and we have marshalled such facts and drawn such conclusions as must necessarily be drawn, I think, under the circumstances.

Q. Then, Mr. Fyshe, of course you surely would not be a party to a report that would unfairly reflect upon officers?—A. I would not.

Q. Then, that being so, you must necessarily have had in your mind some particular officer and the particular act of that officer?—A. I had.

Q. Then, to what officer or officers aid that refer?—A. I cannot name them.

Q. Can you give any information identifying the officers?—A. No, not other than we have already given in our report.

Q. Do you mean, it is through absence of memory?—A. No, there is no defect in my memory.

Q. Then you did know at that time that you wrote that?—A. Know what?

Q. The officials that were referred to?—A. I had in my own mind some idea.

Q. Will you tell me who they were, please?—A. No.

Q. Why not?—A. Because I am not called upon. That is not within the scope of our commission.

Hon. Mr. CASSELS.—Will you kindly ask him if he will give the names?

The WITNESS.—We were not appointed detectives.

Hon. Mr. CASSELS.—Will you ask him if he knew the names of any official he did not blame?

By Mr. Watson:

Q. Did you know the names of any officers at that time whom you did not blame? —A. Yes.

Q. Will you mention them, please?—A. No.

Hon. Mr. CASSELS.—I cannot make him hear, but, Mr. Watson, you may tell him it seems to me, as a matter of fairness to the character of the gentlemen whom he did not think ought to be blamed, he ought to name them.

By Mr. Watson:

Q. His lordship asks me to call your attention to the fact, having regard to the character of the gentlemen whom you did not blame, that in fairness you ought to exculpate them now. Who are they?—A. I do not think we are called upon to do anything of the kind. We neither accuse nor exculpate.

Q. But in this paragraph you do accuse, do you not?—A. No, we do not.

Q. Did you not wish this to be understood as an accusation?—A. I wished it to be understood as a statement of the case—of the fact—that was all.

Q. Do you understand it now as an accusation?—A. I do not.

Q. You do not?—A. No.

Q. Do you think or did you intend that this should carry with it an implication of wrong-doing on the part of any officer?—A. I did, most emphatically.

Q. Then that was an accusation?—A. It was not.

Q. It was not. I am sorry that I can hardly follow you?—A. Well, my mind is clear enough on the subject.

Q. Then I come again to the point. Taking them severally throughout, and dealing with the deputy minister as the head of the department under the minister, whether now you can say to his lordship whether any accusation is made against him? —A. I have to repeat what I have already said, that we neither accuse nor exculpate any individual.

Q. Is that your only answer?—A. Yes.

Q. Then you are aware, I think at all events, as I understand the matter, that this commission to his lordship is based upon your report. You understand that, do you not?—A. I may understand it. I understand that it is said so, that the government say so, but if you want my opinion about it, I do not understand how it ever was appointed. I mean I do not know why it ever was appointed.

Hon. Mr. CASSELS.—You have no personal objection, I hope?

Mr. WATSON.—Mr. Fyshe has not understood my question, I fear.

Q. Then do I understand you think that your report did not justify any further inquiry into the honesty and conduct of the officers?—A. My colleague and myself both think that our report is somewhat in the nature of a judgment of a lower court. It can be appealed against, but the higher court of appeal is parliament, who granted us the authority to make the investigation. We do not think that our report should be made the subject of investigation by any other court, except in this way, that the circumstances on which we decided and have made our report, may be gone over by a second court, and they may come to a different conclusion, as one superior court would of a lower court, but to take our judgment——

Q. Then you refer to this as your judgment?—A. Yes.

Q. And your judgment upon officers of the department?—A. The department.

Q. And upon officers of the department?—A. Well, simply the department, including the officers.

Q. Then you have passed judgment upon officers of the department?—A. We have not; we passed judgment upon the department's management.

Q. Then did you intend this observation, ' There would also seem to be a lack of conscience,' as a judgment upon the officers?—A. That is our judgment of the department, and it does not make any distinction as to any officers.

Q. Then do you include all the officers in that charge?—A. No.

Q. You do not?—A. No.

Q. How many do you include?—A. We do not know.

Q. Do you include one?—A. More than one.

Q. How many?—A. We did not know.

Q. Give me the names?—A. We cannot do it.

Q. You cannot do it. I understand you are unable to do it? Is that the fact?—A. Well, we won't do it, anyway.

Hon. Mr. CASSELS.—Do you think you are going to gain much more, Mr. Watson?

Mr. WATSON.—With your lordship's permission, I would ask Mr. Fyshe kindly to withdraw for the present, and I would like to call him later on.

Hon. Mr. CASSELS.—Yes.

Mr. WATSON.—Later on I would like to have the benefit of some further information from you, Mr. Fyshe.

PHILIP J. BAZIN, examined by Mr. Watson :

WITNESS.—It seems so important, I would like to be questioned in French.

Hon. Mr. CASSELS.—How far can you give your evidence in English? Have you a knowledge of French, Mr. Watson?

Mr. WATSON.—I regret to say not sufficiently accurate to conduct the examination. I would like the opportunity of conducting it in English.

Hon. Mr. CASSELS.—Will it answer to give the evidence in English, and if you feel that you are not expressing yourself as you would like to do, then give it in French. We would then require a French stenographer. What Mr. Bazin states is this, and I quite appreciate his feelings: You can talk in English and express exactly what you want to state. Mr. Bazin may be able to answer questions in English, but at the same time he may not thoroughly appreciate the purport of the question.

Mr. WATSON.—I have but a very few questions to ask.

The WITNESS.—Before going into the merits, I beg the liberty of making a few remarks, as a kind of protest.

Hon. Mr. CASSELS.—I do not think you quite appreciate Mr. Watson's idea. Mr. Watson is calling you, and calling Mr. Fyshe, not with the idea of coercing you into answering anything, but with the idea that this is a public inquiry. We want to get what is right and fair, and his notion in examining you is to procure all the assistance he can, not to impeach your report, or attack your report, but if possible to get the assistance of Mr. Fyshe and yourself, in order, so far as possible, to exculpate whatever individuals of the Marine Department ought to go free of suspicion at the earliest moment. That is the whole object?

Mr. WATSON.—Quite so.

WITNESS.—If you think I should proceed, before doing so, I just want to ask you something.

By Hon. Mr. Cassels:

Q. You take the objection that you are appointed commissioner by the government?—A. Yes.

Q. And that you have made your report, and that as commissioner you ought not to be under review in the court?—A. Yes.

Q. That is your objection, taken broadly. You take your objection, but have you any objection to facilitating this commission by giving any information that you can give?—A. Well, I may tell you right away that I do not think I am called upon. My answers will be just about the same as those of Mr. Fyshe.

Q. You may be quite right, but look at the other side of it. Here are a large number of officials; they are all charged, whether intended or not, and they are all under a cloud. Now, as between man and man, outside of any legal objection, or anything else, do you not consider it fair, that if you can exculpate some, that you ought to do it?—A. I do not think I can exculpate any, because I do not accuse any. I think I do not accuse any.

Hon. Mr. CASSELS.—That is the whole thing in a nutshell. I think, Mr. Watson, Mr. Bazin takes the position that he was a commissioner, appointed to do his work. He has done his work, and he has signed the report. It is quite evident he never intended that the report as signed should carry the interpretation which has been placed upon it. His notion apparently is, that finding the general administration of the Marine and Fisheries wrong, he simply throws it upon the officials to exculpate themselves. That is to a great extent the position taken.

The WITNESS.—As I said, we studied and examined the department as a whole, and we came to a certain conclusion, according to which we made our report.

By Hon. Mr. Cassels:

Q. Your conclusion being that the system was defective, and you argued from that that there must be some wrongdoing by somebody, and you left it to somebody else to find it out?—A. I cannot express it in English.

Q. You cannot put your finger upon any individual?—A. No.

Q. But you feel that everybody is guilty? You talk English better than I do French. However, I think if he wants to give his evidence in French he ought to be allowed to do so.

Mr. WATSON.—I quite understand that. At the same time, I thought perhaps, I could make myself clear to him in a few statements.

Hon. Mr. CASSELS.—Try.

(The witness is now sworn.)

By Hon. Mr. Cassels:

Q. Have you followed Mr. Fyshe's evidence?—A. Pretty much.

Q. And understood it?—A. Yes.

By Mr. Watson:

Q. Having understood his evidence you also understood my questions?—A. Well, I may have understood them, but I am not perfectly satisfied that I may have done so perfectly well.

Q. You have a memorandum there which you would like to read. Can it be deposited?—A. Well, I just took it in pencil.

Q. So that it may be interpreted?—A. I want to have it consigned with the registrar.

Q. My friend, Mr. Perron, might translate it into English?—A. He can do that if you wish.

Mr. WATSON.—Will you do that, if it is not asking too much?

Hon. Mr. CASSELS.—Translate it yourself to the reporter.

The WITNESS.—I beg respectfully the privilege of your honour not to be examined upon the execution of my duties as commissioner. The government of Canada did me the honour to name me as a member of the Royal Commission on the Civil Service. With my colleagues I have executed my mandate to the best of my ability or faculty. We have examined, as much as possible, the state of things as a whole, and we have made our report to the Governor General in Council, with appendices to the report, and this report is now in the hands of or submitted to parliament, which should be the sole judge.

By Mr. Watson:

Q. I am much obliged to you. Then, you have read this report, of course?—A. Yes.

Q. Since it was printed?—A. Well, I read part of it; not much of it since.

Q. And you were a party to the making of this report, you and Mr. Fyshe especially?—A. Yes.

Q. That is, as I understand, the result of personal examination at the department?—A. Yes.

Q. This, therefore, is based upon the information which you obtained in the department?—A. Well, what do you mean by information obtained?

Q. The facts that you became aware of in the department. I forgot I was not addressing Mr. Fyshe. I was speaking too loudly?—A. Well, of course what we got from the department—information we got.

Q. Then you introduced into your report in the first place this sentence, ' There would also seem to be a lack of conscience?'

Hon. Mr. CASSELS.—Did Mr. Bazin read that before it was issued?

By Mr. Watson:

Q. Did you read this before it was issued?—A. Certainly, I read the manuscript.

Q. Was it then in English?—A. It was.

Q. And you have in mind that sentence, ' There would also seem to be a lack of conscience?'—A. I had it in mind, certainly.

Q. Did you intend to make that a part of your report?—A. Certainly, it is a part of the report.

Q. You intended that. Then being so intended, it was also intended to reflect upon some individuals, was it not?—A. Not specially; on the whole as a department.

Q. Do you mean all the officials of the department?—A. Well, the department as a whole; that is what I mean.

Q. Died you find any one particular instance where an individual——?—A. Excuse me, now. When I say the department as a whole, I do not know if you mean from the minister down. I would not lead anybody to believe that I meant the minister as well. I did not. I spoke of the department as a whole.

By Hon. Mr. Cassels:

Q. A reflection on the system?—A. On the 'system,' that is the word.

By Mr. Watson:

Q. Then did you intend that that should apply to any particular officials?—A. No, sir.

Hon. Mr. CASSELS.—I fancy what Mr. Bazin means is this: whether rightly or wrongly, he found a waste of money, and the system all wrong, and some or other of the officials must be guilty.

The WITNESS.—I regret, but I must reply, our report is there, and we want to stick by it, and no more or no less.

By Hon. Mr. Cassels:

Q. Why do you want to stick by it?—A. Because we believe it is right, according to the facts as a whole.

Q. It is based on the system?

By Mr. Watson:

Q. Then did you find that any individuals were guilty of a lack of conscience?—A. Well, I must say I do not want to reply. I do not have anyone specially.

Q. You do not have anyone specially in your mind?—A. No.

Q. Had you at that time anyone specially in your mind?—A. No.

Q. Then take the last sentence, 'In other words some of the government officers are serving two masters and apparently succeeding with both, Scripture notwithstanding.' Is that your expression, 'Scripture notwithstanding?'—A. I do not think it is.

Q. Well, then, you intended to apply it at all events.

(Witness laughs).

By Hon. Mr. Cassels:

Q. What you meant there was serving God and Mammon?—A. Yes. I beg your pardon. I think I did not catch exactly what you said, if it is going to be recorded. I do not think I caught exactly what you said.

Q. By 'Scripture notwithstanding' is meant, I fancy, serving God and Mammon? —A. Well, that is not exactly what I think.

By Mr. Watson:

Q. What did you mean?—A. I say that is one of the points I want to put in French.

Mr. WATSON.—'Scripture notwithstanding.' What is your interpretation in French?

The WITNESS.—He cannot serve two masters at the same time.

Mr. WATSON.—Then, did this sentence have your full approbation: 'In other words, some of the government officers are serving two masters'?

Hon. Mr. CASSELS.—I do not think you can ask that, Mr. Watson.

Mr. WATSON.—It is assumed it did.

Hon. Mr. CASSELS.—He has signed the report.

The WITNESS.—I signed the report.

By Mr. Watson:

Q. Of course that as it reads contains a very serious charge as against officials? —A. Well, it is a matter of appreciation, I suppose.

3262—2

Q. In your mind was it intended to convey a charge against officials?—A. No. We did. not want to charge—to accuse anyone. We have put some evidence—what we call evidence, forward.

Q. You do not accuse anyone. Then can you name any officers to whom that applies?—A. No, sir. That is, I told you I had none in my mind.

By Hon. Mr. Cassels:

Q. He charges the system generally?—A. The system generally.

By Hon. Mr. Cassels:

Q. Mr. Bazin, did you make any personal enquiries into the charges on any contract prices paid?—A. No.

Q. Did you make any investigation yourself into the prices charged?—A. No.

Q. Who did that?—A. I fancy Mr. Fyshe did.

Q. The report is signed by a third party, Mr. Courtney?—A. Yes.

Q. Did he adopt your views?—A. I understand he does. Of course, I have no authority to speak for him.

Q. Your report speaks for itself?—A. For the reason he signed it.

Q. Were all the investigations into the prices, the difference between the price of flour at Sorel and Quebec—was that your investigation?—A. No, sir. Well, of course we took that from the documents. They were departmental documents.

Q. How did you get the market prices? From the documents in the department or did you go on the market to find out?—A. We did not make any difference; it is between Sorel and Ottawa or Quebec, I forget which. The selling people made the comparison in prices.

Q. You took them from the departmental prices?—A. Yes.

Q. And you found there was a difference in prices?—A. Yes.

Q. Between flour purchased at Quebec and flour purchased at Sorel?—A. I forget which especially.

Q. Did you find out, for instance, whether at Sorel the prices were lower?—A. The documents are there.

Q. Merely from the information you had before you, that is what Mr. Watson is asking?—A. As I said, I must say the same thing, everything is contained in the documents.

Q. Have you any other information beyond these books?—A. No.

Q. Then this is simply your conclusion from the effect of the evidence which these blue books contain?—A. Exactly, that is about it.

By Mr. Watson:

Q. Then I understand, or may I understand, that you are not able now to give his lordship any assistance in ascertaining what officers, if any, were serving two masters?—A. I cannot give any more than the report gives.

Hon. Mr. CASSELS.—He has drawn his own conclusion from whatever is contained in the blue books. That may be right or it may be wrong. You and I can judge, as well as he can, whether the conclusion is correct.

By Mr. Watson:

Q. You found there in your investigation many officials who had to do with the expenditure of money?—A. I suppose. We met the officials, some of them.

Q. Now, in justice to these officials, and the inquiry in regard to them, I would like to ask you, did you find anything in your investigation which led you to the conclusion that there was any dishonesty or lack of conscience on the part of the deputy minister?—A. I cannot reply to that, sir.

Q. Do you mean you have not the information?—A. I mean all the information we can give you is in the report.

Q. Did you intend to include him in this part of the report to which I have referred?—A. The department as a whole.

Hon. Mr. CASSELS.—I think he has stated that.

Mr. WATSON.—I wanted to ask particularly to see what he has to say as to the individuals.

Hon. Mr. CASSELS.—He found the system wrong, and in his judgment, upon the evidence in these blue books, he came to the conclusion more money was spent than ought to have been spent; he therefore concluded the system was wrong, and there must be some members of the Marine Department who were guilty of that expenditure, but he has not put his finger upon anyone.

The WITNESS.—I want to be respectful. I think it is all the same question, and he can get the same answer.

By Mr. Watson:

Q. Were you then able to, or did you put your finger upon any one official who was guilty of wrongdoing?—A. No, sir.

Q. That is your position?—A. That is it.

Q. That is the position you take now upon this commission, that you cannot point to any wrongful act of any official? Is that so?—A. We were not called upon, as I said in my small memorandum——

Q. Not called upon to do that?—A. We were not acting as detectives or anything like that, not as to special individuals. It was on the department as a whole.

Q. And do you understand that a charge or reflection of that kind, upon the department as a whole, in connection with the words used, make it apply to all the officials?—A. Well, to the department. That is what I mean.

Q. But you are not able now to give any statement of fact or information which would lead to the conclusion of a wrongful act on the part of any individual?—A. I consider I am not called upon to answer that. I beg to refer you to all these documents.

Q. Did you find any wrongful act on the part of anyone?—A. I cannot say that.

Q. You cannot say that you did?—A. No.

Q. Then I may have to ask you to come at a subsequent appointment again, sometime at your convenience. I suppose you will be able to do so?—A. I belong to Quebec. I am a business man. It is now time for our business. I would be glad and appreciate very much if I could get away to-day.

Q. I mean that. I was going to ask his lordship that you be not detained longer to-day. I am merely saying that we may wish to call you at another time. We will meet your convenience.

Hon. Mr. CASSELS.—It may not be necessary.

The WITNESS.—Mr. Judge, if you please now, as I said, I am a business man. I do not think I can furnish any more information. I might talk the whole afternoon. I have my business to attend to. I have two clerks away just now and I am suffering. I would not like to be asked again.

By Hon. Mr. Cassels:

Q. You want to get away on the four o'clock train, and do not want to be called again unless it is necessary?—A. If you please.

Q. And you have no other information than is contained in your books?—A. No.

Q. As I understand, you find what you think is a defective system in the department, and without naming any individuals as being guilty or not?—A. That is it. We have mentioned it in our report.

Q. You simply joined with Mr. Fyshe in his Scripture, that is the English Church version of the Bible?—A. Well, I think we have the same thing in French.

Mr. WATSON.—Then that is all we have to-day. I am afraid I will have to ask you to come at some other time, but I will endeavour to meet your convenience.

Hon. Mr. CASSELS.—If necessary we will take your evidence in Quebec.

The WITNESS.—Thank you. Do I understand I can go away now?

Hon. Mr. CASSELS.—Yes.

The WITNESS.—Thank you.

Mr. WATSON.—All I can say is we have endeavoured, my learned friend and I, to make the best start·we could to-day.

Hon. Mr. CASSELS.—You have done very well.

Mr. WATSON.—I am much obliged to your lordship. We would like, therefore, that your lordship would now adjourn to some subsequent occasion.

Hon. Mr. CASSELS.—It depends upon what you are going to do.

Mr. WATSON.—Will your lordship be able to proceed any time during next week?

Hon. Mr. CASSELS.—I have three trade-mark cases fixed for Monday. I have a very heavy list fixed for Toronto for Wednesday, Thursday, Friday and Saturday. I have to go to Charlottetown. I will be free, I think, Monday and Tuesday. I have to be at St. John on the Friday. I would have to leave here at all events on Wednesday. There are several cases there. Then I have to go to Halifax. I have to be in Sydney on the 21st May, where there are twenty cases, and court will last three or four weeks. As I have said, the court work takes first call.

Mr. WATSON.—Your lordship's appointments almost equal now what they were at the bar. You have in mind that you may be free on Monday and Tuesday, the 11th and 12th.

Hon. Mr. CASSELS.—I think so. We will telegraph and find out. The eastern court has been tied up and it must be attended to. I doubt if there are any cases at Charlottetown; if not there will be two days free. After all, it just depends upon whether I make a drudge of myself, and of the Exchequer Court, or whether there is going to be any relief.

Mr. WATSON.—Then within two or three days we can determine whether we will proceed on those two days, Monday and Tuesday, 11th and 12th?

Hon. Mr. CASSELS.—You have relieved the officials already to a certain extent to-day. I mean to say they will not feel so very depressed.

Mr. WATSON.—Then if it may stand in that way, contingently for Monday and Tuesday, the 11th and 12th, and we will ascertain in the course of a couple of days.

Hon. Mr. CASSELS.—Yes.

Adjourned contingently as above stated.

IN THE EXCHEQUER COURT OF CANADA.

In the Matter of the Investigation of Certain Statements contained in the Report of the Civil Service Commission reflecting upon the Integrity of the Officials of the Department of Marine and Fisheries, or some of them.

Continued before the Honourable Mr. Justice Cassels, at Ottawa, May 11th and 12th, 1908.

Dr. CHARLES MORSE.
Deputy Registrar Exchequer Court.

NELSON R. BUTCHER & Co.,
Official Reporters.
(Per F. Berryman.)

GEORGE H. WATSON, K.C., and J. L. PERRON, K.C., appear as counsel assisting in the investigation.

Hon. Mr. CASSELS.—What do you propose to do this morning, Mr. Watson?

Mr. WATSON.—I propose to introduce Mr. Anderson as a witness, my lord.

WILLIAM P. ANDERSON, sworn.

By Mr. Watson:

Q. Colonel Anderson, you are the chief engineer in the department?—A. Yes.

Q. How long have you been in that position?—A. Since 1880.

Q. 1880?—A. Yes.

Q. Well, you have been there a fairly long time. Have you an assistant?—A. Yes, several assistants.

Q. Anyone in the position of assistant engineer?—A. Yes, Mr. B. H. Fraser.

Q. How long has he been in that position?—A. Since 1895.

Q. And as chief engineer, your branch, as I understand, gives you direct and personal charge of the construction of lighthouses and fog alarms?—A. I should like to qualify that 'personal' with the understanding that the whole direction of my branch is under the direct control of the deputy minister, of course.

Q. The direct control. I suppose you mean——?—A. I have no authority separate from the authority given me by the minister through the deputy minister.

Q. I see. He is, of course, the superior officer?—A. Yes.

Q. And in that way you are subject to his directions?—A. Yes.

Q. As the deputy minister. Apart from those superior directions, it is within your branch, the charge of construction of lighthouses and fog alarms?—A. Yes.

Q. What else? Chartering steamers for icebreaking and removal of wrecks?—A. No, not chartering steamers for ice breaking. Removal of wrecks, yes; and general constructive work in connection with the department.

Q. Constructive work?—A. A good deal of other technical work, such as reporting on applications for water lots.

Q. Water lots?—A. Yes; reporting on schemes for improvement of navigation, and matters of that kind.

Q. Then, in your position you come into association, communication, with the heads of other departments, I assume?

Hon. Mr. CASSELS.—Other departments of the Marine and Fisheries?

Mr. WATSON.—Yes, my lord.

By Mr. Watson:

Q. Other departments of the Marine and Fisheries?—A. Yes, with our agencies.

Q. With your agencies?—A. Yes, and many resident engineers.

Q. You said that, of course, at all times you are under the direction, the orders of the deputy minister. And you have communications, business communications, directly with the other officials and heads of departments; for instance, the commissioner of lights, Mr. J. F. Fraser?—A. No, not with the commissioner of lights. His branch is altogether separate from mine.

Q. Then have you, as chief engineer, anything to do in connection with that department?—A. Well, the work is inter-related to a certain extent. For instance, in building a lighthouse I have charge of putting up the building, and the commissioner of lights is charged with the provision of the lantern and illuminating apparatus, and after the work is completed the whole management goes into his branch for maintenance.

Q. For maintenance, yes. Then, so far as the constructive work is concerned, you are in consultation with him?—A. To a certain extent, yes.

Q. To a certain extent. I would like to know—the reason I ask this is I would like to establish a basis as much as possible to see where your work lies and with whom your business communications are directly. Now, to what extent do your business communications exist with the commissioner of lights, apart from what you have mentioned in the matter of construction of lighthouses?—A. I think that limits our relations.

Q. Construction of lighthouses?—A. Yes, so far as I can call to mind at the moment. That is to say, in construction of a lighthouse I provide for the building, and he provides for the apparatus and lantern. Then, of course, my building has to be made to carry his lanterns.

Q. Yes. Then do you have all to do with the construction of the building?—A. Yes.

Q. That is solely with you?—A. Yes.

Q. Then, just a word in connection with that. That is pursued upon what line or policy, the construction of lighthouses—that is a matter of contract, is it, in each case?—A. Each case is decided on its own basis. In most cases we let the work by contract; in a few cases where the opportunities of private parties for doing the work are poor, we found it necessary to do the work ourselves.

Q. Then, that is a matter of discretion for the time being, is it? Is there a rule or policy that applies?—A. No; each case is decided on its own basis, with the general understanding that the policy of the department is to let the work by contract.

Q. Yes, you let the work by contract. And usually, just in a word—I will touch upon it afterwards—the construction of the lighthouse amounts in each case to an expenditure of about how much money?—A. Oh, it varies very greatly, from a couple of hundred dollars up to possibly $10,000 or $12,000.

Q. $10,000 or $12,000? I see. I see in connection with this matter that it is stated to me that the average annual expenditure in your branch is about the sum of three-quarters of a million, about that sum?—A. It has been for a very few years past.

Q. Yes. Then I will refer to this again. Now, take another department, Mr. Doutre is in charge of the wireless telegraphy, the establishment of wireless telegraph stations. Will you just state what you have to do in connection with that branch, what your duties are?—A. I have no recollection that I have done any work in connection with that.

Q. Not at all?—A. I think not.

Q. Not a matter of consultation or direction with you as engineer?—A. No, I think not.

Q. I see. Then the next is contracts and purchasing of supplies for lighthouses.

Mr. Stumbles is the head of that branch, I am informed?—A. I have nothing to do with that; that has nothing to do with construction; that is a matter of maintenance.

Q. That is a matter of maintenance?—A. Yes.

Q. And you distinguish between maintenance and construction?—A. Yes.

Q. Then the chief hydrographer, Mr. Stewart, in charge of hydrographic surveys. Do you come in communication with him in connection with your duties?—A. I do; and until about two or three years ago he virtually worked through me; but he has been made independent of me, and the branch is now a separate one.

Q. Then when did that change take place, about what time?—A. Roughly speaking, two or three years ago.

Q. Up to that time what did you have to do with that branch?—A. I advised with him and also advised the minister with regard to the work that was in progress, as to what should be done the next season, and that sort of thing. I never attempted to interfere with his management of his own work.

Q. That was a matter, then, of consultation?—A. That was a matter of consultation.

Q. With you?—A. Yes; and some portions of what are strictly hydrography still remain in my office. For instance, issuing notices to mariners, the issue of hydrographic notices, and that sort of thing, is done from my office.

Q. That is in a general way you speak of that?—A. Yes.

Q. Then, what have you to do with the branch over which Commander Spain is in charge?—A. Nothing whatever.

Q. Nothing whatever?—A. No.

Q. He is in charge of Dominion steamers, fisheries protection steamers, and so on. You do not get into communication with him at all in the ordinary course?—A. There have been occasions when we have consulted together with regard to repairs to steamers and matters of that kind; but with regard to the management of steamers I have nothing whatever to do.

Hon. Mr. CASSELS.—How about the purchase of steamers—A. That is not done through my branch at all.

By Mr. Watson :

Q. Then, with Dr. Dawson in charge of the Tidal Survey Branch?—A. Dr. Dawson reports to me, and I am still virtually head of that branch, although I have never attempted in any way to interfere with his management of his own work.

Q. I see. And Mr. Cunningham in charge of fish culture, establishment of fish hatcheries?—A. Some plans for fish hatcheries have been made in my office, but the work of construction, I think—I should like an opportunity of correcting myself on this—but the work, I think, has been done under his direction.

Q. The work of construction?—A. Yes.

Q. After consultation with you, I assume?—A. Yes, I have prepared some of the plans, possibly all of them; I am not quite sure about that.

Q. But your duties in his department, then, are what, closely speaking?—A. Closely speaking, to prepare plans on which the fish hatcheries are built, or to check them if they are prepared by others.

Q. Then, Mr. Roy is in charge of the stationery branch. I assume you have nothing to do with that?—A. Nothing whatever.

Q. And Mr. Cowie in charge of the St. Lawrence ship channel, what about him?—A. Nothing whatever.

Q. Nothing at all?—A. Nothing at all.

Q. Now, in which of these branches do you have to concur in matters of expenditure, or recommendations for expenditure?—A. Chiefly, if not altogether, in the construction of lighthouses branch work.

Q. I see; that is under Mr. Fraser?—A. Yes.

Q. Then, is there other expenditure in that branch in connection with which your concurrence is obtained? You have spoken of lighthouses; does it extend to anything else?—A. Yes, fog alarms.

Q. Fog alarms?—A. And the past two years when the work has been every extensive we have not had enough steamers of our own, and we have been obliged to charter steamers.

Q. Yes.—A. In that case the rent of the steamer has been paid for out of the construction vote, out of the vote for the construction of lighthouses, if that is what you are referring to.

Q. Yes; and in that way it affects you?—A. Yes.

Q. You have to do with it in chartering steamers. Anything else? You will understand, Colonel Anderson, I want to trace how far you have any connection, directly or indirectly, with the expenditure of money or the recommendation for the expenditure of money in the different branches. You see what I desire to obtain ?—A. I cannot call to mind anything that you have not touched on just for the moment.

Q. Then, as I understand you, your connection and recommendation has to do with expenditure for lighthouses, fog alarms, and occasionally in connection with the chartering of steamers?—A. Well, at the moment I do not recall anything——

Q. Yes. Of course it has been suggested to me that there is some occasional work in ice breaking at Fort William and Georgian Bay?—A. Oh yes.

Q. These matters will occur afterwards?—A. Yes. For the past two years the department have undertaken to keep the ice broken in Georgian Bay and Lake Superior at the close and beginning of the season. The expenditure on that account has been under my branch.

Q. Yes. Well now, for the most part, if not entirely, your connection with money matters is limited to the one branch?—A. Yes.

Q. For the most part. Now, that being so, and just as a matter of system, I will leave that for the moment and take the other branches and the heads of the other departments for the purpose of asking you a few direct questions, if you please. You are aware Colonel Anderson, of the report and the terms of the report made by certain gentlemen acting as Civil Service Commissioners?—A. In general terms, yes; but I have not read the report.

Q. You have not read the whole report?—A. Yes.

Q. No. You know the one important part of the report which reflects upon the integrity and want of conscience of officials in the department ?—A. Yes, I read that.

Q. Yes, you know of that. Just to recall your attention to it I would like to read that paragraph, because I want to ask you some direct questions, if I may, upon the matter. This report says: ' There would also seem to be a lack of conscience. In connection with the enormous expenditures which are deemed necessary the word ' discount ' never appears. It is tacitly assumed there is no such thing; but the whole commercial world knows otherwise. If no one gets any benefit from trade with the government except the trader, then it must be clear that in these great purchases made for the government, without discount, its officers must be assisting the trader to get better prices from the government than he can get anywhere else; for everywhere else he has to give discount. In other words, some of the government's officers are serving two masters, and apparently succeeding with both—Scripture notwithstanding.' You have heard that before, you know of that?—A. Yes, sir.

Q. Now then, to be altogether accurate, and with you here before his lordship, the commissioner, I want to know whether or not in connection with your own work you have any knowledge, direct or indirect, that relates to matters that are the subject of this portion of the report that I have referred to?—A. So far as my own work goes, I have no knowledge of any purchases being made that were not made honestly and in a businesslike way.

Q. So far as your own work goes ?—A. Yes.

Q. You have yourself to do with the direct actual expenditure?—A. Yes.

Q. Then, I want to ask you in regard to that, without being—you understand the position I am in—without being in any way. offensive or desiring to be so regarded, I want to know particularly of you—as I shall have to ask of the others—in connection with your own expenditure. Do you know in connection with your own particular work of any advantages that have been given to contractors or others, or any gains that have been made by those dealing with the department in connection with matters you have had control of, that you have personally had control of?—A. I do not.

Q. Of course, you understand, I am asking this now as a direct personal question of you and affecting your own acts and your own good conscience, Colonel Anderson? A. My conscience is perfectly clear on that.

Q. Yes; that is your answer. Then, so far as your expenditure is concerned or the recommendations which you make for expenditure, what is the system pursued, advertising, seeking tenders?—A. As I said earlier, the system differs in different cases. Where it is thought possible to do it, we do ask for contracts and work on a contract system.

Q. Yes?—A. A good deal of work has been done on the day labour system, that is, where we consider that we could get either better work or better dispatch by doing that.

Q. Yes.—A. A good deal of construction work between Montreal and Quebec has been done on the day-labour system, and the reason for that was that most of it was concrete work in very difficult situations and where we thought we could insure better work by superintending it ourselves. As you will understand, concrete work is work that depends for its stability on the integrity of the contractor, and if it were done by contract and poor concrete was put in, we should lose the whole work.

Q. I see. Then, where it is not by contract, as I understand you, it has been done by day-labour as a matter of business expediency; is that right?—A. Certainly.

Q. Is that a matter of greater or less expense?—A. Usually it is more expensive work than contract work, but usually the quality resulting is better.

Q. I see. Is the result then to the advantage or disadvantage of the country?— A. In my mind, to the advantage.

Q. To the advantage, I see. Now, in connection with any of those classes or kinds of work have you any knowledge of any discounts being allowed, speaking of your personal expenditure first—I am limiting it to that at the present time—have you any knowledge of any discounts being allowed to contractors, workmen or others? —A. No, I have not.

Q. Have you any knowledge of discounts being asked for or claimed—I mean discounts to the advantage of the person dealing with the government, with the department?—A. No, I have not.

Q. You have not?

Hon. Mr. CASSELS.—That is, referring to this concrete work?

Mr. WATSON.—I was applying it generally, my lord, first; I will come to the specific articles separately.

WITNESS.—Might I interject an explanation here? That in this work that is done by the day; in most cases our materials were purchased by contract. That is to say, our cement was purchased by contract, our piles were purchased by contract, our stone was purchased by contract, and it was the work itself and the carrying of the material to the sites that we paid for separately. Where we could, we made contracts for the material.

By Mr. Watson:

Q. Yes. Now, in this report, to which reference has been made, it is claimed, as I understand it, that discounts should be allowed by the contractors for the cash payments?—A. Does not that refer to supplies?

Q. You think that refers to supplies? Do you understand that has any application to the work you have had to do with?—A. Scarcely. It appears to me that where we are requiring small quantities of a great many different kinds of materials that that system of discount would not apply. It is rather for supplies in gross, such as would be required for the maintenance.

Q. That would not come under your personal supervision?—A. At all events, it did not.

Q. Well, should it in the ordinary course, should the matter of these supplies come under your personal supervision?—A. Well, any question of supplies obtained by contract, I do not see how it could.

Q. I see. You do not see how it could. Then, so far as the report makes reference to the officials, charging the serving of two masters, applying that to yourself, is there any foundation for it?—A. Most certainly I claim not.

Q. Or any lack of conscience or good faith?—A. I claim that I have tried to do my duty.

Q. Yes. Now, take some of the others with whom you have had connection dealing with the department : Wireless telegraphy, under Mr. Doutre. Have you any knowledge in connection with his recommendations or expenditures of any irregularities or want of conscience in the expenditure of money?—A. They have never come under my notice at all, I cannot give you any information whatever.

Q. Yes. Then, have you any information that would assist his lordship, the commissioner, in connection with that branch in the inquiry as to god conscience or lack of conscience, or want of honesty or integrity, in the dealings in that department; have you any knowledge that would assist.?—A. None whatever. All I have is a general impression, and impressions do not count. My general impression——

By Hon. Mr. Cassels :

Q. You need not bother about that, then, unles you have knowledge?—A. I have absolutely no knowledge.

Q. We do not want to know what is in the air; we want facts.

By Mr. Watson :

Q. It is a matter of information. You have something you could speak of, that is, you could speak of any business matter?—A. I can only say this, that in certain instances Mr. Doutre has consulted with me, and in those instances my opinion has been that his arrangements were very businesslike.

Q. Yes. Then, with regard to contracts and purchasing of supplies for lighthouses through Mr. Stumbles. Have you any information that would bear upon his conduct in the regularity of his proceedings in the department?—A. None whatever.

Q. None whatever?—A. None whatever.

Q. That is, just affecting the matter in the report as well, can you give any information?—A. None whatever, nothing but impressions.

Q. Then, Mr. W. J. Stewart, chief hydrographer, have you any information?—A. None whatever.

Q. None whatever. And with regard to Colonel Spain and his branch or department?

Hon. Mr. CASSELS.—Captain Spain.

By Mr. Watson:

Q. Yes, Captain Spain?—A. I have no information, as the work has not been under my cognizance in any way.

Q. I see; and you have no information at all. You do not know of anything that would assist in this inquiry, affecting as it does the integrity and the conscience, or lack of conscience, of the officials, and that particular official?—A. I know nothing.

Q. Then, Dr. Dawson, tidal survey branch. I do not want that the question should seem to you too narrow. I want, if you please, any information that you have that may touch upon a want of conscience, want of business honesty.

Hon. Mr. CASSELS.—What does the colonel understand, Mr. Watson, by the question, want of conscience? The department may have paid, for instance, 50 per cent too much, say for supplies. Now, that may have been done under the orders of somebody at headquarters, and the official making the expenditure cannot be accused of lack of conscience himself; nevertheless, there might be lack of conscience somewhere. What do you understand by this question of Mr. Watson's?

By Mr. Watson :

Q. Yes?—A. Well, with reference to that, my lord, I have only a general knowledge of the work that Dr. Dawson has been doing. I am absolutely aware that his work is carried on extremely well, and that Dr. Dawson himself is a man who is above suspicion in every way. I cannot tell you anything about the supplies, because I do not know the system under which they are supplied to him.

Q. Then, referring to him and referring to the others I have particularly mentioned to you, have you any knowledge or information of any excessive expenditure or excessive prices being paid——?—A. I have not.

Q. For work on contracts, material or otherwise?—A. I have not.

Q. You have not. Or of any advantage to any of the individuals or to others with whom they had been dealing?—A. No, none, none.

Q. I will go this far, if his lordship will permit it; have you reason to suspect, reason for suspicion against any of the gentlemen I have named?—A. The conditions are such that I have no business connections that would put me in a position to suspect.

Q. I see. Then pass to Mr. Cunningham, in charge of fish culture, establishing of fish hatcheries?—A. I have no knowledge whatever of the manner in which that work is carried out.

Q. No knowledge at all ?—A. No. I have not certified any of the bills for construction, and I know nothing about his administration of that branch.

Q. And no information that bears upon that?—A. No.

Q. Then, with regard to Mr. Roy, you have not, you said before ?—A. Nothing whatever to do with him.

Q. And Mr. Cowie ?—A. The same thing.

Q. Then the one branch of which you have spoken of a more intimate connection and knowledge is in regard to the commissioner of lights, Mr. J. F. Fraser. Now, just define, if you please, accurately what you have to do with the expenditure, that is, the system, the procedure in connection with the expenditure ?—A. In his branch ?

Q. In his branch?—A. I have nothing whatever to do with it.

Q. Nothing whatever to do with it ?—A. Not with it. It is a separate vote and I have nothing to do with the expenditure of it or administration of it.

Q. Or with the application of it ?—A. No.

Q. You have to do with the construction of lighthouses, fog alarms and chartering of steamers ?—A. Yes.

Q. And that is in that branch ?—A. Yes.

Q. And you therefore have some connection with him, I assume, some business connection ?—A. Only to the extent I have explained to you already. I get from him the lanterns and apparatus for the lighthouses. I take them and put them on to the lighthouses, at least——

Q. Now, the expenditure made for those purchases is recommended by whom ?—A. It is recommended by the officer in charge of the purchase.

Q. Mr. Fraser ?—A. In Mr. Fraser's case recommended by Mr. Fraser, I presume finally by the Deputy Minister, and sanctioned by the minister.

Q. Yes. But the recommendation originally—I am limiting my question now to that branch of the commissioner of lights—the recommendation is by the commissioner of lights, Mr. Fraser ?—A. The recommendation is by the commissioner

of lights, and I presume he is guided by the recommendations of the lighthouse
board which have been approved by the minister.

Q. Yes. Then so far as the construction work is concerned, you are consulted, are
you not ?—A. Yes.

Q. As to the expenditure ?—A. Not as to the expenditure on the lanterns and
apparatus.

Q. Well, what does construction work include ?—A. I think there has been a
little bit of——

Q. Confusion ?—A. Confusion in that matter.

Q. All right. Clear it up, if you please ?—A. Well, as I say——

Hon. Mr. CASSELS.—I understand the Colonel has said, Mr. Watson, he superintended the construction of those lighthouses. I do not know whether he superintended
the contracts for the materials put in them.

Mr. WATSON.—That is just what I want to ascertain, my lord.

WITNESS.—Except the expenditure for the lantern and illuminating apparatus.

By Hon. Mr. Cassels :

Q. Yes, but everything for the erection of the lighthouse came under your supervision. Have you made contracts for supplies and superintended the erection, and
then handed over the building for the lanterns to be put in ?—A. The lighthouse
lanterns are put in by the commissioner of lights, and as soon as the lighthouse is
finished the whole is handed over to his branch for management.

Q. Yes ?

By Mr. Watson :

Q. Do you yourself make the expenditure for the lighthouse itself ?—A. Yes,
for the lighthouse itself, but not for the lantern.

Q. Quite so. And you make the recommendation for the expenditure on the
lighthouse, do you ?—A. Well, yes, yes.

Q. You make that recommendation ?

By Hon. Mr. Cassels :

Q. Do you let the contracts, Colonel Anderson, for the materials that are required
to build the lighthouse ?—A. Yes.

Q. All that is done by you ?—A. Yes.
such as cement?—A. I was referring then, your lordship, to the work in the ship

Q. You have mentioned certain things that had to be purchased under contract,
channel between Montreal and Quebec. Where I said we had let particular work by
day work I was referring to that work at the time.

Q. But all these contracts for supplies were made or recommended by you ?—A.
Yes.

By Mr. Watson:

Q. But as to the lighthouses themselves, those you estimate, you make your
estimate and your recommendation as to the expenditure for those ?—A. Yes.

Q. And is that with or upon consultation with the commissioner of lights, or is
that done by you independently ?—A. The way it is done is this, as a rule: The recommendation is made by the lighthouse board, which is a separate body of officers, and
when a recommendation of the lighthouse board has been approved by the minister
it is tantamount to an order to proceed with the work, and then, as a matter of routine,
the plans are prepared and tenders asked for the construction of the work in question.

Q. Yes. What is the origin of the expenditure in each particular case, or who is
the originator ?—A. Well, the minister, of course.

Q. Of the expenditure in each particular case, that is the recommendation. A
lighthouse is to be erected or constructed; who makes the investigation as to the amount

to be expended, and who makes the recommendation as to the amount of expenditure?
—A. Originally the lighthouse board, but that is revised by the two officers, that is,
by the chief engineer and the commissioner of lights.

Q. By yourself?—A. Yes.

Q. Then, it originates with the lighthouse board ?—A. Yes.

Hon. Mr. CASSELS.—That is, the recommendation of the work, which is necessary?

By Mr. Watson:

Q. Yes, the recommendation of the work which is necessary. And then it passes
on to you and to Mr. Fraser?—A. Yes; and then I——

Q. And then from you to the deputy minister, and so on through the regular
course?—A. Then there is the understanding between the commissioner of lights
branch and my branch as to what is required, and he gives me a memorandum of the
lantern and apparatus to be supplied, and my tower must carry that lantern.

Q. Yes. Now, in connection with that expenditure, you have already spoken for
yourself so far as your own acts are concerned. I want to know specifically, so far as
your knowledge and information go, as to the acts and conduct of Mr. J. F. Fraser,
the commissioner of lights, in that respect; do you know of any irregularities or ill-
conduct or misconduct on his part in connection with any or those matters?—A. You
will understand that his branch being entirely separate from mine, and his expenditure
being entirely separate from mine, I am not in a postion to know.

Q. Have you any information upon that subject?—A. No; nothing more than
impressions.

Q. Nothing more than impressions. Are your impressions based upon business
relations and transactions?—A. No.

Q. Upon what are they based, the impressions?—A. I am afraid they are based
on nothing more than hearsay.

Q. Nothing more than hearsay. Is that hearsay in the department or outside of
the department?—A. Both.

Q. Both. In respect of any particular matters?—A. No.

Q. In respect of any particular lighthouse or contract?—A. No.

Q. Have you any information, then, in respect of any one or more particular
transactions bearing upon his want of integrity or want of conscience?—A. No sir,
I have no information.

Q. Or irregularity of his course?—A. No, I have no information.

Q. You have no information at all?—A. No.

Q. Have you always been in concurrence with him in expenditure, in matters of
recommendation for expenditure?—A. No.

Q. Want of concurrence?—A. Yes.

Q. What is the reason for it?—A. In some cases I considered his ideas extravagant.

Q. I see. Now, just tell me, if you please, or tell his lordship, if you please, what
you refer to. We wish to see, or his lordship wishes to know, how far this may bear
upon his conduct and want of conscience and integrity. Mention the instance, will
you, please?—A. I should find it very difficult to do so, because I cannot call to mind
any instance at the moment.

Q. Any one?—A. No, I do not think of any at the moment.

Q. Well, you rather spoke of that being a distinct view and you have said, as I
understand it, that there was a want of concurrence and your objection to this expenditure. Do you wish to apply that generally?—A. I am afraid I should find it difficult
to apply it at all, but, as I say, as I told you before, it is merely an impression; I am
afraid I cannot bring it down to concrete instances.

Q. Any instance ? Take within the last year, Colonel Anderson, or if you like,
within the last three months to be more specific, your memory may be more fresh and
distinct ?—A. To give you an idea of the kind of thing I have been referring to ?

Q. Yes ?—A. I can call to mind a case of a lighthouse at Flower Ledge.

Q. Where, please ?—A. Flower Ledge.

Q. Where is that?—A. In the Strait of Belle Isle, where the commissioner of lights proposed to change the illuminating apparatus, and this change would involve a change in the lantern. My claim was that the existing lantern would contain an illuminating apparatus sufficiently strong for the construction ; his claim was that the best apparatus obtainable should be placed there. This would involve the changing of the lantern and considerable additional expense.

Q. Yes?—A. This is one instance that I call to mind of the kind of thing I am referring to.

Q. Where his recommendation was for the purchase of a new lantern, in your opinion a new lantern not being necessary ?—A. Yes.

Q. That is the way you put it, concisely, is it ?—A. Yes.

Q. Now, in connection with that, was it a subject about which there might be in your view an honest difference of opinion ?—A. Why not ?

Q. Eh ?—A. Why not ?

Q. I am asking you if it was ?—A. I think in any case of that kind there might be room for honest difference of opinion.

Q. In that case was there ?—A. In that case there might be.

Q. In that case had you reason or ground to attribute any other than an honest difference of opinion on his part ?—A. No ground.

Q. No ground? It would be a matter of an expenditure for a new lantern of how much money ?—A. Really, I could not say without——

Q. About how much—I am not particular for a little in the price for the purpose of the question ?—A. Perhaps 1,000 pounds.

Q. A thousand——A. Pounds.

Q. That is a very large expenditure.

By Hon. Mr. Cassels :

Q. $4,000 or $5,000 ?—A. $5,000.

By Mr. Watson :

Q. For the new lantern ?—A. Yes.

Q. I should call that a large amount.

By Hon. Mr. Cassels :

Q. Would that cover the lantern only, or the changes necessarily incident ?—A. The lantern only.

Q. What other changes were required ?—A. The difference in the price of the apparatus. The modified apparatus that I would advocate, that I did advocate in that case, would be somewhat cheaper than the larger apparatus that the new lantern would contain.

Q. What would the whole change in dollars have amounted to ?—A. Probably the difference in the price of the apparatus would be another 1,000 pounds.

Q. That would be $5,000. Who would be the judge between you ?—A. The minister.

Q. The minister, or the deputy ?—A. The minister, I imagine, because in a case of that kind the deputy would surely refer a matter of that——

Q. I know, but from you ?—A. All my communications with the minister are through the deputy minister.

Q. So far as you are concerned, it would be the deputy who would pass upon it; he could consult the minister or not as he chose?—A. Yes. I would always accept the deputy minister's decision.

Q. I understand that.

By Mr. Watson :

Q. Your direct communication is with the deputy minister?—A. Yes.

Q. You have no direct communication with the minister ?—A. Certainly I have, if the minister calls me in and consults me; but my proper channel of communication is through the deputy minister.

Q. Now, Colonel Anderson, if you will pardon me for saying so, it occurs to me in my view—I may be quite wrong—that where an expenditure is to the amount that you speak of, $10,000, and whether or not that total expenditure should be made, my view is that that ought not to be a matter merely of difference of honest opinion. It is a large amount ?—A. I do not agree with you in that.

Q. You do not?—A. For this reason, that I do not see why two men cannot differ about that. One man will take the ground that he will get the best, no matter what it costs, and the other man will say, ' I will get no better than is absolutely required and save money.'

By Hon. Mr. Cassels:

Q. What was done in that case; was it changed or not?—A. I do not recollect at the moment. I do not think it was changed.

By Mr. Watson:

Q. In a case of that kind, what would become of the lantern that was disused?—A. Our usual practice is to dismantle it carefully and use it at some minor station.

Q. I see. It is not rendered useless?—A. Not unless it is broken in being taken apart or is old enough to be thrown aside.

Q. In a case such as this, where your recommendation was for its continuance as being sufficient, if it was discontinued, what would become of it?—A. It would be utilized elsewhere.

Q. And to advantage?—A. Yes, to advantage.

Q. Then, would the purchase of a new lantern mean a loss to the country of the value of the first lantern?—A. No, not altogether.

Q. Would it mean any loss?—A. Well there would be——

Q. Is there a demand for supplies, a continuous demand for supplies of lanterns? —A. Yes.

Q. And would a lantern displaced or disused at points such as that be in demand for use in other places?—A. Yes, our plans are always to utilize things of that kind.

Q. Now, in connection with that particular matter about which there was a difference, do you know of any possibility of gain personally to Mr. Fraser by reason of the change and his recommendation of a new lantern?—A. I have no knowledge.

Q. Have you any ground for suspicion?—A. I have——

Q. It is only fair to say that you seem to hesitate?—A. I have no knowledge whatever.

By Hon. Mr. Cassels:

Q. Where would the new lantern be purchased?—A. I think that most of that apparatus is purchased either from Chance Brothers of Birmingham or from a French firm

Q. Who would make the purchase—A. The commissioner of lights branch.

Q. He would make the purchase?—A. Yes.

Q. So that if the new lighting apparatus had been put in at this particular place, the purchase for the new light would have gone through him?—A. Yes.

Q. You would have had no supervision over that?—A. No.

Q. In your view, the light then in existence was good enough?—A. No, not the light. I was in favour of a better illuminating apparatus, but I was in favour of an illuminating apparatus that would fit into the existing lantern.

Mr. WATSON.—The continuance of the lantern?

Hon. Mr. CASSELS.—Suppose your ideas had been carried out, would the difference in cost over and above the carrying out of your notion have been $10,000?—A. Yes, that is my impression.

Q. In other words, if they had carried out your new illuminating light, as between that and Mr. Fraser's recommendation, the difference would be about $10,000? —A. Yes.

Mr. WATSON.—The difference would be about $10,000?—A. Yes.

Q. Now, to be more specific. I think—pardon me if I remind you—you have not yet answered my question as to whether you had any ground for suspicion or any improper motive on his part?—A. Suspicion is not evidence.

Q. No, but I am asking?

Hon. Mr. CASSELS.—What Mr. Watson wants is this, Colonel Anderson: Here is a recommendation which involves an expenditure of $10,000, which you thought unnecessary under the circumstances?—A. Yes.

Q. Well, at the present moment we will assume Mr. Fraser thought that necessary, that is, whilst not necessary, yet, in the interests of navigation work, it should be done. Had you any reason for refusing to give concurrence based solely on the excessive cost, or had you any information that too much was being paid for it?—A. It was based solely on the want of need for so great a change, so radical a change.

Q. Then, what Mr. Watson wants is this: Had you any idea or thought that the alleged need was going to something that Mr. Fraser was to benefit from? That is what the point of the question is?

Mr. WATSON.—You see, Colonel, you make it more embarrassing, if I may say so——

By Hon. Mr. Cassels :

Q. It is very embarrassing, we all understand that, for any one in the department to give evidence against other officials, but nevertheless, we have to get at the truth. You have to bury your feelings and give us what you really thought.—A. I am not trying to fence.

Q. I am not saying that for a moment. I appreciate that. But if you have any information, no matter how distasteful, let us have it?—A. I have no information.

By Mr. Watson :

Q. Colonel, the question I have asked I think is a fairly simple one As to whether or not you had any grounds for suspicion?—A. No, I had no grounds for suspicion.

Q. As to any improper motive on his part?—A. I had no grounds for suspicion.

Q. None whatever?—A. Nothing more than, as I said before, hearsay.

Q. Nothing other than hearsay. Then is that based upon reasonable foundation, that hearsay, what you regarded as reasonable foundation?—A. That I cannot tell you. What I mean is this : You take that particular instance. I had no suspicion whatever that Mr. Fraser was impelled by any dishonest motive in the matter.

By Hon. Mr. Cassels :

Q. Had you reason from other and different things from this to suspect his honesty, and therefore——

By Mr. Watson :

Q. It would lead him to this?—A. Well, sir, I am in this position : If I have a general suspicion that the man is extravagant, that he is purchasing unnecessarily large quantities, unnecessary expense on apparatus, that is not any evidence, that is not a thing I can stand here and condemn a man on.

Hon. Mr. CASSELS.—It seems to me that if you see a man, extending over perhaps a year, two years or three years, buying very extravagantly, purchasing articles not needed, and so on, you might naturally form a conclusion in your mind that there was something behind which led to it. You might or might not, I do not know.

By Mr. Watson :

Q. Then, that makes it necessary, Colonel, that we should be possessed of the instance that you refer to so as to enable us to put one and one together and two and two together to reach a conclusion. Now, you say in this particular instance, as I understand you, that you had no ground for suspicion as to improper motives ?—A. I can furnish no concrete instance. What I am trying to explain is this : That if I have any suspicion that the man was unduly extravagant with dishonest motives, it is nothing more than an impression ; I cannot give any concrete instance that would support that.

Q. Well, then, you can go this far, I think, from what you have said, that you can give instances where in your opinion there has been extravagant expenditure recommended by him. Now, let us have another instance than the one you have mentioned. While you are thinking and leading up to it it may assist : Have you reported to the deputy minister, the head, under the minister of the department, your view as to extravagant appropriations or expenditure by Mr. Fraser ?—A. Yes, I have on several occasions.

Q. You have on several occasions reported to the deputy minister ? Have you made any such report to the minister ? I am speaking now, if you please, of the present minister ?—A. I cannot be sure.

Q. You cannot be sure ?

By Hon. Mr. Cassels :

Q. Were these repairs in writing?—A. Some of them certainly are.

By Mr. Watson :

Q. That is to whom, to the deputy minister ?—A. To the deputy minister, yes.

Q. Have you ever made any such report to the present minister that you recollect of ?—A. I cannot think of any.

Q. Or any verbal report to him ?—A. I cannot think of any at the moment.

Q. Perhaps after luncheon you will be able to refresh your recollection, because we want to know about these matters. Did you make any such report to the former minister, Mr. Préfontaine ?—A. Yes, I did.

Q. You did ; in writing ?—A. I think so.

Q. In writing. Many such reports ?—A. I do not recollect at the moment.

Q. Well, then, to his predecessor, that would be the late Mr. Sutherland, did you make any such reports?—A. If I am not mistaken, Mr. Fraser was appointed commissioner of lights by Mr. Préfontaine, and in Mr. Sutherland's day he was not in the position.

Q. I see. Then you think you have made reports in writing to Mr. Préfontaine, and you will be able to give a record of those, will you, by reference to your department——?—A. I shall try.

Q. During lunch time, because that is important. And you say, as I understand, you made frequent reports, I rather gather, to that effect to the deputy minister; is that so?—A. Verbally, certainly.

Q. Verbally, certainly; yes. Then, have you any record in your books or in your office bearing upon those reports or upon the occasion of the reports?—A. Well, I doubt it, for this reason, that I keep no records, the records are kept in the general records branch of the department.

3262—3

Q. I see. Then, you will appreciate that, if possible, we would like to have the dates and the occasions of such reports, if you will try meantime and refresh your recollection, will you?—A. Yes.

Q. Then just another general question. Have you made any such reports with regard to any other official than Mr. Fraser, that is, as to what you deem extravagant expenditure?—A. I think not.

Q. Eh?—A. I think not.

Q. You think not?—A. I think not.

Q. I would like very much if you could go further than that and rememoer with accuracy if you can, because that may be important?—A. It is a very difficult thing to answer in this way. I was not expecting any such——

Q. I know. I had not an opportunity——?—A. Any such examination.

Q. And my learned friend, Mr. Perron, had not an opportunity of consultation with you about that?—A. And I was not anyway prepared for it.

Q. But you will have an opportunity?—A. I have no recollection.

Q. Not with regard to any other official?—A. No; subject to correction if it is brought to my memory.

Q. Then, apart from such reports, did you have in your mind from information that you possessed that any other official was recommending extravagant expenditure? —A. Not to my recollection.

Q. Not to your recollection. I see. Well, now, can you now, without further reference, give the subject matter of such expenditure that you deemed extravagant, the recommendation of which you deemed extravagant? You have spoken of the one, the Flower Ledge. Now, any other instance that is in your mind?—A. Nothing in connection with my own branch.

Q. Nothing in connection with your own branch, nothing at all?—A. Subject to refreshing my memory.

Q. Subject to further review. That may well be so, I quite understand. Then, what are your relations with Mr. Fraser, your personal relations, always friendly?— A. My personal relations are extremely unsatisfactory. I have not spoken to the man since he has been appointed.

Q. I see?—A. Except officially.

Q. Is there personal reason for that?—A. Yes.

Q. In connection with the performance of his duties as an officer or official?— A. Yes.

Q. In that connection. Then, that becomes important, that being so, I think?— A. I think it is of no importance.

Q. You think it is of no importance ?—A. No.

Q. Does that relationship bear at all in connection with his misconduct or ill-conduct?—A. Not at all.

Q. It is purely a matter of personal relation with you, you mean?—A. Yes; tnat is to say, I consider the way in which the man got his position was dishonourable, and I have considered him a dishonourable man, and I would not have anything to do with him.

Q. I see. That is in connection with the way in which he obtained his appointment?—A. Yes.

Q. That appointment, I think you said before, was under Mr. Préfontaine ?— A. Yes.

Q. Upon the recommendation of the deputy?—A. I have no idea.

Q. Then, what you have spoken of refers solely and entirely to that matter?—A. Yes.

Q. And in no way with what you deem misconduct, ill-conduct, apart from that as an official ?—A. No.

Q. I see. That relation has made it, perhaps, more difficult in business transactions between you and him ?—A. It certainly has not made it more pleasant.

Q. I suppose it would go as far as I say, it made it perhaps more difficult. Does the unpleasant relationship exist between any other official and you ?—A. No.

Q. Any one else at all ?—A. No one else at all.

Q. Then, just in connection with that, your relations with the deputy minister ? —A. Have always been friendly .

Q. Harmonious; I see. I did not ask you specifically, I wish to ask you about that so as to cover it before adjournment. I have asked you in regard to other officials. Have you, Colonel Anderson, any information or knowledge bearing upon the question of any irregularity or misconduct or want of conscience on the part of the deputy minister in the performance of his duties or any of them?—A. I have no knowledge.

Q. You have no knowledge ? Have you any information upon the point—do you distinguish between knowledge and information ?—A. I have no information.

Q. Can you give any assistance at all upon that subject ?—A. I am afraid not.

Q. You are afraid not ?—A. I do not know whether I should say 'afraid,' but I think not.

Q. You think not. Has anything come to your knowledge, directly or indirectly, in the department or outside the department, bearing on that, which you are able to speak of ?—A. Nothing.

Q. Well, then, it will be necessary to go through——

Hon. Mr. CASSELS.—How long do you want to adjourn for ?

Mr. WATSON.—Would your lordship mind if we adjourned until a quarter past two ?

Hon. Mr. CASSELS.—Very well. I want to ask one question for my own information. The deputy is who ?—A. Colonel Gourdeau.

Q. He has resigned, apparently, has he not?—A. I have no knowledge of his status at the moment.

Q. Has he charge of all the papers in connection with the whole of this department ?—A. I think as the permanent head of the department he has charge of all records.

Q. Since this investigation was mooted, to your knowledge have any papers been destroyed in the department ?—A. Not to my knowledge.

Q. You have no reason to suspect so. Everything will be produced, I mean so far as you know ?—A. So far as I know, yes.

(Adjourned from 12.45 to 2.15 p.m.)

By Mr. Watson :

Q. A subject, my lord, that was touched upon before the adjournment. I wish to ask one or two questions about.

Q. Colonel Anderson, you were asked before adjournment if you had any knowledge or information bearing upon the loss or destruction of any official documents or papers in the department. I understood you to say that you had not ?—A. I have not.

Q. Have you any information indirect upon the subject?—A. None whatever.

Q. Have you heard of anything of the kind ?—A. I have not.

Q. Have any statements been made, to your knowledge or in your presence, upon the subject ?—A. The only statement is a statement that I heard from my chief assistant, Mr. Fraser, to the effect that anonymous letters had been received by somebody, I don't know who, to the effect that the files had been tampered with.

Q. That is B. H. Fraser ?—A. Yes.

Q. And when did he say that to you ?—A. I think it was on Saturday.

Q. Saturday of this last week ?—A. Yes, certainly since my—yes, it must have been Saturday ; it was since my return to Ottawa.

Q. Will you please give me the whole of the conversation with him ?—A. I do not remember it. It was nothing more than the statement of a rumour.

Q. Yes. Did he show you an anonymous letter ?—A. He did not.

Q. Did he say who had received it ?—A. He did not—if he did, I forget it.

Q. You forget it ?—A. Yes.

Q. Did he say by whom the destruction had been made, how papers had gone astray or been destroyed ?—A. As far as I recollect the matter his statement was something like this : That an anonymous letter had been sent either to you or to his lordship, I do not remember whom, to the effect that the whole staff of the department were working after hours going over files and destroying everything incriminating.

Mr. WATSON.—I am sure, your lordship, I have not had any such communication.

Hon. Mr. CASSELS.—Neither have I.

The WITNESS.—The thing was the merest gossip.

By Mr. Watson:

Q. Is Mr. B. H. Fraser here?—A. Yes; that is he there (pointing).

Q. Do you know anything more about it?—A. No.

Q. Have you any ground of suspicion upon the subject?—A. Not the least.

Q. Have you any reason to suggest anyone in regard to that?—A. No.

Mr. WATSON.—Would your lordship mind if I ask the colonel to stand aside? I regard this as a matter of so much importance that I would like to get at the bottom of it. Mr. Fraser is here. Let us see what he has to say.

Hon. Mr. CASSELS.—Certainly.

BASIL H. FRASER, sworn.

By Mr. Watson :

Q. Mr. Fraser, I understand that you are assistant to the chief engineer ?—A. Yes, sir.

Q. Or, perhaps, you are assistant engineer?—A. I think the order in council said assistant chief engineer.

Q. And how long have you been in that office?—A. About twelve—I cannot remember just exactly how long that is.

Q. Twelve or fourteen years, were you going to say, or months?—A. I have been chief assistant some time—why, I think the order in council appointing me was——

Q. Ten or twelve years?—A. No, not so much. I think I took the position when Colonel Anderson left for some time; it must have been four or five years ago.

Q. I will have to call you later. I want to ask you at the present time about this matter of papers, and whether you have any information bearing upon the question as to destruction of papers in the department?—A. Nothing, except what Colonel Anderson has just said. I cannot remember where I heard it, but there was a rumour around my office—I have a large staff up there—that some such communication had been received.

Q. I want the information specifically stated, if you please, as distinct as you can state it?—A. The rumour was that the officials were up there at night removing papers from the official files, and I particularly—hearing such a rumour I particularly called the attention of every man on my staff, because we were working there procuring information for the purposes of this investigation, and I wanted everybody's attention particularly called to it, so that they could be brought forward if necessary to state if anything of the kind had been done.

Q. From whom did you hear that?—A. I could not tell you at this moment, but the rumour was going round.

Q. Can you mention any names?—A. I could not. There were so many stories flying round the department lately.

Q. That is your department?—A. Yes.

Q. Was it a man or woman?—A. I could not say. I am quite sure it must have been a man. I have no ladies in my branch at all.

Hon. Mr. CASSELS.—A woman would be likely to spread it.

Mr. WATSON.—Yes.

By Mr. Watson:

Q. Then have you any knowledge of any such act being done?—A. Certainly not.

Q. Eh?—A. Certainly not.

Q. Have you any ground or reason for suspicion?—A. Not in the slightest.

Q. In your department or any other department?—A. In mine or any other. In my own, hearing such a rumour, I was very particular to call everybody's attention to it in case that question might come up again.

Q. What did you say to Colonel Anderson?—A. Exactly what he told you.

Q. I want your own words, please?—A. I had heard there was an an anonymous letter received by somebody, I don't know who, stating that the officials of the department were busy fixing up the file, removing any documents that might be prejudicial to anybody. As near as I can remember this is the kind of general statement.

Q. An anonymous letter. Do you know by whom it was received, according to hearsay?—A. No, I have not any idea. It might have been any of the officials of the department or some of the commissioners or something of that kind.

Q. Would it be possible in your branch that that should be done without being known by you or Colonel Anderson?—A. Oh, I think so.

Q. It would be possible?—A. I think so.

Q. Would it be possible to detect any such omission or loss?—A. It might not if the——

Q. Do you say it might not?—A. It might not.

Q. Well, I would like to know about the system in your department, the system of record, and whether or not it is possible under that system that papers might be taken out of a file and you, as the assistant chief engineer, not be aware of the fact afterwards by reference to the file?—A. The file is in our possession only a very short time.

Q. Where is the file?—A. Kept in the record office.

Q. And who has charge of the record office?—A. Whoever is chief of the records branch. We only get the file for our particular uses for the time being and are required as soon as we have used it to return it. If anybody went and tore out a page, unless the file was paged it might be very difficult to trace it back.

Q. But by reference to the file and re-perusing it would you not become aware of some missing part?—A. Well, it is not absolutely certain.

Q. Not absolutely certain?—A. No.

Q. I see. Have you gone over the file since?—A. Well, there are some 30,000.

Q. Have you done so to any extent—you say you have been working at it?—A. Well, I have looked over some of the files.

Q. Has there anything come to your information or knowledge to lead you to suspect that any part has been taken away?—A. Not in the slightest degree. I have no reason to believe any such thing has been done.

Q. Then will you step aside for the present.

The DEPUTY MINISTER.—I want to get to the bottom of this if there is anything in it, my lord.

Hon. Mr. CASSELS.—Yes.

F. GOURDEAU, sworn:—

By Mr. Watson:

Q. Colonel Gourdeau, you are deputy minister?—A. Yes.

Q. And you have been in that office for a very long time?—A. Over 40 years

Q. I will have occasion to ask you to attend at a subsequent time on other matters. —A. Certainly, sir.

Q. I am going to ask you particularly now on this subject that has just been referred to?—A. Yes.

Q. It has been stated that there is a rumour that papers in your office or in the department have disappeared or are disappearing and being destroyed. If anything of the kind has occurred or should occur, would you in the ordinary course be aware of it?—A. No; but it would be found out.

Q. How would it be found out?—A. Anybody knowing the system of correspondence in the department would see it is absolutely impossible to remove any document from a file on account of the way in which it is treated. For instance, a letter is received in the department, and there is double entry; there is the day book and there is what they call the matter book—I don't exactly know the name—but as soon as that letter reaches the correspondent there is a note taken on the subject, the name of the writer and whatever it is, the document in itself, so that there is a double check. Then that is put on the file, and it is a matter there that it is impossible to remove.

Q. So that apart from the particular document, letter, contract or otherwise——? —A. Yes.

Q. There is an entry of record referring to that?—A. A double entry, sir, so as to be absolutely sure. It is utterly impossible to tamper with it, unless it is burned, unless the file is burned, then you would know the file had disappeared.

Q. Then, let me understand this: Everything is supposed to be in the file, is that right?—A. Certainly.

Q. Then, apart from the file, have you a written record of——?—A. A complete, an absolute record.

Q. Listen, please. Have you a written record of everything that is contained in each file?—A. Yes.

Q. You have?—A. Yes.

Q. So that by reference to that record you could tell by examination if anything was missing?—A. At once. You would only have to indicate what file. Mr. Mc-Cleneghan, the officer in charge of the records, is here. I think he will bear me out.

Q. So, in order to make the destruction effectual, it would have to be of the record as well as the file, that is, the record book?—A. Yes, and have to be done by a person not knowing the seriousness of the matter and not at all acquainted with the ways of the department, because he would know that it could not be done, it would be found out, it is utterly impossible.

Q. Now, have you any information or suspicion of any such attempted act or acts by anyone?—A. Not the slightest, not the slightest, because in the preparation——

Q. Have you heard any such rumour?—A. No. I heard it this morning when the gentleman came up to the office.

Q. Then, have you any knowledge at all, directly or indirectly, of any such act? --A. No, none whatever.

Q. You of course, and everyone else are aware that it is a most serious offence, a crime under the code?—A. Yes.

Q. And if anything of the kind occurs it would be necessary to place the matter in the hands at once of the Crown Attorney?—A. Certainly.

Q. Then, have you anything to lead you to give information on the subject?—A. No. If I had, I would have reported to the minister at once, because I am the officer responsible, as the deputy minister, for the correspondence itself, and if I heard any such thing I would have reported it at once.

Q. Who is your immediate assistant?—A. Mr. Stanton.

Q. In the department?—A. Yes.

Q. Has he a knowledge of the records?—A. Oh, he knows perfectly well the system.

Q. And who is the official?—A. Mr. McCleneghan.

Q. Then, have you any knowledge of destruction of any papers or entry whatever? —A. None whatever.

Q. With respect to yourself, the minister or any official?—A. No official, minister or myself.

Q. Or any past minister or official?—A. No.

Q. That will do.

By Hon. Mr. Cassels:

Q. Have you destroyed any of your private papers within the last two months?— A. Oh yes. Private letters and all that kind, but nothing bearing on the department.

Q. I am just asking you the question?—A. Yes.

Q. Were those letters up in the department when they were destroyed?—A. My secretary was with me when I was destroying——

Q. I am not asking you that. I am just asking you whether those were letters or papers in the department?—A. Nothing referring to the department.

Q. I am not asking you that. They were up there, in point of fact?—A. Yes, with my private papers.

Q. Did you go over those with your secretary?—A. Yes.

Q. And were many papers destroyed between you and your secretary?—A. No.

Q. Private papers?—A. No.

Q. To what extent was the destruction?—A. I could not tell.

Q. How long were you occupied in going over and destroying them?—A. Oh, it was during the office hours, I was just getting my drawers emptied.

Q. I just wanted to see. There might be a distinction between official papers and private papers.

Mr. WATSON.—Yes, my lord. That did not occur to me.

By Mr. Watson:

Q. Now, in connection with what his lordship has asked, did these private papers have any relation to anyone who had business with the department?—A. No.

Q. Were those documents or letters from any contractor or anyone who had business relations?—A. Absolutely not.

Q. Eh?—A. Absolutely not, no.

Q. Then, they were papers of what character?—A. Oh, receipts of accounts and private letters. My secretary is here and can verify that.

Q. Private letters?—A. Yes; letters that had gone through the hands of my secretary, too.

Q. Have you been in the habit of receiving private communications?—A. In connection with?

Q. With departmental matters?—A. No. I may mention whatever private letters were received where official mention might have been made of something, they were transferred by my secretary before I had seen them to the correspondence and treated by him.

Q. Then, are letters sometimes addressed to you individually, distinct from your official capacity, in connection with departmental matters?—A. No.

Q. Eh?—A. No.

Q. Then, have you ever received personal communications from contractors or others dealing with the department?—A. No. Whatever letters I would have received from them would go on the file.

Q. I see. Are you sure of that?—A. I am perfectly sure.

Q. Were any such letters destroyed?—A. No.

Q. Has anything been destroyed that bears upon departmental matters?—A. No.

Q. Or upon your conduct?—A. No.

Q. Or the conduct of any official?—A. None whatever.

Mr. WATSON.—Anything further, my lord?

Hon. Mr. CASSELS.—No.

Mr. WATSON.—Then, your secretary.

ANGELA H. THOMAS, sworn.

By Mr. Watson:

Q. Mrs. Thomas, I understand you are the secretary of the deputy minister?—A. Yes, sir; I suppose you call it that, stenographer.

Q. How long have you been in that position?—A. I have been 11 years in the department, 11 years last February, and with the exception of a few months when I first came there, all the rest of the time I have been in the deputy minister's secretary's room.

`. I see. I may have occasion to ask you to return upon other matters later. Meantime I wish to know from you whether or not you have any information, direct or indirect, upon the subject of destruction of papers in the department?—A. No, sir, except what I heard in Mr. Perron's office the other day, that there was a sort of rumour.

By Hon. Mr. Cassels:

Q. Whose office?—A. Mr. Perron's office.

By Mr. Watson:

Q. What did you hear?—A. I simply heard the rumour that people were destroying documents off the files.

Q. Whom did you hear that from?—A. In Mr. Perron's room.

Q. From whom?—A. I heard Mr. Perron talking with Mr. McCleneghan, chief of the record room, and he was asking if such a thing was possible. I was doing secretarial work for Mr. Perron.

Q. Mr. Perron, who is counsel here, was asking Mr. McCleneghan?—A. If such a thing could be possible for any official to remove documents off the files. I heard it in that way, sir.

Q. What did Mr. McCleneghan say?—A. As far as I heard Mr. McCleneghan say, he thought it would be an impossibility. He said that if anything were removed off the official file that the register they had in the record room, any person turning up this register could verify everything that should be on a certain file, and if anything was removed he could verify that from the register. That is what I understood him to say.

Q. That was a matter of inquiry by Mr. Perron, as counsel, of Mr. McCleneghan? —A. That is the way I understood it.

Q. Then did you hear anything else about it?—A. No.

Q. Nothing else?—A. No.

Q. Then, have you any personal knowledge of anything being done?—A. None whatever.

Q. If anything of the kind was done would you have information?—A. No. I am not connected with the records or anything connected with that.

Q. Well, if anything was destroyed in the department of the deputy minister you would know?—A. You mean private documents?

Q. Of any kind?—A. I do not know. I cannot say anything of the official. Private documents I know, there have been some destroyed.

Q. What do you mean by private documents, please?—A. Personal things, private letters of the deputy minister's, entirely personal matters we file there and nothing else, sir.

Q. I do not understand what is meant in the department by the expression 'private document.' I do not see what a private document has to do with departmental work myself?—A. No, it has nothing whatever to do with it.

Q. Then what do you mean by the reference to private documents?—A. Well, any matters from his relatives, any matters concerning his own private personal things. You understand what I mean.

Q. I see. What had you to do with those matters?—A. We usually file the deputy minister's private correspondence in our room.

Q. You are speaking of yourself and someone else?—A. We are always two or three in our room. I am the longest there now, but there has always been two or three in our room, and when I am not there, of course, the other clerk does the work.

Q. You mean those personal and private letters he received passed through your hands?—A. They always pass through our hands.

Q. Do they always?—A. As far as I remember they always have.

Q. Do you make any record of those?—A. Simply nothing, except to answer the letters and file them away.

Q. Personal letters?—A. Yes.

Q. Is there any record made of those?—A. Nothing, except back them, put from whom it is, and file them away alphabetically; that is all.

Q. Who opens the private correspondence?—A. In our room?

Q. You do?—A. Yes; that is our orders.

Q. Do you mean personal, private letters are not opened by Colonel Gourdeau himself?—A. Not as a rule. Our instructions are these: Of course, several letters come there to be opened by us, which are, of course, departmental, but anything addressed to Colonel Gourdeau, Deputy Minister, Marine and Fisheries, come to our office—our instructions are to open the mail the moment it comes to us in the morning, and anything departmental or official, anything relating to departmental matters, we hand in immediately to the records; anything personal from relatives we hand in to the deputy minister. Formerly we used to hold all the mail until he came, and he used to glance through it. Then he gave instructions, to avoid delay, not to bring the departmental mail to him, except anything we knew he wanted to look at immediately and then bring it to him to see.

Q. How long have you pursued that course of opening personal communications? —A. As far as I remember we always did that.

Q. You mean 10 or 11 years?—A. For 10 years anyway.

Q. Ten years past?—A. Yes.

Q. Then, you mean to say you have personal knowledge of his private correspondence?—A. Well, everything passes through our hands, sir; yes.

Q. Is there any class or any kind of letter from any source that you received different instructions about, that you did not open?—A. No, sir. There are a couple of letters I know, say, for instance, from his brother, I know his handwriting, and for that reason if I know it is from his brother I do not open it. I simply pass it into the deputy minister. Anything else we open in our room, whether marked personal or not. The deputy always allows us to open it and bring it in to him.

Q. Let me ask you—I did not anticipate this—have you in any of this correspondence of a personal nature seen any reference to departmental matters?—A. Departmental?

Q. Yes; that is, official matters?—A. Well, in this connection I may say this: A member may write to the minister in regard to a certain thing, and before they answer this member perhaps the official minister may request the deputy minister to please write to the agent and ascertain if those are the facts and what reply I can give to the member. In that case the deputy minister would write privately to the agent. Some things like that. Of course, they affect the department in a way.

Q. I see. From some agent?—A. Yes, and so on. Sometimes a minister wants certain information with regard to a matter, and before anything is done officially sometimes the minister may want to have the agent's opinion, or the captain of a vessel about a certain trip they want to make for the Governor General, and so on. Sometimes they are not put on the official file, and we have got heaps, I may say, of such letters as that. You may perhaps call them semi-official, but they are, of course, written privately, not officially.

Q. Now, have you seen letters from contractors or others outside dealing with the department written to the deputy minister?—A. No, sir. Anything written by outsiders, everything goes on the private file.

Q. Have you ever known any exception to that?—A. No, sir.

Q. Are you sure?—A. I am quite—well, of course, I cannot say perhaps for the last ten or twelve years, but we have the deputy minister's correspondence there for six years back, everything we have stored away, and of course anybody referring to that can see exactly what is in there. I cannot remember every single letter written for the last ten years.

Q. Now, have you any knowledge of the destruction of any papers, private or otherwise, in the department?—A. Well, the only recollection I have of any documents being destroyed is this: When Colonel Gourdeau expected to get his leave and Mr. Debrou was coming in as acting deputy minister, the deputy minister, of course, was ridding out quite a few things from his room.

Q. When was that, please, how long ago?—A. Possibly four or five weeks ago. I cannot say exactly, somewhere around there.

Q. Then what occurred, please?—A. I know I helped the deputy minister on two or three occasions to take old things out, some documents he had for twenty or thirty years, things about the formation of the Princess Louise Dragoon Guards, and lots bearing on that. Everything he burned to my knowledge were things he had for twenty years; nothing of recent date was burned to my knowledge, nothing whatever.

Q. Did you have personal knowledge of what was destroyed?—A. Well, I cannot say, perhaps, every document, but the deputy minister took up, say a bundle of old stubs, 1875 to 1879, and some old cash books, 1879 to 1880. He said it was no use keeping these, and we burned them.

Q. Yes. Was anything destroyed that had any bearing upon departmental matters?—A. Not to my knowledge, sir, nothing whatever.

Q. Or in connection with any transactions with anyone whatever about departmental matters?—A. Not to my knowledge, sir, not a thing, not to my knowledge.

Q. Mrs. Thomas, is there any reservation at all by you in respect to that?—A. No, sir, none whatever.

Q. Anything else, my lord?

Hon. Mr. CASSELS.—Yes. I will ask a question or two.

By Hon. Mr. Cassels:

Q. Who judged, Mrs. Thomas, whether the letter was official or supposed to be private when you opened those letters?—A. Well, if they were marked personal and of an entirely personal nature, I would judge whether they were private, and sometimes possibly——

Q. I did not quite, perhaps, catch your meaning, but did you say private letters coming from a member of parliament?—A. I meant from the minister, sir.

Q. Well, from the minister?—A. And requesting the deputy minister to write a personal letter.

Q. The minister would write a personal letter stating that some member had been asking in regard to some person?—A. No, excuse me, your lordship. I say sometimes the minister might receive a personal letter or receive a letter from a member, and perhaps they thought they could not get the information readily in the department, and perhaps in connection with a trip, say for the Governor General, or some such thing—I can't remember everything just now—he would request the deputy minister to write the agent or captain of a certain vessel and so on, and ask if it were possible to do such and such a thing, before the minister would reply to that letter.

Q. That would be called a private letter?—A. Yes.

Q. And that would be answered privately?—A. Yes.

Q. That would have relation to trips on those steamers?—A. Various matters like that.

Q. Perhaps to the purchase of supplies on those steamers for the comfort of the Governor General?—A. I cannot say.

Q. You cannot speak on that. But that class of letter, you say, would be marked private?—A. I cannot say whether about supplies, but anything like that, any information they wanted to get privately from the agent or captain and so on, perhaps before the minister would decide a certain thing or take any action.

Q. And those letters were private letters?—A. They are all up at the department.

Q. Are they on the official records or the private file?—A. If private letters they are on the private file.

Q. The private file there?—A. Yes.

By Mr. Watson:

Q. They are there now?—A. As far as I know we have all the deputy minister's private correspondence for the past six years.

Q. It is there now?—A. Yes. About six years ago, for want of room, we did burn some things, but to my knowledge nothing has been burned for six years; we have all the private correspondence.

Q. I see. And that can be examined and inspected?—A. Yes.

Q. And may be produced?—A. Yes, sir.

Q. So that it will be available for inspection?—A. Yes, exactly. Accounts, the deputy minister's file, and so on; everything is there, that can be inspected.

James E. McCleneghan, sworn.

By Mr. Watson:

Q. What is your position?—A. I am in charge of the records of the Marine and Fisheries Department.

Q. The records?—A. Yes, sir.

Q. How long have you been in that office?—A. I have been——

Q. About?—A. Well, about 23 years.

Q. Oh, a long time?—A. I have been 25 years in the department.

Q. You look a young man yet. When did you first hear any rumour or statement——A. The first time that I heard——

Q. With regard to the destruction of papers, when?—A. The first rumour I had heard was from Mr. Perron.

Q. When was that?—A. Last week.

Q. What did you hear?—A. Mr. Perron stated to me that he had been approached in Montreal with the statement that this whole affair would be a farce, that the clerks were still in the department, and they were manipulating the files and removing things, destroying evidence of guilt, and all that sort of thing, and he asked me if it was possible.

Q. Mr. Perron stated that to you?—A. Yes; and he asked me if such a thing was possible. I stated a letter might be removed from the file, but it was a very dangerous proceeding, because we could detect it in the record room.

Q. You could detect it in the record room?—A. Yes.

Q. Then, what is the system?—A. The majority of the official letters addressed to the deputy minister are opened in the record room, and they are stamped with the date on it, and entered in a day book and numbered consecutively.

Q. Yes?—A. They are shown to the deputy or his representative and they are afterwards classified and attached to files. They are then entered in a register into the file number. It constitutes a double entry.

Q. So that, in addition to the file, there is a record in a book?—A. In the register.

Q. In a register?—A. In the file register.

Q. A record of the communication?—A. Yes. It is similar to a ledger, in accounting. It not only records the letter received, but the outgoing letter and the memorandum.

Q. That is a very extensive system, and a pretty burdensome one, I should think; however, that is a matter for yourself?—A. It is so.

Q. Perhaps that accounts for such a large staff?—A. No. There are six clerks in that room and they deal with 195 files in one day; that is, we get 195 communications, put them on file and index them.

Q. Now, you made an observation there that the 'majority' of the letters—what about the minority, what about the rest?—A. Well, the messenger, when he receives the mail in the morning, discriminates between what he considers official and what he considers private. Some letters in small envelopes that are not marked official, that are not in official envelopes addressed to the deputy minister, are handed in to the deputy minister's private secretary or to his room. If the deputy minister is absent—in fact, they are opened there and they are eventually sent to our room and recorded in the usual way, and all letters addressed to the minister officially are sent in, are opened in the minister's private—by his private secretary, and forwarded to the record room and entered in the same way.

Q. Then, have you any knowledge of what has been termed here private correspondence or private communications?—A. I have no knowledge at all with regard to private correspondence that Mrs. Thomas has referred to. I never saw, I do not know anything about it.

Q. Is there any correspondence directed to the deputy minister or to any one else which is of a personal or private nature bearing on departmental matters?—A. Well, letters addressed to the chief engineer—there are certain letters addressed to the chief engineer, to the commissioner of lights and to the accountant.

Q. Yes. Are those not opened by the staff in the usual way?—A. They are not opened in the record room; they are opened by the staff in those various departments.

Q. I see?—A. These letters are eventually sent to our room and entered. When we get them we stamp them with the date we receive them, and enter them in our day book and treat them in the usual way, and they are attached to the file.

Q. Such as are sent back to you?—A. Such as reach us.

Q. There may be letters received by you that do not come back to your place or knowledge?—A. Yes. There would be letters, but I would suppose they would be strictly private. If they want them to be treated or have any bearing on the file, they must go on the file in order to effect it.

Q. Then, have you knowledge of any attempt to destroy?—A. I have no knowledge of any attempt.

Q. Have you heard anything except the communication made to you by Mr. Perron?—A. That is the first. I was surprised at that statement.

Q. Is there any foundation for it, as far as you know?—A. No foundation whatever.

Q. And you say if anything did occur bearing upon departmental matters, that it would be easy of discovery?—A. Easy of discovery.

By Hon. Mr. Cassels:

Q. With departmental papers on the file?—A. We could compare the file with the register record, and then if we had sufficient suspicion, if we thought a paper was put on recently——

By Mr. Watson:

Q. What is that?—A. If a paper was put on recently that we had reason to suppose was not there, that is a new addition to the file, the letter number, we could verify that by examining the day book; because they·would have to forge a letter number, because each letter is entered and numbered consecutively. ·

Q. I see. Then have you any personal knowledge of private communications by the deputy minister?—A. I have no personal knowledge.

Q. Have you ever seen any such?—A. No, I never saw them.

Q. Do you know anything about the destruction of any such letters?—A. I do not know anything about it, except what I heard here to-day.

Q. And is there any information you could give, is there anybody else than those I have asked now to appear before his lordship in the department?—A. My first assistant can corroborate.

Q. Would he know anything but what you know?—A. He would know nothing different.

Q. You have first knowledge?—A. Yes.

Q. You have the best knowledge?—A. He is almost equal in every respect to that; and the third assistant—in fact, the files pass through three or four hands.

Q. They pass through your hands?—A. Through my hands. Every departmental file in the Marine branch is examined by both myself and the third assistant before it is put away.

Q. Is there any reason to think your assistant would have any knowledge you have not?—A. I have no reason to think so.

Q. Because I do not wish to take up the time of the commissioner unnecessarily.

Mr. WATSON.—Does your lordship think it necessary to call him?

Hon. Mr. CASSELS.—No. The real point is this : What goes to the official records are there, no doubt; the point is, whether anything that was not official, that might bear on this inquiry, reached the record office.

Mr. WATSON.—That is another matter.

Mr. PERRON.—We wanted to intimate to your lordship that nothing could be destroyed. I made sure when I heard this rumour, I wanted to know whether it was possible. ·

Hon. Mr. CASSELS.—If anything went to the official record it would probably be there.

Mr. PERRON.—That is what we wished to make sure of.

Hon. Mr. CASSELS.—The thing is, if not official the paper or document might go in the way Mrs. Thomas suggested, and not be forthcoming.

Mr. PERRON.—Your lordship will understand that as soon as I was made aware of this I wanted to find out whether it was really possible to destroy any of the records without its being detected. I sent for Mr. McCleneghan to find out of it really could be done, and I found out it could not be.

F. GOURDEAU, recalled.

By Mr. Watson :

Q. With regard to correspondence that is on file and is departmental, I want to ask you plainly and distinctly whether or not anything has ever been received by you bearing upon departmental matters, directly or indirectly, that has not been made of record and put on the files ?—A. No ; I absolutely state that nothing of the kind has been done.

Q. Then, is it possible——A. Will you excuse me, sir ? That was one of my reasons for asking my secretary to open my correspondence, every single letter, there was no restriction. While she kept a few letters I recived from my brother—she knew his handwriting perfectly well—I might have received two or three, but outside of that I wished every letter to be opened, and if there was anything pertaining to business, to be sent right into the room.

Q. What I wanted to know as to the fact——A. Yes, sir.

Q. And without any possible reservation at all——A. Yes.

Q. Whether any letters have been received by you of a private nature that bear directly or indirectly upon your conduct as deputy minister or as official——A. Yes.

Q. Or that bear upon departmental matters ?—A. Yes.

Q. That are not put upon file and made of record ?—A. No.

Q. Do you say no ?—A. No.

Q. You say no. Then all matters of that kind are still on file, Mrs. Thomas says? —A. They must be, certainly.

Q. Have any such letters been destroyed ?—A. No, no, no.

Q. Then I will have occasion to call you again.

By Hon. Mr. Cassels :

Q. I would just like to ask you a question, Colonel Gourdeau ?—A. Yes, sir.

Q. As I understood Mrs. Thomas, she discriminated between what was official and what was non-official. Now, she says letters would come in from the minister stating he had received a personal request from a member of parliament in regard to certain matters in the department ?—A. Yes.

Q. Those she did not treat as official ?—A. Yes.

Q. Those she gave to you ?—A. Yes.

Q. Are those letters still in existence, or have any been destroyed ?—A. They must be in existence. I had no reason to destroy them.

Q. Where should they be, on your private files ?—A. Kept by Mrs. Thomas herself.

Q. They ought to be there ?—A. Yes.

By Mr. Watson:

Q. Have you any knowledge of the destruction of any such papers as those ?—A. No.

Q. That will do. Then we will have an opportunity of further search and getting that file. And Mrs. Thomas—are you there ? Would you be kind enough to get that file in preparation so that we may have it here for precaution and production ?

Mrs. THOMAS.—They are not on file, but in separate bundles.

Q. Have them all collected so as to be available to be produced here to-day.

Mrs. THOMAS.—Yes, sir.

Mr. WATSON.—Unless there is something else that occurs to your lordship, I will proceed with Colonel Anderson.

Hon. Mr. CASSELS.—No.

Mr. WATSON.—I was very glad to hear what has been said.

Hon. Mr. CASSELS.—I have only asked a few questions to bring out the matter clearly.

Mr. WATSON.—This is an exceedingly serious matter.

Hon. Mr. CASSELS.—According to Mrs. Thomas' statement, you see, there may be private requests coming from contractors or others wanting to sell goods and who want to know whether they cannot get help, or that sort of thing. We do not know whether that went on the official file or not. That will develop.

Mr. WATSON.—We will have that file produced at once, my lord.

WILLIAM F. ANDERSON, recalled.

By Mr. Watson:

Q. Then, in respect to the same matter, Colonel Anderson, have you made any statement to any one as to information you had received about destruction of papers or possible destruction of papers ?—A. I have not.

Q. You have not made any statement to any one?—A. I made no statement.

Q. I see. And have you any information bearing upon the subject?—A. Not one word.

Q. Not one word; I see. Have you any ground for suspicion upon that subject? —A. None whatever.

Q. Now, you were good enough to say before the adjournment for luncheon that you might have heard of matters that would carry with them grounds for suspicion against the good conduct of some officials. I am sure that you desire to give every possible assistance and information——?—A. I do.

Q. In regard to the matter. I am sure you do. Then I would like to know, if you will be good enough to state, what information you may have received, even by hearsay or otherwise, bearing upon that matter of want of good conduct or proper conduct as to any of the officials?—A. I do not think there is anything I can tell you with regard to that. You understand perfectly that the air is full all the time, all the time. It has always been the case ever since I have been a public servant that there are rumours about in the air all the time imputing motives to this man, that man and the other man.

Q. Now, then, Colonel Anderson, my learned friend and I are here to assist his lordship in endeavouring to fix that or to clear it up so that it may be solved, so that the truth may be known. Now, we want your assistance at that, if you please?—A. Yes, but it is no assistance to you to mention idle rumours that——

Q. It may help to lead us to ascertain the truth, even if you do not know it?—A. I think I have heard accusations against every man in the department at one time or another, myself included.

Q. Yourself included; yes. Now, bearing upon maters that touch or concern the expenditure of public moneys, and in connection with that affecting their honesty, what have you heard in regard to the deputy minister? Would you rather that the deputy minister was not here?—A. No.

Q. There are several officials here?—A. No, I have nothing to say that I am anxious any of them should not hear. And I may say this, I will not give what is nothing more than street rumours and say that they have any weight. What can I say? I have heard that every man in the department is a thief and a liar. That is no evidence. I cannot quote instances.

Q. Have you any reason to think that it applies properly to any one?—A. No, because I have no proof whatever; I have no reason.

Q. Of course, your long connection with the department and your intimate association with other officials should enable you to be a fairly good judge of these matters, that is, to know the truth pretty well. For that reason, I do not want to seem to press you unduly, but I want to know all you know, if you know anything about it?— A. I know nothing, I know nothing.

Q. That is your answer. Then, have you at any time made statements to any-one that you did know anything that would reflect upon any of the officials?— A. No. I never made a statement that I knew anything.

Q. Or that you heard statements that reflected upon the integrity of officials?— A. I am quite sure I said that.

Q. I see. You have said that?—A. Yes. But, my lord, I must protest against the line——

Q. I do not want to press you too closely.

By Hon. Mr. Cassels:

Q. I think, colonel, you are not bound to answer the question about rumours that you heard on the street charging this man, that man and the other man. If there is anything that you have heard that might help Mr. Watson to clear those men, let us know. Mr. Watson's position is this: He is not trying to convict men; he is trying to relieve them from the accusation under which they lie. That accusation appears in this blue-book, and the accusation has been made by rumours apparently. All Mr.

Watson is trying to do is to relieve those who are innocent and follow up the guilty, and if possible to try to shorten the investigation, I presume, by taking up the most flagrant cases. Now, if you can give any assistance we want it, although we are not taking away the character of these men?—A. My position is simply this: I can say conscientiously, and do say, that I know nothing of any cases of misconduct. If it comes down to a question of rumour, then the air is full of rumours.

Q. Have you heard of any rumours in your own department as to wrong-doing of any officials? I am not taking the street rumours, but rumours in your own official department?—A. Not based on any evidence.

Q. I do not ask if it be based on any evidence. Have you heard any rumour in the department, two or three men talking of someone doing this and someone doing that? While not evidence against them, it might help to clear them up?—A. I should be very loath, sir, to say anything against a man's character that must to a certain extent reflect on him, when it is merely the idle gossip of the street.

Q. You see, Mr. Watson is trying to clear up their character.

By Mr. Watson:

Q. I am trying to clear up or bring home to them misconduct, if it exists; either one or the other?—A. Is it not a fair position to accept my statement that I know nothing against them?

Q. I am not challenging your statement, Colonel Anderson, but I am just trying to pry in to see whether there is any possible reservation or anything you have a suspicion about, because we have to approach it from that standpoint. That is the only way we can get on to matters, to get information, by prying into these elements or matters of suspicion or doubt. Is there any matter of suspicion or doubt that you have any reason to think has a foundation in fact? Now, that is going just as far as I can possibly go, perhaps further than his lordship thinks I ought to go?—A. I think I must say to that that I do not know of anything.

Q. You do not know of anything; I see. Well, then, I take it that you are not in a position to assist us further directly in that way. Then, Colonel Anderson, you mentioned a matter in the forenoon that an official, Mr. J. F. Fraser, had procured his appointment in a dishonourable way—I think those are your words?—A. I think so.

Q. Yes. Now, that may be a matter of importance. I would like to know in what respect it was dishonourable and discreditable to the official?—A. In this way: In my opinion, the man was an assistant of mine. Without saying anything to me, without consulting me in any way, he was made commissioner of lights, and took over quite a portion of my duties, and put the work in such a position that it has been maimed ever since; and I considered that in the way he had accomplished this that he had not acted in a straightforward way. I thought that both of us as civil engineers should have been mindful of the ethics of the profession, and that in arranging for his promotion he should have consulted his chief. I also felt that he was put there for a purpose, and that that purpose was not an honourable purpose.

Q. I see?—A. My explanation of that is, that I believe that he was put there to exploit the use of—what is it you call it—carbide in the department.

By Hon. Mr. Cassels:

Q. What is that?—A. Carbide.

By Mr. Watson:

Q. Carbide?—A. Yes; that it was for the purpose of introducing and extending the use of acetylene gas in the department that he was put in there, and I was bitterly opposed to the introduction at that time under the circumstances which then existed, because I considered that the use of it was fraught with danger to life.

By Hon. Mr. Cassels:

Q. Was that carbide in the buoys?—A. In buoys and beacons, yes; and also to a certain extent in lighthouses.

By Mr. Watson:

Q. Now then, let us see, colonel. In the first place, you thought it was a breach of professional etiquette?—A. Yes.

Q. That is, as between you and him?—A. Yes; I said that.

Q. In the second place, you thought it was a matter of non-observance of professional honour between you and him?—A. That is the same thing.

Q. The same thing, you think. Well, it was not honourable. It leads a little bit further, I think, than a matter of etiquette.

Hon. Mr. CASSELS.—A breach of professional etiquette.

By Mr. Watson:

Q. Then you touch upon a matter of more importance. Those two are matters between you and him personally?—A. Yes; I said so before.

Q. You did. Then comes a different basis, more serious, if I may say so, as you no doubt think so, that you think he was placed there for a wrongful and improper purpose?—A. Yes.

Q. By whom?—A. Well, I always imagined—and it was only imagination, I have no proof that he was—that the influence that put him there was the influence that was interested in the sale and manufacture of calcium carbide.

Q. And define, please, the individual?—A. Well, I believe that Mr. T. L. Willson is the man principally interested. I believe it is a company.

Q. T. L. Willson; I see. Placed there in the interest of the company. Still, that is not reaching far enough, as you appreciate, because Mr. Willson could not place him there, could he?—A. I do not know.

Q. Whose wrongful act was it in placing him there?—A. I want to qualify that. Why wrongful?

Q. I understood you to say wrongful purpose?—A. The person who placed him there may not have acted wrongfully; the person who placed him may not have realized or appreciated the influences that were at work.

Q. I am glad to have the information you are giving, and I do not want to criticize your form of expression at all, but I thought you said he was placed there, you thought, for a wrongful purpose?—A. Very well. If Mr. Willson and his friends had sufficient influence with the then Minister of Marine to have the appointment made, that would not argue that the Minister of Marine or the Department of Marine was acting with any wrongful intention.

Q. I see. Then what minister was it that made the appointment?—A. Mr. Préfontaine.

Q. When was the appointment made?—A. I think it was in the autumn of 1903.

Q. Did you have any personal communications with Mr. Préfontaine on the subject?—A. I did.

Q. What were they?—A. I pointed out to him that in my opinion the plan would never work. I also pointed out that the division of authority would entail, in my opinion, a waste of energy in the working of the department.

Q. It was, of course, taking from you part of your jurisdiction?—A. Yes, and Mr. Préfontaine's reason for doing that was that he considered the work was too great for one man to perform.

Q. Too great for one man to perform?—A. Yes.

Q. Up to that time Mr. Fraser had been associated with you as your assistant?—A. Yes.

Q. Then you told him your views and differed with him in his result, the opinion that he had as to the duties being too onerous for you ?—A. Mr. Préfontaine, yes.

Q. Did you ?—A. Yes, very strongly.

Q. You did that very strongly; and you told him you thought the division would be disadvantageous ?—A. Yes.

Q. That the work could not be as efficiently well done ?—A. Yes.

Q. Anything else that you told him ?—A. Well, I think that was the purport of the communication.

Q. Did you tell him that there was any improper motive or purpose being served by that ?—A. I did.

Q. You did ?—A. I did.

Q. What did you tell him ? I want the whole facts.—A. I told him what I have told you, that in my opinion he was being put in there to exploit the use of calcium carbide.

Q. You told Mr. Préfontaine that ?—A. I did.

Q. You thought it was being done for that purpose ?—A. Yes.

Q. What was said to you ?—A. My recollection is that Mr. Préfontaine assured me it was not the case and that I might rest easy in the matter.

Q. Yes. Did you give Mr. Préfontaine any facts or evidence bearing upon that serious matter ?—A. I cannot recollect at this distance of time.

Q. Well, that would be a matter you might recollect. Was any information or statement given to him in writing ?—A. I have not been able to find a statement in writing, although I am almost positive that there is one.

Q. Did you receive any statement or letter from him that is in writing ?—A. I received a statement from him. I received a letter from him to the effect that he intended to make this change.

Q. Have you got that ?—A. Yes, I have it.

Q. Have you got it here ?—A. I am not quite sure.

Q. Will you look and see, please ?—A. I am quite sure I saw it at luncheon time.

Q. Yes. I asked you to be good enough to make such investigation as you could during the short time that was given you?—A. Yes. I can produce it, though—no, I am afraid I have not got it.

Q. Have you other letters there that bear upon it that you found?—A. Yes, to a certain extent.

Q. Now, let us come to them in a regular way. What have you got that bears upon it, this particular matter; is it of that change?—A. No, not with regard to that change.

Q. I do not want to get off that until we complete that. It is important to preserve some system. This bears upon some other matter?—A. It is a memorandum pointing out to the minister some difficulties that would result from the change.

Q. That is important?—A. After I had accepted the fact that the change had been made.

Q. I see. That bears upon it fairly directly. Then, will you let me see it, please. I will read it, my lord. (Reads memorandum; memorandum marked Exhibit No. 3.)

Q. Have you another one bearing upon that?—A. No, not upon that.

Q. Then we will come to that later. Did you get any answer to that?—A. I cannot tell you.

Q. At all events, you say you think you have a letter from the late minister?—A. That is prior to that, that is, announcing the change he proposed making.

Q. Prior to that, yes. Now, did you put it to Mr. Prefontaine directly that in your opinion there was attempted wrong-doing on the part of Mr. Willson?—A. I did.

Q. You did?—A. I did.

Q. Flatly in that way?—A. Flatly in that way.

Q. Did you speak to Mr. Willson about it?—A. I did not.

Q. Did you speak to the deputy minister about it?—A. I did.

Q. What did you say to him?—A. Practically the same thing. He has known my opinion on the matter for——

Q. Did you write him any letters?—A. Not that I know of—no.

Q. Eh?—A. Not that I am aware of.

Q. Did you receive any written communication from the deputy minister?—A. Not that I am aware of.

Q. What did the deputy minister say to you when you made that charge?—A. Well, my recollection is—but it is subject to correction—my recollection is that he advised me that it was the policy of Mr. Prefontaine to improve the lights, that he considered that the lights would be improved by using the acetylene, and that it was the settled policy of the department to use it.

Q. To improve the lights by the use of acetylene?—A. Yes.

Q. I see. Is that a matter about which difference of opinion might fairly and honestly exist?—A. Certainly.

Q. You think so?—A. I think so.

Q. Did you at that time doubt the sincerity of the opinion expressed as to the wisdom of introducing that, did you doubt the sincerity of that opinion?—A. I am not competent to answer that question after so long a lapse of time.

Q. You cannot. Was there anything that came to your knowledge that led you to believe or to suspect collusion or wrong-doing on the part of the minister or any one else in connection with the department upon the subject?—A. No; I——

Q. There was not, you say?—A. No.

Q. Did you have any view that it was other than an honest difference of opinion as between you and the minister and the deputy minister?—A. It was no more than a suspicion.

Q. Eh?—A. It was no more than a suspicion.

Q. Were there any grounds or any foundation that you can speak of for that suspicion?—A. Well, the only point was the always haunting suspicion that the commissioner, in my opinion, having been put there for a specific purpose, was carrying out the policy for which he was placed there.

Q. That is, the commissioner of lights?—A. Yes.

Q. And that was a suspicion that it was not rightly done, not for a proper purpose. Is that so?—A. In my opinion, the policy was a bad one; it was an expensive one and a dangerous one.

Q. Yes. And did you continue of the opinion that it was not only introduced, but maintained, for a wrongful purpose, or that it was a matter of difference of opinion?—A. I have always been of the same opinion, that it was done with the intention of exploiting the use of calcium carbide.

Q. And you are of that opinion still?—A. I am of that opinion still.

Q. And that carries with it a very serious charge and reflection.

Hon. Mr. CASSELS.—Mr. Watson, would you bring out what the carbide took the place of, and how the carbide came to be used after that appointment, in quantities or money or expenditure.

By Mr. Watson:

Q. Will you just answer that, Colonel Anderson? What did that take the place of, in the first place?—A. Acetylene gas made from the carbide in the gas buoys took the place of a gas made from petroleum.

By Hon. Mr. Cassels:

Q. Did it require a change of buoys?—A. Yes.

Q. Did it require new buoys?—A. Yes. When I say yes, I must qualify that. At first it was used in the buoys that were previously used for the Pintsch gas, but the system has since been changed probably—no, I won't say that either—it has since been changed, but between the time that it was introduced into the Pintsch buoys and the present there were at least two explosions with fatal results, which rather impressed upon the people in charge the necessity of making the change. The whole system has been changed.

By Mr. Watson:

Q. What whole system?—A. The whole system of using carbide in the buoys.

Q. Has been changed since it was introduced?—A. Has been changed since it was introduced.

Q. Now, the change to carbide, did that involve additional expense?—A. Yes.

Q. In what respect?—A. That the acetylene light is a more expensive light.

Q. To what extent?—A. I cannot tell you, because I have no figures at all with regard to acetylene light.

Q. Can you give any proportion of the difference in expense?—A. I cannot.

Q. Then, apart from the additional expense of the material itself, was there any other element of increase?—A. The necessity of changing all the apparatus.

Q. That became necessary, did it?—A. Yes.

Q. Did that involve much expense?—A. That work having been done in the branch of the commissioner of lights, I have no figures.

Q. You have no figures?—A. No.

Q. So that was a matter you always strongly disapproved of, personally?—A. I did.

Q. And what did the deputy minister say to you as to his opinion?—A. I have no recollection.

Q. Did he make any personal recommendation upon the subject, do you know?—A. I am not aware.

Q. You are not aware whether he did or not?—A. No.

Q. Did you discuss the matter with him upon the merits?—A. I certainly have mentioned it upon certain occasions.

Q. But would it not be proper for you to discuss it on its merits with the deputy minister?—A. Yes.

Q. Did you do so?—A. Yes.

Q. With what result as to his position?—A. With, so far as I know, with the result that he consulted the commissioner of lights with regard to my objections and was satisfied with the explanations of the commissioner of lights.

Q. He was satisfied?—A. Yes, sir.

Q. I see. Then, let me inquire what have been the personal relations between you and the deputy minister?—A. Quite cordial.

Q. Quite cordial?—A. Yes.

Q. Never anything to the contrary, no friction between you and him?—A. No.

Q. You spoke of misunderstandings, of difficulties you had with the commissioner of lights always existing?—A. Yes.

Q. Did anything of the kind occur between you and any other official?—A. No.

Q. Or between you and the minister?—A. No.

Q. Or either minister?—A. No.

Q. So, between you and the minister, Mr. Préfontaine, was there mutual confidence?—A. Of course, I always felt sore about the way he had acted with regard to the appointment of the commissioner of lights.

Q. I see. You were always somewhat personally aggrieved about that, on that subject?—A. Yes.

Q. I see. And you made that known ?—A. Did I ?

Q. I am asking you. Did you make that known to the minister ?—A. Not that I am aware of.

Q. Oh?—A. Oh, to the minister.

Q. Yes ?—A. Certainly I did.

Q. Yes. Well, did that affect the mutual confidential relations between you and him ?—A. Apparently not. Up to the day of his death he always consulted me with regard to my own work.

Q. And you always made all proper reports to him?—A. Yes, I did.

Q. And never withheld any information from him ?—A. Certainly not.

Q. And you said, before the adjournment, you have made reports in writing to him ?—A. Are you speaking of Mr. Préfontaine ?

Q. Yes.—A. And with regard to what ?

Q. With regard to the commissioner of lights and his work?—A. I do not remember anything.

Q. That he was extravagant in his expenditure was the subject, you said you had made reports to the minister upon that subject, that you considered the commissioner of lights was extravagant in his expenditure, according to my recollection. You will correct me if I am wrong ?—A. I do not remember the matter coming up in that way, I do not remember the matter coming up especially with Mr. Préfontaine.

Q. Well, did you make your report to any one else ?—A. The matter has come up in some instances within the last year or two, that matter of the Flower Ledge I referred this morning.

Q. Now, did you find any reports in writing ?—A. I found that one with regard to Flower Ledge (producing).

Q. Let us see that, please ?—A. (Witness hands document to Mr. Watson.)

Q. This is directed, 'Memorandum for minister *re* new lighthouse asked for Flower Ledge island. (Reads.)

(Memorandum marked Exhibit No. 4.)

Q. That is the report that you made. That is dated, I see, the 18th of October, 1906. Did you get an answer to that ?—A. Yes. The answer was that the lighthouse was not changed.

Q. An answer in writing ?—A. No.

Q. That what ?—A. No. A memorandum of that kind on the department files is never answered in writing, except that the minister's action is placed on that in the form of a memorandum in a word or two.

Q. Yes. Then you got an answer in that way, that the lighthouse had not been changed ?—A. No, the lighthouse had not been changed.

Q. That met with your view ?—A. Certainly.

Q. So that your view in that respect was accepted, adopted ?—A. Yes.

Q. Then, what change was made ?—A. I am not very sure, but I think no change in the apparatus has yet been made.

Q. I see. Has the lantern been changed ?—A. No.

Q. That expenditure has not been made, then?—A. No.

Q. Apparently the view that you expressed has been adopted?—A. Apparently.

Q. Apparently so. Then, that being so, it shows the departmental course of obtaining advice, and the advice that you gave, and that that has been acted upon, apparently?—A. Apparently.

Q. And you commend that action ?—A. Naturally.

Q. Then, what other documents have you that bear upon it, colonel? You have some others there?—A. I do not think it is anything that bears on the commissioner of lights in any way. I have a memorandum here about another change at Musquash, but as far as I recollect that is a question that was discussed at the lighthouse board.

Q. Yes ?—A. And I am not sure, because I had not time to follow the matter up. I would have to look through the lighthouse board record. This was another question of change of lanterns.

Q. I see. Now, with regard to that lighthouse board, who composed that, who are the members ?—A. The deputy minister was chairman, the chief engineer of tho department, the commissioner of lights, the chief of the marine service, commander of the marine service, were the departmental officers. Mr.——

Q. Then you are on that board, of course?—A. Yes. Mr. Andrew Allan, of Montreal, representing the shipping interests on the east coast, and Captain Troup, of Victoria, representing the shipping interests of the Pacific coast.

Q. Those are the heads of some important branches along with those gentlemen you name from the outside?—A. Yes.

Q. Then, what jurisdiction did that board possess to act finally in the matter?—A. None; it is merely an advisory board. They consider applications for aids to navigation and make reports to the Minister of Marine and Fisheries, either recommending or refusing to recommend these applications. Their duties then end there.

Q. It is a matter of consideration and recommendation?—A. A matter of consideration and recommendation.

Q. And, of course, one would anticipate that the recommendations of such a board would be usually adopted?—A. It has been the practice of the minister to adopt them usually.

Q. Yes. Of course, one could hardly see why a board of that kind would be constituted except for action. Have there been exceptions to that where their recommendations have not been adopted, or do you know of any exception?—A. Yes. I am afraid I cannot particularize, but if my recollection serves me rightly, the board has recommended larger expenditures than we had money to carry out, with the consequence that some of them, at least, have been deferred.

Q. Deferred by the minister by reason of that?—A. Yes.

Q. I see?—A. In a few cases where——

Q. Then, how do you account for the board making such recommendations? You are a member of the board?—A. How do you mean, how do I account for it?

Q. For the board making recommendations for too large an expenditure, more than could be approved of?—A. Well, because the board had no function to apportion the expenditure or to make its recommendations with any reference to the amount to be expended; that is to say, there was nothing to prevent us as a board recommending an expenditure of $10,000,000 if we chose to do it, whereas there might be only half a million dollars available for construction. That was a matter for departmental consideration afterwards.

Q. I see. Then did the board not take into consideration the appropriations that had been made?—A. No.

Q. It did not?—A. No.

Q. The recommendations were made without reference to the funds available?—A. To the monetary considerations involved.

Q. I see. That led to the occasional difference or difficulty?—A. No, I do not think that had anything to do with it.

Hon. Mr. CASSELS.—You tried to educate them up to that?

Mr. WATSON.—The board was?—A. Yes, my lord.

By Mr. Watson:

Q. Then did the board consider those matters you spoke of there, that Flower island and the other matter?—A. I shall have to consult the records of the board before I can answer.

Q. Those were matters that would come before the board?—A. Yes.

Q. So that the board possesses very large powers and functions?—A. Advisory powers only.

Q. Yes, by way of recommendation?

By Hon. Mr. Cassels:

Q. Did the board recommend the substitution of carbide, did that come before them?—A. I really cannot tell you, sir.

Q. Can you find out?—A. Yes, I fancy I can find out.

By Mr. Watson:

Q. Do you think that is a matter that would properly come before the board for consideration?—A. No, I think not. That is a matter for departmental regulation.

Q. But you can find out whether it did come before the board for consideration? —A. Yes.

Q. Well, now, when you made the statement to the late minister as to the improper purpose that you had in your mind, I would like to know exactly what he said?— A. As well as I can recollect, he laughed at me.

Q. I see. Who was there to gain by that, did you think or have in your mind? —A. The owners of the carbide.

Q. That is Mr. Willson and Mr. Willson's company?—A. Yes.

Q. And was there any one in connection with the department who had to do with that company?—A. Not that I am aware of.

Q. Did Mr. Fraser recommend that course, do you know?—A. You will have to ask him.

Q. Do you know?—A. No.

Q. Have you any information as to whether Mr. Fraser has made a gain by reason of any dealings in carbide with that company?—A. No information whatever.

Q. Have you any suspicion with reasonable grounds for it that such existed or exists?—A. No grounds whatever.

Q. Or that anyone else in connection with the department has made any gain, directly or indirectly, by that change?—A. No grounds for it.

Q. No grounds. Have you ever discussed the matter with Mr. Willson?—A. No.

Q. Who else is there besides Mr. Willson who is interested in the company?—A. I have no idea. I have heard—I do not know whether it is true or not—the Bronsons are interested in it.

Q. Now, I do not want to press you unduly, Colonel Anderson, but I would like if you would assist a little bit more in stating the reasons that you had for thinking or believing that the placing of J. F. Fraser had to do with this improper purpose and a gain to Willson; what led you to that belief, what facts or information had you?— A. The fact that Mr. Fraser began using the carbide on a stretch of river between Montreal and Prescott, and that the adoption of the acetylene system of lighting was pressed so strongly by him.

Q. By him?—A. Yes.

Q. That is the fact, that he advocated it so strongly——?—A. Yes.

Q. Created in your mind the suspicion or doubt?—A. Yes.

Q. Anything else than that?—A. I cannot call to mind anything.

Q. Did you ever seek to test or inquire as to whether the prices paid were such as to lead to the inference that he gained by it?—A. No. The matter was taken out of my hands entirely; all the transactions in regard to carbide were done directly through the commissioner of lights branch. I never saw an account.

Q. And I suppose it is fair to yourself and to every one else to say that you have felt somewhat sore about that ever since?—A. I do not think so.

Q. You do not think so. Then I am mistaken about that. You were aggrieved at the time, but you do not feel that now?—A. I feel the same conviction, that it has not been in the best interests of the department to make that change?

Q. I see. That is by reason of additional expenditure, is it?—A. Yes; and by reason of the danger and by reason of the loss of life that has occurred.

Q. You spoke of one or two occasions of accidents?—A. Yes.

Q. Of course, we do not want to go into that. I suppose his lordship will not want to go into that matter?

Hon. Mr. CASSELS.—Oh, no.

Mr. WATSON.—You call attention to that, you think it is less safe. Now, colonel, there are some matters in the report——

Hon. Mr. CASSELS.—Before you drop that, Mr. Watson, I would like to ask the colonel a question.

By Hon. Mr. Cassels:

Q. This Willson you speak of in the company, had he any interest whatever in anything other than carbide?—A. Yes. They are manufacturing buoys on a very large scale. I am not quite sure whether it is the same company, but the same Willson is interested in a large factory of buoys for the use of this——

Q. Carbide?—A. Carbide.

Q. But were these buoys got from the company Willson was engaged in?—A. I understand so; but you will understand, my lord, that they were got through the other branch.

Q. I understand that. I just want to get it for my own information. Have you the slightest notion approximately of what the expenditure per annum would be for these buoys and for the carbide occasioned by the change?—A. I have not.

Q. You cannot give us that?—A. I cannot at all.

By Mr. Watson:

Q. Someone in the department could give us that?—A. Oh, yes.

By Hon. Mr. Cassels:

Q. We will get that. One other question. Are you acquainted with the system called the patronage list in your department?—A. Yes.

Q. Will you explain what that is? Perhaps Mr. Watson will get it. I would like to have that in the report?—A. The patronage list is a list of firms and individuals who are recommended to be patronized for the purchase of goods in their lines of business. There is a list, I believe, in every department of such firms.

Q. Who makes the recommendation?—A. The minister.

Q. That comes direct from the minister?—A. From the minister.

Q. Are the contracts with those people on the patronage list made without tenders or given straight to them?—A. I think that the usual procedure is to ask for tenders from different individuals on the patronage list.

Q. Supposing there is only one on the patronage list?—A. Then it is up to the officer to certify that the prices are reasonable if things are purchased.

Mr. WATSON.—What officer?—A. The officer who is responsible for the purchase, in the case of my branch, myself; in the case of the commissioner of lights branch, the commissioner of lights, and in the case of the wireless telegraph branch, Mr. Doutre, and so on.

By Hon. Mr. Cassels :

Q. In your branch what precaution did you take to see that the man on the patronage list was not getting a higher price than he could get elsewhere?—A. I simply have to use my judgment about the matter, and if I consider the prices are not reasonable, then I so report on their offer.

By Mr. Watson :

Q. Who are on that so-called patronage list in your branch, how many?—A. I have not the slightest idea.

Q. How many, about?—A. I do not think I have ever seen the list. If I wanted to purchase articles in my line and did not ask for tenders, which I usually did, I would ask Mr. Stanton to tell me who were on the patronage list for those articles.

Q. Mr. Stanton, that is you assistant?—A. No, Mr. Stanton is the gentleman in charge of the correspondence branch.

Q. Oh, of course, the correspondence branch. How long has that condition of affairs——

Hon. Mr. CASSELS.—Mr. Watson, that is a very important branch of this inquiry. I have to adjourn at 4 o'clock on account of the work of the Exchequer Court. What hour to-morrow will suit you ?

Mr. WATSON.—Half-past ten.

(Adjourned at 4 p.m. to 10.30 to-morrow morning.)

OTTAWA, May 12, 1908.

Examination of W. P. ANDERSON continued by Mr. WATSON.

By Mr. Watson :

Q. Did you have a separate so-called patronage list in your particular branch ?— A. No. So far as I know there is only one patronage list in the department.

Q. And that is in the records branch, do I understand ?—A. Yes. May I correct the statement I made yesterday ? I said I understood it was in the hands of Mr. Stanton. I have learned since that Mr. Stumbles has had charge of it.

Q. Mr. Stumbles ?—A. Yes.

Q. And I suppose Mr. McCleneghan would have to do with it as well ?—A. I really do not know.

Q. I understand that he has. Then your lordship inquired about that last evening. I find, I am sorry to say, that it will take a little time to complete those lists. They are partly made up by reference to the records in the hands of the different agents, my lord, as well as by reference to the records in the department here. I have therefore so far only been able to obtain a copy of the patronage list commencing in 1890 and going on to 1895, and that may not be complete of itself. I think perhaps I had better not put that in in the meantime.

Hon. Mr. CASSELS.—Just adopt your own course, Mr. Watson, you are going into it very thoroughly.

Mr. WATSON.—I will take care to have all produced.

Hon. Mr. CASSELS.—Just adopt your own course.

Mr. WATSON.—So as to have them accurately prepared, I think I had better not put them in in a partial way. This is the only one I have this morning, commencing in 1890 and running on to 1895. The others will be produced in regular course, and this will be filed at the same time.

By Mr. Watson :

Q. What has been the general system or method adopted in making contracts, by advertisement and tender or otherwise ?—A. Both systems have been adopted. In some cases, indeed in most cases in my branch, advertisements have been published and tenders invited publicly. In some cases instructions have been given to ask tenders of parties that we knew to be in the business.

Q. That you knew to be in the business ?—A. Yes.

Q. Then, is there any line of distinction as to amounts, that is, where tenders are not solicited is that limited to smaller sums or not ?—A. The general practice has been where any considerable sum was involved to invite tenders publicly.

Q. I see. That has been the general practice. And in your department has that been pretty faithfully observed?—Yes.

Q. In any respect has the non-observance of that led to the prejudice of the country, the public?—A. Not that I am aware of.

Q. You are not aware of it?—A. No.

Q. That is what you say, is it?—A. That is what I say.

Q. Then, just another question. Where contracts have been let in the instances that you refer to without public tender, have the prices of the contracts been excessive to your knowledge?—A. Not to my knowledge.

Q. Not to your knowledge?—A. Indeed, if I had any suspicion that they were excessive I should report to that effect.

Q. Does it lie with you in all such matters to make a recommendation?—A. I believe so, I think——

Q. You do not know?—A. Well, it is so general a question that I am a little bit——

Q. I will put it a little more specifically. Assuming that an expenditure is to be incurred on your branch, you are required, are you not, to report úpon that expenditure?—A. Yes.

Q. And to report the estimated amount of the expenditure?—A. Yes.

Q. And then you negotiate for the contract, the work to be done?—A. Yes, I prepare plans and specifications and ask for tenders.

Q. You ask for tenders. And do you report upon the tenders, as to whether or not they are at proper prices and in other respects regular?—A. Yes.

Q. And expedient?—A. Yes.

Q. You do?—A. I may add to that that in a case where tenders were asked for publicly, even if the lowest tender exceeded my estimate, I should have no hesitation in recommending its acceptance.

Q. Yes; where it was the lowest tender?—A. Yes, where it was the lowest tender.

Q. Then, in all such matters do you assume a personal responsibility?—A. Yes.

Q. You do. And your report is made directly to the deputy minister?—A. Yes.

Q. And you receive word back from him as to whether or not it should proceed, I assume?—A. Usually the contract is awarded without my knowing anything further about it, and it is only after the contract has been awarded that I am advised the contract has been awarded and I can go ahead with the work.

Q. That is following upon your report?—A. Yes.

Q. And do you know of any departure or variation from your report by the deputy minister that may be the subject of comment?—A. I do not know of any, I cannot call to mind any now, and I think I should if there had been any.

Q. Then, let me ask you, if you please, another word about the deputy minister. Did I understand you to speak yesterday about your personal relations with him, and as to whether or not they were quite satisfactory?—A. I answered a question, yes.

Q. And your answer, I think, was that the relations were quite cordial and satisfactory?—A. Yes.

Q. Not any friction existing?—A. No.

Q. I see. Has there been any, so to speak, side-taking as between you and Mr. Fraser, because you spoke yesterday of serious personal difficulties between you and Mr. Fraser? I would like to know whether or not you have felt there has been any taking sides with you or against you, in these personal matters between you and Mr. Fraser?—A. There has been no feeling on my part. I do not know exactly how to answer your question. I am quite willing to.

Q. It is pretty plain and direct. Have you felt embarrassment by reason of that condition?—A. Naturally.

Q. You have. Then, those personal differences between you and him have led to embarrassment in the public service?—A. I am not aware of that.

Q. Well, if it leads to your personal embarrassment, would that not operate more or less as a prejudice in the public service?—A. I think not.

Q. You think not. It occurs to me it would be almost impossible to avoid it. Perhaps I am quite wrong?—A. Well, our work is so distinct we have very little in common.

Q. Very little in common; I see. But you have to work along with him in connection with many matters, do you not, Mr. Fraser?—A. No.

Q. For instance, in lighthouses, you do a part and he does a part in the completion, do you not?—A. He furnishes the lantern and apparatus.

Q. And that is a material part?—A. Yes.

Q. And the design has to be made with respect to these appliances?—A. Yes.

Q. So that that would necessarily bring you in very close communication, should bring you in close communication with him; in fact, you should work as practically one mind and one hand; is that not so?—A. Well, if my designs have to be made to suit his lanterns, is that not working together?

Q. That would be working together, yes. Then, that working together would be essential, as you say. Now, in the working along with him do I understand that you have lacked personal confidence in him?—A. Always.

Q. Always?

Hon. Mr. Cassels.—I do not understand, Mr. Watson, that Colonel Anderson works with Mr. Fraser at all. What he stated yesterday, and what he meant to convey, I think, is this: The lanterns are designed for a particular lighthouse.

The Witness.—Yes, my lord.

Hon. Mr. Cassels.—Then instructions are given the colonel to build his lighthouse with reference to this lantern, to receive this lantern, and when that lighthouse is completed he passes it on. I think that is the substance of his remarks.

The Witness.—Yes, my lord, that is exactly what occurred.

Mr. Watson.—Just now he was indicating his designs would have to be complied with usually.

Hon. Mr. Cassels.—I did not understand the colonel to say that he would direct what kind of lantern should be used.

By Mr. Watson:

Q. I suppose that is so, colonel?—A. Quite so.

Q. But at the same time your designs for construction would have——?—A. To be adapted generally to the lantern adopted.

Q. To the appliances, including the lantern?—A. Yes.

Q. And that would necessarily make a combination of forces, or should, so that you should work together in that respect?—A. To a certain extent.

Q. And you say that in this co-operation and working together you had not, and still have not, personal confidence in him?—A. I said that, yes.

Q. You are speaking of his judgment, or honesty and integrity, or is it both?—A. I am speaking probably of his experience.

Q. Probably of his experience. Can you be any more definite? Do you speak of his want of integrity, reliability?—A. I know nothing about his want of reliability. It is no more than a suspicion.

Q. No more than a suspicion; I see. Now, as I think it is rather a serious matter, Colonel Anderson, I would like to know whether that extends to anyone else than to Mr. Fraser?—A. Nothing that I have any ground for proof of.

Q. Then, evidently you have a feeling, some feeling, that it may extend?—A. One may have a feeling that cannot be proved.

Hon. Mr. Cassels.—Well, we are going to try and prove it or disprove it.

By Mr. Watson:

Q. As his lordship says, that is important. I would like to have your assistance in that respect, colonel, if you please. Now, what is the feeling about that, to whom does it extend?—A. The feeling all runs back to the superintendent of lights in this way, that he apparently has the final say in the department, he apparently can have his own way.

Q. He apparently can get his own way, that is Mr. Fraser?—A. Yes; and can have his own plans with regard to lights and buoys or anything he is connected with adopted. Then that naturally gives rise to an impression in my mind that he has undue influence in the department.

Q. I see?—A. And to place that personally is a difficult or impossible matter.

Q. Still, it is no less serious; in fact, it is perhaps more serious by reason of the circumstances that you say it is difficult to trace. Does that extend in your experience or feeling to the deputy minister, that influence that he has?—A. Merely in this way, that the deputy minister and Mr. Fraser appear to work so cordially together. A feeling of that kind is so impalpable, it is so impossible to prove, that one hesitates to speak of it.

By Hon. Mr. Cassels :

Q. You have had large experience there, and you have got it on your mind that Mr. Fraser had undue influence. Now, that feeling must arise from things that are going on in the office, undue expenditures, unnecessary expenditures, and things of that sort. That is what Mr. Watson wants you to state, if it is so ?—A. But I hesitate to say so, for this reason, that a matter of that kind is so absolutely incapable of proof. If there were any feeling that there was friction between the two branches and that things were done against my advice and against my will, I would be the very last man to know of it.

By Mr. Watson :

Q. I see. That is unfortunately the condition that exists ?—A. That I feel exists.

Q. And you feel that has been existing since the time of his appointment ?—A. Yes.

Q. And up to the present time ?—A. Yes.

Q. And exists to-day ?—A. I think not. I fancy the fact of the suspension of the commissioner of lights would indicate that there is a different feeling.

Q. The reason of its non-existence to-day then, is the circumstances that the commissioner of lights has been suspended ?—A Possibly that the minister has become imbued with the same impression I have always had.

Q. Then, where matters of difference have existed between you and him, are those matters in which you have a joint jurisdiction ?—A. There is no joint jurisdiction as I understand it.

Q. Well, a joint obligation then, or a mutual obligation?—A. Well, those are the only portions in which he and I have come in contact. He has other duties that I have nothing whatever to do with.

Q. For instance, you have spoken about the buoys and the like ; have you anything to do with them ?—A. Nothing whatever now.

Q. And you have not had since his appointment eight or ten years ago ?—A. No.

Q. And yet you feel that he has been actuated by improper motives more or less in the adoption of these buoys and appliances and in the expenditure made for them ? —A. Yes.

Q. I see. Well, that is a very serious matter, colonel, is it not?—A. I think so.

Q. And you think that that improper motive, as I understand you, on his part, has led to an additional and unnecessary expenditure?—A. I think so.

Q. You think so. In the way of purchases, of course, that is, that too high a price has been paid. Any thing else?—A. Many unnecessary changes made, in my opinion.

Q. Yes. Unnecessary changes and excessive expenditure. Do I cover it in that way ?—A. I think so.

Q. And that the contractor would directly benefit by reason of those conditions ? —A. That is a very difficult question to answer. A contractor would naturally benefit by selling twice the quantity of material in any case.

Q. Yes. Now, these are matters in conection with which you have no personal responsibility ?—A. None whatever.

Q. They pertain wholly and entirely to another branch ?—A. Yes.

Q. So that it is your expression of opinion——A. May I correct you there ? They affect my branch in this way : for instance, if a larger lantern is ordered for an existing tower than that tower will carry, it means I have to build a new tower to carry the new lantern. In connection with that in many cases I have protested against the necessity for this change, as indicated by that one protest which was handed to you yesterday.

Q. Yes. But, apart from that, it is a matter for which you have no personal responsibility, but it is your opinion in regard to the conduct and management of another branch by the head of that branch ?—A. Yes.

Q. Does that opinion or does that feeling of criticism extend to other branches on your part ?—A. I do not think there is any other branch with which I have any connection.

Q. Are you able to, and will you if you can, express your opinion—and it is by way of criticism, I understand—in regard to any other branch in the departmenté —A. I——

Q. Let me put it this way, then? Have you a feeling that unnecessary and excessive expenditure is occurring in any other branch?—A. I have not that feeling, but I have so very little knowledge of other branches.

Q. Well, I want to know whether you have that feeling, whether it is a subject of criticism or remark from you?—A. No; I think not, but, as I say, the other branches do not come in touch with me.

Q. You say you think not. I think the form of expression may carry with it a little reservation possibly?—A. I did not intend it to. So far as I know, the other branches are fairly well managed.

Q. Fairly well managed; I see. That branch, you think, is not fairly well managed?—A. I certainly think it is not.

Q. And all those matters, I understand, that you now refer to, you have repeatedly brought to the attention of the deputy minister?—A. Yes.

Q. And have you brought them to the attention of any other officials in the department?—A. It was not my duty to.

Q. I am not speaking of that for the moment. But have you done so?—A. Not that I am aware of.

Q. Not that you are aware of. Has that been the subject of rumour and general discussion and as emanating from you, more or less?—A. As emanating from me?

Q. Yes?—A. Not that I am aware of.

Q. Did you discuss the matter that you have now spoken of with regard to that branch with the Civil Service Commissioners or any of them?—A. I did not.

Q. You did not. Not with Mr. Fyshe or Mr. Bazin?—A. I was not called as a witness by the Civil Service Commissioners at all. I was called down one day by a message from Mr. Fyshe, and Mr. Fyshe spoke to me for possibly ten minutes, giving me his opinion of the department. As far as my recollection goes he never asked me a question, nor did I volunteer any information to him.

Q. I see. What I want to know is this—the present commission is based upon the report of the commissioners—as to whether or not you conveyed to any one of the commissioners the information which you have now given here?—A. Not one word absolutely not one word.

Q. Or——?—A. When that interview between Mr. Fyshe and me occurred the whole of the evidence had been taken, it was only two or three days before the report was handed in; and, as I say, I volunteered nothing; I was asked nothing, as far as I know. The whole conversation consisted of Mr. Fyshe giving me his opinion of the department's conduct.

Q. I see. Of course, this portion of the report, the so-called appendix, as Mr. Fyshe stated, is not the result of evidence given, but the result of personal investigation and information in the department?—A. Well, I want to make it as plain as I possibly can that in no way, in no way whatever, was any hint conveyed to them by me, was any evidence given by me, or was anything originated from me that was in that report.

Q. Well, I am very glad to have you make your statement, Colonel Anderson?—A. If I knew how to make it more strongly I should do so, because——

Q. Yes. Then that brings it directly to the matter of the report and to your evidence. Now, upon this portion of the report, as to whether you feel that this report which is the basis of the present commission, is justified, wherein the commissioners say that there would seem to be a lack of conscience on the part of the officials——?—A. I think that is very much too broad an assertion.

Q. Is that justified, in your opinion?—A. I think it is justified in regard to at least one officer; I think it is not justified in regard to the majority of officers.

Q. With regard to the majority. Well, 999 would be a very large majority, that is, out of a thousand. You say you think it is justified in regard to one officer. I assume that you are referring now to Mr. Fraser?—A. I am.

Q. That is J. F. Fraser. Then you say you did not think it is justified as to the majority?—A. I do.

Q. Then give me, if you please, the names of the others constituting the minority?—A. I have nothing to base my evidence on with regard to anybody else, simply because——

Q. It is a mater of suspicion, is it?—A. If it is even suspicion.

By Hon. Mr. Cassels:

Q. You are talking about the Ottawa officials for the moment?—A. I was only thinking of them for the moment.

Mr. WATSON.—Yes, that is the officials in the head department, my lord. I am much obliged to your lordship for limiting it; I so intended it.

By Mr. Watson:

Q. Then, as I understand you, it is a matter of suspicion with regard to some other officials. I would like very much, if I may say so again, that you would render us assistance in these matters of suspicion?—A. I absolutely refuse to do it, for this reason: That if I have suspicions they are based on nothing tangible; they are based on nothing I feel justified in naming a man in connection with.

Q. But the suspicions are such as have formed themselves in your mind as a result of business dealings and associations?—A. If they exist.

Q. Yes, if they exist. And those business dealings and associations are, of course, often the best kind of test, are they not?—A. I think not.

Q. Why, sometimes one reaches very accurate conclusions from associations and business dealings?—A. I think one is always willing to give another person the benefit of the doubt until one has some tangible proof.

Q. I see. It is a matter then now of the benefit of the doubt. Then, will you tell us, please, to whom it is you are giving the benefit of the doubt?—A. No, I will not.

Q. Will you not?—A. No, sir.

Q. Are there many?—A. I refuse to answer.

Q. I would like very much if you would assist, Colonel Anderson. I do not want to press you too urgently?—A. I do not consider it is fair to ask me such questions. If I have suspicions and I cannot prove them, I consider I have no right to mention any names, and I refuse to do it.

Q. You take that position, do you?—A. I do.

Hon. Mr. CASSELS.—I think the colonel is quite right, Mr. Watson, about that. I do not think he has to impute wrong to others on suspicion.

Mr. WATSON.—I will not press it, my lord, of course, in that way.

By Mr. Watson:

Q. Just this one further question: Have you communicated those suspicions to the Minister of Marine and Fisheries?—A. I have not.

Q. Then, Colonel Anderson, I find in this report of the Civil Service Commissioners that in many instances it contains references to work more or less under your supervision and direction?—A. So I found last night in looking it over.

Q. And more or less a matter of criticism on their part?—A. Yes.

Q. And for that reason I would like to just run over some parts of it with you to see how far these may be important, relevant to the inquiry. That is, my lord, an extract from the references in the report, with one or two exceptions, to Colonel Anderson. Has your lordship the report there?

Hon. Mr. CASSELS.—Yes.

Mr. WATSON.—Then I thought that would facilitate if your lordship had that extract in application to my questions.

(Extract put in, marked Exhibit No. 5.)

By Mr. Watson:

Q. Then I find in connection with the lighthouse board's recommendations that your name, colonel, appears frequently in the report, and at page 106—have you a copy of the report? (Hands witness a copy of the report.) Page 106 of the report, about the middle of the page, have you the reference there? The heading is, 'Memorandum by chief engineer for minister, protesting against above memorandum by J. F. F.'?—A. Yes.

Q. And there it is said that affects this matter, 'Memorandum submitted for the minister's information re new lighthouse apparatus recommended by lighthouse board in connection with the memo. prepared by the commissioner of lights, objecting to the action of the lighthouse board in proposing to place improved illuminating apparatus in the present lanterns at seven light stations. The undersigned begs to submit his reasons to the minister for objecting to the conclusions of the commissioner of lighthouses.' And then you say, 'The present lanterns at the seven stations are as follows:—' Now, if you will look at that again, for the moment, the first part of it, this memorandum refers as well to the recommendation by the lighthouse board?—A. Yes.

Q. Then do I understand that this was a protest by you against the recommendation by the lighthouse board?—A. You may consider it a minority report if you choose.

Q. A minority report to the recommendation of the lighthouse board. You gave us the personnel of the board yesterday?—A. Yes.

Q. And I understand from this that the board adopted the report or recommendation of the commissioner of lights?—A. Yes.

Q. And then your protest was against that adoption?—A. Yes.

Q. Now, were you present at the meeting of the board when the adoption was recorded?—A. I am not quite sure.

Q. You are not able to refer to the minutes of the board?—A. I have not got them here.

Q. Well, we will not take up time. You are not sure about that. Was that a matter of irregularity in your opinion on the part of the board?—A. Not at all; that was merely a difference of opinion.

Q. Merely a difference of opinion?—A. Yes.

Q. The majority was against you there?—A. I may say I very often differed from the majority of the board, but in most cases where there was nothing serious involved, no serious expenditure or anything that I did not consider worth making a determined protest about, I let the matter go and did not record my dissent. Where I found the thing was sufficiently important to have my own views put before the minister I made a special memorandum, as I did in this case.

Q. A minority report?—A. You can call it that.

Q. Yes; that is how you spoke of it yourself?—A. Yes.

Q. The way this is put, as I take it, it was intended by the commissioners here to indicate that you reflected upon the decision of the board; it is a very positive opinion that you have expressed ?—A. I do not understand it in that way.

Q. You do not ?—A. What I mean is this : The board meets, I find myself in a minority. If I think the question is sufficiently important to draw the minister's special attention to it,, I put in a memorandum drawing his attention to it and ask to have my dissent recorded on the minutes of the board.

Q. I see ?—A. If I think it is not a matter of any great consequence I do not ask to have my——

Q. Does that course occur with other members of the board as well, do they put in minority reports ?—A. I think I am the only one who has ever recorded any dissent from the majority.

Q. I see. That is the exception, you are the exception in that respect of making a report ?—A. Yes.

Q. You do not know of any instance when another member of the board has reported against the conclusion of the board ?—A. I know of no other instance.

Q. Then, have you found it necessary in your opinion often to dissent ?—A. I think, possibly, six or seven times.

Q. Six or seven times. And on each occasion have you made a separate memorandum ?—A. Yes.

Q. To the minister ?—A. Yes.

Q. I see ?—A. In some cases I have asked to have my name recorded as dissenting, but I have not made any memorandum. I think I saw in here one case where there is a memorandum, ' W. P. A. dissents,' or something of that kind.

Q. Then it is not a matter after consultation or discussion of being convinced by the others ?—A. Well, the way it has generally occurred has been this : The matter has been argued in the lighthouse board, it has come to a vote, I have found myself in a minority. I have then announced that in my opinion the matter was sufficiently important to draw the attention of the minister to it and I intended to make a separate memorandum.

Q. Yes. With a view of inducing the minister to act differently ?—A. With a view of putting my own position in the matter clearly before him; that is simply all.

Q. I see. Then in this matter you refer to the present lanterns at seven stations, the first one at east head of Musquash, a ten-foot cast-iron lantern of Canadian manufacture. As I understand, the proposition was to change that, was it not ?—A. Yes. That is, or is being carried out.

Q. And in your opinion the change was wholly unnecessary, is that right ?—A. I would like to leave out the word ' wholly.'

Q. All right. Was unnecessary. At all events, you had a very firm opinion, it was not a matter of doubt, or you would not have made your separate report. That is the reason that led me to use that word ?—A. With regard to Musquash my opinion was that it was merely a harbour light, it was not necessary to go to the expense of putting on a new tower, a new lantern, a new illuminating apparatus.

Q. And it was the same in regard to the other six. We need not go over them in detail and take up time.—A. May I correct you ? It looks to me——

Q. Certainly. I would be glad if you would do so ?—A. As if the initial protest came from the commissioner of lights, that is to say, that he objected to the stand taken by the lighthouse board meeting, at which he was not present, and that my memorandum is based on his protest against the action of the lighthouse board. I think that is the way.

Q. Well, the lighthouse board was working, adopting his recommendations ?—A. No, not at first.

Q. Not at first ; but afterwards. I see you observe at the foot of that page, or at least the commissioners observe : ' The commissioner of lights wishes to condemn —— ?—A. This is taken from my memorandum.

Q. Yes. 'These lanterns and provide new English lanterns with illuminating apparatus, including upper prisms, and against this proposal I most strenuously protest on the ground that a change in the lanterns is not required, and that such change would not only entail very heavy expenditure for new lanterns, but would also entail rebuilding most of the towers to carry the heavier and larger English lanterns.' That was the basis of your objection ?—A. Evidently.

Hon. Mr. CASSELS.—What is the meaning of that first clause, 22nd of April, 1907? —A. It concludes in this way: 'The undersigned begs to submit his reasons to the minister for objecting to the conclusions of the commissioner of lighthouses.' The earlier part of it would almost give the idea the commissioner of lighthouses dissented from the board.

WITNESS.—So he did, my lord.

Mr. WATSON.—That is what the colonel was referring to. The board adopted the recommendation of the commissioner of lighthouses ?

WITNESS.—No. The board adopted the changes in the illuminating apparatus without adopting the new lanterns.

Hon. Mr. CASSELS.—Yes, without adopting the new lanterns. Then the commissioner, as I understand——

WITNESS.—The commissioner said that the new illuminating apparatus which was suggested by the——

Hon. Mr. CASSELS.—By the board ?

WITNESS.—By the lighthouse board was not sufficient for those stations.

Hon. Mr. CASSELS.—If you read the whole thing it is rather doubtful. It looks as if the commissioner of lighthouses was dissenting from the action of the board.

WITNESS.—That is the case.

Hon. Mr. CASSELS.—And claiming new lanterns. Then Colonel Anderson is protesting against the commissioner desiring that change.

By Mr. Watson:

Q. He says there, my lord, 'I most strenuously protest on the ground that a change in the lanterns is not required, and that such change would not only entail very heavy expenditure for new lanterns, but would also entail rebuilding most of the towers to carry the heavier and larger English lanterns.' Were the changes made?— A. In some cases, yes; in other cases, no. In most cases, no. At Musquash we are building a new tower to take the lantern and apparatus recommended by the commissioner of lights, I think.

Q. Then you say, following upon that: 'The commissioner objects to the central rings only being provided on the ground that about one-third of the lighting power is lost by omitting the upper prisms. I deny emphatically that one-third of the light comes from the upper prisms.' There you are at grave difference with him?—A. Yes.

Q. 'They only transmit a very small percentage of the light, and it has been the best practice of lighthouse apparatus makers to omit them altogether in many recent installations on the ground that they are not worth the extra expense involved, and that the lantern was more compact without the extra height of glazing required to accommodate the upper prisms.' The board, as a board, was possessed of knowledge, I assume, upon all these subjects?—A. The board relies very much on the opinions expressed by the commissioner of lights and myself in reaching conclusions, because we are the two men who are supposed to have intimate professional knowledge respecting these matters.

Q. Yes. Of course, that would make it perhaps a little more embarrassing by reason of the personal difference between you and him?—A. I have never found it to work out so. I have always spoken freely in the lighthouse board, and I think Mr. Fraser has too.

3262—5

Q. Then you say, going on: 'I would point out the general objections made to our Canadian lanterns is the fact that they have vertical sash bars and flat glazing. The cry against our Canadian lighthouses has been raised by European makers of lanterns simply so that they could supply their own more expensive styles of manu_ facture.' Do you mean by that that the Canadian makers have been exercising improper influence upon the board?—A. Canadian makers?

Q. Yes?—A. No.

Q. 'The cry against our Canadian lighthouses has been raised by European makers'—I should have said that the European makers have been making improper representations?—A. Nothing improper, no. Is it not natural in trade and business?

Q. To blow your own horn?—A. To blow your own horn. If I were selling lan_ terns I would try to pick up all the holes I could in the other man's lantern's.

Q. I see. That is the way you feel about all these matters and about individuals in that position, that each should blow his own horn?—A. Each does blow his own horn.

Q. Each does it, I see. Then you say: 'As a matter of practical use of the lan_ terns there is no great difference in the efficiency of the flat glazing and the curved glazing. The lights under discussion are none of them main sea coast lights, most of them are in narrow channels where the distance to be covered is quite restricted.' You have that before you. Will you look at that page?—A. Yes.

Q. You make some other remarks that I need not dwell upon, perhaps, but I want to allude to the last sentence: 'Therefore the undersigned sees no reason to condemn lanterns and buildings that will serve every practical purpose, for the mere purpose of incurring useless additional expense.' That is a very serious charge, is it not?— A. Worded in that way it appears to be. Of course, you will recollect that when that was written I had no idea it was going to appear in this.

Q. But this was written to the minister?—A. Yes.

Q. And is against the board.

Hon. Mr. CASSELS.—It would be more likely true.

WITNESS.—This is my opinion as contradistinguished to the opinion expressed above.

Mr. WATSON.—But you say there it is in your opinion done, that this change is made, 'for the mere purpose of incurring useless additional expense.' It is that I want to draw your attention to?—A. I did not say that.

Q. Yes. You say you see no reason to condemn lanterns and buildings 'that will serve every practical purpose, for the mere purpose of incurring useless additional expense.' You see that, it is the third line from the end of that paragraph?—A. Yes. That is rather an unfortunate way of expressing it.

Q. I see. Well, now, against whom was that aimed?—A. Against nobody.

Q. Against no one?—A. No. What I mean——

Q. Do you say now this is made a matter of record in the report of the Civil Service Commissioners, do you say now, or can you apply that sentence, that remark to any one?

Hon. Mr. CASSELS.—It applies on its face to the commissioner of lights, as far as it appears.

WITNESS.—What I meant to express was, it would have the effect of incurring useless additional expense.

By Mr. Watson:

Q. That is quite different from saying 'for the mere purpose.'—A. I have got some Irish blood and very often express myself very differently to what I intended.

By Hon. Mr. Cassels:

Q. You see, colonel, you started off on page 106, 'The commissioner of lights wishes to condemn these lanterns and provide,' and so on. Now, the language has all reference to the commissioner of lights?—A. Well, I should like to change those words, 'For the mere purpose,' and put in 'with the——

By Mr. Watson:

Q. You think those are not correctly introduced, they are liable to misconstruction?—A. I see now they are liable to misconstruction.

Q. You had no such intention, apparently?—A. No. What I meant was, with the effect of incurring useless expense.

By Hon. Mr. Cassels:

Q. Did you intend to convey the impression that Fraser being mixed up with these contractors was advising changes in order to benefit somebody else connected with them?—A. I did not intend to convey that impression. The impression I intended to convey was this: That if that change he advocated was made, it would have the effect of involving the department in unnecessary expense.

By Mr. Watson:

Q. Well, then, in that did you attribute any improper motives to any one, or intend to?—A. I did not intend to.

Q. You did not intend to. Had you ground or reason for attributing motives which were improper?—A. Exactly the same ground, the same reason I tried to explain yesterday, that my feeling has been that the commisisoner of lights' administration has been an extravagant one.

Q. His administration has been an extravagant one; that is the position. Then this report of the commisisoners manifestly is based, partly at all events, upon this memorandum by you?—A. No, no.

Q. You think not?—A. No, because my memorandum is a later one, made after his, which was referred to me.

Q. When was this report made, the one we are speaking of now?—A. The 22nd of April, 1907.

Q. Of course, that was before the report of the Civil Service Commissioners?—A. Yes.

Q. That is what I mean. And this was before them no doubt, or before Mr. Fyshe and Mr. Bazin?—A. I beg your pardon?

Q. This no doubt was before Mr. Fyshe and Mr. Bazin?

Hon. Mr. CASSELS.—It is printed as part of the report?

Mr. WATSON.—Yes.

Hon. Mr. CASSELS.—I would like to ask the colonel how many of those changes were made.

Mr. WATSON.—How many of the seven?

Hon. Mr. CASSELS.—Yes.

WITNESS.—My lord, I could not answer that without referring to the several files. Musquash is being changed; Cape Spencer has not yet been changed.

By Mr. Watson:

Q. Has the policy been changed?—A. I think that the decision of the lighthouse board has been adhered to.

Q. Yes?—A. Cape Jourimain I don't know about.

Q. Miscou you do not know about?—A. No. Escuminac I don't know about. Fowler Island has not been changed. Point Le Preau I do not know about, without looking it up.

Q. Then in two instances the changes have not been made?—A. In one instance it has been made I know.

Q. And the others you do not know about?—A. No.

Hon. Mr. CASSELS.—Except Flower Island.

Mr. WATSON.—Yes, my lord. He spoke about that yesterday.

By Mr. Watson:

Q. Now, I think that is all there is there. Then, if you will look further on, I think the report proceeds from that on to page 173, where reference is made to your matters. At the middle of that page, contract No. 57, 1906—to be completed October 20th, 1906?—A. Yes.

Q. That is contract August 18th, 1906, made with E. A. Wallberg personally, and he writes Colonel Anderson, chief engineer, as follows:—' We have to-day mailed our tender for the three lighthouse towers which you are calling for on Monday. I trust that you will be able to recommend our tender, as I fear that there may be some people who do not understand this class of work who may quote less than it is worth, and I think that it would be a great mistake to let a construction so important and where heavy loads have to be carried, to any one who are not thoroughly familiar with both theory and practice of reinforced concrete, and who have not the proper experience and organization to carry it out. We will be glad to call on you at any time if you consider it advisable.' And then we have another letter he writes to the deputy, matters of detail. I think that contract was recommended by you?—A. Yes, sir.

Q. Now, that is a subject of observation there by the commissioners. It continues on. Is there anything in that or arising out of it that is fair subject of comment as to irregularity or acts of dishonesty or otherwise?—A. Nothing that I am aware of.

Q. Is there any reason or foundation for criticism of matters in connection with that contract?—A. Not that I am aware of.

Q. Is there in that answer any mental reservation?—A. None whatever.

Q. None whatever. If you then refer to Mr. Wallberg—he is apparently mentioned very frequently throughout in this report?—A. Naturally, he was the contractor.

Q. The contractor. Mr. Wallberg is of Montreal, I am told?—A. He is of Montreal, he is either manager or owner of the Steel Concrete Company, Limited. He represents them.

Q. And are many contracts made with him or his firm?—A. He has built six towers, I think, for us in reinforced concrete.

Q. At considerable expenditure?—A. Very reasonable.

Q. Reasonable expenditure?—A. Yes.

Q. But as to amount, is it a large amount?—A. Not very large.

Q. The total amounting to about how much?—A. Roughly, six times $3,000, about $18,000 or $20,000. I won't—probably I had better say six times $4,000.

Q. Yes, about $24,000. Then the references made to him throughout in this report, I understand from you, are in respect of these six lighthouses; is that right—A. Well, I think in this case they are in regard to three only of them, are they not?

Q. Perhaps so. Then has he any other contracts?

Mr. PERRON.—Four.

Mr. WATSON.—Mr. Perron says four. Has he had any public contracts with this department?—A. Besides the six lighthouses?

Q. Yes.—A. I do not remember of any. I am subject to correction.

Q. Subject, of course, to correction. As a matter of recollection you do not remember of any. Now, is there any matter of suspicion in your mind in regard to the regularity of these contracts?—A. Not the slightest. I am absolutely——

Q. What about the prices paid to him?—A. The prices are reasonable.

Q. Do you say so?—A. I say so.

Q. Are they the result of application, soliciting tenders?—A. In some cases yes; in some cases no. The first tower he built for us was the tower at Cape Race. That was built by agreement with the department on my recommendation.

Q. Yes?—A. Then the next three were these three under discussion now: Cape Magdalen, Matane and Little Metis. In these cases tenders were invited from contractors in reinforced concrete work. Wallberg was awarded the contract because he wast he lowest bidder.

Q. I see?—A. At Little Hope the work was awarded to him, I think without tender, on my recommendation, as to the reasonableness of the price.

Q. Then, do you know how that price compares with ordinary current prices?—A. You cannot compare prices for work of this class with ordinary current prices, because the conditions are so absolutely different.

Q. The conditions?—A. The conditions in each——

By Hon. Mr. Cassels:

Q. Take the price of labour and so on?—A. In each place. The situation is so isolated that it was necessary to make special arrangements to send men and material there, and in each case the position was such that it was impossible, or almost impossible, to get any competition.

By Mr. Watson:

Q. I see?—A. The only comparison of prices we could reasonably make in that case was a comparison between the prices at which Mr. Wallberg would do the work and the price at which we could do the work ourselves, and in each case we were obliged to transport Mr. Wallberg's men and material in our own steamers to get to these out of the way places, they were off the general routes of navigation.

Q. Then, have you any reason to think, or to know rather, that in such cases in dealing with others than the department or government that discounts are usually allowed by him?—A. These were not matters of discount at all; they were matters of set prices for set work. It was not a price for material by measurement or anything of that kind.

Q. Summing it up, would it not be reasonable that he should allow discount upon the price paid?—A. No, it would not.

Q. You say not?—A. No. It was certainly a matter of fixed price. If I ask a man to say he will do a piece of work, he is not going to say he will do it for $100 and take off 5 per cent, unless he is going to give it to me.

Q. Have not the Civil Service Commissioners expressed an opinion that in matters of that character it is well known that a discount is allowed?—A. In matters of that character, or are they referring there to the purchase of supplies?

Q. Which do you think?—A. I should say to the purchase of supplies.

Q. You think to the purchase of supplies. Was that discussed with you by them as to the matter of purchase of supplies?—A. It was not.

Q. Just in a word and while you are here now before his lordship, is it to your knowledge the practice of business men in that position to allow discounts to others in connection with such purchases?—A. The only way in which I have ever known of discounts being allowed is this, where a firm had trade prices published for certain articles and where they would offer to a party in consideration of purchasing articles in larger quantities than usual—'If you purchase to such an extent we will allow you so much discount off our price list.' And of course in many trades the wholesale prices are fixed with a trade discount or with two or three trade discounts.

Q. Yes. Then have you known of any discounts being allowed by supplymen to the department?—A. I have had occasion in my branch to purchase in that way.

Q. How do you purchase?—A. Usually by contract after tender. But in a matter of this kind this is altogether a matter of fixed price for fixed work.

By Hon. Mr. Cassels :

Q. That is for building work?—A. Yes.

By Mr. Watson :

Q. So that it is impossible that any such element should enter in there ?—A. I think it is altogether impossible.

Q. Now then, further it is imputed, as I take it, that commissions may have been allowed by the contractor?—A. I know nothing whatever of it.

Q. Have you heard of any such matter ?—A. Nothing except rumours.

Q. Except rumours. Are you willing to state what they were, or to whom they apply, rather?—A. Well, I have heard them applied to nearly every transaction in the department.

Q. I was including those of your own ?—A. Not that I am aware of. But I should not be likely to hear that if there were any rumours of that kind.

Q. Any foundation for them at all ?—A. I have no idea.

Q. Well now, in connection with those lighthouses that you have been referring to, Little Metis and Matane and Cape Magdalen, have any changes been made since the construction, have any changes been made in the lighthouses since originally constructed ?—A. Not that I am aware of.

Q. Or recommended?—A. No, not that I am aware of.

Q. Have any changes been made in the lanterns since then?—A. Of those towers?

Q. Yes.—A. No, I think not.

Q. You think not ?—A. I think not.

Q. You know of no reference to those ?—A. No.

Q. Have any changes become necessary to be made by the contractor in those that you are aware of ?—A. Not that I can call to mind.

Q. The reason I ask is this : It has been the subject of comment, as I understand, by the commissioners that some changes have become necessary, and I have here on file—that is referring to Little Hope. Yes. There is one here particularly I have Little Hope. What have you to say about that?—A. My recollection of that is that after the contract was let and the work begun the size of the lantern was changed, a larger lantern was put on it than was originally intended to be put there. I am speaking now subjection to correction, but that is my impression, and that in consequence of that it was necessary to corbel out the tower and enlarge the lantern platform to receive the larger lantern.

Q. Then was there any difference as to the size of the lantern ?—A. Yes. A larger lantern was put on.

Q. At the time of the construction was there any difference of opinion about that? —A. I should have to refer to the files.

Q. I see one letter here of the 21st of March, 1907, directed to you by Mr. Wallberg, as chief engineer, saying: ' We beg to quote you for alterations in the reinforced concrete lighthouse tower at Little Hope Island for which we have contract, the sum of $2,300 for alterations.'?—A. Yes, that was for buttresses to carry the enlarged top and the enlarging of the top.

Q. This says, ' The original tower was designed to carry a third order light '?—A. Yes.

Q. ' The lantern to weigh 12,500 pounds and the apparatus 6,000 pounds. The tower as now altered is designed to carry a second order light, the weight of the lantern 24,000 pounds and the apparatus 12,000 pounds resting on a pedestal of about three feet six inches diameter. The outside dimensions to be 11 feet 6 inches. The diameter of the gallery to be 18 feet 6 inches. You will note that we have doubled both the horizontal and vertical reinforcement in the walls and have doubled the strength of the top floor and its supports. ' Now, that expenditure would seem from this letter to arise from some misconception in the construction.

Hon. Mr. CASSELS.—The size of the light, the change of the light.

By Mr. Watson :

Q. Yes?—A. The change in the intention of the department in regard to the lantern and light that was to be carried on that tower.

Q. Well, are these not matters, and was this not a matter, in which the original design for construction would include, or should include, the size of the lantern?—A It did include the size of the lantern originally intended, then the intention was changed.

Q. And changed by whom?—A. I must really refer to the files before I can make sure on this point.

Q. See if you can tell about that by reference to that file. This is one of your own files. (Handing file to witness.) I mention that just to give you a fair opportunity about it, because I understand it has been commented upon as being one of the matters of useless expenditure, that additional $2,300.

By Hon. Mr. Cassels:

Q. Where is Little Hope?—A. An island off the couth coast of Nova Scotia, I think off Shelburne county, out in the open Atlantic; a very difficult place to land at all times.

By Mr. Watson:

Q. I mention to you quite frankly about that, that that has been intimated as a matter of criticism of your work, of an expenditure said to be an unnecessary and useless expenditure?—A. But you will appreciate the fact that I had to make the change to suit the change in the lantern; the change in the lantern was not made by me.

Q. But this was a change immediately after the construction. Why was the design not complete in the first place?—A. It was.

Q. So that no change would be necessary?—A. It was complete for the third order lantern.

Q. Then, how does it happen that a change would become necessary, at the very commencement of its use, in the lantern?—A. It was not at the very commencement. The tower was partly erected in the autumn; the change was made next spring.

Q. Yes. And who ordered the change?—A. That is what I don't know—the change was ordered by my branch.

Q. By your branch?—A. Yes; but why the lantern was changed I do not know.

Q. Well, did that same thing occur with other towers?—A. There was one case.

Q. Matane, has it occurred there?—A. No; it occurred with none of these towers under discussion. There was one case of a wooden tower where I had to make a change after the tower was begun.

Q. That did not occur, then, at Little Metis?—A. No.

Q. You have no knowledge recently of a necessity for any change in matters that are not referred to?—A. I cannot call to mind any other instance at the moment.

Q. And you are not able by present reference to the file to explain the reason for the change beyond the fact that the lantern was to be changed, or rather that the tower was not constructed for the size of the lantern that was necessary to be used?—A. It must be on the apparatus file. I find here a memorandum from my assistant. 'I understand there is to be some change in the lantern and apparatus for Little Hope lighthouse. I should be glad to have full particulars as to weight and dimensions so that the top of the tower can be finished off to suit. There will be no trouble in doing this if we are advised at once. The height of the present tower is designed for a second order light. If a lower order light is to be installed the tower need not be so high, and this will be an advantage.' But apparently the details are not on this file.

Q. The details are not?—A. I can look that up.

By Hon. Mr. Cassels:

Q. Who are those lanterns purchased from?—A. My lord, you will have to ask the commissioner of lights. I think most of them are purchased from Chance in England and from a firm in Paris. There are only three or four firms that make those lanterns and apparatus.

By Mr. Watson:

Q. You have not any personal knowledge about those?—A. No.

Q. Now, Colonel Anderson, just leave that for the present, will you, and refer to that printed report again? There are headings there at the foot of that page saying, ' Can complete them all in one month.' And on the next page, 174, ' Tender accepted and tenderer to prepare his own specifications.' That seems to be introduced as a matter of comment?—A. That is very easily explained.

Q. Why did you not prepare your own specifications?—A. For two reasons: One was, pressure of time, the other was, facility in doing the work. The matter had been talked over very fully between Mr. Wallberg, and Mr. Fraser and myself. Mr. Wallberg proposed to furnish his own plans as a matter of facility for doing his own work and subject to our approval.

Q. Yes?—A. It is a very ordinary way of doing work for any man in special work that he could provide his own plans and specifications, which must be, however, approved of by the officer who is in charge of the work. This is so usual that we never thought twice about the matter, and we invited Mr. Wallberg, in fact Mr. Wallberg proposed to furnish his own plans that would suit his own method of doing the work and make his plans and specifications satisfactory to the department. That was, of course, adopted. We invited him to submit plans and specifications, and he did so.

Q. You say that is not out of the regular and proper course?—A. No, it is a very usual thing to do.

Q. Then it may be passed?—A. I may say that every large railway company ask for bids on what is called general specifications and the bidders are obliged to provide their own plans and detail specifications, and then those plans and detail specifications are passed on by the engineering officers of the corporation and the work let on them. It is a very usual thing, and a very proper thing, I think.

Q. Then we have a reference on that same page 174 to the ' Shipment of material doubtful.' Why that comment?—A. That also is very easily explained. As I said before, these situations were very isolated, out of the regular route of travel, and it was necessary that we should send the materials there in our own ships. We were doing so much work that our own ships were more than busy, and as a matter of fact there was a great deal of difficulty in our being able to transport the materials and workmen for Mr. Wallberg, and a good deal of delay was necessitated.

Q. Then in connection with that matter was there any default on the part of anyone in the department?—A. I think not.

· Q. It pertains to your own branch?—A. I think not. It was a matter that was absolutely beyond our control. We had only limited steamship accommodation and there were many demands on the steamship and we had to fit them in as best we could.

Q. Then look there, on page 175, there is there comment in respect to the diameter of towers. Is there anything in that that calls for explanation?—A. That is a mere question of detail of an inch or two, with regard to exact diameter. The exact diameter had to be arranged to suit the bolting down of the lantern, and Mr. Wallberg simply asked for detail information to enable him to work to plan.

Q. Yes. Then perhaps we are spending too much time with these minor matters. Look at page 176. There is comment there that affects you, I think. ' Sixty-two days after awarding of contract—he knowing this—resident engineer had not received copies of plans.' Why had he not received those from you?—A. There was no necessity for him to receive them until the work was begun.

Q. Why that comment then?—A. Ask the commissioners.

Hon. Mr. CASSELS.—That is the commissioners' comment.

By Mr. Watson:

Q. I see. I want to give you an opportunity to explain these matters. Then at the foot of the page there is a reference again, 'Resident engineer to blame as he was aware of the necessity of the case from the first—see his communication with Wallberg, 14th September last.' Who was the resident engineer?—A. I imagine this refers to Mr. Parent, the resident engineer at Quebec.

Q. Was he to blame in connection with those matters?—A. Allow me to read this. (Witness peruses report.)

Q. Then in connection with that let me ask you, if you have read it, is that one of the minority upon whom certain suspicion may rest as to misconduct on his part?—A. This refers to Mr. Parent.

Q. Can you answer that first?—A. Yes, I can answer that. I have no reason to suspect Mr. Parent of not being absolutely impartial in his desire to serve the interests of the department. He is one of my officers.

Q. And served one master only?—A. Yes.

Q. You know of no act of misconduct on his part, then?—A. I do not.

Q. Then, is this a matter of criticism of his judgment or of yours?—A. I cannot see any criticism of Mr. Parent in this, for this reason, that Mr. Fraser evidently wrote this letter to Mr. Parent under the understanding, under the impression that he had full control of the *Aranmore*, but if I recollect rightly the *Aranmore* was diverted from the construction work and used that autumn for maintenance, for sending down supplies to lights and bringing up lightkeepers, things of that kind, and diverted from the work we expected her to be employed on, that is construction work. Those were details of management that come under the Quebec agent.

Q. That is under—— ?—A. Mr. Gregory.

Q. And on the next page, passing over some of those other headings which more or less reflect on your branch, I think, I see, 'Mr. Parent's defence to acting chief engineer's indictment.' This is rather a serious heading.

Hon. Mr. CASSELS.—What heading is that?

Mr. WATSON.—178, my lord.

A. The acting chief engineer's indictment is that indictment at the foot of page 176 and the first part of 177, and, as I have tried to explain to you, that was written under the misapprehension that Mr. Parent had full control of the *Aranmore* at the time.

Q. That is based wholly upon a misapprehension?—A. Of the facts, as I understand it.

Q. There was an indictment laid, an official indictment, I mean.

Hon. Mr. CASSELS.—That is the commissioners' interpretation of an indictment. They are not criminal lawyers.

Mr. WATSON.—Yes, my lord. Then reference is made here to your assistant, that is Mr. B. H. Fraser?—A. Where?

Q. In this correspondence throughout?—A. Yes.

Q. Is there any reason to apprehend the regularity and propriety of his conduct and acts?—A. I may say, in short, I have no reason to apprehend the regularity of any member of my own staff.

Q. Are you including the outside staff as well as the inside in that?—A. I am.

Q. In connection with that is Mr. Gregory on your staff?—A. He is not.

Q. Then, these headings are a little troublesome in a way. Your lordship will observe them throughout. I do not know it is necessary to go over them all, but I do not want to be in the position of seeming to pass over them.

WITNESS.—Take these headings, 'Wallberg has to send prints of lighthouses to Parent.' 'Department telegraphed to for plans and specifications.' 'Specifications sent by chief engineer.' 'Wallberg applied to for plans.' Those all arose out of the arrangement with Wallberg that he was to supply plans. Wallberg having the originals was to supply blue prints without charge and as a regular matter.

Hon. Mr. CASSELS.—We are not interested in the manner the department carried out its building operations, unless there is something behind.

Mr. WATSON.—Leading to misconduct.

Hon. Mr. CASSELS.—Not technical misconduct.

Mr. WATSON.—Yes, my lord. The only trouble I have in connection with that is that the explanations are not given here, and it may be said those indicate acts of misconduct. For that reason I do not like to pass over them.

Hon. Mr. CASSELS.—I think you are quite right.

WITNESS.—I think through his correspondence, my lord, the indications are an implication throughout of the management of my branch, of the handling of that work. I would respectfully explain that I think that if the commissioners had called on me for explanation that they would have got such explanations on those points as would have prevented them ever making such criticism.

By Mr. Watson.:

Q. Do you mean they did not call on you for explanation ?—A. Not one word. I did not have an opportunity of explaining one word of this to them.

Q. Take for instance at the top of page 180, 'Inspection of Little Metis by Parent —apparently none before this date, and now too late.' Any comment to be made about that ? That is cartainly a reflection of want of care, at all events ?—A. My recollection is that the light keeper here was instructed to act as local inspector and that we depended on his inspection and on the occasions of the inspections of resident engineer for this work.

Q. Yes. Well then, look at the next, at the foot of that page nearly. 'Departmental blunder. Deputy replies that it was a mistake.'—A. That refers to the accountant's branch.

Q. Just that. That is apparently a mistake there. Then there is this: 'Deputy replies that it was a mistake.' Then it says, 'The cheque should have been addressed to the Steel Concrete Company, Merchants Bank Building.' Is that a mere matter of mistake in the address of the communication ?—A. I really cannot tell you. That is outside of my branch altogether. What I mean to say is, I never looked into it.

Q. Then take the foot of the next page. We have some strong language there. 'Gregory's scathing criticism of management with regard to transport of Wallberg's materials.—Query: Who is responsible for it?' What defence have you got to make to that? Is there any substance in that?—I do not want to be spending time uselessly, Colonel Anderson?—A. I do not recollect the exact circumstances, but I may say in general terms that this is part of the general difficulty we had of providing transport for the materials in consequence of the number of different jobs that were going on at the time and the limited steamboat accommodation that we had. I may say, however, that there was a suggestion there from Mr. Gregory that we should hire another boat to transport materials for Mr. Wallberg. We refused to do this, and the materials were eventually carried down by the regular steamers that we had employed.

Q. Now, you see the language that he uses there, he says, 'It seems ridiculous to make special trips costing over $700 each simply to save the cost of $50 worth of scaffolding.' There are two misapprehensions. In the first place, on the part of Mr. Gregory to the effect that we intended to make a special trip, which we did not intend to do, and did not do. In the second place, a misapprehension on the part of the commissioners in supposing that we had ever intended to do or that we did make a special trip.

Q. I see. Then you simply displace those circumstances, the facts ?—A. Well, Mr. Gregory built up a house of straw and then fought against it.

Q. But he says further down, ' I consider it my duty to lay these facts before the department prior to incurring such heavy expenses, as schooners can do the work better than we can with our steamers——A. No expense was incurred, as a matter of fact.

Q. Was that the result of his protest?—A. Not at all. Mr. Gregory misapprehended the position.

Q. Then we can pass it at that. This would indicate a great deal of anxiety on the part of Mr. Gregory in regard to these matters ?—A. Probably, that was natural.

Q. That was in the ordinary course of the execution of his duties, do I understand ?—A. I understand it so.

Q. Then at the top of page 183, the heading. 'What special motive produced this unusual bit of foresight?' Do you observe that?—A. Yes.

Q. You observe that comment by the commissioners——'Produced this unusual bit of foresight ?' That may be——A. I do not feel——

Q. That is hardly commendation ?—A. I hardly feel called upon to comment upon that.

Q. Is there anything in it ?—A. It appears to me the memorandum is—they are such precautions as we usually take in the branch.

Q. But it is said by the commissioners that it is unusual ?—A. I am not responsible for it.

Q. For what ?—A. For their comment.

Q. Oh, for the statement, I see. Now, there is a reference to an application by Mr. Wallberg for a patent ?—A. Yes.

Q. You observe that, ' And on the strength of it wants more business from the department.' Now, it is indicated throughout on the following pages that this application for the patent and its issue was supported for the purposes of enabling him to get greater advantages ?—A. There is not the slighest ground for any such——

Q. Imputation ?—A. Imputation.

Q. Is there not ?—A. No, there is not.

Q. Then, what do you say as to the patent, the application for it, was it bona fide or not ?—A. Mr. Wallberg, I understand, did apply for a patent. My assistant Mr. Fraser, advised me that he had done so. I objected to it on the ground that the use of reinforced concrete in towers was not patentable, having previously been used.

Q. Yes ?—A. I drafted a letter, which was signed by the deputy-formulating that objection.

Q. Yes?—A. There was considerable correspondence and some interviews between Mr. Wallberg and myself and Mr. Fraser and the minister with regard to this question of patenting.

Q. And with the result?—A. With the result that—I think the result was he told Mr. Wallberg if he was entitled to a patent he could go ahead and get it; if he was not, we would continue to employ that method of construction.

Q. If he was entitled to it according to the rules of the department and the statute, you could not prevent the issue of it?—A. We could not prevent the issue of it, and in that case if we employed his patent process we would be responsible to him for the royalty.

Q. Did you withdraw your objections?—A. No, not that I am aware of.

Hon. Mr. CASSELS.—They seem to have come to an agreement to get the work done, notwithstanding the patent, at a reasonable price.

By Mr. Watson:

Q. His lordship intimates that?—A. Mr. Wallberg proposed such an agreement. He proposed that in the event of our making such an agreement he would not charge any royalty on the work done by the department, but he wanted to be protected in regard to outside parties in respect to towers for other purposes.

Q. And was that a proper arrangement?—A. I did not think so, and I recommended to the minister that we should allow the matter to stand on its regular basis, that we should not sign any agreement. My assistant was of a different opinion and he made a recommendation to the minister that such an agreement should be signed to protect the department. But that was done while I was away, and the reason for the apparent clash of opinion between my assistant and myself was the fact that he acted in my absence and I acted in his absence.

Q. I see. There was a difference of opinion there?—A. There was a difference of opinion, that it was more a difference as to the process by which Mr. Wallberg's claim should be met.

Q. And you explained that. Otherwise one would not expect, as you indicate, that your assistant would send a formal communication differing with your opinion as head of the branch?—A. That is the explanation. I was absent from Ottawa. Whenever I am absent from Ottawa he acts for me.

Q. That explains that. We have a reference there emphasizing that some letter is missing, there is a special reference to it?—A. Where is that?

Q. Page 183, about three-fourths of the way down. 'More omissions.' Is there anything significant in that? It looks so on its face?—A. No. It is very likely Mr. Fraser wrote a personal letter to Mr. Wallberg. There was a good deal of correspondence to and fro, and very often anything that was not strictly official was written possibly in a hurry, by myself or Mr. Fraser and sent out without any copy being kept of it.

Q. And is that the course which is pursued in your branch of personal or private communications sometimes?—A. Not generally; but in small unimportant matters where there is nothing depends on it we very often send a memorandum—I very often.

Q. You very often do yourself?—A. Yes. I have a memorandum form. For instance, just where a few words will suffice on something that nothing depends upon where I may send it out.

Q. And no record is kept of it?—A. No record is kept of it.

Q. And that is regarded as a personal or private communication?—A. It is regarded as an unofficial mem.

Q. And does your assistant do the same?—A. I have no doubt he does.

Q. And other officials in your department?—A. I have no doubt of it.

Q. That, you will appreciate, may lead to grounds of suspicion by reason of personal and private communications going in that way?—A. I do not know, it does not seem so to me.

Q. You say those are matters in the ordinary proper course of business communication?—A. It has been our universal practice.

Q. For how long back?—A. Ever since I have been in the department.

Q. That is for a great many years, I understand?—A. Yes. Any small item, for instance, a man wants some dimension or something of that kind.

Q. But the feature is that these are sent in the same way to contractors, those dealing with the department. Is there not an exception in their cases?—A. Of course. I cannot tell anything about this letter. The letter is Mr. Fraser's. It may be found on some other file for all I know.

Q. But directly in answer to my remark, there is not any exception as to these personal or private communications to contractors, where they may be deemed necessary?—A. No; but I would be very careful not to send a private note to a contractor on anything that in any way involved either me or the department.

Q. Of course, we would expect that. I suppose that would apply to all of the others?—A. I hope so.

Q. Now then, look at the next page where you are challenged by the heading——A. Page?

Q. 184. 'Wallberg's proposals find favour with the department.' 'Wallberg so informed. What does chief engineer say to this?'—A. I tried to explain that. That is Mr. Fraser's memorandum with regard to his application for a patent, and I have tried to explain what was the outcome of that.

Q. What you have said covers that having reference to the patent, is it ?—A. Yes.

Q. And there is some further reference to that—you have explained that. There a some comment at page 188 about Mr. Wallberg's tender for Little Hope lighthouse ower. That is what we have been referring to, is it ?—A. Yes.

Q. Now, that says: 'Wallberg, for Steel Construction Company writes B.H.F.' Why should he write to him ?—A. Probably I was away.

Q. 'Quoting for a lighthouse tower for Little Hope Island in reinforced concrete, 4,950, 10 feet 6 inches diameter and 75 feet high, and will be built exactly similar to he other towers which we are constructing for you. We can begin the construction of his tower at once and complete it very promptly, and in order to do so we trust to have your acceptance at very earliest moment.' Is there anything for remark there ?—A. I think not.

Q. On the next page, 189: 'Assistant chief engineer talks of temporary arrangenets, but is apparently willing to let Wallberg decide.' Do you observe that ?—A. I see that, yes.

Q. What explanation have you to offer on that comment ?—A. As I understand, his was a question of Mr. Wallberg's deciding whether he would begin the work late n the autum or postpone it to the spring of the year. That naturally would be a question for Mr. Wallberg to decide.

Q. Why should that be left to him ?—A. There was no use beginning the work unless he could finish it in the same autumn. It was a question of time. It was a question for him to decide whether he had facilities to build the tower before frosty weather set in.

Q. I see. Then is there any matter that properly reflects there upon conduct or discretion ?—A. I think that was a matter proper for Mr. Wallberg to decide.

Q. Then in the next few pages there are comments. Now, at page 194, 'Memoandum for Mr. Noble. Change in Little Hope light. Query: Who discovered the reason for this and who was responsible for the original costly blunder ?'—A. That is a matter I was looking up that file for. I am afraid I cannot answer that at present.

Q. Yes. Who is Mr. Noble ?—A. He is assistant commissioner of lights.

Q. Assistant commisioner of lights ?—A. Yes.

Q. Then, why were those communications with Mr. Noble ?—A. I imagine that Mr. Fraser must have been either ill—he had an attack of typhoid fever some time about then—or he was absent. You see, when Mr. Fraser was away Mr. Noble acted for him.

Q. Then, was it the practice or occasionally the course that communications might be sent to Mr. Noble, the assistant, by reason of the fact of personal differences existing with Mr. Fraser ?—A. Never. All my communications were addressed to the commissioner of lights. Then they were acted on by either the commissioner——

Q. Then, was he made the means of personal communications, that is Mr. Noble? —A. No.

Q. The medium of personal communications ?—A. Between me and the commissioner ?

Q. Between you and Mr. J. F. Fraser ?—A. No.

Q. Now, that speaks of the matter of responsibility for the original costly blunder. You say you will look up that portion of the file ?—A. If I may, yes.

Q. I will be glad if you will, please. Will you look at the bottom of the next page ? 'Resident engineer telegraphs to department for plans 27 days after these had been accepted by them.' That looks an exceedingly irregular course ?—A. Yes. I do not see the——

Q. Was there anything irregular in connection with that?—A. I do not see the reference.

Q. What I have read—you mean at the foot of page 195, the last paragraph ?— A. Yes.

Q. All these headings are in special type there. (Reads heading again.) Do you see that ?—A. Yes, I see.

Hon. Mr. CASSELS.—What is the reference ?—A. The reference on the top of the next page, my lord. ' J. A. Legere telegraphs to B.H.F.'

By Mr. Watson :

Q. Yes. Is there anything fairly for criticism in connection with that matter ? —A. I think not, for this reason; the plans were sent to Mr. Legere before the work was resumed on the altered plans.

Q. Yes. Then at the next page, 197, towards the foot of that page, ' chief engineer '—referring to you—' objects to unnecessary cost transporting broken stone.'—A. Well, that is with reference to a report by Mr. DeMiffanis, who was one of my staff sent down to inspect and oversee the work. He stated that the stone was being transported in a small vessel at some expense, and the action was taken.

Q. Was that maintained, was it found to be supported afterwards ?—A. When we learned of it we wrote to this effect: We have no objection to landing the stone in one trip with our own boat, as we did at Cape Race, but we must absolutely refuse to pay any such charges as I understand are being incurred by these men at Little Hope. Mr. DeMiffanis states that it will cost at least $1,000 to transport the stone to the station in the way it is being done now.

Q. Yes. Was he information given by Mr. DeMiffanis ?—A. I do not know. I know we did not pay anything extra for the transportation of the stone.

Q. Then you do not know whether that was well founded ?

Hon. Mr. CASSELS.—There is a subsequent letter at the foot of page 198 showing the government sent it in their own steamers.

Mr. WATSON.—Yes my lord.

Q. Who was responsible for that ?—A. For what ?

Q. For what might have been the excessive cost of transport ?—A. We undertook to transport the stone, but we also had an understanding with Mr. Wallberg that we could only transport the stone when our own vessels were available. This was aparently some other proposal to use some other means of transporting the stone.

Q. Who made that transportation ?—A. Apparently Mr. Walberg's men did, and apparently is was refused.

Q. Was not this a communication to any official in the department ?—A. That was based on a report from Mr. DeMiffanis to me.

Q. But did any officer in the department or outside officers recommend this course which you protested against ?—A. Not that I am aware of.

Q. Then that was being done at the instance of Mr. Wallberg ?—A. Naturally he would want the best possible facilities for transporting the stone.

Q. And that was not carried out. Then you see at page 199 with reference to the work at Little Hope that, ' Wallberg explains and minimizes roughness of work.' Was there a defect there ?—A. It was merely a question of the outside finish. It did not affect in any way the stability of the work, but it affected the appearance of the work. Mr. Wallberg offered to put on a coat outside that would give a uniform finish in appearance.

Q. Yes. Was there anything—— ?—A. That was referred to the engineer on the work at the time, and what his decision with Mr. Wallberg was at the moment I do not know. I can find out.

Q. Was there reason to think there was anything improper intended by that?—A. Oh, no, a mere question of looks.

Hon. Mr. CASSELS.—Just a wash ?

Mr. WATSON.—It is worded in such a mysterious way——

WITNESS.—If they had consulted the responsible officers most of these things could have been satisfactorily explained. I really think we ought to be given credit for the amount of work done under very difficult circumstances where there was pressure of work all over the Dominion, and we had to split up our forces as we could get opportunity——

Q. I am seeking to give you an opportunity now——

Hon. Mr. CASSELS.—That is what Mr. Watson is doing.

Mr. WATSON.—To explain those comments that are of record. Then page 201: 'Parent explains why work at Matane was not inspected by him.' Was there default on his part there?—A. No, he had other work to do.

Q. He had other work to do. But was there an absence or want of inspection?—A. No. I may say that at Matane I had an opportunity of inspecting the tower myself.

Q. Yes. Then in respect of any and all of these matters on page 201, I think perhaps that covers all the references made to you. Yes, it does, the analysis that I have had made, or the abstract that I have made, covers all these matters. Now, then, in so far as those headings and written statements convey reflections more or less serious against you and against those in your department, what have you to say generally?—A. That I consider that they were made under a misapprehension of the facts and want of sufficient knowledge of the peculiar circumstances that existed at the time that this work was done, and that they are all capable of explanation. I hope that my explanation to you in the matter has shown you that.

Q. Yes. Now, then, reference has been made to purchases by you and in your branch from the Canadian Fog Signal Company?—A. Yes.

Q. What do you purchase from that company?—A. The machinery of fog alarms.

Q. Fog alarms?—A. Operating machinery.

Q. What?—A. Operating machinery of fog alarms, fog signals.

Q. How long have you been dealing with that company?—A. I think about seven years.

Q. Seven years; that is near enough. Who compose that company chiefly, those with whom you have to do?—A. Those with whom I have to do are Mr. John P. Northey, who was formerly of the Machinery Manufacturing Company, and the secretary of the company, Mr. F. S. Mearns. I do not know who compose the company, although I did see a statement of the shareholders lately.

Q. That is sufficient. I just wanted to know with whom the transactions were. Now, to what extent are contracts made with them?—A. Practically we get all our fog alarm machinery from them now.

Q. And the estimate of that per year would be about how much?—A. I really could not tell you without preparing it. The thing is capable of preparation.

Q. Well, just in a general way? Is it a matter of $100,000 or $200,000?—A. I think it is less than $200,000. I cannot give you figures at all; I can prepare them.

Q. You cannot give the figures?—A. Mr. Fraser possibly has them prepared.

Q. Who makes those contracts?—A. They are made in the usual way in the department.

Q. In the usual way in the department?—A. Yes.

Q. But are they the subject of tender?—A. Yes, they are now.

Q. For how long have they been so?—A. Four or five years, I think.

Q. That is by direction of the minister, I believe?—A. Yes.

Q. And what other companies or firms deal in the same articles?—A. No other company. They have the patent rights of what we consider to be the best fog alarm in existence to-day.

Q. Yes?—A. And that is the reason they are dealt with.

Q. That they are dealt with?—A. Yes.

Q. And is that company dealt with exclusively in the purchase of fog alarms?—A. It is now.

Q. Exclusively?—A. Yes.

By Hon. Mr. Cassels:

Q. Are these on lighthouses?—A. No, it is a separate installation, my lord. A fog alarm station we consider as an altogether independent installation from a light station. As a matter of fact, they are usually combined at the same station, but we keep the one pretty well separate from the other, both in construction——

By Mr. Watson:

Q. They are very numerous, of course, they are used to a very large extent?—A. Yes.

Q. And those contracts have your personal supervision?—A. Yes.

Q. Your responsibility carries to them?—A. My responsibility carries.

Q. And to the prices?—A. I do not consider that my responsibility carries to the prices in that case, because as soon as a contract is let, as soon as the work is done under the contract system, I consider that the minister assumes the responsibility.

Q. But do you make as head of the department, a recommendation?—A. I do.

Q. Then you assume the responsibility of making that recommendation?—A. Certainly.

Q. And you expect the recommendation to be regarded as a commendable one, a proper one?—A. Yes.

Q. Then you have that responsibility?—A. Yes, in that way, yes.

Q. And your recommendation, does it include the prices to be paid—it would necessarily?—A. It would necessarily after tenders are invited, yes.

Q. Now; I see by the reference that my learned friend, Mr. Perron, hands to me that the prices paid for these are pretty high?—A. Yes, sir.

Q. Running from $4,400 each article——

Hon. Mr. CASSELS.—Mr. Watson will you allow me to ask a question?

Mr. WATSON.—Certainly, my lord.

Hon. Mr. CASSELS.—Do you know of any instance where higher prices have gone into the contracts than the prices you recommended?—A. No, I do not.

Q. Just so as to bring it out, Mr. Watson.

Mr. WATSON.—Yes.

Q. Do you know of any highr prices than those recommended?—A. No.

Q. This is not a matter of responsibility of Mr. B. H. Fraser now?—A. I assume responsibility for anything that Mr. B. H. Fraser does.

Q. Now, in a word, I may just say to you that the information that has been given to my learned friend and to me is that the prices that are being paid for these fog signals is in every case over $4,000, in many cases running much higher than that, and that the cost of those articles is in the neighbourhood of $300 or $400, putting it plainly and straight?—A. I think there is some justification for that statement.

Q. You think there is?—A. Yes, I believe it is the case. Possibly not to that extent, but it is the case.

Q. Have you had personal knowledge of that?—A. I have.

Q. And notwithstanding that you have recommended the purchases?—A. I have.

Q. At those prices?—A. At those prices.

Q. Well, although it is about the time of adjournment, colonel, I would prefer his lordship would not adjourn until you are given an opportunity to make any explanation you may wish. It is hardly fair there should be an adjournment without your having that opportunity?—A. I was going to ask for that opportunity, my lord.

Hon. Mr. CASSELS.—Just explain it.—A. The point is this, my lord: We are looking for the best sound producer that it is possible to obtain. We consider that in the diaphone which is produced by this company we have the best sound producer that has yet been invented. The prices are based on the cost of the operating machinery and then a price is added for the sound producing device, which is patented.

The cost of the machinery has always been based on the market price of such machinery, and is reasonable. The only point on which there has been any excessive price, or any price that could be considered excessive, has been on the sound-producing patented portion. In that matter we are absolutely in the hands of the company.

Q. Why?—A. Because there is nobody else can produce this machinery under the patent laws, and it has been the practice of the owners of patents of this kind throughout the world to ask excessive prices for their inventions. The prices we pay compare favourably with the prices paid by the government of Great Britain and the government of Scotland for their sound-producing machines.

Q. You do not seem to understand the difference in the patent laws. In the old country a patentee can exact any price he chooses; here under our Patent Act if he asks for an excessive price, a price that is not reasonable, his patent would be void.

WITNESS.—I was going on to explain, my lord, that I have called the minister's attention to the large price claimed by the patentees for these inventions, and he has been quite seized of the fact that the price charged for the sound-producing device was not any representation of the cost of manufacture of it. That is to say, that in making the recommendation to the minister it was accompanied by the explanation that the price of the sound-producer was not the commercial value of the manufacture.

Mr. WATSON.—Would you just let me see that report? I would like to have your report to the minister.

By Hon. Mr. Cassels:

Q. I may say, colonel, for your benefit, that the construction placed on our Patent Act has only been a late one. It has been so held by the Supreme Court within the last 6 or 8 months only. That is a point that is now going to the Privy Council, I may say?—A. Whether that exists in writing I am not at the moment prepared to say.

By Mr. Watson:

Q. I thought you said in the recommendation you made you embodied in that recommendation, which is, of course, in writing, reference to the fact that the price was in excess of the cost?—A. I shall probably find it.

Q. I wish you would?—A. But I am not at the moment prepared to say it exists in writing. I am quite satisfied, though, I can get evidence from the minister that the thing has been brought to his attention.

Q. Yes?—A. And the matter is exactly as I have stated.

Q. Was that recently or some time ago?—A. At the time tenders were last asked for, and within the last month it has been again dealt with, and I may say at the moment I am engaged preparing plans and specifications asking for new tenders, and in those new tenders we ask especially for separate prices for the operating machinery and for the sound-producing device.

Q. Yes. Then I would like if you would get those reports?—A. I will see what I can find.

Q. You say they are recent, within the last month, I understood you?—A. That, I know, was a verbal communication with the minister.

Hon. Mr. CASSELS.—Mr. Justice Burbidge held that under our Act, unlike the Patent Laws of England, the patentee was bound to sell for a reasonable price and to sell out and out for cash.

Mr. WATSON.—Yes, my lord, I remember.

Hon. Mr. CASSELS.—We differed in our office from that view and took the case to the Supreme Court. The Supreme Court has upheld the views of Mr. Justice Burbidge. That is only within the last few months.

Mr. WATSON.—It is a new law for the time being, in a way.

Hon. Mr. CASSELS.—Well, that is the present view of the statute. What time do you want?

3262—6

Mr. WATSON.—Say a quarter past two?

Hon. Mr. CASSELS.—Very well.

WITNESS.—I should like to point out, my lord, in this case the circumstances are peculiar in this respect, that the company has only one customer, that is the Government of Canada, and that all the cost of developing the machine must be paid by that customer.

Hon. Mr. CASSELS.—A great many elements enter into what is a reasonable price. You have got to pay for the invention and you have got to allow large sums. It is a question of fact largely.

By Mr. Watson:

Q. Do you say the price paid, having regard to the circumstances, was reasonable and proper?—A. I say it compares favourably with the price of similar fog alarm machinery paid by other governments.

Q. And yet that is not quite an answer to the direct question?—A. It is a high price; there is no question about it.

Q. Was it reasonable and proper to make the payment you recommended?—A. I must have thought so when I recommended it.

Hon. Mr. CASSELS.—I think what is entering on the colonel's mind is that they could exact whatever price they chose, having the patent; that while charging an excessive price, still, there they were——

By Mr. Watson:

Q. Do you mean, as his lordship rather suggests, that it was a matter of a hold-up?—A. No, it was not a matter of hold-up, but I admit at once that the price is excessive if you take into consideration only the absolute cost of the metal that goes into the device.

Q. But having regard to all the conditions?—A. Having regard to all the conditions, I fail to see how we can make any better arrangement. I can possibly save a few hundred dollars by adopting the English siren. Then I am in this position: I pay nearly as much for the machinery and do not get as good a sound-producing device.

Q. Then, if you will kindly have those reports, colonel.

(Adjourned from 1 to 2.15 p.m. and then resumed).

By Mr. Watson :

Q. Just a question, Colonel Anderson. Were you able to find any reports in writing?—A. I have only been able to got the files since I came back from lunch. These were in there. I have not found anything up to now.

Q. Then I would be glad to give you further opportunity—of course you will be here available—I would like to have the pleasure of recalling you further after to-day. I think then, my lord, Colonel Anderson might be excused for the rest of the day upon this matter. There is some further material I want him to get.

WITNESS.—This letter from Mr. Prefontaine which you asked me and I promised you I would turn in (producing). I should like the opportunity, Mr. Perron, later of consulting these files, if I may.

Mr. PERRON.—Provided you tell Mr. McCleneghan; he is responsible for them.

Mr. WATSON.—The letter which the colonel has handed to me, my lord, is one dated the 16th October, 1903, addressed to him by Mr. Prefontaine, and reads as follows. (Reads).

Letter put in, marked Exhibit 6.

Mr. WATSON.—(As witness is leaving room). We are not asking you to leave, colonel.

WITNESS.—Not at all.

Mr. WATSON.—We are just excusing you from the witness stand, that is all.

Mr. WATSON.—I would like to ask Mrs. Thomas a question or two.

Mrs. THOMAS recalled.

By Mr. Watson:

Q. Mrs. Thomas, you were examined yesterday in regard to correspondence, including matters of so-called private or personal correspondence, and you said that this personal correspondence of a personal or private nature was on file and of record in the department, with some exceptions, which you mentioned, of letters from relatives and so on. What do you now find and produce (referring to several baskets of papers)?—A. All these letters here, Mr. Watson, are the deputy minister's correspondence, which are not to be found on the official files of the department, but all the correspondence which was filed in our office.

Q. All that was filed in your office?—A. In our office, sir.

Q. Now, what course was adopted when that was received, what was done with it? Is that correspondence which you opened?—A. I cannot say it all is, sir.

Q. But opened by you and others?—A. Yes, sir.

Q. Opened by the deputy minister?—A. Well, by ourselves and our office.

Q. By yourselves and your office?—A. Yes, sir.

Q. Then what did you do with it after it was opened?—A. Well, after we opened the correspondence, if it is anything official it will go on the official file, we bring it out to the record room; and anything purely personal or private, and anything very urgent which may be official, which we think the deputy minister should see before it is placed on file, we bring in to him.

Q. Now, what is not placed on file the regular official file is disposed of in some way. What is done with that?—A. Well, as I say, all the deputy minister's correspondence which passes through our hands, letters received by him, or letters that we reply to, we file in our office.

Q. Have you a system in connection with that?—A. We have not got any more system than we docket those, as we call it, we back them and put them alphabetically in pigeon holes.

Q. You do pursue that system, arranging them alphabetically and in chronological order of dates?—A. Yes, sir.

Q. Then you have there now six baskets full?—A. Yes.

Q. And are those arranged with reference to periods or years?—A. Well, everything is muddled up at the present time. You see, I took everything out, 1902, 1903, 1904, you know the very little time we had this morning. We put them in the baskets as quickly as possibly to get them here. Everything is there since 1902.

Q. Since 1902?—A. Yes, everything.

Q. Why not before 1902?—A. Because we have not got them. As far as I can recollect, about six years ago we destroyed private correspondence of that nature for want of room, we had no place to put it.

Q. Then, I want to know if what you have there includes everything of that nature since 1902?—A. To my knowledge everything is there.

Q. To your knowledge everything is there?—A. Yes, sir.

By Hon. Mr. Cassels:

Q. There seems to be drafts of your answers as well here?—A. Yes, sir. We always keep a duplicate of every reply that we prepare.

Mr. WATSON.—Now, my lord, my learned friend and I have not had an opportunity of going over these, except to pick out one or two papers at random.

Hon. Mr. CASSELS.—You and Mr. Perron can go through them at your leisure.

Mr. WATSON.—What I would like, my lord, is that they should be identified now by Mrs. Thomas, the witness, who has personal knowledge of them, and in a way impounded, or, at all events that the witness should be responsible for them. Will you undertake that, you to be responsible for them, Mrs. Thomas ?—A. Are they to be kept here ?

Hon. Mr. CASSELS.—Mr. Morse, have yo uroom in your vault?

Mr. MORSE.—We can make room for them, they will have to go in.

WITNESS.—I could not take the responsibility of them if I am not here.

Mr. WATSON.—At all events, we will go over them as much as we can, at all events sufficiently to show the nature of them, and then produce some portions.

Hon. Mr. CASSELS.—There are lots of letters, for instance, written to Mr. Gregory, to his subordinates, not private correspondence, ostensibly private.

Mr. WATSON.—Quite so.

Q. Then, that is all, you are quite sure that includes all?—A. That includes to my knowledge everything that we have had filed in our office since 1902.

Mr. WATSON.—Then my learned friend calls Mr. Wallberg.

EMIL A. WALLBERG, sworn.

By Mr. Perron :

Q. Mr. Wallberg, you were summoned to bring with you all books, papers, documents, correspondence, cash books, cheque books, counterfoils of cheques, and any other documents having any reference to your transactions with the Marine and Fisheries Department or any of its officials for the years 1904-5, 1905-6, and 1906-7. You received a copy of this subpœna?—A. Yes, sir.

Q. You are the Mr. Wallberg who is mentioned in many instances in the report of the commissioners?—A. I am.

Q. It appears that you have been dealing extensively with the department?—A. As an officer of the Steel Concrete Company, I have had dealings with the department in connection with six towers of reinforced concrete for lighthouses.

Q. Will you please state where those towers were built?—A. Cape Race, Little Metis, Matane, Cape Magdalen, Little Hope and Heath Point.

By Hon. Mr. Cassels:

Q. Where is Heath Point?—A. That is the east point of Anticosti Island.

By Mr. Perron:

Q. Would it be possible for you, Mr. Wallberg, to state about the price of each of those towers now—about, of course?—A. Yes, sir. The Cape Race tower was $4,800; the Little Metis, $3,900; Matane, $3,600; Cape Magdalen, $3,300; Little Hope, $4,950, with the change involving an addition of $2,300; Heath Point, $4,950.

Q. Now, for system's sake, you have just mentioned that a change had been made at Little Hope?—A. Yes, sir.

Q. Will you kindly state to his lordship what that change consisted of?—A. —After the tower had been begun we were advised by the department that they wished to change from one style of light to the next higher, involving weights of approximately twice as great, and they asked us to submit a plan showing the alterations with the accompanying price, which we did. This involved strengthening the tower, doubling practically the strength of it up to the top and running a number of reinforced concrete buttresses to the very top of the tower and reinforcing the connection of the top platform to the tower and strengthening, practically doubling the strength of the top platform.

Q. You have been stati.ng that you had been requested by the department to prepare those changes. Will you state by whom, acting on behalf of the Department of
Marine and Fisheries, you were requested to make those changes?—A. That would be
by the chief engineer, as I recollect.

Q. Colonel Anderson?—A. Yes, sir.

Q. Well, in all these contracts, which you mentioned a minute ago, who was representing the Department of Marine and Fisheries in all your dealings?—A. My dealings came under Colonel Anderson as chief engineer.

Q. Did you have occasion to interview anybody else in connection with those
works?—A. I interviewed Mr. B. H. Fraser, his assistant; Colonel Anderson referred
me to him on certain details.

Q. So do I understand then that the only officials of the Department of Marine
and Fisheries with whom you had dealings, were Colonel Anderson, the chief engineer,
and Mr. B. H. Fraser, his assistant?—A. Those are the only officials here. At the
branches in Quebec and Halifax my men particularly came in contact with the officials
there about transportation. I did not have any business with them except as it came
to an arrangement for steamers and transportation of supplies.

Q. But in Ottawa the only persons with whom you dealt were, as you stated,
Colonel Anderson and Mr. B. H. Fraser?—A. Yes, sir.

Q. Now, personally, did you have occasion to interview some of the agents? You
have just been mentioning the two agencies at Quebec and Halifax?—A. Well, I
believe on one occasion I went to Quebec in connection with the teaming of our supplies for the first shipment by steamer from there, and at that time I met Mr. Gregory.

Q. Mr. Gregory? He was then, I understand, in charge of the Quebec agency?
—A. Yes, and I believe I was introduced to Mr. Parent, an engineer; but this was
only for a short time with either of them, and I don't think I have seen them since.

Q. Well, by the correspondence exchanged did you have occasion to know some
of the officials other than those you have just mentioned?—A. I had some correspondence with Mr. Legere, the engineer in charge at Halifax, as we shipped the Cape Race
and Little Hope supplies from there.

Q. Is that all?—A. That is the only official I have met.

Q. You stated that you had obtained a contract of $2,300 of exras for changes
at Little Hope?—A. Yes, sir.

Q. Can you tell us how far the original plans had been carried out when those
changes were asked for from you?—A. Oh, the original plan for the tower was carried
about 15 or 16 feet above ground, and to this elevation buttresses were to be carried
according to the first plan, so that the change did not involve taking out anything that
we had done; it merely added to it.

Q. Increased the quantities?—A. Increased from there on.

Q. And those instructions were received from, you stated, Colonel Anderson himself?—A. Yes, sir, as I remember it.

Q. Well, then, I understand that there was four lighthouses, six—four or five?—
A. Six altogether.

Q. That there were six lighthouses. Are those the only works which you performed either by contract or otherwise for the Department of Marine and Fisheries?
—A. That is the only work.

Q. Covering a period of how many years?—A. Oh, approximately two years.

Q. Two years?—A. And a total expenditure, as I have named, of something over
$20,000.

Q. Yes. What is the first contract that you obtained from the department?—A.
Cape Race tower was the first contract.

Q. Was this contract awarded to you after tenders had been asked for?—A. There
were no tenders publicly advertised on that contract. I submitted my plans with
specifications and prices with a view to doing some business in this line, which was, of
course, our line of business, reinforced concrete.

Q. How did you come to learn the department intended to build a tower of re inforced concrete there?—A. I interviewed the engineer's department.

Q. Who was that, whom did you see?—A. I saw Colonel Anderson, as I remem ber, I think that is all.

Q. I understand that this tower was the first one to be built with that process of reinforced concrete?—A. Yes, sir.

Q. Before they used to be built——?—A. All of stone.

Q. So this one was a trial?—A. Yes, it was a new system.

Q. Well, now, you have stated that this first contract was awarded to you without tenders being asked for. Do I understand that the same answer applies to the other work?—A. No, sir. This first one, no doubt, proved successful, and when other towers were to be built they were publicly advertised and we tendered, and after a time we were notified that our tender was accepted.

Q. Have you read this report of the commissioners?—A. I have.

Q. Have you got one before you there?—A. I have.

Q. If you have one will you take page 34—just take this one.   (Hands witness print of report). About the middle of the page?—A. Yes, sir.

Q. 'There would also seem to be a lack of conscience. In connection with the enormous expenditures which are deemed necessary the word "discount" never appears. It is tacitly assumed that there is no such thing, but the whole commercial world knows otherwise. If no one gets any benefit from trade with the government except the trader, then it must be clear that in these great purchases made for the government, without discount, its officers must be assisting the trader to get better prices from the government than he can get anywhere else; for, everywhere else, he has to give discount. In other words, some of the government's officers are serving two masters, and apparently succeeding with both, Scripture notwithstanding.' Have you read that?—A. I have.

Q. You understand to whom that applies?—A. I do.

Q. It applies to, according to you?—A. It applies to the officers of the department.

Q. Of the Marine and Fisheries Department?—A. Yes, sir.

Q. Well, now, Mr. Wallberg, in all your dealings with the divers officials of the department, will you state if you found out any facts which would justify the statemet I have just read to you?—A. Not in the slightest. My dealings with the department have been practically the same as with any private concern, and all this work was carried out, sometimes under great difficulties, and they never allowed one cent of extra on any contract. My dealings with the department's officers have been absolutely businesslike in every way, and absolutely above suspicion. My prices are as low as I can do that work for, and I have done it right. The towers are in commission, there is no fault to find with them that I know of, and the profits have been smaller than they have been on my average work. As far as discount is concerned, I may say that I have done business for over 10 years with private firms all over the country before I ever did public business, and I, during that time, executed several hundred contracts and I have carried out quite a number with the government, and, as far as discount is concerned, I cannot recall one instance where there has been five cents discount or of any discount whatever.

Q. You mean discount granted by you to the purchaser?—A. I mean discount granted by me to the purchaser.

By Hon. Mr. Cassels:

Q. Did you ever allow any commissions to anyone for bringing you the work?—A. Never. Not only as regards the officers of this department, but as regards the officers of any department of the government, not one cent.

Q. You see, the word 'discount' would also mean commissions to the men bring ing the work.

Mr. PERRON.—Yes, no doubt.

By Mr. Perron:

Q. Now, Mr. Wallberg, we will take first Colonel Anderson, who is the chief of this branch?—A. Yes sir.

Q. You have, of course, had many interviews with him?—A. Yes, sir.

Q. Many dealings with him?—A. Yes, sir.

Q. You have had to have your work approved by him?—A. He has had to approve as chief engineer.

Q. And I suppose that no warrants for payment could be issued without his authority, without his approval?—A. I believe that is right.

Q. Well now, whenever you went to Colonel Anderson for any reason whatever in connection with your contracts or otherwise, was there ever any question between you and him of commission or what is commonly called 'rake-off,' or any improper conduct whatever?—A. Nothing whatever, absolutely nothing. I want to emphasize that, because I want to say it just as forcibly as I can say it that as regards him and as regards every officer of the department there has never been one hint or one word either way or anything that could lead anyone to suspect or hint at such a thing.

Q. In any way, sense or form whatever?—A. Absolutely in no way, sense or form. I say that most solemnly and most emphatically, and that appertains to all the business with all the officers.

Q. Now, take Mr. B. H. Fraser, he was practically in charge of supervising your work?—A. He had a great deal to do with it.

Q. He was preparing plans, at least, approving of them and going over them?—A. Yes.

Q. Specifications also?—A. He had detail work to do.

Q. The detail work was in the hands of Mr. B. H. Fraser?—A. Yes.

Q. And, of course, if he had felt like being nasty towards you he could have been so?—A. Well, of course, we had certain plans and specifications to carry out. A man may, if he has any spite, make it difficult for a contractor to do his work.

Q. That is what I mean?—A. Undoubtedly.

Q. You have seen those things occurring before in your long experience as a contractor?—A. Yes.

Q. Now, did you ever find that Mr. B. H. Fraser was, as you said, causing you unnecessary trouble in the performance of your contracts?—A. No, not any unnecessary trouble. I believe I got fair dealing; that is all.

Q. From him?—A. From him.

Q. And also from Colonel Anderson?—A. And nothing more. We stood absolutely on contract conditions. In every case I know of I got no favours, not the slightest I know of.

Q. Well, Mr. Wallberg, did you or did you not notice that in the course of your construction anybody else—we will take Mr. Fraser for the present—was rather inclined to be severe with you, too severe?—A. Well, I know in cases where as regards transportation—there is one case particularly from Halifax in a shipment of our men and materials to Little Hope. They were under contract to supply us with transportation on their boats, and they sent our crew on a schooner. While it is probably a one day trip, our crew was 20 days before they landed at Little Hope Island, due to unfavorable weather. All that time I had to pay all the wages and all the board for the whole crew of men, the foreman and so on, which was a heavy expense, I had not contemplated such an expenditure, it was entirely extraordinary, but Mr. Fraser would not allow anything whatever as compensation, as additional compensation, and I could not under my contract go any further or press the point.

Q. Well, did he hint to you that under certain circumstances compensation might be awarded to you for this trouble or delay?—A. Absolutely nothing of that kind, nothing.

Q. Well, when you found that Mr. Fraser was getting rather severe on you did you take some means of making him a little more lenient?—A. No, sir. I cannot say that he was more severe than the conditions would warrant. Perhaps if matters had been reversed, I, or any officer who looks sharply after the business of the department, we would natually stick up for the department in every particular.

Q. Well, now, I suppose in the course of your dealings with the department you must have met 'the deputy minister, Colonel Gourdeau?—A. I have met Colonel Gourdeau.

Q. Yes. Talked business with him?—A. No, I do not think we· ever had any business talks. Any tenders I had before the department, after they went in,·any talks I had were with 'the chief engineer, and after we got through with our portion I never knew anything about the tenders until they were either acepted or rejected.

Q. Yes. But the colonel, you know, was the head of the 'department, and surely you must have talked some matters over with him concerning the contracts with the department or the condition of 'your work?—A. I do not recall any talks. I have met him there and I have talked perhaps for an instant, but never· regarding any details of the work that I can remember of; 'in fact, I have had but very little to do with the deputy minister in such matters.

Q. You never had any conversation with 'him regarding·your tenders or the contracts being awarded to you?—A. No, sir.

Q. Never asked him to let you have the contract 'or see that your tender be accepted?—A. I believe I wrote him one letter in the beginning of your transactions calling attention to the facilities of our 'company, and so on. I believe that is the only communication. I do not recall anything else.

Q. Well, have you seen this letter mentioned in the report of the commissioners, or printed rather in the report?—A. That is the letter——

Q. Have you the page there, is it on page 173, August 18, 1906?—A. Yes, sir, that is the letter I had reference to.

Q. This is to Colonel Anderson, not Colonel Gourdeau. Was a similar one sent to Colonel Gourdeau?—A. Well, the second paragraph.

Q. You are right. So this is the letter you speak of?—A. That is the letter.

Q. Well, did you see him after you had written this letter?—A. No, sir.

Q. You did not meet him?—A. Not while this matter was pending.

Q. You had no occasion to talk to him of the contents of this letter or the subject matter of this letter?—A. No, sir, I did not.

Q. Well, do I understand you to swear that you had nothing whatever to do with Colonel Gourdeau with reference to divers contracts you had with the department?— A. That is what I say.

Q. You swear that?—A. I do.

Q. Well now, let us take the outside agents or representatives of the department with whom you personally or your foreman or other employees had dealings ?—A. Yes, sir.

Q. You stated, you mentioned Mr. Gregory a minute ago, the agent in Quebec?— A. Yes, sir.

Q. And also Mr. Parent, the resident engineer in Quebec?—A.· Yes, sir.

Q. Anybody else in Quebec with whom you personally or your agents or employees had dealings?—A. Those were the only two.

Q. Well, now, Mr. Wallberg, did you yourself or anyone of your employees to your knowledge pay any commissions to these people, either Mr. Gregory or Mr. Parent, with reference to your contracts or otherwise for any cause or reason. whatever?—A. Nothing whatsoever. I did not pay him and no one else nor any employee. That I am absolutely certain, absolutely certain, and there was never any question about anything of that kind. In fact, those men, all they had to do was to see our goods went on the steamers according to contract, that is all. We were under no obligations to them, we were not asking them any favours nor anything of that kind.

Q. Mr. Wallberg, you have noticed in the appendix to the report of the commissioners that it is stated there, or it appears, that you have delayed the shipping of some material and unduly retained the ships. Have you noticed that in the report? —A. I noticed something of that kind.

Q. Yes. Now, we might take 174. For instance, 'shipment of material doubtful'—about the middle of the page—September 14, 1909?—A. Yes, sir.

Q. Now take 176, please, about the middle of the page also ?—A. Yes, sir.

Q. 'Charter party for use of *Aranmore,* dated 17th September; she has therefore been under charter for six weeks.'—A. Yes, sir.

Q. Well, do I understand, Mr. Wallberg, that you had detained this ship for six week?—A. No, sir. In the first place, we shipped materials to Metis and went on with the construction of Metis tower. There was no delay in the shipment of that material. All our materials were got on the ship just as fast as the men could load them on; but then our materials were not shipped to Matane at that time, they were shipped to Matane, in fact, late in the fall at the convenience of the ship. The ship was never held to my knowledge for any time whatever waiting for us any more than was necessary merely to load materials from the wharves.

Q. Do I understand you to say that the *Aranmore*—we will take her for the present—was not detained by you at all?—A. No, sir.

Q. Well, how do you explain these statements?—A. I do not explain them. If the *Aranmore* was there, it was there without any knowledge on our part, and certainly was not waiting that time for our materials.

Q. Well, take the *Champlain,* for instance, page 177, about November 9, 1906, 'Vessel waiting for stone. W. P. Anderson telegraphs E. A. W., Steel Construction Company.' Of course, that is your company?—A. Yes.

Q. 'Resident engineer, Quebec, reports *Champlain* waiting for your broken stone.' Is that yours ?—A. Yes, sir.

Q. 'Must insist on materials being furnished without further delay. We hold you responsible for delay in completion of contract.' Then you were holding the ship, were you not?—A. Our broken stone came from near Quebec, and it was a question of carting in the stone, and if there is any delay in the cartage that is the only delay which there could have been.

Q. Then your contention is you never delayed ships of the government on account of your contracts?—A. Nothing whatever more than was neccessary to cart and put our stone and materials on board.

Q. And that you never paid a cent directly or indirectly to any one of the agents for the purpose of getting delay to ship your goods or material ?—A. I swear that most positively, most positively, nothing of that kind.

Q. Well now, you stated also that you and your employees had some dealings with Mr. Pearson, is it, the agent in Halifax?—A. I don't know the agent at Halifax.

Q. You do not know the agent there. Have you had anything to do with him?—A. I never met him.

Q. The only one you met was Mr. Legère, the resident engineer?—A. Yes.

Q. Now, did you obtain some favours from Mr. Legère?—A. I did not.

Q. Did you ask for them?—A. No. I asked for what we required under our contract, that is the transportation of materials.

Q. And you got it?—A. We got it.

Q. Well, did you have to, or did you voluntarily, give him something for the advantage?—A. No.

Q. No advantage whatever?—A. There was no advantage. In fact, we got what I considered very slow service from the steamers there, but no doubt it was the best they could do, because they did not have steamers available. In fact as I said some time ago, one expedition was put on a schooner and I had to pay the cost of the twenty days. It would not have occurred if a steamer had been available.

Q. Have you directly or indirectly, any transactions whatever with any one of the officials of the department?—A. Absolutely——

Q. I mean outside of the contracts?—A. I have had no dealings particularly outside of the contract work.

Q. You have not endorsed notes for them?—A. Never, I am positive.

Q. When I say endorsed notes, I mean you never signed notes for any one of them?—A. I am positive I never done anything of that sort.

Q. And you never asked them to negotiate notes or negotiable paper?—A. Nothing of that kind.

Q. With any one of them?—A. Not a transaction of any kind with any one of them.

Q. Then, do I understand you to swear that you never had a transaction, outside of departmental business, with any one of the employees?—A. That is what I swear.

Q. Would their names appear in your books, the name of any one of the officers in your books?—A. No, sir. There is not the slightest transaction, outside of carrying out straight contract work, with any man connected with the department.

Q. You know, of course, Mr. J. F. Fraser, the commissioner of lights?—A. I do.

Q. Well, did you notice any difference between Mr. J. F. Fraser and Colonel Anderson, any trouble whatever between the two?—A. I did not.

Q. It never occurred to you that there was such difference existing between those two employees?—A. I did not know anything about that. It would never come to my attention, anything of that kind.

Q. You never noticed anything, you never noticed such a difference between them?—A. No.

Q. Did you have any dealing with Mr. J. F. Fraser?—A. No, sir.

Q. None whatever?—A. No, sir.

Q. Business or unbusinesslike?—A. None whatever.

Mr. PERRON.—I have nothing else, my lord, unless your lordship has anything to ask.

Hon. Mr. CASSELS.—I do not want anything more.

Mr. PERRON.—I think Mr. Wallberg may go home now, if he wishes.

Hon. Mr. CASSELS.—Certainly.

THOMAS L. WILLSON, sworn.

By Mr. Watson:

Q. Mr. Willson, I understand you live here at Ottawa?—A. I do, sir.

Q. How long have you resided here?—A. Since about 1898 or 1899—1899 I should say.

Q. Eight or nine years, then?—A. Yes, sir.

Q. What is your business?—A. Electrical engineer, chemical engineer, manufacturer, inventor sometimes.

Q. What?—A. Inventor sometimes.

Q. Pretty good at inventions?—A. I have been very successful, sir, at inventions.

Q. Well then, what is the business you make money out of?—A. I make money out of two things, calcium carbide, its manufacture, and the manufacture of gas buoys.

Q. Gas buoys and calcium carbide?—A. Yes, sir. I say I am the discoverer of calcium carbide, such as is known to the world and of use to mankind.

Q. You do not mean your are the original discoverer.?—A. Yes, sir, the original discoverer of crystalline calcium carbide.

Q. Perhaps the discoverer of a particular application of it?—A. No, sir, of crystalline calcium carbide.

By Hon. Mr. Cassels:

Q. What is that first word?—A. Crystalline calcium carbide.

Q. What does that mean?—A. Crystalline means this, that a substance is broken and will have cleavage and a smooth surface at points showing crystal. It may not appear to the eye to be actually like a regular form, such as a cut diamond, but it is crystalline. That substance which I discovered was fused crystalline calcium carbide.

reviously there had been none in the world, only an amorphous powdery mass or arbide due to scientific experiments.

Mr. WATSON.—I am glad I did not ask the question.

Hon. Mr. CASSELS.—I understand.

WITNESS.—Amorphous means not crystalline.

Q. What is the gain of the crystalline, that you let the water on the carbide, or he carbide on the water?—A. No. The existing degree of purity. That which had reviously been known was only 15 per cent pure; this is 90 per cent.

By Mr. Watson:

Q. You must have written a book at some time?—A. My life is given to scientific ork, and I am very successful and my name is known throughout the world.

Hon. Mr. CASSELS.—Just try and get at the evidence.

By Mr. Watson:

Q. Are you doing business by yourself, or with a company?—A. Doing business st by myself in all these works, and then after it was progressed far enough it was ut in the form of a company.

Q. When?—A. Which do you refer to?

Q. The company?—A. Carbide?

Q. I did not know that there was more than one?—A. Carbide and gas buoys are works I made successful.

Q. Are they incorporated in one company?—A. No, separate entirely.

Q. What are the names of the companies?—A. Of the carbide companies?

Q. Give us the names of the companies?—A. In the first place I organized the Union Carbide.

Q. Give us the present names?—A. In Canada?

Q. Certainly ; that is all we are concerned with, I think?—A. The Willson Carbide Company, of St. Catharines.

Q. That is one company?—A. That is one. The Ottawa Carbide Company, of Ottawa, the Shawinigan Carbide Company, of Shawinigan Falls, Quebec.

Q. How many carbide companies?—A. Three in Canada.

Q. I see. Then how many buoy companies?—A. One, the International Marine Signal Company.

Q. I see. Now, you know the object of your being called here, no doubt. Have you had individual transactions and dealings with the Department of Marine and Fisheries, apart from your companies?—A. I have had, first, individual transactions with the Department of Marine in the furnishing of gas buoys ; second, as a company, the International Marine Signal Company, which——

Q. That is gas buoys?—A. Gas buoys ; which continued the business, and I may say, personally, my only relations with the Department of Marine have been in connection with gas buoys.

Q. Gas buoys?—A. Yes, sir.

Q. Then what about your carbide and your carbide companies?—A. In the first place, the Willson Carbide Company, in which I am principally interested and principally own, has never had any dealings with the Department of Marine to any material extent. I notice in my statement——

Q. Wait, please. Just be specific in your answers, please. Then, do you mean that the carbide companies that you have mentioned, three of them——?—A. Yes, sir.

Q. That there have been no transactions between any one of those companies and the department in question?—A. I was proceeding to say that the next company, the Ottawa Carbide Company of Ottawa, has had transactions with the Department of Marine.

Q. Yes ; and what about the others ?—A. The Shawinigan Company, I don't know, I don't think they have had very many transactions ; it is a new company.

Q. You are, I suppose, president and perhaps general manager of all these companies ?—A. No, sir. I am only the president of the Willson Carbide. Company at St. Catharines.

Q. And the others ?—A. I am vice-president of the Ottawa Carbide Company.

Q. And are you the largest shareholder in all these companies ?—A. I am not. I am the largest shareholder only in the Willson Carbide Company, named after myself, of St. Catharines, which has never had any material dealings with the Department of Marine.

Q. What do you mean by 'material' ?—A. We might have sent them a few tons of carbide in an emergency, but we have not had any regular supply, they have not been supplied regularly by the Willson Carbide Company; the regular supply has come from the Ottawa Carbide Company.

By Hon. Mr. Cassels:

Q. When was the Ottawa Carbide Company incorporated?—A. I think it has been incorporated seven or eight years, something like that.

Q. Who are the members of that ?—A. The Hon. E. H. Bronson, Frank Bronson, Walter Bronson, Levi Crannel and myself.

By Mr. Watson :

Q. Is that the company which has had most of the transactions in carbide with the government ?—A. They have wholly.

Q. And you have named those who are shareholders of that company ?—A. Practically. There is another shareholder at the present time, Mr. Little.

Q. Who is Mr. Little ?—A. Henry A. Little, barrister of Woodstock.

Q. Who is he ?—A. He is a lawyer in Woodstock.

Q. From whom did he acquire his shares ?—A. He acquired his interest from me or from his uncle.

Q. And who was his uncle ?—A. The Hon. James Sutherland.

Q. Why do you say, from you or from his uncle ?—A. Because I gave that interest to them, that is all.

Q. When did you do that?—A. When the company was organized, 8 or 9 years ago.

By Hon. Mr. Cassels:

Q. What interest was it you gave them?—A. It was a quarter of my interest, which was a fifth of the whole thing.

By Mr. Watson:

Q. What did that pan out in figures?—A. One-twentieth.

Q. How many shares?—A. The company was organized for $200,000.

Q. How many shares did you give?—A. I received a fifth of that, which was $40,000.

Q. I did not ask you how many you received. How many did you give Mr. Sutherland or Mr. Little?—A. $10,000.

Q. $10,000?—A. $10,000.

Q. And had yourself how many?—A. $30,000.

Q. You gave a third of your holding?—A. No, sir; a quarter.

Q. You said you had $30,000 and you gave $10,000?—A. I had $40,000, I have $30,000 left.

Q. You gave $10,000?—A. Yes.

Q. Did the $40,000 comprise the whole paid up capital?—A. No; $200,000.

Q. I am not speaking of the nominal capital, but the paid up capital?—A. The paid up capital was $200,000.

Q. How was it paid up?—A. $160,000 in cash.

Q. In cash?—A. Yes, sir. Paid in cash by the Bronson family and $40,000 given to me for my patents.

Q. I see, $40,000?—A. Yes, sir.

Q. And you gave a fourth to Mr. Sutherland?—A. For negotiating the sale of my patents to the Bronson Company. That is how I gave him that.

Q. You gave them to him for negotiating the sale?—A. Of my patents.

Q. Yes. What was that, a commission?—A. No, it was an interest which he had with me.

Q. But did you give it as a commission?—A. Well, no; he was practically interested with me in initiating the work at St. Catharines.

Q. Yes. But I do not understand your answer exactly. I thought you said you gave them to him for negotiating the sale?—A. Correct, sir.

Q. Then in that event it would be a payment for services by way of commission? —A. Correct, sir, to that extent.

Q. Then there is another extent, apparently, that it is not correct about?—A. He has an ownership in the general business with me at St. Catharines.

Q. An original ownership?—A. Yes.

Q. I see. Then it was not on the basis of commission?—A. Not solely, no, sir.

Q. Then we will have to go slowly. Do I understand from you that the late Mr. Sutherland was a shareholder in that company from its origin, from its formation? —A. In the Ottawa Carbide Company?

Q. Yes?—A. Yes, sir.

Q. I see. In that company?—A. Yes, sir.

Q. And then, who else got shares and commissions in that company?—A. No one else to my knowledge.

Q. No one else. Have you got the books of that company here?—A. The books of the Ottawa Carbide Company?

Q. Yes?—A. They are in Ottawa, sir; yes, sir.

Q. Have you got them here?—A. No, sir; I have not the books of the Ottawa Company, and I was not asked to produce them.

Q. I think you were, at least I am told so. You may be strictly correct. It says: ' All books, papers, documents, correspondence, cash books, cheque books, counterfoils of cheques, and any other documents having any reference to your transactions with the Department of Marine and Fisheries or any of its officials.' Perhaps you are strictly correct; it does not refer to the books of the company?—A. It does not refer to the books of the Carbide Company at all.

Q. We will pass that. We can get them another time?—A. Yes, sir.

Q. They are here?—A. In Ottawa.

Q. You are president of that company?—A. No.

Q. Who is?—A. The Hon. E. H. Bronson.

Q. What office have you in that company?—A. I am nominally vice-president.

Q. Why do you say ' nominally '?—A. Because I really have no business connection with it.

Q. With the company at all?—A. Well, that is only nominal.

Q. Perhaps you would not mind handing over your interest?—A. I will gladly hand it over to anybody who will pay anything for it. It is not profitable. The stock is not worth anything, it never has been, sir.

Q. You mean that is the company that has been having transactions with the department?—A. On the carbide, yes, sir.

Q. And what else above the carbide?—A. Nothing else, sir.

Q. Then do you say there has not been money made by that company in its transactions?—A. Absolutely no. From the very beginning that company has lost money on its sale of carbide, and to-day it is very seriously out. I have no objection to telling you——

Q. Wait, please. Very seriously out. When did the transactions with that company begin in the department?—A. I have here a list of all the carbide sold by that company to the Department of Marine, which I asked for only this morning at a quarter to nine.

Q. If you will just answer the question directly we will get on a little better. When does it begin?—A. From July 1, 1902.

Q. I see. Then there was a contract, was there, to what extent?—A. From July, 1902, to June 30, 1903, they furnished 31 tons and a decimal fraction at a value of $2,044.25.

Q. You mean to say that was the total amount of the transaction?—A. In that year, in the whole year.

Q. Then take the next year?—A. From July 1, 1903, to June 30, 1904, the total transactions were $8,245.25.

Q. Yes?—A. From July 1, 1904, to June 30, 1905, the transactions were $8,638.50.

Q. Go on?—A. From July 1, 1905, to March 31, 1906, the transactions were $11,687.

Q. Yes?—A. From April 1, 1906, to March 31, 1907, the transactions were $19,314.50.

Q. Yes?—A. April the 1st, 1907, to March 31, 1908, the total transactions were $19,768.25.

Q. Yes?—A. If somebody will get me a glass of water, I can speak better. That is the total transactions from the beginning to the present.

Q. It is in the neighbourhood of $60,000?—A. A total of $69,697.75.

Q. A total of about $70,000 of transactions?—A. Correct, sir.

Q. Eh?—A. Correct.

Q. Now, what was this carbide used for, or as a substitute for?—A. The carbide was used for the purpose of making acetylene gas for the purpose of illumination.

Q. As a substitute for what?—A. As a substitute for oil gas, which had previously been used.

By Hon. Mr. Cassels:

Q. Related to the use in buoys?—A. In buoys and lighthouses, some lighthouses only.

By Mr. Watson:

Q. Lanterns in lighthouses?—A. Some lanterns in some of the lighthouses.

Q. Now then, when did your transactions begin as to the buoys?—A. The transactions begin as to the buoys?

Q. That is, with the department?—A. With the department in August, 1904.

Q. August, 1904. Now, I will leave that for the moment. And about this carbide, how did you get on to this carbide proposition?—A. Do you mean furnishing carbide to the government?

Q. I did not mean that. Its introduction, its use?—A. Originally?

Q. Yes?—A. I, as an inventor, discoverer, was working to produce electro-metallurgical productions, and carbide was one.

Q. That will do. And then when was that first introduced as the subject of discussion to any official or head of a department?—A. Well, I presume it must have been prior to July 1, 1902, because carbide was then furnished to the government. I have no recollection otherwise.

Q. Then, with whom was the first discussion?—A. I think it was with the officers of the Department of Marine.

Q. With whom, what person?—A. I think that I have discussed the thing with the deputy minister and with the chief engineer.

Q. That is, with Colonel Gourdeau and with Colonel Anderson?—A. Yes, sir.

Q. Then, with whom did the negotiations begin; can you distinguish?—A. I could not tell with whom the began. There were no negotiations on my part. I found when I was here that some purchases had been made of acetylene.

Q. At that time?—A. Before I had gone to them at all.

Q. At that time who was the minister of the department?—A. I do not know. I think perhaps Louis Davies might have been; I am not sure.

Q. In 1904?—A. Prior to 1902. I don't know who was prior to 1902.

Q. But I thought you said negotiations began about that time?—A. I said prior to that time.

Q. Do you mean much earlier than that?—A. It must have been earlier than that or otherwise they could not have used it in that year.

Q. I know. But was it that year or the year before?—A. It must have been the year before.

Q. Then we will take 1901. Did you discuss the matter with the minister?—A. I do not know, I do not think so. I think the first discussion in the matter was with the same departmental officials.

Q. Then with whom?—A. So far as my recollection goes, it was Colonel Gourdeau and——

Q. Colonel Gourdeau?—A. And Colonel Anderson, too.

Q. Colonel Anderson?—A. I think so.

Q. Then what took place between you and Colonel Gourdeau?—A. Nothing took place between us, sir. The thing was simply a generic discussion, that it was advisable to use high candle power gas.

Q. And do you not remember who the minister was at that time?—A. No, I do not remember who was minister at that time.

Q. At that time was Mr. Sutherland interested in the carbide?—A. Mr. Sutherland was always interested in the Willson Carbide Company of St. Catharines.

Q. Always was, yes. Then, had you at the time influence with the department? —A. Not the slightest, sir.

Q. How long before you obtained a contract after you began your negotiations? —A. I never obtained a contract, sir.

Q. The company; I am not distinguishing?—A. The Ottawa Carbide Company?

Q. Yes?—A. I do not know. They began to furnish carbide in 1902.

Q. Well, then, it is within a comparatively short time after, is that right?—A. It must have been some considerable time before that; they could not have begun to use it.

Q. With whom was the contract made?—A. With the Ottawa Carbide Company, if any contract was made.

Q. With what official?—A. Mr. Crannell.

Q. With what official of the department?—A. Oh, I do not know the purchasing department; I knew nothing of it.

Q. What?—A. I knew nothing of the particulars of it..

Q. Who did?—A. The department and the Ottawa Carbide Company.

Q. But you were the prime mover, the head and front?—A. Not at all. I simply talked of this thing generically to the department.

Q. You mean you talked it up and somebody else put it through?—A. I might have talked it up.

Q. And with whom did you talk it up?—A. Well, as I say, with Colonel Gourdeau, who is deputy minister, and somewhat with Colonel Anderson.

Q. I see?—A. Just generically.

Q. Any one else?—A. No, sir, no one else.

Q. With the then minister?—A. No, sir, not with the then minister.

Q. Then, that was used in substitution at that time for what?—A. Oil gas.

Q. It was manufactured by the Ottawa company?—A. Yes, sir.

Q. And what customers did you have?—A. The Ottawa company?

Q. How many customers?—A. They had a great many customers, sir.

Q. A great many customers?—A. Yes, sir.

Q. So that you were doing a large business, do I understand?—A. Yes.

Q. Apart from the business with the department?—A. Certainly. The business with the department is insignificant in comparison with the general carbide business in Canada.

Q. Now, I observe that the late Mr. Sutherland was Minister of Marine and Fisheries from November, 1901 till the 11th of November, 1902 ?—A. Yes.

Q. Then, have you a memorandum showing that there too ?—A. No, sir ; I have no memorandum in reference to it whatsoever.

Q. Then, your negotiations were probably with him ?—A. No, sir, they were not.

Q. At that time Colonel Anderson was at the head of that branch, as I understand ?—A. I understand he was the chief engineer.

Q. Chief engineer ?—A. Yes, sir.

Q. And at that time was he in charge of the position as well as commissioner of lights ?—A. I understand so, I do not know. I do not know when the change was made.

Q. When was it the change was made ?—A. I do not know, sir.

Q. What ?—A. I do not know.

Q. You do not know?—A. No, sir.

Q. You know that Mr. Fraser was appointed commissioner of lights ?—A. J. F. Fraser ?

Q. Yes.—A. Yes, sir, I knew of it afterwards.

Q. When did you first learn of that ?—A. I don't recollect now.

Q. How did he happen to be appointed ?—A. I don't know.

Q. Was it upon your recommendation ?—A. I had nothing to do with it whatsoever.

Q. Before that had you discussed with him a change to carbide from oil gas ?—A. I probably did. I think he was in the department as engineer there.

Q. And before that had you discussed with Colonel Anderson the change ?—A. I think so.

Q. You had ?—A. Yes, I did.

Q. You were anxious to promote it ?—A. Certainly I was.

Q. In order to promote the interests of your company ?—A. The sale of carbide.

Q. That is what was upon your mind, the sale of carbide ?—A. It was, certainly.

Q. And you discussed it with the deputy minister ?—A. I did.

Q. Then, why was it that you recommended the division of the department ?—A. I did not recommend the division of the department, and I had no power, interest or authority in the department whatsoever.

Q. Well, to whom did you make the suggestion ?—A. I made no suggestion to any one, sir, in reference to that.

Q. Why not ?—A. Well, it is not my business to recommend a change in a department.

Q. Colonel Anderson, as I understand, was not favourable to the substitution of this carbide for oil gas ; you knew that, did you not ?—A. Not at the time, no, sir.

Q. Did you not ?—A. No, sir.

Q. Why, you had interviews with him ?—A. I believe Colonel Anderson, if my recollection is right now, made the first experiments in the Department of Marine that were ever made with acetylene.

Q. And you knew he was against the change ?—A. I did not know so.

Q. You had reason to think so ?—A. I had no particular reason to think so.

Q. Did he not tell you his views were against it, try and think ?—A. Quite frankly, engineers generally in government departments are against any change, and I found not only Colonel Anderson so, but other people throughout the world in the same similar positions.

Q. Well, then, we come back to it in that way of yours, that Colonel Anderson was against it to your knowledge ?—A. Not specifically to my knowledge, generally.

Q. You mean on general principles ?—A. General principles probably.

Q, Well, there is no difference whether it was on general principles or personal articular conviction. He was against it?—A. I cannot say that he was against it, sir.

By Hon. Mr. Cassels :

Q. Is this gas of yours used in the buoys ?—A. It is, sir.

Q. Are the buoys a profitable business ?—A. The buoys, I might say there has een no profit whatsoever taken out of the business to this present moment, your lordhip.

Q. I did not ask you that. I asked you if it was a profitable business ?—A. We ope it to be profitable. I have not found it so yet, sir. On the contrary, I have a ot of money in it, it will take a great many years to get out anything.

By Mr. Watson:

Q. I understand in any and all of these companies as the result of the development of all these inventions, so far you have derived no pecuniary benefit or advantage? A. I did not say so. I will say for your benefit that this carbide company of St. Catharines is a profitable organization and always has been from the beginning.

Q. It deals in carbide?—A. It does, but it does not deal with the government.

Q. Why does it not deal with the government?—A. I never made any offer.

Q. Why do you want to shut the door against them?—A. In the first place, we never had carbide sufficient to supply carbide to the government.

Q. And for that reason the Ottawa Company was formed?—A. To take up and make extra carbide.

Q. For the government?—A. No, sir. The government was not in the minds of the company.

Q. Which is the subsidiary company?—A. Neither one; each is independent.

Q. The St. Catharines is the parent company?—A. Only to the extent of being the pioneer in the work.

Q. But they are all members of the same family?—A. Not at all, sir; absolutely distinct and different.

Q. You mean a distinct charter?—A. A distinct charter and nobody connected with the thing, except myself with the various companies.

Q. You are in all of them?—A. Because I am the patentee and own the patent and derive this interest.

Q. So that, in a word, you have said to me that there never was any profit or money in that way made to advantage out of the carbide business, and to his lordship you have said that there is no profit making in the manufacture and sale of the buoys.

Hon. Mr. CASSELS.—He does not go that far.

The WITNESS.—I did not say so.

Hon. Mr. CASSELS.—He said they had not applied any profit. They are laying up a nest egg, that is all.

Mr. WATSON.—I see. I should judge that Mr. Willson has a pretty contented look.

Q. Well, then, Mr. Willson, it is in connection with these businesses, before we leave them, that your large fortune has been made?—A. My fortune was made in connection with calcium carbide wholly and solely.

Q. I find that you are referred to here as a man very successful in business and fortunate, a milionaire, I suppose, then ?—A. I suppose that is true, sir.

Q. That is true; I see. Generally millionaires deny it in my experience. Well then——?—A. I may say for your benefit and for the court that it was made in the United States and brought to Canada.

Q. I see. You are a Canadian?—A. I was born in Canada, Oxford county, Ontario.

Q. Then, when Mr. Fraser was appointed, or it was after he was appointed the

Willson Company obtained its first contract, did it not, or the Ottawa Company?—
A. The Ottawa Company.

Q. As a matter of recollection can you say?—A. I do not know when Mr. Fraser
was appointed. If you will tell me when he was?

Q. November, 1903?—A. The Ottawa Company obtained its first contract from
July 1, 1902, to June 30, 1903.

Q. Running to that year?—A. But that is previous to Mr. Fraser's appointment,
sir.

Q. Now, you were aware, were you not, that Colonel Anderson not only protested
against the substitution, but protested against the division of his branch?—A. No, sir,
I was not aware——

Q. That answers the question. So you are not aware now. Colonel Anderson has
stated that in his belief the change was made to promote and further your purpose,
the purpose of your business in the use of carbide. You are aware of that, are you?
—A. I have read the statement in this morning's ' Citizen.'

Q. To that effect. That is undoubtedly the result to some extent, at all events, of
personal communications with you. Do you doubt that?—A. I do not understand
your question.

Q. That that statement is made by him no doubt to some extent as the result of
personal communications with you?—A. No, sir.

Q. What?—A. No, sir. Colonel Anderson never got any such inference from me.
Absolutely untrue.

Q. What?—A. Absolutely untrue that he ever got such an inference from me.

Q. What did you do to further or promote the change, the division of the department and the appointment of Mr. Fraser?—A. Absolutely nothing.

Q. Did you favour it?—A. I did not have anything to do with it.

Q. Did you favour it?—A. I did not know of it.

Q. Had you knowledge that it was in contemplation?—A. I had no knowledge
of the matter until it was done.

Q. Did you discuss the change with the then minister?—A. I did not discuss
the change with the then minister.

Q. Did he speak of it to you?—A. He did not speak of it to me.

Q. Did you discuss it with the deputy minister?—A. I did not discuss it with
the deputy minister.

Q. Were there any communications, verbal or written, between you and either
of them on that subject?—A. There were none.

Q. Then, what is the reason for the statement of Colonel Anderson?—A. It is
an absolutely unfounded inference.

Hon. Mr. CASSELS.—I think, Mr. Watson, Colonel Anderson merely stated he had
that suspicion in his own mind. I do not think he stated it as a fact.

Mr. WATSON.—I think he was quite firm in the expression of his belief about the
matter. It was a little more than suspicion; it was a belief. I did not intend to put
it any stronger than that, his belief on the subject.

Hon. Mr. CASSELS.—Yes, that was all.

By Mr. Watson:

Q. Well, then, Mr. Willson, you appreciate that Colonel Anderson is a gentleman
who was not likely to make a statement of that kind without reasonable ground for
it, and it is a statement upon its face and substance which directly concerns you?—
A. If Colonel Anderson said or intimated that I gave him the inference in any way
whatsoever that I was in any way connected with the division of his work, he has made
a misstatement of fact.

Q. He does not say he obtained it directly from you. It might well be as the
result of what you were doing and saying and your general course of procedure?—A.

It was nothing that I ever had to do in connection with him in conversation or otherwise that he could gather such an inference from me.

Q. But you knew Mr. Fraser was favourable to your project?—A. I did not know that.

Q. I thought you told me before that you did?—A. I did not say so.

Q. You did not. You knew Colonel Anderson was against it. It was important, therefore, for you that there might be a change, is not that so?—A. No.

Q. It would serve your interests?—A. Not from any knowledge of mine.

Q. There would be a strong probability that way, is not that so?—A. There might be.

Q. There might be. That was present to your mind, was it not?—A. It was not.

Q. Did you act upon that basis?—A. I did not.

Q. Did you discuss the subject of the change with any one whatsoever?—A. I did not. I did not know of the change until it was made.

Q. Did any one on your behalf?—A. No, sir, that I know of.

Q. It has been, has it not, to your advantage?—A. I cannot say so. The result would have been absolutely as it is to-day, whether Mr. Fraser had ever lived or not, Mr. J. F. Fraser.

Q. In connection with the department?—A. In connection with the department, yes, sir.

Q. Why do you say that?—A. For this reason, that acetylene has seven times the illuminating power of the gas that was used, and it must of its own merit force itself into the position it occupies to-day. Every other country to-day, as well as Canada, is recognizing that and adopting this system, this system of mine.

Q. Stop, please. That is your reason, you think?—A. It is the sole reason why acetylene is in use to-day.

Q. Nothing like having a friend on the spot, they say?—A. It has nothing to do in the world with it, sir.

Q. Then, who were there in the department that knew the great merits of your invention and product?—A. After Mr. Fraser's appointment he handled the matter.

Q. Before that who knew, who had knowledge of the great merit of it?—A. Every engineer in that department should have known of it.

Q. Mr. Sutherland, of course, knew of it?—A. He was not an engineer.

Q. He knew the merits?—A. He knew of the merit of carbide, certainly.

Q. Yes. Well, your contracts in that carbide began in 1902, and we have the total of those contracts apparently?—A. You have, sir.

Q. Why did you charge to the department higher prices than to other consumers or users?—A. The department has always paid the same price that other consumers have paid.

Q. Do you say so?—A. I say so absolutely as a fact.

Q. Is it not a fact that higher prices have been paid?—A. No, sir. No higher prices have been paid by the department.

Q. Have you a record of your prices?—A. We have a record.

Q. Will your books show?—A. Our books would show.

Q. From year to year?—A. From year to year.

Q. Have you any objection to produce those books?—A. Absolutely none. But I cannot produce them ; you will have to get them from the Ottawa Company. I understand they have the books.

Q. They will do according to your direction, they will do as you wish?—A. Why, certainly. I asked them for this this morning, and they got it.

Q. This just gives the prices?—A. Yes, sir, during each year.

Q. But this is the price to the government?—A. Yes, sir. I may say the prices to the public are higher.

Q. These are the prices to this government or to this department and to the governments of the provinces?—A. Correct.

3262—7½

Q. Perhaps you are able to deal with one government in the same way as you do with another, but this has all been sold to one department. This memorandum does not contain a record of prices to any one else ?—A. No.

Q. I understood it did ?—A. But the prices to others were the same during those years in like quantities.

Q. But when you have a wholesale customer, such as the department, why did you not give a reduction ?—A. They did have a reduction.

Q. How much reduction ?—A. Generally it is $500 a ton lower to the government than to the public.

Q. And what discount did you allow ?—A. No discount.

Q. Why not ?—A. It is not a business of discounts ; it is a business of spot cash. You pay your cheque over the counter before you get the carbide.

Q. Do you not give discounts ?—A. Absolutely not.

Q. To other customers ?—A. No, sir. No discounts are allowed in the carbide business.

Q. The books will show whether or not your memory is accurate ?—A. Certainly, sir.

Q. Who has been bookkeeper ?—A. Levi Crannell.

Q. Crandell ?—A. Crannell. C-r-a-n-n-e-l-l.

Q. Is he here ?—A. Yes, sir.

Q. Resident here during all this time ?—A. During all this time.

Q. Why did you say to his lordship, as I understood you, that there had not been any gains ? You have had your own prices, have you not ?—A. Yes; but the cost of production of carbide has been about what we have been selling it for in Ottawa.

Q. Why is that, how do you account for that ?—A. They could not get any more for the carbide, and their location is not the most advantageous in the world ; freight rates on the raw material are too high against them in the city of Ottawa.

Q. Then, you mean to advance the statement, to make it, that the business that you have had with the government and with others on the part of the company, has not been a profitable business ?—A. It has not. They have lost $135,000 on the sale of carbide since their organization.

Q. Will you let me see the last annual statement ?—A. I will secure and show it to you. I have not it here.

Q. For each year ?—A. Yes, sir ; I have not it here.

Q. For each year ?—A. Yes, sir; I will secure that for you.

Q. There was no one to compete with you in this ?—A. No.

Q. You had it all your own way ?—A. Yes, two companies.

Q. You fixed your own prices ?—A. Fixed our own prices.

Q. No beating down ?—A. No beating down. Simply a question of what the cost of production of carbide could be made.

Q. What do you mean by the other company?—A. The Willson Carbide Company.

Q. Did one compete against the other ?—A. No.

Q. Did one set up against the other ?—A. Not at all. Lately the St. Catharines Company could only produce about 1,000 tons of carbide a year, and they sold it all retail at a higher price and did not care to go into the wholesale bsuiness. That is the reason they got a higher price.

Q. Now, then, Mr. Willson, Mr. Sutherland's name has been introduced, and he was minister of the department; you recognized that at that time?—A. At one time, yes, sir.

Q. That upon its face is a subject for comment, is it not?—A. I would say that if Mr. Sutherland did have anything to do with the introduction of carbide it would have been the most creditable thing for him to have been connected with, something that is of such great benefit to mankind and especially to Canada.

Q. Was that the way in which it was introduced and the business began?—A. No, I cannot say how it was introduced.

Q. Did Mr. Sutherland gain by that?—A. He gained nothing by it.

Q. Why not?—A. Because there was no gain at the time in it.

Q. Was not that the means of introduction to other markets?—A. Not at all.

Q. Why not? You were then in your infancy, so to speak?—A. We were producing at that time probably in the neighbourhood of 3,000 tons a year, and we sold 3,000 tons a year. That would bring nearly $200,000. We sold $2,000 worth to the government that year.

Q. Where were your sales made?—A. All over, to the general public of Canada.

Q. Were you dealing outside?—A. No, sir, not at that time. We shipped——

Q. I mean to say the United States?—A. Different companies deal in the United States.

Q. Which?—A. Neither of these companies.

Q. But your circle of companies?—A. The company I originated in the United States was dealing there, another company of mine.

Q. You are just doing business in this circle of companies?—A. Yes. I was the only one connected with the entire circle.

Q. It was more in your interest to have it that way?—A. I sold my patents in the United States and companies were organized on them; I sold them in Canada and the companies were organized here.

Q. When did you begin in the United States?—A. It began in 1895, between 1894 and 1895, and the company was organized there. They began business and it has been continued successfully ever since.

Q. Was there every any gain to you or to your company by reason of that business in 1902-3 with the department?—A. Absolutely not one cent of gain.

Q. Or to anyone connected with the company?—A. Or to anyone connected with the company.

Q. Why were you so very urgent, as Colonel Anderson has stated?—A. I was not very urgent, sir.

Q. Who was the spokesman beyond yourself, anyone else that is equal to you?—A. Well, I do not know of anybody else who can introduce a thing so forcibly as I can, sir.

Q. You are not confining yourself to carbide?—A. No, sir.

Q. That extended to the buoys, at all events?—A. It does.

Q. Well, you are a pretty dangerous man I should think from that statement. Now, then, that has continued up to the present time. Has the interest of Mr. Sutherland in these companies continued?—A. Mr. Little——

Q. It did to the time of his death?—A. Up to the time of his death, yes. He never had any connection with the International Marine Signal Company.

Q. I have not got to that yet?—A. You said companies, and I mentioned the International.

Q. Then your great profit, as I understand you, has been in connection with the manufacture of the buoys?—A. Whatever profit I have had in dealing with the government or Department of Marine is solely in connection with the buoys.

Q. And that began in what year?—A. 1904.

Q. August, 1904, I think you said?—A. Yes, sir.

Q. With whom was that contract made?—A. The contract was made with the Department of Marine.

Q. With the Department of Marine?—A. Yes, sir.

Q. With whom, what person?—A. The matter was brought up by myself in a letter to the deputy minister, announcing that I had made some buoys which I would submit to him for test on the representation that they had certain features of advantage.

Q. That is the way it was introduced?—A. That is all, sir.

Q. Now, my learned friend and I have not that letter yet. Have you a copy of that?—A. I think I have.

Q. Have you got it here?—A. Yes, sir. (Witness procures letter.)

Q. What have you brought with you, Mr. Willson?—A. I have brought letters and correspondence which were asked for and books which were asked for specifically.

Q. Would you mind letting me have them?—A. I have no objections, sir.

Q. Thank you. Then, we will take good care of them and see they get back to you.—A. When will you return them?

Q. When we get through with them.—A. Do you mean you will keep them after to-day?

Q. Yes.—A. All right.

Q. You have given me one letter, this is the letter you speak of, August 6, 1904 (reads).

(Letter marked Exhibit No. 7.)

Q. That is your first communication?—A. That is my first communication.

Q. You say that is the first?—A. Yes.

Q. Did you talk it up beforehand?—A. I spoke of it, certainly.

Q. And this is nothing, I suppose, to what you said, so to speak?—A. That is authoritative.

Q. I see. What is written is authoritative. And there is a letter in answer to that ?

Hon. Mr. CASSELS.—Who is that written to?

Mr. WATSON.—To the deputy minister, Colonel Gourdeau. And there is a letter back. This is dated the 12th August, 1904 (reads).

(Letter marked Exhibit No. 8.)

Q. And you got the result of having them applied to a test?—A. Yes, accepted for test.

By Hon. Mr. Cassels:

Q. Those are carbide buoys?—A. Automatic carbide buoys.

Q. Carbide sold from Ottawa?—A. Carbide put in the centre of the buoys.

Q. But sold from Ottawa?—A. Sold from Ottawa, the carbide was.

By Mr. Watson:

Q. Just before I leave that. You said you had some books there. Will you kindly let me have them?—A. (Witness produces books.)

Q. You do not object to leaving those with us?—A. I object to this one, because our current account is running here; it is the regular book——

Q. Of the company?—A. Of the company. This is my own private book which contained the business up to 1906, from 1904 to 1906, and from that date this book contains everything.

Q. Do you object to leaving that?—A. Not to this, no, sir.

Q. Then may they be marked, my lord?—A. This is the other one they use every day.

(Ledger marked Exhibit No. 9.)

By Hon. Mr. Cassels:

Q. It is the Ottawa book?—A. It is our book here of the Ottawa Carbide Company.

(Synoptic journal marked Exhibit No. 10.)

By Mr. Watson:

Q. Then whose aid and influence did you procure to assist this introduction and to obtain this testing?—A. To obtain which, sir?

Q. The test which is referred to in the deputy's letter?—A. Nobody's, sir. I wholly and solely am responsible for that.

Q. Was that recommended by the minister?—A. The minister at that time, I believe, was Mr. Préfontaine. I had never spoken to him on the subject at all then, sir.

Q. Do you say so?—A. I say so.

Q. Up to the time that test was made?—A. That that letter was written, sir.

Q. Do you say you had had no communications with Mr. Prefontaine?—A. I had no communications whatsoever with Mr. Préfontaine up to the time of that letter.

Q. Verbal or otherwise?—A. Verbal or otherwise.

Q. Then with whom in power or position did you have the communications?—A. Only with the deputy minister, sir.

Q. He was the power?—A. He was the power, and the only power, I ever communicated with.

Q. With Colonel Anderson?—A. No, the deputy minister.

Q. Then did you have the assistance and recommendation of the late Mr. Sutherland?—A. I did not, sir.

Q. Had he any interest in this company?—A. He had none whatever.

Q. Dealing with buoys?—A. He had none whatsoever. Mr. Sutherland never knew of the subject. Mr. Sutherland left—this is now within my own knowledge—Mr. Sutherland left Ottawa a sick man in May, 1904. I did not see or communicate with him in any respect whatsoever, except on a visit to him at the sanitarium, where I saw him just by permission of the doctor in the afternoon. No business was mentioned, and I left him with the feeling that that man was dying. In May of the next year he died, and I never saw him afterwards. (After the laughter had subsided.) After that visit to the sanitarium.

Q. There is nothing like saying a lot. Then, that has been an extensive and important connection?—A. Which has, sir?

Q. That business connection with the buoys?—A. It is a very extensive business.

Q. With the department?—A. With the department, yes, sir.

Q. How much has that amounted to per annum since, about?—A. Oh, up to the —I could not tell you up to the time of the end of that fiscal year, 1907; I could not tell you from my memory.

Q. But about, within $50,000?—A. It has been about a million dollars.

Q. A year?—A. No, sir; altogether. Since 1904 it may be a little more than that, perhaps.

By Hon. Mr. Cassels:

Q. How many buoys would that represent?—A. That represents 219 or 220 that were sold to the department.

Q. How much for each?—A. They run from about $2,000 up to $8,500 for some of the big ones, and two very large ones ran $15,000 apiece.

Q. How much do they cost you to make?—A. That is a question I am trying to find out myself.

By Mr. Watson:

Q. Well, those are interesting buoys?—A. They are.

Q. So that the business each year would amount to something over a quarter of a million dollars?—A. In round figures, yes, sir.

Q. Are you the only manufacturer?—A. I am the only manufacturer of the automatic gas buoy in the world, it is my own invention and patented by me.

Q. Then, when did you form this company?—A. In November, 1906.

Q. Who compose it?—A. First, myself, because I am the largest owner.

Q. Never mind the because's?—A. Henry Little, of Woodstock, his wife and my wife and bookkeeper. The other, Mr. Little and I myself were the only ones who really own the stock.

Q. How did Mr. Little acquire his interest?—A. By payment for it in cash.

Q. How much did he pay?—A. He subscribed $300,000 in cash.

Q. And paid it?—A. It is not all paid in yet, but it is being paid in. He has paid in up to the present $150,000.

Q. Out of the profits?—A. No, sir; no profits have been made yet.

Q. No profits have been made?—A. That is, none have been computed or taken out of the business.

Q. So that the position, the interest of the wives is practically nominal?—A. Nominal.

Q. The business practically belongs to you and Little?—A. It does, sir.

Q. Beyond the interest of Mr. Little's $300,000, what is yours?—A. $300,000 also.

Q. $600,000 is the paid-up capital?—A. $600,000 is the paid-up capital.

Q. So that he has an equal interest with you?—A. He has, sir.

Q. I see, that is the position; and a quarter of a million dollars worth of transactions each year with the department?—A. With the department, yes, sir.

Q. And you fix your own prices?—A. I do fix the prices, sir.

Q. You fix the prices?—A. Yes, sir.

Q. What has the department to say about it?—A. Nothing to say about it in the world, nor has any other government in the world anything to say about it. The prices are uniform to every government.

Q. What is that?—A. The prices are uniform to every government in the world.

Q. What do you mean by that?—A. I am selling to other governments exactly as I am to Canada, at a uniform price.

Q. Yes; and the prices vary, I understand, according to the size?—A. They do, sir.

Q. That is, from $2,000 to $10,000 each?—A. Up to about somewhere around $8,500.

Q. From $2,000 to $8,500 ?—A. Yes, sir.

Q. And the little buoy that you sell for $2,000 costs you how much about ?—A. I don't know.

Q. Oh, your are a good business man ?—A. Exactly, and I put in a cost system, I started at it a year ago, and we are trying to find out what is the cost to us to produce.

Q. Give me your idea within $100 ?—A. No, I haven't any idea.

Q. You have an idea within a thousand ?—A. Well, we sell some buoys for $15,500.

Q. I am speaking of the little ones you sell for $2,000. How much does one of those cost you ?—A. I don't know, sir.

Q. Be fair to us and to yourself.—A. I don't think it is a fair question to ask, for this reason, we are dealing with governments throughout the world——

Q. Listen. And that is the reason, and not because you do not know ?—A. It is partly because I do not know.

Q. Then you do not know for the most part what it costs ?—A. I know that there ought to be a profit in it.

Q. You know more than that. Of course, you know practically what it costs, Mr. Willson. We give you that credit. You would not be willing that it should not be given to you, I think?—A. In the first place that is not a question to ask, for the reason that we are manufacturers and competing with German companies throughout the world with different governments, and to reveal the cost of our productions which we sell to different governments throughout the world is not a fair thing to ask, your lordship. We are not middlemen, we are manufacturers, directly, sir.

Q. Why do you think you can place yourself or your company on a higher basis or standard than other companies that do business with the department of the government, how do you distinguish, simply because you do a larger business ?—A. No, sir. We are not contractors or middlemen. We are furnishing articles which we sell to every government in the world.

Q. You are contractors, you make and sell ?—A. We are selling a suitable article, and to every other government too.

Q. Will you tell me the cost ?—A. Not unless his lordship forces me to tell.

By Hon. Mr. Cassels:

Q. I do not think you are bound to tell if you do not wish to ?—A. Then I will not tell.

Q. Will you not give any information about the amount ?—A. I will not give any information about the cost of production of these buoys, sir, as it is contrary to the public interest of Canada to do so.

Q. Is there any other competition in Canada, Mr. Willson ?—A. There is competition in the old general buoys.

Q. But in these particular buoys ?—A. No, sir. I am the patentee of it throughout the world, and, your lordship, it has just been accepted by the United States government and various foreign governments, whom I will mention to you, Brazil, Great Britain——

Mr. WATSON.—My lord, in connection with this matter I deem it of importance that it should be pressed, and I would say to lour lordship quite respectfully that I have a strong view to the opposite to what your lordship has expressed. I would like to be permitted to refer your lordship later on perhaps, not to-day, to some references.

Hon. Mr. CASSELS.—I should like to have some authority for it. The position of the matter strikes me in this way, Mr. Watson : This company has got a patent in Canada for this particular invention. Now, nobody else can sell it, nobody else can manufacture it. He might make a large profit out of it. It is not very material to this inquiry whether he makes a large profit or not, except as indicating there was something passing between the company and the officials of the department.

Mr. WATSON.—I quite understand that, my lord.

Hon. Mr. CASSELS.—However, if you have any authority I will see it later on.

Mr. WATSON.—Yes, my lord.

Q. Then, the profit increases of course with the increasing business. That is not divulging anything, is it ?—A. No, that is not correct, because as we increase our business we lower our prices.

Q. You lower your prices ?—A. We do, sir.

Q. But the cost of construction lessens as the volume increases ?—A. As the facility of manufacturing increases the cost of production decreases. As we improve our factory we can produce at lower cost.

Q. Then the cost decreases?—A. The cost decreases then.

Q. Do you say you have decreased the prices?—A. We have, sir.

Q. To the department?—A. To the Canadian government, yes, sir. And we are selling to-day at less prices than we sold a year ago.

Hon. Mr. CASSELS.—Mr. Watson, how long do you propose to go on now? It might facilitate further examination after you have been through the papers.

Mr. WATSON.—It might. I did not know it was so late, my lord. I would ask your lordship not to sit beyond 4 o'clock. I was not aware it was beyond that hour.

Your lordship will see the volume of material and the difficulty of getting at the matter concisely, boiling it down. It will help us very materially after we have gone through the documents and papers, my lord.

Hon. Mr. CASSELS.—Yes.

Mr. WATSON.—Then, we would like to know, my lord, as to further sittings. We are entirely in your lordship's hands.

Hon. Mr. CASSELS.—Well, you see, I am entirely in the government's hands. The position I am in is this: that as far back as April I was informed that assistance would be given to perform the judicial work of the court. Nothing has come of that, and I have to go off to New Brunswick to-morrow, after that to Nova Scotia and after that to Sydney, Cape Breton, so I shall probably be away six weeks.

Mr. WATSON.—So long?

Hon. Mr. CASSELS.—I am very sorry for you and for Mr. Perron; it is very hard on you both. After that I have already cases standing for judgment, and I will probably have a few more when I get back. As soon as I get back I will let you know when I get through the work. Then vacation comes along, then I have to be in Manitoba about the middle of September, and from there on to British Columbia. I am only too willing to help on this inquiry, it is important to the country's good apparently, but I can do no more than just wait.

Mr. WATSON.—Then we will have to await a further communication from your lordship on your return from the east?

Hon. Mr. CASSELS.—From Sydney.

Mr. WATSON.—And that will probably not be for some weeks?

Hon. Mr. CASSELS.—One can never tell what may happen. There are twenty cases at Sydney, they will probably take a month, but they may shorten down. However, I will let you know at the very earliest moment.

Mr. WATSON.—We would be very glad if the work could be made continuous.

Hon. Mr. CASSELS.—I am very sorry for you and Mr. Perron. These breaks involve a great deal of labour.

Mr. PERRON.—It is nobody's fault.

Hon. Mr. CASSELS.—It is not my fault.

(Adjourned at 4.15 *sine die*.)

IN THE EXCHEQUER COURT OF CANADA.

IN THE MATTER OF the investigation of certain statements contained in the Report of the Civil Service Commission, reflecting upon the integrity of the officials of the Department of Marine and Fisheries, or some of them.

Continued before the Honourable Mr. Justice Cassels, at Ottawa, June 15, 16, 17 and 18, 1908.

Dr. CHARLES MORSE,
  Deputy Registrar, Exchequer Court.

NELSON R. BUTCHER & Co.,
  Official Reporters.
  (Per F. BERRYMAN.)

GEORGE H. WATSON, K.C., appears as counsel assisting in the investigation.

J. M. GODFREY, appears as counsel for Mr. J. F. Fraser.

Mr. GODFREY.—My lord, I appear for Mr. J. F. Fraser, the commissioner of lights.

Hon. Mr. CASSELS.—Mr. Fraser has not yet been called.

Mr. WATSON.—He has not been called, but probably he will be called. I had a message sent to Mr. Fraser on Friday asking him to be here. Will my learned friend be good enough to have him here to-morrow?

Mr. GODFREY.—I will telegraph to him to-day.

Hon. Mr. CASSELS.—Then I do not think it would be right to deal with anything connected with Mr. Fraser until he is here.

Mr. GODFREY.—I do not object to that, my lord, so long as I hear it personally.

Hon. Mr. CASSELS.—You have no objection to anything being dealt with that reflects on Mr. Fraser?

Mr. GODFREY.—Oh, no, my lord. I rather prefer it, if there is anything against Mr. Fraser.

Hon. Mr. CASSELS.—I do not know anything of him. The way I ruled was that if anyone is affected he has a perfect right to appear.

Mr. WATSON.—Then I have to express regret on behalf of Mr. Perron that he is not able to be here to-day. It was not quite anticipated that your lordship would be able to finish your sittings in the east until the end of the month. The result was that both Mr. Perron and I made a number of peremptory appointments. Mr. Perron unfortunately has not been able to cancel his; I was able to cancel mine at considerable inconvenience and sacrifice.

Hon. Mr. CASSELS.—There are sacrifices all round. I have had to cancel my salmon fishing.

Mr. WATSON.—Yes, my lord. Then I propose to proceed a little further with the evidence of Mr. Willson, I have asked Mr. Willson to be here. He is here. Will you come forward, Mr. Willson, please.

THOMAS L. WILLSON, recalled.

By Mr. Watson:

Q. Mr. Willson, you were to produce some further books upon the return of the appointment?—A. I have these books in the other room.

Q. Will you be good enough to bring them with you to the witness box?—A. (Witness procures books.)

Q. What books have you there?—A. I have my ledger.

Q. Is that the book that was marked No. 9 at the last hearing?—A. Marked No. 9 C.M.

Q. That is the ledger of what company?—A. My ledger before a company was formed, the beginning of my transactions with the department in 1904.

Q. That is with you individually?—A. With me individually.

Q. Then at this time you had the St. Catherines Company in existence?—A. Yes, sir, the St. Catharines Company had been in existence for some years.

Q. You did not tell me the capital stock of that company, the amount?—A. The issued capital stock of the St. Catharines Company is $300,000.

Q. $300,000?—A. Issued and fully paid.

Q. And who was interested in that besides yourself?—A. Besides myself there is William MacKenzie, of MacKenzie & Mann, the Toronto railway men.

Q. Yes?—A. Sir William Van Horne, of Montreal, the Honourable Mr. Gibson, of Beamsville.

Q. Yes?—A. And Mr. Sutherland and myself.

Q. And Mr. Sutherland and yourself compose the company?—A. Yes. My wife has some stock in that also.

Q. And that company was organized about what time?—A. Oh, about 1898 or somewhere——

Q. That will do, 1898?—A. Yes, about that.

Q. Did that company have any transactions with the department?—A. No, sir.

Q. Not at all?—A. Never.

Q. Not of any kind?—A. Not of any kind. The Department of Marine?

Q. Yes, the Department of Marine?—A. Correct.

Q. The Department of Marine and Fisheries. I assume, my lord, we have nothing much to do with that directly?

Hon. Mr. CASSELS.—No. I think we are confined to the Department of Marine and Fisheries.

By Mr. Watson:

Q. Then, incident to the existence and business of that company the business relationship with the department began, is that not so?—A. No, sir.

Q. Are you quite sure? Was the connection and business arrangement with the department not originated in the Willson Company?—A. No, sir, it was not.

Q. Was it not the subject of consideration there?—A. Not at all.

Q. What I want to know specifically from you is as to whether or not the Ottawa Carbide Company was not an offshoot of the Willson Carbide Company for the most part for government purposes?—A. No, sir, it was not, absolutely not.

Q. Then who suggested the Ottawa Carbide Company?—A. It was suggested by the Bronson family wanting to find another means for the use of their power, and they came voluntarily to St. Catharines and looked at my works and asked for a license.

Q. And that you knew was for the purposes of the department?—A. No, sir. The department had not been thought of at that time.

Q. Do you say there was no discussion?—A. No discussion whatsoever.

Q. And in the Willson Carbide Company was there not discussion with the other members of that company as to the expediency of the Ottawa Company for marine purposes?—A. No, none whatsoever.

Q. None whatever. Then, do you undertake to say that it was wholly independent of the Willson Carbide Company and not originated for the purposes of government business?—A. It was wholly independent of the Willson Carbide Company and was not originated for the purpose of doing business specifically with the Marine Department.

Q. Who had before that suggested to you the wisdom of opening up negotiations with the department?—A. Nobody had.

Q. With whom did that originate?—A. With me.

Q. With you?—A. Yes, sir.

Q. After consultation?—A. Not at all, no consultation with any one.

Q. I ask this because it has been disclosed in your evidence before given that Mr. Sutherland became interested in the Willson Carbide Company—in the Ottawa Carbide Company, being a considerable holder I assume in the Willson Company; that is right, is it not?—A. He is a holder of stock in the Willson Carbide Company.

Q. Then you will observe at once the connection and perhaps the natural inference that it might arise from suggestions by him and by reason of his connection with the government?—A. Mr. Sutherland had nothing to do with suggesting the use of carbide by the Marine Department. I myself am wholly responsible for that.

Q. After consultation with him?—A. Not at all, after consultation with no one.

Q. Your statements are pretty strong, Mr. Willson, having in mind he was interested largely with you and with others and that others were also interested with you? —A. I was the principal one interested. All the rest put together, all those stockholders did not have any more stock than I did.

Q. That is in the Willson Company?—A. In the Willson Company.

Q. You had at least half of the stock in the Willson Company?—A. I had, I and my family.

Q. Then you have already stated to his lordship who composed the Ottawa Company. We have that of record and the interests of the several parties. Now then, in the Ottawa Company who suggested the relations with the government?—A. So far as my recollection goes I would state that the matter was one between Mr. Crannell, who was the general business manager, being secretary of the company, and the department, of course at my instigation.

Q. At your instigation?—A. Yes, sir.

Q. Now, at that time Mr. Sutherland was minister of that department, I think? —A. I believe you told me so at the last meeting of this court.

Q. Then did you discuss with him these matters before introducing them to his department?—A. No, I did not, not specially.

Q. Not specially ?—A. No, sir. It might have been mentioned offhand that I had asked the Ottawa Company to come into business relations with the Marine Department.

Q. Was any objection made by reason of his connection with that company ?—A. Not the slightest, neither for nor against.

Q. Do you mean it was not referred to ?—A. It was not referred to.

Q. Was it not referred to by him ?—A. Not that I recollect, sir. Mr. Sutherland had very little to do with the management of the carbide companies, sir.

Q. I quite understand that. But he had a more or less substantial interest?—A. I would not call his interest in the Ottawa Carbide Company a substantial interest.

Q. His holding was $10,000?—A. One-twentieth.

Q. I suppose that was 100 shares?—A. That was 100 shares.

Q. $100 a share?—A. $100 a share. One-twentieth of the total stock of a company is not a very substantial interest, sir.

Q. Still, it is not a very mean proportion either, one-twentieth. One-twentieth of the profits would amount to considerable under some circumstances. Now, you undertook to state on the last occasion that although the transactions with the government by that company were very considerable there were no profits made?—A. There have been no profits made by the Ottawa Carbide Company.

Q. How do you account for that?—A. The cost of the raw product, the carbide, is so high in comparison with the selling price that there is no profit.

Q. What was the selling price to the government or the department?—A. If my recollection is right it began at about $60.

Q. Will the books show?—A. Their books will show, and the statement of their own shows. (Producing statement.)

Q. This is from July 1, 1902. Was that the first?—A. That is the first, sir.

Q. July 1, 1902. I see that he was minister from November, 1901, to November 11, 1902?—A. Yes.

Q. So that the relation started during his being in control of the department. Now, does this show the prices, $65 ?—A. These prices marked $65 per ton, Ottawa.

Q. Yes.—A. Until March 31, 1907, when the price was $60, and then one item of $65, then $60, and so on.

Q. That is down to the present time, apparently?—A. Yes.

Q. So that with four or five exceptions the price per ton has uniformly been $65?—A. It has been with those exceptions marked.

Q. Why the exceptions?—A. The price varied.

Q. It does not seem to have varied very much?—A. That is the statement the Ottawa Carbide Company gave me.

Q. Now, that price I should think upon its face would appear to be an excessive price?—A. It is not an excessive price; it is, on the other hand, a very low price.

Q. Why do you say so?—A. Because in the United States where carbide is sold at $70 a ton to the United States government, costing less than it does to make here.

Q. Do you mean that you sell it?—A. The American Company in which I am interested.

Q. The American Company?—A. Yes.

Q. Sells at $70 a ton?—A. To the United States government.

Q. Under more or less favourable circumstances?—A. Under more favourable circumstances.

Q. That is more favourable circumstances to the company?—A. As to the cost of production.

Q. To the company?—A. To the American Company. It costs them less to produce than it does here and they sell at a higher price, and they are only getting a fair price.

Q. Now, you sold the material as well, the carbide to others?—A. Yes.

Q. To whom else did you sell? Let me see from your book?—A. This book has nothing to do with the Carbide Company.

Q. Where is the book of the Carbide Company?—A. You have just sent for it.

Q. That is the one telephoned for?—A. Yes, sir.

Q. Have you any personal knowledge of others to whom it was sold?—A. I can say this that the price to the general public was $5 higher than this price to the government.

Q. What do you mean by the general public?—A. Anybody who would buy carbide.

Q. Do you mean sold for retail?—A. Yes, sir.

Q. And for consumption?—A. Yes, sir.

Q. What amount?—A. Oh, anywhere running from 100 pounds up to a ton. At a ton and over there was a price of $5 a ton less.

Q. A ton and over?—A. Yes, up to any quantity, carloads or 100 tons.

Q. Then you sold to retailers at a lower price?—A. A very few dealers.

Q. That would be contrary to the rule?—A. Not less than to the government.

Q. I think you said $5 less?—A. No, sir. $5 less than the retail price to the consumer.

Q. You sold to the consumer at $5 less?—A. More. $5 more than we sold to the retailer or to the government.

Q. $5 more?—A. Yes.

Q. Then who were the others who purchased at smaller prices?—A. Nobody in the country purchased at a lower price than the government.

Q. Is that so?—A. That is correct, sir.

Q. Then, did you have a monopoly?—A. There is no monopoly in the manufacture of carbide. Three companies in Canada exist——

Q. No monopoly?—A. Absolutely independent of each other.

Q. That is the three companies with which you are connected?—A. Yes, sir.

Q. That is the Willson Company——?—A. The Ottawa Company and the Shawinigan Company.

Q. Those three companies. No monopoly?—A. No monopoly.

Q. Then what is the cost about per ton of the carbide?—A. I have told you that the cost to the Ottawa Carbide Company was about what we have been selling it to the government for.

Q. But that is almost inconceivable?—A. It happens to be the fact.

Q. Where did you procure it?—A. The carbide?

Q. Yes. I mean how do you make up the cost?—A. We manufacture——

Q. How do you estimate the cost?—A. The cost of our material, the coal or coke and lime, the carbons, the labour, the expense of machinery running, the repairs, the breakdowns, everything that enters into the cost up to the selling of the stuff and putting it on the cars.

Q. And what proportion of your output went to the department, the larger proportion?—A. A very small proportion.

Q. I see. You do not mean to suggest that you are doing bsuiness for the benefit of the public?—A. I mean to suggest this, this will be an explanation to you, that after having started a large works and having many hundreds of thousands of dollars in it, you cannot shut up because it is not profitable. You will run on for years until the increase of production may bring about a profitable condition.

Q. Then it has become profitable by this time?—A. The Ottawa Carbide Company is not profitable by this time.

Q. It has not become so?—A. It has not become so.

Q. Well, it is being continued?—A. It is.

Q. Last time you promised me you would produce your annual returns. Have you got them?—A. I have not them with me, I did not know I was to be called until fifteen minutes before this.

Q. I sent you a message on Friday ?—A. I was out of town. I received it this morning.

Q. I am sorry. Have you any returns with you ?—A. Not here.

Q. Have you a book here showing the annual statements ?—A. I have no returns or statements in connection with the carbide company. You will have those in a few minutes.

Q. Can you state from memory what those returns showed ?—A. Well——

Q. The result, I mean?—A. A. Oh, practically from 1,500 or 1,400 to 1,7000 tons.

Q. As to profit what do they show ?—A. There is no profit in the Ottawa Carbide Company.

Q. No profit at all ?—A. None whatsoever.

Q. Was there a loss ?—A. There was a loss, as I told you, of $135,000.

Q. Then, perhaps the profit was distributed in salaries before it reached the end of the year ?—A. No. The only cost of production is, first, the carbide company's works——

Q. I am not asking you about that. Just keep strictly to the question, please. Is that so, that there was a large distribution ?—A. No, sir.

Q. Of salary and income ?—A. No, sir, no distribution whatsoever to the officers of the company.

Q. What did you get out of the company yourself?—A. The company did not give me any salary whatsoever. I do not work for salary.

Q. You do not work for salary?—A. No, sir.

Q. Then who gets salaries in the company?—A. Mr. Crannell and Mr. Bronson.

Q. Anyone else?—A. The bookkeepers, the typewriters and sales——

Q. Do you mean any of the other shareholders as officers?—A. No, sir.

Q. No one but Mr. Crannel and Mr. Bronson?—A. No one but them.

Q. Have you any objection to stating what they were paid?—A. $2,000 apiece.

Q. Well, it seems to me rather an extraordinary proposition. What is the explanation of it, that you make it in some other way?—A. No, sir; that the carbide cost of production in Ottawa amounts to the figures I have given you.

Q. What did the minister get out of the company by way of income?—A. Absolutely nothing, sir.

Q. Then the negotiations were introduced, as you say, by you to the department through the deputy minister?—A. Yes, sir.

Q. You have your letter books coming?—A. There were no letters written about that time. The letter books are coming, but no letters were written by me.

Q. I want to know what communications you have had in writing with the deputy minister on behalf of the carbide company?—A. I have had none, sir.

Q. Do you say so?—A. I do.

Q. What communications have you received from him by letter?—A. I have received none from him, sir, about the carbide.

Q. In connection with the business relationship?—A. That is so.

Q. Have you ever received letters from him?—A. No, sir.

Q. Has your company?—A. Not in connection with the carbide question.

Q. In connection with what then?—A. Only in connection with my gas buoy business.

Q. I am coming to that afterwards.

Hon. Mr. CASSELS.—This carbide company was formed in order to make the carbide for this other work. They were apparently making an enormous profit out of one and a loss in the other.

Mr. WATSON.—Yes, my lord.

Q. Then, as his lordship suggests, your profits may have been made by what you supplied to the International Company?—A. By what carbide we supplied to them?

Q. Yes?—A. No, sir.

Hon. Mr. CASSELS.—The suggestion was that he might make very large profits by the supply of his gas buoys, and in order to run that he might be able to suffer a loss on the carbide.

Mr. WATSON.—Quite so, my lord: I will exhaust this question of correspondence while we are at it.

By Mr. Watson:

Q. In connection with the carbide company, I want to know whether there was any correspondence with the deputy minister?—A. Not by myself.

Q. By any one else to your knowledge?—A. There must necessarily have been by the secretary of the company.

Q. Was there any private correspondence with him?—A. Not that I know of.

Q. Have you ever seen any such?—A. I have never seen any such.

Q. Did you have any private communications with him with regard to the business?—A. I have had no private communications with him with regard to the carbide business.

Q. In what way did he facilitate the introduction and continuance of your relations?—A. I could not say.

Q. Do you know that he has?—A. I do not know.

Q. What communications did you have with the former minister or acting minister in the promotion of your relations?—A. I do not know.

Q. Have you had any communications or intimations to that effect?—A. I have had none.

Q. Now, then, just a word again. Did you hear the evidence of Colonel Anderson?—A. I heard some of it.

Q. I suppose you have read reports of other parts of it?—A. Yes, sir.

Q. Wherein he stated quite distinctly his belief that the relationship arose at the instigation of and was promoted by Mr. J. F. Fraser. Are you aware of that?—A. I have some recollection of that.

Q. Now, what personal communications did you have with him?—A. I had no personal communications with Mr. J. F. Fraser, except such as I would go into the public office and discuss any question which might arise.

Q. Then why did you ask him to favour and facilitate your proposals?—A. I did not ask Mr. Fraser to favour or facilitate my proposals.

Q. Then why did he do so?—A. I suppose as his duty to the department.

Q. As his duty to the department?—A. Yes, sir.

Q. You know that he did?—A. I know that carbide was used, sir.

Q. And you know that he promoted and facilitated your business relations?—A. I do not know that, sir.

Q. Who did, then?—A. All I know is, he was the officer, as commissioner of lights, who would use the material.

Q. Then why the positive statement of belief by Colonel Anderson that this had been done in order to assist you?—A. I am not accountable for any ideas of Colonel Anderson.

Q. Quite so. But why the statement made?—A. I cannot account for what runs in his mind.

Q. Is there foundation for it?—A. There is none so far as I am concerned.

Q. Now, in connection with the carbide——

Mr. GODFREY.—Just at that point, my lord. I think we ought not to go into the question of Colonel Anderson's opinion; that is not evidence. I would have objected if I had been here at the time. It only arises indirectly here, still I think my learned friend should not press Colonel Anderson's opinion as not being evidence.

Hon. Mr. CASSELS.—I do not know what status you have yet, Mr. Godfrey.

Mr. GODFREY.—Well, my client has.

Hon. Mr. CASSELS.—Yes. I will be very glad to have your assistance in any way available.

Mr. GODFREY.—I would have objected, had I been here, to the opinion of any person. I think this ought to be based entirely on evidence, not on opinion.

Hon. Mr. CASSELS.—This is a different thing. There is a statement made which has gone abroad. Now, that evidence has to be sifted, and it will be better for Mr. Fraser that it should be brought out.

Mr. GODFREY.—Except, of course, it is no evidence against Mr. Fraser as yet.

Hon. Mr. CASSELS.—Go on, Mr. Watson.

By Mr. Watson:

Q. Then, where did Mr. Fraser accompany you in connection with the carbide company, on what occasions did he accompany you on visits?—A. I do not know of any visits in which he accompanied me.

Q. Just try and think?—A. He would naturally go to the carbide works to inspect the manufacture of carbide.

Q. What works?—A. The Ottawa Carbide Company's works.

Q. But where else?—A. Since the gas buoy business started he has been down at the factory to supervise the inspection of gas buoys.

Q. Where is that factory?—A. We have several of them. The present one is at the corner of Albert and Wellington.

Q. Here, you mean?—A. In Ottawa, yes, sir.

Q. But where, outside of Ottawa, have you factories in connection with the international company?—A. We have worked done at various places in Canada and at the Continental Iron Works in New York.

Q. The Continental Iron Works in New York. How many times has he accompanied you there?—A. I could not tell you how many times.

Q. About how many times?—A. I have a recollection of his being there once.

Q. Of his being there once?—A. Yes.

Q. When was that?—A. I could not tell you.

Q. Well, about what year?—A. Probably 1904 or 1905.

Q. Why did you pay his expenses?—A. I did not pay his expenses.

Q. Just try and think?—A. I did not pay his expenses.

Q. What provision did you make for him on that occasion?—A. I never made any provision for him on that occasion.

Q. How many occasions have you paid his expenses on visits?—A. I never paid his expenses on any occasion whatsoever.

Q. Who has in your company, then?—A. No one has, sir.

Q. Are your books here now?—A. Yes.

Q. Let me see them, please?—A. You may be getting mixed on the carbide company and the international.

Q. Oh, I thank you, I am coming to the international.—A. Which was that latter question applied to, to the carbide company?

Q. That was intended to apply generally. Did you so understand it?—A. Yes, I do now.

Q. But did you when you answered?—A. I thought you referred particularly to the business done by the Continental Iron Works, the making of the buoys.

Q. That is the international company?—A. Yes.

Q. It was led up to in that way. It was in connection with that my question was asked. Apparently you distinguished between the two companies. Then, on what occasion have the international paid his expenses?—A. It has never paid his expenses at all.

Q. Then why did he go at your request?—A. I could not answer that. He went down to see the process of manufacture of buoys at the Continental Iron Works.

Q. Then who accompanied him?—A. I was in New York at the time and went to see the Continental Iron Works.

Q. Yes. You were in New York at the time, and who else in your company ?—A. Nobody.

Q. Then do you know of his being there with others ?—A. I do not.

Q. Or at other places with others in connection with the company ?—A. I do not.

Q. Then what benefit did he get from you directly or indirectly ?—A. Absolutely none.

Q. On any occasion? I am speaking of any one of your companies?—A. From no company whatsoever.

Q. Why did you pay commissions, and to whom ?—A. I never paid commissions.

Q. Eh ?—A. I never paid commissions, nor has any of my companies paid commissions.

Q. Now, do you mean that Mr. Fraser has not had commissions on purchases from your company ?—A. He has not, sir.

Q. Let me see the ledger with the index, if you please, for the last three years. Where is the government account here, will you show me?—A. Page 247 of the ledger.

Q. Thank you. Then with what other party have you been dealing, what other person or official have you been dealing with directly other than Mr. Fraser?—A. I may say that I have not been dealing with Mr. Fraser, but with the deputy minister, and under him with Mr. Fraser.

Q. But I understood from you on the last occasion that your communications were for the most part with Mr. Fraser ?—A. I meant always through-the deputy minister.

Q. Through the deputy minister. Then that comes to the deputy minister. Has he accompanied you on some occasions to the different works or factories ?—A. He has accompanied me to the gas buoy works.

Q. Yes?—A. And I believe the carbide works on various occasions.

Q. To New York ?—A. No, sir, never.

Q. What works do you mean, here in Ottawa ?—A. Here in Ottawa.

Q. Outside of Ottawa ?—A. No, sir.

Q. Not outside of Ottawa?—A. Not outside.

Q. And what benefits has he received indirectly ?—A. He has received none, no benefits whatever from me or from any one in connection with my company.

Q. How do you know not with any one else ?—A. Well, I can know because I ascertained from the carbide company. I know positively there has been no distribution of money for any private distribution.

Q. I am not speaking so much of distribution of money as about commissions and advantages ?—A. Or favours. I will say broadly favours of any nature whatsoever, commissions or anything you can imagine.

Q. Will you please have in mind that I am extending this now to the international company ?—A. Yes, I have that in mind.

Q. Where are the books of the international company ?—A. Here is the synoptic journal marked Exhibit 10.

Q. Will you show me the index, please?—A. I do not believe there is an index to that book. Complete details are there of every transaction.

Q. During each year?—A. Yes, sir.

Q. Then tell me this, if you please, to what extent have you discounted paper of any official or assisted in banking arrangements with any official?—A. I have never done either.

Q. You have heard of it, have you not?—A. Not in our company, no one responsible or in connection with it.

Q. Then in what company have you heard about it?—A. I have never heard of it so far as I have any knowledge of any of this business. I have no knowledge beyond that.

Q. Have you heard of it in connection with others?—A. Marine Department officials ?

Q. Yes?—A. No, sir; I have never heard of such a thing.

Q. I thought from your answer you had, but that you were seeking to exculpate your company?—A. Not at all. I have never heard that such transactions have taken place.

Q. Then the prices that were charged for the international company's buoys, it would appear, are very large prices; that is so, is it not?—A. In respect to the value of the goods the prices were very low.

Q. Very low?—A. Yes, sir.

Q. I think on the former occasion you gave a minimum and a maximum, did you not?—A. Yes.

Q. My recollection is that it was from about $2,000, was it not, up to $8,000?—A. Up to the average the buoys run about $8,500. As I explained to his lordship, there were two buoys that were sold, they are extraordinary buoys, they were sold for $15,000.

Q. $15,000?—A. Yes.

Q. Now, that company was formed, the international company?—A. Yes, sir.

Q. And that consists of?—A. I have answered that question. It consisted at the time of its formation of the gentlemen whom I gave you at our last examination, Mr. Little and his wife, myself and my wife and my bookkeeper.

Q. And no one else?—A. No one else.

Q. Why was that formed?—A. Because the business required more capital than I personally could put into it.

Q. That is the business with the government?—A. The business generally of the manufacture of the buoys.

Q. And that business is limited to business with the department?—A. With all departments of the world.

Q. In Canada limited to business with the Department of Marine and Fisheries?—A. Naturally. It is only useful for navigation.

Q. So that department is your only customer?—A. In Canada.

Q. That is all we are speaking of, Canada?—A. Yes, sir. We have numerous customers out of Canada, numerous governments.

Q. There is no competition?—A. There is none necessarily.

By Hon. Mr. Cassels:

Q. This company is a Canadian company?—A. A Canadian company organized under our Dominion laws.

Q. Do you sell abroad any that you manufacture?—A. Yes, sir; we sell abroad to the United States government.

Q. What is made in Canada?—A. To every government, except the United States, the buoys are made wholly in Ottawa, but to the United States we are making at the Continental Iron Works.

By Mr. Watson:

Q. That is in New York?—A. New York.

Q. So you have a factory in New York from which you supply the United States government demands?—A. Yes, sir.

Q. And to what extent do you supply the Marine Department of the United States?—A. We have so far put in nine buoys at various points.

Q. That is very limited, then?—A. At the entrance to New York we have three or four, maybe more, six.

Q. Your business with them is very limited?—A. No, sir. We are commencing a large business with them.

Q. It has been limited up to this time?—A. To get it started, but we have this year $150,000 in the estimates in the United States for our work.

Q. But that is small as compared with what is in the estimates here?—A. Yes.

3262—8½

Q. How much have you got in the estimates here?—A. I could not say.

Q. About how much?—A. I could not say.

Q. Last year, how much?—A. I do not know.

Q. The year before, then?—A. All I know is how much was sold.

Q. But how much was sold?—A. I think we received about a quarter of a million on the average or more. One year may have run into the two years mentioned on my subpœna, $360,000. For your lordship's information let me state that we have sold nearly two hundred thousand or over in dollars to Brazil, we are selling to all the South American countries, we have buoys in Great Britain, we have buoys in Germany illustrating their usefulness, we have shipments now ready for India, Corea and other countries. So it is a world's business we are actually doing, and those prices are all the same as we are allowing to the Canadian government.

Q. Where are those goods manufactured?—A. In Ottawa.

Q. Those go to all places except the United States?—A. Except to the United States.

By Hon. Mr. Cassels:

Q. Have you patents in foreign countries?—A. Every country in the world, 45 countries.

Q. What do you expect in those countries in regard to price?—A. They have not a regulation in their Patent Act such as we have in Canada.

Q. Their laws are diffierent?—A. Great Britain's has just been changed.

Q. Yes ?

By Mr. Watson:

Q. Then why have ou on some occasions made a reduction of price to the depart-ment here?—A. I explained that to you.

Q. Will you answer again please?—A. It was because our facilities for production were increased so that we could lower the cost of production, and we made a proportionate lowering in the selling price to the governments.

Q. What proportion of decrease of price?—A. I think we have reduced it about 25 per cent.

Q. You think so?—A. Yes sir.

Q. And has that been entirely of your own motion or suggestion?—A. It was entirely of our own motion.

Q. Why, you are very gracious, generous, rather, in that way ?—A. Not at all.

Q. You were not asked to do so?—A. We were not asked to do so by the Canadian Government.

Q. Have you been asked by any representative of the department to make any reduction?—A. I have not been asked by any representative of this department to make any reductions whatsoever.

Q. Have your prices ever been questioned?—A. I believe our prices were questioned.

Q. By whom?—A. The deputy minister and his commissioner.

Q. Who was his commissioner?—A. ᴍr. Fraser.

Q. Just tell what took place first with the deputy minister?—A. I asked three thousand five hundred dollars for our standard buoy, $3,750 to be exact and they pointed out this price was perhaps disproportionate to the price of the old buoy. I said, 'We do not know the cost of manufacturing these yet, but I will venture to do so so as to make them for you at $3,000' and I did so.

Q. That was quite a handsome reduction offhand, that is on a venture?—A. I venture to say it cost me more to make the first buoys than I got for them, sir.

Q. You made a reduction, then, upon an apparently very mild suggestion, from the way you put it, of the deputy minister, that it might be furnished for the $750 less?—A. They asked me if that was the lowest prices I could make. I volunteered then to do that.

Q. Does it not strike you as a very free and easy sort of buying?—A. I will explain the cost of those buoys in proportion to the others to the government. Those buoys produce 4 times the amount of gas over the same buoy they were previously getting in the previous gas system, the Pintsch system.

Q. What was the cost of the other buoys?—A. They had made none so large as those, but the cost of a standard buoy at that time was running from $1,800 or $1,760 up to $2,600 or $2,800, according to the size.

Q. Now, do you say that this buoy had four times the capacity?—A. It has four times the capacity, and we are selling it at about double the cost for the individual buoy to the government. But that buoy——

Q. Now wait, please. Is not that capacity for the most part a waste in use?—A. It is not; it is an absolute essential.

Q. That may apply perhaps occasionally, but as a rule is not that additional capacity a waste?—A. That additional capacity is not a waste, but is the reason——

Q. It is a reserve power which is not called into use?—A. No, sir. It increases the light of the buoy and its life.

Q. Its life?—A. Yes, sir. The old buoys had to be charged several times during the season. These buoys are put out at the opening of navigation, for instance, in the St. Lawrence river, and taken up at the close with one charging, and if there is ever a case that one of the buoys has to be charged a second time it is very rare, due to some accident.

Q. Yes?—A. So those buoys require less service attention and give a greatly increased light and have a very much greater value for each dollar paid for them than the buoys previously purchased from the German company.

Q. From what company were they purchased?—A. The Pintsch company.

Q. Where?—A. Through a New York agent called the Safety Car Heating and Lighting Company.

Q. Then according to your statement, if it is accurate—I am not challenging its accuracy for the moment at all—there was really a material saving in the transactions with you. Do you venture to make that statement?—A. I state that positively. There has been a very material saving. To obtain the service you are getting from these buoys now would have required at least double the expenditure on the old system.

Q. Do you mean double the expenditure of your system?—A. That is the capital stock, maintenance by them.

By Hon. Mr. Cassels:

Q. Labour?—A. Capital cost, maintenance, your lordship.

By Mr. Watson:

Q. What additional expenses of labour, that is maintenance?—A. Charging the old buoys was a very serious operation. You have to make gas on the shore, compress it into tanks, and a boat would go out to the buoy and fill it, and then go back and get more gas. Now, these tanks only hold enough to charge two or three, maybe four buoys, and they have then to repeat that operation, and if you put it in the buoys it only lasts for a couple of months.

Q. Now then, Mr. Willson, it has been intimated to me that in connection with the prices you have been and are charging you are imposing upon the department and charging them quite improper and excessive prices by reason of the circumstance that you are there with practically a monopoly?—A. That is not true. Our prices——

Q. Will you let me know to what extent it may be estimated as accurate or inaccurate, and you can only let me know that by stating to his lordship what the cost of these is?—A. I am unwilling to give any information as to wnat the cost of my buoys is.

Q. In Canada I am speaking of?—A. In Canada especially for this reason, we have competition.

Q. You have no competition in Canada?—A. We have competition in Germany.

Q. I thought you said you have your patents everywhere?—A. We have, but we have competition in Germany with the old style buoys.

Q. Oh yes, the old style buoys· Is that the only country where you have competition?—A. There are some buoys made in England, a very few.

Q. In the meantime, Mr. Willson, with your large experience, you understand, we have in the meantime to attempt to look after the interests of the public of this country if Canada without regard to Germany or any parts of England. Now, that being so, I want you to reconsider, if you please, the matter of your feeling as to not giving the cost of these buoys, because it is a very serious matter. You are aware the public so consider it, are you not?—A. I do not regard it as a serious matter. I make these prices myself. I make them fair and reasonable.

Q. That is, they are arbitrary prices, arbitrarily fixed by you?—A. They are arbitrary prices.

Q. Arbitrarily fixed by you?—A. Yes, sir. I make them reasonable, I consider, and the government can take them or let them alone.

Q. You say from your other evidence already given that the government practically is obliged to take these buoys from you in the interests of the country and the public?—A. I say so and repeat that statement emphatically.

Q. Then you are in a position to hold up the government if you are so minded?—A. I am not.

Q. If you are so minded?—A. I am not so minded.

Q. If so minded you might perpetrate a hold up as to charges?—A. If I charged greatly higher prices than I am charging now it might be unreasonable.

Q. Yes, it might be unreasonable. Then the unreasonableness depends upon the cost of manufacture as compared with the selling price?—A. It does depend upon the cost of manufacture, and if the price of raw materials rise we would to-day have to raise the price correspondingly.

Q. Yes. You appreciate, of course, now that the government might take over your patent by reason of the fact that you are not charging reasonable prices?—A. Not by reason of that reason, sir.

Q. By what reason?—A· That they have simply the power. The prices are not unreasonable.

Hon. Mr. CASSELS.—On the last occasion when I ruled that the witness was not obliged to give evidence of price, that was based upon this idea, that until there was some imputation made against somebody that they were getting something out of it the price would not have any relevancy. There is another aspect if you press it—I do not know what may or may not turn on it—if under the Patent Act this company were asked for prices, and they were not reasonable, then the government could refuse to pay such prices and void the patent, and go on and do what they like.

Mr. WATSON.—It is just that. This commission is intended, of course, and designed for useful purposes for the future as well as securing information as to the past, my lord.

Hon. Mr. CASSELS.—There is just this about it: It might be that the prices paid mght be so unreasonable that the official of the department should simply refuse to take them, and then go on and manufacture the buoys. If you proceed on that line I think Mr. Willson ought to tell.

Mr. WATSON.—Yes, my lord. I have led up to that somewhat by showing that no inquiry has even been made of this gentleman apparently as to the reduction of the prices or as to the cost.

Hon. Mr. CASSELS.—That might or might not be important later on. It is only within a very recent period that it has been held by the Supreme Court that if an unreasonable price is asked then the patent can be voided· That aspect if you wish may be gone into.

Mr. WATSON.—I conceive it is my duty.

Hon. Mr. CASSELS.—I think Mr. Willson ought to give the details.

WITNESS.—The details as to the cost?

Hon. Mr. CASSELS.—What it cost and what the selling price is. You see, it may or may not appear exorbitant. It might be an official of the government had no right whatever to pay what might be an exorbitant price, because the government could turn round under the Patent Act and say, ' very well, your patent is void.'

WITNESS.—I would be willing to give privately to, say, Mr. Watson, so long as it does not become public, and your lordship, of course, and, say, to the Finance Minister of Canada and the Minister of Marine.

Hon. Mr. CASSELS.—You could do it in this way——

WITNESS.—But I am not willing to make it public.

Hon· Mr. CASSELS.—You could do it in this way: Give it to Mr. Watson, and then later on if it becomes relevant, it will have to be made public. If in the course of this inquiry no relevancy attaches to it, it will remain private.

WITNESS.—I may say there is only simply a manufacturing profit left in the business.

Mr. WATSON.—Why make it a mystery?

By Hon. Mr. Cassels:

Q. You will have it shrouded in suspicion. You ought to clear it up. I do not see it will do any harm?—A. It does harm to us in foreign countries.

Q. But if this thing is only being purchased at double what the other buoys cost, and by reason of the reduction in maintenance and its increased capacity it is worth four times as much, then you get the benefit immediately in that way?—A· Yes.

Mr. WATSON.—Mr. Willson, you quite appreciate I am not in a position to receive any private information from you that is of any value. I could not receive that and keep it to myself here in a public capacity.

Hon. Mr. CASSELS.—I think if you wish to follow it up by showing that the price paid would be unreasonable within the Patent Act, then he is bound to answer the question.

Mr. WATSON.—Yes, my lord.

Q· Then, Mr. Willson, will you please tell me the range of cost, about, as compared with the range of price?—A. I am not prepared to tell you that offhand.·

Q. About. You can give within a few hundred dollars?—A. We cannot go into that until I look that matter up. I would have to take time, my lord, to make an investigation myself.

Hon. Mr. CASSELS.—That is reasonable, there are all kinds of elements entering into it.

WITNESS.—I will make out a statement· I have very many different companies to attend to and I cannot remember details of that kind. I would say this, that the cost would run from 60 to 75 per cent of what we actually received for the buoys.

By Mr· Watson:

Q. From 60——?—A. To 75 per cent.

Q. That is, you received from 25 to 40 per cent profit?—A. According to the nature of the article. -

Q. According to the nature of the article?—A. Yes, sir.·

Q. 25 to 40 per cent?

By Hon. Mr. Cassels:

Q. That covers an allowance for interest?—A. No, sir, that does not cover those things. That would be the maximum profit.

Q. But you cannot get your maximum profit unless you get at the capital put in and allow a percentage on the capital for working expenses?—A. That does not mean our net profits were 25 to 40 per cent. We do not have any such profits, but that is the actual cost of manufacture in comparison with the selling price.

Q. What Mr. Watson wants to get at is, is the profit reasonable? To get at that you have got to take everything into account?—A. I hold myself responsible for that statement. Is not that sufficient for your lordship? You realize then we have only a manufacturing profit, and I may say to your lordship, if you have never made an inquiry into the manufacturing cost in a factory, any factory that lives on anything less than 25 per cent profit must become in time bankrupt, because there are unknown expenses that arise that eat that up.

By Mr. Watson:

Q. Never mind going into that general question of a manufacturing business. Just confine yourself to this particular matter, if you please. Then a buoy that you sold for $15,000——?—A. I would rather not have that one brought up. Take the regular goods we manufacture.

Q. It would be larger upon that?—A. It would be larger upon that because that was an extraordinary thing.

Q. So just dealing with that isolated case, there were two of those at $15,000, and just for a general understanding it would be quite fair, I assume, to understand that in circumstances like those your profits were probably 60 per cent or more?—A. It is not fair to pick out an isolated case of a single buoy, that is impossible.

Q. Never mind about the fairness or unfairness. Having regard to what his lordship has already stated——?—A. It would not be true.

Q. It would be true?—A. It would not be, sir, with reference to a case, by taking cut an isolated case. You have to take the whole production of your factory.

Q. I know people may figure in such a way, taking in all sorts of collateral and indirect elements, that although they are making immense profits apparently the cost is almost equal to the selling price.

Hon. Mr. CASSELS.—What Mr. Willson means is this: They sell that buoy for $3,000 but they had to start and make these two buoys separately in this particular case.

WITNESS.—That is correct, sir.

By Mr. Watson:

Q. But that is in connection with your whole business, and taking your business as a whole and having regard to the way it is run and to your plant, your appliances and your advantages, you are able to produce that buoy at less than half the selling price; is not that so?—A. No, sir, that is not correct. Your statement——

Q. I understood a moment ago there might be 60 to 70 per cent profit?—A. I did not say so. You are twisting that.

Q. Please do not say that. My statement to you was originally—perhaps you did not hear me—you probably made 60 per cent profit on that?—A. No, sir I did not make any such statement at all. What I said was the cost of production of those buoys in reference to the selling price was 60 to 75 per cent.

Q. I know. But I asked you a specific question. You may not have attended?—A. I am attending.

Q. I asked you a specific question with regard to those two buoys at $15,000 each, whether it would not be fair to reach the conclusion that your profits were 60 per cent on those two?—A. If the cost was 60 per cent?

Q. I did not say cost; I said profit?—A. You cannot make it out to be 60 per cent; 40 per cent.

Q. Profit?—A. The profit would be 40 per cent in that case. Now that cost 60 per cent of the——

By Hon. Mr. Cassels:

Q. What Mr. Watson asked you is this practically: Take these two big buoys, was the cost more than 40 per cent, thus leaving you a profit of 60 per cent?—A. Your honour, that is wrong again. I said the cost of production would be 60 or 75 per cent of the total cost.

Q. I know that, Mr. Willson. What you said was that that was taking the ordinary buoy. But in regard to these two particular ones, the profit might be larger, might it not?—A. It might have been.

Q. Mr. Watson was asking: Would the cost of production of those be more than 40 per cent?—A. It might be about half.

Q. That is the question?—A. I am willing for your own——

Q. That was 50 per cent instead of 30?—A. In that special case.

By Mr. Watson:

Q. Would that apply to others that are priced say from $8,000 up?—A. No, sir. There would be very much less profits in all of those from $8,000 down.

Q. You can produce a statement, but meantime, apparently from what you said, there would be an average of about, will you say 35 per cent profit?—A. There might be. I would say there is.

By Hon. Mr. Cassels:

Q. You understand Mr. Watson put it in that way. I would like to clear it up. I did not understand Mr. Willson to say there was a profit of 35 or 30 per cent at all. It is the manufacturing profit he is referring to, as I understand his evidence?—A. I only referred to the manufacturing cost, the difference between the cost of production in the shop and the selling price. But you have to deduct from that expenses.

Mr. WATSON.—You have very little expense in selling?

Hon. Mr. CASSELS.—You have interest on capital, repair of plant and wear and tear, every manufacturing business has to make allowances for that sort of thing in arriving at the profit. I understand this witness has given strictly the manufacturing cost.

WITNESS.—That is so, my lord. They could never write out such a profit all the year or for any term of years, because they might have to renew tne whole of their shops.

Q. You have to allow interest on the capital?—A. Yes, and everything.

Q. And insurance?—A. Yes.

By Mr. Watson:

Q. That company was formed when?—A. November, 1906.

Q. What were the profits of the business for the year ending 1907?—A. There have been no profits, sir, that we have declared.

Q. You mean they have not been declared. You had an annual statement, you had your regular meeting and your regular report, had you not?—A. We had actually no profits that would show.

Q. I am speaking about reports. You had an annual report?—A. I have no reports.

Q. Eh?—A. No, sir.

Q. There was a report made, was there not?—A. There was a verbal report made; there was no——

Q. No written report?—A. No report that was made in the shape of an annual statement.

Q. Where is your ledger of that company?—A. I will show you.

Q. Show me.—A. I know nothing about the accounts.

Q. Is your bookkeeper here?—A. No.

Q. That is your ledger?—A. That is the main book of the whole company, that is the synoptic journal, every detail is there.

Q. No. 10, every detail. But what does this show, the amount of receipts for the year?—A. The amount of the receipts for the year. I could not tell you anything about it. I am not a bookkeeper and have never seen a set of books.

Q. But you have some idea. Who is the gentleman who brought them here?—A. That is not the man at all. That is the carbide company, this is the international.

Q. Well, who knows about these books?—A. The bookkeeper down at the office.

Q. What is his or her name?—A. Mr. Scott.

Q. What is his first name?—A. A. M. Scott.

Q. Who is the secretary?—A. Well, the secretary—he is the assistant secretary and has charge of all this work.

Q. Who is secretary?—A. The actual secretary is Mr. H. A. Little. Mr. Scott is practically the secretary.

Q. Would you mind telephoning to him at luncheon time to attend here? There is no necessity to serve him wth a subpœna at all?—A. None at all.

Q. If you will kindly ask him to come here after the adjournment?—A. All right.

Q. So that is the information you give to his lordship with regard to the cost of these goods?—A. Yes, sir. That is within practical range.

Q. Within practical knowledge?—A. Yes, sir. Somewhere between 25 and 40 per cent would be, and probably it is under the 35 per cent his lordship suggests, but that does not take into account——

Q. Now, have you ever been asked by any official of the department wnat the cost was or about what the cost was?—A. I have never been asked by an official.

Q. You have never been asked with the one exception you have spoken of at the commencement of your dealings, the interview with the deputy?—A. Yes.

Q. When the reduction was made from $3,750 to $3,000. Has the price ever come in question since?—A. It has never come in question.

Q. Not by the deputy minister or anyone else?—A. Nor anyone.

Q. That is not the usual way of transacting business, is it?—A. In this class of work, yes.

Q. Do you say that? You do not do business in that way in the United States?— A We do business that way all over.

Q. Do you mean to say your prices are not questioned?—A. Oh, they have been questioned, but our prices are made, and they can take the goods or let them alone.

Q. I can understand that. But purchasers usually do not pay fancy prices without some inquiry or question, do they?—A. I may state that those prices are not fancy prices and have never been so.

Q. We will have to judge of that. 35 per cent profit is a pretty fancy profit?— A. No, sir, that is not a fancy profit. That is a very low price as far as profit is concerned.

Q. I see. What do you call a fancy profit?—A. Well, it depends upon whether your——

Q. What do you call a fancy profit?—A. I would like to have 150 per cent.

Q. I see. I thought we would get the measure of Mr. Willson somewhere. You think 150 per cent might be a fancy profit for you?

Hon. Mr. CASSELS.—He might fancy he would get that profit.

By Mr. Watson:

Q. Yes. That has been your object apparently to work up the profits?—A. No, sir; I have been working down the profits.

Q. Voluntarily?—A. Voluntarily, in order to establish a world's business.

Q. I see. Then do you sell identically the same buoys or practically the same. I mean in construction and design, in the United States as here?—A. Our designs are changing.

Q. Never mind about whether they are changing?—A. Practically, yes.

Q. Take those sold last year in Canada and the United States, are they practically the same design?—A. Practically.

Q. And practically the same cost?—A. Practically the same price, selling price.

Q. I am leading up to that. The same design and the same cost. And what is the price over there in the United States?—A. The prices are the same as in Canada.

Q. Let me have a schedule of your prices?—A. I have not any here.

Q. Have you any schedule of prices?—A. We have no schedule of prices. We simply send out a circular.

Q. Have you a circular showing that?—A. The Department of Marine have. We do not have such a thing as a printed list of prices.

Q. That is what I want to get at?—A. In that sense there is no schedule; it is a quotation.

Q. How many different sizes are there?—A. Practically half a dozen.

Q. Varying, as you said before, from $2,000 up to $15,000?—A. Yes.

Q. Yes, $2,000 up to $15,000. Now, how much less do you get in the United States, about what percentage less for the same class of buoys?—A. We are selling the same buoy at the same price in the United States and throughout the entire world.

By Hon. Mr. Cassels:

Q. Is the cost of production in the United States greater or less than in Canada? —A. It should be less, my lord, and when we have our own factory there we hope it will be less.

By Mr. Watson :

Q. But taking last year, this year up to the present time, how does the cost compare of those that are sold in the United States and here?—A. We have no means of comparing the cost of the goods in the United States with the cost in Canada.

Q. About?—A. For this reason, that we are not having our own factory there and we get the work done on time work, and it is perhaps more expensive.

Q. I see?—A. And then this, my lord, is outside of Canada anyway, and he has no right to ask a question about the United States.

Q. Never mind that. I am testing it for Canada to see how far we are imposed on here?—A. I have made a statement under oath that we are charging the same prices to every country in the world. That is absolutely true.

Q. You mean there is no qualification of that?—A. No qualification of that.

By Hon. Mr. Cassels:

Q. Perhaps Mr. Willson means that temporarily by means of their having no factory in the States they may make no profit, but that is being corrected by time and they will eventually make the same profit as here.

WITNESS.—That is correct.

By Mr. Watson:

Q. Perhaps you will make more profit?—A. I hope so, because we are nearer the raw material.

Q. Then has there been any system of contracts between you and the department? —A. No, simply a letter ordering the goods.

Q. No contract?—A. No contract.

Q. I see. For instance I have here produced to me a letter written by you on the 15th of October, 1904. 'I beg to tender for supplying the Board of Marine and Fisheries with the Willson Automatic Gas Buoy in different sizes, as follows:—No. 5, Automatic Gas Buoy'—and describing it in some detail, my lord, I need not read that—'for the sum of $2,000, No. 7, at $3,000, No. 9, at $5,000, all as illustrated by the accompanying blue prints.' Have you got those?—A. They were furnished to the department.

Q. 'It being understood the prices quoted above for buoys of different types are based on the entry free of duty of the material which it may be necessary to import for use in their construction.' So you got that advantage?—A. Correct.

'Counter weights to be varied in weight and strength to meet the requirements of yourselves without extra charge.' That is to the deputy?—A. Yes, sir.

Q. Now, do you mean to say wnen you put in a tender such as that,—and did you put them in every year?—A. I would notify them, yes, sir, as to the change in price, if there was a change in price, not otherwise.

Q. How often have you increased the price?—A. We have never increased.

Q. Then when you got a letter of that kind there was a simple plain acceptance and no question ever raised as to the price you asked.—A. The deputy would write a letter asking us to supply certain buoys after that; that is all.

Q. Of course, you manufacture a certain quantity for sale each year?—A. We are manufacturing all the time.

Q. So you have a supply always on hand?—A. We have.

Q. And you are always looking for a market?—A. We are.

Q. Your supply exceeds the demand to a considerable extent?—A. No. We make a number sufficiently to run the factory economically.

Q. Yes. I like that word 'economically' from you. That is in connection with the sale. Then you are bound to sell in order to do business and make profit?—A. Certainly we are bound to sell.

Q. And if you cannot get the price you ask you are bound to take such price as you can get, you are bound to do business?—A. No, sir.

Q. You are bound to do business?—A. We always sell at the price we ourselves make.

Q. And what if the price were not agreed to—of course, you would take the best price you could get, would you not?—A. No, sir. We will not lower our prices any more.

Q. What is that?—A. We will not lower our prices any more.

Q. You will not?—A. We will not.

Q. Then do you wish this as an authoritative and final statement by you that the prices of these buoys to the government will not be lessened?—A. I say that the price now charged is so low in relation to its cost of production that it is not possible to lower it.

Q. That is not an answer to my question, because it is rather important perhaps, and I would like to know?—A. I would answer your question then by stating, unless the price of raw material falls considerably below what it is now we cannot lower the price.

Q. Then you say you will not supply the department with buoys at a less price than you have heretofore been charging?—A. We will not supply these buoys at a loss to produce.

Q. I did not ask you that. You do not answer quite in line. At a loss—35 per cent profit is one thing, 25 per cent is a little different?—A. Yes.

Q. 10 per cent would make quite a reduction on these articles, many of them?— A. It is the difference between continuing or stopping.

Q. Do you mean you cannot continue in business without making 35 per cent profit?—A. I mean to say that is correct.

Q. And you will not?—A. I did not say we will not.

Q. Sufficient for the day, I suppose you think is the exigency of the day, leaving out the evil?—A. The evil only exists in men's minds.

Q. I see. A great many people would like to have the same evil existing, I think, in their pockets. At all events that is the position you take. You are not prepared to say what you will or will not do in the future.—A. Why, certainly not. I am not prepared to say what I will or will not do.

Q. It depends on what price the government or the department may say they will give or will not give, that has considerable to do with it, of course?—A. I cannot answer that question.

Q. Well, I think almost anyone can answer that for you.

Hon. Mr. CASSELS.—You will find that printed in the report.

Mr. WATSON.—Yes, my lord. I was just going to refer to that report. I have a couple of pages particularly where reference is made to that. Page 153, my lord, is one reference.

By Mr. Watson:

Q. Have you gone over this report of the commissioner, Mr. Fyshe, and the others? —A. I have read over parts of it, yes, sir.

Q. Yes. It is stated here that 'The light branch of the department has within the last three years come to be almost entirely bound up with a private concern in Ottawa called the International Marine Signal Company, of which Mr. T. L. Willson is president and chief proprietor.' Now, you observe the language?—A. Yes.

Q. That this branch of the department has come to be almost entirely bound up with this private concern. The course of dealing justifies that, I understand, from the commissioners?—A. I do not know what would justify such a thing.

Q. Well, it is not the fact that you have become bound up with that branch of the department?—A. We are not bound up with that branch of the department, no, sir.

Q. How does that arise then, that statement or inference?—A. I cannot explain the peculiarities of the minds of Mr. Fyshe and Mr. Bazin, who wrote that report, or Mr. Courtney.

Q. 'It is based on a patent for automatic low pressure acetylene gas buoys, taken out by Mr. Willson, which is supposed to be a great improvement on all other buoys formerly in use by the department and still used by other countries.' There the statement is, Mr. Willson, that the buoys formerly used by the department are still in use in other countries. Is that the fact?—A. They are still used in Canada, sir.

Q. That is the buoys that were formerly used here?—A. Yes. These are supplemental to what they had.

Q. Then, is it a fact, that the design or pattern of buoys formerly used is for the most part still used in other countries?—A. They are. We have not supplied all the buoys in the other countries yet; there are many thousands of buoys wanted.

Q. Then the implication here is, it is not an improvement so generally recognized? —A. It is an improvement generally recognized by all people connected with mariner's work. Mariners themselves and the different governments of the world are recognizing this as an improvement, and it is only because these men's minds were not right when they made that report that we get such an improper imputation as that.

Q. Was there any account of the test of the new buoy printed or made public? There was a test of the buoy in August, 1904?—A. In the blue book, the Canadian blue book.

Q. Was that made public?—A. It is public. If a blue book of Canada is public it was public.

'We have not seen any account of the test,' the commissioner says. You say there was an account of the test?—A. Why, certainly in the Department of Marine record.

Hon. Mr. CASSELS.—It goes on to say that.

Mr. WATSON.—Yes, 'And the deputy wrote Willson October 7th and 11th, 1904, saying that the commissioner of lights, who had tested the buoys, advised that they possess a number of advantages over the types previously in use; and that these automatic gas buoys would now be used exclusively by the department, concluding his letter by ordering 46 buoys at Willson's own prices, amounting to $148,000.' That is correct?—A. The statement is correct.

Q. Including the statement that they were ordered at your own prices?—A. No; because there is where there was a discussion of the price for that order.

Q. I see. I thought that was only in regard to one buoy?—A. No, sir. There is the first order, that is your first order of a large number. The buoys I sent first for test were not in that, and I do not know, I do not think——

Q. Do you mean the price of these supplied at a total of $148,000 was reduced?—A. There was discussion of that price.

Q. Then I ask you, Mr. Willson, if you had been told by the department that they would pay you $100,000 instead of $148,000 would you have supplied the buoys?—A. I would not, sir.

Q. It is just a question of how much less you would have taken?—A. I would not have taken $1 less for those buoys at that time.

Q. That is making a very strong broad statement?—A. Yes. I know what I am talking about.

Q. Because there is added to this, ' This was a good beginning for Mr. Willson and, with the splendid facilities extended to him by the department, he has not been slow to better it.' Including the relief from duties, of course?—A. I would say that is all an improper motive exhibited in that, sir.

Q. I am just asking for facts, not for your opinion?—A. I am stating the facts That is improper, that statement.

Q. ' It may seem that in taking up with a new idea so largely and so suddenly, the department were hardly acting with tne prudence required by the circumstances. New ideas are not apt to reach a perfect development all at once, and the most ordinary considerations would seem to have called for more caution.' Now, let me understand, to what extent have improvements been introduced since then?—A. Very little improvement. Whatever there was I furnished to the department free of cost. Very little improvement.

Q. You did not expect an order like that, $148,000 in the first instance?—A. Why, certainly. I asked them to give me all they could for supplying any districts they might have where lacking.

Q. Of course, you ask for a lot?—A. Yes. I am going to ask for very much more.

Q. Do you mean in price or quantity?—A. No, sir, in quantity.

Q. And do you expect to get it?—A. I may state I have made improvements in aids to navigation to these buoys which will compel the government to adopt them for saving of life, and that these things have been completed within the last two or three weeks.

Q. So you are in a position practically, as you say, of compelling the government to take these goods?—A. By creating a new class of goods superior to anything in use. This is a new epoch in the whole business.

Q. And in connection with that also you will compel them to pay the prices you desire?—A. I cannot compel them to pay any price.

Hon. Mr. CASSELS.—Public opinion would compel the adoption of improved life-saving methods.

Mr. WATSON.—Yes.

By Mr. Watson:

Q. Then this dealing and this transaction to the extent of $148,000 went through Mr. Fraser?—A. It went through the deputy minister and Mr. Fraser's department.

Q. Upon Mr. Fraser's report?—A. I presume so.

Q. Do you know if the deputy minister exercised any independent judgment or merely confirmed the report?—A. I cannot answer details of internal operation.

Q. What interview led to the acceptance of that order with the minister, Mr. Prefontaine, at that time?—A. I cannot recollect that I had any particular interviews with Mr. Prefontaine.

Q. Did you have any?—A. I cannot tell.

Q. Was it your persuasion or the reasons you advanced to him that procured you this order?—A. No, sir. I made no representations to Mr. Prefontaine in connection with that order.

Q. None at all?—A. No, sir.

Q. In connection with this order?—A. No, sir. That is the beginning of the business with the government.

Q. That carries the implication you have had interviews in connection with other orders?—A. I would naturally talk it over with the minister.

Q. Did you?—A. I certainly asked the minister to visit the premises where we made the buoys, and he did so in conjunction with different officers of his department; he did so a number of times.

Q. Now, this says, ' The buoys first purchased consisted of three types, designated No. 5, No. 7 and No. 9 respectively, costing $2,000, $3,000 and $5,000 respectively.' That is in accordance with that letter the prices are, I think. Then it is stated here, ' By March 31st, 1905, Willson had shipped to the order of the department 16 buoys, No. 5 and a No. 7 to Prescott, three No. 7's and a No. 9 to Halifax, eight No. 7's to Quebec, and one No. 5 stored to the order of the department. As early as March 6th, 1905, the commissioner of lights appeared to be animated by very progressive ideas with regard to these buoys.' What do you know about that?—A. All I know is the facts, that the buoys were ordered, made and delivered, and paid for.

Q. This refers to particular reasons for such animation, probably as emanating from you?—A. Nothing emanated from me, most positively, for his actions.

Q. Then it is said here, ' The salient points were the recommendation to provide 40 standard automatic lighting whistling buoys at $3,750 each. The matter was not acted upon at the time, but the supplementary estimates for 1905-6 contain an amount of $360,000 to provide for these changes.' You recollect that, do you?—A. I do not recollect it, sir.

Q. Is it in connection with that the reduction was made?—A. No reduction was made before we first shipped that lot of buoys.

Q. You practically got the same price afterwards, $3,750?—A. That, sir, is for a bell buoy, $3,000 for the buoy and $750 for the bell .

Q. You got up to $3,750 then?—A. That is for a new buoy of different type, that is for the addition of an automatic bell arrangement in connection with the buoys.

Q. Yes.—A. I might say likewise in reference to the whistling buoys which we named at $5,000, these are very large and heavy buoys and whistle as well as give a light.

Q. ' It will be observed that he was alive '—page 154 towards the bottom of the page—' to the great improvement already claimed to have taken place in the manufacture of the buoys; so much so that he wanted the whole year's appropriation, amounting to $360,000, invested at once in new buoys, without apparently having considered beforehand where they should all be placed or if they were really required.' Did you know of that fact?—A. I did not know.

Q. Did you know they were not required at the time they were ordered?—A. I did not know.

Q. Or at the time they were furnished or at any time since?—A. I know since they were furnished they have been reported upon as of the greatest aid to navigation around the Nova Scotia coast.

Q. I know. But do you know that after the buoys were delivered by you they remained idle a great length of time and were not put in use?—A. Such a statement is absolutely untre.

Q. How do you know?—A. Because the goods manufactured were shipped by us from the factory and immediately placed in service.

Q. Do you say that applies in connection with all the buoys?—A. With all the buoys furnished to the government. They were applied for specific purposes and locations.

Q. And not left out of us ?—A. No, sir.

Q. How do you know that ?—A. Because we sent our own men to aid in installing our buoys. My lord, there is another expense we never charge against the government. We furnished our men all over the country to install those buoys or look after them afterwards. These buoys were all installed by us and reports made by our men, and they were all placed as rapidly as facilities for handling them were afforded us. To my own knowledge that statement of the commissioners' is absolutely untrue.

Hon. Mr. CASSELS.—What page is that statement on ?

Mr. WATSON.—Page 154. That they have not been in use appears in another place; it is not there.

WITNESS.—My lord, of course, you understand there have been certain reserve buoys to take the place of those that might be damaged, and I may say that the reserve of buoys held in Canada is less than in most countries in the world. This is of my own knowledge again.

Hon. Mr. Cassels :

Q. I do not understand your statement made a few moments ago, that by reason of the new improvements you have made the government will be obliged to take the buoys. I understand what the meaning is, but I would like to know this : Do you mean they would have to disuse the buoys they have in existence ?—A. No, sir. They are additional and supplementary buoys with large and powerful whistles.

Q. And the present buoys ?—A. They will be attached to some of the present buoys. For those which will require to be larger we will make new buoys. That is the most important improvement.

Q. They can be adapted to some of the present buoys, and other larger buoys will be required ?—A. Yes. That is an explosive whistle. You will hear it next week if you happen to be in town.

Q. Here ?—A. Yes, sir.

Q. Where will it go off ?—A. It will go off at the point every day, it will be an explosion.

Q. We might have it for the lunch hour if it is to continue.

By Mr. Watson:

Q. Now, then, there is this: 'Prescott writes about charging cost of buoys which they have reshipped. May 9th, 1905. W .H. N. assistant C. of L.'—Who is W.H.N.?—A. W. H. Noble, probably.

Q. Oh, yes. '*Re* account of T. L. Willson, writes asking if $9,000 charged for buoys shipped to Lévis'——?—A. Point Lévis, opposite Quebec city?

Q. Yes. ' Are to be charged to Quebec buoy service from Prescott and the amount credited the advance of $30,000 charged against this depot.' Do you know anything about that?—A. No, sir; I do not recollect. Was it a letter to the department or me?

Q. That is *re* your account.

Hon. Mr. CASSELS.—What page is that?

Mr. WATSON.—Page 204, my lord, about three-fourths of the way down.

By Mr. Watson:

Q. Then another letter, ' your letter of the 19th *re* gas buoys shipped to Lévis, I have to inform you that the buoys have been inspected and passed at Ottawa and the accounts certified here. The advance of $30,000 charged against the Prescott depot should be charged to general account, and only those buoys which were actually used between Moncton and Kingston charged to Prescott. I have made a memo. to this effect for Mr. Owen.' Then, speaking generally, you in all cases just make statements of what prices you will charge, and those prices have been accepted without question or inquiry?—A. Yes, sir.

Q. That is the position?—A. With the exception I have already noted to you.

Q. And you say you have no personal knowledge of any excess of expenditure—I am not speaking of price now—as to the quantity or number of buoys?—A. I have no knowledge of such excess or any excess. On the other hand, I think the amount of buoys ordered was absolutely necessary.

Q. You were always, of course, pressing for further orders, were you not?—A. I was asking for further orders, certainly.

Q. As far as your influence or efforts were concerned you were seeking to sell goods and getting as many orders as you could?—A. Yes, sir.

Q. And I see by a letter written to the deputy minister, page 211, it is stated there: 'Ottawa, February 10, 1908. We find that a letter was addressed by you to Mr. T. L. Willson, on July 12, 1905, to the effect that the "department will require 12 No. 5 automatic gas buoys to be placed in hand, and advise when the department may expect delivery of the same. Shipping directions to be given later." On July 19 Mr. Willson acknowledges receipt of the order for 12 No. 5 automatic gas buoys. On January 9, 1906, the commissioner of lights instructs Willson to "ship the 12 automatic gas buoys, which you have held for some time for this department, to the Dominion Lighthouse Depot, Prescott." 'We can find no subsequent trace of these buoys, and shall be glad if you can explain what became of them.' Now, how do you account for those 12 buoys being ordered and shipped and out of use?—A. In the first place, after the order is given it takes some time to make them, then after we get shipping directions they are distributed to the places ordered. I do not know that those buoys were out of use.

Mr. GODFREY.—See the next letter.

Mr. WATSON.—Out of use?—A. I do not know they were out of use.

By Mr. Watson:

Q. The letter written by the deputy minister might seem to carry that conclusion. Your lordship will find that on page 211. 'I have just received your letter with reference to the disposition of 12 No. 5 gas buoys ordered by this department from Mr. T. L. Willson on January 9, 1906, and stating that you are unable to trace the disposition of these buoys. I must say that I was surprised that there should not be a proper record of this matter, and took occasion to look into it personally, and I send for your information files Nos. 27122 and 26860, together with the official record of automatic gas buoys, book No. 1, which belongs to the commissioner of lights' branch, and I have marked the portions of the files and of the record book referring to the disposition of these buoys. You will observe that instructions were given to the manufacturer to ship these buoys to Prescott, that later directions were given to the lighthouse depot at Prescott to ship certain of these buoys to New Brunswick, that to avoid expense the lighthouse depot directed the manufacturers to make the shipment from Ottawa, and further, that the remaining buoys, covering the buoys not directed to be sent elsewhere, were sent to Prescott. I have no objections to give the Civil Service Commissioners any information which may be required with reference to the operation of this department, but at the same time I am advised that the facts upon which you want information are not within the scope of your inquiry.' That certainly indicates there were buoys floating about out of use?—A. No. I remember some buoys of that order having been shipped to New Brunswick, and they were at once put in service. I think we sent a man down there and aided in putting them in service.

Q. Those 12 buoys No. 5, the regular price would be $3,000 each?—A. No, sir I think they are $2,000 each.

Q. I am taking your previous letter?—A. If you will refer to it you will see it is $2,000. No 9 was $5,000.

Q. But I thought it was $3,000, not $2,000 each?—A. No. No. 7 was $3,000.

Q. Well then, in effect you say that the supply has been according to the demand, and that the goods were put in actual use to your knowledge?—A. Yes, sir.

Q. As soon as received by the department?—A. I do. With reasonable time to get men to the place and facilities for handling them.

Q. And now there is another company. What is the other company, the Quebec Company?—A. For what?

Q. Your third company. I have got this Willson Carbide Company and the Ottawa Carbide Company. Then there is the——

Hon. Mr. CASSELS.—The Shawinigan Carbide Company.

By Mr. Watson :

Q. The Shawinigan Carbide Company?—A. Yes.

Q. As apart from the St. Catharines?—A. That is entirely apart and on the same basis as the Ottawa Company.

Q. Where is that situated?—A. It is located at Shawinigan Falls.

Q. And what transactions has that had with the department?—A. None that I know of.

Q. Do you know that it has or not?—A. It has not had any until very recently.

Q. How recently?—A. Within the last month or two.

Q. What does it supply?—A. Nothing but carbide.

Q. And makes its own prices in the same way?—A. It does.

Q. I see. All your companies deal in the same way with the government, you make your own prices, there is no trouble, no questions asked?—A. I do not think that is a fair statement at all.

Q. Do you not?—A. No, sir.

Q. I am taking it, I thought, from your previous answers?—A. That was only in reference to the gas buoy business, sir.

Q. I see. That does not apply to the other?—A. No.

Q. But from what you said in effect it does?—A. The price has been uniform

Q. Has there ever been any question of prices there?—A. Never.

Q. Well then, that carries on to the statement I made to you. You fix your own prices, or at least you tell them what your prices are, no inquiries are made, no questions asked, no efforts to reduce your prices; that is the fact?—A. I think that is correct.

Q. With all your companies?

Hon. Mr. CASSELS.—When do you want to adjourn, at one o'clock?

Mr. WATSON.—Yes, my lord.

Hon. Mr. CASSELS.—To what hour?

Mr. WATSON.—Say a quarter past two, my lord.

By Hon. Mr. Cassels :

Q. Then, Mr. Willson, all these buoys that were supplied to the government were furnished with carbide practically by the Ottawa Company?—A. The Ottawa Company did furnish carbide to the government.

Q. And that was used for these buoys?—A. Only partly, my lord. They used carbide for various purposes, lighthouse purposes as well, and it was their general supply out of which they took sufficient for the buoys.

Q. Can you tell me what amount of carbide was taken for that?—A. The total supply the government has been using and asking tenders for was 350 tons last year. I imagine 287 to 300 tons every year.

(Adjourned at 1 p.m. to 2.15 p.m. and then resumed.)

By Mr. Watson:

Q. Then, Mr. Willson, I see by the Auditor General's report, 1904-5, that that year the total purchased from you amounted to $192,500. Now, that was much in excess comparatively of your sales to any other government?—A. At that time, yes, sir.

Q. In fact, it was your chief business?—A. Chief business at that time, yes, sir.

Q. So that your buoys were adopted for use here much more speedily and to a greater extent than in any other country, and that remains so to the present time?—A. Up until recently in accordance with the needs of the country.

Q. Yes. It is true even at the present time?—A. I would say not.

Q. What other countries are using your buoys?—A. I think Brazil, in accordance with their needs, is buying equally, if not more.

Q. You cannot mention any other country than Brazil, though?—A. Well, we have all the other countries started.

Q. Yes, started, but I am saying not to the same extent?—A. Not to the same extent. The work is educational; you have to deliver the buoys and have them tried, and so on.

Q. Then 1905-6 it increased very extensively. According to the report of the Auditor General for that year, I see it was $336,000, and more?—A. I believe that is correct, sir.

Q. So that the use was growing very rapidly. And then in 1906-7, according to his report, the amount was $238,000, not quite so much?—A. I believe that is correct, sir.

Q. $238,000. Now, you have explained the system of prices, the profits and the conditions, and also the circumstances with regard to the fixing of prices by yourself, and that there was no dickering as to prices, using that form of expression as is usual now-a-days?—A. That is substantially correct.

Q. That is substantially so?—A. Yes.

Q. And you say with regard to the different officials, high and low, that you know of nothing done by them improper?—A. I certainly say that I know of nothing done by them improper.

Q. And you say there have been no advantages or gains to them?

Hon. Mr. CASSELS.—What do you mean by that expression improper? You see, the commissioners' report, Mr. Watson, is based to a very great extent on this, not that anything wrong has happened, but that there was such very great carelessness, and the officials went into this without knowledge. From the standpoint of Mr. Willson it may perhaps be proper.

Mr. WATSON.—Yes, my lord.

By Mr. Watson:

Q. Now, we have here the fact of the early and quick adoption to a very large extent of your system and of your buoys?—A. Yes, sir.

Q. And you admit that that is very unusual and extraordinary?—A. I do not admit any such thing, sir.

Q. As compared with other countries?—A. Not as compared with other countries.

Q. You have just given your answers. Barring Brazil, it is very unusual and extraordinary?—A. One country is sufficient outside of Canada to have done the same thing to render this not extraordinary.

Q. That is your opinion?—A. That is in accordance with the facts, sir.

Q. To what extent has property become practically valueless and been disused that was theretofore in use, have you any idea?—A. I don't know, and I do not think very much property that the government had formerly in use will be disused, not used.

Q. But your buoys have taken the place of others that were in use?—A. The other buoys were used for other purposes by this department.

Q. What other purposes?—A. I understand for——

Q. Of your personal knowledge?—A. No, I cannot say from personal knowledge.

Q. You have no personal knowledge ? Could you not have made use of those other buoys, the old material ?—A. We are trying to do so now, and we have formulated a tender to the department or are doing so for the purpose of altering those buoys.

Q. Precisely. Why did you not do that before?—A. We were never asked to do so.

Q. I see. But now you think that may be feasible ?—A. It may be.

Q. And if it had been adopted it would have meant a saving of a large amount of money ?—A. No, sir, no saving whatsoever.

Q. Why not ?—A. Because the buoys which were purchased from us were needed for the specific places they have gone to.

Q. But to take the places of other buoys ?—A. They can only be useful when they are prepared for subordinate positions. The buoys they have at the present time at the department when converted to our system can only be used for subordinate positions.

Q. Subordinate positions. But meantime they have been displaced and disused ? —A. A few of them only.

Q. And by reason of that the orders to your company have been increased, is that so ?—A. They might be, but only temporarily.

Q. Do not get away from the facts. That is the result ?—A. I would say no in answer to your question broadly.

Q. That is not quite consistent with what you said before.

Hon. Mr. CASSELS.—What Mr. Willson states is, the places where these buoys bought from him were located could not be utilized for the other buoys, but in other places they can change them and perhaps use them ?—A. That is absolutely correct, my lord.

Mr. WATSON.—I understand the statement, my lord, but at the same time the buoys he supplied took the place of those old buoys at the same points.

Hon. Mr. CASSELS.—But those old buoys never could have been altered to be put back in their old places.

Mr. WATSON.—I am not so sure.

WITNESS.—That is absolutely correct, my lord. Most of these buoys are great ocean buoys, of which they never had any before of any kind whatsoever.

By Mr. Watson :

Q. Well, now, to what extent are these ocean buoys, because it seems inconceivable to me—perhaps it is want of knowledge and experience—that buoys for 1905 and 1906 to the extent of $336,000 should have been bought for ocean purposes in one year ?—A. I may say that they put 30 of the largest buoys we have ever made around the Nova Scotia coast. They did not have any such buoys out before on the Nova Scotia coast; they only had some whistling buoys. They had no combined gaslight and whistling buoys, and these large buoys were gotten up for that purpose.

Q. Then there is the fact that all of a sudden some one came to the view that this large quantity of buoys was necessary where none had been used before. How do you account for that ?—A. They are a necessity. I may say to you that the American government also, through their division on the Maine coast, have requested information from us and tenders for duplicating that Halifax system along the whole northern coast of the United States. My lord, it is a sudden conclusion there too.

Q. Well, it is not so sudden, they are doing it many years after. At all events, your lordship understands the position, what was done about it, and I suppose that is the reason for comment by these Civil Service Commissioners in their report.

Hon. Mr. CASSELS.—I think the Civil Service Commissioners' report is based more upon the negligance of the department in not making thorough investigation before they bought. It may be it has turned out all right. Nevertheless, Mr. Fyshe and Mr. Bazin think it was not business not to have made a proper investigation.

Mr. WATSON.—Yes.

By Mr. Watson :

Q. What do you say as to the necessity of such further investigation before this large expenditure was made ?—A. I say there is no necessity for such investigation. A greatly increased light was offered, it was needed, the department accepted it and put them out.

Q. Yes. Of course, you appreciate as well as we do that you are speaking more or less from an interested standpoint ?—A. I am speaking from the standpoint of the testimony of those who use the lights, the mariners. I have that here to the absolute proof of, my lord. There is not any question, it is not a matter of private opinion, it is a matter of public knowledge now.

Q. Well, at all events this was done upon your movement and advocacy, they were led to embark upon this large expenditure and, as you say, greater benefits for safety and otherwise followed ?—A. On my representation that the lights would fulfil the requirements and be superior to anything they had or known of otherwise in the world.

Q. Now, how much did the late minister make out of these transactions with the International Company ?—A. To whom do you refer ?

Q. The late Mr. Sutherland ?—A. He made nothing. He was not connected with this company, he knew nothing about the business of this company.

Q. That descended to Mr. Little ?—A. It did not descend to Mr. Little. Mr. Little came into this of his own free choice and idea.

Q. As the result of the previous connection ?—A. Not at all.

Q. He was one of the heirs-at-law to it, so to speak ?—A. Absolutely no heir-at-law in this respect to this International Company.

Q. You were yourself ?—A. I was not an heir-at-law. It was an absolutely new and original idea which I developed.

Q. It is the result, then, of the connection with you ?—A. It is the result absolutely and solely of my representation to him that I desired him to come into it.

Q. It has been extending over this long period of years ?—A. No, sir. I had no connection with Mr. Little until I started this. This is his first effort with me.

Q. Now, then, are your bookkeepers here ?—A. My bookkeepers are not; one of them is, Mr. Cole.

Q. I may have to ask you something further later on, but I will give you notice. Is there anything further your lordship would like to hear from Mr. Willson ?

Hon. Mr. CASSELS.—No, Mr. Willson is going to give a statement of the cost of these.

By Mr. Watson:

Q. Yes. When will you be able to give us that, Mr. Willson ?—A. I will have to look that up.

Q. I would like to have it Wednesday morning ?—A. I will look into it immediately. Then you will not require me until Wednesday ?

Q. At half-past ten o'clock Wednesday morning.

HARRY COLE, sworn.

Mr. GODFREY.—My lord, before taking this witness, there is a matter mentioned by Mr. Willson, which I think perhaps affects my client. That is the statement he made that he has evidence to show the efficiency of this service, and he tells me now he would like to put that before the commission.

Hon. Mr. CASSELS.—Anything he wants to say.

Mr. GODFREY.—I think that is only proper to show the efficiency of the service.

Hon. Mr. CASSEL.—Anything you wish to ask, Mr. Willson?

Mr. WILLSON.—I will gather this evidence together and place it in your lordship's hands Wednesday morning.

Mr. WATSON.—What evidence?

Mr. WILLSON.—As to the efficiency.

Mr. WATSON.—You had better make your statement if you have any statement. We do not want written reports about matters of that kind.

Hon. Mr. CASSELS.—He will be here in the witness box on Wednesday morning.

Mr. WATSON.—That is all right on that point.

Mr. GODFREY.—I suppose it is in the form of written recommendations?

Mr. WILLSON.—It is original records purely.

Mr. WATSON.—Written records from whom?

Mr. WILLSON.—From the different mariners using these aids.

By Mr. Watson:

Q. You are secretary of what company, or bookkeeper?—A. Bookkeeper of the Ottawa Carbide Company.

Q. Have you got the annual report of that company for the year 1904-5?—A. Yes, sir.

Q. Let me see it, please?—A. It is in our letter book. It may take a moment to get it. (Witness refers to letter book.) May I be permitted to state, my lord, that I do not think it is fair that we should be asked to produce our balance sheets and other statements showing our cost of production? We are in competition here in Canada with two other different companies. One, at least, would be very anxious to get these figures if I give them as Mr. Watson asks.

By Hon. Mr. Cassels :

Q. Well, you see, we have heard your company has been losing money from year to year. I doubt whether any other company would like to lose money in that way?—A. We do not like to either.

Q. I do not think it will hurt you much. Nobody will try to emulate your procedure. Perhaps Mr. Watson will show you how to make a profit?—A. I wish he would.

By Mr. Watson :

Q. That does not relate to it?—A. That is merely the auditor's certificate.

Q. What does this show?—A. The balance in the ledger at the end of the year.

Q. December 31, 1905. I want the one before this, please?—A. There it is. (Turning up page.)

Q. Well, your profits that year were $43,000?—A. No, sir.

Q. What do you mean by that item then, $43,235?—A. That is the amount of debit of profit and loss, it is on the debit side of loss.

Q. Loss for that year?—A. A loss up to that time.

Q. That is 31st December, 1904?—A. Yes.

Q. That runs through the previous years?—A. That runs through the previous years.

Q. And where is the statement for that year's business?—A. (Turning up page.) I think it is that.

Q. This shows a loss, that is intended to show a loss?—A. This for the year shows a gain, it shows a gain for that single year, I think the only year since we began operating, a gain of $5,000.

Q. A gain of $5,321?—A. That is one year.

Q. What is that last item, 'Department of Marine and Fisheries experimental'?

—A. We were carrying on some experimental work for the department, testing lights for them. That was a charge we wrote off.

Q. With whom did you come in contact for the most part ?—A. How do you mean ?

Q. In the Department ?—A. We did all our business through the deputy and Mr. Fraser his commissioner.

Q. Through the deputy and Mr. Fraser. Then the next year is this one?—A. Yes.

Q. 1905 ?—A. You have got marked here a loss of $2,871 ?—A. Yes.

Hon. Mr. CASSELS.—What are the items of expenditure ?

Mr. WATSON.—I was just looking. Wages, $16,000; power, $12,000; office expenses, $6,000; taxes and water rates, $2,000—the total expenses amount to in round figures, $99,000, practically $100,000; and the extent of the business was about $96,000.

Hon. Mr. CASSELS.—Sales ?

Mr. WATSON.—Merchandise.

By Mr. Watson :

Q. What do you mean by merchandise ?—A. Covering carbide sales for the year.

Q. There is some other report in connection with it ?—A. The other annual statement.

Q. I see. The profits were evidently put in plant, were they not, $195,000 plant ? —A. Where ?

Q. There (indicating), that is it, is it not, license, $40,000; plant, $195,000 ?—A. That plant account has nothing whatever to do with the profit and loss account.

Hon. Mr. CASSELS.—What is your capital account ?

Mr. WATSON.—$200,000.

By Hon. Mr. Cassels :

Q. Paid in in cash ?—A. Paid in in cash with the exception of $40,000 to Mr. Willson.

Q. Is the other $160,000 in the plant ?—A. The other $160,000 and an amount of $70,000 over that we use in our present plant.

Q. Where did the $70,000 come from ?—A. That is indebtedness by our loan from the Bronson Company.

Q. How much of your receipts were utilized in buying that plant ?—A. Practically none, because we have had to borrow from the Bronson Company to carry on the business since the time we started.

Mr. Watson :

Q. I see by this statement of 1905 you owe the Bronson Company $111,000?—A. Yes.

Q. Is that over and above the $160,000 you say they paid ?—A. Yes. That is the $160,000 was paid in in cash to capital account.

Q. Have you any record of that?—A. How do yo umean?

Q. Of the payment in of the $160,000?—A. Yes, it is in the ledger.

Q. Let me se that, please. Is not that the fact, in the meantime you have been accumulating largely in stock apart from plant?—A. How do you mean ?

Q. Merchandise, stock on hand ?—A. No. Our merchandise stock varies at different times.

Q. Let me see that ?—A. Here it is.

Q. Where?—A. Account of stocks, credit $40,000 to stock account.

Q. I know. But where is the entry of the payment ?—A. Here are the subscriptions.

Q. But where is the entry of the receipt of $160,000 ?—A. The $160,000 was paid in. Here is the stock account of the parties who subscribed.

Q. These may be just cross entries showing payments. Where are the receipts of the moneys ?—A. Here, take this, see, it is here in one item. There is the entry there (indicating). It is necessary to refer to each account.

Hon. Mr. CASSELS.—Thre ought to be annual balance sheets showing from time to time the produce of the company.

WITNESS.—What he asks, my lord, is individual entries.

By Hon. Mr. Cassels : ·

Q. I tindersand that. But to see whether you really have been augmenting your plant your balances sheets from year to year should show the returns or ought to show that ?—A. We certainly have, slightly.

By Mr. Watson :

Q. The actual payment of cash ?—A. Here is the entry charging the Honourable Mr. Bronson with his proportion, $83,000. Here is the charge to him, here are the amounts he paid in in cash. For instance, take page 1.

Q. That is all right, that is enough. I wanted to see whether there was any record of the actual things. You say at page 9 the ledger shows actual payments of $83,900 ?—A. Yes.

Q. You say the rest of that is all paid in ?—A. Just the amount of one subscription, the amount from one subscriber.

Q. Let us see the statement of 1906 ?—A. (Witness takes up another book).

Q. That is another book, is it ?—A. Yes.

Q. December 31, 1905. Where is your summary ?—A. Here it is. (Producing.)

Q. The statements are getting quite exhaustive. Now, 31st December, 1906, you have got marked a loss there ?—A. Yes, sir.

Q. $6,859. Who was Mr. Lamont ?—A. Mr. Lamont who is a chartered accountant practising in Ottawa here.

Q. Let us see how much you added to that plant in that year ?—A. Those are simply stuck together with his statement.

Hon. Mr. CASSELS.—Compare the assets of 1906 with the assets of 1907.

Mr. WATSON.—Yes. Let us have 1907. This is 1906. Let us have 1907.

Hon. Mr. CASSELS.—See how the two stand out. If they increased in 1907 it was because the plant was more valuable.

WITNESS.—That 1907 is in our current letter-book. You will have to bring it up, because we are referring to that every day.

By Mr. Watson :

Q. What profits were there in 1907 ?—A. There was a loss.

Q. How much ?—A. Offhand I could not say.

Q. About how much ?—A. A loss of about $7,000.

By Hon. Mr. Cassels :

Q. That is made by balancing one against the other ?—A. Yes, the difference.

Q. The difference between your assets—— ?—A. And our liabilities. The difference between the assets of one year and the assets of another.

Q. I would like to see whether the assets increased.

By Mr. Watson :

Q. Yes. How much have the assets increased, where is the statement of assets here for 1906 ? Let me have 1904 again. How much are the assets there ?—A. $166,000.

Q. Now, 1906, the assets?—A. The assets here are $334,000, less $52,900.

Q. Why less $52,900?—A. Because that is a loss that year.

Q. Of $52,000?—A. Not the loss for that year, but the loss up to that time, 1906.

By Hon. Mr. Cassels:

Q. You might borrow $200,000 or $300,000 from the Bank of Montreal, you might put that into new plant, and you might carry that into your balance sheets as a debt or that year, but it would have increased the plant or the buildings. You cannot get that thing unless you know the details. I am not for a moment suggesting that you have done anything of the kind?—A. We do not do business in that way.

Q. I am not suggesting you do. I mean a balance sheet is of no use at all unless e know what you are doing. It is very easy to make a deficit.

Mr. WATSON.—Taking the plant at 31st December, 1904, it is put at $195,000, nd in 1906 it is $198,000. Not much increase there.

Hon. Mr. CASSELS.—No. They might not make an increase on the balance sheet f they borrowed from the bank.

Mr. WATSON.—The liabilities in 1904 at the end of that year——

The WITNESS.—If you had done that, my lord, that would show on the liabilities.

By Mr. Watson:

Q. Were $309,000, including capital, and the liabilities on 31st December, 1906, were $334,000, including capital—$25,000 difference.

By Hon. Mr. Cassels:

Q. Of course, the balance sheets speak for themselves if they are correct balance sheets?—A. They have been audited by a chartered accountant each year.

By Mr. Watson:

Q. Then take 1906. Where are the salaries for that year?—A. The salaries are shown here. Office expenses, salaries and legal expenses, $6,396.

Q. Wages, $18,343. What proportion of your business was with the government? —A. A very small proportion. For instance, we manufacture annually in the neighbourhood of 1,500 tons. The business with the government since we started totals somewhere—the total is in the statement of Mr. Willson, we are prepared to give to Mr. Willson—we manufacture annually about 1,500 tons. We have sold to the government since we started to do business with them 1,086 tons, that is running over six years.

Q. I see. That is comparatively small. Then, were you here this morning?— A. Yes, sir; I came in about half-past eleven.

Q. How much more do you charge the government than others?—A. We never have charged them more. We have sold to the government at lower prices than we have sold to our other commercial customers.

Q. I see. You say there has been no excess in price?—A. No excess in price. We sell to the government the same as to other commercial customers, except, as I say, on one or two occasions we charged less.

Q. What is the reason for that?—A. Well, on one occasion there was a difference of opinion as to when the fiscal year ended. We quoted the government a certain price of $60 a ton, and we then to the government and public raised our price to $65 a ton. The fiscal year——

Q. That was a mistake on your part?—A. I beg your pardon?

Q. That was a mistake on your part?—A. In what way?

Q. Was it a mistake as to when the fiscal year ended?—A. No, it was not.

Q. Well, you gave them an advantage that time?—A. No. We gave them an advantage that time because all others from a certain date paid $65. Instead of the fiscal year ending the 30th of April, because of a misunderstanding, there was a difference of opinion, whether on our part or on the part of the officials of the department, and we extended that price and gave them the benefit of it until the 1st of July. In that matter the departmental officials treated us in a more harsh way than we would have tolerated treatment from any commercial company with which we do business.

Q. Very extraordinary ?—A. That is a fact, sir.

Q. Then, with what individual did you have to transact business ?—A. We came in contact personally with no individual, you might say. All our business was done by letter. Occasionally, if the government were in a great hurray for carbide, they would call us up over the telephone.

Q. Who communicated with you ?—A. Sometimes Mr. Fraser, sometimes Mr. Stumbles.

Q. Which Mr. Fraser ?—A. Mr. J. F. But it was only occasionally that would happen. Sometimes they would run short of carbide at a certain branch, and we would get probably a hurry call for it.

Q. You do occasionally allow commissions to purchasers ?—A. No, sir. We have never allowed commissions since we started manufacturing.

Q. To ordinary purchasers ?—A. No. We have wholesale and retail prices.

Q. You have intervening agents ?—A. No, sir.

Q. You have no middlemen ?—A. We sell direct everything we manufacture.

Q. Never at any time had middlemen to whom commission goes ?—A. No, we have never had middlemen since we began.

Q. Have you had with the government, with the department ?—A. No.

Q. Has any commission been paid or allowed in connection with these government contracts ?—A. Not a cent.

Q. What advantage has any official obtained ?—A. Any government official ?

Q. Yes.—A. None, so far as we are concerned.

Q. Have you had to do with either of the other companies ?—A. No, sir, I am entirely confined to the Ottawa Carbide Company.

By Hon. Mr. Cassels :

Q. Have you aver given any benefits of any kind to any official ?—A. We never have.

Q. As distinguished from money ?—A. Nothing of any kind. We have done a perfectly straight business, and no one with whom we have ever dealt with has benefited personally by one cent that I know of and I know practically of every cent expended by the company.

By Mr. Godfrey :

Q. Just a question. Did you ever allow a less price to anybody ?—A. No. We have certain prices per ton, we have certain prices for quantities of less than a ton. From those prices we make no departure.

Q. To people outside the government ?—A. Outside the government as well as the government.

Q. So that the same rule the commissioner objected to applied to all the trade?—A. It applied to all the trade. Every person who buys from us buys on the same basis, whether they be the government or a private individual.

Mr. GODFREY.—I would like to ask Mr. Willson with regard to the International Marine Signal Company whether any discounts were allowed to anybody.

Hon. Mr. CASSELS.—Mr. Willson will be here on Wednesday morning.

Mr. COLE.—May we remove our books ? They are our entire office records.

Hon. Mr. CASSELS.—Do you want them, Mr. Watson ?

Mr. WATSON.—I do not think that we require them any more at present.

Mr. COLE.—They are available any time they are wanted.

Mr. WILLSON.—I make the same request with regard to ours. I will bring the ookkeeper and the books together.

Hon. Mr. CASSELS.—Can't you bring him this afternoon ?

Mr. WILLSON.—I tried unsuccessfully during the lunch interval. I will telephone gain.

FRANK STEWART MEARNS, sworn,

By Mr. Watson :

Q. Mr. Mearns, you live in Toronto ?—A. I do.

Q. And you are a member of the bar ?—A. I am.

Q. And you are connected with this Fog Signal Company ?—A. Yes, sir.

Q. What is your position in the company —A. I am a stockholder and director nd secretary-treasurer.

Q. Stockholder, director and secretary-treasurer. When was that company ormed ?—A. In the spring of 1903, early in 1903.

Q. I ask you about it because the company has had large transactions with the epartment in question, has it not ?—A. Yes.

Q. When did those transactions begin?—A. They began—I think 1902 was the first.

Q. 1902?—A. Yes.

Q. And continued to the present time?—A. Up to the present time.

Q. And do you recollect about how much of the transactions were in 1902?—A. I annot recollect. It was before the formation of our company, at the time when the business was being done by the Northey Manufacturing Company.

Q. I have not got the Auditor General's report here earlier than 1904-5. I see for the year 1904-5 the amount paid to your company was $428,000, getting on to half a million of dollars for that year?—A. All that, I presume, would take in work done in 1902 and 1903.

Hon. Mr. CASSELS.—What page?

Mr. WATSON.—1904-5, page 99, my lord. The Canadian Fog Signal Company. Three-fourths of the way down.

The WITNESS.—That would cover work done in 1902, 1903, 1904 and 1905.

By Mr. Watson:

Q. There is nothing to indicate that?—A. That, I think, is correct.

Q. There is nothing to indicate that there on the face of that. Then 1905-6, that is just the fiscal year. I think you are mistaken about that; however, we will see. How was it, do you recollect, in 1905-6?—A. Oh, it was very small.

Q. Not such a figure as 1904-5, apparently?—A. Well, it would be very very small, it would not be anything at all in comparison with that, because that was intended to cover several years.

Q. I see in 1906-7 one item of $54,720?—A. That would be the entire——

Q. No, I think not. Ninety-six and 66, well, it is nearly $218,000. Who is president of your company?—A. John P. Northey.

Q. Of Toronto?—A. Yes.

Q. Formerly of the Northey Manufacturing Company?—A. Yes.

Q. What is the capital stock of your company?—A. $100,000.

Q. And you sell these alarms or fog signals?—A. Yes.

Q. Anything else?—A. No.

Q. They are practically horns, are they?—A. Sound-producing devices.

Q. In what quantity do you sell, about what number?—A. During the six years we have been dealing with the department, the 3-inch, that would be the standard size, the size that is usually adopted, they would average about six or eight a year, spread over the six years time.

Q. Now, Colonel Anderson stated before his lordship that the cost of these signals, as he understood, was somewhere between $300 and $400 each, and the average price that you have been collecting from the department is about ten times that amount for each. Is that so, speaking generally?—A. I do not understand that Colonel Anderson has made that statement. Pardon me for saying so.

Q. Never mind about reasoning about it, please. What is the price, the average price of those articles as sold to the government?—A. I have the contract here.

Q. Never mind about the contract. Just tell me what is the average price as sold? —A. The average price for the plant and phone, which have always been purchased. together, is $8,500.

Q. For each?—A. For each plant.

Q. $8,500?—A. $8,500; and with two phones at the one station, $8,950.

Q. But what is it that is sold at about $3,000 or $4,000?—A. We have not made any sales of a diaphone separate from the plant; we sell the diaphone as part of the plant.

Q. Is there any part of it for which a price of $3,000 or $4,000 is obtained; because he made that statement?—A. No, that is not strictly correct.

Q. Well, not strictly correct?—A. It is correct——

Q. Never mind splitting of hairs, if there is any splitting of hairs. What portion of the goods sold adds to it the price of $3,000 or $4,000?—A. We put in the plant at less than cost price.

Q. I did not ask you that at all, Mr. Mearns. I am just trying to get at the explanation of Colonel Anderson's statement. Something was purchased by them and sold by you. He understood it cost between $300 and $400 and that it was sold for about ten times that amount. What does that refer to?—A. I understand he referred to the cost of the metal when he stated $300 or $400.

Q. Never mind about that. I am referring to the article. What was it?—A. The instrument, the diaphone.

Q. The diaphone?—A. Yes.

Q. What is the selling price of the diaphone?—A. We quoted it here at $4,600 in the contract.

Q. The diaphone?—A. Yes.

Q. I see. That is what I wanted to get at before. And how much does that diaphone cost by itself?—A. By itself?

Q. Yes?—A. Do you mean the metal?

Q. The diaphone itself, how much does it cost, that particular article?—A. I cannot very well state that, for this reason: we have spent six or eight years in developing.

Q. Never mind, leave out the years, leave out the time. What is the actual cost of producing that at the present time?—A. You mean the cost of the metal and the manual labour in making the machine?

Q. Yes?—A. I cannot tell you, but it may not be more than $400 or $500.

Q. It may not be?—A. No. With the trumpet it would be possibly $1,000.

Q. But I am not speaking of anything else with it. I am speaking of the one thing, the diaphone?—A. Very well, $400 or $500. That is the metal and the manual labour of making the machine.

Q. That is sold by you at $4,800?—A. That is not correct.

Q. That is sold along with something else, you said that a minute ago?—A. We never make or sell a diaphone separate from the plant.

Q. Oh, no. You have already said you quoted the department the price of the diaphone?—A. Yes.

Q. How much is the price mentioned there?—A. $4,600.

Q. That is what I was trying to get at?—A. If it is alone, separate from the lant.

Q. That is what I am getting at?—A. But we give two diaphones for the same rice.

Q. Never mind about arguing the matter?—A. I simply wish to state the facts.

Q. I know. But you are advancing too far. It excites doubts and suspicions the ay you advance. I think so, the way you are jumping ahead trying to excuse the mpany before you are asked?—A. I do not think so.

Q. I see. What is this paper?—A. That is the original contract with the depart-ent.

Q. Made the 10th of May, 1906?—A. Yes.

Q. Did you have any contract before this?—A. The tenders were——

Q. Did you have any contract before this?—A. Yes.

Q. Where is it, please?—A. Not under tender.

Q. Never mind whether it is under tender. Let me see the contract made before his?—A. We have no contract of that kind.

Q. I did not say this kind. Any contract made before this?—A. I have not a ontract, save an ordinary letter that came from the department.

Q. Well, I asked you if there were contracts before this. You said yes. Now, let s. see them without explaining?

By Hon. Mr. Cassels :

Q. Those were patents?—A. Oh, yes, we have eight or ten patents.

Q. I presume you add the value of the patent device, and so on?—A. Yes.

By Mr. Watson:

Q. I asked you exactly the cost to produce, and so on. You need not explain the reason why. Now, where are the contracts?—A. Here is one dated 1903 (producing).

Q. This is a bundle of correspondence to and from the department, is it?—A. Yes.

Q. Commencing on the 23rd December, 1902. Here is an offer dated 24th March, 1903: 'I hereby offer to supply for Belle Isle Fog Alarm Station all the machinery for operating a five-inch and eight-inch diaphone, the machinery to be operated by steam of sufficient capacity' and so on 'for $15,600. I agree to supply same plant as quoted for the above, omitting steam boilers, for $13,780.' And a letter from Colonel Gourdeau of 3rd of April, 1903: 'I beg to advise you that your offer to supply fog alarm station and all the machinery for operating a three-inch and two-inch diaphone, plant to be operated by steam of sufficient capacity to give a $3\frac{1}{2}$-second blast per minute for $7,400 is accepted, and I have to request you to proceed with the immediate con-struction of the plant.' Is not that the first contract you had?—A. That is all I know of.

Q. Now, you stated about the diaphones and the actual cost at the present time in the making and production of the diaphones and the selling price of the diaphones. Now, what else do you manufacture and sell, apart from the diaphones, anything else ?—A. Nothing but the accessories to the diaphones, that would be the timing device.

Q. The what ?—A. The timing device, the operating valves and the trumpet.

Q. Yes. And do those add to the cost ?—A. Decidedly so.

Q. How much, to what extent ?—A. I cannot tell you that.

Q. About how much ?—A. That I cannot tell you, Mr. Watson.

Q. I see. Well then, it would appear from this contract that you produce, follow-ing upon the correspondence, that is the contract of May, 1906, that that was made for a period of three years; is that right?—A. That is right.

Q. How much did you supply during this present year under that contract ?—A. Oh, I cannot tell you that. It would be a very small amount.

Q. About how much during the present year?—A. I don't know we have received any contracts during the present year.

Q. During the present year. How much last year, 1907 ?—A. Well, that I cannot tell you.

Q. About how much,—you are secretary of the company ?—A. I really do not know, Mr. Watson.

Q. Within $100,000 ?—A. $40,000 to $50,000.

Q. How much then, you can tell, about $40,000 to $50,000, is that right ?—A. I cannot say accurately.

Q. I am not asking within $100 or within $1,000. $40,000 or $50,000 last year, and how much in 1906?—A. Oh, altogether I suppose, taking all the years and totaling all the years it would not be more than $550,000.

Q. So on the same basis that you have spoken of the actual cost to you would be the odd $50,000 and the profits $500,000 ; is that right ?—A. Quite inaccurate.

Q. Why so?—A. Because we have spent so much money in developing the instrument ? Oh, yes, in developing the instrument, but you have got it. And do you use it in any other countries ?—A. No.

Q. Eh ?—A. No. We have had some sales in Newfoundland, and we are now beginning to place it upon the English market.

Q. Well, you are going to get the benefit of your development ?—A. We may, we may not.

Q. What is that ?—A. We may, we may not.

Q. You mean it may not be acceptable there ?—A. They may invent something better there.

Q. You have not been successful in introducing it anywhere else, apparently?—A. Yes, we have been successful.

Q. Where else ?—A. We have installed one in the British battleship *Dominion* within the past month.

Q. Yes?—A. And we hope to install more.

Q. You are just seeking to introduce them elsewhere ?—A. Quite so. We have installed some in Newfoundland.

Q. What did they take the place of here ?—A. The Reid horn, I understand.

Q. What ?—A. The Reid horn and the English siren.

Q. And what is the cost of the Reid horn ?—A. That I cannot tell you.

Q. What was it bought and sold for ?—A. That I cannot tell you. I do not know what I have here. I have got a record of what they pay in England for what would be used here.

Q. Never mind. You do not know ?—A. No, I do not know.

Q. You have no idea?—A. I have no idea what they paid here. I know what they paid in England for the same instrument.

Q. Then are you in competition here with others?—A. Excepting with what had been in use.

Q. What is that?—A. Excepting what had been in use here.

Q. Well, I say are you now in competition here with others in the supplying of these signals?—A. Not of our kind.

Q. Not of your kind?—A. Not of the design.

Q. Are there others similar to these? You mean yours is just the same but it merely has a little improvement?—A. No. The principle is entirely different. The siren is on quite a different principle from the diaphone, it is quite different.

Q. Then are you without competition?—A. Quite so.

Q. You are without competition?—A. So far as the diaphone is concerned. That is, we have the only patents.

By Hon. Mr. Cassels:

Q. What is the diaphone, Mr. Mearns?—A. My lord, permit me, I will show you diagram of it explaining our patent.

Q. Is that your patent?—A. Yes, sir. (Hands same to his lordship.)

By Mr. Watson:

Q. Can you describe it?—A. I am not a mechanic, Mr. Watson.

Q. Well, it is a great deal more expensive than the signal that was therefore in se?—A. I do not understand so.

Q. You do not understand so?—A. No.

Q. Has it taken the place of other signals?—A. Quite so.

Q. Here?—A. Quite so.

Q. Entirely so?—A. I understand so.

Q. You understand so?—A. Yes.

Q. And then of course the fact is you have been making immense profits out of e business?—A. I do not think so.

Q. What?—A. I do not think so.

Q. Well, you make a percentage of 300 or 400 per cent?—A. We are not making at, Mr. Watson, that is not a proper interpretation of our contract, for we supply e plant at less than——

Q. The contract fixes the price, the contract does not say anything about profits, oes it?—A. No; but we supply the plant, we have no profit upon the plant.

Q. I am not talking about the plant. I am talking about the diaphone?—A. We o not furnish the diaphone separate from the plant. We never have done so yet.

Q. You never have done so yet?—A. They never purchase that way. They urchase——

Q. You have been without opposition in making contracts, that is so? I under-tand you have got no competition?—A. We have competition from other classes of nstruments, sound-producing devices; we have no competition so far as the diaphone s concerned.

Q. You say yours superseded them?—A. Quite so.

Q. So that you are without competition, then?—A. Because it is a much more powerful instrument, a much more efficient instrument for service. That is recognized not only here——

Q. How did you happen to get it introduced, do you know?—A. I do not know. t was before I became connected with the company. It was after a long series of competitive tests with the siren. Colonel Anderson was the person who first adopted t, and it was after a long series of tests on the St. Lawrence in competition with the siren.

Q. How do you know Colonel Anderson adopted it?—A. I think that is so. Colonel Anderson will admit that.

Q. That he adopted it?—A. Yes.

Q. Did you have personal interviews?—A. I had no interviews. Mr. Northey had, of course.

Q. Who?—A. Mr. Northey. The diaphones were being sold to the government before our company was formed.

Q. By whom?—A. The Northey Manufacturing Company. The Fog Signal Com-pany came in after. The Northey Manufacturing Company had been sold to the Canada Foundry or the Canadian General Electric, and this part of the business of fog signals was continued by Mr. Northey, Mr. Forbes and myself.

Q. What Mr. Forbes?—A. A manufacturer of Hespeler.

Q. Mr. Northey, Mr. Forbes and you constitute the company?—A. We were also directors and stockholders of the Northey Company.

Q. Never mind that. You constitute the present company, the three of you?—A. No, there were five, Mr. Wadsworth and Mr. P. E. Northey.

Q. What Wadsworth?—A. T. P. Wadsworth.

Q. T. P. Wadsworth. Is he a brother of W. R.?—A. Yes.

Q. Then the capital stock, I suppose, was by the transfer of the patent, the patent was put in at that amount?—A. Yes; but the value of the patent——

Q. Never mind about the value of the patent for the moment. The capital is $100,000 paid up capital upon the transfer of the patent, and then you have been dealing in that way?—A. No. We have acquired new patents since.

Q. I know. But doing it that way there was no cash capital put in?—A. Oh, yes, there was.

Q. When?—A. It was cash capital when the company was organized.

Q. That is $100,000 was the paid-up capital for the patent?—A. Oh, no; there was cash paid in. Mr. Forbes paid in cash.

Q. You see, I cannot make much headway.

Hon. Mr. Cassels:

Q. How much of the capital went for the purchase of that?—A. The patents were valued at $100,000—only one patent. That was a small patent in connection with——

Q. What was the total of your capital?—A. $100,000.

Q. Did the patent absorb the whole of it—that belonged to whom?—A. The patent belonged to Mr. Northey.

Q. Very well. He got $100,000 for that?—A. Yes.

Q. How did the others pay for their stock?—A. In cash.

By Mr. Watson:

. How much did they pay?—A. The full value of their stock.

. How much money have they paid in?—A. Mr. Forbes paid in $10,000 in cash.

. Did anybody else pay in anything?—A. I paid in mine.

. How much?—A. I paid in full. You mean——

Q. Never mind. How much?—A. $10,000.

Q. Did you pay $10,000?—A. No, but in value.

Q. We are asking about cash now.

Hon. Mr. CASSELS.—You see, if Mr. Northey got $100,000 somebody else must have put in the money to pay for it.

By Mr. Watson:

Q. He says the whole capital stock was $100,000?—A. That is so.

Q. You are getting away beyond the $100,000 capital stock. Mr. Northey got $100,000 stock for the patent. The capital stock was $100,000. What did the rest of you get? Did he give each of you a few shares?—A. No. Mr. Forbes paid his money to Mr. Northey.

Q. Oh, I see, as additional——

Hon. Mr. CASSELS.—He bought an interest in the patent to the extent of $10,000, and this witness bought an interest to the extent of another $10,000.

By Mr. Watson:

Q. How much did you pay?—A. Full value.

Hon. Mr. CASSELS.—Then Mr. Northey took that?

By Mr. Watson:

Q. Yes. Mr. Northey put in his pocket the cash he got?—A. Quite so. He had the patents, of course.

Q. Well, then, how much did you pay to Mr. Northey?—A. I paid him up.

Q. How much?—A. I paid the full amount.

Q. I know. But I am asking how much the amount is?—A. $10,000.

Q. $10,000 in cash?—A. No, not in cash.

Hon. Mr. CASSELS.—He said in kind and cash.

By Mr. Watson:

Q. I see, in kind and cash. Did anybody else pay anything?—A. The others are, of course, nominal.

Hon. Mr. CASSELS.—How did you get your working capital?

Mr. WATSON.—They have not got any, apparently.

By Mr. Watson:

Q. How did you get your working capital, you never had any, had you?—A. We advanced from time to time personally to the bank.

Q. You borrowed from the bank?—A. We did not borrow. Practically, I suppose, that is equal to it. We did borrow from the bank and gave our personal undertaking.

Q. So that you have no working capital, but what working capital you require you get advances for from the bank. That is the position. What bank do you do business with? If you would answer up a little more plainly I would not have to ask so many unpleasant questions, Mr. Mearns?—A. I am quite free to answer anything within reason.

Q. Then what bank do you deal with?—A. The Royal Bank.

Q. Is that the only bank?—A. We did, I think, a short time deal in the Imperial Bank.

Q. The Royal Bank is your banker now?—A. Yes.

Q. I see. Well now we have got on that far. And you are charging very high prices, of course that is manifest?—A. I do not think so.

Q. Eh?—A. I do not think so.

Q. You do not think so?—A. No.

Q. Well, you have got articles here costing $4,600, which cost to manufacture about $400 or $500, and the articles at $8,500 in the same proportion, I suppose?—A. We are not getting that.

Q. Eh?—A. We are not getting that.

Q. Here it is, $8,500 for each two-unit plant with standard 3-inch diaphone complete; $8,950 for each two-unit plant with two standard 3-inch diaphones complete. Here are the prices mentioned here.

Hon. Mr. CASSELS.—What he says is the diaphone costs $400 if they have to supply them apart, but they supply the plant as well.

The WITNESS.—At less than cost.

By Mr. Watson:

Q. Let us see the statement?—A. I cannot tell you, I will show you my book.

Q. Let us see the books. We will have this correspondence and this contract marked.

(Correspondence marked Exhibit 11.)

Q. Who knows most about the business?—A. Mr. Northey, I suppose, more than I would.

Q. I expect him down to-night. He has returned now?—A. Yes.

By Hon. Mr. Cassels:

Q. Take the balance sheets?—A. I do not know the first thing about books.

Q. Take the balance sheet?—A. I do not think we had a balance sheet.

By Mr. Watson:

Q. You must have a balance sheet, you know?—A. I don't think so.

Q. There is an annual statement?—A. We have had no annual statement. W have not completed our development.

Hon. Mr. CASSELS.—What percentage is the dividend ?—A. We have simply drawn money from the bank and divided it pro rata according to the amount of stock.

By Mr Watson:

Q. How much?—A. I cannot tell you.

Hon. Mr. CASSELS.—You know whether 20——

Mr. WATSON.—Or 35 or 40 per cent?—A. I cannot tell you that.

Q. You cannot tell whether it is 5, 20, 40 or 50 per cent?—A. I cannot.

By Hon. Mr. Cassels :

Q. Your interest is $10,000?—A. Yes.

Q. What did you get last year ?—A. I could not tell you that, my lord, without referring to my bank book.

Q. Have you no knowledge?—A. I have a general idea.

Q. What is your general idea?—A. It would be 6 years.

By Mr. Watson:

Q. Never mind 6 years, take last year?—A. I could not possibly do it.

By Hon. Mr. Cassels:

Q. How much do you get during the six years?—A. Well, it might run to about $15,000.

By Mr. Watson:

Q. For your interest?—A. Yes. That is salary and everything else, wages and everything else in connection.

Hon. Mr. Cassels:

Q. Annual dividend?—A. It might possibly run that, but at the same time we are personally responsible for the development account.

Q. Never mind that. You know what your wages or salary is. How much do you get a year?—A. We are supposed—I was supposed to get $5,000 for the first two years and then $3,000.

By Mr. Watson:

Q. How much did you get last year for salary?—A. It has not been drawn yet. We have not made an adjustment of the amount.

Q. Bless my soul! I do not think you are doing yourself justice. I know you so well, I know you are thorough and accurate in your business matters, we all know that. Come along now, and give us a little better information. There is not anybody who does business in a more systematic way than you do; that I know personally.

Hon. Mr. CASSELS.—150 per cent spread over the six years. Then to get at that you have to deduct what he was entitled to draw.

(Contract marked Exhibit 12.)

By Mr. Watson:

Q. You received $5,000 for the first two years. That is beginning with what years?—A. 1903.

Q. And four?—A. And four.

Q. 1903, 4 and 5—— ?—A. Yes.

Q. 1905, 6 and 7, how much salary?—A. I have not drawn my salary yet.

Q. How much salary were you to get?—A. There was an understanding.

Q. How much on the understanding?—A. I understood I was to get $3,000 a year.

Q. That would be for three years $9,000, plus $10,000; that is $19,000 in salary in five years, is it not?—A. Yes.

Q. Now, how much did you get besides that for dividends?—A. Well, I have not got——

Q. About how much?—A. I have not drawn my salary.

Q. Never mind about the salary. About how much have you got for dividends?—A. Oh, altogether—I cannot tell you without referring to my private bank book.

Q. Let us see the book?—A. I have not the book here.

By Hon. Mr. Cassels:

Q. What did Mr. Northey get out of it?—A. Mr. Northey has not adjusted the matter.

By Mr. Watson:

Q. Never mind that. How much has he got out of it?—A. I cannot tell you.

Q. He got $5,000 for two years. How much did he get for those two years?—A. He was supposed to get a salary of $10,000.

Q. Now, we are coming to it. $10,000 for each of those two years. Then how much did his brother get, $5,000?—A. He got nothing.

Q. How much did Mr. Wadsworth get?—A. He was an employee, he got $1,200.

Q. That is Mr. Wadsworth. And who is the other man?—A. Forbes.

Q. How much did Mr. Forbes get?—A. I do not know. He was paid a salary. He was paid two years, I think, something.

Q. How much?—A. About $2,000.

Q. $2,000 a year?—A. Yes.

Q. Then who else was there?—A. No person.

Q. Then it has been maintained for the most part for Mr. Northey and you?—A. Not quite so.

Q. Well, you are the chief drawers. Then you were just secretary, were you?—A. Quite so.

Q. Then you know a great deal about the business, you are very familiar with the business, getting that salary of $5,000 a year would give a man a lot of knowledge about a business?—A. I was engaged in professional work.

Q. I am talking of the $5,000 a year?—A. That included professional work done for the company in getting out the patents. We secured 8 or 10 patents, and I had to look after the legal work of the company as well.

Q. Well then, do you know anything about the business of the company?—A. In a general way.

Q. I see. How much did the company make in 1902?—A. The company was not formed then.

Q. In 1903?—A. I cannot tell you that.

Q. Eh?—A. I cannot tell you that.

Q. What other book is there besides the one his lordship has?—A. I think cash books.

Q. Let us see. You make us feel like dentists. We would not be sorry if we felt like the patients. Well now, I see this cash book is for just one year, 1907, is it not?—A. Yes.

Q. And here is J. P. Northey's account. October 3rd, 1906, he got the handsome sum of $20,000 cash. What was that for?—A. I cannot tell you. That will be, I suppose, profits of the business standing back for some time.

Q. Where is the cash book before 1906 to see whether it belongs to any other year?

I see on March the 4th, 1907, he got another $8,000, several small sums meanwhile, and then September 7th, 1907, he got another good sum, $20,000.

Hon. Mr. CASSELS.—Are those carried into the ledger?

Mr. WATSON.—Cash. Let us see, are these carried down into the ledger? This is a fine business. Then April 1st, 1908, $20,000 cash again.

Hon. Mr. CASSELS.—If it goes on much longer he will be paid off.

By Mr. Watson:

Q. And the government is the only customer?—A. Quite so.

Q. Quite so, the government the only customer. Well, it looks as if what Colonel Anderson said is pretty correct. The department has been held by the nose pretty well. Somebody is getting money. Where is this carried forward in the ledger—this is the cash book—have you got the ledger here?—A. Yes.

Hon. Mr. CASSELS.—There would be Northey's account in the ledger.

Mr. WATSON.—Yes. This is Northey's account in the cash book. I have mentioned fully $70,000 there in 1906 and '07. There is no ledger number. Is that all his share out of the business? Don't blush, Mr Mearns. Come along, you have got a good thing, tell us about it.

Hon. Mr. CASSELS.—There is a ledger there. These are all down in the ledger?

Mr. WATSON.—There is, my lord.

Hon. Mr. CASSELS.—40 ledger B, whatever that is.

By Mr. Watson :

Q. This is all out of the business?—A. I am not familiar with the books. As I explained to you before, if you will give me time to go over the books I will answer you intelligently.

Hon. Mr. CASSELS.—Where is the ledger?

By Mr. Watson :

Q. Is this the ledger, is Northey's account here ?—A. It would be the other one, I presume. I am not familiar with these books.

Hon. Mr. CASSELS.—Turn up the ledger. They may have been advances.

By Mr. Watson:

Q. Is this the ledger?—A. Yes.

Q. Here, this corresponds.

Hon. Mr. CASSELS.—Now, take that $20,000.

Mr. WATSON.—October 3rd, to cash $20,000.

Hon. Mr. CASSELS.—That refers back to some book that will show what it is for.

By Mr. Watson :

Q. Page 40, where does that refer to? Whose writing is that?—A. Mr. Wadsworth's.

Hon. Mr. CASSELS.—See what that is paid for.

Mr. Watson:

Q. I thought the secretary kept the books. Then we will see. Page 40. By the Department of Marine and Fisheries cheque J. P. Northey bonus $20,000, October 2nd, 1906——That is a cash bonus—F. S. Mearns, bonus $2,500, Forbes $3,500. Who is the other man, this man?—A. Yes.

Q. Just the three of you got bonuses?—A. Yes.

By Hon. Mr. Cassels:

Q. The three stockholders?—A. Yes.

Mr. WATSON.—So those were bonuses?

By Hon. Mr. Cassels:

Q. Northey ought to get 8 times what you got?—A. Yes.

By Mr. Watson:

Q. That was profit bonus, of course ?—A. Or dividend.

By Hon. Mr. Cassels:

Q. A dividend of 25 per cent?—A. Quite so. It extended over a period of time.

By Mr. Watson:

Q. Where is the ledger before this ?—A. Is not that it there ? (Indicating.)

Q. You got bonuses from 1902. Does it go back that far? Have you anything here before this day book, this cash book, this ledger commencing September 1st, 1906? —A. Yes, I have got one book here.

By Hon. Mr. Cassels:

Q. Surely you can give us how much you have paid in bonuses since the commencement. You call it a bonus; it is 25 per cent dividend?—A. I cannot offhand.

Q. You ought to be able to show what profits you have been making. That bonus of 25 per cent is a dividend of 25 per cent.

By Mr. Watson:

Q. That is the cash book. Have you got the ledger before 1906?—A. That is all I have here.

Q. Well, where is Mr. Northey's account in this ledger, have you got an index to it?—A. There ought to be one.

Q. See if you can find it?—A. I am not familiar with the books. I have explained that to you.

Q. $5,000 a year ought to make you familiar with something?—A. I did not get $5,000 a year, Mr. Watson.

Hon. Mr. CASSELS.—What we would like to get is the bonus that has been paid from the time the company commenced.

By Mr. Watson:

Q. Yes. Now, which is the first book you have here?—A. This is the first book, the cash book.

Q. Let us see it. When does that start, June, 1903, that is right, is it?—A. Yes.

Q. That is the first cash book.

Hon Mr. CASSELS.—Now, what is the capital account?

By Mr. Watson:

Q. It does not say at all. Northey cheque $4,000. Have you got any other books than these?—A. That is all I have here.

Q. All you have here; but where are the others?—A. That gives all the entries up to date. Those are the original entries, the books with all the original entries.

Q. Where is the entry here of the payment to you of $5,000 in 1902? We will get at that system ?—A. It was paid in 1904.

Q. 1902 and 1903, $5,000 each year ?—A. Oh no, there was not any $5,000 each year.

Q. 1903 and 4?—A. $5,000 for the two years.

Q. No?—A. Pardon me.

By Hon. Mr. Cassels:

Q. I have no doubt you meant that, but you said $5,000 for each year?—A. For the two years.

By Mr. Watson:

Q. Not for each year?—A. I said for the two years.

•

By Hon. Mr. Cassels:

Q. It has gone down as if for each year. You mean you got $5,000 for the two years?—A. That was $5,000 for the two years and $3,000 for two years. It was a tacit understanding.

Q. It has gone down as if it was per year.

Mr. WATSON.—Well, we will have to have the books marked and get someone who knows more about them.

- (Cash book marked Exhibit No. 13.)

By Mr. Watson:

Q. Mr. Northey, I suppose, will know more about it?—A. I do not know. Possibly he might.

Q. Then who would know more about the business than Mr. Northey and you? I am awfully sorry to have to ask you a question like that, Mr. Mearns. Somebody must know about it, you know. You are holding back like thunder?—A. No, I am not. I simply do not know.

By Hon. Mr. Cassels:

Q. Were the bonuses over and above the salaries? You know that surely?—A. Yes.

Q. Now how often did you get a bonus?—A. I cannot tell you. I can tell you all I got altogether.

Q. That is what?—A. I have stated. Somewhere between $15,000 and $20,000.

Q. Was that all bonus?—A. No, salaries and bonuses.

Q. That is no use to us until we know the amount of salary?—A. There was an understanding I was to get $3,000 for salary. That has not been continued. There was $5,000 a year paid for two years.

Q. That would be $5,000. Now, how much more?—A. I have not been paid that.

Q. I know. We have three years at $3,000, $9,000 and $5,000—$14,000, and you have got altogether $15 000?—A. Between $15,000 and $20,000. That was taking salaries and dividends and everything else.

Q. You know what your salary was. You got for two years $5,000?—A. Yes.

Q. And for three years $9,000?—A. I have not been paid.

Q. We will see whether you have been paid or not. You are to get $14,000. How much of the salary has been paid?—A. $5,000.

Q. Then they owe you still for the balance of salary?—A. Yes.

Q. And you got $20,000 inside of five years?—A. Well, six years.

Q. Well, you got $15,000 in bonuses, you call it; you got 150 per cent dividend? A. That is salaries as well.

Q. I am not tying you down. During the six years you have been in operation you have got 150 per cent, in the neighbourhood of $15,000?—A. For salaries and bonuses.

Q. Not salary, as I understand it. What you say is they still owe you salary except $5,000?—A. No, I would not like to put it that way.

Q. Supposing you got $14,000 for salaries, that leaves $6,000 dividends?—A. Yes.

Q. For the six years?—A. Yes.

Q. That is about a thousand dollars a year?—A. Yes.

Q. That would be 10 per cent of the stock. If these are the correct figures Mr. Northey has got his salary and his bonuses, and you each got 10 per cent on that basis of operation.

By Mr. Watson :

Q. I see in 1906, from September 1, 1906 to April 21, 1908, a little more than a year and a half, Mr. Northey has aparently drawn out between $65,000 and $70,000 and between the same date, Mr. Forbes has drawn out $8,500 and Mr. Mearns has drawn out between the same dates $8,500.

Hon. Mr. CASSELS.—Northey on $80,000 and the others on $10,000.

Mr. WATSON.—$8,500 in the last year and a half. Now, how much did you draw before that?

Hon. Mr. CASSELS.—That is at the rate of 50 per cent a year after deducting what he is entitled to for salary.

By Mr. Watson:

Q. I suppose so. That is the way it is, is it?—A. Apparently so from what you say. I would have necessarily to go over the books. I have not ascertained it accurately.

Hon. Mr. CASSELS.—Unless that ledger is examined to see whether they get salaries in addition.

Mr. WATSON.—These are bonuses, my lord; these are not salaries. These are evidently bonuses, not intended to be on salary account.

By Mr. Watson:

Q. Now, then, that shows an immense profit on no capital except the patent; that is the position?—A. Nine patents.

Q. Eh?—A. Nine patents.

Q. But as distinguished from cash capital?—A. And——

Q. Have you got any statement of the assets of the company ?—A. And the expense of developing during six years.

Q. That is all gone, that is paid for?—A. It is not paid for.

By Hon. Mr. Cassels:

Q. It is equal to 50 per cent a year?—A. It is not paid for at all. The cost of developing in England has certainly been paid by this company. We are continuing development.

By Mr. Watson:

Q. You are making contracts there now, that is the idea. Now, who obtained these contracts?—A. Which ones have you reference to?

Q. The contracts with the department?—A. The department made the contracts, the officers of the department.

Q. Who in the department made the contracts?—A. Colonel Anderson——

Q. Anyone else?—A. Fixed the prices and the orders were given through the deputy minister.

Q. Did you have any personal interviews with Colonel Anderson?—A No.

Q. You did not?—A. No.

Q. Did you have any personal interviews with anyone?—A. No.

Q. No personal interview with anyone at any time in respect of the business?—A. At any time?

Q. That is what I am asking?—A. You are speaking of the first contracts, I understand.

Q. In respect of the business did you have any personal interviews with anyone? —A. Oh yes.

Q. With whom?—A. I have had with Colonel Anderson.

Q. With Colonel Anderson?—A. Yes.

Q. Anyone else?—A. With Mr. Fraser.

Q. That is B. H. Fraser?—A. Yes.

Q. What were your interviews with Colonel Anderson about?—A. Oh, in reference to details in connection with the work.

Q. Details?—A. Yes.

Q. Eh?—A. Details in connection with the work.

Q. Yes. Then you were attending personally to these matters of detail, were you? —A. Sometimes, occasionally.

Q. Where did you see him?—A. Here.

Q. At Ottawa?—A. Yes.

Q. How many times, do you suppose?—A. Not possibly more than half a dozen times in six years.

Q. Was there ever any dickering between you and him as to the prices—you understand the expression?—A. The prices were originally fixed by Colonel Anderson and Mr. Northey.

Q. Eh?—A. The prices were originally fixed by Colonel Anderson and Mr. Northey.

Q. Did you have anything to do at all in fixing the prices?—A. Not originally.

Q. What did you have to do it with it? You are not a mechanical man?—A. Quite so.

Q. What did you have to do with it?—A. Subsequently matters of detail in carrying on the work.

Q. That is a matter of mechanics. What did you have to do with details in carrying on the work?—A. Trifling, it would not be of any importance.

Q. What did you discuss with him, matters of contract?—A. Sometimes complaints would come in as to the operation and working of plants.

Q. You knew nothing about those matters?—A. I gave attention to certain things. For instance, complaint was made of the efficiency of the alarm at Cape Race last year, and after a good deal of communication and interviews we sent our engineer down there. He remained there possibly a month and a half at a good deal of expense to the company, and I took that up with Colonel Anderson.

Q. Well, anything else you took up with him?—A. There are other matters in connection with complaints.

Q. Can you remember anything else you took up with him?—A. Offhand I could not without thinking over.

Q. Did you ever see him anywhere else than in Ottawa?—A. Not particularly. I have met him in Toronto, he has come to our office.

Q. He has come to your office in connection with what?—A. In connection with work.

Q. Did you ever discuss the question of price at all?—A. No.

Q. Did he ever complain to you that it was too much?—A. I have heard him complain that the prices were high.

Q. That is Colonel Anderson complained that the prices were high?—A. Yes.

Q. To whom and when?—A. Oh, that would be some time ago. I have heard him complain, in fact to myself, that the prices were high.

Q. What did he say?—A. That he thought the prices were high.

Q. And what did you say?—A. I said I did not think they were high, considering the cost we had been put to in regard to developing the instruments, because that cost had been very very large.

Q. Did you tell him you never had any capital stock, any cash capital? That stands out pretty prominently when you talk about the cost of development. You have got no cash capital and never had.—A. We are paying royalties.

Q. Well, that shows more profits. Whom are you paying royalties to?—A. To company who control the basic patent.

Q. Who is that?—A. The Hamilton Foster Fog Signal Company.

Q. How much royalties do you pay?—A. It is graded according to the instrument.

Q. But how much does it amount to?—A. I could not just offhand te.. you.

Q. About how much?—A. It would range from $150 to maybe $1,000 an instrument.

Q. A year?—A. No, each instrument·

Hon. Mr. CASSELS.—Do you pay royalties on what you sell or do you pay annual fee?—A. No, on what we sell, on the small instrument. That was only a very y small instrument.

By Mr. Watson:

Q. The sums you have made are after you paid those royalties. Then how often you see Mr. Fraser?—A. B· H. Fraser?

Q. Yes?—A. Occasionally, not very often.

Q. Did you ever see J. F. Fraser?—A. Yes, I have seen him.

Q. What about?—A. He has called simply at the office·

Q. Had he anything to do with it? I thought it was not in his department?—A. one time he had.

Q. At what time?—A. That was 1903 or '04, I think it was.

Q. Then that was before the division of the department, was it?—A. Yes.

Q. He was acting then under Colonel Anderson?—A· Yes.

Q. Yes?—A. No, no. After, it was when he was commissioner of lights for a ort time.

Q. What did you have to do with him?—A. I had nothing particular to do with m.

, Q. Why did he call upon you?—A. He called at the office; he did not call upon e particularly.

Q. He called at the office, where?—A. In Toronto.

Q. In Toronto?—A. Yes.

Q. Did you ever ask him to come there?—A. No.

Q. How did he happen to be there?—A. He came there, I presume, in connec-on with the work.

Q. And what was done for him?—A. In what way?

Q. Any way?—A. I do not know.

Q. Was he entertained freely?—A. No.

Q. What?—A. No.

Q. Where else did you see Mr. J. F. Fraser?—A. I have seen him here.

Q. Did you come here to see him?—A. No, not particularly.

Q. That was a matter of entertaining, then, more or less?—A. No.

Q. Eh?—A. No.

Q. What about it, then?—A. Nothing.

Q. What did he get or what did you do for him?—A. He got nothing.

Q. He got nothing?—A. No.

Q. What took place between you and him with regard to encouragement of the usiness, encouragement of contracts?—A. Nothing at all.

Q. Eh?—A. Absolutely nothing.

Q. Were prices decreased or increased after he ceased to do with it?—A. The rices were fixed by Mr. Anderson originally, dealing with Mr. Northey, before I ecame connected with the company. These prices were continued up to the time nders were asked for and that contract made.

Q. Tenders, that is a pure matter of form. There was nobody else to tender?— ., There were other firms.

Q. For different kinds of articles altogether?—A. Sound devices.

Q. But there was nobody else to tender on this article?—A. Quite so. Our patent prohibited that.

Q. What was the object of asking for tenders?—A. There were other devices, and the plant was open to the world to tender upon it.

Q. Well, then, how often did you see Mr. B. H. Fraser?—A. Occasionally.

Q. Whereabouts ?—A. I met him here occasionally. I would come down sometimes with Mr. Northey on other business and would occasionally see him, not very often.

Q. You would occasionally see him?—A. Yes.

Q. Ever see him in Toronto?—A. Sometimes.

Q. What did he go there for?—A. He came to the office in connection with the work.

Q. Was that a matter of entertainment ?—A. No.

Q. Eh?—A. No.

Q. Did you say not?—A. No.

Q. I ask you directly because I am informed it was so, otherwise I would be the last to ask you this question?—A. I cannot credit that.

Q. You cannot?—A. I cannot.

Q. Then when did you see him in New York?—A. I do not remember seeing him in New York.

Q. You do not remember seeing him in New York? Now, do you say that ?

By Hon. Mr. Cassels:

Q. Surely you cannot forget this, Mr. Mearns?—A. I may have.

By Mr. Watson:

Q. You may have seen him in New York?—A. I have seen him once in New York, and once only.

Q. How long ago was that and how many days did you spend with him? Now come along?—A. That may have been within the last year.

Q. And how many days did you spend with him?—A. I did not spend very many.

Q. Eh?—A. I did not spend any time with him.

Q. How many days?—A. I was in New York, a day, two days.

Q. Friday, Saturday, Sunday and Monday, and how much longer? Now, do you mean to say you have forgotten it, the early part of this year and you have forgotten it? Come now, Mr. Mearns?—A. Oh, I did not see him all that time there, Mr. Watson. What is the use putting it that way ?

Q. Did you see him during those days in New York?—A. I saw him a portion of those days.

Q. Why not say that before? You could not have forgotten that. That is within a month and a half or two months. Now, what was he doing with you there in New York during those four days?—A. He was there, I presume, upon his own motion.

. Do you know what he was doing?—A. I do not.

. Who paid his expenses?—A. I did not.

. Who paid his expenses at the hotel?—A. Himself.

. Eh?—A. Himself.

Q. Eh?—A.—Himself, I presume; I did not pay them.

Q. How did he happen to be there with you those four days in New York?—A. I cannot tell you that.

Q. You cannot tell. How did you happen to be there?—A. I went there on my own business.

Q. In connection with this business?—A. In connection with our business in New York.

Q. In connection with your business in New York?—A. Yes.

Q. And what was he doing there at the time ?—A. I cannot tell you that.

Q. He was staying at the same hotel?—A. Possibly so.

Q. Was he not?—A. I could not prevent him.

Q. I did not ask you that. Was he not staying at the same hotel?—A. Yes.

Q. What was he doing there?—A. I cannot tell you.

Q. You spent nearly all the time, the four days together?—A. I did nothing of the kind. I went there in connection with our United States Company. I went there to attend their annual meeting. I was there on other business. I was there in connection with purchasing plant. Mr. Northey was in England. I was not there to have any clandestine meeting with him.

Q. Eh?—A. I was not there for the purpose of having any clandestine meeting with him. It is not fair to say that Mr. Watson.

Q. You were with him most of the time?—A. I was not there most of the time with him. I casually met him there.

Q. I am asking you those questions from reports I have, so I do not want any misunderstanding between you and me, witness. Now, just tell us what it means. It seems extraordinary your being there with that officer for four days and obtaining these large prices?—A. I was there attending to my business.

Q. That is business of the company?—A. Business of the United States Fog Signal Company.

Q. And the business of this company?—A. Partly so.

Q. Partly so. The business of this company?—A. Yes.

Q. Now, tell me what Fraser was doing there?—A. I cannot tell you that.

Q. Have you any idea how he got there or what he was there for?—A. He did not go with me. I simply casually met him there.

Q. You have no knowledge of what he was there for?—A. No.

Q. What hotel was it?—A. The Manhattan.

Q. You have no idea how he hapepned to be there?—A. I have not, not the slightest idea.

Q. You were visiting him and down town with him?—A. I did not.

Q. You were down town with him?—A. Certainly, I walked down the street with him.

Q. Certainly you did. Now, then, do you think those matters require any explanation?—A. I do not, Mr. Watson. I am quite free to say I was not there for any improper purpose; I was there for my own business.

Q. You have no idea how he happened to be there?—A. I have not, not the slightest idea.

Q. Not the slightest idea?—A. No.

Q. Was business with the company discussed during that time?—A. No, I do not think so.

Q. What?—A. I do not think so.

Q. You do not think so?—A. No.

Q. Were you trying to get his ear?—A. No.

Q. His favour?—A. No.

Q. Were you particularly friendly with him?—A. Oh, as friendly as I would be with you or any person else.

Q. Well, you are putting it pretty broad, with any person else. That is, with any one else you happen to meet, no more than that?—A. That is all.

Q. That is no friendship at all, is it?—A. The ordinary friendship that one person would have for another.

Q. Then how many other times did you see him in New York?—A. I have no recollection of seeing him at any time.

Q. Just try and think. How many other times have you met him in New York?—A. I cannot recollect.

Q. You cannot at present recollect. How many other times in other places, Boston and other places?—A. I never saw him in Boston.

Q. Where abouts have you met him last besides New York?—A. Oh, I met him in Toronto.

Q. It is the fact, is it not, that he has been making visits along with you and Mr. Northey from time to time in the same way ?—A. No, I do not understand that.

Q. You do not understand. What do you understand about it ?—A. It is just possible he went to New York with Mr. Northey in connection with some compressors, I think, and I may have been possibly there at the time. I am not quite sure of that, I think possibly I was.

Q. When was that, last year ?—A. No, it was before that.

Q. You could not forget an occasion like that ?—A. I have been down there frequently with Mr. Northey.

Q. Yes. And frequently with Mr. Fraser ?—A. Oh no.

Q. How many times with Mr. Fraser when he was there ?—A. I have no recollection at present excepting once.

Q. You have just told us about another occasion ?—A. I am not clear as to that, Mr. Watson.

Q. Who paid his expenses on those different occasions?—A. Himself, so far as I am concerned.

Q. Himself ?—A. Yes.

Q. Out of his own pocket ?—A. So far as I am concerned.

Q. Not departmental ?—A. Well, I presume it would be departmental.

Q. Do you know whether it was or not ?—A. I do not know. I know I did not pay his expenses.

Q. How much did Mr. B. H. Fraser get from time to time ?—A. Nothing.

Q. What ?—A. Absolutely nothing.

Q In any way. Absolutely not a copper.

Q. Commissions ?—A. No commissions.

Q. In what way was he remunerated ?—A. He was not remunerated in any way.

Q. What advantages or gains did he get ?—A. He got no advantages.

Q. Eh ?—A. Absolutely none.

Q. Does his name appear in the books anywhere ?—A. No, so far as I know.

Q. Not as far as you know ?—A. I do not think his name appeared in the books at all.

Q. Will you undertake to say it does not ?—A. I will.

Q. You take your oath on that ?—A. I will.

Q. What discounts were allowed to him ?—A. None whatever.

Q. What discounts were allowed—— ?—A. None whatever.

Q. To anyone ?—A. No one.

Q. No discounts allowed. What commissions ?—A. None.

Q. How did you make it up to him ?—A. Make it up to him ?

Q. Yes.—A. We made nothing up to him.

Q. For the friendly help he was giving. You recognize he was your friend ?—A. I recognize certainly he was not our enemy, he was not antagonistic to us.

Q. You recognize you were pulling along, pulling as much as you could ?—A. Certainly not, we made no contracts with him.

Q. You did not make contracts with him, but he was their second man, and you were pulling his leg as much as you could; is not that so ?—A. It is not so so far as I am concerned.

Q. Then who would do that, Mr. Northey ?—A. I do not think he did.

Q. Eh ?—A. I do not think he did.

Q. You do not think he did ?—A. No.

Q. Did you ever try it with Colonel Anderson ?—A. No.

Q. Or with Mr. J. F. Fraser ?—A. No.

Q. Or with the deputy minister ?—A. No.

Q. How did you do it, then ?—A. We have not done it.

Q. How did you get these large prices ?—A. We do not consider them large.

Q. You do not consider them large. You consider the profits large ?—A. Not hen you take into consideration all the surrounding circumstances.

Q. That is the large cash capital. The cash capital, you know, was a great cir--umstance. Now, do you want to leave this matter between you and Mr. B. H. Fraser efore his lordship just as it stands now without saying anything further ?—A. As to hat ?

Q. As to your relationship and trips and interviews with him?—A. I want to say ositively any trips I ever had with Mr. Fraser I have accounted to you for them, nd there was no improper act on my part, none whatever.

Q. You have got nothing more to say about those New York occasions or trips?— . Absolutely not. I went on the business of the company.

Q. You have no idea what he was doing there?—A. I do not.

Q. Not at all?

By Hon. Mr. Cassels:

Q. Did you know the report had been made by the commissioners when you were n New York the last time?—A. Possibly I did.

Q. Did you discuss that fact with Mr. Fraser?—A. I may have casually referred ᴏ it, but there was no specific discussion, because the report does not refer to our ompany, my lord. There is no criticism of our company at all in the report. I was ot at all concerned about it.

By Mr. Watson:

Q. Now, you have not any incorporated company in New York city?—A. We bave in the State of New Jersey.

Q. None in New York. Who owns that in New Jersey, the same parties?—A. Oh no

Q. Who?—A. Mr. W. H. Gains, Mr. T. E. Northey, and Mr. J. P. Northey, of course, has an interest.

Q. And yourself?—A. No, I have no interest.

Q. You have no interest in the business in New York city or the United States? —A. No.

Q. That is right. You have nothing to do with that company's business over there?—A. Any more than I was looking after the business of the company and drawing contracts and all that kind of thing.

Q. What is the capital stock over there?—A. $150,000.

Q. Has any money been put in over there?—A. Of that I cannot speak.

Q. That means it has not, of course, does it not, none to your knowledge?—A. The patents would be——

Q. Would be the assets. And the same in the foreign companies, the patents are ㇋he assets ?—A. No, that is not correct. Mr. Northy would have to speak of that. I am not a stockholder in the English Company, but capital has been advanced there, I understand.

Q. You saw Mr. Fraser when he got there in New York that time, you went to ㇋he station with him to see him off? You recollect that meeting with him at the ㇂tation?—A. Possibly I did—no, I did not meet him at the station.

Q. You went to see him off?—A. Possibly I did.

Q. Possibly you did?—A. I think I did, yes.

Q. Nothing in it at all, I see?—A. Oh no.

Q. Well, we will have to follow it up with Mr. Northey and Mr. Fraser.

By Hon. Mr. Cassels:

Q. Does this company possess any works, or was everything made by the Northey ᴐompany?—A. Made by the Northey Company, then by the Scholfield Holden Company. But our work principally was development, we do the testing.

Q. I know. But I want to know whether you had any plant of your own or whether the whole thing was made for you by somebody else?—A. It was made by us for——

Q. Then you supplied the government?—A. The principal part of our work was the casting. We had to have that built by the Polson Iron Works for $15,000, and we had to have that——

Q. Is not that in your ledger as part of the expenses of operation?—A. It has not been adjusted, it has not been carried on. A part of it has, but——

Q. Why did you pay bonuses until you knew what your profit was?—A. We did that, we simply did that because we were all personally liable on our personal paper. Frequently I gave my own personal obligation to the bank. Within the last two weeks I have done that.

Q. When you paid the Northey Company or this other company that made these things for you, did they give them to you at cost price, or did they get their profit first?—A. They gave it at a close figure·

Q. Well, they make a profit on it?—A. They would.

O. Then the next step is, you furnish to the government?—A. Yes.

Q. Then you had the expense of testing?—A. Yes.

Q. Then you made a bonus or dividend—we will call it dividend—which was profit?—A. Every instrument was made complete, we had to put it under a system of tests.

Q. Can you form any opinion or give any information by starting at the beginning of 1903 whether the bonus was paid each year, or whether the bonus in 1906 covered three years back?—A. I fancy that is correct. We were not paid in that way. The government paid—possibly just in the early part of our work the payments came in very irregular, we had to wait possibly eight or nine months. Then when the money came in we simply distributed it, whenever the money came in we distributed, and frequently distributed more than we should have.

Q. You deducted that and distributed the balance?—A. Yes. Sometimes we overdrew our bank account possibly $80,000 or $90,000, and Mr. Forbes——

Q. I should think it would be very easy by getting to work at the beginning of 1903 to show what profit was made from year to year?—A. It would be. The whole business has not been conducted for the purpose of investigation; it has been carried on for their own private purposes.

Q. Is there anybody would know from your books what profits you have made during the last five or six years?—A. I do not think so without going into the books.

Q. Have you had any contracts this current year for this department?—A. We are building the same as last year. I do not think we have any this year.

Q. You contracted last year, 1907?—A. Yes.

Q. At the same price?—A. Yes.

Q. When you made this contract last year you must have known you were making large profits. This particular signal cost about $4,000 and you got about $4,600.

Mr. WATSON.—Costing about $400.

By Hon Mr. Cassels:

Q. Costing about $400?—A. My lord, we put in the plant at less than cost price. If we had a profit on the plant then that would be quite right, but we put in the plant at cost price.

Q. How much? That is what we want to get at?—A. A considerable sum.

Q. Cannot you say?—A. I say the cost of the plant is $4,500; we put in $3,900.

Q. That is $600 spread over how many years, how many plants have you fixed? You say $4,900 for the plant?—A. $4,400. We put in about $3,900.

Q. There is $500 you lost. Now, is that the whole? Then the profit must be very much in the neighbourhood of $4,000 on each one of these things, that is what it comes to. I am not saying you are not entitled to it?—A. It would not be. Your lordship must remember this: During all these years we have been putting out large ms in development, we have had to have engineers continuously at work developing. e have given the government every improvement we have made in the business.

Q. Cannot you tell what expenditure has been incurred?—A. With time I could.

Q. You are entitled to get at all the expenses you have been put to, how much u are out.—A. If I had known your lordship intended to go into that part of the siness I would have been prepared.

Q. What is charged is this: The government has ben paying actually more than ould have been paid, and the contention or point raised is that the government ought have compelled you to furnish these signals at a reasonable price?—A. What we y is, we are not being paid as much as in England for an instrument of less value.

Q. In England it is a different law from ours altogether. That is the contention, all events. To get at that, to deal fairly with you you have got to get the outlay r the period of years, what is a reasonable sum to be allowed for management and erything else, and then what is the balance distributed. Then we will get at the fact hether you were paid reasonable prices or not. The department may not have paid cessive prices, but you see it is only fair to the officials you should give the infor- ation?—A. I suppose we can get at it.

Q. If I had time I would do it in about a night, I think.

Mr. WATSON.—You can work it up.

Hon. Mr. CASSELS.—I should be very sorry to be a lawyer and not be able to take ledger and tell what it contains. However, Mr. Northey may be able to give us the formation.

By Mr. Watson :

Q. Mr. Northey is a business man of large experience. I think we all know Mr. orthey ?—A. Quite so.

Hon. Mr. CASSELS.—What we want to get at is the reasonable outlay so as to certain the profits and what the percentage is.

(Cash book of Northey & Co., marked Exhibit 14.)

(Ledger of Northey & Co., marked Exhibit 15.)

(Ledger of Northey & Co., marked Exhibit 16.)

Mr. WATSON.—You had some idea of these matters, because you were kind enough) give me a memorandum showing the great work done ?—A. Certainly.

Q. And this was in connection with the cost and the price ?—A. Yes.

Q. So it was present to your mind when you made this statement. You will e very glad to hand this in ?—A. I have no objection.

Q. You prefer it should go in, do you not ?—A. Quite so.

Q. That is what I understood you gave it to me for ?—A. Quite so.

Q. It shows the amount of work done, and that is a sort of explanation of the irge cost.

(Statement marked Exhibit 17.)

Q. So that the matter of cost was present to your mind days ago ?—A. In a eneral way it certainly was.

Q. That is the reason I think you ought to have been prepared.

Hon. Mr. CASSELS.—What time to-morrow ?

Mr. WATSON.—Half past ten, my lord.

(Adjourned at 4.30 p.m. to 10.30 to-morrow and then resumed.)

June 16th, 1908.

Mr. WATSON.—My lord, Mr. Northey is here this morning. I will pursue that articular matter, if your lordship please ?

Hon. Mr. CASSELS.—All right.

JOHN P. NORTHEY, sworn.

By Mr. Watson :

Q. Mr. Northey, you live in Toronto ?—A. Yes.

Q. And you were formerly connected with the Northey Manufacturing Company?—A. Yes.

Q. Were you the chief holder in that company ?—A. I had more stock than any-one else had.

Q. In that company, yes. And now you are practically the owner of the International Fog Signal Company ?—A. No, I do not know anything about the International Company.

Q. What is your company ?—A. The Canadian Fog Signal Company.

Q. The Canadian Fog Signal Company. We had some particulars of it yesterday from Mr. Mearns, the secretary of the company. I am sure his lordship would like to get a little bit more accurate information about it from you. That company was formed at what time ?—A. Well, I think it was 1902.

Q. 1902 ?—A. I think so.

Q. And formed by whom ?—A. Mr. Mearns. Do you mean the stockholders ?

Q. Yes ?—A. The stockholders are Mr. Forbes of Hespeler, Mr. Mearns and myself.

Q. The three of you ?—A. Yes.

Q. And how did you come to form that company?—A. Well, to do business, to raise money to do business. We had some orders from the Canadian government at that time.

Q. At that time you had some orders ?—A. Yes.

Q. Who had obtained these orders ?—A. I had from Colonel Anderson.

Q. From Colonel Anderson ?—A. Yes.

Q. So that the first orders then were obtained from him ?—A. Yes.

Q. And that was before you had the patent?—A. No.

Q. When did you acquire that patent?—A. Well, it was some short time before that.

Q. A short time before that?—A. Yes.

Q. You had nothing to do with that kind of business before?—A. Yes.

Q. Where and when?—A. With the Northey Manufacturing Company. We were making for the Canadian Government fog signals.

Q. Of what design, any particular design?—A. Yes. The only design in use, that was the siren.

Q. That was the old design ?—A. The old siren.

Q. That was an old design, was it not?—A. Well, you might call it an obsolete design.

Q. Eh?—A. It was out of date.

Q. That was out of date ?—A. Yes.

Q. Why were you making it?—A. At that time it was out of date—at least now. At that time it was the only thing that could be used, the most efficient.

Q. Were you then in competition with others?—A. Yes.

Q. Many others?—A. There were no patents. There were probably——

Q. No one in Canada?—A. No one in Canada. I only know of two being made.

Q. You mean two——?—A. Signals of the siren type.

Q. Prior to 1902 or after?—A. It was prior to 1902. I think we made them in 1900 and 1901.

Q. Well now, when did you commence making under the patent the new design? —A. Well, I think it was in 1903.

Q. You are not quite sure, apparently?—A. Well, it was 1903. I know that because I sold my business to the General Electric in 1903, and it was just before that we were making them.

Q. From whom did you acquire the patent?—A. From the Hamilton Foster Fog gnal Company.

Q. Of New York?—A. Yes.

Q. How much did you pay for that patent?—A. We agreed to give them royalties.

Q. How much royalties?—A. Well, it ran from a thousand dollars down to a ndred dollars, according to the size·

Q. From $100 to $1,000 according to the size. Your expression was you agreed give them, perhaps carrying with it an implication that that has not been paid?—A. h, but it has all been paid.

Q. Since then?—A. We pay as we go along.

By Hon. Mr. Cassels:

Q. Did you take an absolute assignment of the patent?—A. Yes, my lord. It is istered in Ottawa, England and everywhere else·

By Mr. Watson:

Q. And the consideration for the patent was the royalty?—A. Yes.

Q. That is the only consideration?—A. And some stock in the English company d the American company.

Q. Some stock in the English company and the American company?—A. Yes.

Q. The English company has not yet been formed, has it?—A. It is in the hands the solicitors in London and it is being formed now·

Q. The American company has not been formed?—A. Yes, it has been for years.

Q. With a New Jersey charter?—A. With a New Jersey charter.

Q. But you have not commenced to operate there yet?—A. We have. We are aking in the States.

By Hon. Mr. Cassels:

Q. I do not understand what that has to do with the Canadian company. Is that art of the bargain?—A· It is quite independent of the Canadian company.

Q. The consideration by the Canadian company was merely a royalty?—A. Yes, royalty.

Q. This American company, I believe, has different shareholders?—A. Quite so.

Q. It has nothing whatever to do with the purchase price?—A. Nothing to do ith the purchase price.

Q. Did you get any stock or any consideration in those other companies as part f your bargain with them for the Canadian patent?—A. No.

By Mr. Watson:

Q. You are forming those other companies?—A. I am.

Q. But you said you were to get shares in the American and English companies? -A. Quite so.

By Hon. Mr. Cassels:

Q. You must have had an assignment of all the patents?—A. I have.

Q. In the States as well ?—A. France and everywhere.

By Mr. Watson:

Q. I see. You are giving them a royalty and also shares in the American and nglish companies?—A. Quite so.

Q. That is all?—A. That is all.

Q. No interest in the Canadian company beyond the royalties?—A. No.

Q. Now, then, so as to lead up to the further questions I want to ask you and to put it in a consecutive way, you have since been supplying these diaphones and plant to the government to a very large amount?—A. Here in Canada?

Q. Yes?—A. Yes.

Q. To a very large amount?—A. I think half a million dollars.

Q. Yes. The particulars show that, half a million dollars?—A. That is for plants as well as instruments.

Q. Eh ?—A. That is for plants as well as instruments.

Q. Certainly. And in connection with the supply you have been making very large profits apparently?—A. We have made good profits.

Q. You have made good profits?—A. Yes.

Q. Mr. Mearns stated last evening the profit was in the neighbourhood of 50 per cent. I suppose that is fairly accurate?

Hon. Mr. CASSELS.—50 per cent. Oh, yes, about 5,000 per cent.

By Mr. Watson:

Q. Yes, 5,000 per cent, not 50 per cent. About $4,000 on each diaphone?—A.Well, we made on the two contracts we got from the government we figured on 35 per cent and made 29 per cent, not 4,000.

Q. Well, we will just have to get particulars. The diaphones are made at an expense of something like $400?—A. Yes, but that don't cover it.

Q. Is that so?—A. No, they cost more than that.

Q. How much?—A. What size?

Q. Give me the sizes, please?—A. Well, I suppose that one at Cape Race cost——

Q. What was the size of that?—A. 7-inch.

Q. Yes.—A. I suppose that would cost $800?

Q. $800, that diaphone?—A. Yes. That is, roughly.

Q. Why do you say you suppose?—A. Well, I have not the cost here with me.

Q. $800. And how much was that sold for, the No. 7?—A. That plant I think we got $13,500 for, but that plant cost us $10,000.

Q. Just wait, please. I asked you about the diaphone. The diaphone cost you, according to your statement, about $800?—A. Yes, but we——

Q. Listen, please. How much did that cost you in its construction?—A. That would cost $800, and we gave it to the government for nothing.

Q. You gave that diaphone for nothing?—A. Yes; and also we never got a dollar for that, and also one at Belle Isle Straits.

Q. Then what was the selling price of that diaphone?—A. We have not sold one of these.

Q. Have you made a selling price on any diaphone?—A. Yes.

Q. What?—A. We made a selling price on the 3-inch.

Q. On the 3-inch?—A. Yes.

Q. What was the selling price of that?—A. $4,600.

Q. How many of these have you supplied?—A. Well, I suppose we supplied probably 40.

Q. Forty. And what is the selling price of these?—A. We sold some of these——

Q. For $4,600, you say. And the cost of this 3-inch is how much?—A. But you are leaving out the plant.

Q. Purposely. I am dealing with the diaphone, if you please?—A. Right.

Q. I will give give you a chance to answer any other questions you may think necessary to explain your position. The diaphone you sold for $4,600 cost how much? —A. $600, about.

Q. Mr. Mearns said about $400 or $500?—A. Well, then, it would cost $600 with the royalties, over $600 with the royalties.

Q. So that upon the diaphone itself, the 3-inch, you would have a profit of $4,000? —A. About that.

Q. And you have supplied about 40 of those, not more?—A. Yes, but I do not think we supplied more than ten of those singly. The rest of them had plants on them.

Q. Yes, but I am not speaking of the plants just now?

Hon. Mr. CASSELS.—Mr. Mearns suggested the plant was open to anybody to make and the Northey Company made the plant at——

A. The Canadian Company.

Q. And at a small profit, Mr. Mearns said?—A. We lost money on that contract.

By Mr. Watson:

Q. The plant was made—— ?—A. All of those plants were supplied at a loss.

Q. Just wait, please. Who made the plant?—A. The Polson Iron Works made part, and the Canada Foundry of Toronto and—I forgot the name—the Fairbanks-Morse.

Q. The Northey Company?—A. No. They had sold out at that time. Those three and the Schofield Company made the plant for us.

Q. You had contracts with them?—A. Yes.

Q. Have you got those contracts here?—A. I think we have.

Q. Let me see them, please?—A. Oh, the contracts with the——

Q. With the manufacturers?—A. They were quotations, there were no contracts made by letter.

Q. Let me see them, please. Have you got them?—A. No, we have not those with us. There were no contracts with these people; they were quotations.

Q. Amounting to contracts?—A. Yes, I suppose they would be called contracts.

Q. You are not afraid of the expression ' contracts '?—A. No; but it was not a formal drawn-up contract. We asked those people for prices on certain tanks, air compressors and gasoline engines, and they wrote and said they beg to quote so and so.

Q. Well, that is the way contracts are frequently made?—A. Yes, we call them quotations.

Q. Now, what were the contract prices for these plants?—A. Well, we have that made, I have a list.

Q. Yes. Give me the list of the contracts.—A. (Witness goes for papers.)

Q. Bring the whole bundle so that we will not have to go backward and forward for it, please.

Q. (Witness having returned) What does this show?—A. That is each station and the contract prices.

Q. The contract price of what?—A. For the plants for each station.

Q. You mean as supplied to the department?—A. Yes.

Q. It is not what I asked you, Mr. Northey. I asked for the contract showing the prices paid to the manufacturers?—A. Oh, well, that would take a stack of letters as high as that (indicating about a foot).

Q. Well, have you got any of them?—A. I have not one here.

Q. But you have contracts?—A. We have quotations.

Q. From the manufacturers?—A. Yes.

Q. Why did you produce this?—A. I understood you to say you wanted the cost of each station, what the government paid?

Q. No. I am talking of the cost to yourselves.

By Hon. Mr. Cassels:

Q. Mr. Mearns said the people with whom you dealt made a profit, but a small profit, on the plant. That is his statement yesterday. Now, you say you made that at a loss?—A. Yes. But, my lord, we bought those things from these people and we quoted them to the government.

Q. Did you sell to the government at a less price than you paid the manufacturers?—A. I think we did.

3262—11½

Q. You think. That is a different thing?—A. There was not a penny made.

Q. You may not have made a penny; you did not lose?—A. For example, the last two plants we made I know we lost $100. It was on $1,000.

Q. We want to get the facts now, and the sooner we get to them the better. The point is simply this, that Mr. Watson is asking. You made a profit from the government on this diaphone of $4,000 or thereabouts which cost $600; you went outside to the manufacturers and bought the plant that had to go with that, and you sold that plant to the government at a price which recouped you what you paid for that plant. Apparently at present your profit was about $4,000 on a $600 machine. That is what Mr. Watson is driving at?—A. Quite so.

By Mr Watson:

Q. That is the position?—A. That is right.

Hon. Mr. CASSELS.—That is really what it comes to.

By Mr Watson:

Q. So on the plant part you are practically even, according to the statement you made now to his lordship, and your profits are on the diaphone?—A. That is quite right.

Q. The diaphone is what you have the patent upon?—A. Yes. We have no patent on the plant.

Q. Well, how much profit have you made out of the plant, occasionally $1,000 on each plant?—A. No.

Q. Not quite that much?—A. Our books would not show that, we have not figured that way.

Q. Why do you say your books do not show that?—A. Our books should not show that.

Q. Do you not keep a record of your business transactions?—A. We have a record and I know of no great profit on the transactions with the government.

Q. You mean on the whole transactions ?—A. Yes.

Q. Your books show that profit?—A. I think so.

Q. Let me see the book you were trying to get yesterday.—A. What book yesterday?

Q. The book showing the profit on the transactions with the government ?—A. Well, where are the books ?

Q. Well, Mr. Northey——A. I have not the books in my pocket.

Hon. Mr. CASSELS.—Mr. Mearns had them.

Mr. WATSON.—Yes.

By Mr Watson:

Q. Are those the books, you are familiar with the business of the company?—A. Yes, but I am not familiar with the books.

Q. You are familiar with the business ?—A. I never had my hands on those books.

Q. You were just saying the books would show a profit on the transactions with the government?—A. I had a statement figured at the end of a certain year, we had made 29 per cent on transactions with the government.

Q. Those books show a great deal more than that?—A. At that time they did not.

Hon. Mr. Cassels:

Q. That is 39 per cent on the capital stock?—A. No, my lord. I am speaking of transactions with the government. At that time the profit showed 29 per cent on the total transactions with the government.

Q. Mr. Mearns mentioned a dividend of 150 per cent in one year alone. He calls it a bonus; I call it a dividend.—A. I am not speaking of bonus or dividend.

By `Mr Watson:

Q. Who knows most about the financial business of the company?—A. Mr. earns.

Q. Mr. Mearns knows most about it?—A. Yes.

.Q. He is most familiar—who is most familiar with the books?—A. I suppose Mr. earns. I have not had anything to do with the books.

Q. But you have had a good deal to do, of course, with your own personal receipts rom the company?—A. Yes, I know what that is. I don't know to-day. The books how that.

.Q. You got the patents without any cash expenditure?—A. I got the patent in this manner, if I may explain.

Q. Have you not explained already?—A. No.

Q. Upon a royalty basis?—A. I have not explained how I got them.

Q. I do not care about the different negotiations.—A. I was not going to speak of the negotiations.

Hon. Mr. Cassels:

Q. Did you pay anything for them except royalty?—A. They had to sell their patent to me.

Q. That is not the question. Did you pay anything except royalty?—A. No.

By Mr. Watson:

Q. Then the patent was transferred to you and you sold some interest in it to Mr. Mearns?—A. Yes.

Q. And to Mr.——?—A. Forbes.

Q. Yes. How much did you get from Mr. Mearns?—A. The same as from Mr. Forbes.

Q. Oh, my stars?—A. 100 cents to the dollar.

Q. That is not an answer?—A. Par.

Q. How much money did you get from Mr. Mearns?—A. $10,000.

Q. Did you get that, did you really receive that?—A. Yes.

Q. How much from Mr. Forbes?—A. $10,000.

Q. Not in kind, but in cash?—A. In cash.

Q. In cash?—A. Well it was a note. The note was paid.

Q. And that left you then with $80,000?—A. Yes.

Q. Then you transferred that patent to the company?—A. Yes.

Q. At $100,000?—A. Yes.

Q. That is right, is it?—A. Yes.

Q. And that $100,000 formed the capital of the company?—A. The capital stock of the company.

Q. Then 80 per cent of the stock was issued to you, 10 per cent to Mr. Mearns, and another 10 per cent to Mr. Forbes?—A. That is right.

Q. That is the way it stood?—A. Right.

Q. There was no cash capital put in; that is right, is it?—A. We each put in so much.

Q. I did not ask you that. You put in the patent, you put that in at $100,000?—A. Yes.

Q. And that is the capital stock?—A. Yes, but there was cash put in afterwards to do business with.

Q. Mr. Mearns said you borrowed some money from the bank?—A. Yes, we borrowed from ourselves and paid it back.

Q. Then the company borrowed some money from you; that is right, is it?—A. Yes.

Q. That is the way the business was run?—A. Yes.

Q. There was no cash capital in the company?—A. No, it was all patents.

Q. Yes, all patents. So there was no cash investment in the company. Now, during the last year and a half how much have you drawn out of the company yourself?—A. I cannot tell you.

Q. About how much?—A. Well, it would only be a guess.

Q. Make your guess, please?—A. The last year and a half—well, it might be $50,000.

Q. $50,000?—A. It might be.

Q. It might be $75,000?—A. I do not think so.

Q. It might be in that neighbourhood?—A. I do not know. ⊥ do not know what it is.

Q. Eh?—A. I do not know what we have drawn out the last half year.

Q. The last year and a half?—A. ⊥ear and a half.

Q. I should think a man would be able to state within a thousand dollars what money he has got within a year and a half from the company?—A. I have got money from other concerns.

Q. Eh?—A. From other sources.

Q. In connection with the company?—A. In connection with this company.

Q. Not in connection with this business?—A. No.

Q. You mean you have so much money you cannot keep track of it?—A. I keep track of it, but I am busy. I am in England half my time.

By Hon. Mr. Cassels:

Q. Mr. Northey, you can surely tell within $5,000 for the past year and a half?—A. I could not.

By Mr. Watson:

Q. You could not tell how much profit you have got within $6,000?—A. I could not.

Q. Can you tell within $10,000?—A. No, I cannot, really.

Q. Can you tell within $20,000 the amount you got?—A. No, I could only guess.

Q. What profits that you have made during the last year and a half in the dealings with the Department of Marine and Fisheries?—A. I could not tell you, but the books will show what I have drawn, Mr. Watson.

Q. I see. And everything has been done upon that basis in the transactions between your company and the department that you cannot tell within $20,000 your receipts for a year and a half?—A. I do not know what you mean exactly.

Q. I am just seeking to apply your answer, which is so indefinite. Then how much did you get before the year and a half?—A. Well, I do not know.

Q. How much have you received, $40,000 a year yourself since the company commenced its transactions with the department?—A. I do not think so.

Q. About that?—A. No, I would not think that at all.

Q. Well, how much have you received, do you think?—A. I cannot tell you what I have received.

Q. That is the queerest thing in the world to me, Mr. Northey. You have been a manufacturer?—A. Yes.

Q. Known amongst us as a sharp, accurate, shrewd business man?—A. Not too shrewd, I don't think.

Q. A good financial man?—A. Not a financial man. I have never been a financial man at all.

Q. Can you tell within $20,000 the amount you have received personally in profits during the last 6 years?—I think it might amount to $150,000.

Q. What?—A. It might amount to $150,000.

Q. During what period?—A. During the last 5 or 6 years.

Q. During the last 5 or 6 years?—A. Yes.

Q. You may have received $150,000 yourself?—A. Yes.

Q. That is representing your 80 per cent of the $100,000 for the patent. I see. I see on two or three occasions you have drawn as much as $20,000 each time?—A. Yes, that is right, I think.

Q. What is that?—A. I think that is right.

Q. You think that is right. Was that dividend?—A. That would be dividends.

Q. That would be dividends?

By Hon. Mr. Cassels:

Q. Or bonus?—A. Or bonus.

Mr. Watson:

Q. For instance, I see on October 3rd—I see, Mr. Northey, in this book marked Ledger Exhibit No. 16, commencing in September, 1906, and ending April, 1908, a little more than a year and a half—will you look here, stand up here, please—On October 3rd you apparently received $20,000 in cash?—A. Yes.

Q. That was dividend, was it?—A. Yes.

Q. And then, leaving out some smaller sums, on March 4th you got another dividend of $8,000?—A. Yes.

Q. And then some small drawings, and on September 7th you got another dividend of $20,000?—A. Yes.

Q. So within a year, that is from October 3rd, 1906, to September 7th, 1907, you drew out in the neighbourhood of $50,000?—A. That is right.

Q. $50,000 within a year. And then I find further small drawings, and on April 1st, 1908, you drew out another sum of $20,000?—A. That is right.

Q. This would indicate, then, you are drawing in the neighbourhood of $50,000 a year for yourself?—A. For that one year.

Q. Well, it is coming on into the next year, 1908, the same apparently, and I suppose that is a fair indication of the profits that are being made by the company? —A. Yes.

Q. And your partners, that is Mr. Mearns and Mr. Forbes, are of course drawing the same proportion?—A. Quite so.

Q. And that profit is being made out of diaphones and plant supplied to the department?—A. Yes.

Q. Limited to that?—A. Yes.

Q. No other means of revenue, no other business?—A. No.

By Hon. Mr. Cassels:

Q. And after paying royalty, I understand?—A. After paying our debts and liabilities.

By Mr. Watson:

Q. And in respect of that you have no cash invested in the business. You have your patent and you put in your time, or part of your time?—A. That is quite so.

Q. That is the position?—A. Yes.

Q. No other such profitable business, I suppose, as that in the country. Why do you charge such prices to the government in view of this condition of affairs?—A. Well, we put in one plant in Cape Race, for instance——

Q. Never mind about the illustration. Why do you charge such prices?—A. Because I suppose it is worth it to the government.

Q. What?—A. I suppose the government is willing to pay it.

Q. You mean because you can get it?—A. But we say other governments——

Q. Just wait, please. It is because you can get it?—A. Yes. If they do not pay that they won't get the instrument.

Q. That is, you take the most you can get?—A. That is the usual way in business.

Q. And if you could not get that much you would have to be content with what you could get ?—A. We would not cut the price a penny. I can tell you why.

Q. Just wait please. One at a time. You would not cut the price a penny ?—A. That is right.

Q. Now, this means, you see, at this rate that you are making about $70,000 a year profit ?—A. And why not ?

Q. Of course, why not ?—A. Why not ?

Q. And you say you would not take any less ?

By Hon. Mr. Cassels :

Q. There is no imputation against you; you can get whatever you like. The point Mr. Watson is trying to make is this: The government should have made inquiries through their officers as to what was a reasonable price, and if they had done so you would not have got these prices.—A. I suppose the government did that, my lord.

By Mr. Watson :

. Do you know ?—A. I do not know what goes on.

. Were you ever asked the cost price of these ?—A. I would not have——

. Were you ever asked ?—A. Yes.

. By whom ?—A. Colonel Anderson.

. When did he ask you ?—A. He said it was a big price.

. Was that the question ?—A. You asked me when I was asked:

. Yes.—A. It was back when I made the contract in 1902.

Q. What did he ask you at that time ?—A. Well, he asked us to make him a price for plant for half a dozen different stations, Cape Race and several others, and I made him a price, and he said if we made 25 per cent it would be enough for us to make.

Q. He said so ?—A. Yes. I said it would not. An ordinary manufacturer without any protection made 25 per cent, and I said we should make 33 per cent, and I would not come to his price.

Q. You would not come to his price ?—A. No.

Q. What did he offer you ?—A. He said, ' If you make 25 per cent it is all you should make.' I said, ' An ordinary manufacturer makes 25 per cent,' and even in the business I was in that was not protected by patents at all we made sometimes 40 per cent.

Q. In what ?—A. Hydraulic engineering business.

Q. Of course, when you say the ordinary manufacturer makes 25 per cent, that has not been the condition of affairs for a great many years in this country ?—A. Yes it has. I beg to differ.

Q. An ordinary manufacturer makes 25 per cent profit ?—A. I know a number of businesses—I need not mention them here—that are making 25 per cent.

Q. The average profit is not more than 10 or 12 per cent ?—A. I do not know, I have not seen the balance sheets of a great many concerns, but I know I made—I am speaking of some of the articles we sold the government.

Q. Oh, yes, some special articles ?—A. You are speaking of the volume of trade as a whole?

Q. The volume of trade as a whole. The average profit of manufacturers where they make a profit at all, where they are prosperous?—A. I think they make 20 per cent.

Q. 20 per cent ?—A. I know we did in my business at the end of the year.

Q. Now, reverting. You saw Colonel Anderson in 1902, and he then stated to you he thought 25 per cent should be enough for you ?—A. Yes.

Q. What did you say to that ?—A. I said it was a patent article, and if it would do the work he claimed it would himself it was worth 33 per cent.

Q. 33 per cent ?—A. Yes. We thought over it. I put in prices on that basis, and there was nothing ever put in.

Q. That was in 1902 ?—A. 1902 or 1901 probably.

Q. Now, then, has he ever discussed the price with you since then to your recollection?—A. I do not know that he has. I believe the prices were all based on those prices.

Hon. Mr. Cassels:

Q. How many orders did you get at that time?—A. About six or eight, my lord.

By Mr Watson:

Q. Amounting to how much?—A. $56,000.

Q. That is $56,000 out of half a million. And you say the question of price has never since been mentioned by Colonel Anderson to yourself?—A. I do not think it. I am not sure about that. You know, we never asked the Canadian government for an order.

Q. Wait, please. Now, then, who told him the cost of the diaphone, did you?—A. The cost of the diaphone was not entered into at that time.

Q. Who told him at any time the cost of the diaphone, do you know?—A. I do not know who told him.

Q. Because he made the statement to his lordship that he understood the cost of the diaphone was between $200 and $300?—A. It was not taken into account.

Q. That is, the diaphone you charged in the neighbourhood of $4,000 for, he understood cost about $400?—A. Yes, it cost fully that.

Q. Did he ever speak to you about that, about the disparity?—A. I do not think so, I am not sure.

Q. And have you ever been asked since for a reduction of price?—A. Well, we may have been. I am not sure.

Q. Do you make your annual returns to the government showing the profits of the business?—A. The provincial government.

Q. Where is your charter, provincial or Dominion?—A. Provincial. We made returns, we fill out returns.

Q. I see?—A. I know I have sent half a dozen returns to the government. We send one in every year.

Q. And those show the profits that are made?—A. I do not think you have to in Ontario, have you?

Q. Well, we will not go into that just now. Then at all events that is the course of the business. Now, you recognize, do you not, Mr. Northey, as a business man, that as between vendor and purchaser, if I may use the expression, it is an unconscionable profit?—A. I do not agree with you at all. I do not agree with you at all. When you consider the importance of the instrument.

Q. You do not agree?—A. No, I do not. If you were off the coast of Newfoundland on a foggy day you might think so.

Q. Think what?—A. That it is not a large price.

Q. I am not asking about the usefulness of the diaphone at all. I am speaking about the cost and the selling price?—A. You cannot separate the two, as I understand.

Q. Why not?—A. Because it is the value of the instrument that makes it worth the price, its utility.

Q. That is the value of the instrument wholly distinct from its cost?—A. Quite so.

Q. So if you could get $10,000 for each one you would think yourself justified?—A. I think so.

Q. I see. Instead of $4,000. Why didn't you ask $10,000 instead of $4,000?—A. Because we had to deal with all the governments, and we wanted to deal with them on the same basis.

Q. What other governments have you been dealing with?—A. The British government, the American government, and the Newfoundland government.

Q. When did you commence to deal with the British government?—A. Three years ago, two and a half.

Q. Have you sold diaphones to the British government?—A. They have made tests and are making tests now, I know.

Q. You have not made any sales?—A. No, we have been in treaty.

Q. You have not had any selling price pass between you and the British government?—A. Yes, they have asked for prices.

Q. They probably won't take them at that price, they will be very foolish if they do?—A. It has to be submitted to the board of trade.

Q. So you have not had any transactions with the British government?—A. Only testing and quoting prices.

Q. You know what I mean?—A. We have had no money transactions.

Q. No money transactions?—A. We have as a matter of fact, we have the Admiralty.

Q. You have supplied the Admiralty with these diaphones?—A. Yes.

Q. Have you sold these same diaphones?—A. The Admiralty have ordered one for the battleship *Dominion.* We put it on. It was just erected last week, the week before last.

Q. Why did you tell me a week ago you had not sold any?—A. I was speaking of the fog alarm business. The British government have different branches.

Q. Of course, that is not for the diaphone?—A. Yes.

Q. The same kind of instrument?—A. Quite the same.

Q. How much will you sell that for?—A· We have not quoted a price yet.

Q. So you do not know what you will get?—A. They have ordered and they will pay the price whatever it is.

Q. That is the beauty of dealing with governments?—A. They are pretty hard people to deal with.

Q. They pay any price. Have you dealt with any other government?—A. Newfoundland. We have put in 10 or 12.

Q. Within what period?—A. The last four years.

Q. When did you commence that?—A. I think about four years ago; we have orders now for one or two.

Q. And you have sold 10 or 12?—A. About 10.

Q. And what prices have you got from them?—A. The same prices as we get here.

Q. How much less, Mr. Northey, about how much?—A· Which?

Q. About how much less price have you got upon those than from this department here?—A. We have got more.

Q. Eh?—A. Our quotations there are higher.

Q. I know. Quotation is one thing, cash is another?—A. No, it is the same thing.

Q· What is the difference in price between what you receive from the Newfoundland government and this government?—A. I should think 5 per cent higher. I know we made a point of quoting them 5 per cent higher.

Q. You made a point of quoting them 5 per cent higher?—A. Yes.

Q. And you got what you quoted?—A. Yes. There was no cut of any kind.

Q. What?—A. There was not a cut of a penny·

Q. Any request for a cut?—A. They asked for prices. We gave prices.

Q. I did not ask you that?—A. They only asked, 'is that your lowest price?' We said yes.

Q. That is the only government you have been dealing with?—A. The only government.

Q. So you have had this department, and the department in Newfoundland you have supplied with 10 or 12 diaphones?—A. Yes·

Q. And that has been your whole business up to this time?—A. Yes. That is for fog signal work.

Q. Yes. The prices for the Newfoundland government were based on the prices received here?—A. Yes.

By Hon. Mr. Cassels:

Q. Is it patented there?—A. Yes, my lord.

By Mr. Watson:

Q. Now, have you ever discussed these prices with the deputy minister?—A. No. have only met——

Q. Have you had any communication with him?—A. All the letters you have, signed by him, and our reply goes to the deputy minister.

Q. That is through the branch, I suppose. We know that, as a matter of fact?—A. Yes.

Q. But you have not with any one in the department, except on the one occasion ·ou have spoken of in 1902, had any discussion on the question of prices?—A. I don't hink 't.

Q. You don't think so?—A. I don't think so· We have tendered, you know.

Q. Of course, you would be prepared to take less if you could not get more?—A. o, we would not, because it spoils our business in other countries. We must charge veryone equally.

Q. What?—A. We must charge all countries on the same basis.

Q. Yes. But you fixed your standard here?—A. Yes, and we are going to stand o that.

By Hon. Mr. Cassels:

Q. You see, in England they may amend the patent laws and you will find your-elves out?—A. I offered, my lord, to submit to arbitration the whole thing.

By Mr. Watson:

Q. I see you are willing to submit to arbitration?—A. Yes.

Q. As to what price you will sell for?—A. As to what price we will sell at and what price the government would make it direct.

Q. The government would make it themselves?—A. That is the same as we suggested in England.

Q. No doubt half the price would pay an immense profit still?—A. It depends on the volume of business.

Q. But on the basis of the business already done?—A. I do not know what it is worth to the government. That is our way of looking at it.

Q. You mean the extent to which they can be held up?—A. No, we do not hold anyone up.

Q. What?—A. We are not holding anyone up.

Q. You are demanding a price and refusing to supply the article unless you get that price.

By Hon. Mr. Cassels:

Q. I suppose he meant that owning the patent they can put whatever price they choose on the article?—A. It is a question.

By Mr. Watson:

Q. What is the length it has to run?—A. 14 years.

Hon. Mr. CASSELS.—18 years.

By Mr. Watson:

Q. It began?—A. It began this year, one of them.

Q. And they are likely to continue in force?—A. Until something else comes better we will be able to do business.

Q. And there has not been any improvement upon them during the last ten years or more?--A. No.

Q. You do not anticipate that?—A. I hope not.

Q. I see. So according to your view you have a life legacy in that way?—A. I do not know about a life legacy.

Q. I see. Life premium.

Hon. Mr. Cassels.—It is to be hoped he will live longer than the patent.

Mr. Watson.—I suppose so.

Q. Now then, Mr. Northey, you ask that an opportunity should be given to you to justify this condition of affairs. What have you to say in justification of this extraordinary condition?—A. Well, you seem to think the prices are too high. Now, I came in on the *Victorian* last week at Sydney, and we had 1,500 bags of mail and 1,200 passengers, and we had to lay outside that harbour—there is no fog signal there, at least it is an obsolete type, none of ours—we had to lay out there 8 hours until the fog lifted. Now, if the government put in a fog signal and paid $5,000 or whatever it is, I think it would pay them handsomely.

Q. Yes. Anything else?—A. Cape Race, there have been thousands of lives lost there and millions of money so the wreck chart shows, and we made there $4,000 on that plant, and it has been heard out 45 miles by the *Empress of Britain* or *Ireland,* I am not sure which, and the old instrument could not be heard anywhere, it could not be depended on. This keeps ships off the rocks, and it is surely worth 33 to 35 per cent profit to us out of the government. We have not made any more than that on the turn over, and it think it is remarkably cheap.

Q. What turn over?—A. On the turn over to the government. I think we supplied one diaphone without plant. I am quite satisfied we have not made 35 per cent profit on our dealings with the Canadian government.

Q. I must protest against that statement as I understand the facts.—A. I shall be glad to be corrected if that is not true.

Q. The diaphone costs $600?—A. I am taking the whole transaction with the government.

Q. So am I?—A. We only supplied one at that price, $4,600, without the plant.

Q. I am taking it with the plant. The diaphone you sell for $4,600 costing you $500 or $600?—A. Yes.

Q. The plant with it you make, you come out even on?—A. I do not think we do at the end of the year, we do not apparently.

Q. Well, it is not much either way?—A. There appears to be a good deal one way.

Q. So there is a profit of $4,000 on a sale of $12,000?—A. No. I am saying in our whole transactions with the government we have not made I do not remember 35 per cent. Supposing we got $500,000 from the government, $500,000 worth of work, that would be $170,000 profit, would it not? 35 per cent on $500,000 is $170,000 thereabouts.

Q. Yes?—A. I maintain we have not made more than an ordinary profit.

Q. You have just said you have been drawing $75,000 profit a year?

Hon. Mr. Cassels:

Q. Mr. Northey, the selling of this diaphone is the whole business of your company?—A. Yes.

Q. Very well. That is what you are incorporated and what you are carrying on business for?—A. Quite so.

Q. This thing costs $600 and you get $4,600 for it. The plant you have made by other manufacturers, and you come out about even on that, Mr. Mearns said a little profit?—A. We do not at the end of the year.

Q. How much——?—A. The book will show we do not make——

Q. How much is the cost of the plant at the end of the year?—A. It is easy to estimate the cost of the plant, but at the end of the year it is always a great deal more.

By Mr Watson:

Q. Let us see the books.—A. I will try and figure it up. Can I be called again n a few minutes?

Q. Yes, if you want to be.—A. May I have the books?

Hon. Mr. Cassels:

Q. We want to get at that. You may lose on the plant?—A. We have at the end f the year

Q. Let us know what it is. It looks here as if you were making an enormous rofit. It may be taken together you made a loss.—A. May I do that now?

By Mr. Watson:

Q. In a minute or two when we get through. I was taking for granted Mr. earns knows more about it than you. We have had his statements. Now, your peronal negotiations have been with whom?—A. Colonel Anderson.

Q. No one else?—A. No one else.

Q. During the whole period?—A. We got an order from the commissioner of ights.

Q. When?—A. That was, I suppose, the first order, three years ago.

Q. That is Mr. Fraser?—A. Mr. J. F. Fraser.

Q. An order for what?—A. Well we got an order for—I cannot tell you how many lants now.

Q. Why did not that come from Colonel Anderson?—A. I do not know anything bout that. We got the first order through Colonel Anderson and then apparently hat part of the department was turned over to the commissioner of lights, I don't now why.

Q. You cannot explain?—A. No, I do not know anything about that.

Q. Then the one transaction you had with him?—A. I think there were two.

Q. Then all the other transactions with Colonel Anderson?—A. Yes, those are the only two people I have dealt with.

Q. And how do you get paid, cash?—A. Cheque.

Q. Cheque on delivery?—A. No. After delivery, well, it may be three or four months.

Q. And what discount do you allow?—A. No discount.

Q. Why not?—A. Because it is a net cash deal.

Q. Have you ever been asked for discounts?—A. No, that was the price agreed on.

Q. Eh?—A. That was the price agreed on.

Q. You get a discount from the manufacturer, do you not?—A. The manufacturer quotes us $1——

Q. Do you not get discounts from the manufacturer of the plant?—A. It depends. If selling list price he does not.

Q. I am asking on the prices you pay. You pay those after a discount?—A. No. If we ask a price wor a 12-horse power gasoline engine, which they use in the department, he says $600. That is the price. No discount on that.

Q. No discount?—A. Absolutely none.

Q. You usually get discount?—A. There are lists subject to discount.

Q. Then why do you not allow discount, because you have a monopoly?—A. No. You are on the wrong basis altogether. We entered into a contract with this government to supply them with plants at a certain price. Now, why should they ask us for discounts? It would be laughable after you have put in a price. Whoever would do such a thing?

Q. I see. Have you had a continuing contract since 1902?—A. No. Contracts were called for after that date, and I think they last for a year.

Q. Your last contract apparently is for three years, is it not?—A. Perhaps it was three years.

Q. 1906 ?—A. Three years, likely.

Q. And has that been terminated ?—A. They are asking for tenders again.

Q. I ask you, has this contract been terminated ?—A. What do you mean by that, cancelled ? It terminates automatically, does it not ?

Q. Have you received notice terminating this contract ?—A. I do not think we have. I have not seen any notice. It terminates automatically, does it not ?

Q. I am not asking you that. Have you not received notice within the last 3 months terminating this contract ?—A. I do not know, I have only returned from England. I have been there, with the exception of two weeks, since the 1st of January.

Q. And you say tenders are now being asked for ?—A. Yes.

Q. Tenders from the public ?—A. They are published in the papers. Tenders are asked for fog signals.

Q. What is the use of doing that sort of thing ?—A. I do not know. I thought it was foolish myself.

Q. I think you are the only makers ?—A. They have called for tenders. I noticed it in the papers in Quebec.

Q. On this diaphone, this same design ?—A. I do not know about the diaphone. They have asked for plants.

Q. That is a different thing. They can get plants from any manufacturer ?—A. Quite so. There were tenders asked before.

Q. That would be reasonable then to ask tenders for plants?—A. Yes.

Q. It is not necessary to get them from your company ?—A. Not at all.

Q. That can be obtained from any manufacturer ?—A. Yes.

Q. And you would sell the diaphone without the plant ?—A. Yes. We would be glad to get rid of the plant nuisance.

Q. So the field is open for any amount of competition for that plant ?—A. It was open before.

Q. And has been open ?—A. Yes.

Q. But why ask for tenders on the diaphone if you are the only manufacturer and the only patentee ?—A. I do not know why they did that.

Q. That has been asked for ?—A. I do not know it has been.

Q. I thought you said so ?—A. I have not seen the specification. I understood they asked for tenders for plants and instruments.

Q. Now, what other fog signals are being used besides yours ?—A. Only the sirens and Reids and explosives.

Q. You claim they are a little less efficient ?—A. Considerably less efficient when you can hear ours and cannot hear the others at all.

Q. Well, you claim there is a difference ?—A. Quite a difference in that respect.

Q. But the others are in general use in practically all other countries ?—A. All other countries.

Q. And what is good for other countries, is it not good enough for us ?—A. Yes; but this is new and the others are old, they are now taking this up.

Q. I see?—A. The United States government has asked me to make a test in New York harbour.

Q. So this department took this up——?—A. First.

Q. First; and taking it up first they took it up on the basis and prices you have spoken of, which have been maintained?—A. Yes.

Q. There being no competition. Then do you propose to put in tenders?—A. Yes.

Q. Of course, you will take such prices as you can get, making a reasonable profit?—A. I cannot say what our prices will be. It is hardly fair. There might be some competitors here.

Q. I see. You cannot say what your prices will be. So it is a matter of competition and what you can get and what will be given?—A. A matter of efficiency altogether.

Q. What?—A. A matter of efficiency.

Q. A matter of what?—A. Efficiency; which is the most efficient instrument. If a man has that and is protected, then he gets his price.

Q. What is the price of the sirens?—A. Well, we paid £300.

Q. What does the government pay, do you know?—A. I do not know what the government pay, but I know I bought one as a standard to test by, and they charged me £300 or £350.

Q. That is about $1,500 to $1,600?—A. Yes.

Q. As against $4,500, $5,000 or $6,000?—A. Yes.

Q. Your most expensive diaphone is how much?—A. $6,000, I believe.

Q. Is that the highest?—A. That is the highest we have sold.

Q. So about $4,500 up to $6,000?—A. No. They are from $200 up to $6,000. It depends on the size.

Q. $200 up to $6,000, I see. What commissions do you pay?—A. What commissions?

Q. Yes, upon transactions?—A. Well, I suppose Mr. Millett of New York, he is trying to make arrangements, he probably wants 10 per cent.

Q. Who is Millett?—A. He is a man who travels all round the world and sells this sort of apparatus.

Q. So you are willing to give him whatever you have to give?—A. I think our company in England would give him 10 per cent; I am not sure.

Q. You own that company for the most part, that is yours?—A. Yes.

Q. So you are prepared to pay whatever commission is necessary to be paid?—A. I cannot expect a man to work for nothing, of course.

Q. Of course. And in the same way, commssion, of course, is the same thing as discount, it amounts to the same thing?—A. Not exactly the same.

Q. Well, if you don't pay commission——?—A. You pay commission to a man when he is working for you——

By Hon. Mr. Cassels:

Q. A commission for getting orders?—A. And discount is for buying.

By Mr. Watson:

Q. What commissions have you paid on sales here?—A. I have done business direct here with the department. We have not paid any commissions here.

Q. Why have you not?—A. We don't want to pay commissions to the government.

Q. What commissions have been paid to officials?—A. None. Not a dollar, not a penny.

Q. Not a penny?—A. Not one penny.

Q. What commission has been paid for facilitating your business?—A. We never asked Colonel Anderson for an order. He asked us to come down and quote. We never ran after this government.

Q. Do you mean you were not particular about doing business with the government?—A. We were not quite ready, and he was anxious to deal.

Q. When were you not quite ready?—A. In 1902.

Q. Well, let us get down to modern times, the present time, that was a small transaction in 1902 comparatively?—A. Yes, but it fixed prices for all future dates.

Q. You seeking to do business and soliciting orders?—A. Not at all. We have not solicited one order yet.

Q. You are anxious to sell, it increases your profits?—A. Yes.

Q. You are looking for people in that respect?—A. Yes, a little.

Q. Then, who has done the solicitation?—A. No one; that is from our side.

Q. No one at all?—A. Absolutely no one.

Q. You have been standing back?—A. No, we were not ready at that time.

Q. I am not talking about that time. I am referring to 1905, 1906 and 1907?—A. We were not down here seeking orders, we were not here at all.

Q. It has been a matter of compliment and favour to the government rather than to yourselves, then?—A. Well, they want the instruments.

Q. Well, then, what benefit have any of the officials obtained?—A. There has not been one official who has got one penny of benefit from our company, not one official, not one penny. There has not been one penny given to any official in the government.

Q. Not in that way, you mean?—A. Commission or bribery, whatever you like to call it, there has been no money given them at all. We came here on Colonel Anderson's invitation and closed up those orders. Then Mr. J. F. Fraser came up to our place—it was the first time I think I ever met him—and he said a lot of the plants were obsolete and he wanted quotations for new plants.

Q. That is for new plants?—A. For new plants, and we gave him prices.

Q. When was that?—A. I think that was 1904.

Q. Yes?—A. I am not sure of the year.

Q. Any time since?—A. There was another order came a year afterwards, I think.

Q. And Mr. B. H. Fraser, the assistant of Colonel Anderson, you had to do with him?—A. Only in details. He has never ordered any.

Q. Has he been up to see you, to visit you?—A. Frequently. I have been down to see him to-day. There is a drawing I went to show him.

Q. Frequently to see you. And what provision do you make for expenses of officials?—A. Why, if we go anywhere we get expenses.

Q. What?—A. If we go anywhere we get money for expenses.

Q. You mean you pay expenses?—A. No, if I go anywhere. You say what provision do we make for expenses?

Q. But the officials?—A. The government can pay.

Q. I know they can do so; but why do you pay the expenses of the officials?—A. We never paid a dollar expense of the officials.

Q. Do you mean that?—A. Certainly. Why should we? The government pay their expenses.

Q. That is your answer?—A. That is my answer.

Q. The government is able to pay?—A. You know my answer is I have not paid. I do not know who paid their expenses, I suppose the government did.

Q. Now, you are aware that officials have been already charged with having committed dishonest and unfaithful acts?—A. That is common report. That is all I know.

Q. Now, I want to know to what extent you have personal knowledge of that?—A. I have no personal knowledge, absolutely none.

Q. What presents have you made to officials?—A. Never. Perhaps a cigar. I have not made a present to the value of $1 to any official either of this government or any other.

Q. You have asked them to go with you to different places?—A. No. They have asked me; I never asked them.

Q. They have been with you to New York, some of them?—A. I think we went down there to see an oil engine—yes, Mr. B. H. Fraser went.

Q. Why did he go down there to see an oil engine?—A. He wanted to see the same engine adopted by the department. He went to Chicago also.

Q. He wanted to have one adopted by the department?—A. He was sent there by his chief, I understand.

Q. Colonel Anderson?—A. I don't know. He gave him authority, I suppose.

Q. When was that?—A. Perhaps 4 years ago, perhaps 5.

Q. Any other occasion?—A. Yes, Chicago.

Q. When was that?—A. About the same time.

Q. Any other occasions?—A. Well, he has been up to Toronto, of course, a number of times.

Q. And you frequently go on trips together?—A. We did at that time.

Q. And continue to do so?—A. No, we do not now.

Q. You pay his expenses on those occasions?—A. I do not.

Q. Do you not?—A. Why should I?

Q. I am not asking you why you should.—A. I do not pay his expenses. I have ever paid a dollar of his expenses, except perhaps to pay for a lunch and he would ay for a lunch.

Q. Then, did you see the commissioners, Mr. Fyshe and Mr. Bazin ?—A. Did I ee them ?

Q. Yes?—A. No.

Q. While they were making their investigation ?—A. No.

Q. How does it come that that report contains no reference whatever to transac-ions with your company ?—A. I suppose they thought the transactions were clean.

Q. I see. Not worthy of comment. Because you are aware that that report con‡ ains no reference whatever to transactions with your company and the large prices eing paid ?—A. I suppose they thought they were right.

Hon. Mr. CASSELS.—Is that correct, Mr. Watson ?

Mr. WATSON.—Yes.

Hon. Mr. CASSELS.—I was under the impression they do refer to those transactions.

Mr. WATSON.—No, my lord.

Hon. Mr. CASSELS.—Perhaps it is the other one, the gas buoys.

Mr. WATSON.—Yes. The Willson Company; there is no reference to this at all nywhere.

Q. Now, can you account for that discrimination, because apparently it is dis-rimination ?—A. Which is discrimination ?

Q. The discrimination in your favour that there is no reference made in that eport to these transactions with you, and your company has been getting much the ighest profit apparently of anyone dealing with the department so far as ascertained t present ?—A. I cannot swear to anything. I suppose they looked through all the apers and found the business is straight.

Q. At all events it appears that Colonel Anderson knew of the profits that were eing obtained ?—A. Well, he is an intelligent man. Of course, he knew about the rofit. He did not know anything about the royalties, of course.

Q. I think that will do.

By Hon. Mr. Cassels :

Q. I want to ask you a question, Mr. Northey. I would like to understand vhat that plant is that goes with the diaphone, what is the nature of it ?—A. I can ;ive you a drawing, my lord.

Q. Cannot you describe it?—A. It is composed of in most cases two gasoline ngines, some two or three compressors and one to six tanks, large air tanks, and the iping and fittings to connect up all this plant, and the instrument.

Q. Could the old plant used for the siren be used for your siren ?—A. Oh yes.

Q. The same plant ?—A. Yes. but the Canadian government had not any of hese plants in existence.

Q. I am just asking the question, the same plant was used formerly for the siren? —A. They had only two.

Q. They could get it in the market, and then buy from you the diaphone ?—A. Yes, the diaphone.

Q. You were not bound to sell the plant only for the horn ?—A. I think the law eads that way.

Q. It is the other way?—A. I think the law reads that we have to sell at a reason-ble price. The matter is, what is a reasonable price for the duty performed ?

Q. That is a question. You think $4,600 for a thing that cost $600 is a reason-ble price ?—A. When you consider the duty performed, the benefit.

Q. That is your solution ?—A. Yes.

By Mr. Watson :

Q. Then I understand, Mr. Northey, you are to prepare that statement ?—A. Yes, I will do that at once.

By Hon. Mr. Cassels :

Q. Would you say what loss you have suffered from the plant ?—A. I can swear there was no profit.

Q. You swear there was no profit ?—A. From the plant ?

Q. Yes?—A. I mean not loss from the whole business. I do not know I can find that from these books. What I propose is to show the net profits on the transactions with the government.

Q. The net profits on the balance. You say that is counterbalanced by a loss from the plant?—A. Yes.

Q. I would like to find what that loss is. It is only fair to set that off against the profit.—A. If I find out the net profit, would not that show? You cannot do that in an hour.

Q. Do it in your own way, and Mr. Watson can bring it out.

By Mr. Watson:

Q. Yes. That is the financial result as to the plant. We have the other.—A. I would like also to tell you the net profits on all the transactions with the government.

Q. We have all the profits on the diaphone.—A. We will try and find it.

Mr. WATSON.—Is the bookkeeper here for the International Marine Signal Company? That bookkeeper was to be here this morning, my lord.

It is a little bit out of order, my lord, but there are some officials of the department that are being detained here pending the inquiry, and they are very anxious to be relieved so that they may get away to their duties. I will call Captain Demers.

Hon. Mr. CASSELS.—Very well.

LOUIS ARTHUR DEMERS, sworn

By Mr. Watson:

Q. What is your position in the department?—A. Chief examiner of masters and mates.

Q. Chief examiner of masters and mates?—A. Yes.

Q. Have you to do with financial matters, the recommendation of expenditure? —A. I have a little in the way of marine instruments for different officers.

Q. Instruments for different officers?—A. Under my control, yes.

Q. The annual expenditure in your branch is about how much?—A. Well, the sum voted is $10,000, but it is never expended altogether.

Q. I have here in a statement before me that the annual expenditure is about $13,000?—A. Is it combined with the marine schoolsé

Q. Yes?—A. Yes.

Q. Would that be right?—A. Yes, sir, about right.

Q. That is the examination of masters and mates and marine schools?—A. Yes.

Q. How long have you been in the department?—A. As chief examiner?

Q. How long have you been in the department?—A. Since 1891.

Q. 1891?—A. Yes, sir.

Q. How long have you been in your present office or position?—A. Beginning the fourth year.

Q. Before that where were you?—A. I was in the government cruisers.

Q. Where do your duties take you?—A. While in the government cruisers?

Q. Where do your duties from day to day take you, where do you perform your duties?—A. Right in the office here.

Q. Do you have to go outside?—A. Yes, I have to make trips of inspection.

Q. Inspection of what?—A. Annually of all the offices.

Q. Of what offices?—A. Victoria, Vancouver, Nelson, Quebec, Montreal, Charlottetown, Halifax, St. John and others.

Q. What offices are those?—A. Examiner of masters and mates.

Q. So that that takes you away?—A. Yes, sir.

Q. And what do you find your average daily expenditure is when you are away? A. It depends on which way. If I am travelling west it is more than when I am travelling east, and if I perform the work during the day and travel during the night, putting in 24 hours altogether, it exceeds one day more than another.

Q. Now, just recollect my question and kindly give me an answer. What do you find your average daily expenditure is, your average daily expenditure, when you are away?—A. It amounts to $8 or $10 per day.

Q. Including travelling expenses?—A. Yes, sir.

Q. Do you say that much?—A. Yes.

Q. $8 or $10 a day?—A. Yes, sir.

Q. Do you say that much?—A. Yes.

Q. Do you keep a record of it?—A. I do not.

Q. Eh?—A. I do not.

Q. You keep no record?—A. I simply send in any bill. I make my bill and send it on to the department.

Q. Do you not keep a personal record of expenses?—A. Yes.

Q. That is what I asked you, do you keep a record of your expenditure?—A. That is what I make my accounts from.

Q. From what?—A. From the record I keep myself in a diary. I make my bill out at the date and send it to the department.

Q. How often do you send it in?—A. As soon as I return from a trip.

Q. Then how is the money expended which you have to do with, the $13,000 a year about that, $10,000 or $12,000?—A. Well, the examiners of masters and mates get $300 a year for their services as such and get $250 a year as lecturers in marine schools, of which there are 12, and then the rest of the money is expended for rent.

Q. So that accounts for the expenditure?—A. Yes, sir.

Q. I see. They get their money direct?—A. Yes, direct monthly.

Q. Now, you are aware of the report of the Civil Service Commissioners, are you not?—A. I glanced over some pages. I did not read it, I was not interested.

Q. Why do you say you are not interested?—A. It has not the same attraction for me.

Q. This report, as you will recollect, charges a want of conscience on the part of officials, not distinguishing. Now, what do you say as to your acts in that regard?—A. I am not concerned in that.

Q. What is that?—A. It does not apply to me.

Q. It does not apply to you?—A. No.

Q. To whom does it apply?—A. I do not know, sir.

Q. This says, ' There is not only a lack of efficient organization and method in the department. There would also seem to be a lack of conscience.' What do you say about the inefficient organization of your branch?—A. Nobody could pass an opinion upon the efficient organization of my branch, because I was never questioned about it. No questions were asked by the commissioners who made that report. I never saw anyone of them.

Q. But it might be asectained without going to you directly?—A. It would not refer very much to my branch. I am positive about that.

Q. Is it not a fact that the organization of your branch is inefficient?—A. It is not a fact.

Q. It is not a fact?—A. Not my branch.

Q. What do you say as to organization?—A. My branch is efficiently well conducted to the best of my ability.

Q. Why is the expenditure an unusually abnormal expenditure?—A. Not at all.

Q. What do you say as to it?—A. Because we have an improvement, I call it. Previously the examiners used to get a fee, now they get a salary which causes the extreme expenditure.

Q. They used to get fees?—A. Yes.

Q. That was less?—A. Well, it was less, and they made it a business to make it more because it carried more remuneration for them.

Q. The officials got more?—A. The examiners of that time.

Q. Why do they get more, why did you recommend more?—A. I did not recommend more.

Q. Who did?—A. I recommended less by allowing $200 salary.

Q. Instead of fees?—A. Yes.

Q. I took it the other way from what you said that the salary amounted to more than the fees previously?—A. There are officers and more examiners appointed, which has caused extra expenditure.

Q. Then the individual payments, have they increased or lessened, that is payments to individuals for work performed?—A. In cases they have, in others they have not.

Q. What is the net result?—A. On the whole the expenditure has increased in the way of salaries.

By Hon. Mr. Cassels:

Q. What receipts have they got to get from this department?—A. Apart from the fees for the certificate there are no other fees. $5,000 or $6,000 a year altogether, I think.

Q. That formerly used to go to the——?—A. It was voted for the benefit of the public.

Q. It was given to the officials?—A. Yes, half of the fee was given to the officials.

Q. Now the fees are retained by the government?—A. And salaries paid instead.

By Mr. Watson:

Q. Now, then, the officials, the officers of the department are charged in this way, 'In other words, some of the government's officers'—the report does not designate which—'some of the government's officers are serving two masters and apparently succeeding with both.'—A. I served only one, that is the minister.

Q. What is that?—A. I served only one, the minister, so that does not apply to me at all

Q. You say that does not apply to you?—A. No.

Q. Have you any knowledge, being in the department as long as you have——?—A. No, sir.

Q. Of any irregularities?—A. No, sir.

Q. Or improper conduct or acts?—A. No, sir. My work takes up my time. I do not meddle with other officials. I keep my own counsel in my own offices and have no dealings with others

. From whom do you obtain your directions?—A. The deputy minister.

. Anyone else?—A. The minister

. The minister through the deputy?—A. Yes.

. You do not go directly to the minister?—A. Sometimes

. But ordinarily from the deputy?—A. Through the deputy.

. And you have not to do with any other official?—A. No, sir.

Q. In any way at all?—A. No, sir, well mostly.

Q. Well, being in the department and living in the department as you do, can you give any assistance or information to his lordship as to what this refers to?—A. None at all, my lord, not a word. I do not know anythin gat all beyond the rumours; of course, the rumours I cannot state. There are no facts.

Q. Do you know to whom these things apply?—A. I do not sir.

Q. What favours, advantages or gains indirectly do you get from those with hom you come in communication outside?—A. None at all.

Q. Do you know of others getting any such?—A. Formerly there were.

Q. Eh?—A. Formerly there were.

Q. Who?—A. Some of my examiners used to get favours or gratuities. When I ound it out I dismissed them. Now I think we have a good staff of men, I have no ault to find

Q. Formerly, you mean?—A. Before there was any head directing it, there was no hief examiner.

Q. They used to get gratuities as the result of the examinations?—A Yes.

Q. From those they passed?—A. Under the system of fees.

Q. When did that prevail?—A. Four or five years ago, four years ago.

Q. Four years ago?—A. Yes

Q. Was that known?—A. I do not know.

Q. What is that?—A. I do not know.

Q. How did you find out about it?—A. Because I went around.

Q. And what did you do with the officials?—I dismissed them, or recommended heir dismissal.

Q. And were they dismissed?—A. Yes, they were.

Q. Do you know any such who are now in the service?—A. None under my con- rol now. They are all straightforward men.

Q. Do you know any officials or employees of the department who have been ilty of such acts?—A. I do not sir.

Q. Or other improper acts?—A. I do not.

Mr. WATSON.—I am not aware of anything else that may be asked regarding these atters, my lord, affecting Captain Demers.

By Hon. Mr. Cassels:

Q. I understand, Captain Demers, formerly these officials were paid by fees?— A. Yes.

Q. Their salary was an increase on the fees formerly?—A. They had no salary; hey received $4 per candidate.

Q. The present salary is less than the fees?—A. In some cases.

Q. On an average?—A. Yes.

Q. They were paid salaries and the government get the fees?—A. Yes, my lord.

Q. That will do.

COMMANDER O. G. V. SPAIN, sworn.

By Mr. Watson:

Q. How long have you been in the service?—A. I came in 1892.

Q. 1892?—A. 16 years, and 12 years in the navy, 28 years' service.

Q. What has your position been?—A. I am a wreck and pilotage commissioner or Canada.

Q. Wreck and——?—A. And pilotage.

Q. And pilotage, that is of the Dominion steamers?—A. No. I have been relieved of the command of the Dominion steamers for about a fortnight by Admiral Kingsmill.

Q. Then prior to a fortnight ago what were your duties?—A. I was wreck com- missioner, pilotage commissioner and commander of the marine service.

Q. And commander of the marine service?—A. Yes.

Q. Then I understand from what you say that your branch has been divided or subdivided?—A. My branch has been divided into two. Admiral Kingsmill has harge of one and I have charge of the other.

Q. Was that upon your recommendation ?—A. That was done upon my own recommendation.

Q. I see. The duties were too heavy ?—A. The duties were too much for me to properly attend to.

Q. Then your department has had an expenditure of about how much money ?—A. In the Dominion steamers ?

Q. The department that you have been in charge of up to a fortnight ago. Might it be separated ?—A. Yes. Dominion steamers, I think it is under.

Q. How much for the Dominion steamers, an annual expenditure of about how much ?—A. I think it is probably $350,000, something like that.

Q. Something like that ?—A. Yes.

Q. I have nearly double that, $600,000, annual expenditure on maintenance of Dominion steamers about $600,000 ?—A. That is probably right, sir.

Q. That is probably right ?—A. No doubt it is right.

Q. Then the other branch, the fisheries cruiser fleet, an annual expenditure of about how much do you say ?—A. I should think about $200,000.

Q. $250,000 I have got it here. You have been under the mark rather as to your estimates of the expenditures—the expenditures have been over the mark, perhaps. Then to whom have you made your recommendations ?—A. In reference to all matters ?

Q. Yes.—A. To the department, to the deputy.

Q. The deputy ?—A. The deputy minister.

Q. What have your relations been with him ?—A. In what way ?

Q. Personal relations?—A. Very good indeed.

Q. What is that?—A. Very good.

Q. Very good ?—A. Very good.

Q. Where is the friction that has existed in the department ?—A. I do not know of any friction at all in my branch.

Q. On your part ?—A. No.

Q. But you have been there a great many years?—A. Well, I have been there, but I have been away a very great deal.

Q. Where has the friction been found to exist ?—A. I do not know of any friction.

Q. Eh ?—A. I do not know of any friction.

Q. As between the heads of the department ?—A. Not personally.

Q. Not personally ?—A. Not personally, no.

Q. Well, what do you know of it ?—A. I do not know anything about it, sir.

Q. What has been your relation to other heads of other departments ?—A. Excellent.

Q. Excellent?—A. All round.

Q. With whom do you come in contact in the course of your business ?—A. With the deputy minister.

Q. Anyone else ?—A. And the minister.

Q. Anyone else, any of the heads of the department ?—A. No.

Q. You have nothing to do with them ?—A. No.

Q. No association with them in business matters?—A. No.

Q. Now, in connection with your duties do you have to travel much ?—A. I have travelled a great deal, a very great deal.

Q. A very great deal?—A. Yes.

Q. Where?—A. All over Canada. I am supposed to inquire into every shipping casualty of any importance that occurs in the Dominion.

Q. Now, the matter of your expenditure has been the subject of comment before to-day, has it not?—A. So I understand.

Q. You understand so?—A. Yes.

Q. Has it ever been challenged, to your knowledge?—A. Yes, I think it has, sir, I know it has.

Q. When and where, in the department?—A. No, not in the department.

Q. Not in the department?—A. No.

Q. Whereabouts then?—A. I think it was challenged by the Auditor General 4 5 years ago.

Q. And what did the Auditor General say as to your expenditure? He spoke to u personally, I assume?—A. Yes. He told me he thought it was very high.

Q. What was your expenditure at that time when it was challenged?—A. I think e expenditure amounts to somewhere between $8 and $10 a day. I am allowed $6 day by order in council.

Q. Yes. When was the order in council passed?—A. Oh, a long time ago, I think 1901.

Q. 1901?—A. I think so, 1901 or 1902.

Q. That is not so very long ago. And that was passed upon your recommenda-n, I suppose?—A. No. It was passed on the minister's recommendation, I presume: was away at the time; I did not know anything about it.

Q. As a limitation on you?—A. No. I am wreck commissioner and have to do a eat deal of work with the general public and lawyers, and have my own court room Montreal.

. Your own what?—A. My own court room in Montreal.

Q. What kind of cases do you decide?—A. I decide all shipping casualties.

Q. Shipping what?—A. Shipping casualties.

By Hon. Mr. Cassels:

Q. You mean the admiralty court room?—A. No; my own court room.

By Mr. Watson:

Q. A separate court room?—A. Yes.

Q. One might think you are a judge.

Hon. Mr. CASSELS.—And so he is.

By Mr. Watson:

Q. Under the Act?—A. I do not know how you take it. I presume under the Act am a sort of judge.

By Hon. Mr. Cassels:

Q. You inquire into accidents?—A. Shipping accidents, and find out who is at ault. That is my particular business.

By Mr. Watson:

Q. Now, of course my question was as to your expenditure, not as to your quasi-idicial duties or functions. Has that anything to do with your expenditure?—A. I link so, yes.

Q. Do you mean it increases by reason of those duties?—A. Well, it is increasing ore or less by reason of those duties, because I have to meet certain people whom I ould not meet otherwise.

Q. Whom you have to meet. You do not have to spend money on people who me before you?—A. No. But it costs you money to be away from home. I can live uch cheaper in Ottawa than when travelling.

Q. I am not talking about your living in Ottawa. I am speaking of your travell-g expenses outside.

By Hon. Mr. Cassels:

Q. I suppose the $6 is over and above living expenses?—A. It is supposed to cover l hotel bills.

By Mr. Watson:

Q. And travelling expenses?—A. No, not railway expenses.

Q. And have you gone beyond that?—A. No, I cannot go beyond it. If I am away for five days I put in an account for $30 for the five days.

Q. You put in that account?—A. Yes.

Q. Whether you spend that much or not?—A. I am allowed that. Sometimes I spend more.

Q. And sometimes you do not spend as much?—A. Sometimes I spend more, sometimes not the whole $6.

Q. Although you do not spend $6 you send in your account for the $6, is that right?—A. Certainly, that is what I am allowed.

Q. You are allowed that irrespective of actual expenditure, do you mean that?—A. No, I do not mean that. That has to cover hotel bills. It just depends on where I am. If in Quebec or Montreal it costs a little bit more; if in a small place it costs less.

Q. I suppose it depends on the opportunities, the facilities—perhaps the temptations?—A. I do not know what you mean by that exactly.

Q. I am very glad to hear you are in that position. Then I observe in 1904-5 that your travelling expenses during that year are reported at $4,627?—A. Well, I do not know whether that is correct or not, I am sure.

Q. That is a pretty large sum, is it not?—A. I should think a very large sum. I do not think that can be correct. I am not sure, though.

Q. It is quite correct as taken from the account?—A. I think if you look over the account a large sum of that is for assessor's fees, stenographer's fees, and all sorts of fees.

Q. This is the Auditor's report which contains this reference. Is this the time he objected to it? The Auditor's report of 1904-5. Travel and disbursements from September 8 to July 27, 1905, $4,627.15. That is that, that is?—A. I think the probabilities are there is about $1,800 of that for stenographer's fees.

Hon. Mr. CASSELS.—Are those itemized?

Mr. WATSON.—No.

Hon. Mr. CASSELS.—Do they reach the Auditor itemized?

Mr. WATSON.—Oh, yes, they are itemized.

The WITNESS.—You will see there are witnesses' fees and stenographers' fees included in that.

By Hon. Mr. Cassels:

Q. You send in a regular account?—A. Yes, my lord. And the big expenditure there—I remember one account of some $300 for detaining vessels which I had arrested at Father Point; United States vessels.

Mr. WATSON.—Is it not a fact that the Auditor General objected to your expenditure?

Hon. Mr. CASSELS.—Does he object to any specific item?

Mr. WATSON.—I do not find it of record, my lord.

The WITNESS.—He spoke to me about it. You might say he did object. He thought it was high.

Q. He thought it was high?—A. Yes.

Q. What do you say as to it?—A. Well——

Q. That would seem exceedingly high?—A. I have travelled a very great deal, I do not think I can do it for much less.

Q. You do not think you can do it for much less?—A. No.

Q. The fact is your expenditure has been pretty free and easy?—A. I would not call it free and easy, no.

Q. It has not been limited to actual necessities?—A. Well, I think it has in the places I am in, yes.

Q. Having regard to the places you are in?—A. Yes.

Q. I cannot understand how an official in the performance of his official duties has any obligations upon him except for necessary expenditure.

Hon. Mr. Cassels:

Q. He has to keep up the position of a gentleman, that is what he means. That involves expenditure that might not be suitable for a mechanic?—A. That is what I mean exactly. It is hard to explain it to you. That is exactly what I mean.

Mr. WATSON.—You mean it depends upon your taste in travelling?

Hon. Mr. CASSELS.—It depends upon his station in life.

By Mr. Watson:

Q. What profit, if any, have you made out of these items of expenditure?—A. None at all.

Q. Eh?—A. None at all.

Q. The report of the commissioners may include you as an officer where it has reference to lack of conscience in the performance of duty and in expenditure. What do you say to that?—A. I say it does not include me.

Q. Has any complaint ever been made against you in the department?—A. No.

Q. Eh?—A. No.

Q. Has the deputy minister ever challenged your expenditure?—A. No.

Q. Never on any occasion?—A. No, not as far as I remember, never.

Q. Not even after it was challenged by the Auditor General?—A. When it came back from the Auditor General he spoke to me about it.

Q. Then what took place, were you not challenged then in matters of expenditure?—A. I say I was, that is the time I was.

Q. And what was the result of that, a limitation?—A. There has been no limitation. This $6 a day was given to me in 1901, but it was not given on that account at all.

Q. Then you mean to say the $6 a day has included everything expended by you except for actual travelling expenses?—A. Yes.

Q. Does not that $6 include travelling expenses?—A. No. It includes hotel bills, but not travelling expenses.

Q. I see. Then you make quite a little money out of that sometimes?—A. No. I told you I did not make any money whatever.

Q. I see, you did not. Then do you go sometimes on duties other than official duties?—A. No, except when I am on leave.

Q. Except you are on leave?—A. Yes.

Q. And when on leave are your expenses paid?—A. Certainly not.

Q. Eh?—A. No, sir.

Q. Not paid?—A. No.

Q. Complaint has been made—I assume you are aware of it, of course you are aware of it—of expenditure by you on trips to New York and the like?—A. I have heard that, yes, I heard it in the House of Commons.

Q. Eh?—A. I heard it in the House of Commons.

Q. Yes, you have heard that?—A. I have, in the House of Commons.

Q. And you have been at New York and other places not engaged in business of the department, and expenses have been charged up to the department; is not that so?—A. No, it is not so.

Q. What?—A. No, it is not so.

Q. It is not so?—A. No.

Q. Is it not so that you spent a considerable time in New York city in connection with personal and domestic matters?—A. Not that was charged up to the department. I think you will find a bill charged up to the department of $33.75 for the passage to New York and back again, and that is the charge in the Auditor General's report.

Q. Why did you charge up expenses?—A. I was down on duty.

Q. Were you not down on personal and domestic matters?—A. No, I was down on duty, Mr. Watson.

Q. We want to be perfectly plain and frank and open with each other, and there is no reason why the same language that has been used elsewhere may not be used here, I assume, and it has been stated that in connction with certain domestic matters, divorce matters, expenditure was incurred by you?

Hon. Mr. CASSELS.—As I understand, the commander went down on official busi-ness. What he says is he charged the fare, which is right. While there, I suppose he stayed on some few days, not charging the government, attending to private business.

WITNESS.—Exactly, my lord.

By Mr. Watson :

Q. That is what you say. How long were you there?—A. I think I was there probably four or five days.

Q. Four or five days ?—A. Yes.

Q. What duties did you perform on that occasion ?—A. I was sent down to attend to pilotage duty, to see how the pilots shipped and transhipped on the ocean liners in New York.

Q. Who instructed you ?—A. I was instructed by the minister.

Q. By the minister or the deputy ?—A. I suppose it came from the minister. It came through the deputy.

Q. And when was that ?—A. I forget when that was. It must have been——

Q. How long ago?—A. Three years, perhaps a couple or three years ago.

Q. Then, at all events your statement is that nothing was included in your account to the department of expenses relating to your personal matters; is that what you say ?—A. Yes.

Q. Did you have to do with the wireless telegraphy or system ?—A. Yes.

Q. Through whom ?—A. Through the company, I suppose.

Q. Through what individual ?—A. Through the manager.

Q. What is his name ?—A. The manager now is a man called Oppe.

Q. Oppe ?—A. Yes.

Q. Then how long has he been manager ?—A. He has been manager probably three years, perhaps more, I do not remember.

Q. And what is the relationship between you and him, a business or personal one?—A. I know him very well indeed, I have known him for years.

Q. You mean he is an intimate personal friend ?—A. Certainly.

Q. An intimate personal friend. So it is beyond the business relationship ?—A. Between him and I ?

Q. Yes ?—A. Very much so; he is a personal friend of mine.

Q. You understand the reasons of my asking that, I assume. This gentleman is the official of the company with whom you have business transactions ?—A. I have not had anything to do with the Wireless Company for two years, I think.

Q. With whom you had business transactions before, I assume ?—A. Yes. He was not manager all the time, though.

Q. And this genaltman is the manager of this company with whom you have large business transactions ?—A. With whom I have had business transactions.

Q. Yes, with whom you have had business transactions. He takes a very active interest in your personal and domestic matters, that is a fact, that is the subject of comment ?—A. He is a personal friend of mine.

Hon. Mr. CASSELS.—I think, Mr. Watson, I would leave out domestic matters.

WITNESS.—It is pretty hard to bring in that, I think.

By Mr. Watson:

Q. They are matters not introduced for the first time. I do not wish in any way to be offensive to you, not in the slightest degree. Those are matters of record. I want the record to be as full and complete as may be thought necessary. Then what business advantages have you had from him, from this company?—A. None whatever.

Q. What commissions have you received?—A. None.

Q. What discounts?—A. None, none whatever.

Q. How many shares have you got in the Marconi Company?—A. Not a single share.

Q. Have you not had shares in the company?—A. No.

Q. You have had large dealings with that company?—A. I have had dealings from my position as looking after that.

Q. Quite so. But you say you have not had——?—A. I have not had anything from them whatever.

Q. Then what gains indirectly have you participated in as the result of your official duties?—A. None, none whatever.

Q. Presents?—A. Nothing.

Q. Nothing of that kind?—A. Nothing.

Q. Then wherein does the statement of want of conscience lie as applying to you? A. I do not know where it can lie. I have not the faintest idea.

Q. And it is said in the same report to which I referred that some officials at all events are serving two masters?—A. Yes. I do not know what that refers to.

Q. You do not know what that refers to?—A. No.

Q. Have you any knowledge of irregularities on the part of other officials?—A. None.

Q. Eh?—A. None, whatever, none.

Q. Any knowledge of advances or gains directly or indirectly to other officials?—A. None.

Q. You state it does not apply to you?—A. Certainly it does not apply to me, and I have not any knowledge of any other.

Q. And you had to do with the *Anticosti* lightship?—A. She was one of the ships.

Q. What repairs were done to that ship?—A. We have two inspectors, a boiler and machinery inspector and a hull inspector.

Q. Yes. The expenditure there was said to be very excessive. Was that under your direction?—A. No; it was under the two inspectors' direction.

Q. Who were they?—A. Mr. McConkey and Mr. Smith.

Q. Who are they?—A. Both of them are in Halifax now, I think.

Q. Halifax?—A. I think so.

Q. Had you anything to do with that?—A. No. The repairs were all done in Quebec.

Q. Were they not made upon your recommendation?—A. No.

Q. Did you recommend the main expenditure?—A. No.

Q. Do you mean you had nothing whatever to do with it?—A. Nothing whatever.

Q. What do you know about it?—A. The reports came to me from those two inspectors—at least they came to the deputy.

Q. Through you?—A. No. From them to the deputy.

Q. And then how did they reach you?—A. They came to me——

Q. From the deputy?—A. From the deputy.

Q. Did you observe the expenditure was excessive?—A. The expenditure was large on the *Anticosti*, but there was a very good reason.

Q. Did you observe the expenditure was excessive?—A. On the *Anticosti*?

Q. Yes?—A. Yes, I think I did.

Q. And that excessive expenditure was by whom, these two officers you have named?—A. There was a reason for the excessive expenditure.

Q. Yes. What was the reason?—A. The reason was she had to have her hawse pipe and stem all changed.

Q. Anything else?—A. She had to have other anchors and chains on account of the changed hawse pipe.

Q. Anything else?—A. I do not think there was anything else.

Q. What was the total expenditure on that?—A. I do not remember.

Q. About how much?—A. I do not remember.

Q. Did you criticize it?—A. Criticize it,—no, I don't think I did.

Q. You don't think you did?—A. No. I noticed it was a high price. I don't think I criticized it, because it was necessary.

Q. Was it not your duty to inquire into it?—A. I did inquire into the reason for the expenditure.

Q. And as the result of that inquiry what was your report, that it was not justified, or justified?—A. No. I think the report I made was that it was necessary.

Q. That is what you say?—A. I think so.

Q. Not only necessary, but proper?—A. Yes, absolutely necessary. It was absolutely necessary to change that hawse pipe.

Q. And did you report it was necessary and proper and not excessive?—A. I expect I did.

Q. You expect you did. Do you remember?—A. I don't think I should probably say anything about the expenditure. I should report on the necessity for the repairs.

Q. Would you not have to do with the amount?—A. I would, but the two inspectors are there for that particular purpose, to estimate the amount of the cost. I am not an engineer, and it was outside me to know how much things are going to cost.

Q. Now, the Civil Service Commissioners comment upon that, and say that expense was no consideration, it was an invitation to extravagance?—A. I do not think that is correct at all.

Q. What?—A. I do not think that is correct at all.

Q. Did you give them information?—A. They never came near me. The only thing I had to do with the Civil Service examination was that one gentleman asked me how it was that 250 years ago the aids to navigation at Montreal did not cost what they did now.

Q. 250 years ago?—A. Yes.

Q. You are not using the words given to you?—A. Yes, the words given to me.

Q. That was asked by whom?—A. I don't know which. It was upstairs in the accountant's room, and I was asked how it was that 250 years ago the expenditure on the ship channel was not anything like it was now. I told them I supposed a canoe might have come up 250 years ago.

Q. This was a joke?—A. Certainly, no doubt a joke. But that is all the conversation I had.

By Hon. Mr. Cassels:

Q. A jocular remark on Mr. Fyshe's part?—A. I don't know whether it was Mr. Fyshe or not. I think it probably was. It was intended simply as a joke. I am only saying this as it is the only conversation I had.

By Mr. Watson:

Q. No other comments to you?—A. No.

Q. Were you asked for information about this lightship?—A. No. They never came near me.

Q. Then you had not to do personally with the expenditure upon that ship?—A. No.

Q. Then do you know as a fact that the expenditure has been unreasonable and excessive?—A. No.

Q. What do you say?—A. No.

Q. Has it not been increasing?—A. In the department, you mean?

Q. I do not mean in the department. Higher prices, more money is being spent upon the same class of work?—A. I do not think so. There is much more money spent because everything is on a much bigger scale.

Q. Oh, yes, that is understood, that is appreciated. But what I mean is, what I am asking is, whether or not money is not paid much more freely, in fact extravagantly, unnecessarily?—A. No.

Q. What do you say?—A. No.

Q. What supervision exists over you, through the deputy minister?—A. Through the deputy minister. Everything had to go to the deputy minister.

Q. By you?—A. By me.

Q. Are your recommendations approved by him?—A. Sometimes approved, sometimes not.

Q. That is, disapproved, you mean?—A. Sometimes they would not be approved, sometimes they would be. I have not a free hand at all.

Q. That is, you are subject——?—A. To the department.

Q. To the deputy minister?—A. Certainly.

Q. Then you come into contact with contractors to a considerable extent?—A. No, not at all.

Q. Not at all?—A. No. I have nothing to do with it.

Q. Nothing to do with it?—A. Nothing whatever.

Q. That will do, your lordship.

By Hon. Mr. Cassels:

Q. Have you anything to do in connection with supplies?—A. No, my lord, nothing whatever.

Q. Have you anything to do with the fitting out of any of the vessels?—A. They are fitted out at the different ports under the agent.

Q. You do not do it yourself?—A. I am responsible for the discipline, cleanliness of the appointments, discipline of the men.

Q. But the supplies and everything——?—A. Are bought by other people entirely.

Q. That will do.

WILLIAM STEWART, sworn:—

By Mr. Watson:

Q. What is your department, Mr. Stewart?—A. Hydrographic survey.

Q. Hydrographic survey?—A. Yes.

Q. What is your annual expenditure, about?—A. Between $110,000 and $120,000 a year now at the present time.

Q. How long have you been in that branch?—A. I have been in the hydrographic survey since 1884.

Q. 1884. You have been there a very long time, then?—A. Yes, quite a while.

Q. What are your duties just in a very general way?—A. The general conduct of all hydrographic surveys in the Dominion of Canada.

Q. The expenditure that you recommend is made in what way and through whom?—A. I beg your pardon?

Q. How is the expenditure made?—A. It is made for each survey party. There are five or six parties out in the field, and we make an expenditure for each party separately. A sum is asked; we ask for a certain amount for each year.

Q. Just employed on survey work?—A. On survey work altogether.

Q. The parties go from Ottawa, they are made up at the department?—A. They are all in Ottawa in the winter making up their notes, except one part which remains in British Columbia; the others all come to Ottawa.

Q. The money is expended, then, for expenses and——?—A. Salaries and the maintenance of two or three steamers and the pay of the crews and the men employed in the survey work.

Q. And under whose branch, in whose department, were you; until recently your department was under the chief engineer's branch?—A. For a few years.

Q. When was that?—A. Between 1893 and 1903, I think.

Q. During that time?—A. During that time, yes. It was a differenct survey then to what it is now. It was then only one party, there was just one survey party going on at that time.

Q. And then it was in charge of the chief engineer, that is Colonel Anderson?—A. Yes.

Q. And you were in his department?—A. I was in his department.

Q. And the department was separated from his?—A. It was enlarged, practically a new department was formed. That is, there were survey parties conducted by two or three in the Public Works Department and in the Railways and Canals Department. They were transferred to the Department of Marine. Then we took over some of the Admiralty survey parties, that is, we took over the work they were doing, and that made quite a large branch, and it was separated from the chief engineer's branch.

Q. Now, was that change made upon your recommendation?—A. No, sir.

Q. Upon whose recommendation?—A. I do not know, sir. I was just notified.

Q. Was it made upon the recommendation of Colonel Anderson?—A. I saw no recommendation.

Q. Eh?—A. I saw no recommendation. I simply was notified that this branch was formed.

Q. Was it after consultation between you and him?—A. I had no consultation with him about the matter at all.

Q. You mean before the division took place there was no consultation between you and him?—A. Not on that subject, no.

Q. Not on that subject?—A. Not on that subject.

Q. Well, that just opens the door a little bit to what I wanted to inquire about. Has friction existed throughout in the department?—A. Not with me, sir; I don't know of any.

Q. You have no knowledge of it?—A. Not at all, and I had no friction with Colonel Anderson at any time.

Q. Not at any time. I see. Was there a difference between you and him as to the taking over of that department or as to the subsequent taking it back?—A. Not a word.

Q. You have no knowledge of anything of that kind?—A. Not a word.

Q. Then, in these matters that are referred to in the report of the Civil Service Commissioners, Mr. Stewart, what have you to say?—A. Which special ones, about the——

Q. You know what this report is and that it practically is a charge against the staff of the department. It refers to a lack of efficient organization and method in the department, and that there would seem to be a lack of conscience. What do you say as to that?—A. I can only speak about my own conscience. I think I have quite as much as any one else. As to the organization of the survey, I think it is quite as good as any survey on the face of the globe.

Q. And what about the expenditure?—A. The expenditure is about normal; I do not think it is any worse than any other hydrographic survey.

Q. Not any worse than any other ?—A. Not any worse.

Q. Do you mean from that it is pretty bad ?—A. No. I do not think the hydrographic survey is badly conducted. The hydrographic survey is more expensive than other survey work from the fact that we have got to maintain steamers. We cannot get on the waters without them. Our work is on the water, we have little or nothing to do with shore work.

Q. Is it done with efficiency ?—A. It is.

Q. What do you say as to economy ?—A. The economy is all right. I don't think it is extravagant.

Q. Well, you have to do with that expenditure, the recommendation of it ?—A. I have.

Q. One might expect a pretty clear cut expression from you as to whether the expenditure is justified or not ?—A. The expenditure is justified.

Q. This report indicates that considerable expenditure may not be justified ?—A. It does not apply to the hydrographic survey.

Q. I do not find the commissioners say it does ?—A. They did not come near me. I don't know them at all, I don't know them to see them.

Q. No information was obtained from you ?—A. Not a word.

Mr. WATSON.—I think that is all I have to ask, my lord.

By Mr. Cassels :

Q. Is Mr. Dawson of that party?—He is in charege of the tidal survey.

CAMERON STANTON, sworn.

By Mr. Watson :

Q. What is your position, Mr. Stanton ?—A. I am chief clerk in the Marine Branch.

Q. Chief clerk in the Marine Branch. And do you assume other duties at any other time ?—A. By the minister's orders I act as deputy in his absence.

Q. In the absence of the deputy minister ?—A. Yes.

Q. Then what duties do you have to perform particularly in that respect ?—A. I have no defined duties like the chief engineer or the accountant, no defined class of duties, but I have the duty of chief clerk, a certain amount of supervision.

Q. Over what or whom ?—A. Over the correspondence and the—for instance, in the deputy's absence a file will come to me for approval and recommendation.

Q. Yes. Now, comment is made about that by the Civil Service Commissioners and about that system of correspondence. What do you say as to that ?—A. The system is, I believe, the same as obtains in all other departments, a similar system.

Q. I am not speaking about other departments ; I am speaking about this department particularly ?—A. What particular department ?

Q. The commissioners' say, ' The custom has been '—page 130, my lord—' to assume that everything has to be formally settled by the head of the department, the deputy. Each letter has to be answered by someone in the department who is supposed to be *au fait* with the subject, or at any rate to give his attention to it. A letter is prepared by him, but the deputy signs it, knowing often little or nothing about it, and having no time to inquire. Hit or miss the letter goes, and in many cases it is found later on that it was written in ignorance of or conflicting with previous correspondence or instructions, and therefore calculated to bring reproach and discredit on all concerned. But nobody is the wiser for all this. It is regarded as unfortunate perhaps, but more or less inevitable in the nature of things. Certainly nobody is punished for it. The rush of unorganized work and the consequent jumble goes on as before.' Now, that comes home to you, does it not ?

Hon. Mr. CASSELS.—Of course, Mr. Watson, I am not sitting here to try whether the system of the department is effectual or not, except so far as is necessary to bring that out within the scope of the commission. The commission is limited in its particular objects.

Mr. WATSON.—Yes, my lord, except so far as this may affect or be read along with the statement in the report of general lack of conscience.

Hon. Mr. CASSELS.—I understand. But I am not here to sit in judgment on the methods of carrying on the business of the Marine Department, otherwise we shall be here all our lives.

Mr. WATSON.—I quite appreciate, my lord, it would be a lengthy undertaking to go into all the details, it would mean an immense amount of work.

Q. In a word, is the organization sufficient to enable the work to be done properly and conscientiously?—A. In my opinion it is.

Q. In your opinion it is. This report indicated that it may not be done conscientiously and it may have been done in ignorance by reason of the general confusion that exists?—A. That is not my opinion.

Q. Well, I have no doubt you have personal knowledge in your position as chief clerk?—A. I have. I do not think that remark is justified, at least the commissioners' remark, I mean.

By Hon. Mr. Cassels:

Q. Does the manner in which the business is carried on leave it open to any of the clerks to be guilty of improper conduct in the way of receiving money or bribes?—A. I do not think so, my lord.

By Mr. Watson:

Q. Have you ever found any such thing existing?—A. No.

Q. Have you any knowledge or information as to improper conduct or acts on the part of any of the officials?—A. None, whatever.

Q. Have you ever heard of such things in the department?—A. No.

Q. Of any lack of bona fides, good conduct or good conscience?—A. No.

Q. Eh?—A. No.

Q. What have been the difficulties in the performance of duties there, any?—A. None with me.

Q. Or with others to your knowledge?—A. Not to my knowledge.

Q. Then it is said the expenditure is excessive, and to the extent as indicating want of honesty?—A. I have no knowledge of that whatever.

Q. You have a pretty intimate knowledge of the expenditure, I assume, in the Marine Department?—A. No, I should say not.

Q. Would you not as chief clerk?—A. No.

Q. That would not come within your realm?—A. No, sir.

Q. You deal for the most part with the correspondence?—A. With the correspondence, yes, sir.

Q. And necessarily dealing with the correspondence you would be familiar with the subject matter?—A. Well, you see, I do not see all the correspondence.

Q. Yes?—A. For instance, I see all the correspondence when the deputy is away, because I would have to sign it.

Q. Then you have correspondence with contractors?—A. No, I have nothing to do with contractors.

Q. Nothing to do with them?—A. No, nothing.

Q. Your correspondence is with whom?—A. Well, where the letters are prepared for me to sign them, but I have no personal relations with contractors; my work does not bring me into relation with them.

Q. No; but does it not bring the correspondence between them and the department before you?—A. Yes, I should have the letters to sign if the deputy is away, that is all, perhaps for a day.

Q. Yes. Now then, in this correspondence have you ever seen or observed any evidence of any improper dealings between contractors and the department or any official of the department?—A. None whatever, no.

Q. And in connection with that what reference have you observed, if any, to matters of discount or commissions in the correspondence?—A. No reference whatever.

Q. Has it ever been referred to, to your knowledge?—A. Not to my knowledge.

Q. Have you any knowledge of any discount being allowed or improperly obtained?—A. No, no knowledge whatever.

Q. Do you know of any discount being allowed in the first place?—A. No.

Q. Or of any commission being obtained?—A. No.

Q. Or of any other advantage or gain?—A. None, whatever.

Q. To yourself or any official?—A. Not to myself. I have never received a present or an offer of a present.

Q. Do you know of any such to anyone else, any other official high or low?—A. No.

Q. No knowledge of any such thing?—A. No knowledge whatever, no.

Mr. WATSON.—I think there is nothing else, my lord.

Hon. Mr. CASSELS.—I just want to ask him one question.

By Hon. Mr. Cassels:

Q. Do you know of any perquisites of any kind received by any officials of the department from outside people, contractors?—A. No.

Q. You do not know?—A. No.

(Adjourned at 1 p.m. to 2.15 p.m. and then resumed.)

CHARLES HECTOR GODIN, sworn:—

Mr. WATSON.—I should state to your lordship in respect to Dr. Godin and a number of other officials, who consider themselves more or less reflected upon by the report, that I have not anything specific against them, but partly in the discharge of my duty in performing this investigation, and also in justice to these officials, I consider it is only right to give them an opportunity to explain and exculpate themselves or otherwise. I want to put a number of them in so that they may get back to their usual work and be free from interruption.

Hon. Mr. CASSELS.—Or the reverse.

Mr. WATSON.—Yes, my lord. Either one or the other.

By Mr. Watson:

Q. Dr. Godin, what is your position?—A. I am medical superintendent of the marine hospital service.

Q. And I observe from a memorandum I have that the annual expenditure of this service is about $50,000?—A. About that.

Q. Under your direction?—A. Under my direction.

Q. And under your recommendation to the deputy minister?—A. Yes, sir.

Q. And where are your duties performed, here or in different places?—A. Here in Ottawa.

Q. Here entirely?—A. Yes.

Q. Where are the marine hospitals?—A. In various places. Down in the maritime provinces and one in British Columbia, Victoria.

Q. I suppose you visit them?—A. Sometimes.

Q. Sometimes?—A. Yes.

Q. Just in connection with that and arising out of one or two answers of some of the other witnesses. When you go out what do you find your daily expenditure amounts to on an average?—A. Well, it depends whether we travel east or west, it is quite a deal different.

Q. Well, east, what do you find it to be?—A. You mean transportation?

Q. Transportation with hotel, your average expenditure?—A. With the transportation, well, it depends altogether on what city we are going to.

By Hon. Mr. Cassels:

Q. Suppose you went to the Royal, St. John?—A. In St. John?

Q. Yes?—A. Between $5 and $6.

By Mr. Watson:

Q. The average expenditure?—A. Yes.

Q. And you find that to be so, speaking generally?—A. In the eastern parts.

Q. Then in the west?—A. More expensive.

Q. How much?—A. Probably about $8 or $10. I suppose it would be about that.

Q. Well, now, you have other officials under you, of course, employees?—A. Just a clerk and stenographer.

Q. That is all?—A. That is all.

Q. That comprises your branch, I see. Any excessive or extraordinary expenditure within the last four years in your branch?—A. Not that I know of. I have just been appointed since 1906.

Q. 1906?—A. Yes, in July.

Q. How do you find it compares with previous expenditure?—A. The vote is about the same each year.

Q. The vote is about the same?—A. Yes.

Q. And is there anything abnormal in it?—A. Not that I know of.

Q. Then, with respect to the observations which have been made by the Commissioners of Civil Service, do you know anything about a lack of efficient organization in connection with looseness and carelessness?—A. None whatever.

Q. Or in connection with want of good conscience or want of accuracy?—A. None whatever.

Q. To the extent, I mean, of recklessness?—A. None whatever.

Q. Nothing of that kind?—A. No, sir.

Q. Any of those observations that you have all heard so much of; do they have application to your or to your department, can they have?—A. What observations?

Q. The observations of the commissioners about the officials serving two masters, and expressions of that kind?—A. No, sir.

Q. Were you applied to for any information regarding your department?—A. No, sir.

Q. None at all?—A. None at all.

Q. By the commissioners?—A. Mr. Bazin asked me once what was my duty; that is all.

Q. That is all that occurred?—A. I met him in the hall. That is just what he asked me.

Q. Any criticism upon your department by the Auditor General?—A. Not since I have been appointed.

Q. Now, then, do you know of anything irregular on the part of other officials in the department?—A. No, sir.

Q. Have you any information that bears upon any such matters?—A. No, sir.

Q. Any evidence or information of dishonest conduct or acts on the part of any one?—A. No, sir.

Q. You have not. That will do, sir.

REGIS ROY, sworn.

By Mr. Watson:

Q. Mr. Roy, you are in charge of what?—A. I am in charge of the printing and stationery branch just now. I had been private secretary for the deputy minister for many years before.

Q. Private secretary for the deputy minister?—A. Yes, sir.

Q. From what time to what time?—A. From 1884 up to 1904.

Q. From 1884——?—A. To 1904.

Q. That is 20 years?—A. Yes. I have been 26 years in the service.

Q. So you have been——?—A. I have been 24 years in that department.

Q. Already 20 years as secretary of the deputy minister?—A. Yes, sir. Well, not the same deputy. There used to be another deputy before, the late Mr. Smith.

Q. The late Mr. Smith?—A. Yes.

Q. Then, when did the present deputy assume his duties?—A. 1896, I think it was.

Q. Now, then, just in connection with that matter, before referring to your own matter. As secretary of the deputy you have had to do with the correspondence more or less?—A. Yes, sir.

Q. In fact, with all the correspondence so far as it goes out?—A. Yes, sir.

Q. And how about the correspondence coming in to him, did you have to do with that; did you open the letters, read the letters?—A. Not under this deputy.

Q. Not under this deputy minister?—A. No.

Q. I see. Then we need not go into the other. Mr. Smith, he is not living?—A. No.

Q. It is just the correspondence that goes out?—A. Yes.

Q. Did you take all of that correspondence from him, all the dictation from him?—A. Well, a god deal of it.

Q. Who took the other?—A. Well, towards the later years, Mrs. Thomas was secretary.

Q. It would be confined, then, to you and Mrs. Thomas?—A. Yes.

Q. Now, in regard to letters that were dictated to you in the capacity that you occupied, did you find much private correspondence between the deputy and the contractors, as a matter of recollection?—A. No, there was none at all that I recollect of.

Q. What?—A. There was none at all. It was all official correspondence or semi-official correspondence, but none with contractors.

Q. None with contractors?—A. None whatever. I had none at all whatever to do with contractors, no correspondence of any nature.

Q. Did the deputy have correspondence with contractors?—A. I do not know. I did not see any.

Q. Was there any such correspondence passed through your hands?—A. None.

Q. No private correspondence passed through your hands?—A. None.

Q. Well, who took his private dictation?—A. I took private dictation myself.

Q. From him?—A. From him.

Q. That concerned what kind of subject matter?—A. Well, matters about the department of an official and semi-official character, but there was none about contractors work, none at all.

Q. None about contractors work?—A. No.

Q. But that correspondence more or less may have had to do with subject matters of contract?—A. None that I can recollect of.

Q. None you can recollect of?—A. No.

Q. Well then, from that correspondence, as a matter of recollection—and I think you would be apt not to forget—you would judge of the relationship betwen the deputy and the contractors or those with whom he was corresponding. Did you find an intimate personal relationship between them?—A. None whatever.

Q. Do you mean that?—A. Yes, I do mean it.

Q. Do you recollect of letters which would naturally arouse suspicion or doubt as to transactions or dealings?—A. No.

Q. Nothing of that character?—A. None at all.

Q. At any time?—A. At any time, while, of course, I was in the office.

Q. Well, I am limiting it to that. I am asking you as being there?—A. Yes, I understand. There was none at all.

3262—13½

Q. Did anything of that kind ever occur that would excite the suspicion or doubt of a reasonably minded person ?—A. No.

Q. Or your doubt or suspicion, assuming you are reasonable ?—A. No, there was not.

Q. Do you say that positively ?—A. I say that positively.

Q. Do you know of any favours granted in any way to the deputy by outsiders with whom dealings were taking place?—A. There were none while I was there, to my knowledge.

Q. I see. You are speaking quite positively ?—A. Oh, I am.

Q. Have you talked this matter over with the deputy ?—A. With nobody.

Q. Then with regard to your own expenditure, the stationery branch, since you assumed that office—that was when again?—A. 1904.

Q. 1904? Do you make contracts for stationery?—A. No, sir.

Q. Who does ?—A. The superintendent of the government stationery office.

Q. Who is that?—A. Mr. Goldthrite.

Q. I do not see his name on the list ?—A. He is not in our department.

Q. Then what do you have to do with it ?—A. I simply make requisitions on the government stationery office for anything required in the office, and we get it from the government stationery office. We have nothing to do with the prices or contracts.

Q. You know what prices are paid ?—A. Of course, because the accounts come at the end of the month and I check them over.

Q. What do you say as to the prices being paid ?—A. They were all right. If they were not I would certainly have had an official letter written to the government stationery office.

Q. That duty comes on you of seeing that the prices are proper ?—A. Yes. .

Q. Have you known of any excessive or unreasonable prices being paid ?—A. No, there have been none.

Q. Do you know how the prices are as compared with prices paid by other people in business ?—A. With a general knowledge of prices I know they are fair.

Q. Are they at all in excess of prices paid by others?—A. No, they are not. I believe in fact in some cases, in a few cases, they are cheaper than persons could get them individually.

Q. I mean business people ?—A. Yes, I know, business people.

Q. And do you know of any irregular acts that have occurred in the past in regard to the department or the officials ?—A. None to my knowledge.

Q. While you were acting as secretary of the deputy you must have more or less come in touch with the other departments or branches, would you not ?—A. Certainly, I would be in touch with all the officials and so on.

Q| And what were the difficulties that came to your knowledge ?—A. None came to my knowledge.

Q. None at all?—A. No. The deputy was upon good terms with every official in the department, and there had never been anything, no hitch or anything at all. I would be in a position to know.

Q. What would be the chief subject of complaint against officials?—A. I have never heard of any complaint against officials.

Q. You have not?—A. No.

Q. Perhaps there ought to have been?—A. Perhaps there ought, but during the time that I was there I did not hear of any.

Q. Any complaints as to prices, conduct or acts?—A. No, I did not hear of anything.

Q. And have you any knowledge of the matters referred to in the report which reflect upon officials of the department?—A. The only thing I can say is this, that about the correspondence being signed by the deputy, the reflection is cast there by the commissioners that it was signed by him without looking at the letters. I have to say I do not believe it, because it is to my knowledge that the deputy minister has many and many a time corrected letters and sent them back for correction because they were not right, so I do not see where they could get that assertion.

Q. And what about the imputations of dishonesty or want of conscience on the part of the officials?—A. I have never heard of any in the twenty-four years.

Q. Has anything of that kind come to your knowledge or information?—A. No.

Q. Did you ever hear anything about discounts or commissions?—A. I never heard anything of that kind.

Q. What were the differences that existed between Mr. J. F. Stewart and the deputy?—A. J. F. Stewart?

Q. Mr. J. F. Fraser and the deputy?—A. I do not think there have been any differences. I did not hear of any.

Q. What differences between him and Colonel Anderson, between J. F. Fraser and Colonel Anderson, do you know anything about those?—A. I do not know anything about that. I think it was about that time I was transferred to another branch of the service, so if there was anything I did not see there was anything. I do not believe there was anything.

Q. It has been said, or suggested rather, that Mr. J. F. Fraser could do practically what he liked with the deputy?—A. I do not believe it.

Q. Did you ever see any evidence of it, any indication of it?—A. No. But from my knowledge of his character I do not think anything of that kind could be done.

Q. Anything else, my lord?

By Hon. Mr. Cassels:

Q. The orders relating to purchasing of supplies come before you?—A. No; only just the ordinary office supplies, before I used to see it in an official way.

Q. For instance, from Quebec if they wanted to purchase supplies of steel and that sort of thing, would that be referred to Ottawa?—A. I would see the supplies in an official way. If there had been anything wrong——

Q. I did not ask you if there had been anything wrong. I am not suggesting there is anything wrong. What I want to know is whether the correspondence relating to purchases of supplies came within your jurisdiction?—A. I would see it, being attached in that office.

Q. Did it come before you?—A. Just in that character.

Q. Do you know anything of the patronage list?—A. I never saw anything wrong.

Q. I never said there was anything wrong. Answer the question. Do you know anything of the patronage list?—A. No.

Q. Did you ever, in the letters you had to take or sign, see any references to the patronage list?—A. No.

Q. Had you any knowledge of any letters written to purchase from so and so, say in Quebec, Halifax or elsewhere?—A. I would certainly see some, but I could not recollect any names.

Q. I am not asking whether you recollect names or not. I want to know did that come under your view?—A. Yes, I have seen some letters like that.

Q. Are those letters all official?—A. Yes, they were all official.

Q. Did you see any letters not of an official character?—A. I have never seen any.

Q. No private letters?—A. No, my lord.

Q. Nothing but official letters. And those are of record in the department?—A. Yes, they would be on record in the department.

Q. Thank you. That will do.

MARK R. McELHINNEY, sworn.

By Mr. Watson:

Q. Captain McElhinney, you have to do with the life-saving service?—A. Yes, sir; lately I have had to do with that.

Q. And before that with what branch?—A. I was appointed as nautical adviser and second-class clerk. I just attended to what was sent to me by the deputy.

Q. What was sent to you by the deputy?—A. Yes, sir. Letters, correspondence. I answered letters of a nautical character, you know. I was appointed as nautical adviser, you see.

Q. Yes. And you have to do with the correspondence upon that subject?—A. Upon those subjects.

Q. And how long were you there in that position?—A. Well, you see, I came in in '82.

Q. You are not excited, are you?—A. In '82 I came in.

Q. How long did you continue in that particular work?—A. Oh, I think last year —well, I was promoted several times from second-class up to first-class, and last year——

Q. Never mind. I want to know how long you have been in that particular work? —A. I could not designate it distinctly, because it come right along during my whole service, I have been right in that up to now.

Q. From 1882 in the nautical——?—A. Nautical adviser.

Q. In different positions there?—A. Different positions.

Q. What did you reach to in that department?—A. A year ago I was appointed chief clerk.

Q. But in some other branch?—A. No.

Q. In that same branch?—A. In that same branch.

Q. I do not seem to be getting very close in touch with you and with your work somehow or other. It is my fault, no doubt?—A. Well, you refer to the——

Q. I want to know what your work was?—A. You refer to the life-saving service. I have always had a little to do with it in advising the deputy minister and writing letters in regard to that.

Q. Yes. Well, then, you were in the position you speak of and you had to do with a certain portion of the correspondence?—A. Yes, sir.

Q. That is directly under the deputy?—A. Directly under the deputy. He signed all the letters I wrote.

Q. Did those letters have to do with the expenditure of money?—A. Not much.

Q. Not much?—A. Not much. Some had to do with prices.

Q. With prices?—A. But very little, once in a while.

Q. And in connection with that part of the correspondence dealing with prices or the expenditure of money, was any portion of it of a private nature?—A. None.

Q. The correspondence?—A. None whatever.

Q. And were you familiar with the prices that were being paid or proper to be paid?—A. In that matter, yes.

Q. What do you say as to the prices?—A. So far as I know they were all right.

Q. But you do know, don't you?—A. I know.

Q. Then why do you limit it in that way?—A. Well, so far as I know, anything so far as I had to do with it they were all right.

Q. They were all right?—A. Yes.

Q. Do you know how the prices being paid by the department compared with prices being paid by others, or would similar work be done?—A. Similar work.

Q. More or less?—A. More or less, yes.

Q. But were the prices more excessive, the prices paid by the department?—A. I am not aware of any.

Q. Eh?—A. I am not aware of any prices paid.

Q. You are not aware of any?—A. No, sir.

Q. Can you say whether or not they were excessive, yes or no?—A. I can say they were not excessive.

Q. I see.

By Hon. Mr. Cassels:

Q. What do you mean by prices, what do you refer to by prices, contract work or purchases?—A. Oh, the prices of goods that were bought that came in the correspondence that I had to do anything with.

By Mr. Watson:

Q. What class of goods, what kind?—A. Ship stores and that kind.

Q. And from whom were those purchases made?—A. Oh, some were bought in Halifax, some in the United Kingdom.

Q. Were they limited to certain sellers or vendors?—A. Not at all.

Q. Purchased in the best market?—A. Not at all, not any what I had to do with.

Q. Were they limited to a certain patronage list?—A. No, sir.

Q. They were not, eh?—A. Not what I had to do with.

Q. What you saw or had information about?—A. Yes, sir.

Q. That is so?—A. That is so.

Q. Then, what were the difficulties in the department that were apparent to you?—A. I am not aware of any difficulties.

Q. Not aware of any difficulties?—A. No. sir.

Q. What were the subjects of complaint or comment?—A. I don't know of any complaint, only from rumour outside, and that I don't know anything about.

Q. And how long have those rumours been going on?—A. Oh, well, rumours, rumours——

By Hon. Mr. Cassels:

Q. Ever since Ottawa existed?—A. I cannot say.

Mr. WATSON.—Ottawa is not a place for rumours, surely?

Hon. Mr. CASSELS.—I was only interpreting what he had in his mind.

By Mr. Watson:

Q. Ottawa is too big for that, surely?—A. I don't know when gossip and rumour will cease.

Q. Against whom were those things circulated?—A. I cannot say.

Q. Do you know if there was any foundation for those?—A. I do not.

Q. Eh?—A. I know of no foundation for them.

Q. You seem a genial soul. You must have lots of friends about there?—A. They are all friends, I believe, so far as I know.

Q. Then you know about everybody. What are the irregularities and difficulties you have heard about there?—A. I could not specify anything.

Q. You could not specify anything?—A. No, sir.

Q. Any improper act or acts of dishonesty on the part of any one?—A. Not that I am aware of.

Q. In the department anywhere?—A. I am not aware of any.

Q. Not on your part?—A. None that I know of.

By Hon. Mr. Cassels:

Q. What is the nature of those stores that were purchased? You are referring to ships' stores, what do they consist of?—A. Just in furnishing the ship.

Q. Describe what you mean by that?—A. Provisions.

Q. Yes?—A. Coal, provisions, engine stores, &c.

Q. Everything connected with the running of the vessels?—A. With the running of the vessels, yes, sir.

Q. Did that all pass through your department?—A. Well, I had to do with that a few years ago; I superintended the building of vessels on the other side, so several—

Q. But what about the equipment?—A. I had to buy the stores there.

Q. Now, did you know anything about current market rates? You have been secluded there for 26 years. Had you any knowledge of the current market rates for flour?—A. Well, I generally know pretty nearly what flour was in the market.

Q. Had you in your position any occasion to know what the current market rates for goods were at the time these orders were given?—A. Oh, yes. I always looked at the prices.

Q. Did your correspondence that you are referring to state what prices were to be paid?—A. Oh yes.

Q. Is that correspondence on the files of the department?—A. I think it is.

Q. You think it is?—A. Yes.

Q. Personally did you make any investigation as to what these goods could be bought for in the open market?—A. When in Glasgow I asked for tenders from the different dealers.

Q. When was that?—A. Oh, that was in 1901—1888 and 1889.

Q. Was that for the department?—A. For the department.

Q. You asked for tenders ?—A. For tenders.

Q. For what class of goods?—A. Just ship's stores, fitting out for the ship.

Q. Well, what about the purchase of flour ?—A. For flour ?

Q. Yes. Did you know anything about the market rate of a barrel of flour ?—A. I did then.

Q. At that time ? But since during the period of years ?—A. Yes.

Q. Have you kept tally of that at all ?—A. Not since.

Q. You assumed that everything was all right as far as you knew ?—A. I am sure it was all right.

Q. Well, it depends on what the market rates were and what prices were paid ? —A. Yes.

Q. So far as you know it was all right ?—A. All right as far as I know.

Q. That will do.

CECIL DOUTRE, sworn.

By Mr. Watson :

Q. When were you appointed and to what position ?—A. July 23, 1906, superintendent of government wireless stations.

Q. Superintendent of government wireless stations ?—A. Yes.

Q. You were not in the department, then, before July, 1906?—A. No.

Q. Then in what branch were you, who was the head of your branch?—A. I was.

Q. You were. Was that separated from some other branch at that time, some other department ?—A. No, it was always a separate branch.

Q. That was always a separate branch ?—A. Yes.

Q. Who was your immediate predecessor?—A. Commander Spain.

Q. There must have been a division then in his work?—A. He had charge of the wireless work previous to that time.

Q. Then his branch was divided or subdivided?—A. The work was taken, yes.

Q. The work was taken ?—A. It was taken away from his branch and I was appointed to take charge of the work.

Q. Do you know how that division came about ?—A. Well, I understand the reason was Commander Spain did not have sufficient time to devote to the work which he had charge of at the time, and for that reason it was decided to appoint someone to look after that.

Q. Now in connection with that work what were your duties?—A. To supervise generally the work of the wireless stations which the government owned, and which were under contract at the time by the Marconi Company.

Q. By the Marconi Company ?—A. Yes. Since then we have built some stations but that is subsequent.

Q. Has there been any change in your position ?—A. Yes.

Q. What?—A. Oh, I occupy three positions: Superintendent of wireless stations, cting accountant of purchasing and contract agent.

Q. What ?—A. Purchasing and contract agent.

Q. That is a very important position, I should think?—A. Yes, I think it is.

Q. For the whole department ?—A. For the entire department.

Q. Of all goods?—A. Of all goods.

Q. When that was formed did you take the place of someone else ?—A. No, it as an entirely new appointment.

By Hon. Mr. Cassels :

Q. Since this investigation ?—A. Yes. The appointment only dates from May 4, I think.

By Mr. Watson :

Q. That is of this year ?—A. Yes.

Q. I see. So that is a new office ?—A. A new office entirely.

Q. And do you mean to say now you have sole superintendence of all purchases ? A. Yes, I will have. Not at the present time, for the system we intend inaugurat- ıg is not in operation. At the present time we are simply keeping the department oating buying our supplies as we require them, and the agents are doing the same hing in the different agencies for the same reason that the organization is not per- fected to take charge of that; but the intention is to purchase everything for the department from one end of the Dominion to the other.

Q. Then the heads of the different branches or departments will make their requests through you or to you ?—A. They will make requisitions, and if they are approved by the deputy minister they will be forwarded to me and I will supply their requisitions.

Q. You supply their requisitions?—A. I do.

Q. And do they make any recommendations or reports as to prices?—A. I would not accept any.

Q. Do they?—A. They have not at the present time.

Q. Is that the intention?—A. I do not think so.

Q. That will solely be in your judgment and discretion?—A. Entirely so.

Q. And what experience have you had for it?

Mr. WATSON.—Perhaps I am getting into the matter of system your lordship has prohibited?

Hon. Mr. CASSELS.—This is a new system, I understand, doing away with the patronage list.

Mr. WATSON.—Yes.

By Mr. Watson:

Q. Now, in connection with that, just in reference to the observation from his lordship about the patronage list, are you going by the patronage list?—A. No.

Q. Not at all?—A. Yes, to a certain extent. If I find there are a sufficient number of people on the patronage list from whom I can obtain competitive prices I will utilize the patronage list; if not I will have to go outside them.

Q. That is a matter in your discretion?—A. I think it is left largely in my hands.

Q. Then how many would you say were enough, one or two?—A. No, not by any manner of means.

Q. What is your rule in regard to that, or have you a rule?—A. Yes, I have. I would consider if I got prices from ten different houses I was getting competitive prices.

Q. I should think so?—A. But I would not consider three to be competitive prices by any manner of means.

Q. You would not?—A. No.

Q. What is the lowest you would consider?—A. Not three taken from the patronage list.

Q. You would not?—A. No.

Q. What is the lowest number?—A. It would depend on the nature of the goods and the quantity.

Q. I suppose that might be so. What do you mean by patronage list?—A. The patronage list is generally understood in the department—I cannot speak with any degree of knowledge—to be a list of people recommended to the department as capable of supplying certain classes of goods.

Q. Generally, I suppose, friends of the government for the time being?—A. That might be.

Q. Do you know that?—A. No; because I know we have a large number of so-called Conservatives on the list. So I am told. I am told every day that so and so is a Conservative.

Q. I suppose that is a matter of complaint?—A. No, I do not think so, it is simply cited as a matter of fact. Whether they are or not I do not know.

Q. But somebody has been complaining, that is the case, is it not?—A. No; it is simply mentioned as a fact.

Q. Then do you discriminate?—A. No, I never have, because I do not know one from the other.

Q. The political complexion?—A. No, I do not, and I have no desire to.

Q. Well, you may be a Daniel come to judgment?—A. I may be.

Q. We have heard of a patronage list for a very great many years, most of us. At all events, that is the course that you are pursuing. And do you know what course has been pursued in the past in the department with regard to that patronage list, is what you are now stating any different from what has heretofore been in vogue?—A. I could not say definitely, but I understand that is generally what has been practiced, if they could get sufficient competition from the patronage list they would, if not they would go outside of it.

Q. How do you ascertain that the prices given to you correspond fairly with the market prices?

Hon. Mr. CASSELS.—I do not think you need follow that up, because it is not in force here.

Mr. WATSON.—I see.

By Mr. Watson:

Q. Have you put it in use yet at all?—A. Yes.

Q. To much extent?—A. As far as possible with the limited organization we have.

Q. And as far as you have used it have you ascertained the market prices?—A. I have a general knowledge of prices myself. Any other knowledge I do not possess myself I obtain elsewhere.

Q. How do the prices compare with the ordinary regular strict business market prices?—A. Provided the purchasing is done properly the government can buy cheaper.

Q. Can they?—A. Yes.

Q. Why don't they buy cheaper then?—A. I really do not know.

Q. Is it not a fact that the government does not buy cheaper, but buys at the dearest prices?—A. No, I would not admit that.

Q. Have you a knowledge with regard to that?—A. That they buy at the dearest prices?

Q. Or prices that are not the cheapest prices, that are not fairly cheap?—A. No, I do not know. This government as a general rule pay pretty fair prices.

Q. I am speaking of your department?—A. For the simple reason that the government buy the best class of goods Very probably for commercial purposes so high a ade of goods would not be purchased, but the government generally buys the best rade of goods obtainable.

Q. And pay prices accordingly?—A. They pay for what they get, naturally.

Q. Well now, what have you to do with the Marconi Company?—A. Well, the Iarconi Company are operating the government stations under contract. I have to se that they perform the service and that their accounts are rendered in accordance ith the service which they render the government. If they are, why the account is assed and paid; if they do not render the service, why deductions are made from hat account.

Q. That is a matter of contract with the company?—A. Of contract with the ompany.

Q. And what has Commander Spain to do with that?—A. At the present time?

Q. Yes?—A. Nothing.

Q. Up to this time he had?—A. Up to the date of my appointment, yes, he ccupied the same position as I occupy.

Q. And is Mr. Oppe the manager of the company?—A. I understand he is.

Q. Then you have been there now for getting on two years?—A. Practically.

Q. In the matter of supplies?—A. What way?

Q. Do you know that the people from whom you purchase frequently give discounts on sales?—A. Well, all the supplies I have bought, most of the supplies that I ave purchased have been bought at net prices, it being the custom of the trade to upply goods in that way. It is not every firm will send a list price with discounts nd it is not every class of goods that are sold in that way. Take the matter of upplies from people I do business with very largely. I think only two companies end us a list price, they invariably sell at net prices.

Q. The commissioners speak of their knowledge of a rule applying to discount?— \. Yes.

Q. What do you say, is that correct?—A. No, absolutely not correct.

Q. You say that is not correct?—A. Absolutely so.

Q. Then to what extent does that discount prevail?—A. Well——

Q. I mean in the proportion of business people?—A. Exactly. As acting account- int I have always made a practice to scrutinize as far as I possibly could all accounts vhich were paid. I introduced a new system after I took the position of acting iccountant. I refused to sign a cheque unless the cheque was attached to the account, ind in that way the account passed through my hands. Of course, I naturally have 1ot time to go through every account, but I noticed cases where there was discount, 1ot cash discount, but trade $discount$, and sometimes cash discount.

Q. Well, do you mean that that was allowed?—A. I beg your pardon?

Q. Do you mean that that was given or allowed?—A. Yes. Trade discount and tlso cash discount, if we cared to take advantage of it.

Q. That is for cash as distinguished from what credit?—A. As distinguished from rade discount. For instance, if you buy——

Q. A discount for cash?—A. As distinguished from trade discount.

Q. As discount from a credit purchase, a time purchase?—A. No. People selling o the government consider they do not take advantage of cash discount and very requently it is not mentioned, but a certain proportion of accounts you will find offer i cash discount provided the government take advantage and pay the account within 80 days.

Q. Then——?—A. Then you have a trade discount, that is a trade discount given rom a list price.

Q. That is given irrespective of cash or credit?—A. Yes, irrespective of cash liscount.

Q. But where there is a discount for cash that is a payment within 30 days?— \. A payment within 30 days.

Q. And if not paid within 30 days, if you don't take the discount what credit do you get?—A. Practically——

Q. Four months?—A. No, depending on when the account reaches the accountant to be paid. Invariably all invoices which have cash discount on them we always take it off, whether the account is paid in 30 days, 60 days or 90 days. That is the practice I made. I take it off in any of them.

Q. And the reduction was accepted?—A. It was never complained of to my knowledge.

Q. Never complained of?—A. No.

Q. Well, that is a good system to adopt?—A. You have to do it.

Q. That system you speak of, do you recognize it as being materially different from the system heretofore in vogue or use?—A. No, not materially different, but I presume it is brought to a greater degree of refinement.

Q. I see?—A. Heretofore the purchasing has been largely left in the hands of the officers at the head of the different branches, all of whom are very busy with other duties and probably did not have the time necessary to devote to the ascertaining of what the proper prices were.

Q. And it is manifest that is a material advance forward for accuracy?—A. Undoubtedly.

Q. I suppose so, if you keep in touch with market prices generally. But is it the practice for one man to keep in touch with market prices of all goods that come in?—A. Certainly.

Q. Now, then, during the time you have been there what have been the difficulties that have existed in this department and the subject of comment and criticism?—A. It is very difficult to say.

Q. What?—A. Very difficult to say. A multiplicity of reasons, I should imagine.

Q. What do you mean?—A. I mean to say you cannot state any one cause or reason for the so-called difficulties the department has been labouring under.

Q. What difficulties are you referring to?—A. Well, the difficulties that have generally been referred to in the department.

Q. Irregularities?—A. No, I would not call them irregularities.

Q. Where have they existed?—A. I do not know of any irregularities.

Q. Do you not?—A. No, I do not. The only irregularities I know of and can call to mind are very minor irregularities.

Q. What do you refer to, please?—A. I refer to advances made on account of payments. Those are the only irregularities I can bring to mind at the present time.

Q. I see. Advances made——?—A. On account of payments.

Q. Advances made to whom and by whom?—A. Sometimes the department has purchased goods from parties on which advances have been made.

Q. Before delivery?—A. Yes, before delivery.

Q. Before delivery of the goods?—A. Before delivery of the goods.

Q. Yes?—A. And I presume in a department it might be considered irregular, but I know it is frequently—I should not say frequently—but sometimes it is done in commercial circles. That is the only thing I could possibly recall as an irregularity, and, as I say, it is a minor irregularity.

Q. Where has that existed?—A. In the department.

Q. I know; but in what particular branch?—A. I really could not tell you.

Q. What?—A. I really could not tell you.

Q. What instances have you in mind?—A. An instance that came to my knowledge in the accountant's branch, I think of an account for some sulpho-naphthol. I understand it is a deodorizer or disinfectant.

Q. What was it, please?—A. An order for some sulpho-naphthol and advances made before some of the goods were delivered, if I am not mistaken.

Q. Advances made by whom?—A. By the department.

Q. Through whom?—A. I do not exactly understand.

Q. Through what individual ? The department does not act except by an official?
A. I could not say. The cheque was issued by the accountant's branch, like all
eques.

Q. That was in charge of Mr. Owen?—A. Yes, he was accountant, I think, at the
me.

Q. He was accountant ?—A. I think so.

Q. And to whom was it paid ?—A. To a man by the name of Eyre.

Q. And when was that ?—A. I could not say.

Q. About what year ?—A. I think it was last year.

Q. Last year. And what was the amount of it, about ?—A. I think it was about
150, somewhere in that vicinity.

Q. I see. That was to Eyre. Eyre represented what company ?—A. The Win-
ate-Johnston Company.

Q. The Wingate-Johnston Company ?—A. Yes.

Q. Where from ?—A. Montreal.

Q. And who got the benefit of that ?—A. No one.

Q. Were the goods afterwards delivered ?—A. All.

Q. And to whom was the payment made ?—A. Eyre.

Q. Payment was made to Eyre ? Eyre was the agent ?—A. Eyre was the agent.
e subsequently died, and I think there was a balance still due to Eyre at the time,
ad I think he was indebted to Wingate-Johnston & Company. I think we paid the
alance to Wingate-Johnston & Company, or the Wingate Chemical Company—that
as it, the Wingate Chemical Company.

Q. I see. Then did any of the goods go to individuals?—A. Not that I am aware
f.

Q. Not that your are aware of?—A. No.

Q. Have you seen the correspondence ?—A. I have.

Q. Have you got it ?—A. No.

Q. Can you produce it ?—A. I can.

Q. That is the correspondence between the department and Eyre, or the Chemical
Company ?—A. The Chemical Company, I think.

Q. I see. Did Eyre pay the Chemical Company ?—A. No, I don't think so. I
think there was still a balance due them when he died, and the department paid over
the balance which was due Eyre at the time.

Q. From what you are referring to, as I understand, advances were made by that
department for goods, those advances were made to the agent, and the agent did not
pay the company for the goods ?—A. That is something we have absolutely nothing
to do with.

Hon. Mr. CASSELS.—$150 was advanced ?

Mr. WATSON.—Yes, my lord.

Q. That is all there was in it?—A. That is the only thing I can mention as being
at all irregular, and that is a minor irregularity, which I would not consider an irregularity.

Q. And is there ground to suspect something wrong by individuals?—A. I do not.

Q. Did any individual in the department get any advantage by reason of that
kind of transaction ?—A. Not that I know of.

Q. Have you any reason to think so ?—A. No, I have not.

Q. You have not ?—A. No.

Q. Then do you know of any other irregularities ?—A. None whatever.

Q. Do you know of any act that might be designated unconscientious ?—A. No,
I do not.

Q. Not faithful ?—A. No.

Q. Were you applied to for information by the Commissioners of the Civil Service ?—A. No. I never met any of them. They never asked for any information whatever.

Q. Do you know of the Marconi Company making any gifts, presents or advances to any one in the department ?—A. No.

Q. Eh?—A. No, I do not.

Q. Have you ever heard of anything of the kind?—A. Yes, I have.

Q. What have you heard?—A. I have heard that they had given stock to some members of the department. I never heard who, though.

Q. Did you hear any names?—A. No.

Q. They did it through Mr. Oppe?—A. Yes.

Mr. WATSON.—I heard the same thing, my lord. That is the reason I am asking. Mr. Oppe will be here to-morrow. I am not asking these questions in a blind way, my lord.

WITNESS.—That is a general rumour that has been round the department ever since I have been there.

Q. Ever since you have been there?—A. Yes, sir.

Q. But you are not able to apply it?—A. No, I have absolutely no information whatever.

Q. Are you able to apply that to any one else?—A. In connection with the Marconi company?

Q. In respect of that or any other company, contractor or supply people?—A. No, absolutely.

Q. Has anything ever occurred that has come to your knowledge between officials and supply men or contractors which is the subject of comment, of criticism?—A. No. I never heard of anything any more than just as a general rumour, which all the witnesses have mentioned here more or less, the rumour that some of the officers of the department had been lacking in conscience or something of that kind, but absolutely nothing of a definite nature.

Q. But did you ever hear of that before it was published in this report?—A. Oh, yes.

Q. You heard that before?—A. Yes.

Q. What foundation is there for it?—A. I cannot imagine. I have never seen anything to warrant it.

Q. Is that something that attaches to this department as distinguished from other departments ?—A. No, I do not think so.

Q. You know nohing about that, then?—A. No.

Q. Any other information you can give his lordship upon the subject?—A. Absolutely none whatever.

Hon. Mr. Cassels:

Q. One thing. Have you had sufficient experience in your new position to make an estimate of what the new method of purchasing will save the country in future pe rannum?—A. Well, I have never given the matter very much thought. I expect, I have no doubt the saving will be large.

Q. What do you call large, $100,000, a million?—A. Hardly.

Q. $1,000?—A. Yes.

Q. What do you think the difference will be under the new system?—A. I should say $50,000, if not double that, a year.

Q. Then your trade discount you get now as against the past means you get wholesale prices?—A. We get wholesale prices; and apart from that——

Q. One moment, please. The trade discount is what a wholesale purchaser gets from a manufacturer?—A. Yes.

Q. That they never got in the past?—A. Oh, yes.

Q. I want to know that. They have always got wholesale prices?—A. When they have bought from wholesale people. When they have bought from retail people they have paid retail prices.

Q. But buying from wholesale people they got wholesale prices?—A. Yes.

Q. That is what you call wholesale discount?—A. Yes.

Q. And under your new system——?—A. We expect to buy larger quantities olesale.

Q. With the additional saving in the discount?—A. Not only that, but in the cise requisitions from the officers.

Q. And the competition?—A. And the competition.

Q. That will do.

B. H. FRASER, recalled.

By Mr. Watson:

Q. You are sworn, Mr. Fraser?—A. I was sworn on a previous occasion.

Q. Oh, yes; I beg your pardon. What is your position?—A. Assistant to Colonel derson.

Q. Assistant to Colonel Anderson. Then, are you an engineer?—A. Yes, sir.

Q. An engineer?—A. Yes, sir.

Q. How long have you been in the department?—A. Nineteen years this year.

Q. And in his department all the time?—A. All the time under Colonel Anderson.

Q. Then you were there before it changed, before there was a division?—A. Oh,

Q. Before there was a division in the department. And Mr. J. F. Fraser was in at department at that time?—A. He had been there some considerable time.

Q. He was superior to you?—A. No, he was junior to me. I was there some years ead of him.

Q. He was your junior?—A. While he was in my branch or in the branch I was nnected with.

Q. I see. Is he a relative of yours?—A. No connection whatever, no relation.

Q. And you were appointed nineteen years ago?—A. Yes, sir.

Q. How did the division of the office come about?—A. I have no idea, I am sure. was not consulted, I know nothing about it.

Q. You know nothing about it?—A. No.

Q. Was that by reason of excessive work in the department, too much work in the epartment?—A. I forget now. It seems to me I heard Colonel Anderson say in his ridence something to that effect. I did not pay much attention to it. I have quite rgotten the reason if I ever knew.

Q. It was said by Colonel Anderson that that was by reason of the recommenda-on and influence to some extent of Mr. J. F. Fraser. What knowledge have you of ıat?

Hon. Mr. CASSELS.—And of Mr. Willson.

By Mr. Watson:

Q. Yes?—A. I have no knowledge whatever of that. I could not tell you any-ıing at all about it. I was only in a subordinate position. I would never be con-ılted in anything of that kind.

Q. But you were superior to Mr. J. F. Fraser?—A. Not at the time that division ame about. Before that he had been taken from the inside and placed in the outside ervice, where he was entirely independent of myself. I had only charge of the draft-ıg room at that time.

Q. The drafting room?—A. Yes.

Q. Then what do you know of the influence of Mr. J. F. Fraser with the superior fficers?—A. Of the department?

Q. Yes?—A. Nothing whatever. I have no knowledge of any influence that he ıight have possessed, if he had any.

Q. You have no knowledge of it?—A. None whatever.

Q. But you had been working there intimately associated?—A. With Mr. J. F. Fraser?

Q. Yes?—A. For the short time he was in the drafting room, but not a very long time.

Q. Then afterwards he was in your branch or department?—A. Yes, but he was on outside services all the time.

Q. That brings you into close communication, contact?—A. No, not the work he was in; I had no connection with it whatever.

Q. Then do you know any reason for the suggestion or statement that that change was the result of influence or pressure on the part of any individuals?—A. I could not say anything about that.

Q. What?—A. Nothing came to my mind, nothing of that.

Q. Did you have any information of those matters?—A. No information.

Q. Did you hear anything of them at the time?—A. Not that I remember. I never paid very much attention.

Q. You say you did hear something, that is what that means?—A. No. I mean I did not pay much attention to the appointment, except that it appeared to me the division in the branch might at some time affect my prospects. I was in hopes of working up in the department.

Q. You thought that might be to your advantage?—A. It might be to my advantage or disadvantage. I knew that could not happen without affecting the status of everybody connected with the branch.

Q. Then it might follow that everybody would favour those divisions?—A. It was more a question of the scope of the department. If the department increased it was evident more officials would be necessary. It was sure to be an advantage to somebody at some time.

Q. Then who complained,—Colonel Anderson said be complained?—A. He certainly would not complain to me.

Q. Did you hear about that?—A. No, excepting everybody there could see there was a little feeling about it.

Q. That was apparent?—A. There was no question about that.

Q. When was that?—A. I presume since.

Q. I mean what year did that take place? I have forgotten for the moment?—A. I could not say offhand.

Q. About how many years ago?—A. I should think four or five years ago, perhaps longer.

Q. And that condition existed from that time forward, more or less?—A. I have not seen much of it lately.

Q. Not much lately?—A. Practically none at all lately.

Q. And how did that affect the operations in the department?—A. I do not think it had a bad effect at all.

Q. You do not think it had?—A. Not as far as I could see.

Q. Was anything done by Mr. J. F. Fraser that appeared to be reprehensible or censurable in regard to the matter?—A. Nothing, except I myself might consider his action a little bit unprofessional.

Q. What do you mean?—A. Well, one of the ethics of engineering is to be extremely loyal to your chief, and while I am not exactly acquainted with it, I have an impression he had been promoted without the usual formalities being gone through.

Q. Without the usual formalities, that is, Colonel Anderson had not been sufficiently considered?—A. That is the impression I got at the time. If he had first resigned his position under Colonel Anderson and then been appointed, that would have been more professional.

Q. You are speaking of it from the ethical standpoint?—A. Entirely so.

Q. That rule of ethics prevails to a high degree in the department?—A. As far as I know. I have seen nothing to the contrary.

Q. It sometimes costs a lot?—A. Loyalty to your chief?

Q. Oh, no. Then at that time were you dealing in carbide with the Willson Company?—A. I never dealt in carbide.

Q. Did you have any knowledge of that?—A. Very little. I think just about that time the question of the use of acetylene was being considered:

Q. By whom?—A. By the chief engineer. That is my recollection.

Q. Did you know what his view of it was?—A. I always thought he was rather favourable to it.

Q. You thought he was favourable to it. Now, it has been suggested that the introduction of it was promoted, perhaps unduly promoted, by Mr. J. F. Fraser. Have you any knowledge of that?—A. None at all. After he passed from our branch I had quite enough work on my hands.

Q. And it has been plainly suggested or stated that Mr. Willson had too much to do with that, it was through his influence?—A. I have no knowledge whatever of that.

Q. Have you any knowledge of that at all?—A. Nothing at all. My office is in a different position from his.

Q. Have any circumstances come to your knowledge that bear upon those matters?—A. None at all.

Q. What has been the relationship between Colonel Anderson and the deputy minister, do you know?—A. They have always been very friendly whenever I have seen them together.

Q. You know nothing to the contrary?—A. Nothing, no.

Q. Where has friction existed in the department?—A. I have seen practically none.

Q. Practically none. Where has it existed as a fact?—A. I do not know any, except Colonel Anderson certainly had feeling against Mr. Fraser, as I judge, but latterly I have seen nothing of it.

Q. And where have the jealousies and rivalries existed?—A. I have not seen any.

Q. Have you not?—A. Not at all.

Q. Have they not been too common there?—A. There have been no jealousies that I know of.

Q. Everything in harmony?—A. Apparently so, as far as my work is concerned.

Q. Then have you any knowledge at all about the business transactions with the Carbide Company or with the International Gas Buoy Company?—A. Absolutely nothing, sir. I never had the slightest, I know absolutely nothing.

Q. Then you do know something about this Canadian fog signal?—A. Yes, I had a good deal to do with that.

Q. I see. Did that commence under your recommendation?—A. Oh, no. I had—

Q. Who introduced that, what official, the chief?—A. I would just like to understand what you mean by the question? Who introduced the Canadian Fog Signal Company?

Q. Into the department, yes?—A. I think it was the outcome of work that had been done by the Northey Company before. Before the Canadian Fog Signal Company ever was in existence the Northey Company had done some work for us. I was not in charge of the whole thing, but I had a good deal of technical work in connection with that, so my memory is fairly good on that. There was some work done by the Northey Company at the time it went out of business and this work was then taken over by the Canadian Fog Signal Company at that time.

Q. Taken over?—A. I mean they continued. The Northey Company went out of business, but whatever work was going on the Fog Signal Company continued.

Q. There was very little work with the Northey Company?—A. Not a great deal.

Q. And that was purchasing what from them?—A. They supplied the fog signal that was installed at Louisburg.

3262—14

Q. What was that called ?—A. It was a Scotch Siren.

Q. I see. Then at that time the purchases of signals were of the design known as sirens, were they ?—A. No, sir. That was the first one of that kind.

Q. Then we need not go into that. The prices being paid then for the signals were comparatively small, were they not ?—A. I am inclined to think that that one cost us quite as much as any one of the same power put in since. I could not say offhand, but I think it did.

Q. And was that being manufactured by others ?—A. It was manufactured in the old country.

Q. So that up to that time there was competition in the manufacture and supply of the signals ?—A. Well, I know very little about that.

Q. But you know about that ?—A. I was in a very subordinate position. The work was done by the chief of the branch, and if he told me this thing was built by the Northey Company——

Q. Colonel Anderson had everything to do with that ?—A. Absolutely. At that time he was superintendent of lights and had charge.

Q. When did he cease ?—A. At the time the change was made and that branch went over to the commissioner of lights.

Q. What branch ?—A. All the supply of lighthouse apparatus and fog signal apparatus, and everything of that kind.

Q. But these fog signals are bought in your department now ?—A. Yes, sir ; that is a fact.

Q. Then why speak of them going over to the other department ?—A. They did go over and stayed over there a year or two, perhaps two years.

Q. But where did the negotiations or purchases for the present diaphone system originate ?—A. Oh, there had been some diaphones purchased before it went over to the commissioner of lights.

Q. You are not unloading them on the other department in regard to the introduction of that ?—A. Absolutely not at all

Q. Why not ?—A. Why should I ?

Q. You do not seek to do so ?—A. Not the slightest.

Q. You take the responsibility of that ?—A. I cannot take the responsibility, I am only a subordinate.

Q. I see. But that began and was introduced under Colonel Anderson ?—A. Undoubtedly so.

Q. Now then, more pointedly. You knew about the cost of these diaphones. When did you first learn of that ?—A. I learned more about it to-day than I ever knew before, I think, in some ways. At that time I don't think we ever considered the diaphone as a sound producing device alone ; it was a question of the whole plant the same as it had been before.

Q. Well?—A. I am perfectly candid with you. That is what I mean to say. We never considered the price of the diaphone as a single instrument alone, the instruments that were purchased from the Fog Signal Company.

Q. Are you making this now in explanation and excuse?—A. Not at all.

Q. Then just keep to the one point. When did you first learn the cost of the diaphone?—A. The diaphone alone, separate from the plant?

Q. Yes?—A. I never took that question into consideration until tenders were called for the thing and a special price was put in for the diaphone.

Q. When was that?—A. I should think about 3 years ago.

Q. It must have been before that?—A· No, sir.

Q. The cost of the plant never varied materially, you had been using the same kind of plant before?—A. Of course the plant now is very much smaller than it was originally.

Q. It is smaller, but the cost of that has not changed very materially?—A. Undoubtedly as the plant became smaller the price became smaller too.

Q. Proportionately?—A. Yes.

Q. And there are many manufactures of the plant, we have heard?—A. No.

Q. Not many manufacturers of the plant?—A. I doubt if there is any one single manufacturer. It is a thing that has to be composed of various members.

Q. Mr. Northey has stated there are many manufacturers from whom plants can be obtained?—A. That is, I doubt whether one manufacturer can supply the whole plant.

Q. I am not including the diaphone?—A. No, not the diaphone· This air compressor, pipes, tanks.

By Hon. Mr. Cassels:

Q. One man assembles the whole thing. He makes a contract for it and goes to some other person for the parts?—A. That is the only way it can be done.

By Mr. Watson:

Q. They could do the same as the Northey Company. That company does not manufacture them, but it assembles them, as his lordship put it?—A. Yes.

Q. There is no difficulty about that· There is plenty of competition in that?—A. As to supplying the different parts?

Q. Yes?—A. Oh yes.

Q. There is no question about that. So there has been no monopoly except in regard to the diaphone?—A. In connection with this plant?

Q. Yes?—A. That is all.

Q. And that has been known to you?—A. It was adopted·

Q. That has been known to you in the department?—A. I don't know whether you call it a monopoly. The department always had the option to throw the thing out.

Q. Always had the option?—A. Certainly.

Q. And did you know you could get diaphones from anyone else?—A. It never occurred to me we could.

Q. I see. It never occured to you that there was competition or might be competition in regard to that?—A. No, I do not think it did.

Q. It did not occur to you, for instance, that these were manufactured under exclusive patents, that did not occur to you?—A. That is what I am trying to make out. Owing to the fact I knew this thing was patented I had a good deal to do with that thing from the time it first came into the country in a technical way.

Q. That is what I am informed you had?—A. I don't deny it.

Q. I am informed you had too much to do with it from the other standpoint?—A. I will be very glad to have you question me on that as much as you can·

Q. I will do so. Then at all events did you know the diaphone could not be purchased from anyone else?—A. That was my impression, undoubtedly.

Q. You were not accurate about it?—A. I think I was pretty accurate. It never occurred to me to go to anybody else.

Q. It looks as though it might be a matter of indifference, then?—A. No. If you will allow me to explain.

Q. I do not want any long speeches.—A. There will be no long speeches. The fact is this department was trying to get a good fog signal. We had been a great many years without one on account of our system being a little bit old, and the chief engineer put me largely in charge of the development of this instrument when it came into this country first.

Q. Which instrument, the diaphone?—A. Yes. Acting under his directions it never occurred to me to look anywhere else. This concern had charge of it, we were developing it, and I simply acted under my instructions in connection with the technical parts of that thing. I had no knowledge of the price or anything of that. It was purely a question of development.

3262—14½

Q. You mean to say you did not consider the matter of price?—A. It was not my business.

Q. Whose business was that?—A. My superior officer's.

Q. Did you obtain any information about that?—A. Not at that time.. My business was to——

Q. You obtained no information, and the recommendations you made were irrespective of cost?—A. Well, I would have to look over the correspondence to see, I would not like to say offhand.

Q. That is your recollection?—A. Now we are speaking of the time the thing came into the country first?

Q. Yes.—A. Absolutely; I never questioned it.

Q. When did you first begin to think of the cost?—A. I think after the work came back again from the commissioner of lights branch.

Q. Yes, three or four years ago. Then it was you became aware that it cost about $400 or $500?—A. Yes, sir.

Q. And you knew the same things were being sold to the department for $4,600? —A. No. That question of $4,600 never came up until tenders were called for.

Q. What price had you paid for it before, the same price?—A. As I tried to tell you before, we bought those things entirely as plant.

Q. Never mind that. You get back to the plant the same as Mr. Northey does?— A. There is no distinction between the diaphone and plant, the whole thing was a fog signal plant, that diaphone and everything else.

Q. I know. But you became aware 3 or 4 years ago that the diaphone itself only cost $400 or $500?—A. Somewhere in that vicinity.

Q. And about the same time, putting one and one together and two and two together, the result was you were paying between $4,000 and $5,000 for the diaphone, and you knew the cost of the plant—you can add and subtract?—A. But I don't think at that time we were paying that much.

Q. The evidence shows that?—A. I think not.

Q. Has there been an increase in the price during the last 3 or 4 years?—A. No, but in the last 3 or 4 years it has been a contract.

Q. Then do you mean to say that the prices have been increased in the last 3 or 4 years, because that is news to us?—A. I would like to be perfectly clear about this thing. Up to the time tenders were called for this plant the price of the diaphone had never been considered separately.

By Hon. Mr. Cassels:

Q. What did you pay for the siren with the plant?—A. I could not tell you offhand.

Q. How much less then you paid for this one?—A. I think, in fact, I feel quite satisfied, but I would have to look it up to see, that siren cost us as much complete as the diaphone costs us now.

By Mr. Watson:

Q. But Mr. Northey has stated the siren cost about £300 or £350?—A. It takes a great deal more machinery to drive than the diaphone.

Q. But his lordship asked the cost of the diaphone.

Hon. Mr. CASSELS.—I asked about the whole thing.

Mr. WATSON.—Yes. Then what was the cost of the siren?—A. Mr. Northey is better posted. If he says the cost——

Q. Have you any idea?—A. None whatever.

Q. Then it seems to me inconceivable, Mr. Fraser, that you having the introduction, going into the matter and considering it as you did for the purpose of applying it, you would make no consideration of the cost at all. It was a new matter at that time, was it not, not adopted in other countries?—A. No, but Colonel Anderson had examined it very closely

Q. But do you mean to say you adopted a new system or article of that kind without reference to its cost?—A. I presume he went very fully into that.

Q. Have you any knowledge?—A. You would have to ask him.

Q. Have you any knowledge?—A. I do not know what he did about it.

Q. And you have no knowledge of the cost, but yet I think it was delegated to you for the most part?—A. About the cost?

Q. Not about the cost, but the introduction of it and the working of it?—A. The mere testing of it.

Q. The testing of it?—A. Yes.

Q. You knew it was new?—A. Undoubtedly.

Q. You knew it would involve large additional expense?—A. I do not know I was interested in that at the time.

By Hon. Mr. Cassels:

Q. Did you know it required a cheaper plant than the old siren plant?—A. Undoubtedly.

Q. Did you know that from the outset?—A. From the outset it was evident.

Q. That the plant required for this diaphone would cost very much less than the plant required for the siren?—A. That was the first diaphones we had, they were very much smaller.

Q. Take the corresponding sizes, you were aware from the commencement——?—A. No. At the start—I must correct myself a little bit there—at the start when they made bigger sized diaphones they took a good deal more plant than now.

Q. Corresponding with the plant of the siren, you say the plant of the diaphone cost very much less?—A. Not when they made the first very big diaphone.

Q. When?—A. When the diaphone had been changed from double pressure.

Q. When was that?—A. Within the last 3 or 4 years.

By Mr. Watson:

Q. The fact is, as far as I can ascertain from you, this has been adopted and proceeded with practically without regard to cost; that is the long and short of it?—A. I would not like to say that.

Q. So far as you were personally concerned?—A. I was only a subordinate.

Q. But a subordinate and engineer, the man who was supervising this. Did you not make any report or recommendation to the chief?—A. About the cost?

Q. Yes?—A. No.

Q. Did you have any communication with the deputy minister?—A. No.

Q. Or the minister?—A. No.

Q. You never mentioned any of these matters. Do you not mention matters of price in your department to the deputy minister or the minister?—A. I deal entirely with the engineer.

Q. Do you know what course he takes?—A. I am bound to know now after being there so long with him, yes.

Q. The recommendations of the heads of the departments under the system are usually adopted, necessarily so, is not that so?—A. I would think so.

Q. That is almost a necessity?—A. It is in my opinion a necessity to carry on work of that kind.

Q. The deputy minister is seldom, perhaps, an engineer?—A. Colonel Gourdeau was not.

Q. And necessarily the deputy, and over him, the minister, would have to rely on the heads of departments?—A. Necessarily, in my opinion.

Q. Then these matters of price, such as we have had here now of these diaphones, to your knowledge were never brought to the attention of the deputy minister or the minister?—A. I would not exactly say that.

Q. To your knowledge?—A. I am satisfied that Colonel Anderson must have brought——

Q. I am not asking you that. I say to your own knowledge. I am not asking you to reason about it?—A. No, I cannot say.

Q. No. Then three or four years ago you knew there was this extraordinary profit on the diaphone, it costing $400 or $500 and being sold for as many thousands. Did you rebel against that at all when you learned that as an official?—A. Yes, sir. I want to make that clear to you. I did call the attention of Colonel Anderson to the thing.

Q. You called his attention to it?—A. Yes.

Q. You are a man getting considerable remuneration. What is your remuneration. about?—A. I think it is $2,700.

Q. Well, you are getting very substantial remuneration, involving considerable responsibility. In connection with that you drew this to his attention?—A. I certainly did.

Q. Three or four years ago?—A. I think probably at the time the tenders came in.

Q. And commented upon the excess of price?—A. Of course, my opinion is the thing cost more than $300 or $400.

Q. I am not asking you that?—A. I think I have a right to say that.

Q. Are you trying to excuse the manufacturers?—A. No, not to excuse exactly, but I want to say that. You are trying to make it appear I knew it was a very excessive charge.

Q. I am taking my premises from you, witness; that is, you knew the cost was $400 or $500 and that the selling price was as many thousands; I am taking those premises from you?—A. I tried to tell you a moment ago I thought the cost was more than that.

Q. Did you not know the cost was $400 or $500?—A. That is the manufacturing cost, but I could not tell what the cost would be to the manufacturer.

Q. That is rather argumentative and is a little bit of advocacy, I think, I do think so.—A. Possibly it may be so.

Q. I am asking you as to the actual cost of the manufacture of that, and you knew it was $400 or $500. Now, why do you want to build up to the manufacturer, or do you?—A. Only to the extent I really thought the thing did cost more than——

Q. But you were told that was the cost?—A. I am told that now; I did not know that then.

Q. I think you told me you knew 3 or 4 years ago.

By Hon. Mr. Cassels:

Q. When did you see the price list?—A. I say I knew 3 or 4 years ago they intended to charge $4,600.

Q. When was that?—A. Only after the tenders were called for, probably.

Q. How long ago?—A. I think in 1905.

By Mr. Watson:

Q. It must have been before that. You have been paying that price right along? —A. The tenders are there on the file.

Q. Well, before the tenders what prices had you been paying?—A. I am trying to tell you we paid the price for the plant complete then, and that price I had nothing to do with.

Q. But anyone would distinguish between the two. You knew the prices of the plant, you knew that years and years before. You see, that is the simplest matter in the world?—A. That matter was under the chief engineer, and when he said it was a fair figure, as his assistant I had nothing further to say.

Q. Did he say it was a fair figure?—A. I am satisfied he did.

Q. Are you speaking from recollection?—A. I would have to refer to the file to be sure. I know it could not be done any other way.

Q. Now then, at all events you do not take any responsibility in regard to that, I understand?—A. Up to that time, no.

Q. Up to what time?—A. Up to the time tenders were called for.

Q. Do you assume responsibility since then?—A. To this extent: I made a report then as to the cost of the plant then put in, and I am satisfied the cost of the plant was all right. As to the cost of the diaphone I never had one word to say.

Q. You never had any objection or complaint as to that?—A. Pardon me. I said I called the thing to Colonel Anderson's attention, the price of the diaphone. I said it was high, he said that was a fair price.

Q. Then what has been your relation with these manufacturers?—A. Purely techincal.

Q. Eh?—A. Technical.

Q. Technical?—A. That is it. In regard to the question of manufacture it is a study in itself, it is a science in itself.

Q. You were here yesterday. Would you tell me why you spent four days with the secretary of that company in New York?—A. I do not see why I should not.

Q. You do not see why you should not. That is a fact, as I understand, you spent four days there with him?—A. Three days, I think, to be exact, not the whole time.

Q. That was a matter of entertainment and pleasure, more or less, I suppose?—A. It was on my part, I went there on a bit of pleasure at my own expense, it was holiday time.

Q. At your own expense?—A. Yes.

Q. You were not there on the business of the department?—A. Not at all.

Q Did you get leave to be absent?—A. I mentioned it to the deputy minister. I forget whether I got Tuesday—Monday was a general holiday—I certainly mentioned to the deputy I would not be there on Saturday, I told him I was going to New York.

Q. You went there to meet Mr. Mearns, did you?—A. Well, I had an idea I would meet him there, I knew he was going to be there.

Q. That is creating a sort of personal relationship between you and the manufacturers, who are enjoying what is here shown to be an extraordinary and immense profit. Did that occur to you?—A. It never occurred to me. I must say I never thought of any thing of the kind, absolutely not, no sir.

Q. Then what benefit have you received from this company?—A. I have received no benefits from that company.

Q. What?—A. No benefits whatever.

Q. What favours or advantages?—A. None whatever.

Q. Who paid your expenses on that occasion?—A. I paid them myself.

Q. Part of them?—A. I am absolutely positive, I am swearing that.

Q. All of them?—A. Every cent of them.

Q. I see· Then your influence and assistance have been sought by the company, more or less?—A. I don't think so, certainly not in an improper way.

Hon. Mr. CASSELS.—Mr. Watson, unless you can get the Supreme Court to sit somewhere else I will have to adjourn; they are coming in.

Mr. WATSON.—Your lordship will see we can hardly, I think, transfer to the other court this afternoon conveniently. Would your lordship be willing, in view of this earlier adjournment, to sit at 10 o'clock to-morrow instead of 10.30?

Hon. Mr. CASSELS.—I will sit at 9 o'clock if you like.

Mr. WATSON.—I would prefer 10, if your lordship pleases.

Hon. Mr. CASSELS.—All right.

Adjourned at 3·45 p.m. to 10 a.m. to-morrow and then resumed.

JUNE 17, 10 a.m., 1908.

Mr. WATSON.—My lord, I will break in upon the conclusion of Mr. Fraser's examination just for a moment, if your lordship pleases.

Hon. Mr. CASSELS.—Before you start I want to make a suggestion as to the way this thing occurs to me and the course of procedure we had better take.

This diaphone business has assumed very grave importance. The evidence that has been given so far, although not too explicit, would indicate this state of facts: that during the past 3½ to 4 years the diaphones with the necessary machinery, whatever they call it——

Mr. WATSON.—Plant.

Hon. Mr. CASSELS.—With the necessary plant have been sold to the government, the government paying an amount of about $500,000. Now a statement is made that of that $500,000, $150,000 is for the diaphone and $350,000 for the plant.

The way it strikes me on the evidence at present is this: Under the Patent Act the government had a right—when I talk of the government I mean the officers of the government—the government had a right to ask for this diaphone, and the patentee or manufacturer was bound to furnish it at a reasonable price. If he failed to do so the patent became void. Under another section of the Patent Act the government had a right to manufacture the patented invention, and it is more a question of paying reasonable compensation.

The evidence, so far as it has gone, shows this state of facts; the cost of the diaphone is $400. It could hardly be said that a manufacturing profit of 50 per cent would be an unreasonable compensation to allow any manufacturer. That would bring it up to $600. The patentee received a royalty in the neighbourhood of $100, so that the cost, with the manufacturer's profit at the rate of even 50 per cent and the patentee's royalty, would be $700 altogether on the present evidence, and if not furnished at that price the patents could be voided and the government could have it manufactured and save the patentee's royalty.

Now, if $150,000 is the sum attributable to this diaphone business, all the government should have paid is the sum of $25,000, and the result is that they have paid $125,000 in excess of what should have been paid. That over-payment may have arisen from negligence, or it may have arisen from a misconception altogether of the rights of the government. Nevertheless, there is the fact. It may have arisen from other motives into which we have not yet probed.

I think the evidence on the cost ought to be gone into more explicitly. There are several points I think ought to be brought out. One is, what is the agreement between the Northey Company—I do not know the name of the company now, I have forgotten —and the patentee. I should like to see that agreement. I should like to see what royalty has been paid. The company represented by Mr. Northey had no right whatever to exact anything further. Therefore I think it of importance we should see the agreement so as to know exactly the terms upon which the company was manufacturing and the royalty which was to be paid.

Secondly, I think it ought to be ascertained what relative proportion of the $500,000 is applicable to plant and what to the diaphone. It may turn out that a larger sum is applicable to the diaphone or a smaller sum.

Then, I think, we ought to get in more detail the cost of manufacture so as to see what sum has been overpaid.

I think it calls for very careful and rigid inquiry under the facts. I suggest, therefore, the line of cross-examination you are about to proceed with should be in the meantime held over until we get this information.

Mr. WATSON.—Yes, my lord. I had in mind that your lordship might anticipate some of these matters that have now been referred to, and having that in mind I had a special consultation with Mr. Northey about these matters. Your lordship is aware that the books that were produced are so made up that although it may be quite in eir ordinary course of business—I am not saying it is not so—still one cannot make nything out of them at all. They are not even in the witness box able to give any formation.

Hon. Mr. CASSELS.—On the evidence it appears the cost would run to about 100.

Mr. WATSON.—Yes, my lord. I found Mr. Northey was not able to give me any ore explicit and definite information than was stated the other day, so I have asked im to have statements prepared and to search and see if there are not some other ooks which bear on the subject of cost and that agreement.

Hon. Mr. CASSELS.—Have you a statement showing the number of purchases?

Mr. WATSON.—Yes, my lord. The royalty was not brought down; it was intended o be.

Hon. Mr. CASSELS.—The matter requires very careful investigation, and it becomes mportant to those concerned, whatever officials they are, that they should explain why his sum of money has been overpaid.

Mr. WATSON.—Quite so. It is apparent it is necessary to have more definite nformation than the president and the secretary of the company are able here to give.

Hon. Mr. CASSELS.—Unless their memories are revived.

Mr. WATSON.—Yes, I have asked them to refresh their memories.

Hon. Mr. CASSELS.—Mr. Mearns may be able to give better information.

Mr. GODFREY.—I may say that Mr. Mearns went to Toronto last night. He asked e to mention that he would like to be notified if anything came up.

Mr. WATSON.—I will see to it.

Hon. Mr. CASSELS.—That is how it occurs to me at the present moment. I do not ay at the present time there is anything wrong with the officials. There is this over-payment that requires to be explained.

Mr. GODFREY.—He also stated that he would submit the whole price to arbitration.

Hon. Mr. CASSELS.—That is for the future· I think the question of price need not be submitted to arbitration; the statute provides for that. If he does not submit a reasonable price the patent can be voided.

Mr. WATSON.—Then I may not be able to proceed to-day or to-morrow——

Hon. Mr. CASSELS.—Excuse me one moment. You will find, Mr. Godfrey, in the Supreme Court reports a case in which McCormick was the defendent· It came from London. The court upheld the late Mr. Justice Burbidge's judgment as to the meaning of the statute.

Mr. GODFREY.—That is 37 S.C.R., I believe.

Dr. MORSE.—That is the case of Hildreth v. McCormick· It was decided by Judge Burbidge, and his judgment was confirmed on appeal to the Supreme Court.

Hon. Mr. CASSELS.—There they construed the statute.

Mr. WATSON.—Mr. Merwin is here.

Hon· Mr. CASSELS.—Will you not be able to· sit beyond to-morrow night?

Mr. WATSON.—Not, my lord, I am sorry to say, during this week. And in connection with that matter, now you speak of it, I have understood all along your lordship would not be able or disposed to use any part of the summer vacation from the 1st of July.

Hon. Mr. CASSELS.—I was under the impression counsel could not assist me, and I could not see how I could do the work alone.

Mr. GODFREY.—I am extremely anxious Mr. J. F. Fraser should be given an opportunity before this session is over to state his position.

Hon. Mr. CASSELS.—You see, it is impossible for Mr. Fraser to get through until this other information comes out.

Mr. GODFREY.—I do not think he is really interested in this.

Hon. Mr. CASSELS.—That has to be seen.

Mr. WATSON.—I told my learned friend I intended to call Mr. Fraser before your lordship rises on this occasion.

Hon. Mr. CASSELS—He is not out of the country?

Mr. WATSON.—He is here.

Hon. Mr. CASSELS.—I mean to say he can be recalled again if anything turns up?

Mr. GODFREY.—Except that he is here under considerable expense, and he is under some suspicion.

Hon. Mr. CASSELS.—He may be, but we have got to get to the bottom of this. I assure you I am not doing it from any pleasure.

Mr. GODFREY.—I am quite sure of that, my lord.

Mr. WATSON.—Mr. Merwin is here.

GEORGE T. MERWIN, sworn.

By Mr. Watson:

Q. Mr. Merwin, you are able to attend here and to produce the books of account relating to matters between yourself and the department. Have you brought with you the books?—A. No, sir. Our books are all in the general office. I do not keep any books here at all.

Q. You do not?—A. No, sir.

Q. But are you not in business for yourself?—A. No, sir; I am an agent for the company.

Q. An agent for what company?—A. The Safety Car Heating and Lighting Company.

Q. You have books, I understand, in connection with your agency here?—A. No accounts, only stock records of our material.

Q. Nothing else?—A. Nothing else.

Q. And is the head office of that company at New York?—A. New York, yes, sir.

Q. Then you have also been a representative of Brooks & Company, or are you Brooks & Company?—A. I was a member of that firm at one time.

Q. Are you not now?—A. No, sir.

Q. And have you brought with you the books of that company?—A. No, sir. I had no subpœna to do that. My subpœna reads for myself.

Q. Then you control the books of Brooks & Co.?—A. No, Brooks does that.

Q. Who is Mr. Brooks?—A. At present he is——

Q. He is in Montreal part of the time?—A. Frequently. I understand he is expected to come back at noon on Monday.

Q. And are the books with his firm in Montreal?—A. I do not know. I presume they are.

Q. You were representing, or at least you were a partner in that firm until quite recently?—A. Yes, sir.

Q. Within the last few months?—A. Within the last few months. I had no interest in the business for over a year.

Mr. WATSON.—Then, my lord, I find from the investigation of such material as I have been able to obtain in connection with contracts between the department and Mr. Merwin and the firms that he represents, that in order to assist your lordship to do the work at all effectively and, I think, properly it will be necessary to have the books produced. Therefore I am not prepared to proceed with the examination of Mr. Merwin, or any, in fact, of these witnesses who are in the position of contractors for large amounts with the department, without production of their books. It is absolutely essential.

Hon. Mr. CASSELS.—Where do these gentlemen live?

Mr. WATSON.—Mr. Merwin is in Montreal.

Hon. Mr. CASSELS.—And the others, where?

Mr. WATSON.—The books of one of the companies he represents are in New York, it they may be produced here.

WITNESS.—Well, I will ask my principals to have them here. I have no doubt ey will.

Hon. Mr. CASSELS.—How many gentlemen from Montreal are there here?

Mr. WATSON.—There is no other gentleman from Montreal here.

Hon. Mr. CASSELS.—How many do you expect to examine in Montreal?

Mr. WATSON.—Well, my lord, there will be 8 or 10, perhaps more.

Hon. Mr. CASSELS.—My suggestion will be this: You want to cause as little inconvenience as possible. I have no doubt whatever we will have to be in Quebec some time or other if we are spared, and we can accommodate those gentlemen by taking their evidence at Montreal on the way.

Mr. WATSON.—I am glad to hear your lordship's suggestion. I think it will be more convenient in every way for the purpose of examination of the books.

Hon. Mr. CASSELS.—I want to make it as convenient as possible. If we can do it that way we can stop at the court house there.

Mr. WATSON.—Yes, my lord. But my difficulty meantime is, it is quite impossible for me to give the assistance necessary without having the books beforehand and having an opportunity to examine them.

Hon. Mr. CASSELS.—I would suggest you get an accountant to give the information you want.

Mr. WATSON.—Yes, my lord.

Q. Can you give us an undertaking that the books of Brooks & Co. will be produced?—A. I cannot give that personally.

Q. Or that the books of the other company will be produced?—A. I am quite sure of that.

Q. That is, the books showing the dealings between you and your firm and by you as an agent with the department will be produced?—A. Yes.

Q. Subject to inspection and examination?—A. I do not doubt for a moment that they will be perfectly willing to do it.

Q. That will be necessary.

Hon. Mr. CASSELS.—It will facilitate matters if an accountant goes through and gets the information you want. It will shorten things.

Mr. WATSON.—I will not detain you further. You have not anything now you can give us, I see?—A. Nothing at all.

Q. That will do for the present. We will give you further notice. Meantime we will call upon you for the books.—A. Then I am excused for this session?

Q. Yes, subject to that undertaking for the production of the books, if you please. Then is there anybody else here from Montreal?

W. F. B. HENRY sworn.

By Mr. Watson:

Q. What firm are you connected with?—A. Watson, Jacques & Co.

Q. Of Montreal?—A. Yes.

Q. Are you a member of the firm?—A. No, I am an employee.

Q. Is there not any member of the firm?—A. I am the manager.

Q. I see. Have you personal knowlenge of the dealings between your firm and the department?—A. I have.

Q. As intimate knowledge as any one else, or more so?—A. Probably more so.

Q. Have you produced the books of the firm or company?—A. I have got three baskets full at the station, and I have all the contracts here with me.

Q. You have?—A. Yes.

Q. Is there any objection to leaving them here?—A. Well, they are in use all the time.

Q. You mean the books?—A. Yes.

Q. Is that so?—A. They are current books, you see.

Hon. Mr. CASSELS.—Mr. Watson, would not the same suggestion apply much better?

Mr. WATSON.—I think so. I just want to know particularly about the production, that is what I am most anxious about, to know how far they are producing and are willing to produce the books; that is absolutely essential.

WITNESS.—We are quite prepared to produce any books.

Q. And they may be subject to inspection at any time?—A. By any one representing your department or any department.

Q. Will you kindly make out a list of the books you have produced and a list of the contracts?—A. Yes.

Q. If you will kindly do that to-day, leaving with me such list so that they may be identified from such list?—A. Yes.

Q. I will be obliged. And upon that being handed to me I think you may also be released for to-day.

Hon. Mr. CASSELS.—Yes. There is no use keeping him here.

Mr. WATSON.—Others from Montreal have been subpœnaed. I suppose they are not here yet.

B. H. FRASER recalled.

By Mr. Watson:

Q. Mr. Fraser, are we to understand that you have given as full information and particulars as you are possessed of with regard to the matters of price of the diaphone, nothing else than what you stated yesterday?—A. I do not quite understand.

Q. Well, yesterday you said that there had been no inquiry into the matter of cost, that the statement of price had been accepted and acted upon without reference to the cost, there had been no effort made to obtain any reduction of price; that is the fact as you understand it?—A. No, I do not think I said that, sir.

Q. What do you mean to convey now, then?—A. I would like to say this: When the thing was first installed, as I say, I was not in charge, but I had a working knowledge. I think you have got the details from Colonel Anderson, and I am quite certain he went into prices. In fact I know he did, Mr. Northey says he did.

Q. Never mind reasoning about it or what Mr. Northey's evidence shows. I am just asking about your own personal knowledge?—A. I know perfectly well prices were gone into.

Q. Did you personally do anything?—A. I can hardly remember now.

Q. I am only asking of your own personal knowledge?—A. I do not remember I did anything.

Q. Then others will have to speak for themselves?—A. Yes, the records.

Q. Now, the fact is, as I understand, that during the absence of Colonel Anderson you are in actual charge of the branch or department?—A. Yes, sir.

Q. And to what extent does that occur, what proportion of the time are you in charge?—A. A very small proportion. He is not away very often.

Q. So that would not amount to much?—A. Anything that I would consider of very much importance I would not deal with until he came back.

Q. So that the responsibility, as I understand you, in regard to the prices paid sts upon your chief, that is the head of the department, Colonel Anderson?—A. es, sir. My functions are——

Q. That is what you say. We have gone over that matter with you last evening. there any further explanation you wish to make of matters that were elicited yester-y evening, stated by you, that you have in mind?—A. No. I would only like to say at it appears to me the only point I could see that I think should be plain was as to e fact that I was aware of the excessive profits being made and that I did not bring e department's attention to it. As far as I can see—I do not know whether I have right to say this or not—but thinking the matter over on the profits of the diaphone ing excessive for a patented article, I had absolutely nothing to do with fixing that ·ice. I never made a recommendation regarding it, and the price was not fixed by me accepted by me, nor had I anything to do with it. As I said before, when I saw ie prices I called the attention of the chief engineer, who was my chief, and I con-dered my duty done then. After that I only had to see the contractors carried out e contract according to the terms, and I have certainly never been lax in regard to at.

Q. That is what you have to say yourself with regard to that matter. You cannot sist at all, as I understand, in giving any information as to the actual cost of the aphone or plant which accompanies it? Have you ever gone into that at all?—A. ell, the plant was entirely a question of contract. I never went into it very care-lly. We called for tenders.

Q. We have heard before, of course, that the plant was made, or might be made, ʳ many manufacturers, and that it was a subject of competition, always so. Now, st in regard to the other personal matter.

By Hon. Mr. Cassels:

Q. Before you leave that, Mr. Watson, I would like to ask a question. When ʳere these fog signals first introduced?—A. The diaphone fog signal?

Q. No, the common fog signal?—A. Oh, the fog signals have been in use for ·ery many years, long before I came into the department.

Q. I mean by the department?—A. Before I came into the department.

Q. Then when was the siren introduced?—A. The first siren was introduced, I uppose, 6 or 7 years ago, perhaps a little more.

Q. You stated yesterday that the plant required for the diaphone cost very much ess than the plant for the siren?—A. At the present time. We have been cutting lown the price of the plant right straight along.

Q. You say it is a less costly plant?—A. It is getting so all the time.

Q. But when did you know the plant was less costly?—A. That would be about he time tenders were being called for. It would depend largely on the size.

Q. Did you notify the minister or his deputy, or Colonel Anderson that the plant onnected with the diaphone was much less costly than that connected with the siren? –A. I feel certain that that must have been known to Colonel Anderson.

Q. Feel is one thing. Do you remember it?—A. I do not remember saying that. ir.

Q. It would occur to almost any reasonable man that if a plant which is the ʳreater proportion of the cost was of very much less cost, you should not go paying he same prices?—A. I called Colonel Anderson's attention to that matter, that I hought the proportion for the diaphone was too large, I certainly did.

Q. When was that?—A. The first time I knew they were charging this.

Q. Can you fix the date?—A. The only date I can fix is when the tenders were ent in.

Q. As one of the commissioners have you anything to do, irrespective of Colonel Anderson, with respect to the purchase of these things?—A. I have not.

Q. When was the department separated?

By Mr. Watson:

Q. 1903, was it not?—A. Probably it was about that time.

By Hon. Mr. Cassels:

Q. And from that time on who had charge of these particular buoys?—A.Buoys?
Q. Signals?—A. Fog signals?
Q. Yes; which department?—A. It was in the commissioner of lights' department at first, and then about a year or two——
Q. Well, how long in the commissioner of lights' department?—A. I expect about a year.
Q. You were the commissioner of lights?—A. No, sir.
Q. Who was?—A. Mr. J. F. Fraser.
Q. Oh, Mr. J. F. Fraser

By Mr. Watson:

Q. Of course, Mr. Fraser, it started in your department, that is, the purchase of the diaphones commenced——?—A. In the chief engineer's branch.
Q. In the chief engineer's department?—A. Yes, sir.
Q. There is no question about that, that is where it originated. And it was continued for some time, and then afterwards you say it was under the direction of Mr. J. F. Fraser for about a year?—A. As near as I can recollect now.
Q. Then it came back again to your department?—A. Yes.
Q. Was there any increase of prices during the time it was in Mr. J. F. Fraser's charge, or were the prices maintained as they had been before?—A. I had nothing to do with that.
Q. I see?—A. What was done by his branch.
· Q. I see. You disown liability, responsibility rather, perhaps quite properly, in regard to those matters. You said something to his lordship about the decrease of price arising partly from the smaller size?—A. Lesser consumption of air requires a smaller plant to supply it.
Q. That is not the only reason for the lessening of the price, is it?—A. That is the primary reason, the less consumption.
Q. There was the matter of competition, was there not?—A. In the price of the plant?
Q. Yes?—A. Well, I would expect that that would have a difference.
Q. Well, do you know?—A. I cannot say that I know.
Mr. WATSON.—Now, then, perhaps, my lord, we will have to get the further information from these parties and from Colonel Anderson. Mr. Fraser apparently has not personal knowledge.
Q. Have you taken occasion since last evening to make an inquiry as to the personal matter that I referred to, namely, the expenses, your expenses when you were at New York for four days in April of this year?—A. There was no necessity.
Q. No necessity?—A. No.
Q. What I want to get your definite answer upon is whether you found that those expenses were charged to the department?—A. Oh, no.
Q. Are you quite sure?—A. I am absolutely certain.
Q. They are not included in any account of yours?—A. Not in any way.
Q. Now, is it not a fact that frequently there were occasions of visits by you similar to the one you refer to?—A. Never.
Q. As between you and the members of this firm?—A. Never before.
Q. Never before, you say?—A. And not likely ever to be again.
Q. I see. That is what you say?—A. I do not like to get into trouble any more than I can help. It seems I have made a mistake this time.
Q. Now, were you here when Mr. Wallberg was giving his evidence?—A. Yes.

Q. You had to do personally, I understand, with the contracts made between him and the department, had you not?—A. Well, I have my routine work in connection with that. I ask for the plant and figure out the strength of the structures and see they are satisfactory and that sort of thing, and report to the chief engineer.

Q. And report to the chief engineer?—A. Always to the chief engineer.

Q. Were you promoting business relations between him and the department?—A. I would think so.

Q. That is not a satisfactory answer, I should think?—A. No. I will say I was not, and I had no reason to do anything of the kind. I did not promote his interest.

Q. You would not think so. Were you assisting him in obtaining a patent?—A. I was not assisting.

Q. Were you not recommending him to obtain a patent?—A. No, sir.

Q. You know the result of his obtaining a patent would be that he might then claim additional prices, you know that as a matter of fact, you knew that would follow?—A. I thought it would follow, that was my opinion. I find I am not at all posted on the patent law, in fact I know nothing about it.

Q. I ask you quite plainly were you not assisting him in obtaining a patent, assisting him in the Patent Department?—A. Oh, no. I could not assist him in the Patent Department.

Q. Making recommendations?—A. I made a recommendation to our own department to withdraw objections to his obtaining a patent.

Q. Why would you do that?—A. Because I thought if he ever did get his patent we would have him in our hands, instead of us being in his hands.

Q. How would you have him in your hands?—A. Because he was willing to make an agreement putting the prices entirely in our hands.

Q. Who was?—A. He was.

Q. How long ago?—A. I think last summer.

Q. Earlier than that. Was not that two or three years ago?—A. Last summer, not more than a year ago.

Q. Last summer?—A. Not more than a year ago.

Q. At all events, then, a year ago you know that such an agreement was practicable and might be arrived at with patentees. Now, just apply that to the case we have alluded to for the moment, the Fog Signal Company. Why did you not apply that to them? It is evident you had present to your mind these matters?—A. No, I think not.

Q. You had with Mr. Wallberg?—A. Yes.

Q. Why not apply that to the other patentees?—A. Because we were in the habit of constructing lighthouses ourselves; we were not in the habit of constructing fog signals, also machinery, ourselves.

Q. Yes. But you knew the signal company obtained the manufacture of the fog signal by another person, they were not in the course of manufacturing themselves, you were aware of that?—A. I think they were.

Q. Oh no. That company does not manufacture the diaphone or the signals, they have someone else to manufacture for them; were you not aware of that fact?—A. Well, I did not go into that at all.

Hon. Mr. CASSELS.—Is that quite so?

Mr. WATSON.—Yes, my lord, it is the fact. I found it out only last evening from Mr Northey.

Hon. Mr. CASSELS.—I understood yesterday the company was formed to manufacture the diaphone.

Mr. WATSON.—I was under that impression when I made inquiries. And in regard to that I want further information to see how much they pay for it, so I have asked for that specifically.

Hon. Mr. CASSELS.—Yesterday he stated he formed a company to take over this business for the purpose of manufacturing this diaphone.

Mr. WATSON.—Quite so. But since the court adjourned I got a little further information and made inquiries, and I ascertained that is not so. They have another person to manufacture for them.

By Mr. Watson:

Q. Then was there any other patentee that you dealt with?—A. Not that I remember just now.

Q. At all events you were, were you not, in a particularly friendly attitude towards Mr. Wallberg personally?—A. Not at all. I do not know him at all outside of business.

Q. Outside of business. You are in the habit of visiting him?—A. Never.

Q. These visits, or the one at New York that you have referred to, going there on purpose, you will have well in mind, is apt to create some suspicion, Mr. Fraser?—A. I see that now.

Q. And leads me to ask further questions in regard to other men?—A. I do not object at all.

Q. Have such things occurred with others?—A. Never at all.

Q. And what about prices that have been paid to Mr. Wallberg, any limitation upon those—the patent was not obtained—what prices are you paying him?—A. We have done no work with him since.

By Hon. Mr. Cassels:

Q. What is the patent for?—A. For a tower, not necessarily a lighthouse tower, but for a tower constructed of reinforced concrete.

Q. A tower in the lighthouse, connected with the lighthouse?—A. It can be used for that purpose as well as other purposes, my lord.

By Mr. Watson:

Q. Now, in the construction of the towers and the piers, that is done by contract for the most part?—A. We likely get it done that way.

Q. You likely get it done that way?—A. It is less trouble for us as a rule.

Q. Do you mean because it is less trouble?—A. From my point of view.

Q. I see. These things are not done by day work?—A. Quite frequently.

Q. I wanted to inquire in regard to that. There were some towers, or piers rather, in Lake St. Peter?—A. Yes, sir.

Q. Many there?—A. There were four.

Q. Four?—A. Actually in Lake St. Peter.

Q. And I understand that three of those have been swept away by reason of defective work or design. Now, was that done by a contractor?—A. That work was all done by the department.

Q. All done by the department?—A. By day labour.

Q. Under whose direction?—A. Under the direction of the chief engineer.

Q. Or under yours, which?—A. No. I am under him entirely. I do not want to shirk any responsibility in connection with that matter at all. I had a good deal to do with the design of them, and I assure you it is no pleasure to me to know some of those towers have been damaged.

Q. I want to know whether anyone in the position of a contractor had responsibility in regard to those matters?—A. No. We would have to take all the responsibility on ourselves in the department for that.

Q. In the department?—A. Yes, in the engineer's branch of the department. I do not see how we could possibly avoid it.

Q. Those three piers were swept away as the result of defective materials and entailed a loss of hundreds of thousands of dollars, I understand?—A. I would not admit on account of defective material or defective design.

Q. You would not?—A. No, not defective.

Q. At all events it was found they would not stand the ice pressure of that year? —A. That is a fact.

Q. Yes. They were so constructed that they would not stand the ice pressure in the spring?—A. They stood one year, and two of them are standing yet in very fair condition.

Q. And the loss by reason of the construction so that they would not stand that pressure, what is it, many hundreds of thousands of dollars?—A. No.

Q. $200,000 or $300,000?—A. I would not think $100,000.

Q. What is the cost of those piers?—A. I could not tell you.

Q. About what is the cost of those piers?—A. I could not tell you offhand at all.

Q. You can tell me within $10,000? You are there in the department. What are you there for?—A. I would not like to give the cost offhand.

Q. Within $20,000, the cost of the three piers?—A. The three piers that were damaged?

Q. Yes?—A. You are not quite right. There were four piers in the lake; two of them are still standing there undamaged.

Q. There are three piers damaged, two entirely swept away and the other two in use?—A. No. Those two can be used to-morrow.

Q. On being repaired?—A. Without spending another cent on them, for their original purpose.

Q. Not impaired?—A. No, not for actual use. Two of those piers are perfectly good to-day.

Q. What was the cost of those three piers, about?—A. I should think they would cost about $50,000 apiece on an average.

Q. Then at all events that was constructed through departmental management and work; that is right, is it not?—A. Yes.

Q. And men were paid by the day?—A. By the day.

Q. Were the superintendents paid by the day, or were they regular employees of the department?—A. The superintendent was a regular employee of the department.

Q. What is his name?—A. When those towers were built, Mr. Roy.

Q. Mr. what?—A. Mr. Roy.

Q. Is he in the department still?—A. I understand he resigned some short time ago.

Q. I have a statement here saying there is no doubt the three piers which were damaged, that the piers were not built on a sufficiently large basis to withstand the ice shove of last year. Two are in consequence tilted some degrees out of level, and one which stood in much deeper water was tilted so far as to be rendered dangerous to navigation, and the top was removed?—A. That is perfectly true.

Q. That is perfectly true?

Mr. WATSON.—My lord, that is all I have to ask Mr. Fraser for the present. I will have to ask him something further at another sitting of the commission. Has your lordship anything further to ask?

Hon. Mr. CASSELS.—No. Mr. Godfrey, do you wish to ask him anything?

Mr. GODFREY.—No, my lord.

Mr. WATSON.—I have told Mr. Fraser he will not be required any further this month, my lord.

Then, have you your bookeeper here, Mr. Willson?

Mr. WILLSON.—Yes, sir. I would like——

Mr. WATSON.—I would like the bookkeeper first, please.

CECIL GARRY, sworn.

By Mr. Watson:

Q. What is your name?—A. Cecil Garry.

Q. Mr. Garry, you are the secretary, are you, of this International Marine Company?—A. No, sir

Q. Bookkeeper?—A. Ledger-keeper.

Q. Just ledger-keeper. Who was the secretary of the company, Mr. Crannel?—A. No, the secretary is Mr. Little.

Q. Mr. Little of Woodstock is the secretary. And how long have you been bookkeeper or ledger-keeper?—A. I have been ledger-keeper for several months.

Q. Just several months. Don't you go back of that?—A. I don't know.

Q. Who was bookkeeper before you?—A. Mr. Scott, I believe.

Q. Where is Mr. Scott?—A. I don't know

Q. Then you have no knowledge of matters beyond the last two or three months?—A. No, sir.

Q. Or is it a month?—A. Oh, 3 or 4 months probably.

Q. That is all?

Mr. Watson.—That is not quite the witness I anticipated, my lord, would be given to us by Mr. Willson.

Hon. Mr. Cassels.—It is possible he is here to produce the books only.

Mr. Willson.—I can make a statement.

Mr. Watson.—I will refer at present to the written records, my lord, and then proceed upon those.

By Mr. Watson :

Q. What are the books you produce?—A. The current ledger and synoptic journal.

Q. The current ledger. That commences when, there is no number to it?—A. No number.

Q. When did it commence?—A. At the commencement of the business of the International Marine Company, I presume.

Q. Does it?—A. I suppose so.

Q. You suppose so. The first entry I see here is 1907. Is that when the business commenced?—A. I could not state with any degree of accuracy when it is started.

Q. So you are not able to give any information about that?—A. No.

(Current ledger marked Exhibit 18.)

Q. And what is the next book you produce, what is this book?—A. A synoptic journal.

Q. Why do you call it a synoptic journal, have you any idea?—A. No, I didn't name it.

Q. You did not name it.

By Hon. Mr. Cassels:

Q. I suppose you know what it is?—A. It is the general day's business.

Q. Day by day?—A. Yes.

Q. A synopsis of the business day by day?

By Mr. Watson:

Q. Show me, please, where records of the transactions with the department are entered here, can you?—A. I could not show you that.

Q. Is there a separate account with the department?—A. I don't keep this book, it is not under me.

Q. Who keeps this book?—A. That is not kept by me.

Q. Who keeps it?—A. Mr. Scott keeps it.

Q. You keep this ledger, Exhibit 18?—A. Yes.

Q. The synoptic journal was marked Exhibit 8 at the last sitting. What is the other book you produce?—A. That is an old ledger, Exhibit No. 9 at the last examination.

Q. Where is the account here with the department?—A. Page 291.

Q. And who kept this book?—A. That is before my time.

Q. You do not know anything about that. How many other books are there in your company, a good many others?—A. Those are all the books I have knowledge of.

Q. Just three books?—A. Yes.

Q. Do you know of any other books than those three?—A. There is a merchandise sales book.

Q. Precisely. Why did you not bring that up?—A. Those are the books I was asked to bring.

Q. You were just asked to bring these three?—A. Yes.

Q. The merchandise sales book, and what other books are there there?—A. That is all I know anything about.

Q. Just four books. Then have you produced the annual statement for last year? —A. I don't know anything about the annual statement.

Q. You do not know anything about that at all?

Mr. WATSON.—I understood, my lord, that would be produced as well, the annual statements for several years of this company.

Q. You do not produce those, you do not know anything about them?—A. No.

By Hon. Mr. Cassels:

Q. Does he know where they are?—A. I don't know anything about the annual statements.

Mr. WATSON.—That is not quite satisfactory. What other statements have you, Mr. Willson?

Mr. WILLSON.—Those statements (producing).

Mr. WATSON.—Then, Mr. Willson is good enough to produce to me, my lord, documents which I will put in, and which I will have to take a little time to peruse. I have not had them before, my lord, and I do not know how far they may go.

By Mr. Watson:

Q. Have you got the annual statements, Mr. Willson?

Mr. WILLSON.—No. There is no annual statement, my lord, in reference to this business of the company. It was organized in November, 1906, and the termination of the company's year will be on the 1st day of October, 1907. The business of the company was not at that time in such a settled condition that there could be any statement. I have the figures that your lordship desires to get and which you made a suggestion on Monday that the public ought to know, the costs. I have the figures which I can give the honourable counsel there if you will put me on the stand.

Mr. WATSON.—Will you let me have them, please?

Mr. WILLSON.—I can give them.

Mr. WATSON.—Have you not made them matters of record?

Mr. WILLSON.—I will show you some of the records in the books after this witness retires.

Mr. WATSON.—Well, you will have to let us have charge of those.

Mr. WILLSON.—I have no objection to your having charge of the papers, but the current books of operation we will have to remove and bring backwards and forwards as you may desire.

Hon. Mr. CASSELS.—Certainly.

Mr. WATSON.—Where are the written statements of the business? I am not asking for an explanation at the present time; I merely want the books produced.

Mr. WILLSON.—This is a document showing the number of patents issued, 114 patents.

(Statement marked Exhibit 19.)

Mr. WATSON.—Have you any financial statement to produce?

Mr. WILLSON.—I can make up a financial statement now. I have none to produce.

Mr. WATSON.—Have you made that of record in writing?

Mr. WILLSON.—I have not, sir.

Mr. WATSON.—Will you be good enough to do so.

Mr. WILLSON.—I will do so, sir.

Mr. WATSON.—Will that be equivalent to an annual statement?

Mr. WILLSON.—It will be equivalent to the statement. You will get the absolute cost of production of these goods with the profit to the company. I am willing to give that now at this instant.

Mr. WATSON.—Wait a minute. I will get that from you in writing.

Mr. WILLSON.—I will give it in writing. My lord, counsel has asked me so suddenly to produce things that it is impossible to comply with his request.

Hon. Mr. CASSELS.—You will get all reasonable time. Mr. Watson is not pressing you.

Mr. WATSON.—Then this is a bundle labelled Halifax. Correspondence between your company——

Mr. WILLSON.—And ship masters. Evidence that it was agreed on Monday I should produce to this court.

Mr. WATSON.—Wait. Between ship masters——

Mr. WILLSON.—And mariners in reference——

Mr. WATSON.—They are not officials of the department.

Mr. WILLSON.—No sir, nothing to do with the department. It was evidence I——

Mr. GODFREY.—It was what I asked for on Monday, my lord.

Mr. WILLSON.—It is, my lord.

(Bundle marked Exhibit 20.)

Mr. WATSON.—And then this is marked Pacific Coast.

Mr. WILLSON.—This is absolute evidence of the merits and use of these buoys, my lord.

Mr. WATSON.—From other people?

Mr. WILLSON.—No, sir, by the mariners.

Hon. Mr. CASSELS.—We will have to charge you a large price for getting such advertisements.

(Pacific Coast bundle marked Exhibit 21.)

Mr. WATSON.—What is this?

Mr. WILLSON.—Evidences from the United States.

(Marked Exhibit 22.)

Mr. WATSON.—These are a sort of certificates of value?

Mr. WILLSON.—They are more than that.

Mr. WATSON.—Well, don't tell me, please, at the present time.

Mr. WILLSON.—It is absolute evidence, my lord.

Hon. Mr. CASSELS.—You will come in later, Mr. Willson.

Mr. WATSON.—I will get that later. Then these are marked England, and these are reports from captains.

Mr. WILLSON.—Of the Hamburg-American Line.

(Two bundles marked Exhibits 23 and 24 respectively.)

Mr. WATSON.—You produce a great deal of records of that kind from outside parties. What I am wanting——

Mr. WILLSON.—There is this one which contains this printed account. If you will put that in evidence, I desire that in evidence.

Mr. WATSON.—Those four may go in also. They are, so to speak, certificates of character of the goods.

Mr. WILLSON.—More than that. Blue books of the United States government reporting on this.

(Four pamphlets marked Exhibits 25a, 25b, 25c and 25d.)

Mr. WATSON.—What I want, you understand, is a record of the business of your company from the time it commenced until the present time, showing the cost of production and the selling prices and the profits. Will you be good enough to have that prepared?

Mr. WILLSON.—I will give—my lord, does this inquiry extend outside the years asked for in the subpœna to me?

Hon. Mr. CASSELS.—Not if you object to it.

Mr. WATSON.—All the subpœna asks for is from the beginning of 1904 to the present time.

Hon. Mr. CASSELS.—You might get another subpœna.

Mr. WATSON.—Yes. Is it not wide enough for you?

Mr. WILLSON.—What I am willing to do is this, to aid you in this investigation, to give you the actual sales of the company for the first year of its organization, the profits on the business for that year, the gross profits.

Mr. WATSON.—Will you kindly wait, Mr. Willson. We have not much time this morning. If you will kindly follow my directions for the purposes of production that is all I ask for the present. Your company was organized in what year?

Mr. WILLSON.—November, 1906.

Mr. WATSON.—Your subpœna goes back to 1904?

Mr. WILLSON.—Yes.

Mr. WATSON.—So I think it goes back far enough for that company. If you will be good enough to prepare statements from that company I will be obliged.

Mr. WILLSON.—The statements are here. So far as previous to the company's existence, that is the company's——

Mr. WATSON.—If you will prepare——

Mr. WILLSON.—I cannot prepare anything previous to that.

Mr. WATSON.—A statement of this company's business from its organization.

Mr. WILLSON.—I have that to give you now if you will take it.

Mr. WATSON.—I want that in writing.

Mr. WILLSON.—I can make that in 10 minutes.

Mr. WATSON.—And, Mr. Willson, I would also like to have the secretary or chief bookkeeper of your company.

Mr. WILLSON.—I might make an explanation, my lord. The bookkeeper who was here has become rather elderly, a change was made in our place, and the young man who had charge of the books from February on would know more and would pick out more quickly for you what you want than Mr. Scott.

Hon. Mr. CASSELS.—Send someone, Mr. Willson, who will give the information.

Mr. WATSON.—Yes. Someone who can explain.

Then, my lord, I would like to call the Auditor General.

JOHN FRASER, sworn.

By Mr. Watson:

Q. Mr. Fraser, how long have you held your office?—A. Since the 1st of August, 1905.

Q. And previous to that you were in the department?—A. I was in the Finance Department from 1875.

Q. You are familiar, no doubt, with the report made by the commissioners, the so-called Civil Service Commissioners?—A. I have read it pretty carefully.

Q. Yes. And you are familiar with the commission to his lordship, you know the scope of it. You have been here, I think, and heard his lordship indicate what he conceives to be the proper scope of the inquiry. The report affects the question of the lack of conscience of officials, want of good faith and good conduct on their part, matters of that kind as arising from special paragraphs of the report. In connection with your duties as Auditor General all accounts, of course, come before you for examination?—A. They do.

Q. To be passed. Now, I want, if you please, such specific information as you are able to afford to his lordship, bearing upon the subject matter and upon matters of irregularity, so-called want of conscience, or, more directly acts of dishonesty by officials of the department as far as they have come before you.

Hon. Mr. CASSELS.—If they exist.

By Mr. Watson:

Q. If they exist. I am assuming that, my lord. Now, in the first place, take the deputy minister of the department, Colonel Gourdeau. What, if anything, has come to your knowledge in your official capacity bearing upon acts of irregularity and of that character as issuing from him? If that is too close and specific broaden it if you please. You know the scope of the investigation?—A. Well, I felt he did not sufficiently control or ascertain the manner in which the business was done by his officials although he was the responsible head.

Q. That directly is a matter of system or method?—A. Administration.

Q. Accuracy, yes. Do you pass beyond that in any information that you obtained entering into irregularities or want of conscience? It is a broad expression?—A. It is so very broad that I hardly understand what is meant by it there.

Q. Has there been negligence or remissness to the extent of recklessness, and in that way an absence of good conscience in the performance of duties?—A. It would be hard for me to say that there was negligence, except judging by results.

Q. Then will you just state what you have in regard to the matters as issuing from him?—A. Well, I have had to complain very frequently about the prices, the cost of goods, the manner of purchase, the lack of calling for tenders, and all that sort of thing. I always felt that the business might be done in a better way. Of course, that was a matter of opinion.

Q. Yes.—A. You find in our report a variety of correspondence in connection with the purchase of large quantities of goods that appear to be at retail prices.

By Hon. Mr. Cassels:

Q. Those appear in print, do they not?—A. In print.

By Mr. Watson:

Q. Do you recollect any particular year that you are referring to?—A. Ever since, in the last three reports.

By Hon. Mr. Cassels:

Q. The quickest way would be to hand Mr. Fraser his last three reports.

By Mr. Watson:

Q. Yes. Those are the reports for 1904-5, 1905-6 and 1906-7, those are the copies. (Handing copies to witness).—A. It is pretty hard to select anything from here because they are all a general criticism of their expenditures for the years.

Q. Of the expenditures, yes?—A. For instance, I just see before me now here one headed ' Large expenditure not under contract.' There is F. L. Brooks——

Q. What page is that?—A. Page 208.

Q. What year?—A. 1905. ' I beg to bring to your notice the following payments made during last year from the vote for construction of lights:—F. L. Brooks, of Montreal, $9,930.87; Canadian Fog Signal Company, Toronto, $428,298.12; Mc-Kelvey & Birch, Kingston, $16,092.18; I. Matheson & Co., New Glasgow, $12,385; George T. Merwin, Montreal, $134,005.24; Thomas L. Willson, Ottawa, $192,500. The vouchers sent me in support of these payments do not contain any evidence that such large purchases were made under any special agreement as to prices, or that tenders were invited by public advertisement. I shall be obliged if you will let me know the precautions you have taken in all these cases to assure yourself that the prices charged were the best that could have been obtained even if tenders had been invited.'

Q. Yes. Now, before leaving that, apart from that written report and inquiry, did you make any personal investigation?—A. As to the prices?

Q. Yes; and as to the course of procedure and conduct of the parties. Did anything come to your knowledge to indicate any improper conduct?—A. No.

Q. Or misconduct?—A. No, not any occasion.

Q. Or any advantages or undue advantages and gains?—A. No.

Q. I see that was in 1905?—A. 1905.

Q. Did you get a written answer to that?—A. I do not appear to have.

Q. Are you in the habit of having personal communications?—A. Oh, yes; there is more or less.

Q. Do you recollect any personal communication following upon that?—A. No. It is so long since. I have possibly talked the matter over with some of them.

Q. Those items were officially passed by you as appeared in the books?—A. They were all paid before audit.

Q. That is usually the case?—A. Well, a great deal of the expenditure of the Marine Department, the bulk, is paid before audit.

Q. Necessarily. Was that their system?—A. Yes. We are trying to establish audit before payment now in connection with contracts, but thare is a large part of their business that it would be very inconvenient to do.

Q. To have otherwise?—A. Yes.

Q. So that is not a matter which you would wish to criticise, that fact?—A. No.

Hon. Mr. CASSELS.—What was that, any special thing?

Mr. WATSON.—That is up to 1906. That is one contract that was put in. Prior to that there was no contract. There were a few letters, but not in the form of a contract.

Hon. Mr. CASSELS.—'The vouchers sent me in support of those payments do not contain any evidence that such large purchases were made under any special agreement as to prices.' I thought there was an agreement?

Mr. WATSON.—There was an agreement or understanding, yes, my lord, by letter.

By Mr. Watson:

Q. You understand that, Mr. Fraser, what you meant there was a formal written contract?—A. Yes, no contract, and I did not know at that time it was a patented article that tenders could not be called for. I took some steps to ascertain the form of the company. I recollect applying to Mr. Mearns, the secretary, for a list of the shareholders, which he declined to give.

Q. Which he declined to give?—A. Which he declined to give. However, I got the official list, and it did seem to me to be a pretty small company to handle such a business.

Q. Yes. We have had the evidence since here.—A. Yes.

By Hon. Mr. Cassels:

Q. No objections raised to that payment at all?—A. No objections raised?

Q. Yes?—A. No, the payments were all made before. I was, of course, either, I think, verbally informed that it was a patented article which could not be got for less.

By Mr. Watson:

Q. I see. The information was given to you and the items were passed. Perhaps you had not personally the knowledge that his lordship has indicated from the bench in regard to the rights of the government or the department?—A. I may have, but I had no knowledge of the cost of the article. I did not know whether the price was excessive or not. It was a piece of machinery with which we were not familiar. It might have been worth the money, it might not, and the vouchers had the necessary certificate on them that the prices were fair and just.

Q. Is that upon every voucher?—A. That, or 'According to contract.' There has got to be a certificate of that sort.

Q. Who certifies to that?—A. Usually the officer having the most intimate knowledge.

Q. In this case that would be by the head of that department, Colonel Anderson, I assume?—A. I believe, or Mr. B. H. Fraser.

By Hon. Mr. Cassels:

Q. Are those of record?—A. The vouchers?

Q. Yes?—A. Yes.

Q. Of this fog signal company?—A. Yes. They are in the Marine Department.

Q. With the signatures attached?—A. Yes, with the certificates on

Mr. WATSON.—I will have those produced.

Hon. Mr. CASSELS.—In connection with the fog signals.

Mr. WATSON.—Yes.

By Mr. Watson:

Q. Will you proceed then?—A. I notice another one on page 208, headed 'Silverware, etc., for steamers *Montcalm* and *Champlain.*' 'December 26th, 1905. Sir,—I beg to bring to your notice the accounts rendered by Messrs. B. J. Coglin & Co., for silverware, glassware and other table furnishings to the amount of $3,492.79 for the steamers *Montcalm* and *Champlain*. I should like to be informed of the advantage to the department of purchasing the articles in question through Messrs. Coghlin instead of direct from the trade. I should also like to be informed if it is customary to equip these vessels, which are not passenger carrying vessels, with silverware, cutlery, etc., of such an expensive nature as that which appears in the accounts above referred to.'

Q. Did you get any answer in writing to that as of record?—A. Unless it appears in the next year.

Q. You call attention to those matters in one report?—A. Yes. There may be some replies in the next year after this report was closed perhaps and too late to get in.

Q. Is there anything else that attracts your attention particularly in the report of that year?—A. Well, all the rest is principally in connection with the revenue.

Q. Yes. Then apart from the exercise of sufficient care and caution, business prudence, did you ascertain anything in regard to those matters reflecting irregularity or misconduct of officials?—A. We had a good deal to do in connection with that silverware, for instance.

Q. And what official had to do with that?—A. The deputy minister had something to do with it. I had, I know, a good many interviews with him in connection with it about the prices and the reason for purchasing from Mr. Coghlin, who was not in the silverware trade, but apparently the hardware business.

By Hon. Mr. Cassels:

Q. Is there any check upon the date as to whether the silverware was actually purchased or whether it remained on the steamer?—A. It was not on the steamer at the time, I ascertained.

Q. How long afterwards?—A. It was a year after its purchase before it passed on the steamer.

Q. Where was it meanwhile?—A. When I saw it it was in one of the storehouses at Quebec.

Q. Lying there?—A. Lying there. Some of it unopened. I think it was all unopened until a short time before I saw it.

By Mr. Watson:

Q. Then will you just state as nearly as you can from recollection what occurred between you and the deputy minister with regard to that?—A. I may say the account had a peculiar entry on it. The last entry on it was '5 per cent commission' a charge of 5 per cent commission. I think the account was typewritten and this was written in in ink.

Q. Commission to whom?—A. It did not say. I think that that was the exact wording of it, '5 per cent commission,' and I was in doubt as to what was meant by that, whether 5 per cent commission to somebody for the order, or whether the man was charging simply 5 per cent commission for purchasing the goods. It was a peculiar entry.

Q. That is Mr. Coghlin?—A. Yes, Mr. Coghlin. I asked the deputy minister. I think he said something, he did not know about it first, then he told me afterwards that the agreement with Mr. Coghlin was he should purchase those goods at manufacturers' or wholesale price and furnish them to the department and get 5 per cent commission for handling the business, which seemed a very reasonable proposition, that the reason the business was done through Mr. Coghlin was that he could get better rates from the trade than what the government could get, which was possibly correct too.

Q. That is, Mr. Coghlin could?—A. Yes. He evidently had been purchasing some from those firms before. Well, there was a good deal took place, I can hardly recollect the order of it, but eventually Mr. Coghlin came to see me and said he had some complaints to make about statements made about his business, and I asked him what the bargain was in connection with it. He told me the same thing as Colonel Gourdeau told me. I asked him if he had furnished the goods at the wholesale prices, and he said he had. He was prepared to make a declaration, but in the meantime I had ascertained the original cost of the goods.

Q. Yes?—A. Which was—well, I have forgotten now what percentage he had placed on. I had asked the department for the original invoices. They told me they did not have them, but I obtained them in other ways.

Q. When you speak in that way would you give the name   did you ask the deputy minister?—A. The deputy minister for them?

Q. Yes?—A. If all the conversations were not with him they were with his knowledge.

Q. Yes?—A. I think the dealings were altogether with him.

Q. Yes?—A. I told Mr. Coghlin before making a declaration of that sort that I had in my possession the original invoices, which showed that he had charged a very large profit as well as the 5 per cent commission.

Q. I see, as well as the 5 per cent?

By Hon. Mr. Cassels:

Q. Who was Mr. Coghlin?—A. He was a large hardware dealer in Montreal.

By Mr. Watson:

Q. I should state to your lordship in connection with that—pardon me, Mr. Auditor General—I had him subpœnaed, my lord, for attendance to-day, but I got a message from him that he had been subpœnaed but he was just about sailing for London, England, and under the circumstances, he having taken his passage, I let him go.

Hon. Mr. CASSELS.—Was he dealing in those goods himself ?

Mr. WATSON.—He will be here at the next sitting.

By Hon. Mr. Cassels :

Q. Yes. But was this gentleman dealing in those particular goods ?—A. No. He was a large hardware merchant, he has a large warehouse and deals in supplies a great deal in the way of chains and heavy hardware of that sort.

By Mr. Watson :

Q. I understood you to say before the silverware was not in his line ?—A. No, although he may have had facilities for purchasing. He did buy some few years before, I ascertained, for some other steamers some silverware. When I confronted him with the original invoices he said there must be some mistake, and in fact he did not know what to say. It ended, however, in Mr. Coghlin refunding about $1,100.

Q. Oh, indeed. Mr. Coghlin refunded about $1,100 on the purchase price of something over $3,000?—A. Yes. Taking the contrract to be what Colonel Gourdeau told me, and as it was confirmed by Mr. Coghlin, that they were to be furnished at the original wholesale price and 5 per cent commission allowed.

By Hon. Mr. Cassels :

Q. That would mean he utilized his being in the wholesale business to get from some other trades wholesale prices, that is what that would mean ?—A. Yes.

Mr. WATSON.—But the statement of the wholesale price was not correct.

By Hon. Mr. Cassels :

Q. I understand that. But he was using his position as dealer to get wholesale prices ?—A. Yes.

Q. What did the deputy minister know about the contract originally ?

By Mr. Watson :

Q. Yes?—A. Well, I think if I recollect he had something to do with ordering the goods.

Q. Oh yes, ordering the goods, but about the prices. What information did you get from him as to his personal knowledge about matters of contract ?—A. He said that was the bargain they made with Mr. Coghlin.

Q. I see. The statement you got from him was in the ordinary course as if he
d personal knowledge ?—A. Yes.

Hon. Mr. CASSELS.—But the point, Mr. Watson, is this: Colonel Gourdeau may
ve gone to this Mr. Coghlin and Coghlin told him the wholesale prices which he
uld get the silverware for was so and so. Well, the deputy minister may have
lieved that and so represented it. What we want to get at is, whether he knew
ıat were the wholesale prices.

WITNESS.—I understand they had the original invoice in the department. I
n't know. I could not get it there.

By Mr. Watson :

Q. You mean showing smaller prices ?—A. Yes.

Hon. Mr. CASSELS.—What you mean is, Colonel Gourdeau knew the prices being
arged were less than the prices contracted for?

Mr. WATSON.—More, my lord.

By Hon. Mr. Cassels :

Q. More?—A. I do not know he knew, but I thought that the whole transaction
as unbusinesslike, and it transpired afterwards that the statement was not correct.
a file of papers that was brought down to the Public Accounts Committee there
ıs a letter there stating Mr. Coghlin was to purchase those goods on the same terms
he had purchased some in previous years for some other of the vessels, and turn-
g that up, Mr. Coghlin was to get the trade discount, he was to be allowed the trade
scount. For instance, the goods were made out at certain prices, some of them
ere is a trade discount of 50 to 60 per cent, some 40 per ecnt, some lines of goods,
at he would get that advantage, that was the difference between what they would
ll to the government and what they would sell to the trade.

By Mr. Watson :

Q. Well then, was the department to get the advantage, that he, Coghlin, would
et ?—A. No, not according to the terms on which the previous years' purchases were
ıade. Coghlin was to get these trade discounts.

Q. He would have that for himself ?—A. Yes.

By Hon. Mr. Cassels :

Q. That would be his commission ?—A. Yes.

By Mr. Watson :

Q. Did you reconcile that with the 5 per cent ?—A. That is what I could not
econcile. I wanted to know whether the 5 per cent apparently as an ofterthought
as written on those vouchers.

Q. Then did anything come to your knowledge to lead you to the inference that
nyone else than Mr. Coghlin had participated financially in the matter ?—A. Noth-
g came to my knowledge. I thought that that 5 per cent was for somebody, but I
ıay have been mistaken. I have never been able to ascertain. Mr. Coghlin denies
at he had paid any commission to anybody in connection with it.

Q. I see. The result is that you did not get enough information to quite satisfy
ou, as I gather from what you say?—A. No, I did not get enough.

Q. I see. It is open to the view that there was improper conduct somewhere apart
rom Mr. Coghlin?—A. I do not know whether it is open to that view. That was the
iew I held at the time.

By Hon. Mr. Cassels:

Q. Whose duty was it, Mr. Fraser, to see that prices were correct?—A. In the
rst place, the deputy minister, of course, is responsible for all the purchases of the

department, he has to see that some official or other in whom he has confidence will see that the prices are right.

By Mr. Watson:

Q. Are accurate?—A. And I think—I would not be positive now without seeing the documents—but my recollection is that those vouchers were initialed by Colonel Gourdeau.

Q. I have sent for them.—A. I would not be positive about that, it is so long since.

By Hon. Mr. Cassels:

Q. We had better see the documents, because the point is this: Did the colonel initial that before the larger account came in, did he know what the price was to be?—A. They contended that the prices were low and fair.

Q. I know. But was that the price before the reduction of $1,100?—A. That was the price before the reduction. The amount was paid and all.

Q. What is that?—A. It was paid at the higher prices.

Q. But were the official vouchers at the higher prices?—A. Yes.

Q. Well, have you any reason to think that Colonel Gourdeau knew what the real price was?—A. No. I do not know whether he is a judge of silverware or not.

Q. Do you know whether the silverware is there yet or not?—A. Whether it is there?

Q. Yes.—A. Yes, I think so. I do not think that will be disputed.

Q. Is it for the sailors?—A. Well, at the time I saw it it was locked up in the stateroom and they were building a cabinet on the steamer to lock it up in. It was for entertainment purposes when the board of trade or any public body used the steamer.

By Mr. Watson:

Q. Have you anything further to say about that, Mr. Auditor General?—A. That is all, that is as far as I could get in the matter. It left a doubt in my mind; that was all.

By Hon. Mr. Cassels:

Q. Had you any conversation with Colonel Gourdeau after the refund of $1,100? We want to get all the information you can give us?—A. Yes. Colonel Gourdeau asked me since if we should not pay the $1,100 back to Mr. Coghlin, as it came out in evidence afterwards that he should not have refunded that according to his contract.

Q. That Coghlin should not have?—A. Coghlin.

Q. Coghlin should not have refunded the amount?—A. Yes.

Q. That was the attitude of the deputy minister?—A. The peculiar thing was that they were both agreed on this statement, that the goods were to be supplied at the original cost price and 5 per cent commission charged, and on the strength of that Mr. Coghlin had made the refund of the overcharge, the apparent overcharge. Afterwards, some months afterwards, when the agreement in writing was produced at the Public Accounts Committee he wanted to get his money back. It has always seemed strange to me ever since that neither of them had any recollection of the original agreement, why they should contend that the agreement was one thing, which would mean a lower price to Mr. Coghlin, and it should transpire afterwards that there was the higher price he should have got.

By Mr. Watson:

Q. You say the deputy minister spoke to you about returning that?—A. Yes.

Q. When was that?—A. Possibly a year ago.

Q. What took place in regard to that?—A. I told him if he got a vote of parliament I would pass it.

Q. I see. What did he say, I would like to know?—A. Oh, I forget. 'It is too

ad to keep the poor old man out of his money,' and that sort of thing, and that he
vas pressing for it.

By Hon. Mr. Cassels:

Q. Pressing whom for it?—A. Pressing the department, I suppose.

By Mr. Watson:

Q. To get it back again after having refunded it?—A. Yes.

Mr. WATSON.—Well, we will have the documents a little later, my lord. They are
getting them.

By Mr. Watson:

Q. Then, will you proceed, Mr. Fraser? Anything else in regard to that matter?
—A. No, I think that is about the history.

Q. Of that matter?—A. Of that matter.

Q. Now, any other matters of a similar nature, confining yourself at present to
the deputy minister?—A. No, I do not know of any acts, unless lack of conscience
or want of conscience means something of that sort, what would appear to me to be
extravagance.

Hon. Mr. CASSELS.—Mr. Fraser, what I want to get at is: Do you know any
acts that were done, which might be perfectly harmless and perfectly innocent, and
yet at the same time on another set of facts be the reverse? This last thing you have
spoken of, for instance, may be absolutely clear, and Colonel Gourdeau free from
blame. Nevertheless, there is the fact you have given, and it may be an inference
may be drawn from that the other way. Lack of conscience, I suppose, means pri-
marily dishonesty. If you find a man buying goods at double more than the value
and paying for them, when his duty was to see that the country got the goods for the
proper value, why, it required explanation. It may be perfectly all right.

Mr. WATSON.—In order to discharge his conscience.

By Hon. Mr. Cassels:

Q. Yes?—A. I do not know whether the comimssioners, that is, the Civil Service
Commissioners, had any evidence in view when they made any of these statements.
There was one thing I stated before them there in reference to certificates, that I
was not satisfied with the certificates on the vouchers, and I think there is——

By Mr. Watson:

Q. What do you mean by that?—A. Those certificates are 'fair and just' or
according to contract.'

Q. I see?—A. You see, we have to accept under the Act vouchers as being correct as long as they are properly certified by somebody having knowledge. I might
say we have to accept, we are performing our duty as far as the Act is concerned in
accepting those unless we have other knowledge in connection with it, and I had complained about the certificates, that once having found a certificate wrong that the
basis of my confidence in the voucher was gone.

Q. Yes?—A. And I had in mind three or four officials at the time.

Q. Three or four officials? And will you please state who they are?—A. One of
them was the deputy minister, Commander Spain was another and Mr. J. F. Fraser.

Q. Yes?—A. And my reasons for——

Q. Any others?—A. No, I think not.

Hon. Mr. CASSELS.—I do not see any evidence of Mr. Fraser before the commissioners.

Mr. WATSON.—Yes, my lord. In the report of the Civil Service Commissioners
he is referred to in many places.

Mr. CASSELS.—Yes. But I mean to say no evidence to warrant examination.

By Mr. Watson:

Q. I do not think he was called to give evidence before the Civil Service Commissioners?—A. Yes, he was in two places.

Q. All right?—A. Then my reason for saying that in connection with Mr. J. F. Fraser was the prices that were paid to Mr. Merwin, for instance. I did not suggest anything dishonest with it, but as it was proven afterwards in the Public Accounts Committee that those prices were much higher in a good many instances than what could be obtained, and then a certificate of ' prices fair and just ' being attached to these, his certificate for that purpose would be valueless afterwards, reasoning on those grounds that the certificate either means they are fair and just, or it is of no value.

Q. You mean in one case with Mr. Merwin you know of evidence afterwards which would lead to the conclusion that the prices were not fair and just although certified to by him as such?—A. Yes. That is a matter of record now in connection with the Public Accounts Committee.

Q. Yes, I am aware of that. Now, let us exhaust the information you have in regard to each, first in regard to the deputy minister. You have spoken of one or two matters, is their anything else that has been called to your attention as affecting his position?—A. Well, his certificate came in the same category, after I had found out in the case of the silverware that the prices were not fair and just.

Q. Yes. Then did you get any specific information afterwards which would lead to any inference other than a favourable one as to his conduct?—A. In connection with the silverware?

Q. Yes, other than that?—A. No. It has been in that unsatisfactory condition to my mind ever since, that the matter was never satisfactorily explained.

Q. That is as to the silverware?—A. Yes.

Q. But I am seeking to carry it on to any other transaction by him. Have you a knowledge of any other transaction of a similar character or in which you were not satisfied with the evidence of proper business transactions?—A. Well, I have seen his certificate in connection with the admission of goods free of duty where the certificate was not correct.

Q. Do you mean in favour of importers, contractors?—A. No. This is a certificate that the goods were required for the use of the government, and they were not.

Q. When they were not?—A. Yes.

Q. Yes?—A. To that extent the government was deprived of revenue.

Q. And what do you refer to, what goods, what occasions?—A. A case of silverware purchased through Mr. Coghlin.

Q. Other purchases?—A. One specific——

Q. Is this the one you have referred to before?—A. No.

Q. Another case with him?

Mr. GODFREY.—Against Colonel Gourdeau?

Mr. WATSON.—Yes.

By Mr. Watson:

Q. You found a certificate that goods were required by the government and therefore admitted free of duty?—A. Yes.

Q. But not required by the government. You mean not supplied to the government?—A. Not supplied to the government.

Q. What explanation did you get of that?

By Hon. Mr. Cassels:

Q. What date was that?—A. I think it was in 1905.

By Mr. Watson:

Q. That was with Mr. Coghlin?—A. Yes. I got no explanation, I did not ask or any. I was never asked to pay the bill, the government has not paid for the silver-are.

Q. Do you mean an account was presented as for goods supplied which were not ctually supplied?—A. No account was presented.

By Hon. Mr. Cassels:

Q. A certificate?—A. A certificate, it was for Mr. Coghlin's purposes.

By Mr. Watson:

Q. But I understand now purporting upon its face to be goods supplied to the overnment, and the goods in fact were never supplied?—A. No.

By Hon. Mr. Cassels:

Q. What is the amount of that, do you know?—A. I think possibly the bill would e $70 or $80.

Q. Did you call the deputy minister's attention to it?—A. No, I think not.

By Mr. Watson:

Q. Anything else, Mr. Fraser?—A. No, that was sufficient warrant for me to ake my statement that I had not confidence in the certificates.

Q. But what I want to know particularly is, is there any other specific matter relating to the deputy minister?—A. No.

Q. I see. Then, before we leave him I have this file. Are you sufficiently familiar with that to identify the particular memorandum you are referring to? (Handing file to witness.)—A. That is certified by Mr. Gregory, agent at Quebec.

Q. I see. By Mr. Gregory, that is the silver is?—A. Yes. A correct statement. I had Mr. Gregory's certificate in view, too, at the time I made the other statement.

Q. That would be another official, then. You do not find them certified by the deputy?—A. No.

Q. Then do you find here in this file the original invoice that you had asked the department for and which you were not able to get?—A. No. That is the invoice made out by Mr. Coghlin. I forget where the original invoices are now, whether they are in the Private or Public Accounts Committee. I obtained them at the Custom House at Montreal. Possibly I returned them after.

Q. I think I will have this file marked my lord. (File marked Exhibit 26.)

Q. Then anything else you have in your mind relating specifically to the deputy minister?

Hon. Mr. CASSELS.—Mr. Fraser, if the scope of this investigation requires me to go into anything either to exculpate or incriminate officials, Mr. Watson is entitled to all the help he can get from anybody. You may know of cases that ought to be investigated, where there may be no wrong in them. If you have anything of that nature you ought to furnish it.

Mr. WATSON.—Limiting it first to the deputy minister, because we are dealing with him just now.

By the Hon. Mr. Cassels:

Q. Each of these officers in the Marine Department. There ought to be every assistance given. They may be perfectly blameless, nevertheless there may be suspicions which require investigation.—A. No, I do not know of any cases which have not been pretty thoroughly gone into. I know we go as far ourselves as we can, and the Public Accounts Committee have been through the accounts.

Q. Is there a record kept in the Public Accounts Committee?—A. Yes, it is printed.

Q. We will get that.

Mr. WATSON.—I have got that, my lord.

By Mr. Watson :

Q. Then, if you think of anything else you will be good enough to let us have the benefit of it, please?—A. Yes. And the third one there I mentioned——

Q. Let us take them in order. The next one after the deputy you mentioned was Commander Spain?—A. Yes. I had no confidence in his certificate for the same reason that it was found to be wrong.

Q. Found to be wrong. Now, what instances have you of that?—A. In connection with his travelling expenses.

Q. Yes.—A. I think his account for 1905, after it was certified to by himself and by the deputy minister.

Q. By the deputy minister?—A. Yes.

By Hon. Cassels :

Q. Did you find anything in his account other than over charges?—A. Well, charges for travelling that he had not performed.

By Mr. Watson :

Q. Did you actually?—A. When he was present in the department here.

Q. I see. Well, I asked—probably there was some information that I had not been able to obtain when I examined Commander Spain yesterday, but I intended my questions to cover everything, and I think they did cover everything. His statement was they were correct. What did you find, Mr. Fraser, in regard to that?—A. Well, he had to make a refund of, I think, between $800 and $900 on one year's travelling expenses.

Q. What year was that, 1905?. I see in that year the expenses charged at $4,627. I called his attention to that yesterday. A refund of $800 or $900,—do you mean that expenses were charged for being out when he was in?—A. Yes.

Q. Is that the character of the charge? It is not excessive payments, that is where he paid $2, $3, $4 or $5 a day too much, you don't mean that; you mean, I understand, charges he made for being out when he was inside?—A. Precisely. Railway fares and the ordinary expenses.

Q. And did you ascertain the fact that he was actually in Ottawa when he was charging for expenses outside of Ottawa?—A. Yes, by the record.

Q. And you say that that existed to the extent in one year of $800 or $900?—A. That is as far as I could check it. I could not get the whole of the records.

Q. Why not?—A. I could not find them.

By the Hon. Mr. Cassels :

Q. Did you get the records in the Marine Department?—A. Yes.

Q. Who keeps them?—A. Well, it was the attendance book I asked for, and I don't know, the books usually run a month or two months, something like that, and I could not get the whole of the books for that year.

Q. Was part of that $800 the $6 a day allowance?—A. Not at that time. At that time he got $6 a day or a per diem allowance, I think it was $6, while investigating wrecks; on any other business he got his actual expenses.

Q. This was $800 actual expenses which you say he should never have charged?—A. Yes.

By Mr. Watson:

Q. What did he say as to that in explanation—A. He got mixed on his dates, that was the only explanation.

Q. Then you mean there was no satisfactory explanation?—A. No, I did not consider that was a—it was unsatisfactory, that he had to refund the money.

Q. Had he to certify to that account?—A. Yes.

Q. Any one else?—A. The deputy minister's initials were on it.

Q. Yes.—A. I do not know whether that account is the one on file. I think it was remodelled.

Q. Oh, the account was corrected?—A. I think so.

Q. Well, the original account should remain on record, should it not?—A. Well, they got it back to examine it and see what was the trouble with it, and I think I got a new account.

By Hon. Mr. Cassels:

Q. Was the old account not kept?—A. It was out of my hands then.

Q. What?—A. It was out of my hands.

By Mr. Watson:

Q. You have not any personal knowledge whether that was kept or not?—A. No.

Q. You indicate a doubt?—A. I do not know anything about whether it was kept or not.

Q. I see. Have you knowledge of the system sufficiently to say whether or not the deputy should have personal knowledge that he was in and not out when those expenses were charged for?—A. He should have personal knowledge.

By Hon. Mr. Cassels:

Q. Was this fact brought to the attention of the minister or anybody else?—A. Your lordship, I might be permitted to say just at this point——

Q. What?—A. At this point I would like to say, if it were possible, that I would not like to go into any confidential conversations with the minister.

Q. I don't want any conversations, but it seems to me on the statement you made this morning the first duty of somebody would be to report the fact to the minister? —A. His deputy minister should have done it.

Q. I merely ask you whether to your knowledge it was reported to the deputy minister or the minister?—A. It was reported to the deputy minister, certainly.

Q. Was it reported to the minister?

By Mr. Watson:

Q. By you?—A. Yes.

Hon. Mr. CASSELS.—When was that?

By Mr. Watson:

Q. In writing or verbally?—A. I imagine verbally.

Q. When, his lordship asks?—A. I could hardly say. I have occasionally conversations with the ministers, if there is anything that I think I ought to bring to their attention, even suspicion. That is one reason why I do not like to speak about it.

By Hon. Mr. Cassels:

Q. You have no knowledge whether after the report went to the deputy minister, and after the information was given to the minister, any information was afforded to either of them by Commander Spain, have you any knowledge of that at all?—A. Oh, I do not know what explanation he gave at all.

By Mr. Watson:

Q. You do not know whether the matter was ever attempted to be cleared up. Did you ever get any clearing statement of that afterwards?—A. No. I never had any doubt in my own mind as to the padding of the account.

Q. Because it is inconceivable in the absence of explanation that the matter was not put in the hands of the County Crown Attorney, to my mind. At all events you do not know what explanations were made or were not made afterwards?—A. No, I have no administrative duties at all.

Q. Then anything else in regard to Commander Spain?—A. Oh, I think his next account following that one had two or three items in that had to be struck out.

Q. You mean not excessive charges, but wholly false items, distinguishing them in that way. It would be an entirely false item if he charged an item for expenses out when he was in, would it not ?—A. My recollection is, it was some boat-hire or horse hire, something of that sort, he charged in his next account that I called his deputy's attention to.

Q. Yes?—A. And he ordered it to be struck out.

By Hon. Mr. Cassels:

Q. Was that because it had not been used, or because it was not a proper payment? There would be a great difference between the two?—A. In that case the deputy said it had not been expended.

Q. What?—A. It had not been expended.

By Mr. Watson:

Q. That is, the deputy told you?—A. Yes.

Q. It had not been expended at all. Was that in 1906?—A. That would be 1905 or 1906.

Q. Anything else, Mr. Fraser?—A. Well, I asked the deputy then to keep a record for the next year's audit, that I would require a memoranda at the end stating the dates on which Commander Spain left the department on business, what the business was, and when he returned, to enable me to check his next year's account properly. After the close of the year when I asked to be furnished with that information I was told that it had been kept, but they thought it was not necessary, or something, at the end of the year, and it was thrown in the waste basket.

Q. Who told you that?—A. The deputy minister.

Q. Yes?—A. So his accounts were in that unsatisfactory condition that they may be right or not.

Q. I see. You have the instances which you have given where you learned they were positively wrong, in fact false?—A. Yes.

Q. Did you ascertain that any other items afterwards were false, that is, the next year, 1906 and 1907, did you get evidence of falsity of items?—A. No, I had no means of getting it.

Q. I mean by inquiry or otherwise, you did not get it?—A. No.

Q. Then did you pass it?—A. I had to, certified correct.

Q. I see. Certified correct by whom, by him and the deputy minister?—A. I could not say now what certificates were on.

Q. Then did you learn anything else ?—A. I know they are approved by the deputy minister.

Q. Then did you learn anything else in regard to him ?—A. No, I think not.

Q. I do not know whether you were present or not when I asked him yesterday about some trips outside, trips to New York and other places where personal business or pleasure was entered upon, apart from departmental business. Did anything of that kind come to your knowledge and information?—A. No. There were some trips to New York on those accounts there, but so long as his deputy minister says it was official business that has to satisfy me.

Q. Then did you get any information that would be of assistance here?—A. No.

Q. Judging as to the honesty or dishonesty of the official and anything else that you can state in regard to him? You have already referred to some matters that I think are very serious?—A. No, I do not think there is.

Q. Well, then, if you think of anything else please let us know.

By Hon. Mr. Cassels:

Q. Do you know of any personal relationship between the deputy minister and
he commander which might lead the deputy minister to assist the commander in
assing items that ought not to be allowed?—A. No, I do not know of any reasons
or it. The deputy minister, I think, gave his cheque for about half of the refund,
ut whether he collected it from him afterwards or not I do not know.

By Mr. Watson:

Q. Do you know that of your personal knowledge?—A. He told me.

Q. The deputy minister told you?—A. Yes.

Q. Did you ask him the reason for it, or did he give you any reason for it?—A.
h, he said the other man was hard up, that he had this lying in his own bank account.

Q. He contributed it?—A. Well, no, he did not say he was contributing it.

By Hon. Mr. Cassels:

Q. Have you any reason to suspect it was a refund of half the $800?

By Mr. Watson:

Q. That it was a refund by the deputy minister of half the amount?—A. No, I
would not like to say that. I have no reason at all for thinking that.

Q. I see. It may have been an act of generosity in advancing to an official in
trouble, possibly?—A. That, or they may have had some financial arrangements or
dealings that I know nothing about, a personal matter.

Q. That will explain it. Now, the next official you referred to is Mr. J. F. Fraser.
What did you learn with regard to him?—A. Nothing but what I say about those
prices. I think they were excessive.

Q. That is the prices paid to whom?—A. Well, the prices paid to Mr. Merwin.

Q. That is the gentleman who was here this morning for a few minutes?—A. Yes.
I have forgotten now whether all the machinery was purchased by him—no, there was
some other machinery, I don't recollect who it was purchased from, some under feed
stokers and Worthington pumps. If the evidence given in the Public Accounts Committee was correct, it appears to me the prices were excessive.

Q. The prices were excessive. That is, the prices that were paid were excessive?—
A. Yes.

Q. In connection with that did you get the view that it was known to the official
that the prices were excessive?—A. Well, I held that view myself that it must be
known to the official, because Mr. Fraser's judgment and intelligence and experience all
led me to suppose that he might have known that those prices were high.

Q. I see. By high you mean excessive?—A. Excessive.

Q. To what extent did that exist?—I mean to say was it just a casual matter, a
small matter, or a matter of importance in amount?—A. Pretty large in amount.
These articles run into thousands of dollars.

Q. I did not have this evidence until 11 o'clock this morning. There is a lot of
evidence. I will have to go into it with Mr. Merwin. That is one of the reasons I
could not go on with him this morning until I get the books.

Hon. Mr. CASSELS.—You will have information to enable you to know what Mr.
Fraser is referring to.

By Mr. Watson:

Q. Yes, I will compile it to know what information he had in addition. It was by
reason of getting this information that it was necessary to have further assistance
from Mr. Fraser this morning, as I mentioned to your lordship.

Q. Then to what extent did that prevail in time, in years?—A. Well, of course, I do not know much about anything previous to 1905. My experience with the accounts have been from that time.

Q. Then you say that is in connection with the transactions with Merwin which are partly, at all events, of record, and which we will be able to avail ourselves of afterwards, and also in regard to Brooks & Co.?—A. Brooks & Co., and Mr. Willson.

Q. That is the carbide?—A. Yes, although I learn now they cannot get them any cheaper, according to Mr. Willson's statement.

Q. You mean to say that in 1905 you formed the opinion that the prices were excessive as being paid to Mr. Willson or the Ottawa Carbide Company?—A. Well, yes, because there was no competition so far as I could learn.

By Hon. Mr. Cassels:

Q. Either referring to carbide or the other thing?—A· Well, it was Mr. Willson then; it is now the International Marine Signal Company.

By Mr. Watson:

Q. Yes. Are you referring to the carbide or the buoys?—A. The buoys.

Q. The gas buoys?—A. The gas buoys.

Q. Then did you draw the attention of any official to that?—A. Oh, every year I think we have written to the deputy minister.

Q. The deputy minister, yes. And in consequence of that, what took place, an interview?—A. No, I think if there was any interview it would be with Mr. Fraser himself. The deputy minister, I think, on one or two occasions sent him to explain matters to me.

Q. What was the explanation or the effect of it?—A. Oh, that those were the best terms that could be got under the circumstances.

Q. Yes. Did you know that it was claimed to be covered by a patent?—A. I think so.

Q. The amount of that expenditure, of course, was very large?—A· Very large.

Q. Any reason to question the business prudence of that expenditure? I do not mean particularly as a matter of judgment, but as a matter where it was improper under the circumstances affecting conduct and conscience?—A. Oh no. I did not know how those prices were arrived at or how the business was started with Willson. I presume that with such a large piece of business as that both the deputy minister and the minister would have to concur in everything that was done.

Q. Yes. Colonel Anderson has stated in regard to that he thought it was the result of improper and undue influence and pressure. Did anything of that kind come to your knowledge?—A. No.

Q. Did you get any such information from Colonel Anderson?—A· No, I do not think so.

Q. Then so far as your information goes it is a question of quantum or excess of prices paid?—A. Well, I think goods were ordered in advance of requirements.

Q. Did you ascertain that?—A. Well, I don't think those buoys are all in use yet.

Q. You mean ordered and delivered and paid for and not in use?—A. Well, I know we paid I think about $200,000 to Mr. Willson for buoys that remained for some length of time, I could not say for how long, a considerable period, on his premises.

Q· Do you mean six months or a year or more?—A. I do not think a year.

Q. How many months?—A. I think it was at the close, I do not know whether it was June, 1906, or June, 1907, somewhere along that period.

By Hon. Mr. Cassels:

Q. Do you know whether it is proper to have a reserve of buoys?—A. I do not think it was proper to make a payment of $200,000 to him before the goods were delivered.

Q. I do not quite understand the functions of the auditor. What actually is your duty, simply to represent to the deputy minister, and then if he passes the matter that is an end of it?—A. Well, we have to question anything that we think is not in accordance with the rules and regulations or with the Act, or anything improper.

Q. Well, supposing he says it is all right, is that the end of it?—A. Oh no. We have got to get a better explanation than that, we have got to satisfy ourselves in some shape or form that the matter is all right, or report it to the Treasury Board.

Q. Then certain things you have spoken of to-day you were never satisfied about. Did you report them to the Treasury Board?—A. They are in my report here to parliament, and after parliament has dealt with it my duties end there.

Q. That relieves you?—A. I report to parliament or to the Treasury Board.

Q. I see?—A. Of course where it is ordered before payment we decline to make payment. It is hard to determine that advance of $200,000, because it might be on what is called a progress estimate, there might have been value there for a good deal more than the amount of this money, but I could not see where the department was under any obligation to pay that $200,000 until the goods were delivered.

By Mr. Watson:

Q. Then, in connection with that did you learn anything of the relationship which might lead you to the conclusion of personal advantage or gain to an official by reason of an irregular act——?—A. No.

Q. Or extraordinary act? That is, the payment of $200,000 in advance. Did you get any information or particulars that might lead to such a conclusion?—A. No. There have been all sorts of reports to which sometimes not much importance should be attached. I never heard of anything definite or anything that could be considered evidence in any shape or form.

Q. Then you never knew there was anything in it for the buoy?—A. No.

Mr. GODFREY.—There was always gas in the buoy.

WITNESS.—Of course, we are naturally suspicious, and our work has a tendency that way, and I try to follow up those suspicions as far as I can to ascertain whether there is any foundation for them or not. I may say in connection with Mr. J. F. Fraser that I have never had any foundation, I have never ascertained anything that would be a proper foundation to make any statement of that sort.

By Mr. Watson:

Q. I see. We have got the business relations with Mr. Merwin, Brooks & Co., and Mr. Willson and his companies. Anyone else, any other company or individuals?—A. I think he had something to do with the fog horn.

Q. That is the Canadian Fog Signal Company?—A. Yes.

Q. Yes?—A. I think some plant was ordered by him or during some time that he had control of it.

Q. Well, that was in the same position practically or a somewhat similar position to the first purchases from Mr. Willson's company, except that seems to be, as his lordship says, much more glaring in regard to the transaction.

Hon. Mr. CASSELS.—I did not use that language. I did not use it in connection with Mr. Willson.

Mr. WATSON.—Well, no. An extraordinary condition.

Hon. Mr. CASSELS.—I thought that was an extraordinary state of affairs in connection with the expenditure of $150,000, according to my view.

Mr. WATSON.—Yes.

By Mr. Watson:

Q. Did that matter come to your attention, the Canadian Fog Signal Company, the payment there?—A. Yes. I thought—I do not know just exactly what I did think about it. There was about half a million dollars.

Q. In expenditure?—A. In expenditure, without, so far as I could ascertain, any negotiations or attempt at negotiations for reduced prices, or to ascertain the cost of the article.

Q. Well, that was for the most part in Colonel Anderson's branch. Did you have a discussion with him about it?—A. No. I do not think I have ever seen Colonel Anderson on business at all.

Q. You never have?—A. I don't think so. I know him very well, but I do not think I ever had anything to do with him on business matters.

Q. Did you know that was in his branch or department?—A. Yes, I think I must have at some time seen Mr. B. H. Fraser in connection with it, but.for some reason or other, I do not know why, we are more in touch with Mr. B. H. Fraser than with Colonel Anderson. Possibly it is more convenient. There was no especial reason for it.

Q. Did you ask for particulars, information about that, did you receive same?—A. Well, as far as I can recollect the only particulars I got were that it was a patented article and could not be got for less; they had to pay the prices if they wanted the goods. I thought at the time the purchases were very large, and possibly in advance of their requirements too. However, I might·not be a competent judge there.

Q. That is a matter of method and system in the department?—A. Yes. However, we criticize mostly anything that appeals to us.

Q. Yes, I suppose so. Then anything else you learned in regard to Mr. J. F. Fraser?—A. No.

Q. Or anything with regard to Mr. B. H. Fraser?—A. No, sir. I have no knowledge of anything that is improper.

Q. I do not suppose that either one of them is related to you?—A. No.

Q. They are not related to each other, they say. Then the other official you named was Mr. Gregory, I think?—A. Yes, at Quebec.

Q. Yes?—A. Well, I thought his certificates were very loose. It seemed to me while he certified to the reception of that silverware and prices fair and just, he had never seen the goods at all, he had not seen them for a year afterwards.

Q. Do you know of other improper acts by him?—A. Oh, there would be perhaps matters of administration, excessive buying and extravagant prices. Generally speaking, it seems to me that what they buy at the Quebec agency always costs more than at the—

Q. I see. Have you any knowledge of any misconduct in connection with that, apart from the excessive expenditure, personal gain or advantage in participation?—A. Only by hearsay.

Q. This report also refers to the question of discount and commission. Have you any information to give upon those subjects?—A. No I think the way I understand that report is that they complain the department does not take the ordinary business methods of obtaining discounts on the purchases, for instance, discounts off for cash, as the common saying is. It is not a very usual thing in government business to get a discount off.

Q. You say it is not?—A. No.

By Hon. Mr. Cassels:

Q. You mean with the patronage list or without?—A. Either with or without.

By Mr. Watson:

Q. You mean to say the government usually has to pay more than individuals?—A. Unless they have a contract, I think. It has been my own experience that wherever anybody has any dealing with anybody they know belongs to the government they charge them more, from hotels down to anything at all. That seems to be considered—

Q. You think that is justifiable, it goes upon that basis?—A. I do not think it is justifiable.

Q. I mean to say people seem to do business upon that basis?—A. The whole country seems to have that idea.

Q. Whatever they can get they should take?—A. Yes.

Hon. Mr. CASSELS.—What I want to know is this: Suppose goods are purchased for ·teamers, and the accounts are passed and paid, is there any check kept, as far as you know, on the boat as to whether those goods remain on those steamers? Who is responsible?—A. I imagine the steward would be.

Q. Does it pass out of your hands the moment they are certified?—A. Yes. We have nothing to do with the stores.

Q. Nothing to do with the subsequent dedication of this property, if there is such a thing?—A. No, unless we know that it was sold, or anything of that sort. We would have to see that we get the receipts.

Q. Is he an Ottawa man?—A. Gregory?

Q. No. Is it his business to look after the stores, or is there an officer charged with that duty?—A. I do not know. I do not think the stores of the Marine Department were very well looked after. At the depot at Prescott, now, I understand there is a proper system of store keeping and checking up, so that everything has got to be accounted for, and at Sorel, and as far as I could see at Quebec there was no proper system of ascertaining whether everything that should be in stock was in stock.

By Mr. Watson:

Q. That is Quebec city?—A. Quebec city. That may have been remedied recently. I do not know.

Q. There has apparently been a change within the last few months, Mr. Doutre was saying?—A· Yes. Then I think things are gradually changing. I think, I know the present Minister of Marine has been doing· everything that he could in the way of improving matters, trying to get everything on a good business footing.

Q. Yes?—A. And he must be gradually getting—it is a big· institution to get into shape all in a short time.

Q. How long has this condition of affairs you refer to been existing?—A. Well, Mr. Gregory was in the service 45 years, and he said it was always the same. Now, the business of the department has grown immensely within the last few years in connection with the· ship channel, and the Dominion steamers are increasing, this lighting business has increased very rapidly, they have the St. Lawrence splendidly lighted now, they say it is a torchlight procession, steamers can hardly get astray. All this has necessitated a tremendous increase in the expenditure. So perhaps what was a business system that might have been all right for a small business would not be any good for a large business.

Q. Then have you covered as much ground as you think is useful by way of information, have you anything else that you can state by way of information, Mr. Fraser, bearing upon the matter?—A. No, I do not think so.

Q. Then I would like to impress upon you, if anything else occurs to you, to be good enough to communicate with me so that I may bring it before the court, before his lordship?—A. I will.

Q. That will do.

Cross-examined by Mr. Godfrey:

Q· A few questions, Mr. Fraser. Your evidence regarding Mr. J. F. Fraser's dealings with Merwin and Brooks & Company was all before the Public Accounts Committee?—A. Yes.

Q. And your information with regard to that is simply information which the general public has as taken before the Public Accounts Committee?—A. Well, the general public have the information taken before the Public Accounts Committee.

Q. And it is that upon which you base your opinion here to-day?—A. I may have a knowledge of prices apart from the evidence taken in the Public Accounts Committee.

Q. Do you remember having had that knowledge?—A. Yes, I know in one case, and I can recall a case now.

Q. I see. But you did not know all the surrounding circumstances in connection with the purchase of that machinery?—A. No. What do you mean by the surrounding circumstances?

Q. As to who was really responsible, who was the guiding spirit in giving those prices?—A. No, I do not. All I know is the man who certified to the prices.

Q. But you do not know of the circumstances that led up to the certificate?—A. No, certainly not.

Q. Then with regard to the Willson matter. In your judgment that was such a large matter that it would be a matter of general policy for the minister?—A. It should certainly.

Q. It should certainly be.

Mr. WATSON.—My lord, I am not quite sure as to the status of my learned friend in some of these matters. I understood your lordship gave my learned friend and anyone else a status for individuals whose honesty, conscience or want of conscience was actually attacked, but not beyond that.

Hon. Mr. CASSELS.—Well, it seems to me that Mr. Fraser at the present moment is being charged with what might turn into dishonesty. He has a right to relieve himself in every possible way. It might be a very proper way to relieve himself by showing the responsibility was on somebody else.

Mr. GODFREY.—I do not wish to pursue it any further.

Mr. WATSON.—I just wanted to understand; I am not objecting.

Hon. Mr. CASSELS.—If there is a charge against anyone, he ought to have every possible right to relieve himself.

By Mr. Godfrey :

Q. Then, Mr. Fraser, you did not refer in any of your references to Mr. J. F. Fraser, personally, I understand?—A. Our correspondence is all addressed to the minister.

Q. I see. And your only recollection of any interviews is with regard to those gas buoys?—A. I beg your pardon?

Q. Your only recollection of any interview is with regard to the prices of the gas buoys, in which he said they were the best they could get?—A. That is only a vague recollection. I know we discussed the thing.

Q. Mr. Fraser has just the same sort of vague recollection, I may tell you?—A. Yes.

Q. Now, of course, you have accepted his certificates since this Merwin matter?—A. I presume so.

Q. Without raising any question about them, I understand?—A. I would not say that.

Q. Then you mentioned about $200,000 paid in advance for buoys. Just let me understand that, Mr. Fraser. Was that one transaction of $200,000 paid in advance?—A. I am speaking from memory now. Whether it was $100,000 or $200,000 I would not be prepared to say; it was a very large sum.

Q. I asked Mr. Willson about it when you were giving evidence. He tells me the most he can remember is that there was one occasion while waiting for government inspection that there was about a $40,000 advance on a $50,000 contract, and that is the only recollection he has of an affair of that kind. Now, would you undertake from your present knowledge to contradict that statement?—A. I think so.

Q. You think you would. I suppose you could get at the facts in connection with it?—A. Yes. If I was up in the office I could get them in a few minutes.

Q. But you are not in a position, I suppose, to give any definite date?—A. My impression is it was for $100,000 or over.

Q. I do not want to press you, Mr. Fraser, unless you are in a position to give evidence. And you know nothing of the necessity in the department for a reserve of buoys?—A. No.

Q. That is not a matter, of course, that comes under you purview ?—A. Well, the necessity for purchase does to a certain extent. If I know purchases of goods that are not required are made it is my duty to call attention to it.

Q. Certainly. But you do not know of the necessity as a matter of public policy for a reserve of buoys ?—A. No.

Q. You heard Mr. Willson's evidence—at least, he did give evidence that Canada had the lowest reserve of buoys of any country in the world he knew of ? You would not contradict his statement in that respect ?—A. These were not, as I understood, in reserve, they had not been delivered to the department.

Q. I am now talking about having buoys on hand which were not intended for immediate use. Your suggestion is only a temporary one. You do not pretend to give any evidence with regard to the necessity, as a matter of public policy, to have a reserve of buoys on hand ?—A. No, I would not undertake to go into that. I might have my own opinion about it.

Q. That is not a matter in which you consider your opinions are worth a very great deal ?—A. No. It is my own opinion.

Q. Thank you, Mr. Fraser.

(Adjourned at 12.50 p.m. until 2.15 p.m. and then resumed.)

OTTAWA, June 17, 1908, 2.15 p.m.

Mr. WATSON.—I should state for your lordship's information that I have just received a further communication from my associate, Mr. Perron, regretting exceedingly that he is not able to be here owing to peremptory engagements that he was wholly unable to cancel—not anticipating—being in the same position in that respect that I was in—that your lordship was going to be able to sit further during this month owing to your engagements in the east. The result was other appointments were made by us. Fortunately I was able to cancel mine, but Mr. Perron was not so fortunate.

Hon. Mr. CASSELS.—Tell him, Mr. Watson, nothing has been lost by his absence.

Mr. WATSON.—Well, my lord, I do not feel that way. I miss his assistance very much.

Hon. Mr. CASSELS.—So far as I am concerned. Of course, I am only speaking for myself.

Mr. WATSON.—Then, my lord, there are some gentlemen here from Montreal who are exceedingly anxious to get away. Your lordship's suggestion this morning as to the further later sitting in Montreal, I think, is quite the right one, and I propose to ask these gentlemen to come forward for a minute. I want to get their productions, and they are anxious to get away on the early train. I am unable, owing to not having the productions before, to examine them as I think necessary, but I want to get a few statements from them.

Hon. Mr. CASSELS.—It is a great pity to keep them away from home. We can go to them easier than they can come to us.

JOHN OPPE, sworn.

By Mr. Watson :

Q. Mr. Oppe, you are the agent of the Marconi Company, I understand?—A. I am general manager.

Q. General manager ?—A. Yes.

Q. The head office of that company is in——?—A. Montreal.

Q. And how long have you been general manager ?—A. Well, I have been general manager for over five years, since the company was formed.

Q. So you have personal knowledge of the dealings between the department and your company ?—A. Yes.

Q. In fact all that has taken place through you ?—A. Yes.

Q. You were asked in your subpœna to make certain productions?—A. Yes.

Q. What have you brought with you ?—A. I have my company's books.

Q. May I have them, please ?—A. May I send for them ?

Q. (The books having been brought in by a messenger.) Is this the lot ?—A. No, this is the ledger.

Q. Just ask him to bring the others as quickly as he can ?—A. Yes.

Q. Commencing when and ending when ?—A. It is right up to date.

Q. From the commencement of the transactions ?—A. Yes.

Q. Where is the account with the department ?—A. (Turns up page.)

Q. Not paged ? Oh, yes. Then this book, my lord, may be marked as an exhibit.

(Book marked Exhibit 27.)

Q. Is this book in use by you?—A. Yes.

Q. So that it will not be convenient for you, perhaps, or would it be, to leave it here?—A. No, we could not do that, my lord, without considerable inconvenience in our business.

Hon. Mr. CASSELS.—Do you want to get a list of the stockholders, or——

Mr. WATSON.—This is the regular ledger, showing the different accounts in the business, the whole of the business transactions as ledgerized?—A. I don't think you will need all these.

Q. What are they?—A. Cash books and journals and so on.

Q. Just let me have them, please, the cash book. This is the original cash book.

(Cash book marked Exhibit 28.)

Q. I think we will have this marked. Do you produce the transfer ledger? —A. No.

Q. Are these carried forward, these entries?—A. Yes.

Q. Original entries?—A. Yes.

Q. Then I think it might be marked. (Transfer ledger marked Exhibit 29.) And this book is another cash book.

(Marked Exhibit 30.)

Q. And a second cash book. Is this a cash book as well?—A. Yes

(Second cash book marked Exhibit 31.)

Q. And the original ledger.

(Marked Exhibit 32.)

Q. And four journals.

(Marked Exhibits 33, 34, 35 and 36 respectively.)

Q. Anything else?—A. No, sir.

Q. These books are kept, of course, in the head office at Montreal under your direction?—A. Oh, yes.

Q. And may be subject at any time convenient for inspection and examination? —A. Certainly.

Q. And for further production. So that if you are permitted to take them now you will undertake that they will be available for inspection and subsequent production?—A. Certainly, so far as my power goes.

Q. Yes.

Mr. WATSON.—Then, my lord, under the circumstances, I prefer that the further examination of this witness should stand until your lordship sits in Montreal. I can hardly enter upon it without completing it. It may take a little time.

By Hon. Mr. Cassels:

Q. Have you any other papers outside of these books?—A. No, my lord.

By Mr. Watson:

Q. No letter books?—A. The correspondence is all in the office, I can produce it.

By Hon. Mr. Cassels:

Q. And any transfers?—A. I can produce all that.

Q. The stock book is not among these books?—A. The stock ledger is not here. We have that, and our registrars keep that.

Q. Are there transfers held in trust for anybody not shown in these books?—A. Not in these books.

Q. But I say are there any transfers of stock held in trust for anybody that do not appear in the book?—A. No.

Q. Nothing of that sort?—A. No.

Q. So that all the information as to stock is there?—A. Yes; and our transfers are available and our auditors are available.

Q. Yes. I only ask for information. Well, it will suit you to be examined in Montreal later?—A. Yes, my lord.

Hon. Mr. CASSELS.—I think we had better do that, Mr. Watson.

Wr. WATSON.—Yes, my lord.

BERNARD J. COGHLIN, sworn.

By Mr. Watson:

Q. Mr. Coghlin, have you produced your books of account, your records of business, have you brought them with you?—A. I have not. I was never asked to bring them. I only received the message last night at half-past seven o'clock.

Q. The subpoena called for production of the books. Perhaps you are not able to get them?—A. I was not able to get them at the time.

Q. You understood the subpoena called for them?—A. Yes.

Q. But you were not able to get them?—A. No.

Q. You have them all in your——?—A. All in my office.

Q. All the usual and regular books?—A. Yes.

Q. Containing records of all transactions with the department?—A. Yes.

Q. And I have to ask you if you will undertake to produce them at any time to us or our representative there for the purposes of inspection at convenient periods?—A. I am prepared to do so at any moment.

Q. And to produce them at the further hearing by appointment?—A. Yes, sir.

Q. Were you here this morning when the Auditor General was giving his evidence?—A. Not in the beginning of it; I was here when he was concluding his evidence.

Mr. WATSON.—I am not in a position, my lord, to enter upon his examination either, but I think perhaps it is reasonable to ask him just one question while he is here, in view of what the Auditor General stated, to see what he has to say. With regard to the order which was given to you for some silverware for one of the steamships, do you recollect the order?—A. I do.

Q. It is said in connection with that, that you afterwards made a refund of about $1,100 of money which had been improperly exacted by you, and therefore voluntarily refunded, or refunded after inquiry, perhaps?—A. Yes, in connection——

Q. Just, in a word, have you any explanation in connection with that ?—A. In connection with that I may tell you the Auditor General and the deputy minister imposed upon me, absolutely imposed upon me. They summoned me up here to ask me some questions and they said, 'You have overcharged us on these invoices.' I explained matters to them as best I could from memory and they were not satisfied. Then I said, 'What will you be satisfied with ? I don't want my name to be made public in this connection, I am not doing this sort of business.' I said, 'How much will you want' ? They said so much. I said, 'Give me a cheque,' and I made it out there and then. On inquiry when I got back to the office I found I had not only returned my profit, but $400 or $500 more than the profit I made on the transaction. The goods were specially imported for them, they were specially made, they were made from drafts or description that I gave them of them myself, and I did not charge them what I ought to have charged them. I did not charge them sufficient in the first time, my lord, and I found there were insinuations made that the goods were not supplied at all. I said, 'That is not my fault. They were delivered to you at Quebec.' The Prime Minister went down to inquire for them and he found them in Quebec six months before I was paid for them. Furthermore, I find the deputy minister went about inquiring what prices were charged for such goods and he found he could not get such goods made in Canada, but something similar, and my price was 25 per cent less than the price he could have bought them for in Ottawa or elsewhere. So I demanded a refund of this money I overpaid, and I asked permission from the minister to sue the government to have the money refunded. That is my explanation of the matter. I am prepared to prove it.

Q. Did you ever explain it to the deputy minister or to the Auditor General ?—A. I explained it to the Auditor General, and the auditor told me in my office if I sued the government he would be prepared to recommend the money to be refunded to me. The Auditor General made that statement to me in my office. He saw the injustice both himself and the deputy minister had done me.

Q. Well, will these matters appear from your books, the verification or otherwise ?—A. No, they won't, this is not in the books ; but my entry is in the books of the goods I supplied them with.

Q. Yes. Is there a record in your books showing the prices and the commissions and the whole transaction ?—A. Yes, there is.

Q. With the profits made by you ?—A. No, no. It is not a question of profit. There is an entry made of the invoices. And again, I must tell you, my lord, I think they have found out the original invoices through illegitmate means by going to the Customs House and getting it. I was not aware that original invoices were to be handed about from time to time to anybody and everybody who wanted to see them. I think the Auditor General was over-zealous.

By Hon. Mr. Cassels:

Q. How much were you out of pocket?—A. I was out of pocket about $500.

Q. Over and above what you paid?—A. Over and above what I paid, without calculating my profits upon the transaction.

Q. I understand that. I mean actual cash?

By Mr. Watson:

Q. You mean——?—A. I was $1,100 altogether. Your honour, the Auditor General was over-zealous.

Q. You will have to permit us, having your books in hand, to inquire further into this and test the accuracy of these statements, Mr. Coghlin?—A. Yes.

By Hon. Mr. Cassels:

Q. I would like to ask you one question. Did the colonel refund you half your loss?—A. No.

Mr. WATSON.—That was Commander Spain, my lord.

Hon. Mr. CASSELS.—Oh yes. Pardon me. That is all right, Mr. Coghlin.

By Mr. Watson:

Q. Then I will have to call you again when his lordship sits in commission in ontreal. I was instructed from you to state you were leaving?—A. I am leaving Saturday or Friday.

Q. When do you return?—A. I shall be back the 1st of September or October, t until then. I will be an exhibitor at the Franco-British exhibition; I am an ventor.

Q. You have other representatives at Montreal?—A. Yes, I have clerks.

By Hon. Mr. Cassels:

Q. They could give the evidence?—A. Yes.

By Mr. Watson:

Q. That will do for the present. You will be subject to further examination on is, Mr. Coghlin.—A. Thank you, my lord.

JAMES BUCKLY, sworn.

By Mr. Watson:

Q. Mr. Buckly, you live at Prescott?—A. Yes, sir.

. What is your business there?—A. General merchant.

. You have lived there for very many years, I understand?—A. Yes.

. You deal in coal?—A. Yes, sir.

. To a considerable extent?—A. Oh, yes.

. You supply coal in the locality?—A. Yes.

Q. That is, by retail?—A. Yes.

Q. Not otherwise?—A. Not always.

Q. The report of the Civil Service Commissioners—page 35, my lord—refers to ansactions between you and the department. Are you familiar with those?—A. Yes.

Q. The reference is as follows: ' Another curious memorandum appears on file, ted September last. It is in reference to a letter from a contractor at Prescott mplaining that his contract to supply anthracite coal for the depot there, for one three years, involved a loss to him of 50 cents a ton. Contract price was $5.75 d cost price $6.25, and he begs for consideration. " I am willing," he says, " to ntinue the furnishing of the coal, under the circumstances, at cost price ".'?—A. at is correct.

Q. Is this the letter, September 13, written by you?—A. Yes.

Q. 1907, my lord. ' *Re* anthracite coal for depot here and steamers in connection, beg to submit to your department in the matter of anthracite coal for depot here, d the steamers in connection. The memo. of agreement reads for one or three ars; I have furnished the anthracite coal for one year and over at $5.75 per ton a loss to me of considerable. The coal costs me $6.25, so you can readily see the s to me. I am willing to continue the furnishing of the coal, under the circum- nces, at cost price, say $6.25 per ton. This, I feel assured, when brought to your tice, in all common fairness to me, will be satisfactory. The loss I have sustained the past might be considered. Coal at Ottawa is $7.50 per ton; at Prescott the gular price is $7, Brockville $7 per ton, and I don't think that the department will ject to paying the cost price of the coal at least. I have carried out the agreement r a year and over and stood the loss, and might I beg request for favourable con- deration in the matter. Respectfully yours.' Directed to the deputy minister. at is the letter?—A. Yes, that is correct.

Q. You had a contract previous to that?—A. Yes.

Q. And that contract called for supply by you at $5.75 a ton?—A. Yes, that is right.

Q. And that was to run for three years?—A. One or three years.

Q. Then under the circumstances mentioned in this letter you wanted to get out of the contract?—A. Well, I would just as lief get out of it.

Q. What is that?—A. I would just as lief get out of it.

Q. Your letter indicated you were more than lief, you wanted to get out of it?—A. Yes, because I was selling at a loss.

Q. But people expect to stand to their contracts, do they not?—A. Certainly.

Q. That was a claim for indulgence?—A. Yes. If they would give me cost price for it I thought I was perfectly justified in asking for it.

Q. You thought you were justified in asking for it?—A. Yes; but they refused to grant it.

Q. The commissioners say in the report, 'The memorandum is as follows:'—That is based upon that—'I recommend that the contractor's offer be accepted; and as he has furnished coal at a loss in the past, that 5 per cent profit be allowed him for coal in future. Anthracite coal in Ottawa costs from $7.25 to $7.75, and the regular price at Prescott.' This was agreed to?—A. No.

Q. That is what the commissioners have reported, that that was agreed to?—A. They made a mistake in that, for I never got it nor even any reply to my letter.

Q. You never got a reply to your letter?—A. No.

Q. I find a memo. attached of the 17th of September, 1907, a memo. for the deputy minister signed W. W. S. Who is that?—A. Mr. Stumbles.

Q. 'Mr. Joseph Buckly, of Prescott, who furnished anthracite coal to this department at $5.75 per ton, states that this coal was furnished at a considerable loss to him. The coal cost him $6.25, and he is now willing to continue the furnishing of the anthracite coal at cost price, namely, $6.25 per ton. I recommend that Mr. Buckly's offer be accepted, and as he has furnished coal at a loss in the past that 5 per cent profit be allowed him for coal in future. Anthracite coal in Ottawa costs from $7.25 to $7.75, and the regular price at Prescott is $7 per ton.' That is signed on the 17th of October, 1907, with the initials of the deputy minister, who has endorsed upon that in red ink as follows: 'This will have to be decided on the conditions of the contract;' and underneath that is written 'carry out the contract.' Followed by the initials of the minister, Mr. Brodeur. So that you say that that memorandum or request was not granted?—A. Not granted, no.

Q. That was evidently, then, a misapprehension on the part of the Civil Service Commissioners where they say it was agreed to. It was not agreed to?—A. No, not agreed to. $5.75 is all they are paying me.

Q. Under the same contract?—A. Yes, sir.

Q. The contract is still in existence?—A. Still in existence, yes.

Q. So you are held?—A. They hold me to the contract, $5.75.

Q. Properly enough, I should think?—A. I don't know, I am standing the loss of it.

Q. You hold other people to their contracts, you generally do if you can, I suppose?—A. I don't know.

Q. You take the lean with the fat, the worse with the better. At all events, that is the record of the transaction?—A. Yes.

Q. Have you had much contracting with the department?—A. No, only for coal principally.

Q. Coal principally?—A. Yes.

Q. How long have you been furnishing coal?—A. I think about five or six years.

Q. Usually how much more do you get from the department per ton than you get from your ordinary consumer, purchaser?—A. I don't get as much.

Q. What?—A. I don't get as much from the department.

Q. Do you mean that?—A. Yes, sir.

Q. Have you got your books here?—A. I have my books here.

Q. Let me se them, please ?—A. What books do you want to see ?

Q. Well, what books do you keep?—A: I have got it all down here on paper, the hole transaction.

Q. What book is this?—A. The daybook.

Q. Showing your regular transactions with all customers, including the department ?—A. Yes; and there is another.

Q. This starts in 1899 and runs up to 1905 ?—A. Yes.

Q. This may be marked, if you please.

(Marked Exhibit 37.)

Q. What one is this ?—A. After 1905.

Marked Exhibit 38.)

Q. Are you familiar with the books?—A. Yes.

Q. I do not suppose you are your own bookkeeper?—A. I have got a clerk, you 10w, and go over them.

Q. This starts in 1906 and goes forward to the present time ?—A. Yes.

Q. Now, then, just let me see when was this contract made?—A. The last one?

Q. With the department ? This letter was written in 1907.—A. I have the contact. (Producing.)

Q. That is better. It is a pleasure to see a man of such system and business. es, the contract is here, my lord, dated 31st day of August, 1906. This is the contact ?—A. Yes.

(Marked Exhibit 39.)

Q. This speaks of the price, $5.75 per ton net as required ?—A. Yes.

Q. Then certain other qualities of coal, apparently a little less, and delivered at rescott ?—A. They didn't take it.

Q. Well now, that is in 1906 ?—A. Yes.

Q. Will you please show me in your books a record of sales and deliveries to some her customers about the same time of the same quality of coal ?—A. For 1906 ?

Q. Yes. Take any one ?—A. (Turns up book.)

Q. Take H. B. Benham, pages 76 and 117, take 117. Where is that, is that thracite stove coal ?—A. That is not the same.

Q. That is 1908 ?—A. Yes.

Q. That is on a little too far. Take the earlier page, 76. In 1908 I see you were lling stove coal at how much, $7 ?—A. Yes.

Q. And the nut coal at $7, in 1908, the same kind of coal?—A. Oh, yes.

Q. Here is Mr. Benham, this is April, 1907, about the time of your communica- n, September and October, 1907. Where do you find the prices there ? There is .75 nut coal, $6.75 where he took delivery at the yard ?—A. Yes.

Q. $7. Is that the same kind of coal ?—A. Yes.

Q. And you have entered here coal, $7, stove coal, $7.39, egg coal, $7.49. I see at is during the same period. What about others, take Mrs. Gahan ? Here is $7, t coal, $6.75?—A. Here is Bray.

Q. Bray, 7, half a ton $3.50. I do not think it is necessary to pursue it. I just k those at random, my lord. Now, show me the account of the deputy minister in ur book ?—A. The deputy minister ?

Q. Yes?—A. That is for two cars of coal.

Q. Whatever it is let me see it.—A. 494.

Q. Page 494. That is 1905 or prior to that, Colonel Gourdeau ?—A. Yes.

Q. I find the account here, September 24th, 1904, 20 tons of egg coal at $6.50? A. Yes.

Q. Eight tons of nut coal ?—A. That was in a car.

Q. At $6.50 ?—A. Yes.

Q. And September, 1905, 20 tons of egg coal $5.95 ?—A. Yes.

Q. Chestnut coal $5.95. I see you paid the freight on this ?—A. Yes, but charged it here.

Q. I see you have charged it against them. How much less was that than th current price ?—A. This was in cars, and cartage would be saved on that ; tha accounts for this difference in the price.

Q. A difference of how much ?—A. Say 25 cents, if that had to be carted from the yard. That was the regular price to be sold out of the cars.

Q. You say that was the regular price ?—A. Yes, where sold by the car.

Q. And what was the regular price where delivered ?—A. .$7.

Q. You got $6.50; there would be a difference of 50 cents, then?—A. Well, i would cost 35 cents, about 35 cents to handle that coal. I call it $6.50.

Q. Then did you give him an advantage by reason of his position?—A. No, sir

Q. Why?—A. No, sir. I would have sold that car to you at the same price o: to anybody else.

Q. Thank you?—A. He never asked me for anything.

Q. Eh?—A. He just ordered that car, he telephoned from Montreal to send carload of good furnace coal.

Q. Do you mean Montreal or Ottawa?—A. He telephoned from Montreal.

Q. How do you remember?—A. I remember getting it.

Q. You remember the fact?—A. Yes.

Q. Was that by reason of the connection with the department?—A. Oh, no.

Q. Do you say there was no advantage or gain at all?—A. No advantage or gair at all; it was not taken into consideration.

Q. Did you get paid for that?—A. Yes, sir; there are the credits there.

Q. How much discount did you allow?—A. None, no discount.

Q. Did you allow any discount to the department?—A. What for?

Q. For cash?—A. On their contract?

Q. Yes?—A. No.

Q. Why not?—A. I think their discount would be enough.

Q. I did not intend to hurt your feelings?—A. Oh, no, that is all right.

Q. Well, do you usually allow discount?—A. No, sir.

Q. Do you ever allow it?—A. No.

Q. Now, where is Mr. J. F. Fraser's account?—A. Mr. J. F. Fraser had one ca of coal long ago, I don't know the date, and he paid me for it like a gentleman, gav me a cheque on the bank. Page 405.

Q. 412. J. F. Fraser. This is June 17, 1903. He got it cheaper—$5.50?— The price of coal varies in different years.

Q. Was that the regular price at that time?—A. That was the regular price i car lots.

Q. Quite sure?—A. Yes, sir. I sold to any one at that price.

Q. Eight tons of nut and ten tons of nut?—A. Ten tons of stove.

Q. Oh, yes, I beg your pardon, and 25 tons of egg coal ?—A. Yes.

Q. Quite a large order?—A. That is what he had and he gave me a cheque for i

Q. $238.70, that was paid?—A. Yes.

Q. How much allowance was made to him?—A. Not a cent.

Q. What rebate?—A. What rebate? There is no rebate on coal.

Q. Nothing of the kind, eh?—A. No, sir.

Q. Do you say those are the regular prices charged to others at the same tim —A. Yes, sir.

Q. I see there are other entries in the book apparently agreeing with that?— Yes.

Q. Then what other officials did you sell to; where is Mr. Stumbles' account? A. I did not sell any to him; he never asked me.

Q. What other officials?—A. No other that I know of.

Q. High or low?—A. High or low, that I know of.

Q. That you know of?—A. No.

Q. Those are the transactions?—A. Those are the transactions.

Q. I am much obliged to you for facilitating the inquiry by your ready and proper productions.

By Hon. Mr. Cassels:

Q. Mr. Buckly, what quantity of coal did you sell on this contract, taking it for he year?—A. I don't know.

Q. Don't bother about adding up. Was it a large quantity or small?—A. The boats coal at the different places they go into.

Q. Well, turn me up your book where you say it cost you in Prescott $6.25 cost price; I would like to see that?—A. I could not show you the entry in the book.

Q. But I would like to see why you paid in Prescott $6.25 for your coal?—A. I lon't know where I could show you here.

Q. I should like to be satisfied?

By Mr. Watson:

Q. Yes. You state in the letter what the cost is?—A. There would be about the way it would be (producing statement).

Q. 'Cost of the coal to J. B.'—Buckly?—A. Yes.

Q. 'The coal cost at Ogdensburg per gross ton, $5.75, which is equivalent to $5.13 per net ton; ferriage to Prescott, 15 cents per net ton; C.P.R. yardage charge, 15 cents per net ton; unloading cars, 25 cents per net ton; cartage delivering, 35 cents per net ton. screenings, 17 cents per net ton; weighing, 5 cents per net ton; $6.25.' These added make, $6.25?—A. Yes.

Hon. Mr. CASSELS.—What is that memorandum?

Mr. WATSON.—A memorandum prepared in nice form and shape.

The WITNESS.—From recollection.

By Hon. Mr. Cassels:

Q. But have you any letters showing the contract price at which you bought in Ogdensburg?—A. No. The coal is bought in different places.

By Mr. Watson:

Q. What his lordship asks is, did the coal cost in Ogdensburg per gross ton, $5.75; have you anything in writing to show that?—A. No, I have not anything here in writing, because that is circular prices, you know.

Q. At that time?—A. Yes.

Q. You say so?—A. Oh, yes.

Q. Are you prepared to pledge your oath as to the accuracy of that?—A. Yes. It goes up 10 cents every month. Suppose that was $5.75 the first time, next it would be $5.85, that is the fall of the year.

Q. That is during how many months?—A. It goes up to the first of October, and last year it was $5.85.

Q. But you have entries in your books, I suppose, somewhere, your letters would show the cost price?—A. Well——

Q. For instance, from whom did you purchase?—A. From different people; I could not tell you exactly.

By Hon. Mr. Cassels:

Q. Where is your ledger account showing what you paid?—A. I don't know, it was down here. We take the coal and they draw a draft.

3262—17

Q. I know. But you pay for it?—A. Certainly.

Q. Then you must have it entered. Turn up your ledger and see what it shows?
—A. It aint in this book.

Q. Is it in the other book?—A. No.

By Mr. Watson:

Q. What book is it in?—A. There is another book called the coal book.

By Hon. Mr. Cassels:

Q. Why did you not bring that with you?—A. I didn't think it would be necessary.

Q. It seems to me that is essential?—A. If I were going to get paid the extra
then I would think it would be necessary to show it.

By Mr. Watson:

Q. Well, that is not a matter of argument, Mr. Buckly. You can send that book
down?—A. Certainly.

Q. I wish you would do so?—A. I can send it to you.

By Hon. Mr. Cassels:

Q. We are not doubting your statement, but we want to see it. You ought to
buy it cheaper wholesale?—A. You cannot get coal, my lord, for that now-a-days. It.
goes up 10 cents the whole transaction.

By Mr. Watson:

Q. That is the transaction with the department?—A. Yes, all the coal I bought.

Q. That is showing the places where delivered?—A. Yes.

Q. And the references to the boat?—A. Yes, the boat and quantities.

Q. The boat and the depot?—A. Yes.

Q. Then who got the commission?—A. What commission?

Q. Commission on the sale to the department?—A. I don't know. There was
none.

Q. Was there no commission?—A. No, sir, no commission.

Q. Well, if you please, send down that book. You might leave this memorandum
and this. Do you want the books?—A. I couldn't get along without them.

(Statement of cost of coal marked Exhibit No. 40.)

(Memorandum of coal sold to the Marine and Fisheries Department marked
Exhibit No. 41.)

Q. Send the book down to the acting deputy of the Marine and Fisheries Department. I will get it there?—A. All right, sir.

Mr. WATSON.—I am instructed, my lord, the matter of the work of the department
requires that as many of these officials should be brought before your lordship as soon
as possible so as to let them resume their work in the usual way. I want to call half
a dozen of them in the first place before I take one or two of the more important ones.

Hon. Mr. CASSELS.—That may hurt the dignity of those you intend to call first.

Mr. WATSON.—I mean some of them are of more importance in the matter than
others.

Hon. Mr. CASSELS.—In the way of evidence.

Mr. WATSON.—Oh, yes. I am not referring to their position and their personal
dignity.

EDWARD ADAMS, sworn :—

By Mr. Watson:

Q. Mr. Adams, what is your position in the department? Do you say you are a
it deaf of hearing?—A. That is all, not much. Chairman of the Board of Steamboat
nspection.

Q. And how long have you been in that position?—A. I have been chairman since
394, that is fourteen years come 1st of July.

Q. And do you have much expenditure in your branch?—A. Our expenditure is
omewhere about $40,000.

Q. It amounts to so much as that?—A. Well, somewhere about that. I think our
stimate for this year is about $42,000.

Q. That expenditure is incurred in what way, paying inspectors?—A. Paying the
nspectors' salaries and their travelling expenses, and in some cases where there are no
ublic buildings we pay the rent of the offices out of that expense.

Q. And that is in many parts, I suppose, of the Dominion?—A. Yes, a number
f parts.

Q. You do not make contracts?—A. No.

Q. Except with the inspectors?—A. Only the inspectors.

Q. Are they paid by fees?—A. No, sir. They are paid by salary and their
xpenses are paid by the department.

Q. And is there any limit to the expenses?—A. Well, there is no limit to it other
han they make a return to me monthly of their expenses with vouchers for the actual
xpenses.

Q. For the actual expenses?—A. Yes; and they make returns to me showing
here they have been daily and what they have been doing, the steamers and parts
ey have inspected and the men.

Q. What about perquisites?—A. There are no perquisites. I know nothing about
nything outside of their expenses.

Q. At all events they have to make their returns to you in that way?—A. Monthly.

Q. And in that way the expenses are incurred?—A. That is the way the expenses
re incurred, sir.

Q. I do not find any special reference to you or to your branch in the report of
he commissioners?—A. Not that I have any knowledge of.

Q. No. Have you any knowledge or information of any improper or irregular
cts or conduct on the part of anyone in the department?—A. I have no knowledge
nly of my own branch.

Q. Well, in your own branch?—A. Only my own branch. I know nothing about
ther parts of the service.

Q. You know nothing about other parts of the service?—A. No.

Q. And in your own branch, do you know of any irregularities?—A. In my own
ranch, no.

Q. Well, what about irregularities or improper conduct?—A. That I have no
nowledge of.

Q. In your own branch?—A. In my own branch?

Q. Yes?—A. Are there any irregularities?

Q. I am asking you?—A. Are they accused of any irregularities?

Q. I was asking you?—A. If they are not accused I do not know of any.

Q. I am asking, have you any knowledge of any such?—A. In my own branch?

Q. Yes?—A. Not that I am aware of.

Q. Are you able to say definitely whether or not such exist?—A. So far as my
nowledge goes.

Q. Perhaps it does not go far enough?—A. That may be, but I use every means
o find out.

3262—17½

Q. You do?—A. I do.

Q. And you have a belief one way or the other about it?—A. I believe our service is conducted as fair and straight as it possibly can be done. That is my opinion about it. And I think very great proof for that is that we don't get many complaints about it from the public.

Q. And outside of that and in the department I understand you to say you have no knowledge or information of other matters ?—A. No, I don't know anything about other branches of the department.

Q. Well, I hope you will continue to pursue your good course.—A. I will try to. I have so far.

Q. I am sure you will, that will do, thank you.

Silas B. Kent, sworn.

By Mr. Watson :

Q. Mr. Kent, I observe you are in charge of the fishing bounty branch?—A. Yes, sir.

Q. What does that mean ?—A. It is the disbursing of the bounty to fishermen.

Q. Do you mean money bounties ?—A. Money bounties to fishermen.

Q. What class of fishermen ?—A. Deep sea fishermen.

Q. And what is the annual amount of that, about ?—A. $160,000.

Q. Indeed, $160,000 a year. Do you mean that is to all fishermen whether able or disabled ?—A. No. Certain classes that comply with the regulations governing it.

Q. That is a bounty ?—A. A bounty.

Q. And who exercises the discretion, is the bounty fixed in amount to each ?—A. Well, it is fixed from year to year. It depends on the number of applications received.

Q. And it is fixed by whom ?—A. By the minister.

Q. Upon whose recommendation ?—A. On my own.

Q. On your own recommendation ?—A. And the recommendation of the deputy minister.

Q. Your recommendation is made to the deputy minister ?—A. Yes.

Q. And then he approves or disapproves ?—A. Yes.

Q. And it is finally passed by the minister, is that right ?—A. Yes.

Q. About $160,000 a year. Does that consist of the whole expenditure, there are no matters of contract, then ?—A. No contracts.

Q. Just that distribution ?—A. That is all.

Q. And in connection with that distribution what opportunity is there for peculations ?—A. None whatever.

Q. Returns on bounties or commissions ?—A. No.

Q. Any serving of two masters there ?—A. No, none whatever.

Q. Do you know of any such thing?—A. No.

Q. Have you a staff under you ?—A. I have.

Q. Has anything irregular or improper occurred in connection with your branch? —A. No. The staff have not any opportunity to do anything wrong.

Q. I see. Has there been any criticism or comment by the commissioners or by the Auditor General upon your expenditure or business ?—A. Not that I am aware of.

Q. I see. Do you know of any irregularity—how long have you been in the department ?—A. Upwards of twenty-six years.

Q. Oh, a long time. Where were you before you got in your present office ?—A. I was in the outside customs service.

Q. That is in the Customs Department ?—A. Yes.

Q. Do you know of any irregularities, ill-acts or misconduct by officials in the department outside of your branch ?—A. No, I do not

Q. No knowledge of anything of that kind ?—A. None whatever.

Q. Any information that you can give upon that subject ?—A. No, sir.

Q. I suppose it is no use asking questions in the dark. I have no reason to expect anything here.

Hon. Mr. CASSELS.—How is the bounty given, in what way ?—A. It is based on claims filed by the fishermen.

Q. Is that on the catch ?—A. On the catch and length of time fishing.

Q. That is cod fishing, of course ?—A. Yes; that is all deep sea fisheries, except fresh fish and river fishing.

Q. What is the amount of the percentage, what does each man get ?—A. Well, it varies according to the applications and the class of fishermen. There are what are called vessel fishermen and boat fishermen. The vessel fishermen get a larger sum than the boat fishermen.

Q. Just to encourage the fishing industry?—A. Yes, to encourage the fishing industry.

By Mr. Watson:

Q. As a matter of encouragement? This bonus is not to employees of the department, but to outsiders?—A. Yes.

Q. I would be very glad if you would distribute that bonus around amongst us generally?—A. It would be quite a help.

Q. Any other class that gets a bonus besides fishermen that you know of in your department?—A. No.

Q. That will do, thank you.

ROBERT N. VENNING, sworn.

By Mr. Watson:

Q. What is your branch, Mr. Venning?—A. Fisheries branch. I call it a division, because the department is named the Department of Marine and Fisheries.

Q. What is your position?—A. I am assistant inspector of fisheries, assistant commissioner of fisheries.

Q. Who is your head?—A. Well, the minister, the deputy minister and Professor Prince.

Q. Professor Prince is commissioner?—A. Yes.

Q. I should have called him first, perhaps. Your name happened to be on the list first. So you work directly under Professor Prince?—A. I do and I don't. Professor Prince has been attending to special work recently. The last three years he has been outside attending to special commissions, and I have been responsible for the administration of the fisheries affairs of the department.

Q. Of the branch?—A. Of the fisheries division.

Q. What does it involve, in a few words?—A. The whole of the fisheries branch?

Q. No, your duties ? You speak of yourself as inspector?—A. At least, not inspector, that is a misnomer. I am assistant commissioner.

Q. What are your duties, speaking generally?—A. We attend to the international questions arising between this country and the United States, Russia and other countries, in connection with seizures, fisheries questions that have arisen. Then we have affairs between the province and the Dominion with regard to federal rights and provincial rights in regard to fisheries; we have the general administration of fisheries affairs, statistics, fishery licenses, fishing bounty branch—the gentleman who has just given his evidence is under that also—and we have fish-breeding, fishery protection service, and so on.

Q. I understand?—A. It is divided into many subdivisions.

Q. Yes. How long have you been in the department?—A. Well, I joined th service in 1869. I have been in Ottawa since 1873.

Q. 1869. You must have been pretty young?—A. Yes, I was. I joined the out side service and came to Ottawa in 1873.

Q. Then, what is your annual expenditure, about?—A. Of the fisheries branch

Q. Yes?—A. I should say in the vicinity of three-quarters of a million.

Q. Three-quarters of a million?—A. Yes, possibly that, possibly not quite that That would include the $160,000 which Mr. Kent just gave you evidence on.

Q. Three-quarters of a million. Are you in the habit of making contracts? A. No.

Q. How do you make expenditures, how do you happen to get that much out? —A. Well, it is divided into quite a few services. We have, for instance——

Q. Chiefly in salaries?—A. Yes, one branch chiefly salaries. Fish-breeding, for instance, forms a large portion, and the salaries of fishery guardians, disbursements and fishery officers form a large part.

Q. Outside of salaries what does the expenditure consist of?—A. Well——

Q. Are there purchases?—A. Oh, yes. There are purchases in connection with fish-breeding and purchases in connection with some of the other services.

Q. What class of purchases?—A. Well, there would be——

Q. Do you mean food?—A. Yes, there would be food also and food also in connection with many of our fishery guardians, and I don't know about fish-breeding. It would be in connection with actual operations. We buy boats sometimes and material in connection, and there are fish hatcheries.

Q. And who has to do with that expenditure, the recommendation fixing tha amount?—A. We have an officer, the superintendent of fish culture, who attends t that particular branch.

Q. What is his name?—A. Mr. Cunningham.

Q. I see, Mr Cunningham. Well then, Mr. Venning, what irregularities have you known to exist, improper acts or misconduct on the part of officials in your branch? A. I have none whatever.

Q. Do you know of any such?—A. I know of none, sir.

Q. Any chances of commissions or benefits or gains?—A. No, I do not know where the chances would come.

Q. Are there any such things that have been heard of?—A. Not in connection with the branch I am in.

Q. Or that you know of, anything at all?—A. No, I know of nothing.

Q. Has there ever been any complaint or suggestion of any such thing?—A. Not to me.

Q. Or to your knowledge?—A. Or to my knowledge in connection with our branch.

Q. You do not think you are referred to particularly?—A. I may say I do not think any of the remarks of the commissioners refer either to myself or to anyone of my branch.

Q. Was any information obtained from you?—A. The records are entirely distinct; we keep a separate set of records, we have a separate staff, and the commission—

Q. Did the commissioners ever interview you or anyone else to your knowledge? —A. No one in my branch or myself. They never looked at a record or book in our branch.

Q. Then, apart from your branch, what do you know of the difficulties in other branches and improper acts, if any?—A. I don't know if any exist, and as a matter of fact it takes me all my time to look after my end of the house.

Q. Do you know?—A. No, I don't. I have heard more here to-day than I knew before.

Q. I see. That will do.

EDWARD E. PRINCE, sworn.

By Mr. Watson:

Q. Professor Prince, you are commissioner of fisheries?—A. Yes, sir, I am commissioner of fisheries.

Q. How long have you been connected with that office?—A. I was appointed in 1892, the order in council was dated then, and I commenced my duties within a few months after that.

Q. You have held office since?—A. Yes.

Q. You know of the commissioners' report and the subject of this investigation. What information can you give to us as bearing upon your department or upon the other departments?—A. I have been a good deal away, as Mr. Venning explained to you. I have meetings of my own out of Ottawa, so I have not followed so closely these matters, but I was struck by the fact that the fisheries were entirely left out by the commission. They do not think there was anything to investigate there.

Q. Was there any investigation in that branch?—A. I was never consulted.

Q. You were not spoken to or consulted about it?—A. No.

Q. Well, you are an important official of a very important branch; I think you are within the list, but you say you were not consulted. Then do you know of any irregularities or improper acts in your department, in your branch, by any officials or employees?—A. No. No such irregularities have ever appeared so far as I could see.

Q. Have they ever come to your knowledge at all?—A. Not at all. It seems to me that in our service there is not a possibility of that kind of thing. Our expense was largely regular expenditure for salaries and so on that are, of course, defined by order in council and are regular. There is not a large amount of irregular expense.

Q. Then the contracts that are made are made in what way? I mean to say, are they formal contracts or informal and verbal and by letter, or how are they made?—A. Of course, the salaries are paid regularly.

Q. Of course, I am not speaking of salaries?—A. Building hatcheries and things of that kind?

Q. Yes?—A. Oh, that is done both ways, by contract and by day labour.

Q. And do you know of any such thing as commissions being paid or received by officials or others with whom you have dealings?—A. I never heard of such a thing, it never came to my notice. I don't think there is such a thing. I think our service is kept down economically, in fact too economically sometimes. I think I can vouch for that.

Q. You run to pretty large amounts?—A. Yes.

Q. What is the total expenditure in your whole department?—A. Well, of course the different—I suppose fish culture would be $120,000 to $130,000.

Q. But as commissioner of fisheries how much, what is the total?—A. The whole of those branches. As commissioner of fisheries, all the services, as far as I am concerned I think Mr. Venning was correct when he said——

Q. Three-quarters of a million dollars?—A. It must be approaching that.

Q. And in the other departments and branches you have no knowledge?—A. No knowledge and no interest.

Q. No information at all?—A. No, sir.

Q. That will do, Professor Prince. We do not want to detain you and the other gentlemen any longer from your duties, unless your lordship knows of anything further to ask them.

Hon. Mr. CASSELS.—No.

Mr. WATSON.—Then, Mr. Cunningham.

Francis H. Cunningham, sworn.

By Mr. Watson:

Q. You are in charge of what?—A. I am superintendent of fish culture.

Q. Superintendent of fish culture. That is in the department of Professor Prince?
—A. In the Department of Fisheries. Professor Prince is commissioner of fisheries.

Q. How long have you been in the service in that department?—A. Twenty-five years.

Q. What is your expenditure in your branch?—A. About $250,000 a year.

Q. Is it, indeed?—A. Yes, sir.

Q. That is incurred chiefly in what way?—A. Building of fish-breeding establishments and the maintenance of same.

Q. Do you make contracts?—A. We do in some cases.

Q. Contracts for what?—A. For the putting up of the building. Not in all cases, but only in cases where we can do it cheaper by contract. If we can do it cheaper by day labour we do it in that way.

Q. $250,000. That is all practical work?—A. All practical work, all technical work.

Q. It requires a pretty strong practical head over a branch of that kind?—A. Yes.

Q. What salary do you get?—A. $2,300.

Q. You ought to go in business for some company and get three or four times more than that?—A. I am sorry I am not in business for some company.

Q. Then, we will pass on. In connection with those contracts, are they by tender, or in what way?—A. By tender through the regular contract branch. I make out a specification of what I want and give it to the engineering branch, and the engineer makes out plans and specifications. Tenders are then called for by public advertising through the officer who has charge of the contract system.

Q. Is that so invariably?—A. That has been so all the time. In cases where tenders are not called for, contracts, or tenders rather, have been asked from those living in the locality, and that has been done in the usual way.

Q. Then you have your contractors, you deal directly with them?—A. No, sir.

Q. Who does?—A. The officer having charge of the contract branch.

Q. And who was that?—A. That has been in the past Mr. Stumbles. He has advertised for the tenders, contracts, being prepared.

Q. Do you not make recommendations, you indicate the requirements?—A. I indicate the requirements, the contract is arranged for, and I am notified who is the successful tenderer. Then I see the work is built.

Q. You superintend it?—A. I superintend the work.

Q. And what do you know of commissions being paid to these men?—A. I do not know of any commissions.

Q. Have you known of any such things?—A. No, sir.

Q. Commissions, advantages or bonuses?—A. No advantages or bonuses.

Q. What irregular acts have you information of?—A. I have no information of any irregular acts.

Q. Twenty-five years I am going back?—A. In 25 years I cannot say. I cannot point to any one case that I have personal knowledge where there has been an irregular act. I have passed all through the department.

Q. By anyone?—A. By anyone.

Q. By any minor official or officials?—A. I have heard more here than I knew before that has occurred in connection with the department. Rumours—there have always been rumours.

Q. Always rumours?—A. I can remember rumours the first three weeks I was in the service.

Q. Twenty-five years ago?—A. Twenty-five years ago.

Q. Rumours of what ?—A. The same as you hear in any big concern ; there must be somebody getting money improperly or something of that kind. The civil service has always been a butt all over. You will hear it in any place. It is not only in Ottawa but all over.

Q. What is the reason of that, because they are such good livers ?—A. No, because the civil service in the country seems to be a football ; that is the only reason I can account for it.

Q. Well, have there been any complaints at all ?—A. No, sir, not so far as my work is concerned.

Q. I think you are referred to in some portions of that report, are you not ?—A. No, sir.

Q. Perhaps not.—A. I have not had the pleasure of seeing one of the Civil Service Commissioners.

Q. Were you not communicated with ?—A. Not in any way at all ; and so far as our work in the department was concerned I am informed they did not see a file or make any requisition at all.

Q. Then what do you know of other branches of other departments ?—A. I may explain that the Fisheries Department is just as distinct from the Marine Department as the Post Office Department would be from the internal——

Q. Because you are all there together ?—A No. We are up on the roof pretty near, up on the flat. We don't know what is going on below us.

Q. I think you are the ones who should be below, being among the fish.—A. That is where we would like to be.

Q. At all events, you say you have no knowledge of anything in other departments, irregularities or misconduct or ill-conduct ?—A. I have no knowledge.

Q. Have you anything to do with the deputy minister ?—A. Yes, the deputy minister, and the minister also.

Q. What about the friction and difficulties that exist ?—A. I think that has been exaggerated very largely. The only friction I know of is in rumours that have reached us. That is all I know of. There is no friction that would in any way delay the course of departmental work.

Q. Then in what way do the officials get their promotion, through whom chiefly, who promotes them ?—A. The minister.

Q. The minister ?—A. The minister.

Q. And the minister is prompted by some one under or below, or at least solicited? —A. Well, the manner in which he arrives at his decision I cannot say. He is the man who would have to answer a question of that kind.

Q. I see. And what have been your relations with the deputy minister ?—A. My relations with the deputy minister have always been very friendly.

Q. And what about supplies that you have occasionally made to the deputy minister?—A. Supplies that you have made?

Q. Yes?—A. I have not made any supplies that I am aware of.

Q. You procured supplies for him?—A. I never procured any supplies for the deputy minister.

Q. Do you know anything about any such thing?—A. No.

Q. Is there any other Cunningham than you?—A. Not in the Department of Marine and Fisheries.

Q. Is there here at Ottawa?—A. Yes.

Q. Who is he?—A. I think he keeps a grocery store on Rideau street.

Q. Any relation?—A. No. I think he is an Irishman, and I am an Englishman.

Q. Well, Irish and English do sometimes mix?—A. They do. My wife is an Irish lady.

Q. It is generally better for the English than for the Irish?—A. I don't know. I would not like to say that.

Q. Then, what have you heard about supplies by under officials and favours to the deputy minister?—A. I have never heard of any favours or supplies to the deputy minister. I fail to see where an under official could render a service to the deputy minister by supplies. They would have no means of getting supplies for the deputy minister that I am aware of.

Q. Have you any knowledge of such a thing?—A. I have no knowledge of any such thing whatever, no knowledge whatever.

Q. Any knowledge of requests from superior officials to under officials for favours directly or indirectly?—A. No, sir.

Q. Have you ever heard of any such things?—A. I never heard of any such things.

Q. Quite sure?—A. Quite sure, sir. I have not heard of anything.

Q. That will do for the present. I may have to ask you a word again afterwards. Are you going out of town?—A. I cannot say, sir.

Q. Well, all right then.

JAMES McCLENAGHAN, recalled.

By Mr. Watson:

Q. Mr. McClenaghan, what is your office?—A. I am in charge of the records of the marine branch of the Marine and Fisheries Department.

Q. Of the marine records?—A. The marine records, not the fisheries.

Q. In charge of them. What do you mean by that; you are not bookkeeper?—A. Well, I supervise the registration, classification and distribution.

Q. Of the records?—A. Of the records, letters.

Q. Correspondence, I see. You have been the subject of considerable comment apparently, or your work has, by the Civil Service Commissioners. Why do you allow such confusion to exist?—A. I don't think that applies to the record branch.

Q. Well, I think it does according to the report?—A. In the reading of it I take it to be procedure and policy in connection with the internal work on the files.

Q. Work on the files?—A. Yes.

Q. But, as I understand, communications are not treated with care and with system. Do you know anything about that?—A. I think that our system is practically perfect.

Q. That is since the New Yorkers came in, perhaps?—A. Oh, no, long before. The present system of flat filing was introduced in 1887. I might say I introduced it in 1887 under the late deputy minister, Mr. Smith. Previous to that each letter was entered and docketed individually, numbered individually, and folded up and put away. If you wanted a case you would have to get out a number of letters, put them together, and then when they were disposed of they were distributed in their places. Under the present system of flat filing when a letter on a new subject is received we make a docket of it, and then any subsequent letters are attached to that file. When the typewriters were introduced I suggested that a carbon copy of the answer should be placed on the files, and they have been so placed. At first it was objected to by the typewriters, but it has become universal now.

Q. So that you think that a proper system?—A. It is the only system, I think, the only reasonable and logical system.

By Hon. Mr. Cassels:

Q. You keep letters on any one subject together with the answers?—A. Yes. Of course the file the commissioners refer to is one in connection with the accountants' branch.

By Mr. Watson:

Q. Have you anything to do with that?—A. Well, the letters as a general rule were initialed in the accountants' branch; they were the result of audit of accounts that were sent in from the agents. Those accounts were sent in under cover of a statement from the agents. When the officers in the accountants' branch audited the accounts they might come across an account that they thought was improper or the charge was not according to contract, and they wrote a letter, and, as a general rule, they would quote this number on the challenged acccount filed, and write to the agent for an explanation. The letters would go on, they would be sent down to us with the number quoted, and they would naturally be put on that file by the officers in my branch. Sometimes I have probably examined the files; but Mr. Fyshe called me in in connection with that challenged account file, and he questioned me as to how long I had been in the service, and he went into particulars in connection with the registration of the letters; but he had no suggestion to make that I am aware of, except that all the letters, say from the agent at Quebec, Mr. Gregory, should be altogether on one file for the purpose of examination.

Q. Do you mean without regard to the subject matter?—A. Yes. I said that was impracticable, because Mr. Gregory wrote on thousands of subjects.

Q. You would have to separate to maintain any sort of system, I should think?—A. I said the only way that could be effected would be to get Mr. Gregory to send a duplicate of every letter, then put the duplicate on file and call it Mr. Gregory's correspondence, but he seemed to have in view a yearly inspection by commissions so that he could see all Mr. Gregory's correspondence in one file.

By Hon. Mr. Cassels:

Q. I suppose what you mean is this: You can answer letters much easier when you have got all the letters in connection with that one subject together instead of having to hunt through the whole file?—A. Yes. I thing all the departments try to have all the letters on one subject together.

By Mr. Watson:

Q. You have quite a considerable correspondence?—A. 37,000 letters were received in the Marine and Fisheries branch last year.

Q. In one year?—A. In one year. These letters had to be distributed on 30,000 files—I would not say 30,000 files. Our file numbers run up to 30,000, but a great many of the 30,000 are dead; the old files are superseded, and I must not call the whole 30,000 live files. But I suppose out of the 30,000 files there are 20,000 live. For instance, a lightkeeper's file may begin back in 1887 and be continued after his death by his successor and so on right up to the present. Then in connection with the lighthouse service we have a file; we introduced a system not long ago in which we take the numbers of the lighthouses. The lighthouses are numbered consecutively, beginning at the Atlantic ocean, running from the Atlantic to the Pacific——

Q. Well, that means a great deal of correspondence?—A. A great deal.

Q. I do not want to ask his lordship to hear too much of the details of the system. That perhaps is not necessary.

Hon. Mr. CASSELS.—Every office has that system.

By Mr. Watson:

Q. What irregularities have existed there in regard to money matters?—A. Well, we have nothing to do, my branch, with money matters. We do not meet the contractors.

Q. But you keep charge of the records, you come in contact with those matters if they exist?—A. The files pass through our hands.

Q. And during the last year what instances have you found, what evidence have you found of such things by the records?—A. I have not noticed anything on the files.

Q. Have you not?—A. No.

Q. Do you read the communications?—A. We look at them superficially; we cannot go into them very carefully—when you have 37,000 letters in a year, or 150 in a day, you cannot go into them very carefully—but we audit them in a certain way. When the files are returned we examine them to see if the letters have been answered.

Q. But have you found evidence of improper acts, misconduct, disclosed in this correspondence on the part of officials?—A. No, I have not.

Q. Have you ever found any trace of such?—A. It depends on what you mean by the word 'improper.'

Q. Well, I take it in its ordinary sense as applied to officials?—A. Well, dishonesty?

Q. Let me have your definition of it to see where we are at?—A. Mr. Fyshe asked me that question: If you have noticed any evidences of dishonesty or graft?

Q. What is the distinction you have in your mind between an improper act and misconduct?—A. An improper act would be accepting money that was not earned.

Q. I should think that would be misconduct as well. Tell me what you have found in regard to such matters?—A. I never noticed anything of that kind.

Q. What?—A. Qn the files.

Q. Where have you found it?—A. In no place.

Q. It was not put on the files, you mean?—A. All I see is what goes on the official files; I have no other means of knowing.

Q. Do you not see them before they get on the files?—A. Yes; I classify them.

Q. You classify them. Some communications are put on file, the majority, I have no doubt?—A. All we receive in the record room are put on file.

Q. Everything?—A. Yes.

Q. Then what is there that does not go on file?—A. Nothing. If anything is received by the deputy which is of a private nature I suppose it is kept in his room; we do not see it at all.

Q. That does not come to the files?—A. No.

Q. Who is to decide whether it is of a private nature, the deputy?—A. The deputy or his private secretary.

Q. That rests with them?—A. Yes.

Q. So you may not get all the correspondence?—A. There may be private correspondence that we do not see.

Q. As a matter of fact are you aware you do not get all the correspondence for the files?—A. I am aware from the evidence given by Mrs. Thomas.

Q. On the former occasion?—A. Yes.

Q. Then do those communications that do not go upon file come to your knowledge at all?—A. I never see them.

Q. Do you know anything of them?—A. I know nothing of them.

Q. Then do you know of so-called private communications between the deputy minister and contractors or supply men?—A. I know nothing whatever.

Q. Have you reason to believe such exists?—A. I have no reason that I know.

Q. Have you heard of such?—A. None, except when this investigation began, whatever has been brought out by this investigation.

Q. What do you understand by 'private communications'?—A. Communications of a private nature that any one person may have with another.

Q. Concerning departmental matters?—A. It may be concerning——

Q. It may be. I cannot understand how anything that concerns departmental work could possibly be deemed private?—A. It might be a recommendation to the deputy minister with regard to an official.

Q. If it is to him in his capacity as deputy minister, then it is official; it could not be private or personal. However, that is a matter we need not discuss too much, I suppose. At all events you understand some communications took place of that kind that are thought to be private, whether they are or not?—A. As to whether they are strictly private, of course, I have not seen them and I cannot judge.

Q. I do not see why a private communication should come into the department at all?—A. I know the late deputy had private communications from his relations.

Q. Oh, yes; those are strictly private communications?—A. Well, I think that is all the private communications that, as far as I am aware, the deputy kept in his room.

Q. Now, from any of the records of the files has any information come to you of improper acts or acts of misconduct directly or indirectly ?—A. No, nothing has come to my knowledge.

Q. Is there hesitation about you now ?—A. No. There is nothing that has come to my knowledge.

Q. Have you heard of such things ?—A. Well, just what the other officers have stated, there are rumours.

Q. Here in evidence, yes. Then do you know of favours or advantages obtained directly or indirectly by officials ?—A. I know of no favours or advantages.

Q. Purchases ?—A. No, I know of none whatever. We never meet or see the contractors in our room.

Q. Supplies are purchased in the department ?—A. Yes.

Q. To a very, very large extent; and is it not a fact that occasionally an official gets a supply at the same time ?—A. I have heard so this afternoon.

Q. Have you any knowledge of those things ?—A. No knowledge whatever.

Q. Where did you hear them this afternoon ?—A. This morning, I think it was in the Auditor General's evidence.

Q. Have you ever received any information of any such matter ?—A. I have never received any such information.

Q. Nor seen any indications ?—A. Nor indications.

Q. Are you quite sure ?—A. I am quite sure.

Q. Then do you know of any acts on the part of the other officials—you have been there a long time—that are improper and subject to criticism or comment?—A. No.

Q. As to good conscience or ill-conscience ?—A. What the Auditor referred to this morning is, I think, in connection with Commander Spain. It does not come in my branch.

Q. Have you any knowledge of those things ?—A. No. I have no knowledge.

Mr. WATSON.—Unless your lordship wants to ask something I think the witness may go.

Q. Hon. Mr. CASSELS.—No.

Mr. WATSON.—That will do, then.

JOHN B. BOUDREAU, sworn.

By Mr. Watson :

Q. You are marked here as assistant accountant ?—A. Yes, sir.

Q. Who was acting accountant ?—A. Mr. Doutre.

Q. How long have you been in the office as assistant ?—A. Five years.

Q. And how long in the department ?—A. Five years.

Q. Oh, you have been in just during that time. What are your duties as assistant accountant, in a few words ?—A. Well, I look over the accounts when they come in to see they are paid, that they are proper, that they are not overdrawn, that the money voted is not overdrawn, and signing cheques and doing general work of an accountant

Q. Have you anything to do with the correctness or accuracy of the accounts ?—A. We have the accounts checked in the department by officers.

Q. To see that they correspond with the vouchers and the orders ?—A. Yes.

Q. Have you anything to do with the orders?—A. Nothing to do with the orders.

Q. It is just a matter——?—A. Of checking the accounts.

Q. And checking it with the orders and supply vouchers ?—A. Yes .

Q. That is it, is it ?—A. That is all.

Q. Nothing else ?—A. Nothing else, sir.

Q. Then you pay money ?—A. We issue the cheques.

Q. You are the ones that send them forth ?—A. Yes.

Q. And you often, of course, get requests for speed ?—A. Yes.

Q. And inducements held out to you to accommodate and facilitate ?—A. No.

Q.. Eh ?—A. No. We get a note from a party saying, 'I am in need of money. Kindly send my cheque as soon as possible.' That is all they do.

Q. Where does the rake-off come in ?—A. I didn't see it yet.

Q. I am asking you seriously, in one way at all events, is it not so, that opportunities of that kind frequently arise ? People say 'It is worth some consideration for me to get this through quickly, I want money,' and so on ; does that occur ?—A. No.

Q. Have you ever known that occur?—A. I am not aware of that.

Q. You are not aware of it?—A. No.

Q. Have you ever known that occur in the accountant's branch of the department?—A. No

Q. With anyone ?—A. I am not personally aware of it.

Q. With the accountant or anyone else ?—A. No, I am not aware of any inducement of that kind.

Q. What benefits or gains do you get apart from your salaries?—A. Get anything else?

Q. Have you any knowledge of any such things?—A. What?

Q. Benefits, gains, perquisites to officials in your department ?—A. I know nothing personally. The only thing I know is rumour, and of course I don't give that—

Q. You don't take that into account?—A. No.

Q. But rumours are often pretty accurate, you know ?—A. I don't know.

Q. Those rumours apply to your department?—A. To every department.

Q. And to yours?—A. All likely, yes.

Q. Have you heard them of yourself?—A. No. I suppose I am like the rest of them.

Q. Then do you know of the foundation for any such things, whether there is any foundation for any such rumour?—A. No, I am not aware there are any foundations. The rumour might be created by the report of the commission or something of the kind.

Q. Were you interviewed by the commissioners?—A. Yes. I showed the books in the accountant's branch to Mr. Fyshe.

Q. And what took place?—A. Well, he found that the books were a little large, and it was expensive for the paper. That is about what he told me.

Q. Well, I did not expect an answer like that ?—A. Well, I showed him all the books. He seemed to be——

Q. He made valuable suggestions?—A. He seemed to be quite satisfied with the system established lately. He went over every book. He did not stay there long.

Q. Under whose direction are you?—A. Mr. Owen until lately, and now under Mr. Doutre.

Q. Anyone else ?—A. The deputy minister.

Q. Then, do you get orders and directions from the deputy minister?—A. Sometimes I do.

Q. What has the deputy minister to do in the department?—A. Well, of course, if Mr. Owen was away, and if there was some account payable, he would come to see it was paid promptly and see the work was done.

Q. Then, correspondence with the creditors, middlemen and commission men all comes through you or comes to you for payment?—A. No. They generally address to the deputy minister or to the accountant.

Q. The deputy minister or the accountant, but it comes before you?—A. It is sometimes addressed to the minister also.

Q. And have you seen in such correspondence claims for commission?—A. No, I don't remember.

Q. Eh ?—A. I never saw anything of the kind.

Q. Do you know anything about payment of commission to anyone, middlemen or others?—A. I don't know anything of the kind, I am not aware of anything of the kind.

Q. What discounts appear on the face of the account?—A. You mean——

Q. Discounts for cash or for money?—A. We get some discount.

Q. You get some discount?—A. Yes.

Q. Who gets the discount? That is what I want to find out?—A. The deparment gets it.

Q. I have not heard much of it yet. Discount from whom?—A. I mean Mr. Fyshe made a statement that we never got discount on the accounts. Well, in fact we have.

Q. You do?—A. Yes.

Q. Do you remember anybody who gave you discounts ?—A. On their accounts with the department ?

Q. Yes?—A. We get some.

Q. From whom?—A. Well, I can't say that; I don't know that. I can point out some.

Q. Where discount is allowed for cash payments?—A. Within thirty days of payment.

Q. And how are your payments usually made?—A. They are made as soon as the account reaches the department.

Q. I have heard people say they were sometimes not made at all?—A. They are made sometimes late if we have no money to pay them.

Q. I see. What is the usual period of credit?—A. Well, we have no time limit. Sometimes we are obliged to keep it six months if the money is not voted, sometimes nine months.

Q. You never allow interest ?—A. No.

Q. The government never pays interest?—A. No.

Q. Are you sure about that?—A. I am pretty sure so far as my branch is concerned.

Q. I have known of several people who wanted interest but could not get it. Well, then, what is the irregularity that exists on the part of officials in your department?—A. Well, the irregularities in our department, I have learned more here than I knew in fact before.

Q. But just tell his lordship what you do know of the irregularities existing there? —A. I don't know of any irregularity.

Q. I thought you were going to tell me of some?—A. I cannot tell you, because I do not know of any irregularity. There might be some little error made, but I do not think there is any irregularity.

Q. I thought you started out to tell me the irregularities are so and so. What did you have in your mind?—A. I did not start to tell you.

Q. Did you not?—A. No.

Q. I made a mistake then. Then what do you know of irregularities, improper conduct on the part of officials?—A. I do not know of any.

Q. On the part of the chief accountant what do you know?—A. Well, I know that Mr. Doutre mentioned something yesterday about the payment of $150, and I don't see that is a great irregularity.

Q. What is that?—A. I don't see that is a big irregularity.

Q. Not a big irregularity?—A. No.

Q. $150 is not ?—A. Well, circumstances, they tell you, alter cases.

Q. Circumstances of the case?—A. Yes.

Q. Are you familiar with them?—A. With whom?

Q. With the circumstances?—A. Of that case?

Q. Yes?—A. I am now since I heard of that.

Q. Have you personal knowledge?—A. Of what?

Q. Of the circumstances of the case that Mr. Doutre referred to?—A. Yes, I have.

Q. You have. Well, I will have to ask you one or two questions. Where did your share come in? You say you had personal knowledge of the circumstances of the case, that is right?—A. I mean——

Q. I will show it to you in a minute. (Referring to file.) What personal knowledge have you? Let me have your statement first?—A. That is about the payment of $150, but as to other things I don't know.

Q. Eh?—A. I say about the payment of $150.

Q. About the payment of $150 you do not know?—A. I know about that.

Q. This letter was put on file by you (producing). Never mind reading it. See if you can idenitfy it?—A. I do not remember having seen it.

Q. Who was Mr. Eyre?—A. He was a commission merchant here.

Q. A commission merchant?—A. Yes.

Q. Did you have transactions or dealings with him?—A. No.

Q. None at all?—A. I must inform you this is what was brought to my attention as an irregularity in our department.

Q. Well, this is your department?—A. Yes.

Q. Who was he agent for the Wingate Chemical Company?—A. Yes; but I did not know that up until lately.

Q. Now, I have a letter here. You referred to it. I did not know you had knowledge about these matters. So, I may as well see what you do know. The letter is from Mr. Eyre to his principals, that is, the Chemical Company, and dated 5-11-'07—5th November, 1907: 'I wish you would put in a lot for P. Harty, Ottawa, two extra cans addressed to me tagged. I want them for Mr. Owen, the accountant, and Lieut.-Col. Gourdeau, deputy minister, both Marine and Fisheries. Is Mr. Reid with you yet? I cannot charge anything for above. Yours truly, W. J. Eyre.' This is what you had in mind, was it?—A. Not at all.

Q. What?—A. No.

Q. I thought you were going to give me information about that?—A. No, about the payment of $150.

Q. Had the payment of $150 to do with that?—A. I don't know it had.

Q. What explanation can you give me of that letter?—A. None whatever. I don't know anything about it.

Q. 'Two extra cans addressed to me'—what is that, 'tagged,' is it not?—A. Yes.

Q. 'I want them for Mr. Owen'—he was the chief accountant, was he not?—A. Yes.

Q. 'And Lieut.-Col. Gourdeau, deputy minister, both of Marine and Fisheries. I cannot charge anything for above.' Do you know anything about what those goods were?—A. No.

Q. I thought I was going to get information from you about those things?—A. I didn't know that.

Q. What was it you were going to tell me?—A. About the payment of $150 that was brought out in the course of the evidence of Mr. Doutre as being somewhat irregular. I simply mentioned it to say I knew at the time the evidence was made that an order had been given to Mr. Eyre for $350, and that he got——

Q. Why did you pass that as a payment in advance, why did you issue that cheque?—A. I was instructed to issue the cheque.

Q. Who instructed you?—A. Mr. Owen.

Q. Mr. Owen instructed you to issue the cheque in advance?—A. Well, the order had been given.

Q. Well, how was that explainable, how was that explained?—A. Well, you see, Mr. Eyre had been dealing with the department for a number of years.

Q. Yes?—A. And of course I don't know exactly the circumstances under which e advance was made.

Q. That was irregular and improper, was it not, according to the system?—A. ell, sometimes advances are made once the goods are started before the goods are bsolutely delivered.

Q. Why so?—A. Of course, people cannot be kept waiting for their money. When he goods are delivered they can be checked.

Q. But the goods before delivered you are speaking of. People do not pay for oods before they get them usually, do they?—A. No.

Q. You do not pay for a suit of clothes when you give the order for it?—A. No.

Q. If you have the ordinary cash credit, that is, if you are fit to be out? How do ou account for this, does that sort of thing prevail to any extent?—A. No.

Q. Then it was done at that time under the direction of Mr. Owen?—A. Yes. Did anyone else give directions?—A. Not that I am aware of.

Q. Eh?—A. No.

Q. Did you challenge it?—A. I was instructed to issue the cheque. I didn't know hether the goods had been delivered or not.

Q. That is all there was to it?—A. Yes.

Q. Then anything alse you know of?—A. Not that I can think of now.

Q. Do you think if you had a little time you might hunt up something else or hink of something else?—A. No, I don't think of anything.

Q. I see. In respect of any of the officials, is that right?—A. That is right.

Q. Well then, we will get on. That will do.

JOHN A. MURRAY, sworn.

By Mr. Watson:

Q. What department are you in, Mr. Murray?—A. Marine and Fisheries.

Q. What branch, I mean?—A. Charge of the records.

Q. Of the fisheries records?—A. Of the fisheries records.

Mr. McClenaghan is in charge of the marine records?—. Yes.

Q. You are in the same position in the fisheries records?—A. Yes.

Q. How long have you been there?—A. About 25 years.

Q. And who is your superior officer?—A. Well, after the deputy, Professor Price is commissioner of fisheries.

Q. I see, you are there. Well then, we will perhaps get to the point. What vidence of irregularities have you found in the correspondence in your record depart nent?—A. I don't know of any.

Q. You do not?—A. No, sir.

Q. In the correspondence or otherwise?—A. No.

Q. Do you know of complaints?—A. No—well, in what way?

Q. Complaints against officials?—A. Oh, no, I have no knowledge of any.

Q. Improper acts?—A. None whatever that I know of.

Q. Borrowing money as officials and not paying it back?—A. No.

Q. What do you know about that?—A. I don't know anything. I don't know nybody I know of ever borrowed.

Q. Do you know of officials going out on official trips getting money from other fficers and not returning it, any record of those things?—A. Not in the fisheries.

Q. Where is it then?—A. I don't know. I have nothing to do with any other art of the department.

Q. Does that sort of thing exist, to your knowledge I mean?—A. Not to my nowledge.

Q. Not to your knowledge?—A. No.

3262—18

Q. Do you know of any acts of dishonesty, misconduct ?—A. No, I do not.

Q. What has ben the trouble in your department, your branch I mean?—A. As far as I know there has been no trouble at all as far as the fisheries part of it is concerned.

Q. That will do.

JOHN MACPHAIL, sworn.

By Mr. Watson :

Q. What is your position ?—A. I am at the present time temporarily in charge of the commissioner of lights branch.

Q. Commissioner of lights branch ?—A. Temporarily.

Q. Your duties call you out of the city ?—A. Sometimes.

Q. But within the next day or two ?—A. I think not.

Q. But within the next day or two ?—A. I think not.

Q. I would rather call you after Mr. J. F. Fraser. Then you are occupying the position he occupied ?—A. Temporarily,

Q. I would rather call you after he has given his evidence.

Mr WATSON.—I have another witness, Mr. Noble, but I find by the records that he has been before the Public Accounts Committee, and, unless he has to leave town, I would rather not take him up just now.

Q. You are not required to leave town ?

Mr. NOBLE.—No, sir.

Mr. WATSON.—It does not interfere with the performance of your duties in the matter?

Mr. NOBLE.—No, sir.

Mr. WATSON.—Then I will call hi ma little later, my lord.

Hon. Mr. CASSELS.—How late do pou propose to sit?

Mr. WATSON.—Does your lordship prefer to rest ?

Hon. Mr. CASSELS.—I prefer to sit.

Mr. WATSON.—I have read a letter here which refers to Mr. Owen, and I think it is due to him to call him, also the deputy minister, but I will have to call the latter to-morrow. I will call Mr. Owen for a minute.

ALFRED W. OWEN, sworn.

By Mr. Watson :

Q. Mr. Owen, you were the chief accountant?—A. I am still, I hope, sir.

Q. I beg your pardon ?—A. I am still.

Q. I beg your pardon. You are on leave of absence, then?—A. Yes.

Q. I see. And how long were you accountant ?—A. I was made accountant in 1896.

Q. 1896. What time of that year?—A. I think it was about the 8th of July, if I remember rightly.

Q. 8th of July of that year, I see. And when did you cease to perform your duties?—A. On the 3rd of March of this present year.

Q. The 3rd of March of the present year?—A. The 2nd of March, I think.

Q. I beg your pardon?—A. The 2nd of March, I think.

Q. I will not be able to conclude with you this evening, but you knew Mr. Eyre? —A. Yes, he was a noted character around town here.

Q. Well?—A. He was a commission merchant.

Q. Representing what firm?—A. Well, he represented several firms.

Q. Yes?—A. He dealt in, he sold different lots of goods to the different departments that I am aware of.

Q. To the departments?—A. Several departments.

Q. We are confining ourselves to this department now, you know?—A. Well, what he sold to our department was sulpho-napthol. It was a disinfenctant.

Q. What?—A. Sulpho-napthol. It was a disinfectant.

Q. A disinfectant?—A. Yes.

Q. Was he a personal friend of yours?—A. I knew him very well.

Q. For some length of time?—A. Ten years, I suppose.

Q. You gave him orders?—A. I never gave him any orders, sir.

Q. Eh?—A. I never gave him any orders in the department.

Q. You never gave any orders?—A. No.

Q. You had nothing to do with that?—A. Nothing to do with that.

Q. He was a personal friend of yours?—A. I knew him well, yes.

Q. What do you mean by a 'noted character,' that he was a genial soul?—A. He was a genial soul, yes.

Q. I see. I thought possibly that might be your meaning. Nothing else?—A. That is all, sir.

Q. Too good to himself, and sometimes to others?—A. That is so.

Q. That is what this letter indicates that I read?—A. I don't know about this letter. Oh, yes, I saw that letter on file in the office.

Q. I suppose you did. When did you see it?—A. I saw it some time ago, about a month or two ago.

Q. And did you get the goods?—A. I never got the goods.

Q. Why not?—A. I don't know. I never knew about the goods being sent until I saw that letter.

Q. You never knew about their being sent?—A. No, I never knew about their being sent until I saw that letter.

Q. What were the goods?—A. It says there a gallon of naphthol. It never came to me.

Q. Who got it?—A. I don't know.

Q. The deputy didn't get yours too?—A. He didn't get one either.

Q. How do you know he did not?—A. Well, he has told me so.

Q. Both disappointed?—A. I was not a bit disappointed.

Q. This shows, you see this?—A I see this

Q. Upon its face it is certainly not anything else than a very serious matter?—A. Yes; but I never received it; I never knew the letter was written.

Q. 'I want them for Mr. Owen, accountant, and Lieut.-Col. Gourdeau, deputy minister, both Marine and Fisheries?'—A. I never ordered it.

Q. 'I cannot charge anything for the above'?—A. I never ordered and never got the goods.

Q. Were they delivered?—A. Not to me.

Q. Did he speak to you about it?—A. Not at all.

Q. What?—A. Not a word. I never knew anything about it until I saw that letter in the office.

Q. It was in respect of the same order, or the order with which this was to be included, that you made the advance payment of $150?—A. Nothing at all.

Q. Just try and think?—A. Nothing at all.

Q. There was an advance payment of $150?—A. That was a small matter, $150.

Q. You call that $150 a small matter?—A. The amount of the invoice was nearly $400.

Hon. Mr. CASSELS.—What is the value of it?—A. We have got sulpho-naptho from this man for ten years.

Mr. WATSON.—Who has?—A. The departmenrt.

His LORDSHIP.—What is the value of a gallon?—A. $3.

By Mr. Watson:

Q. $3?—A. Yes.

Q. I see. But goods were ordered at the same time, that is, concurrently with this? —A. The goods were ordered before this.

Q. I have got all the correspondence here?—A. I don't know the time the goods were ordered.

Q. You do not know the time they were ordered?—A. I don't know exactly when the goods were ordered. They were delivered.

Q. Why did you pay $150 in advance?—A. He said he had to pay the Wingate Chemical Company, he had to send them some money. I gave him $150, and I told him that was all we could give him.

Q. That was irregular, of course?—A. It may have been, but that is a small matter out of $6,000,000 expenditure. In our department I don't think you will find many irregularities.

Q. $1,000 is a small matter as compared with a million dollars?—A. This is not a thousand.

Q. This is not. This is comparatively small, but is that the way you justify it by comparison?—A. No. Because we always received the goods from him punctually, and I thought I was perfectly safe in giving that to him.

Q. You know he did not pay that over to his principals?—A. I did not find that out until January.

Q. You did not find that out until afterwards?—A. And the balance of the money was not paid until eight months after the goods were delivered.

Q. What was the balance?—A. I cannot give that from memory.

Q. Do you give that as a justification for paying the $150 beforehand?—A. Oh, no.

Q. That was an irregular act?—A. Yes. I did it to oblige him.

Q. You did it to oblige him?—A. Yes.

Q. Do you oblige your friends?—A. I do nothing of the kind.

Q. With public money in advance? That is what you did on that occasion?— A. Well, that is the only occasion I think you can find out.

Q. Well, what about others we cannot find out?—A. Well, the books are there to find out, all the books in the whole department.

Q. Would you prefer to wait now until the morning to continue?—A. Certainly.

Q. I thought you would?—A. That was a pretty small thing.

Q. We will have to find out about the larger ones to-morrow morning.

(Adjourned from 4.30 p.m. to 10 a.m. to-morrow and then resumed.)

June 18, 1908.

Examination of Mr. OWEN continued:—

By Mr. Watson:

Q. How long were you in the department as accountant, Mr. Owen?—A. I have been in the department as accountant—I have been 27 years in the department altogether. I have been accountant for 12 years.

Q. How long?—A. 12 years.

Q. Then, as accountant, what are your duties, just in a few words?—A. Just to have the management of the whole branch of the accountant's office and the correspondence in connection with it.

Q. The correspondence in connection with it?—A. Yes.

Q. You mean you have charge of the correspondence?—A. Any letters I write in reference to the accounts.

Q. Yes?—A. Any letters in connection with the accounts that require explanation I always dictate, and the letters are sent down for signature.

Q. That is in connection with the payment of accounts?—A. In connection with the payment of accounts.

Q. Then have you anything to do with the certifying of accounts?—A. No, sir.

Q. By whom are accounts certified?—A. By the agents and by the parties who order and receive the goods.

Q. And by anyone else?—A. By contract by the engineers and the assistant engineers, the commissioner of lights, the inspector of lights.

Q. That is, the heads of the different departments?—A. Yes.

Q. I will file this letter from Mr. Eyre.

(Letter marked Exhibit No. 42.)

The WITNESS.—I may say, Mr. Watson, I made a report on that sulpho-naphthol business. I have a copy of it in my hand that I got from the office (producing).

By Mr. Watson:

Q. You made a report?—A. Yes.

Q. And your report, I see, is dated the 21st of March, 1908?—A. Yes.

Q. This purports to be a copy?—A. Yes. I made that for the minister.

Q. Did you make any report prior to this time?—A. Not on that.

Q. Were you asked to do so?—A. No.

Q. To whom was this report made, to the deputy minister?—A. The deputy minister.

Q. This report reads as follows (reads).

(Report marked Exhibit No. 43.)

Q. That is signed by you?—A. Signed by me.

Q. You desire that to be put in?—A. Yes. I thought the original was with the papers there.

Q. I do not find it with the papers I have. Then do you mean to say you did not know for whom Eyre was selling agent?—A. I knew, but we never had any correspondence with him and never did any business with the people at all, and they never came to the department.

Q. But you knew he was an agent?—A. Yes.

Q. Acting for a principal?—A. Yes.

Q. And that the principal would be entitled to the money?—A. But I always paid him before and there was never any complaint.

Q. Usually you pay the principal and not the agent, do you not?—A. Sometimes we pay the agents, sir.

Q. Sometimes?—A. In many cases we pay the agents.

Q. The usual course, I would think, would be to pay the principal?—A. We generally pay the agents; when we give the orders to agents we generally pay them. I have known it in several cases.

Q. You have known cases where it is done?—A. Yes.

Q. Who gave the order for these goods?—A. Well, I think there was some order given by the inspector of lights for the lighthouse service above Montreal.

Q. I am asking about these goods?—A. Mr. Stewart, of the Hydrographic Survey, and some for the Dominion steamers, St. John, New Brunswick, as far as I can remember.

Q. As far as you can remember?—A. Yes; and this order was sent in to me signed.

Q. So you had the verification of the order?—A. Yes.

Q. Then that being so, and before delivery, it was not at all in the regular course to make an advance payment?—A. I almit that, but I considered it was perfectly safe and the department did not lose anything by the transaction.

Q. And that was done upon your own responsibility?—A. My own responsibility altogether.

Q. Did you confer with the deputy minister or anyone else before doing so?—A. Not in this case, I don't think.

Q. That was entirely your own act in making the payment?—A. Yes.

Q. Of course, you do not exercise that discretion in the ordinary course?—A. No, I don't.

Q. That would not pertain to the duties of an accountant?—A. No, sir—well, in some cases sometimes the deputy is a very very busy man and in with the minister or business, and it is not always I can get him, you see.

Q. Well?—A. Then sometimes I take the responsibility on my own shoulders as accountant of the department.

Q. Sometimes you take the responsibility of doing what?—A. Of settling accounts and making payments.

Q. Where they are not certified?—A. Oh, never without a certificate.

Q. Then I understood you to say that the deputy minister does not certify to these accounts?—A. No, sir.

Q. Is that so?—A. Certainly not. He does not certify to his accounts.

Q. Does he certify to any accounts for payment?—A. Certainly. Some accounts I take to him to look over to put his initials on them.

Q. But I want to know what the rule is?—A. We always go to the deputy where there is an application to advance an officer.

Q. For advances?—A. We generally get the sanction of the deputy before I pay it.

Q. I do not quite follow you. I did not understand you to say that advances were made?—A. Sometimes we have to give advances.

Q. How often?—A. We have to give advances to agents.

Q. How often? Do you mean to your own agents?—A. Our own agents, yes. They always have a staff of men to pay every week.

Q. Oh, that's a different thing, that is paying wages.—A. Paying wages; and then we pay the account for it.

Q. That is a different subject matter to the payment for goods and supplies. That is what I am asking you about.—A. I take the certificate of the agents or the responsible officers for the payment of the money. We have many accounts of from $45 to $50 in the year, and I could never take all to the deputy for his signature on every one, I could not do it.

Q. You say it is not the custom?—A. No, it is not the custom.

Q. Then about how often, or, rather, in what proportion of cases are advances made prior to delivery of goods?—A. I think very seldom. There was one advance made.

Q. Do you recollect?—A. Yes. There was one advance made to the International Signal Company before the goods were delivered, but that was by order of the minister.

Q. Yes. How often does that occur, that advances are made?—A. Very seldom.

Q. And under special circumstances?—A. Yes, only under special circumstances.

Q. Then when you deal, that is when you purchase from agents, that is not your own agents, but agents of the sellers or vendors of goods, does the agent get a commission to your knowledge?—A. Not from the department, they may get a commission from their principals.

Q. Have you ever had any knowledge of agents claiming a commission?—A. Never, I never knew it.

Q. Or of anyone claiming a commission?—A. I never knew of any.

Q. Have you ever known commissions to be paid to any official ?—A. In the department ?

Q. Yes.—A. I never heard of any.

Q. What ?—A. I never heard of any.

Q. Would any such thing come to your knowledge if it existed ?—A. Not me at all. I issue all the cheques——

Q. Wait, please. You have the original documents showing the contract or the order ?—A. Yes.

Q. Now, in any cases that you have had, in all cases in fact, the payments are supposed to conform to the original memorandum ?—A. The original memorandum, the documents certified.

Q. The order or contract ?—A. As certified.

Q. Yes. How often have you known that to be departted from from one cause or another?—A. You mean for payments?

Q. Yes. Do you know of any distribution of payments ?—A. I do not know of any distribution of payments at all.

Q. That is, payment in part to one person and in part to another; have you known such a thing ?—A. I have not known of anything like that.

Q. Do you follow what I am referring to ?—A. Yes. Do you mean accounts are all backed up, and the person who makes out the cheques follows the backing of the account and charges to the vote it applies to ?

Q. And the cheques issue ?—A. To the party.

Q. To the creditor ?—A. Yes, to the creditor.

Q. Whose name appears upon the accounts ?—A. Yes.

Q. Have you ever known cheques to be issued to anyone else than the creditor? -A. I have never known of any.

Q. Have you known of cases where a creditor has transferred the account and the payment is made to someone else for him, for the creditor ?—A. I cannot recall a case of that kind.

Q. Then you would know, I should think, whether there was any reduction in the issue of the cheque from the order or contract price?—A. Yes.

Q. Have you ever known of any such thing?—A. I have never known of any such thing.

Q. Are you sure ?—A. I am pretty sure. I never knew of a case of that kind.

Q. And you have been accountant how long?—A. Since July, 1896.

Q. Who was the accountant prior to you?—A. Colonel Gourdeau.

Q. He was the accountant?—A. Yes.

Q. That was in 1896?—A. 1896, sir.

Q. He was accountant prior to you. Then, Mr. Owen, had it come to your knowledge in any way that there have been irregularities on the part of any officials in the department?—A. I have heard rumours, but I have no knowledge of it at all whatever. Just the rumours I have heard since this investigation commenced and I never heard any rumours—I don't know anything at all about it.

Q. In connection with the payment of accounts have you heard anything of discounts or commissions?—A. I just took a note in my pocket in the office this morning of discounts upon an account here.

By Hon. Mr. Cassels:

Q. A promissory note?—A. For $2,200. A discount of 2 per cent at 30 days, and the discount was taken off.

By Mr. Watson:

Q. The discount taken off?—A. Yes.

Q. Well, this is an account of the Canadian Pacific Railway Company?—A. Freight. Here is the account. They are both included here. Here is the account of the Sherwin-Williams Company from Montreal, I think it is.

Q. The Sherwin-Williams Company?—A. Yes. Paid in St. John, New Brunswick.

Q. April 28, 1908. This is a recent one ?—A. Yes.   I told some of the officials in the office to get some more to bring down here in case they were required.

Q. In some cases discounts are allowed?—A. Yes.

Q. What is the rule in regard to that?—A. Well, of course, that is for cash payments within 30 days. Some accounts stay over for several months, and there is no discount taken off them because they have got to go through the usual routine, they go to the agent for a certificate and then to whoever ordered the goods, and then they come back to the department for payment.

Q. Why are not discounts obtained on all accounts that are paid within 30 days? —A. Well, there is no—it is the way the purchase is made, I suppose, by the agents.

Q. Have you not anything to do with that matter, the matter of discounts or commissions?—A. No. Where I see an account where they allow discount for prompt payment I always have it taken off.

Q. In connection with the performance of your duties as accountant have you any discretion to exercise?—A. I have a great deal of discretion.

Q. What ?—A. I take a good deal.

Q. What discretion have you to exercise in regard to the matter?—A. All the accounts come before me.

Q. They come before you either certified or not certified?—A. Either certified or not certified, and those accounts not certified I send back.

Q. That is purely a matter of system. I am distinguishing the system from judgment or discretion on your part. What judgment or discretion have you to exercise? —A. Judgment and discretion in the payment of accounts ?

Q. In the payment of accounts?—A. Yes.

Q. That is, you can stop payment of an account?—A. That I do not think is correct.

Q. On what grounds ?—A. If I think there is an overcharge in the account.

Q. You mean to say, if you think the price is too high?—A. I object to it.

Q. If you think the contract that the head of the branch has made is for too high a price, you have a discretion to exercise, to check that ?—A. To check that.

Q. You have?—A. Yes; and I use that too.

Q. Well, I suppose that is all right if you say so. I do not know of accountants usually having such discretion?—A. Well, I take that responsibility on my own shoulders.

Q. On your own shoulders ?—A. Yes.

Q. I see. Then you are really a superintendent over—you supervise contracts really to see whether the prices are correct ?—A. Not the contracts.

Q. That the prices are right ?—A. If a person makes a contract, I accept the contract if the officers in charge say the work has been done.

Q. But you do not accept the price ?—A. I do not accept the price in the contracts made.

Q. You do not accept the price ?—A. No.

Q. I see. You excercise independent judgment ?—A. That is for goods that are purchased.

Q. And have you always done so ?—A. I have always done so.

Q. So that there is that additional check by you upon the work of the heads of the branches ?—A. Yes. I have got certain officers detailed to check accounts and to bring to my notice any overcharge they think in the accounts.

Q. That is not merely an overcharge in freight or incidental charges but in the contract prices ?—A. Yes, contract prices.

Q. Then, do you keep yourself familiar with the market price of goods ?—A. We have. We take——

Q. Do you keep yourself familiar with the market price of goods ?—A. We have——

Q. Just answer that, please ?—A. Yes.

Q. You do ?—A. Yes.

Q. And do you take the propjer means to keep yourself familiar ?—A. Yes, we have those commercial papers brought to the office every day with the prices.

Q. Now then, has it come to your knowledge in many cases that there has been an excessive price ?—A. Well, I think so. Yes, there have been excessive prices—that is, many cases you say ?

Q. In your own opinion ?—A. Yes.

Q. How did that arise ?—A. Well, I found out what we paid at other places.

Q. Yes. Who were the officials who made contracts at excessive prices ? Give me their names, please?—A. Well, I don't know whether they meant the charge——

Q. I did not ask you what they meant. Just give me the names of those you found making contracts at excessive prices ?—A. Well, I found some in Quebec.

Q. Yes, that is Quebec ?—A. Yes.

Q. That is Mr. Gregory ?—A. In Mr. Gregory's agency.

Q. In his agency ?—A. Yes.

Q. What agents ?—A. Well, he was the agent there.

Q. But anyone else than Mr. Gregory in Quebec ?—A. Well, all the accounts come through him.

Q. I see. He is responsible for those ?—A. Yes.

Q. Then anyone else ?—A. Well, sometimes I would take exceptions to accounts from Nova Scotia.

Q. Who is the official there ?—A. Mr. Parsons.

Q. On the ground of excessive price?—A. That is all, I think.

Q. Who else ?—A. Well, sometimes St. John.

Q. What is his name ?—A. Harding.

Q. Who else ?—A. There is a lot of other agents, several agents.

Q. Anyone else, anyone here in this province or at the head office ?—A. Not in the head office, no, I don't remember. I can't recall at this present moment, but I might if I hunted up my records, I could find out.

Hon. Mr. CASSELS.—Hodn't you better hunt up your records and find it out ?—A. Yes.

Mr. WATSON.—For instance, have you found Colonel Anderson, as chief engineer, making contracts at excessive prices ?—A. I never found him, no sir. I always took Colonel Anderson's certificate at once because he is a very good officer, I always took his certificate.

Q. Then did you discriminate between officials without regard to prices ?—A. Well, if there is a contract price made I take his certificate for it.

Q. Yes. But why didn't you take the certificates of other officers? I want to see what the point of distinction is ?—A. Which officials ?

Q. For instance, Mr. Gregory?—A. That is for supplies purchased; it is no contract. It is just for goods purchased and delivered on board the steamers and to the lighthouses.

Q. Yes. But I asked you a little while ago if you undertook to consider prices mentioned in contracts; you said you did?—A. No, not the contract, because I think when a person makes a contract you have to pay in accordance with his contract, if he does the work.

Q. But supplies are purchased——?—A. Not by contract.

Q. By contract sometimes, are they not?—A. No.

Q. In what way?—A. There are no tenders issued for supplies.

Q. But there are contracts, that is, correspondence?—A. Correspondence, yes.

Q. A contract can be made by correspondence.

Hon. Mr. CASSELS.—These witnesses confound the term 'contract.'

Mr. WATSON.—Yes, they do.

Hon· Mr. CASSELS.—They do not seem to think it is under contract if done by letter.

By Mr. Watson:

Q. Unless it is some document signed and sealed you do not call it a contract?—A. No. I call that a contract.

Q. Of course, a contract by correspondence is perhaps equally as binding as a formal contract?—A. Well, if there is a contract I always read the contract and pay according to the contract, and if the officer's certificate is according to the contract I take his certificate.

Q. But in other cases where supplies are purchased, that is based usually upon correspondence?—A. Well, no. The agent has power to purchase supplies.

Q· I know. But the agent makes his purchases as a result of correspondence, he arranges through correspondence?—A. Not altogether.

Q. No, not altogether. Someone stated here that sometimes that is not done, but it is the rule?—A. It is the rule.

Q. Notwithstanding that rule and notwithstanding agreements made by correspondence, you undertake to exercise a discretion as to the reasonableness of the price?—A. Yes, I do.

Q. I see. And that is part of your duty?—A. Yes, part of my duty·

Q. And what about the accurate performance of that duty?—A. Well, if I think it is an excessive price I write a letter to the agent for an explanation.

Q. And have you ever issued a cheque for goods at excessive prices?—A. I may have.

Q. Why did you do so?—A. But I would not know the price. There are lots of goods I do not know the prices of·

Q. Did you ever do so knowingly?—A. Not knowingly.

By Hon. Mr. Cassels:

Q. Is there a fund, Mr. Owen, in Quebec, applicable for the payment of goods?—A. No, sir. All the accounts are forwarded to the department.

Q. They have to come to you?—A. All come to the department.

Q. And the cheques are all paid from here?—A· All the cheques are returned to the agent for distribution.

By Mr. Watson:

Q. Is everything paid by cheque?—A. Everything is paid by cheque.

Q. No such thing as a cash payment?—A. No.

Q. Every sum, no matter how small, and every account has to be paid by cheque from the head department?—A. And sent to the agent for distribution.

Q· And everything must go through your hands?—A. Yes. I keep a record of every cheque issued.

Q. Then, Mr. Owen, you have had imposed on you great responsibility?—A. Yes, sir; it is quite a responsibility.

Q. And you have assumed that responsibility?—A. I·have, sir.

Q. As to the charges being——?—A. Fair and just.

Q. Fair and just?—A· Yes.

Q. And do you certify to the Auditor General as well?—A. Certify to the Auditor General?

Q. Yes?—A. I send a statement to the Auditor General every month of every cheque issued. Besides I send a weekly statement to the Finance Department.

Q. Just wait, please. Do you certify to the effect that the prices are fair and just?—A. No; I officially account.

Q. That is the same thing ?—A. Yes.

Q. You understand that to be the same thing ?—A. Yes.

Q. Then is the deputy minister called upon to make a similar certificate ?—A. Not in the general payment of accounts, because, as I told you before, he could not attend to that.

Q. Then I understand from you he does not have the responsibility upon him of ascertaining whether the price is just and reasonable ?—A. No, I do not refer to him at all about this.

Q. That does not rest with him, according to your statement ?—A. Just wait. Too much——

Q. No matter what reason you have to think. I just want to know the fact. You say it does not?—A. If I have an account——

Q. I am rather mistaken. I thought the deputy minister was responsible in a way for all payments, all prices by way of supervision.—A. Well, he could not possibly.

Q. That rests upon you for the most part ?—A. Rests upon me; and if I sign a cheque, that is a guarantee to the deputy that the payment is all right before he signs.

Q. That the payment is all right and the prices are right ?—A. Yes.

Q. That is right, is it ?—A. Yes. If I sign a cheque he accepts it.

Hon. Mr. CASSELS.—Mr. Owen, supposing an account comes from Quebec and you are not satisfied with the prices, what do you do ?—A. I send it back again.

Q. Is that through correspondence ?—A. That is through correspondence.

Q. Then you get letters back ?—A. With a full explanation.

Q. Those are all on file ?—A. Yes.

Q. So any correspondence where you have differed in regard to prices will appear of record ?—A. It will appear on the files.

Q. What eventually happened, were the prices reduced ?—A. If they give a satisfactory explanation I pay the account; if not, sometimes I make a reduction myself.

Q. Suppose they pay $4 a barrel too much for flour, what then?—A. That $4 a barrel, I think I made a reduction on flour of 50 cents. On finding out it was a particularly good brand of flour I thought the price too high, and I made a reduction myself of 50 cents a barrel before I paid the account.

Mr. WATSON.—Then did you criticise that account ?—A. Yes.

Q. With what result in the end ?—A. I made a reduction of 50 cents on the barrel.

Q. Why did you not reduce it more ?—A. I thought that was enough.

Q. Did you compare it with the market prices ?—A. I compared it with the market price we paid in Halifax.

Q. That you paid in Halifax ?—A. Yes.

Q. But did you compare it with the market prices of other purchases ?—A. Yes, because it was a particularly good brand of flour, it was a flour down——

Hon. Mr. CASSELS.—You are referring now to some particular case. What do you mean ?—A. I thought you were referring to a case of flour.

Mr. WATSON.—What case have you in mind ?—A. That the commissioners wrote about.

Q. What is the case ?—A. Of flour in Quebec.

Q. Do you remember who they were, the vendors?—A. Lennon & Co., I think.

Q. They were charging more ?—A. Than I thought correct.

Q. And the agent at Quebec certified to more ?—A. Yes.

Q. You reduced it ?—A. I reduced it.

Q. And do you recollect now what explanation was made of that?—A. They said the flour was a particular brand of flour required down in the Belle Isle or some place down there, where the climate was severe, so they wanted a particularly good brand of flour. That was his explanation, but I thought the flour used down at Sable Island——

Q. Why did they require a better quality of flour there than at Montreal or elsewhere ?—A. That is what I thought.

Hon. Mr. CASSELS.—It is to coax their appetite.

Mr. WATSON.—Yes. The air is very fresh down there ?—A. It must be.

Q. Well, at all events that is an illustration of the way that you have performed your duties ?—A. Yes, sir.

Q. You have that responsibility upon you ?—A. Yes, sir.

Q. And do the agents know that ?—A. Yes.

Q. The agents all know that ?—A. Yes, the agents all know that.

Q. About how many purchasing agents are there in the department, speaking generally?—A. Well, the heads of the different branches are considered, like Mr. Stewart of the hydrographic survey——

Q. I know, the heads of the different branches. But apart from the heads ?—A. The heads of the different agencies.

Q. Do you know how many there are ?—A. I think British Columbia and——

Q. I do not want the names of the provinces. What is the number of agents, pseaking generally?—A. I think six agents altogether.

Q. Then it is not very onerous if only six ?—A. They send in a tremendous number of accounts, you know.

Q. I see. About what amount is expended yearly in the payment of accounts of that kind in your department ?—A. Well the whole total, the total of the department I think is about $6,000,000.

Q. Six million dollars ?

Hon. Mr. CASSELS.—Per annum ?—A. Per annum, sir.

Q. Have you any check on whether those goods are received ?

Mr. WATSON.—Do you keep any check upon whether the goods have been received?—A. I just take the agent's word for the goods being received.

Q. Do you have a certificate of delivery ?—A. We have a certificate of delivery.

Q. Or rather of receipt ?—A. Yes.

Q. That is always produced to you ?—A. That is always, sir.

Q. Now, then, in the course of this business of yours, the performance of your duties, have you had any knowledge of any improper act by any official or representative or agent ?—A. It has not come to my attention, sir.

Q. I am not referring now to excessive prices that you have criticised.—A. Yes.

Q. But to benefits or gains received directly or indirectly by any official or employee ?—A. It has not come to my notice, sir.

Q. Have you ever known of such a thing?—A. I have not known of it in my office.

Q. You have not ?—A. No, sir. All the time——

Q. Then have you known of any irregularity or improper act by any officials of the department here at the head office ?—A. I have not heard of any, sir, because——

Q. Never mind about the because.—A. I have always kept very busy. I don't go round amongst the offices.

Q. Why do you say because. Do you think it exists, but has not come to your knowledge ?—A. No. I have to stay in my office so much I don't hear what is going on.

Q. You think if you got out you probably would hear of things ?—A. I don't think so. I never heard of any irregularities, sir.

Q. You never heard of any ?—A. No.

Q. Do they exist ?—A. I don't know, I don't think so.

Q. Eh ?—A. I don't think so, I don't know.

Q. Have you ever said to anyone irregularities or improper conduct existed or occurred ?—A. I never did so.

Q. Eh ?—A. I never made any such statement of that kind.

Q. Against anyone?—A. Against anyone.

Q. To any person whatsoever outside of the department ?—A. Never. I never speak shop outside of the department.

Q. Eh?—A. I never talk shop outside of the department.

Q. Have you ever made statements of criticism, or that would lead to criticism, of the department outside the office?—A. Well, I don't know. They said I made some kind of statement up in the House one night, but I don't recall what it was. That was the time of the long session there when they were up two nights steady, and they accused me of making some statement that they went and told the minister about. I don't recall what it was more than the man in the moon.

Q. You cannot recall it ?—A. I mean I don't recall it. They say it was in connection with the auditors in the office.

Q. Yes. Do you disclaim responsibility?—A. I disclaim responsibility. I don't remember it at all, I haven't the least recollection, and I told the Colonel, I told everybody in the office. I don't know exactly what I said. I might have said something.

Q. What was it you said ?—A. I don't know. That is what I want to find out. It has never been brought to my notice.

Q. Do you mean to say you were in an irresponsible condition ?—A. I was not, I very seldom get in an irresponsible condition.

Q. You see, the reason that I ask the question is that it follows naturally from your statement ?—A. But I cannot recall the statement that I made.

Q. You cannot recall it ?—A. I cannot recall it.

Q. Do you know of anything to give foundation or basis to the statement ?—A. I don't think so.

Q. Do you know ?—A. I don't know. The discussion was going on about the auditors in the department and——

Q. Do you mean the Auditor General?—A. No, no. There were expert auditors came in there to establish a new system of bookkeeping.

Q. Has that new system been established ?—A. Yes.

Q. That will facilitate your work, I presume?—A. It is a splendid system.

Q. A splendid system ?—A. Yes.

Q. Was it necessary?—A. Well, I thought at first it was not, but I found out afterwards it was necessary.

Q. Why has it become necessary ?—A. Well, we have got a double check on the accounts and we have got a controlling ledger.

Q. When had the previous system been introduced ?—A. Somewhere I think about '83 or '84·

Q. And the expenditure has increased much since then ?—A. Oh yes. Ten times as much, five times as much.

Q. Five times as much since then?—A. Yes.

Q. Then do you say there was necessity for a new system ?—A. Yes. At first I thought there was not, but after the establishment of the new system I say it is perfectly correct, and it was necessary too.

Q. I see, it was necessary. What do you say about its being perfect ?—A. It was a perfect system.

Q. As accountant, I judge from what you say that you were rather hostile to that at first ?—A. I was, because they were brought to me as though I did not know a thing about it, you see.

Q. I see?—A. But I gave them every facility.

Q. Now then, as accountant, I am asking you, if you please, with regard to the statements made by Mr. Fraser, the Auditor General, yesterday?—A. Yes.

Q. You have heard what he said ?—A. I heard what he said.

Q. Statements which reflected somewhat upon some of the officials ?—A. Yes. I read it this morning, and I heard it.

Q. Commander Spain ?—A. Yes, I heard him mentioned.

Q. What knowledge have you of the matters that he referred to and of the result that he reached ?—A. Well, the result he reached——

Q. I know the result he reached. What knowedge have you of those matters ?— A. I hadn't any knowledge at the time of those matters.

Q. While the accounts were being passed into you, had you knowledge of any irregularities ?—A. Not at all. I gave them to a special official to examine the accounts.

Q. What is that ?—A. I detailed an official to examine the accounts.

Q. Who was the official ?—A. Mr. Boudreau.

Q. That is the witness who was here yesterday?—A. Yes. He examined the accounts; after he examined the accounts, he took them to the deputy for his initials, and the deputy considered, I suppose, they were all right; but in checking accounts we never go through the attendance books for officers, because we don't think it is necessary.

Q. I see. Then had you knowledge of any improper conduct or acts on the part of Commander Spain ?—A. Not at the time, I had not.

Q. When did you get that knowledge ?—A. From these reports here.

Q. But during the performance of your duty did anything of the kind come to your knowledge ?—A. It did not occur to me at all.

Q. Then the Auditor General stated that the certificates of others, the certificate of the deputy minister of the department, was not considered by him to be satisfactory ?—A. I cannot understand it.

Q. What ?—A. I cannot understand the statement.

Q. You cannot understand the statement ?—A. No.

Q. What do you mean ?—A. I think he is wrong, because I think the deputy is most particular in every transaction I have ever had with him. I think the Auditor General is quite wrong.

Q. Has anything come to your knowledge or information to lead to any such conclusion ?—A. Nothing.

Q. Not at any time ?—A. Not at any time, sir.

Q. Have you found inaccuracies or incorrectness in statements or certificates certified by him ?—A. By the deputy ?

Q. Yes.—A. No, sir, I never did.

Q. Did the Auditor General communicate with you ?—A. No, he did not.

Q. Well, you pass everything on to him ?—A. I send the vouchers over to him every month with a statement of the cheques issued.

Q. Then I should think there would be direct communication afterwards between you and him ?—A. No. It would be officially through the deputy minister himself of the department.

Q. I see. The Auditor General communicates only with the head of the department, that is, the deputy minister ?—A. Yes.

Q. He does not communicate with other officials ?—A. Yes.

Q. That is the system. That, I suppose, would necessarily be so. It did not occur to me for the moment that would be the reason for no communication with you? —A. Yes, sir.

Q. Then have you ever been called upon as the result of inquiries by him or criticism by him to see him to make explanations ?—A. The Auditor General ?

Q. Yes?—A. No.

Q. Have you known of irregularities, misconduct, on the part of Mr. Fraser, J. F. Fraser ?—A. I have not heard, sir, only what I heard of rumours current around since the investigation commenced.

Q. Now, the Auditor General said that as the result of his experience he had not full confidence in his certificates. What reason is known to you for that ?—A. No reason at all. I cannot understand it. I have always considered Mr. Fraser an excellent official in every way.

Q. What about Mr. Gregory ?—A. I don't know anything about Mr. Gregory. I am a long way from Mr. Gregory.

Q. But you are not a long way from the facts, you ought not to be, a chief accountant?—A. His certificates on the accounts, as I explained to you, I took exception to the prices.

Q. Then I gather, in a word, that you have not had confidence in his certificates?
—A. Some I have known to be all right, and I criticised some of them. That is all.

Q. Have you discussed that with the deputy minister ?—A. I have.

Q. With what result?—A. I make a memorandum to the deputy minister.

Q. Yes?—A. And there is an official letter written.

Q. I see?—A. Any criticism of the account I make on a memorandum and write to the deputy at once.

Q. And then what becomes of it, where is the responsibility after that?—A. The responsibility rests—he has to have a satisfactory explanation about the account, and if the explanation is satisfactory, I——

Q. Satisfactory to whom?—A. To the department; I get——

Q. Never mind about the department.—A. Satisfactory to the deputy or the minister, the account is paid.

Q. Then what about any criticism upon yourself, apart from those advance payments which you say have sometimes been made ?—A. Well, the advance payments made were always regular.

Q. Has there ever been a loss by reason of those?—A. There has never been a loss.

Q. You do not say that they are regular ?—A. That one you say was irregular, but I take the responsibility for that. I admit it, but the goods were received and all settled up.

Q. Now then, just in another word, what have you to say this morning in regard to the letter of Mr. Eyre that I read to you last evening; have you thought that over? —A. Which letter ?

Q. Thhe letter I read to you of Mr. Eyre last evening to his company, where he speaks—— ?—A. I don't know anything at all about it.

Q. Where he speaks here about having two cans sent, one to you and one to the deputy minister ?—A. If I remember right, 'tagged, addressed to him,' is it not ?

Q. 'Two extra cans addressed to me, tagged.' What does that mean ?—A. I suppose if tagged the address would be on it. I never saw it and don't know anything at all about that letter.

Q. And he says, 'I want them for Mr. Owen, accountant, and the deputy minister.'—A. Well, Mr. Owen did not get it.

Q. 'I cannot charge anything for them.' How do you explain them ?—A. I cannot explain them at all.

Q. Was there any conversation between you and him ?—A. Never a word.

Hon. Mr. CASSELS.—What was it ?—A. A disinfectant. It is a splendid thing for lighthouses and steamers for the cooks' galley, for washing up grease and keeping the place in good order..

Q. Would he send it to you for disinfecting purposes ?—A. Lighthouses always have it, the inspectors call for it.

Mr. WATSON.—His lordship is not asking about lighthouses, but whether it was for your personal use?—A. I buy it myself at the druggists.

Q. Eh?—A. My wife always buys it from the druggist, when she wants it, in small quantities.

Q. If it got to you it might be useful to the extend of $3 ?—A. Certainly, but I never got it.

Q. Did you ever receive presents from anybody ?—A. No, sir.

Eh ?—A. No, sir. Sometimes a chap might throw a cigar.

Q. I am not speaking of anything of that kind at all. That is not what is meant, but goods or bonuses ?—A. I never got any.

Q. Gratuities?—A. I never got any.

Q. Have you known of any such thing ?—A. I have not.

Q. To any official in the department ?—A. I have not heard of any. I don't come in contact with the purchasing people.

Q. That is not what I am asking you. I am asking you if you have any knowledge, directly or indirectly, of gratuities to any officials of the department ?—A. I have never heard of one single instance.

Q. If you had heard of it you would know of it ?—A. Yes. I have never heard of it.

Mr. WATSON.—I do not think there is anything more, unless your lordship has any questions.

Hon. Mr. CASSELS.—No. I think we had better go through those letters from the outside agent, Mr Owen.—A Yes.

Q. I do not mean now.

Mr. WATSON.—That correspondence ?

Hon. Mr. CASSELS.—Yes. Mr. Owen, we do not want them at present.—A. They have got a batch here.

Q. You can get them together with the answers so that we can see them later.

Mr. WATSON.—I have had those collected and they will come along in ordinary course. I am giving that attention.

Commander SPAIN, recalled.

By Mr. Watson:

Q. Mr. Spain, you stated to me this morning you would like to have an opportunity of making some further statements in evidence. I assume it is with regard to the matter stated by the Auditor General yesterday. Mr. Fraser, the Auditor General, stated yesterday—— ?—A. I heard that statement.

Q. You were here. I am just calling attention to one matter particularly, that in 1905, I think it was, you presented an account which he believed to be padded to the extent of $800 or $900. What have you to say in regard to that matter, anything? —A. Well, I have a good deal to say. In 1904 and 1905, sir, I was continuously away. form the office on duty, continuously. When I came back, some time in June, 1905, I think, I explained to my minister, Mr. Prefontaine, that I lost my note book, my pocket book, and my coat, they had been stolen from me. I said I did not know how I was going to make up my accounts without this information lost in my note book. The minister instructed me to make the accounts as correctly as I possibly could and attach an affidavit to them that I had lost this book and that was the best I could do. These accounts were made up in that way as well as I possibly could at the time, and they were sent over to the Auditor General. The Auditor General returned them with remarks to my clerk—I understand they came to my clerk, Mr. Gordon—that there were several days in this account that I was in Ottawa and that I had got them down in this account as being away from Ottawa when I was in Ottawa. This is explained by the fact that I had lost my books. I did not know the exact dates and I did as nearly as I could. It simply meant on the 23rd of any month I was in Montreal and I have missed it in Ottawa, I have put in Montreal on the 20th or 21st instead of the 23rd. That is exactly how the statement of account was put in. The account was sent back, and it was rectified immediately and returned to the Auditor General, and I understood from him that it was satisfactory. I explained the whole thing to my minister, I explained the thing to the deputy, I told them about the loss of my books. They both knew it; and that was the best I could do under the circumstances.

By Hon. Mr. Cassels:

Q. Have you got the affidavit here ?—A. I don't think it is here.

Q. Is it on the file or taken off ?—A. I don't know if it is on the file. There was an affidavit made.

Mr. WATSON.—An affidavit of what ?—A. That I had lost my pocket book and my account book.

Q. The records in the department would show when you were here, would they not ?—A. The records in the department would show when I was here. They would more particularly show it now.

Q. But at that time?—A. That is nearly four years ago.

Q. At that time the records in the department would show when you were here in the office ?—A. I don't know they would exactly.

Q. Well, there is a record of ins and outs and of attendances—A. Yes.

Q. A regular record, so by reference to that you could ascertain without inaccuracy when you were in the head office here ?—A. Exactly.

Q. And when you were not. Well now, is that all you have got to say ?—A. That is all I have got to say, I think, your lordship.

Q. Well, I think you are leaving it——

Hon. Mr. CASSELS.—What I would like to have explained is this: I understand the account was passed and paid ?—A. No, sir, it was not paid at all.

Q. Well, I may have misunderstood.—A. One is a regular advance, an advance given to each officer in charge of a branch, and these advances at the end of the year, the fiscal year——

Q. I see. You are paid so much money to cover expenses, and you had deducted this amount and then had to refund?—A. No. I refunded to the revenue, as I do every year, the balance of the advance.

Q. I understand—A. That is what I did, and it is done by every official in charge of a branch.

Q. I understand this adjustment. For whatever reason the Auditor General refused to allow that item ?—A. That account was not taken at all. Another one was substituted and the old one was torn up immediately.

Mr. WATSON.—Who tore it up ?—A. My clerk I presume.

Q. What is his name ?—A. His name is Gordon.

Q. Where is he now ?—A. He is unfortunately dead. He was a very capable man. He had been private secretary to the ministers for ten years.

Q. Well, you say the original account, the original memorandum was destroyed? —A. The original account.

Q. How do you account for a new account being put in ?—A. Because we had to put in a new account.

Q. Why ?—A. This account was sent back to be revised.

Q. Why was it sent back ?—A. Because there were some days in it that were wrong. That is what I tried to explain to you.

Q. How do you account for those days being wrong ?—A. Because I lost my books with the whole of my accounts.

Q. But the records in the department would have shown ?—A. I did not go to the records as I should have gone, I did not think of them.

Hon. Mr. CASSELS.—What period of absence did this account cover ?—A. It covered, I think, from August to June.

Q. Nearly a year?—A. Very nearly a year. Your lordship, I was away nearly the whole time, continuously away.

Mr. WATSON.—So, according to your statement, there was a means of accuracy by a reference to the office records, and you did not make that reference before you put in the account ?—A. No I did not make that reference. That reference, anyhow, would be left to my clerk to do.

Q. And as a result your account was sent back, and it had to be reduced by $800 or $900 ?—A. No, there was nothing like a reduction of that sort.

Q. That is what the auditor has stated ?—A. I think the auditor is wrong.

Q. How much was it ?—A. I don't know. It was a considerable sum.

Q. You would have some idea ?—A. I think it was probably $400 or $500. It was very nearly a year's travelling.

3262—19

Q. Yes, I know, but do you mean to say it was not as much as $800 ?—A. No.

Q. Eh ?—A. No.

Q. Now, who contributed to the payment of that reduction, anyone ?—A. No, there was no—it was a refund of a balance of advance.

Q. Yes, but you had received the money ?—A. I had received the money, I had expended the money.

Q. You had made up that much more ?

Hon. Mr. CASSELS.—They gave at the beginning of the year a certain sum to meet expenses.

Mr. WATSON.—Did you have to pay over the surplus ?—A. I did pay the balance of unexpended advance, that is what I did.

Q. Well then, you heard the statement of the Auditor General?—A. Yes.

Q. He said you paid that and you got half of it from the deputy minister?—A. I am afraid the Auditor General is incorrect in that.

Q. What do you say ?—A. I say no, I did not.

Q. Did you get any of it ?—A. I did not get anything from the deputy minister in reference to that matter whatever.

Q. Or from anybody else ?—A. Not from anybody else in reference to that matter, nothing whatever.

Q. Your answer implies or carries with it the inference that you may have got moneys from him in respect to other matters ?—A. That is exactly the case.

Q. Eh?—A. That is exactly the case.

Q. That is exactly the case ?—A. But nothing whatever to do with that.

Q. Eh ?—A. Nothing whatever to do with that.

Q. Then in what kind of matters were you in the habit of receiving money from him?—A. I was not in the habit of receiving money from him in any matter.

Q. Well, you see, you have carried it on to that.

Hon. Mr. CASSELS.—He may have by loan.

WITNESS.—Entirely by loan. It was a loan from the deputy minister in reference to a purely personal matter. The personal matter was the matter you referred to the other day.

Mr. WATSON.—I see. That was in what year ?—A. I think it was probably in 19—, probably the end of 1905.

Q. You say, then, you got a loan as a matter of purely personal convenience?—A. Purely personal between us.

Q. Have you ever received money from him in connection with official matters? —A. None whatever of any sort, kind or description.

Q. Now, further, the Auditor General said that he had found that your statements or accounts certified by you included charges for horse hire and matters of that kind that were not accurate, in fact false charges ?—A. I am afraid I cannot agree with that.

Q. What is the fact ?—A. The fact is, if horse hire was put down in that case I had horse hire. That is the fact of the case.

Q. He was quite firm and positive ?—A. I must be quite as firm the other way.

Q. Have you ever included any such items in your account ?—A. That I have not had ?

Q. That have not been incurred ?—A. Certainly not.

Q. Eh ?—A. Certainly not.

Q. On any other occasion than that one year has your account come back to you? —A. No.

Q. Eh ?—A. No.

Q. Have you had to account for further sums ?—A. No.

Q. Excepting in that one year ?—A. Except in 1904-5.

Q. Except at that time ?—A. Yes.

Q. Anything else that you wish to say, Commander Spain ? You heard the evidence. I give you a full opportunity.

Hon. Mr. CASSELS.—I would like to get some information about this affidavit. Do you think that affidavit was returned with the account ?—A. It may have been, your lordship.

Q. Well, you do not know about that ?—A. I am not certain about that at all. I think the probabilities are that I would have a copy of the affidavit myself in my office. I th'nk it is very possible.

Q. You think you would have a copy of the affidavit on record ?—A. Yes.

Mr. WATSON.—You say you have a copy?—A. I think it is possible.

Hon. Mr. CASSELS.—Can you tell me in a general way what the nature of the affidavit was ?—A. The affidavit stated I lost my note book and was therefore unable to accurately account for my expenses, something like that.

Q. But you did it to verify the account, you swore to the correctness of the account ?—A. Yes.

Q. Why would you swear to the correctness of the account without verification of the figures ?—A. The affidavit is put on the bottom of the account.

Q. I know. But what I want to see is this, I would like to see the affidavit. You had lost your note book, as I understand it, with the result that you were unable to give in detail accurately the dates upon which you were away?—A. Yes, my lord.

Q. Well, the affidavit may swear to any particular things or it may be general. I would like to see how it is?—A. I think it will show 'to the best of my ability.'

Q. I think you had better get the affidavit and then come back.

Mr. WATSON.—Yes. In the department I will have a search made.

Hon. Mr. CASSELS.—Yes. A great deal turns upon how that affidavit was taken.

Mr. WATSON.—Now I call the deputy minister.

Colonel GOURDEAU, recalled.

By Mr. Watson:

Q. How long have you been in the department?—A. I think about 40 years.

Q. Forty years?—A. Before proceeding with my examination I would ask the privilege, my lord, to read a statement I have got here, if there is no objection.

Mr. WATSON.—Just as his lordship may direct. I have not seen it.

By Hon. Mr. Cassels:

Q. What is the nature of the statement?—A. In connection with the way the investigation began with the Civil Service Commissioners. I think the court will be perfectly satisfied that I can read it.

Q. Will you let me glance at it ?—A. Certainly, sir.

(Hands statement to his lordship.)

Mr. WATSON.—Have you a copy ?—A. No, I have not a copy.

Q. I have not seen this, my lord.

Hon. Mr. CASSELS.—You might glance at it.

Mr. WATSON.—After your lordship.

Hon. Mr. CASSELS.—I think that the utmost latitude should be given to any of these gentlemen to clear themselves.

WITNESS.—Will you allow me to read it ?

Hon. Mr. CASSELS.—I think so.

(Witness reads statement down to, 'If he had, much, if not all, of what he has written, would not have appeared.')

Mr. WATSON.—That refers to whom ?—A. Mr. Fyshe.

(Concluded reading.)

3262—19½

(Statement marked Exhibit 44.)

WITNESS.—As I have mentioned in my statement a report, my lord, that I received on my return from Quebec, I suppose I had better read that. This is a memorandum from Mr. Owen. (Reads.)

(Memorandum marked Exhibit 45.)

On receiving that report I thought it my duty to prepare a memorandum, which I submitted to the minister. It reads as follows. (Reads memorandum.)

(Memorandum marked Exhibit 46.)

Hon. Mr. CASSELS.—Why do you desire to retire, colonel, when you can write such vigorous English ?—A. Well, I think I was inspired by the case particularly.

Mr. WATSON.—How long have you been in the department ?—A. A little over forty years.

Q. Before you became deputy minister what position did you occupy ?—A. Accountant.

Q. For how long ?—A. Oh, several years. I could not tell you exactly.

Q. And when were you appointed deputy minister ?—A. 1896.

Q. Were you here yesterday during the time the Auditor General was giving his testimony ?—A. No.

Q. Reference was made by him to some matters affecting you and the performance of your official duties, I think ?—A. Yes, I read it in the papers. I suppose I have not all the details, but I read the pith of it.

Q. He said, amongst other things, that he felt that you did not sufficiently control or ascertain the manner in which the business was done by the officials in the department ?—A. That is the opinion of a gentleman in another department.

Q. In another department ?—A. Yes ; who does not know anything about the department more than he sees the accounts.

Q. What do you say as to that control and ascertaining the manner and particulars in which the business is done by you ?—A. I control the business to the best of my ability, and I consider I controlled it well.

Q. As deputy minister I assume you have quite the chief responsibility in the department ?—A. Naturally it must fall on the deputy.

Q. Why do you say that ?—A. Because he is the deputy head of the department, he is the working officer of the department, and while you must rely upon the honesty and good will of the chiefs of the different branches, still the responsibility will come back to him if there is anything wrong.

Q. I see. Then did you, as deputy, assume responsibility for the administration ? —A. Yes.

Q. The administrative work in the department ?—A. Yes.

Q. Apart from questions of policy ?—A. Yes.

Q. As between you and the minister. How does the matter stand in that respect ? —A. I don't quite catch your meaning.

Q. In matters of administration ?—A. Well, in matters of administration, while the administration of the department is carried on by the deputy, it is always approved of by the minister. I would not undertake anything, as deputy, without first submitting it to the minister, giving him reasons for acting in such and such a way and getting his approval.

Q. In matters of detail ?—A. Detail even.

Q. How far have you become familiar with the administrative work by the different branches, matters of account, for instance, contracts.

Hon. Mr. CASSELS.—Pardon me, Mr. Watson. Commander Spain seems to have that affidavit.

Commander SPAIN, recalled.

By Mr. Watson :

Q. What do you now produce ?—A. The affidavit I put in with my accounts.

Q. Where did you find this ?—A. In my drawer.

Q. In your office ?—A. In my office.

Q. This reads in this way as produced, my lord. (Reads.)

(Affidavit marked Exhibit 47.)

Q. This, I see is, ' Declared before me in 1905 '?—A. That, I think, ought to be 1906. There must be a mistake in the dates, because those accounts are in reference to 1906.

Q. Then do I understand you to say that you are prepared to vouch that this is a correct copy of a statutory declaration which was actually made by you on the 2nd of January, 1906 ?—A. Exactly.

Q. Are you prepared—— ?—A. I am prepared to swear to it.

Q. To vouch for the accuracy of that ?—A. I am.

Q. And you say that this was attached ?—A. To the account and shown to my minister.

Q. And where is the original ?—A. I do not know where the original is, I have not any idea.

Colonel GOURDEAU, recalled.

By Mr. Watson :

Q. Then, matters of detail in contracts made by the heads of departments ?—A. Yes.

Q. Do those details come to you in such a way as to enable you to exercise independent judgment and discretion ?—A. Absolutely not. The contract system, I would like to explain to your lordship, is carried on in this way, especially since Mr. Brodeur assumed control of the department. When tenders are called for they are given to a clerk I may say, which is Mrs. Thomas, who is my secretary, and they are kept under lock and key until they are produced again. On the day on which they are to be opened they are brought into the minister—they have always been brought into the minister—and they are opened by the minister himself in the presence either of his secretary or another clerk. The minister has also exacted from the chief engineer of the department, especially in matters of construction, that he should give him an idea, an estimate of what the cost of that work would be as an engineer, so that the minister at first glance may see himself whether the offers compare reasonably. As soon as these offers or the contracts for that work have been signed by the minister, his clerk and myself, with the date put on, they are sent to the officer concerned, who then makes his report as to whether the lowest tenderer should be accepted, or if another tenderer after that should be accepted, and in a case like that, which is extremely rare, this report to the council is prepared. The council then decide whether they will go over the lowest tender and take the other for the reasons specified. But in no way was I, as deputy minister, able to control further or help a contractor in securing advantages before the department. In the system, the perfect system that has been adopted by Mr. Brodeur it is absolutely impossible. The system that obtains in the department now is exactly the system proposed by the Honourable Mr. Foster in the House sometime ago as being a perfect system for the reception or treatment of contracts.

Q. When do you say that system was introduced ?—A. When Mr. Brodeur became minister.

Q. What date was that?—A. Well, that would be after the death of Mr. Prefontaine, which was in——

Q. 1906?—A. 1906. He died in the Christmas of 1906.

Q. 1905, was it ?—A. Yes, Christmas of 1905.

Q. Mr. Brodeur assumed office, I see, on the 5th of February, 1906 ?—A. Yes.

Q. That is correct ?—A. Yes, about that time.

Q. Then, what was the system before that time?—A. Before that time there was an officer entrusted on that work who had quite a knowledge in the way of construction and the handling of such documents, Mr. Stumbles. They were kept by him just in the same way and brought down to the minister when the time had arrived for opening those tenders.

Q. And how long had that system been in vogue or use ?—A. For several years, as long as I can remember.

Q. As long as you can remember?—A. Yes.

Q. Before you became deputy minister?—A. Yes.

Q. How long back, then?—A. Really I could not say.

Q. I only want to know whether within five or ten years ?—A. Oh, it must have been in vogue for 15 years altogether.

Q. Do you mean 15 years before 1906?—A. No, before Mr. Brodeur took charge.

Q. Before 1906, I see ?—A. Exactly. I might be wrong. I think it is about that.

Q. What was the system before that?—A. It was in the same way, but I really forget what clerk had that in hand.

Q. I mean to say was the system more or less——A. I was under that system, under my predecessor, the late Mr. Smith, when I was accountant.

Q. The same system prevailed?—A. Yes.

Q. Then the contracts and the expenditure of money—in the first place the amount of the expenditure and the purpose of the expenditure emanates from the hea of the department, I understand, the head of the branch?—A. Yes.

Q. Does he certify it?—A. Yes, he certifies the account.

Q. He certifies the account ?—A. Yes.

Q. In all cases ?—A. In all cases.

Q. Are you in a position, as deputy minister, to verify those certificates or recommendations, and do you do so?—A. If a technical matter, a matter of a technical nature, for instance, pertaining to hydrographic surveys or the construction of lights or maintenance and other technical matters, I would not be in a position to know, I would have to rely entirely on the officer in charge of that branch.

Q. Then do you certify those matters to the minister?—A. No. I simply bring those matters before the minister with my concurrence. I get explanations from the officer, they appear reasonable to me, he is in charge of that branch, he has got the confidence of the minister and my own, and I always in every case get the minister's approval.

Q. You get the minister's approval ?—A. Yes.

Q. Do any matters go to the minister involving expenditure without first having your stamp upon it, your stamp of approval upon it ?—A. There might be some during my absence.

Q. That is only during your absence?—A. Yes. Under other ministers there might be in very rare cases.

Q. In rare cases ?—A. Yes.

Q. Then I understand you take upon yourself the responsibility of approving or disapproving ?—A. As deputy minister, if I see anything wrong I bring it to the attention of the minister at once.

Q. That is incident to the office ?—A. Yes.

Q. Now then it has been stated that in the opinion of the Auditor General there has been want of accuracy amounting almost to negligence, judging by results, in matters of expenditure, accounts and contracts ?—A. Yes.

Q. What do you say to that ?—A. Well, that is rather a general satement. Are there any cases mentioned in particular ?

Q. Well, what have you to say to the statement ?—A. I do not think it is correct.

Q. Applying it directly to the evidence given in regard to Commander Spain in 1904 and 1905.?—A. I will tell you my recollection of that.

Q. His travelling expenses ?—A. Yes. I will give you my recollection of that. It is some years ago. The matter was brought to my attention by the Auditor General and I was rather startled by what he told me.

Q. Well, just tell what he said, what took place ?—A. I was so astonished that I went over to his office and I had a long conversation with Mr. Fraser. He told me he was under the impression that teams had been charged for which were never used and that some dates had been put down in his account of his being away from the office while he was in Ottawa at the time. I told him I was very much astonished to hear such a thing from an officer of Commander Spain's standing, and that I would not only inquire into it but would give the auditor every facility of going further into the account. I spoke to Commander Spain about this thing, told him it was a most serious matter, and that unless explanations were given satisfactory to the department and to the Auditor General's office it was a most serious matter for him. I believe he had a long conversation with the auditor and gave the explanation which was given before his lordship this morning. To the best of my recollection the last interview I had with Mr. Fraser about this was that he would be satisfied, provided in future we would give him the dates upon which the commander started and the dates upon his arrival. Well, we have got what we call in French a book d'annoncement, a book in which you sign your name every morning, an attendance book, and I told him we would let him have that and also let him have a memorandum, because I was very particular in enforcing in the department that a statement should be made by every official before leaving for any business, stating the day he was leaving, what he was leaving for, and the probable time he would be absent, in order to control his business, to know where he was going and what he was doing. When that was given me there was generally an application for an advance, and I could easily see whether that would meet the expenditure and the locality where he was going, and I would simply put F. G. on it, and the accountant would give that advance so that it would have to be accounted for. This matter, as I say, was explained to him by Commander Spain, I thought it was accepted by the auditor, and I told him over the 'phone the very day Commander Spain came back and said it was satisfactory, 'Before I will put my initials to this account and let it pass, are you satisfied' ? And he he was.

Q. You said that to whom ?—A. The Auditor General over the 'phone. I would not have passed that account if the auditor had any objections to it.

Q. But is it not the fact that that account was passed by you before it reached the Auditor General ?—A. Certainly. I do not examine those accounts. It would be an utter impossibility for me to examine the accounts. While I said a few minutes ago that I was responsible as deputy head, there was an official placed there for the purpose, the sole purpose of examining accounts for travelling expenses, Mr. Boudreau. All Mr. Boudreau had to do was to send down for the attendance book and examine that account and find out the dates. If there was anything he could not understand he could see Commander Spain about it. When that came to me duly filed as a pro-proper account for payment bearing the signature of the officer charged with that work I, as deputy, simply put my initials on it, but I would never for a moment lead his lordship or the court here to think that I would undertake to go through the travelling expenses or certify myself that a man was in a certain place on a certain day. We have got to leave that to a man's honour and position in the department. I would never for a moment hold myself responsible for anything of the kind.

Q. I suppose you regard yourself in fact as the general manager of that department?—A. Exactly. And if the organization is good and the heads of branches are good, the department is successful; if there is anything wrong in those departments there will be mistakes.

Q. But it is of course a part of your duty as general manager to see that the organization is good?—A. Is good, yes.

Q. And that it is maintained?—A. Yes.

Q. Had you any reason to doubt the accuracy of those returns or statements by Commander Spain?—A. No. I thought myself that some of his accounts appeared a little extravagant in tipping or something like that, and I have had several of his accounts changed in that way, reduced, just after a cursory glance even after presented to me. But I had no idea, and I have none to-day, that Commander Spain would in any way try to overcharge or wrongfully overcharge any amount he had not expended.

Q. Did you say tipping or tippling?—A. Tipping waiters. I mean to say if I saw a tip of 50 cents I would not pass it, I would insist on its being reduced to 25.

Q. Now, then, on that occasion, referring to Commander Spain; it is said he was called upon to refund by the Auditor General an amount of $800 or $900?—A. That is a mistake of memory on the part of the Auditor General. I think it is $630.

Q. $630?—A. Yes, $630; and after discussing the matter again with Commander Spain—I did not hear him mention that—he told me he was out of pocket $350 by the loss of his book and not being able to account for certain expenses which he had made, which he considered were correct.

Q. Now, it was also stated that you paid half of that amount?—A. I never did, I never did, I never did.

Q. At all events the recollection of Mr. Fraser was you stated so to him?—A. Perhaps what misled him—it is quite a misconception of the thing—what misled Mr. Fraser was this: In talking over the matter I said, 'Mr. Fraser, I am very sorry an officer is in such a plight, and if there is anything wrong I do not want to have the thing settled in this way, but if the thing can be explained and Commander Spain is short of money, I will try and help him to get it.' But I did not mention to him, I did not say I would give the money. Next day I heard the amount had been deposited to the credit of the receiver-general, and I never gave him a cent good, bad or indifferent.

Q. Were you applied to by him?—A. Not at all.

Q. Did you make the statement to Mr. Fraser?—A. That I have just mentioned to you?

Q. That you would pay half of it? That was his recollection?—A. That I would help him to pay it. I don't think so, I might have said I would pay part of it. I would have rendered a service. I think it my duty to do what I can for any official in the department.

Q. If it were wrong-doing?—A. No, I would not have touched that at all. I told you before, sir, I would not have touched it at all.

Q. And you say, as a matter of fact, you did not pay any portion of it?—A. Not a dollar, not a cent. It was deposited before I knew it to the credit of the receiver-general.

Q. You see, Colonel Gourdeau, the recollection of Mr. Fraser as to the matter led him, as he says quite openly, to suspect your honour in regard to the matter as well as that of Commander Spain?—A. I do not think that.

Q. That is, in the contribution.

Hon. Mr. CASSELS.—I do not think, Mr. Watson, he threw any imputation on the colonel at all. I think the answer came from a question I put and wanted to clear up.

WITNESS.—Yes, I saw that in the paper.

Mr. WATSON.—It impresses me the other way.

Hon. Mr. CASSELS.—It would naturally give to others the impression that the colonel was was 'divvying' up, and I wanted to get at that, and the question was put by me after.

WITNESS.—I am very much obliged to your lordship. I was not here at the time.

Hon. Mr. CASSELS.—That is the way it came up. I did not understand Mr. Fraser meant he would have half.

Mr. WATSON.—That is the impression on my mind.

Hon. Mr. CASSELS.—I put the question purposely because it would have left the impression on my mind; it might have left the impression on my mind. I thought if the fact warranted it it ought to come out; if the fact did not it was only fair it should come out.

Mr. WATSON.—He put it so strongly that to his mind, he says, it was a padding, and of course is a deliberate act.

WITNESS.—We never spoke in the office.

Q. What is that?—A. There was never any conversation in that way in the office.

Q. Between you and the auditor?—A. I mean to say that it was, as you call it, a padded account. He told me he had discovered the dates were wrong and some charges made for teams which had not been used. That was a matter he had more information about than I had.

Hon. Mr. CASSELS.—What impresses me is this: This $600 odd is a very large sum extending over a year?—A. Yes.

Q. Now, that account goes in verified by affidavit?—A. By whom?

Q. By an affidavit.—A. Yes.

Q. The affidavit accounts for the loss of the book from which the dates can be given.—A. Yes.

Q. As I understand Commander Spain, his account was a detailed account showing the different days and where he was?—A. Exactly.

Q. And he puts in that affidavit to verify it?—A. Yes.

Q. Well, one would have thought before an affidavit is made——?—A. He would have tried to verify the dates?

Q. Yes.—A. Certainly, that seems to be so, and I thought so at the time myself.

Mr. WATSON.—Apparently they were capable of verification, to some extent at all events, by record in the department.

Hon. Mr. CASSELS.—I think before a man takes an oath explaining certain things he should think of some means of verifying his account.—A. Of course, as was explained, I got that explanation myself from him, that he relied a great deal upon his secretary, Mr. Gordon, who might have been negligent and might have made a couple of wrong entries in his private book.

Q. Take $650. That means a very large number of days absent at specific places. Now, I think going back a year I could make out a note of where I was, I could sit down and think it out.—A. Certainly.

Mr. WATSON.—Did you have reason to suspect the honesty of that official?—A. No.

Q. Have you ever had reason to suspect the honesty of that official?—A. No, or I would have reported it to the minister at once.

Q. You spoke of extravagance in his travelling expenses?—A. Yes.

Q. Was that to the extent of personal gain?—A. No, not at all. In choosing expensive rooms, sometimes buying a ticket for one way and being obliged to buy a ticket for the same way returning, while he could have bought a return ticket. I might have been wrong, but I was under the impression that he never had charged anything for the purpose of accumulating his account and profiting by it.

Q. Had you any reason to suspect that expenses were being paid out of departmental funds when engaged otherwise than on departmental business?—A. No. I had heard something about it and spoke to Commander Spain, who explained to me thoroughly and absolutely that he was at a certain place for the department. I could not recollect the place now.

Q. As deputy minister would you be able to follow and judge of the necessity of his being at this place or that place?—A. Certainly. I would not let him go away from the department unless he showed me his programme that he was going to certain places to do certain things.

Q. Does that apply to the business of every official?—A. Yes.

Q. It is after conferring with you?—A. Yes, letting me know where he is going. I might say something. -

Q. Go on?—A. I have forgotten now. I have eaten it up.

Q. I see. Now, the auditor also spoke of some orders that were given, some silverware that was obtained. Was that upon your direction?—A. No.

Q. Who made the recommendation for that ?—A. There were no recommendation made.

Q. Who made the purchase ?—A. The order must have been given, if the purchase had been a regular purchase by the department I should have been informed by the minister in a memorandum telling me to write an official letter to Mr. So-and-so to provide certain things. That was not done. That is an unfortunate thing I have never been able to explain myself. The order was given previous to the minister going to England, and unfortunately he died there, and that was the occasion that there was nothing of official record to show that an actual order had been given from the department. If it had been given from the department it would have been referred to Commander Spain to find out the quantities.

Hon. Mr. CASSELS.—How do you know it was given by the minister ?—A. Well, the minister mentioned a word to me about it a day or two before he went to England that the order had been given.

Q. That was Mr. Prefontaine ?—A. Yes, sir.

Mr. WATSON.—Of course, the Auditor General speaks of direct communications with you in regard to this matter ?—A. Yes.

Q. And he spoke of an order, or a memo rather, showing 5 per cent commission ? —A. Yes.

Q. And that that was discussed with you. That would show the basis of a contract?—A. No. I can explain it, I think, very easily to his lordship.

Q. Just say what there is to say ?—A. When the silverware was received there was a good deal of delay in placing it on the boat. Everything was brought up before the Public Accounts. This is a matter of ancient history.

Q. I beg your pardon ?—A. I say this is an old matter, but my recollection of it is this: That when we had nothing to go upon owing to the death of Mr. Prefontaine, we had to find out upon what conditions that was purchased. I could not tell. I simply wrote to the auditor or spoke to him that it was upon the same conditions that he had furnished silverware for the *Druid, Minto* and *Stanley,* that is, 5 per cent commission, and I really understood that was the case. But I made a mistake and afterwards rectified my mistake with the Auditor General, and all the other dealings followed afterwards. Mr. Coghlin was very much annoyed because forced to return $1,100, and I think, no doubt the Auditor General will have to admit it, he lost a couple of hundred dollars, although he said he lost more, and we got the silverware cheaper than the commonest silverware and delf could be procured.

Q. Why was the refund made of $1,100?—A. Because a great deal of correspondence was passing about excessive prices. They were preparing the annual report. The Auditor General had made a very large list, the items were all particularized, and I thought it better to have an understanding with Coghlin. I got Coghlin up there, and although the auditor says he had mentioned 5 per cent to him also, he denied it in the office.

Q. Who denied it?—A. Mr. Coghlin; and then he refunded the 5 per cent. He said it was a mistake of his clerk in Montreal.

Q. 5 per cent would not amount to $1,100 ?—A. No. That is exactly where the rub is.

Hon. Mr. CASSELS.—Mr. Coghlin's statement is that on the previous purchases a commission of 5 per cent was allowed. On these last purchases the commission was done away with, and instead of that he was to get the difference between the wholesale and retail prices. When he came up to Ottawa he said that, and that was correct. Then you produced other accounts which showed the difference of $1,100. His statement is that without anything further being done he paid the full amount.

WITNESS.—He was excited and did not want the matter to come before the Public Accounts.

By Hon. Mr. Cassels :

Q. That is his statement. I do not know what the facts are?—A. Those are absolutely the facts, my lord.

Mr. WATSON.—What do you say was the reason for the payment of the $1,100 ?

By the Hon. Mr. Cassels:

Q. The repayment of the $1,100?—A. Well, the Auditor General thought the amount was excessive, the order was large and that Mr. Coghlin should make the reduction.

Q. But the Auditor General says that even the departmental accounts of the transaction show that the over-payment was $1,100 too much—A. Why too much?

Q. He says the invoice in the department shows it was too much?

Mr. WATSON.—Will you look at the invoice? This says a commission of 5 per cent.

Hon. Mr. CASSELS.—You remember the Auditor General stating when he came to inquire he found they had invoices on file which showed the difference of $1,100 between the——

Mr. WATSON.—Between the previous prices and these.

Hon. Mr. CASSELS.—Yes; and he compelled them to produce the invoices?—A. The first invoices were from Coghlin's own file. We took those invoices as he was the man who bought the goods.

Q. Where are those invoices?—A. Here.

Q. What do they show?—A. The amount plus the difference making the $1,100, because they were the first prices. Then the Auditor General discovered that the original accounts from England were with the customs, where they had to pay the duty, and there of course there was a great dissimilarity in the accounts, and while the auditor and myself arived at the same amount as to his travelling expenses and some expenses he was put to one way or the other, we might have forgotten something, but we arrived at an amount I thought at the time reasonable, and Coghlin thought reasonable, and he gave us a cheque for the $1,100. Now he says he has lost $400.

Mr. WATSON.—How is it you did not ascertain the same matters that the Auditor General ascertained? You did not ascertain them upon your investigation of the account?—A. Because I had nothing to make me doubt there was anything wrong in that account. They even spread the rumour that that silverware was not delivered. We did not deliver the silverware because I made an express order. The *Montcalm* was a large steamer, the *Montcalm* has a crew of over 70, and it was the intention of Mr. Prefontaine, that that boat, which was an ice-breaker, would also be a boat to convey representatives of all shipping interests and give them an idea of the aids to navigation and other improvements we were making to the river. We already had an excursion at that time of the Board of Trade. It cost a considerable amount to borrow silverware and crockery for the reception of those people, and I do not think at all the quantity is excessive. That is my opinion.

Q. That is, the quantity of silver?—A. Yes, purchased.

Q. And what as to the price?—A. Well, I took the trouble to go to jewellers myself, and I found out that even on the first prices charged by Mr. Coghlin it would cost from 10 to 12 per cent more to purchase the same goods.

Q. Are you speaking of retail or wholesale prices?—A. Retail.

Q. But why should the department buy by retail? Are you not always able to buy at wholesale prices?—A. Certainly; but it is not the policy of the government so far.

Q. What do you mean by that?—A. Because there is a patronage list. We are obliged to go to certain people to buy goods from.

Q. What do you mean by patronage list?—A. When a man is on the patronage list for, say the purchase of flour, or the purchase of lumber, we have got to go to him for lumber. Of course, it is the duty of the officer who examines the account to find out whether that lumber is charged at an excessive price, and if so to challenge the account. We have hundreds of accounts challenged every year, and the result is a large number of accounts have been reduced simply through the good examination of the accounts by the accounts branch. That same flour account was buffeted about between Quebec and Ottawa until a member of parliament, Mr. Power, came up to the minister and laid a serious complaint against me because I was hoolding back payment of the flour account. When I explained to the minister that that brand, called 'Five Roses Brand'—I remember it well, it was such a memorable account—I thought was at an excessive price, the minister asked Mr. Power what it was reasonable to give and when he got down to Quebec to find out what the rates were. We got that reduced finally.

Hon. Mr. Cassels.—Why are you compelled to buy retail?—A. I think we are adopting a much better plan now, but as I mentioned, my lord, up to then, there was a list of people from whom we had to purchase.

Mr. Watson.—What do you mean by had to purchase?—A. If, for instance, Jones, Robinson or White were on the list for flour, we had to go to those people for flour.

Hon. Mr. Cassels.—It simply means you lost the difference between the wholesale and retail price by going to the patronage list?—A. Yes.

Mr. Watson.—How long has the patrongage list been in existence?—A. To my recollection ever since I have been in the department, 35 or 40 years. There has been no difference with any government.

Q. What is that?—A. There has been no difference at all, it has been always the same.

Q. In every administration?

Hon. Mr. Cassels.—Can you give any idea of what amount in dollars and cents the country has lost during the last three years by that method?—A. A very large amount, but I would be very——

Mr. Watson.—Do you mean by higher prices?—A. Certainly.

Hon. Mr. Cassels.—In dollars and cents how much during the last three years? You say a large amount. I want to get some idea of what you mean by a large amount? A—Oh, I would not like to give my opinion. It would be a very large amount.

Q. Would it run into millions?—A. Oh no; no. It might be a couple of hundred thousand dollars.

Q. And that goes to secure the fidelity of the patronage list?—A. I may tell you there is very often keen competition in that patronage list.

Q. But take the loss of $200,000 during the last three years; that really is money spent to secure the fidelity of the faithful, that is what it comes to?—A. I do not know. We have to write for prices to these people.

Mr. Watson.—Do I understand you to make the statement that during the last three years $200,000 has been paid in excess of regular and proper prices by reason of the existence of a patronage system?

Hon. Mr. Cassels.—He does not say that. He says during the last three years $200,000 has been paid by reason of this patronage list, which might have been saved if they had done what might have been done, bought wholesale.

Mr. Watson.—Do you say that?—A. Certainly.

Q. You had to certify the prices were just and reasonable?—A. Yes; but if told to buy from a retail grocer why should we not buy from him? That is a matter of policy.

Hon. Mr. Cassels.—It is a matter of election policy.—A. Then I may tell you there are a great many places where our ships go—your lordship, I would like to reduce that amount, because there are no wholesale places, for instance, where all our protection vessels go on the coast. There you have to buy as you go from little retail merchants, and they often charge very dear. It would not be so much.

Q. What about having storehouses at those places and shipping the stores down and keeping them there?—A. They are very remote places on the north shore and it would be very difficult to keep them from being robbed by the Esquimaux. To keep charge of that would cost a great deal of money.

Mr. WATSON.—How does that compare with other years, other periods, those excessive payments?—A. Not the slightest difference.

Q. Do you mean the whole of the time you have been in the department?—A. Yes.

Q. For the last 40 years?—A. Yes.

Q. There has always been a patronage list?—A. Yes.

Q. Why is not the patronage list enlarged, would it make any difference then? Assuming a patronage list, might it not be extended so as to include 15 or 20 dealers, in that way giving competition?—A. That is what we do. For instance, in Halifax you got a number of names, 10 to 15 grocers. We ask those grocers how much they will furnish us with tea, sugar, coffee, eggs, pork and bacon for the next season, and we hold them to their prices.

Q. But, I understood from your answer to his lordship that the result of the patronage list is a want of proper competition?

By Hon. Mr. Cassels:

Q. Mr. Watson, that is not what the colonel indicates at all. The result of the patronage list is that they do get competition, but competition at retail prices; whereas the loss occurs because the government is doing that instead of going to wholesale dealers and buying at wholesale prices. That is what I understand?—A. Yes.

By Mr. Watson:

Q. That is, competition exists, but exists in the wrong class?—A. Well, if you buy wholesale, naturally you have got to pay much less.

Q. Then to what extent do you buy wholesale as distinct from retail?—A. Well, for the Sorel plant, that is in the $100,000, they are getting very much better prices. When we compared the prices of Samson & Filion, Quebec, with the prices that obtain at Sorel we were told it was unfair for this reason: A great number of the articles which were purchased and were much cheaper to buy at Sorel shipyard were for use in soft water, whereas every article bought from Samson & Filion was for use in salt water, where there is a good deal of corrosion.

Q. Then the difference arises by reason of buying retail as against wholesale?—A. Yes, that is all.

Q. There is competition in that, but the prices are retail instead of wholesale?—A. Exactly.

Q. Now, to what extent does that prevail? Do you mean that applies to all purchases?—A. That diminishes. I started this myself. I considered the provisioning of the boats should be done by the captains themselves and then they should certify the prices. That takes away the grocery accounts and removes a great deal of trouble, but it also removes some of the patronage.

Q. But take the ordinary supplies for the department. How are they purchased?—A. Oh, in different ways; some are purchased of course by tender. Say we want a lot of cement, that is purchased by tender, open tender advertised in the papers. Then we get wholesale prices.

Q. That is wholesale prices?—A. Yes.

Q. I want to know what proportion, the extent of the purchases?—A. That is a difficult thing. There is a considerable amount purchased by retail people——

Q. By what?—A. From retail people.

Q. I know. But I would like to have an idea about what the proportion is?—A. I would not like to give it right off without thinking over it.

Q. Could you do so?—A. Yes, I could make it up. Certainly, I could make it up very exact. I should be very glad to prepare a statement of the kind.

Q. Then it is also stated by the Auditor General that directions were given to admit goods free of duty which were not required or obtained by the department?—A. I do not know of any case. There may have been a case slip through in that way, but I do not now of it. That has been abolished and now we are obliged to pay duty on anything. It is just a payment from one department to another.

Q. He spoke of a specific case?—A. What case is that?

Q. Where direction was given by you, I think——?—A. What case is that?

Q. That goods should be admitted free of duty?

Hon. Mr. CASSELS.—What he has stated was this——

Mr. WATSON.—And they were not obtained by the department.

Hon. Mr. CASSELS.—He stated that certain goods were brought into the country and a certificate given that they were required for government purposes, that relieving them from duty; whereas in point of fact they were brought in for a private person and not for the country at all.—A. I do not know of anything of the kind. Something of that might have passed, because they were given by any officer who would apply for them stating that such and such a thing was wanted in the department, and I would sign a certificate. But that is absolutely abolished now, and everybody pays on everything purchased for the department.

By Mr. Watson:

Q. Yes, but the implication may arise that officials were using their opportunities to get goods for themselves or some of them, without duty?—A. I do not know of any case.

Q. Have you any knowledge of any such case?—A. No, I have not, absolutely.

Q. Have you ever heard of any such case?—A. No; and I have thought over it to see if anything woul dcome to my mind; it might if stated; but I am absolutely unable to recall anything of the kind.

Q. Does anything apply at all in respect of your own personal matters?—A. No. When I was in the active militia I got a great many things without paying, and I got a certificate without paying duty.

Q. Then with regard to officials have you any knowledge of any improper acts on their part, acts of misconduct by which they gained or lost or otherwise?—A. No.

Q. By anyone?—A. No.

Q. Have you any knowledge of any benefits or gains directly or indirectly, passing or being received by officials, yourself or other officials?—A. No.

Q. Any such thing ever occur?—A. No.

Q. During your official life, to your knowledge?—A. No.

Q. Have you any knowledge of officials obtaining or receiving gratuities or presents from contractors or people with whom the department was dealing or the public by reason of official connection?—A. I never pay attention to any rumours.

Q. Have you any knowledge or information?—A. No, I cannot recall anything there because I never paid the slightest attention to rumours or anonymous letters.

Q. Have you yourself been subject to importunity by others, outsiders, in that respect at any time or known others to be?—A. No. There might be amongst my letters some letters that might have asked me to do something or that something might be done, there might be, but I would pay no attention to that whatever, it would remain among my letters and that woud be the end of it. You have got all my correspondence. I never had anybody approach me in any shape or form, nor did I, as put in my statement, by word or deed let anybody believe or think I could in any way further their interest. I never lost sight of the interests of the department since engaged in that department on one single occasion, to my knowledge. I may have erred, made some mistakes through want of judgment, perhaps sometimes—I am getting old—but I never lost an opportunity of doing what I could in the interests of the department.

Q. Did you yourself ever receive any benefits or gains, directly or indirectly, from any source?—A. Not at all, not at all.

Q. Of any kind?—A. Of any kind whatever.

Q. Nor at any time during your official life?—A. Nor at any time during my official life.

Q. And what do you say as to others, have you not known of others?—A. No, I really do not know of any case. As I told you I do not attach the slightest importance to rumours.

Q. Perhaps it is not unfair—it is not unfair to you, and may be considered quite otherwise that it should be stated to you as deputy minister, the head of the department in that way, that it is said by rumour that you have become a wealthy man?—A. Yes, I see.

Q. And that your only source of income should be from your salary, which could not lead to accumulation. You have put something in writing with regard to that. Have you anything else to say?—A. Nothing else to say, nothing else to say whatever. I was left with a considerable amount when my father died in 1895 and I have never lived up to my salary since I have been in the government, for the last 20 years, anyway.

Q. Now, it has been said by Colonel Anderson that the division of his office arose in a way that was somewhat objectionable, and that he thought influences of one kind or another had led to that?—A. Well, I do not think so.

Q. I want to know what the fact is?—A. There was no difference in withdrawing the duties of the channel and the lighting from Colonel Anderson and giving them to Mr. Fraser than there was in withdrawing the hydrographic service which was under Colonel Anderson. It was done in about the same way.

Q. What was the reason for the division?—A. Well, the minister thought that the duties——

Q. What minister are you speaking of?—A. Mr. Prefontaine; that there should be a division, and he naturally took the officer who was recommended by Colonel Anderson himself for his good work, that was Mr. Fraser. He had charge of all the lighting acetylene business and everything on the St. Lawrence, and there is a letter on file from Colonel Anderson which shows that at last they had come to the conclusion that they were getting an absolute good light in that way. These apparatuses were referred to Mr. Fraser as an expert and a man who understood that work thoroughly, and if Colonel Anderson had understood it better than him he would have taken it upon himself to give the information that is on file.

Q. Then had you to do with that change?—A. Nothing whatever.

Q. Except, I suppose, you recommend it?—A. No. The order in council came to me signed by the minister. I had nothing whatever to do with the preparation of the report to the council, I never saw it, and it was handed in to my office I think immediately. I can vouch for that.

Q. I am speaking of the division of the branch?—A. Of the division of the branch, yes.

Q. You say that was upon the responsibility of the minister himself?—A. Entirely.

Q. Was there a recommendation from Colonel Anderson, the chief of that branch, to your knowledge?—A. No, no, no.

Q. What was the justification or reason for it?—A. As I told you, the large amount of work in Colonel Anderson's branch. He had all the building of the lighthouses, the establishment of fish culture——

Q. Was it too much for one man?—A. I really think it was too much for one man to control, I really think it was.

By Hon. Mr. Cassels :

Q. He was not relieved of any salary?—A. I beg your pardon?

Q. He was relieved, but not of salary?—A. Not of salary. On the contrary he got an increase.

By Mr. Watson :

Q. Then, what, if anything that you know of, gave rise to some feeling that existed on the part of Colonel Anderson, which he has spoken of?—A. Nothing more than he felt aggrieved that some of the branches which he had and which he controlled were taken away from him. I do not think anything else than that.

Q. Was the matter ever discussed between you and him ?—A. After it was done?

Q. Yes.—A. That is where I saw it displeased him very much. He felt sore about it.

Q. Was it discussed before it was done with him ?—A. I do not think so. It might have been. I do not remember. That is a good while ago.

Q. Did it affect the personal relations between you and him ?—A. Between Colonel Anderson and myself ?

Q. Yes?—A. I don't think so, because I think he must have found out afterwards that I had nothing to do with it.

Q. What have been the relations between you and him ?—A. Very good, very good. He was rather disappointed when I was appointed deputy minister.

Q. What is that ?—A. He was disappointed when I got the deputyship at the time, but after a little while he was quite satisfied. I think I treated him honestly and squarely, as I did every single man in the department.

Q. And what difficulties, if any, existed between him and Mr. J. F. Fraser?—A. Well, as I tell you, he was very much annoyed to think that work had been taken away from him; but if you will look at the correspondence from the time his appointment was made and what took place between the different interests that were—I think he made a great mistake when he gave his testimony, which was as much as to say that the acetylene was started simply to benefit certain interests here. I think something like that was said.

Q. Well?—A. I happened to look up the files and I found the very first letter addressed to me was from the Prime Minister of Canada, in which he said that there were some firms that were recommending the adoption of this acetylene gas, and that he would be very much obliged if we could make some experiments and see what could be done. That was the first. They were sent to Colonel Anderson as chief engineer. They were very crude matters of their kind, and they were put aside. Afterwards some other person came along with the same light, and the minister recommended Colonel Anderson to put one on the Little Island, Aylmer. They were very effective as far as the light was concerned, but the acetylene would freeze in the cold weather, and some other change had to be made. The electrician made a change by which the whole of the reservoir—I forget the name, but that prevented the freezing. That was an expensive matter, and that had to be left aside. Then came improvements in buoys. They were still under Colonel Anderson and he deputed Mr. Fraser to that work entirely, thinking and knowing—or he would not have done otherwise— that he understood the work, and it was during the time he had charge of all the buoys in the St. Lawrence that correspondence took place which showed ne had every confidence in Mr. Fraser, and he was doing the work and mastered it as far as he could. During all that time experiments were being carried on, and I was even present at experiments by Mr. Willson, in his own private house, at which Colonel Anderson, Mr. Fraser and myself assisted. He had placed a buoy in his back yard where it was thought that light would not work in cold weather. We had about twenty degrees below zero and that buoy had been lighted for 30 or 40 days and gave a brilliant light. That was simply to exhibit to the chief engineer of the department. Then I think there are hundreds of letters testifying to the absolute reliability and brilliancy and effectiveness of this acetylene light. Not only that, but there was a letter from the representative of the Russian government asking the minister some time ago if he would be kind enough to give every assistance to allow one of their engineers to inspect our lighting system, as it had reached their country, and was thought most admirable, from the reports they had received.

Q. Then what do you say as to the change made and the introduction of acetylene?—A. Well, I think there was considerable trouble in arriving at a good buoy, and in order to insure success we know there must be money expended, and perhaps some money badly expended at first.

Q. Was the change necessary and expedient?—A. Absolutely. I think over $2,-000,000 have been saved in insurance since the proper lighting by that system of the St. Lawrence.

Q. $2,000,000. During what period?—A. In insurance alone during a year or two. The shipping interests have those details and are very anxious to bring that before his lordship. There was a statement also made by Mr. Fyshe, Commissioner Fyshe, stating that the lighthouse board was instituted simply as a means to spend money, and he charitably brought in the name of Mr. Allan, stating that he was on the board, and of course it was for the interests of his own ships. Well, I have a statement here which shows about all those buoys. I would like to enter this here because it is a very important statement. There is a statement showing everything that came before the lighthouse board, what was passed and what was refused, and it will be shown to be almost a million dollars. Why, Mr. Fyshe said there was hardly anything refused by the board.

(Statement marked Exhibit 48.)

Q. In a word, what has been the result of the change and the introduction of acetylene as to the amount of expenditure?—A. The expenditure is large simply because we had to change the old installation. Directly you would put one of those buoys in a place a captain would speak to his agent at Montreal or Ottawa and say: 'There is a new buoy fixed, we can see it out from six miles.' As soon as that happened there was a commotion to get those buoys, and we had to replace little by little the old system.

Q. What became of the old system?—A. They are utilized. That will be explained to you by Mr. Fraser, who has perfect control. Allow me for my own satisfaction to say that when I saw all these strictures by Commissioner Fyshe I looked into the matter thoroughly, I worked day and night until I knew the purchase of every single buoy, where it was placed, the number of spare buoys we had in every locality and the accounting for every single buoy numerically. Every buoy has its number. You can tell if No. 238 is down at any particular station, that is every single buoy is accounted for, and the system is a most admirable and perfect one. While I am leaving the department there is nothing I am more proud of than of the success we have had in lighting and establishing aids to navigation. I think this will be corroborated by the shipping interests of the lakes and Montreal, who are most anxious to appear before his lordship. They have written to me about it.

Q. Has it involved much increase of annual expenditure?—A. Certainly, when you diminish the insurance by millions of dollars.

Hon. Mr. CASSELS.—You might increase the expenditure because there is an increase of buoys; but taking buoy for buoy, does it increase the expenditure?—A. Certainly, yes; because the life previously of an old wooden buoy might be a couple of years. Those buoys had to be fixed up and repaired, they were bumped by ships; then we had the can buoys; then the ordinary Pintsch buoys; then finally we lighted on this buoy, which is absolutely perfect.

Mr. WATSON.—You think so. Then will the purchase of them be over a period more or less expensive than the purchase and maintenance of the old system?—A. Oh, naturally.

Q. Which?—A. Naturally the new system will cost a little more.

Q. In the original purchase?—A. Yes.

Q. And having regard to maintenance?—A. I do not believe it.

Q. You don't believe what?—A. You will get a more intelligent answer from Mr. Fraser.

3262—20

Q. What is your knowledge about the matter?—A. I have asked that several times. I would not like to say anything I am not sure of.

Q. Are you an engineer?—A. No. When I first entered the department I——

Q. Now, it is said that first introduction was promoted by Mr. Willson and for the purposes of his gain?—A. I do not think so.

Q. Have you any knowledge of that?—A. I have knowledge in this way. During Mr. Sutherland's time they were juggling around with those primitive acetylene lights which were tried to be foisted on the department.

Q. Tried to be what?—A. Well, they had certain lights which were good for a large institution, any building, but they were not good to be put outside, because, simply as I told you before they froze.

Q. You use the expression, 'Tried to be forced on the department?'—A. Yes.

Q. By whom?—A. The proprietors of those lights. Any man who has got a thing better than the one in existence will do his level best to introduce it in the department. That is what I mean.

Q. Well?—A. And during that time these men were continually coming up before Mr. Sutherland, and finally I believe one particular light which was in a deposit of— I forget. Mr. Fraser is here and he might tell me.

Q. Go on?—A. Mr. Sutherland asked Mr. Willson if he would be kind enough to send on one of his engineers to find out if that light was good. They went on experimenting from one thing to another, the thing worked on until the production of this good buoy, step by step they went on until they got this buoy which is absolutely perfect.

Q. Now, it is said there has been an excessive purchase of these, and that they have been allowed to lie idle for periods?—A. I do not think so.

Q. Have you any knowledge of that?—A. Now, there is all the history of the buoys numerically.

Q. Have you any knowledge of that, Colonel Gourdeau?—A. That there were too many purchased?

Q. And that they were allowed to lie idle for considerable periods, purchased in advance of the demand for use?—A. There might have been a few cases where it looked like that, but that can be explained to you by the engineer in charge.

Q. Have you any responsibility in regard to that?—A. No.

Q. Upon what recommendation were the purchases made?—A. The officer who was in charge of the service, certainly.

Q. And as deputy minister is it possible for you to control that?—A. As much as I can. I took a most lively interest. I was on the lighthouse board and I followed the progress of those buoys just as anxiously as if I had been interested, I was so taken with the possibilities of that buoy, and the result is a complete success, which can be proved by those shipping interests.

Q. Have you any knowledge of improper or wrong influences being exercised in respect of that by any one?—A. No. Most of those things were settled and arrived at before they reached the officers of the department. Now, I would like to put in this statement of the number of buoys, where situated, how disposed, how payments were made and why made.

(Statement marked Exhibit 49.)

Q. Were payments made in advance to the Willson Company?—A. Yes. I think the department was out $100,000.

Q. An advance of $128,000?—A. Instead of $200,000.

Q. Well, he said afterwards it might be $100,000?—A. He made another mistake. It might be $90,000 to $99,000. That was like a progress estimate.

Q. Why did you pay on any estimate?—A. I do not consider we paid in advance. It was like a progress estimate. All these buoys were finished, they were lying in his way. He was actually storing them for us until we paid the amount to get them away.

Q. There was no delivery?—A. He wanted us to take them away. There is nothing in that at all.

Mr. GODFREY.—As a matter of fact the delivery is here at Ottawa in regard to buoys?—A. Yes. They were an incumbrance to Mr. Willson there.

Mr. WATSON.—What about the prices paid to the company for those buoys?—A. I am not an expert.

Q. Did you ever investigate?—A. Yes. I went down to the factory. I not only spoke to Mr. Willson, but to some of the men, to some of the engineers. I spoke to some men outside of the business. I asked them what the buoys were worth. They said it was difficult to say, that the machinery to bend the metal into curves was dear and that the buoy ought to be a very expensive buoy. I asked them if $3,750 was expensive, and they said they would not undertake to build any buoys like that because they had not the means and could not do it. So when we had a talk with Willson his price was——

Q. $3,750 in the first place?—A. I thought it was. I advised him that since the department were adopting that system it would be better for him to make a little concession, and he gladly reduced his buoy to $3,000.

Q. Yes, but after that he said the question of price never arose?—A. Because all the prices were settled as to numbers. They are there in the statement I have given in. They were all settled as to numbers.

Q. That is, settled years ago at the time of the reduction in 1902?—A. No; when they were changed to $3,000.

Q. That would be 1902?—A. I forget the date.

Q. Well, why was no application made or why was there no discussion after that with regard to prices?—A. Because we could not call for tenders on a buoy which was manufactured under a patent. What was the use of calling for a tender from the man who was the only one manufactureing thr buoy?—He would give in his tender just the same price as he gave us in his offer by letter.

Q. Had you any knowledge that prices by a patentee might be regulated?—A. No, I was not sure. I am not up in that kind of thing.

Q. Had you any knowledge of that kind?—A. It came to me lately, from something his lordship said.

Q. But before that had anything of the kind come to your mind?—A. No.

Q. It had not?—A. No.

Q. It was never present to you as deputy minister?—A. No. I did not think I could secure them from Mr. Willson at a cheaper price or I would have tried it.

Q. I see. Well now, in connection with a similar matter, that is, the Canadian Fog Signal Company, the purchase of those signals?—A. Well, on that of course I had several conversations with Mr. Fraser and Colonel Anderson.

Q. With which Mr. Fraser?—A. B. H.

Q. B. H.?—A. Bazil; and while they agreed that really the instrument itself could be manufactured for $300 or $400—I think Colonel Anderson mentioned one at $250 or $300—it was controlled by the patent, and I thought the government themselves had a right to manufacture if they wanted to, and we discussed the matter several times. Colonel Anderson gave his opinion that it was very expensive, but unfortunately no efforts were made to reduce the cost of this.

Q. Then did you know at the time of the early purchases of these horns, signals, what the actual cost was, $300 or $400, and that the price was $4,000 to $5,000?—A. No, I did not at the time.

Q. When did you learn that?—A. About a year ago.

Q. A year ago?—A. Yes.

Q. Do you mean not before that?—A. No. The matter was entirely under Colonel Anderson's branch, and I knew there was a lot of expenditure made in connection with improving that machine, and I even went with Mr. Prefontaine to see the result of that.

3262—20½

Q. Of a test?—A. Yes.

Adjourned at 1 p.m. to 2.15 p.m. and then resumed.

Q. I think that I was asking you at the time of the adjournment about this payment for these diaphones, fog signals?—A. Yes, sir.

Q. Did you ever go into that matter yourself, apart from what you say was told to you by Colonel Anderson?—A. No. It is such a technical matter in itself that I would not have been able to come to any real conclusion that would have been satisfactory to my mind.

Q. Well, did you come to any conclusion?—A. I came to the conclusion that the price was exorbitantly high.

Q. Well, you gave it sanction?—A. I held the technical officer of that branch

Q. Well, you gave it sanction?—A. I held the technical officer of that branch responsible for this expenditure.

Q. That is Colonel Anderson?—A. Yes.

Q. And I understand you thought at that time you have said you did not have in mind that under the provisions of the Patent Act it might be regulated?—A. That it could be appropriated? No.

Q. You did not?—A. No.

Q. And the same with regard to the Willson Carbide Company?—A. Certainly.

Q. Now, was any inquiry made of you by Mr. Fyshe in regard to the carbide matter or in regard to the fog signal matter?—A. No. He never gave me a chance to explain anything. I called upon Mr. Fyshe a couple of times when I notified him the way of proceeding. The minister then sent for me. He said: 'I have had a talk with Commissioner Fyshe and I think everything will go on very well.' I said, 'I am very glad to hear it. Everything I can do to help I will do with the greatest of pleasure in the world.' I took a room from one of the best offices to make the commissioners comfortable. I gave them use of a messenger, and while he received me very politely I never had an opportunity of explaining anything. The messenger told me he used to work himself into a frightful rage and——

Hon. Mr. CASSELS.—Never mind what the messenger told you.—A. All right. What I can say personally myself is that I have heard it myself. I know it. He kept up such blasphemous language that it was something awful.

Q. Every Englishman swears if he chooses.

By Mr. Watson:

Q. Now then, you have heard what has been said with regard to that order by Mr. Eyre?—A. Yes.

Q. And you have heard that letter read?—A. Yes.

Q. That is an extraordinary epistle?—A. It is most extraordinary. I will explain to his lordship the matter as far as I know. The minister sent this letter in to me to ask me if I knew anything at all about it some weeks ago. I had never seen anything about nor did I know anything about the matter at all, and I was so astonished at the purport of the letter—I may tell you, to begin with, Eyre was known to me, but it was simply a nodding acquaintance on the street, because he had been on the patronage list. I forget what he used to sell, and I called upon Mr. Harty, the inspector of lights, who had the distribution of disinfectants. I asked Harty, 'This should have been sent down to the stores. I want you to proceed to the stores and find out if two extra cans were ever delivered there.' He called down to the stores but could not find anything.

By Hon. Mr. Cassels :

Q. You do not think that was sent to disinfect the department?—A. I do not know; but I certainly can tell your lordship that no disinfectant of that style would come into my house. It is a perfectly horrible thing.

By Mr. Watson :

Q. Did you ever receive it ?—A. No.

Q. Did you ever have any knowledge of it ?—A. No. I emphatically deny I ever spoke to the man about it. He is dead and not here to defend himself. I simply say I had nothing whatever to do, good, bad or indifferent, with that thing; it was absolute news to me.

Q. Well, now, there has been a reference to very reckless expenditure in regard to the *Anticosti* ship ?—A. Yes. I think I have got——

Q. Under your direction as deputy?—A. Yes. The *Anticosti* lightship, yes.

Q. What have you to say about that ?—A. Well, there was a contract made with a firm in Levis to change the hawse pipe so that we could have a larger anchor and a larger chain, so that it could have free running through the new hawse pipe. That was as far as the building of the ship was concerned. There are two inspectors in our department, there is a hull inspector or ship's husband and there is an inspector of machinery. That only related to part of the ship, that is the constructed part, and that of course naturally increased the contract which had been taken, which amounted to a little over $3,000, for those changes. So that when the other inspector came to Quebec and found there were other things to be added to the repairs of that ship he naturally said that that would have to be done, and for some reason or other the contract that had been sent down to Gregory, our agent in Quebec, to have signed, was never returned to the department, and the repairs were gone on with without the signature of that contract; but both those inspectors are ready to be examined—and they will probably be examined in Quebec—and explain that not one single cent over and above what should have been spent for the change was paid.

Q. What do you say as to the expenditure being excessive ?—A. No, no, there is no excessive expenditure. If he would have allowed us to explain and would have given us the advantage of having examined both the ship's husband and the inspector of machinery, he would have been perfectly satisfied there was nothing there of any extravagant character.

Q. Then we will have an opportunity of having that evidence ?—A. Certainly.

Q. Then there is comment ?—A. While I think of it, Mr. Watson, would you allow me to draw the attention of his lordship to what I said this morning about the saving in insurance? It is about half a million a year. I consulted the records. It is about half a million saved by the new aids to navigation.

By Hon. Mr. Cassels:

Q. Lower insurances by reason of the extra safety ?—A. Exactly, your lordship. I want to have that corrected. I said a million this morning; it is a half a million.

By Mr. Watson :

Q. That is saved to whom ?—A. The shipping interests, the lowering of their insurance.

Q. I see. You say that is by reason of the introduction of the new system and new signals ?—A. And increased aids to navigation, yes.

Q. Then reference is made to blundering correspondence ?—A. Yes. Well——

Q. Which seems extraordinary that should exist ?—A. That is another thing I assure you if he had given us an opportunity to explain how the correspondence is managed in the department he would be perfectly satisfied, any intelligent man would be.

Q. What do you say as to the system?—A. I say the system is as perfect as it can be in a government department. I may say this, too, that two years ago a gentleman who had been sent to Washington by the department, my lord, came to our department on business. He visited our correspondence branch and told Mr. McClenaghan, the gentleman examined here yesterday, that if he had known our system was so perfect he would have avoided his trip to Washington. It is an absolutely perfect system. There is another thing I would like to add. He said it was impossible for a person to overlook the correspondence and sign all the letters signed knowing what they were ? Well, he did not consider what he was saying for a moment. We will take a case in point. Supposing that the agent in Quebec wishes to expend $50 on the repairs to a life-boat or something like that: That is sent to the officer in the department who has got that in charge, he prepares a memorandum in which he says to the minister, 'I recommend for such and such reasons that the repairs asked for by the agent of such and such a place be granted for the following reasons.' I examine that, I initial it. If it is a large enough amount, that goes for minister's initials also. Then there is a letter prepared. Now, it stands to reason when that letter comes to me to be signed I have only to glance at it to see what it is about, and while there might be an error in the spelling that I might not notice, I would know the purport of the letter. I may say that during the last two years I have worked on an average 12 hours a day, I have rarely taken a Sunday, I have rarely taken a half holiday on Saturday. I attended to my work as much as I could, and it took me an hour and 20 minutes and an hour and a half to sign my correspondence every day, and I knew what I was signing perfectly and thoroughly.

Q. There has been considerable said about Samson & Filion's account ?—A. Yes. That is the account I spoke about this morning, and you will get all the explanation much better in Quebec.

Q. Can you give any explanation ?—A. The explanation I can give is this: We had also challenged that account, we had a lot of trouble and bother, and the people who had furnished the goods were continually asking their friends to bring pressure on the department to pay. Finally, when it was refused, the last time when I was in Quebec I told Mr. Gregory it was better for him to get a technical man of a rival house, selling the same class of goods and doing the same work to pass upon the labour items and examine the articles and get a statement as to the reasonableness of the account. It was after that statement was prepared and received that it was decided in the department, after making certain deductions, to pay it. All the details of that account the commission will get when you are there in Quebec, but it was reasonably settled and challenged entirely by the department.

Q. Then, Mr. Deputy, we heard from Mr. Buckly last evening that you were dealing with him, the dealings being introduced with the department ?—A. How introduced with the department ?

Q. I mean to say the department first gave orders to him for coal ?—A. Yes.

Q. Followed by some individual orders ?—A. Yes.

Q. Including an order from yourself ?—A. Yes.

Q. I want to know whether this is a fact that the coal that was sold to you was shipped to someone else, is that a fact ?—A. Yes.

Q. Is that a fact ?—A. Certainly, on my own orders. There was nothing hidden about it, and I would have continued to buy my coal that way, because the saving was from $15 to $20.

Q. Why did you ship it in the name of someone else ?—A. A messenger of the department. I was absent at the time and did not want it to fall on my family. It was shipped to Chambeau, he was a messenger i nthe department. There was nothing in that at all. I did not want any concessions whatever from Mr. Buckly. I wanted to get coal at a reasonable amount, and there was a combine here in Ottawa two or three years ago which kept the prices up. When the minister told me it might lead to discussion I dropped it, I never bought any more.

Q. That item of shipmnet was in his name in the way you have mentioned?—A. Yes, entirely.

Q. You say that was a matter of personal convenience to yourself?—A. Yes.

Q. And yet upon its face it would seem irregular?—A. Well, it might be interpreted in that way, but there was absolutely nothing more than that. I purchased my coal at a cheaper rate that way, while I could never have bought from the firms in the combine.

Q. How did you pay him?—A. I paid him in bills.

Q. You mean money?—A. Yes. My secretary knows all about it. That thing came up before the Public Accounts Committee, and I showed them actually the money had been paid and I had my receipts for it. More than that, when I heard the thing was to be questioned I simply telegraphed and asked him to make a deposition before a magistrate that I had purchased the coal from him and paid in the regular manner and that I did not owe him a single cent, which he did. That was produced before the Public Accounts Committee.

Q. One further question, was the full payment made by you and was it in the regular course?—A. Entirely made by me. The money was ready for him when he came to Ottawa, I gave it to him in bills.

Q. Then let me ask you, if you please, whether you have been in the habit of dealing personally with supplymen, that is men in business supplying to the department?—A. No, no, no.

Q. Has that condition of affairs existed?—A. No, not at all.

Q. Has it existed at all to any extent?—A. No, no, no.

Q. The reason I asked you that, Mr. Deputy Minister, I do not want to be unduly personal or apparently unduly severe, but it is important in the public interest that the facts should be known and ascertained and the matter cleared up?—A. Yes.

Q. I think you answered the question. I did not make the statement that you are reputed to be a wealthy man, having secured your wealth without any other source or revenue than your salary, and it is generally expected that no honest man can become wealthy in the public service?—A. Well, while I would like that to be examined either by yourself or his lordship, I am quite willing now to state before the court that a part of the money that I recived from my father's estate and what I have been able to save myself and in a couple of lucky speculations in stocks, I am quite sure that I do not—that I own in the vicinity of $20,000.

Q. You mean no more than that?—A. No. $20,000 to $22,000. I think it is about that. That is why I thought it better to mention it in my statement this morning, because I would not like the general impression to prevail that I had profited in any shape or form by my position to add to any property I have got.

Mr. WATSON.—Then, my lord, I find in perusing and considering the matter that it will be probably necessary for me to recall the deputy minister after some further evidence is given in Montreal by the supplymen and merchants there and in Quebec, and I prefer, then, with your lordship's concurrence, to let this further examination stand. I have touched upon important matters of a personal nature; other matters of detail I will follow up afterwards with your lordship's concurrence.

Hon. Mr. CASSELS.—I suppose you want the fullest investigation?—A. Certainly, most assuredly.

Mr. WATSON.—Then I will have occasion to recall you, unless there is something else you want to state now?—A. No, I do not think of anything. I had an explanation about all the report of the commissioners, but I suppose it will be brought out in some other way.

By Mr. Godfrey :

Q. One or two questions. This question, colonel, of the introduction of the new gas buoy, the international buoy, was a matter of general policy with the department?—A. Yes.

Q. You had been experimenting to get a better system of gas buoys for some years?—A. Yes.

Q. And I suppose it was a matter of congratulation to the department when you got this buoy, which you say is as nearly perfect as you can get?—A. Yes.

Q. And then it was adopted as a matter of general policy to introduce that buoy as rapidly as possible?—A. Yes.

Q. Now, did that account for the very large initial expenditure which has been made in the course of a few years ?—A. Yes.

Q. But that is a matter in which you and the minister and the commissioner of lights agreed in?—A. Yes.

Q. Then prior to the introduction of the new buoy what condition was the St. Lawrence ship channel in before these recent aids to navigation ?—A. Well, it required improvements.

Q. It was a dangerous channel, was it not?—A. Well, it had dangers, yes.

Q. Costing largely increased rates of insurance?—A. Yes.

Q. What has been the condition since the introduction of the buoys?—A. It is in good condition. As I have stated, there is a saving of half a million a year.

Q. A large saving of property evidently since the introduction of those buoys?—A. Yes, and security to ships.

Q. Then, who do you think must receive credit for the increased facilities of navigation?—A. I think the officer in charge.

Q. Who is that?—A. The officer in charge of the department.

Q. Who?—A. Mr. J. F. Fraser.

Q. You think credit must be given him for the work done on that channel?—A. I think so.

Q. You spoke of evidence which should be given by the shipping interests?—A. Yes.

Q. There was some evidence taken from the shipping interests in Montreal with regard to the increased aids to navigation?—A. Yes.

Q. When was that ?—A. I forget now ; some time ago.

Q. You think that ought to be before the commissioner?—A. I think so. They are very anxious to be heard.

Q. Whom do you suggest as witnesses to be heard?—A. Representatives of shipping interests in Montreal.

Q. Mr. Hugh Albert Allen?—A. Andrew Allen.

Q. And Mr. Thomas Robb?—A. He is secretary.

Q. And these are the men who can be heard when the commissioner is in Montreal?—A. Yes.

Mr. GODFREY.—I ask Mr. Watson to note that when the commission meets in Montreal to have the examination taken of those gentlemen.

Hon. Mr. CASSELS.—Very well.

JAMES F. FRASER, sworn.

By Mr. Watson:

Q. How long were you in the service?—A. Since October, 1893.

Q. And you were in Colonel Anderson's branch?—A. My first appointment was to Colonel Anderson's staff, yes.

Q. You are an engineer?—A. I am.

Q. And you remained in his department how long?—A. Until his branch was divided in November, 1903, practically ten years after.

Q. November, 1903, I see. Now, what did you have to do with that division?—A. Personally to do with it? Nothing at all.

Q. Was it upon your recommendation?—A. That it was made? No, it was on the decision of the late minister, the Honourable Raymond Prefontaine.

Q. Was it upon representations made by you?—A. By me, no.

Q. Was it after consultation with you?—A. The first knowledge that I had that the branch was to be divided was given to me by the minister himself after he had made up his mind to do so.

Q. I ask you this, Mr. Fraser, because Colonel Anderson has expressed the belief that it was procured, brought about in an unprofessional way, and through your influence partly?—A. Colonel Anderson is absolutely mistaken. The minister himself was responsible for the division, and I had no choice in the matter; I could not have taken any other action at all in it.

Q. Of course, it was a matter that resulted in your promotion or advancement?—A. Absolutely.

Q. What had ben your relations with your chiefs?—A. Up to that time?

Q. Yes?—A. As far as I know, perfectly satisfactory.

Q. And at that time, and after, what about the relationship?—A. He has given evidence on that point.

Q. I want your evidence, if you please?—A. Do you mean my relations with him?

Q. Yes?—A. Professional or personal?

Q. Personal and official?—A. As far as the official relations were concerned, I do not know in fact that there was any difference, as far as I could see the work of the department went along.

Q. The work of the department went along?—A. Yes.

Q. But the personal relationship?—A. I may say I have had no animus or feeling against Colonel Anderson since that time, since the change was made.

Q. Perhaps not quite a full answer?—A. As full as I know how to give you.

Q. Then has there been any friction between you and him?—A. Well, there has been that absence of personal communication, if you call that friction.

Q. Absence of personal communication?—A. Exactly, which exists usually between men.

Q. Eh?—A. I say an absence of that personal communication which exists usually between men.

Q. I do not quite follow.

Hon. Mr. CASSELS.—He means a chill on the colonel's part.

WITNESS.—Exactly.

By Mr. Watson:

Q. That is what you mean?—A. Precisely.

Q. And does your work connect more or less?—A. Generally less. I mean to say there is not very much connection between the two branches in a technical way.

Q. In a technical way?—A. Yes.

Q. But a certain amount of co-operation is necessary, is it not?—A. A certain amount of co-operation is necessary.

Q. You are working practically to attain the same result in connection with the same matters, but in different branches?—A. Different branches, exactly.

Q. That is right?—A. Yes.

Q. And co-operation is necessary?—A. A certain amount of co-operation is necessary.

Q. How can that co-operation exist and contine with the absence of harmony? —A. Oh, well, there is a wide distinction between business matters and personal matters, I think.

Q. I see. Then has it interfered with the performance of official duties?—A. Not to any extent.

Q. Not to any extent. I will just have to leave it that way. Then has Colonel Anderson complained to you of the manner in which your duties were performed?—A. I have never had any complaint from him as to the manner in which my duties were performed.

Q. As to inefficiency?—A. Absolutely none.

Q. As to impropriety?—A. No suggestion of the kind.

Q. What are your duties for the most part?—A. Broadly speaking, the operation and maintenance of aids to navigation, the application and the provision of illuminating apparatus and gas buoys.

Q. And that has brought you into close communication apparently with the carbide companies?—A. Not in close communication, no; in an ordinary business sense, yes. No more with the carbide company than with any other person the department has to deal with.

Q. I understand Mr. Willson is a personal friend of yours?—A. Mr. Willson is no more a personal friend of mine than anybody else that comes to the department in the ordinary way to do business with me.

Q. Was it not through his representations and influence that the dealings with him began and the system was introduced?—A. I do not understand your question.

Q. Was it not through his personal solicitation that the change to his system began or was made?—A. The change to his system began because it was the best system.

Q. Yes; but based upon his statements and representations?—A. Based upon tests made by the department.

Q. Were they not originally based upon his representations?—A. Anybody who has anything to do with the department, if they want to sell gas or anything else, they must represent their product to the proper person. Of course, in that sense

Q. Then your answer would be 'yes,' which is a shorter answer, and a more direct one, is it not?—A. Well, no, I am not prepared to admit that.

Q. You are not prepared to admit that?—A. No.

Q. I see. Up to that time you had used a different production?—A. We used Pintsch gas, oil gas.

Q. Which was much cheaper, and supposed to be sufficient for the purpose?—A. It was sufficient for the purpose because there was nothing else.

Q. The same as was used in other countries?—A. The same as was used in other countries, because there was nothing else.

Q. Then it was deemed sufficient, not merely here, but in other countries, supposed to be much in advance of our new country; that is so, is it not?—A. The other countries are not in advance of Canada in respect to aids to navigation. There is no question about the thing, because the other countries had nothing to try, except what they had, oil gas or Pintsch gas. Canada is far in advance of other countries.

Q. Far in advance?—A. Yes.

Q. Going too fast, is it not?—A. Not a bit; not going fast enough.

Q. Not fast enough for J. F. Fraser, perhaps, is that right?—A. No. I speak of the benefit of the shipping interests.

Q. That is what you mean?—A. Yes, that is what I mean.

Q. Now, then Colonel Anderson has expressed the pretty firm belief that this was brought about by reason of the personal influence of Mr. Willson?—A. I am not responsible for Colonel Anderson's beliefs at all.

Q. I did not ask you whether you were.—A. I beg your pardon if I——

Q. And that was not proper, and at the time not necessary?—A. I think the shipping federation—

Q. And this is in effect his belief, a charge of improper procedure in the department, and improper influence in the department. What do you say to that?—A. I say it is absolutely wrong. There is no basis of fact for his statement or suggestion at all.

Q. Did he ever discuss it with you?—A. He never discussed it with me.

Q. Was it commenced before or after the division?—A. The work was commenced under Colonel Anderson's direction, the experiments in connection with the utilization of acetylene. Colonel Anderson expressed himself on the official files of the department that acetylene would supersede Pintsch gas for the different gas buoy services.

Q. Before the separation?—A. Before the separation, as a matter of record.

Q. Then at that time the late Mr. Sutherland was minister, I think?—A. Before?

Q. At the time of its introduction, was he not?—A. At the time the first experiments were carried out under Colonel Anderson?

Q. Yes, at that time?—A. Yes.

Q. What had he to do with it as minister, do you know personally?—A. I do not.

I may say that the first experiments which I carried out in connection with the utilization of acetylene were made by me without any reference from the department or from Mr. Sutherland. I was not aware at the time my first experiments were made that Mr. Sutherland knew what carbide was, or that any experiments were being carried out concurrently in the department by Colonel Anderson or anyone under him.

Q. Why did you set about it, by reason of your progressive disposition?—A. I think it was pretty much an accident, that I started myself. I found, when we took over the steamer *Scout* from the Department of Railways and Canals, a small acetylene plant on board, and I began experimenting with that in regard to the value of acetylene as a light, and that was my first introduction to acetylene gas. I did not know Mr. Suthreland knew about it or had any interest in it; I did not know Colonel Anderson at that time was carrying out any experiments on the same lines.

Q. I see. Then it is broadly suggested that this was done to further the personal interests of Mr. Willson and those associated with him in his business?—A. Yes.

Q. What do you say to that?—A. How can I answer that question? I am not in a position to answer it.

Q. You do not know whether that was so or not, then?—A. I do not know whether that was so or not.

Q. I thought you knew at the time it was introduced?—A. What?

Q. The use of the acetylene ?—A. I do not understand your question.

Q. The carbide. I mean the use of that. At the time that the change was made I may say it is suggested that the reason for the change was jus to further the personal interests of the proprietors, of the owners of the invention?—A. Well, I don't know.

Q. And it was not upon the merits?—A. There is no question about that. It was introduced upon the merits of the gas itself, absolutely without reference to anything else.

Q. That is what you say ?—A. That is what I say.

Q. It was at considerable increase of expenditure ?—A. With corresponding increase in efficiency, which is the first thing to be considered.

Q. Do you mean to say that the increased efficiency is in full proportion to the increased expenditure ?—A. It is in very much higher proportion. Take the comparison betwen acetylene gas and Pintsch gas; acetylene gas costs 50 per cent more than Pintsch gas, but you get five times the light power from it; that is a much greater proportion than the increase in cost.

Q. What was the proportion of increase about, the increase of cost?—A. Well, I say acetylene gas——

Q. I mean in dollars ?—A. Do you mean to say of the service generally ?

Q. Yes?—A. It is a very difficult thing. You cannot make a comparison of the service now and the service as it was before acetylene was introduced, it is so much greater.

Q. What is the greater service ?—A. The total number of buoys burning acetylene. But, take any part of the service which you would deem a fair comparison, take the ship channel buoy service; there there are 50 buoys installed, approximately, or more. I think that service would cost—it is a very largely guess work, because that data we have not made up—I think that service to maintain would cost about 10 to 15 per cent more than it would under Pintsch gas.

Q. Yes?—A. But the efficiency would be 400 or 500 per cent, as far as the power and light and everything is concerned.

Q. Yes. What was the result as to buoys and material on hand before the change, did they become useless ?—A. We took 39 of the gas buoys out of service which were formerly Pintsch gas buoys, but they were taken out because structurally weak, not because replaced by other buoys. Those buoys are being utilized as unlighted buoys, and consequently without any loss to the service in that way.

Q. They are being utilized ?—A. They are being utilized. They were taken out of service beacause structurally weak. That type of buoy caused the accidents at Kingston and Parry Sound.

Q. Then was there any loss by reason of disuse arising through the change ?—A. Well, take that Pintsch gas buoy, which was costing $12 a piece; you removed 39 of those and use them to mark places where a cheaper buoy could be used; there would be a theoretical loss.

Q. Yes?—A. But it was imperative to carry that out, because the buoys were not of sufficient strength. They would have been removed from service anyway whether Pintsch gas or acetylene had been used.

Q. I see. Then why did you pay the prices that may seem upon their face to be exorbitant for the buoys?—A. We did not pay an exorbitant price. Basing the price of those Willson buoys on the type we bought for the Pintsch buoys, they are much cheaper. That is a matter of record and comes out in the report I made to the department

Q. Have you a copy of that report ?—A. I have not with me. I have nothing with me. The annual report for the department for 1904 and 1905.

Q. Well, go on please?—A. Well, wait a minute. I am mistaken in that. What I want is printed in the commissioners' report, a copy of that order in council, which Mr. Fyshe describes as an exhaustive one.

Q. Well, you were speaking about the prices, go on.—A. I am going to get you the data of it now.

Q. What page are you referring to ?—A. Page 219 of the Civil Service Commissioner's report.

Q. Yes?—A. You will find a table showing the cost and different dimensions of the old type Pintsch gas buoys, and below that is the corresponding table showing the cost of the automatic gas buoys.

Q. Yes?—A. Now, comparing the two, which can be compared properly, you will find on the third line of the last part of the table a type which is marked No. 10, price $3,000, gas cantained 10,000 cubic feet.

Q. It is the price without lanterns?—A. Precisely. They are both the price without lanterns in order to make a fair comparison. That is what is called a standard gas buoy; I mean to say it is the size which is most frequently used. All other sizes are either special, or intended for shallower waters. That buoy carries in the shape of carbide 10,000 cubic feet. Now, the buoy in proportion in the table above which can be properly compared with that will be No. 2.

Q. $1,300 ?—A. $1,300, and has gas contents, either No. 2 or No. 1-C—I don't know why that 'C' is there, compression, I guess—either No. 1 or No. 2, the price being $1,200 or $1,300, the gas contents being 1,760 and 1,690. Now, that works out for each at a price per foot of 68 cents or 77 cents, whereas the Willson buoy gives 10,000 cubic feet and that works out at a rate of 30 cents. That is the basis on which all gas buoys in the past have been paid for, the price per cubic foot of gas contents, and the price is in proportion to the amount of gas they contain. For that reason the Willson buoy is cheaper than the other. It has a further advantage: If you have a buoy which contains 1,690 cubic feet you have to charge that buoy more frequently, that is to say, you have to have the services of a steamer, the steamer crew and equipment to go out and put gas in under compression, whereas the Willson buoy carrying 10,000 cubic feet of gas has in many cases lasted a year, and it does not require attention during that time; therefore the maintenance expenses are less.

Q. Is that materially less ?—A. Yes, it is materially less, but you cannot put it down in dollars and cents, or even in percentage, but you know it is less.

Q. Yes?—A. Now, the same reason will apply to all the other buoys we have there. I have taken the standard buoys as a sample.

Q. Your position is, your view is rather that they are more expensive to the department?—A. No, they are less expensive to the department. The first cost is higher unquestionably, but the maintenance cost, for the season I have given, is less, and the efficiency is much greater. Well now, that is the basis on which those prices were passed by the department.

Q. Then without reference to the cost apparently ?—A. Without reference to the cost of the buoy itself.

Q. Yes?—A. No. The reference to the absolute cost, the number of pounds of metal, and the number of hours of work that went into that buoy did not enter into this.

Q. Then you were paying from $3,000 up ?—A. $2,000.

Q. Up to as high as $15,000 ?—A. Correct.

Q. And did you ever inquire as to the cost, the percentage of profit that the manufacturer or vendor was making ?—A. No. No inquiry was made as to that.

Q. Why did you not ?—A. Why was it necessary to do so ? Here we had something cheaper than anything we had before, and giving us much better results. The price was not unreasonable.

Q. The price was not unreasonable. Would that not depend upon the cost ?—A. Not at all. If we could get a buoy costing $10,000 and giving us better service than we had before, it would be worth while paying for it as a business principle.

Q. But you would not be willing to pay $10,000 for it if you could get it for $5,000 ?—A. But the manufacturer informed us that we could not get it for less. As a matter of fact Mr. Willson——

Q. But you have just said that you never inquired into the price ?—A. No. You mean to say inquired into the absolute cost ?

Q. Yes?—A. No, that is correct. I also added that the manufacturer stated those were his prices, and he would not accept less. As a matter of fact that standard gas buoy of $3,000, his first price on that was $3,750.

Q. Yes. We have heard about that?—A. Yes, that is right.

Q. Then there was a reduction made as to that, but no other reduction was asked for or claimed as to other sizes or other goods at any later day?—A. No. The department accepted that scale of prices because it was much cheaper than the old buoys bought before.

Q. And more efficient?—A. Yes.

Q. And did it ever enter into your mind that the manufacturer might be making a very unreasonable profit?—A. No, it did not appear to me he would be.

Q. But you had made no inquiries? I thought you were an engineer, a practical man?—A. That is very true. That is a business proposition. The manufacturer says, ' those are our prices, accept them or leave them.'

Q. A business proposition always involves a financial consideration as well?—A. Correct. But in this particular case we were getting more value for the money we spent.

Q. As compared with other expenditure, you say?—A. Other expenditure exactly, in the same line.

Q. Prior expenditure in the same line?—A. Yes.

Q. But the fact is you did not make efforts to obtain those goods at less prices after the first occasion?—A. After the first reduction from $3,750 to $3,000.

Q. You did not. What interest did you have in the Carbide Company?—A. Absolutely none, none whatever.

Q. Did you know who were interested in that?—A. Eh?

Q. Did you know, is the question?—A. Did I know? No, I did not know of my own personal knowledge. It is a matter anybody in the street knows, that the Ottawa Carbide Company is controlled by the Bronsons. Beyond that I did not know anything. Mr. Willson, I believe, told me he had some interest in it; beyond that I know nothing.

Q. But you knew of his interest in other parent companies out of which this arose?—A. No, I did not. I suppose he would have an interest in the Wilson Carbide Company on account of the similarity in name.

Q. Did you know Mr. Sutherland had an interest?—A. I did not know.

Q. Did you know?—A. Not in the Ottawa Carbide Company.

Q. What company did you know he had an interest in?—A. I did not know he had an interest in any carbide company.

Q. What is the Shawinigan Company?—A. I do not know, beyond the fact that one exists.

Q. Did you have any dealings with that company?—A. No dealings with the Shawinigan Company.

Q. None at all?—A. I believe the department now has a contract with them, quite recently.

Q. But during your regime?—A. No relations at all with the Shawinigan Carbide Company.

Q. Then was there any competition with the Ottawa Carbide Company?—A. Public tenders were called by the department after, I think, the first or second year.

Q. Why call for public tenders if there is only one company manufacturing and supplying?—A. We had at that time no official knowledge with reference to it. We received tenders from three carbide companies. The relation between those three the department knew nothing about.

Q. But you knew the company was manufacturing this under patent?—A. The carbide?

Q. Yes?—A. I think I knew that.

Q. Then, knowing that, you knew it would not be manufactured by any other company under the same patent, not likely, at all events?—A. I do not know. I have learned since there are variations of the patent law; for example, a man may license another.

Mr. GODFREY.—Did you speak of the buoy or the carbide?

Mr. WATSON.—The Carbide Company.

Q. Did you have any knowledge of that?—A. Knowledge of which?

Q. Knowledge of any possible competition?—A. I suppose on the face of it there would be competition.

Q. Do you say that?—A. I would suppose so, why not?

Q. I am not asking you to reason at all; I am just asking you the fact. Have you knowledge whether that company had the monopoly or control by reason of its patent, yes or no?—A. The Shawinigan Company?

Q. No, the Ottawa Carbide Company?—A. Why, I don't suppose the Ottawa Carbide Company had any monopoly in the matter.

Q. By reason of its patents?—A. It operates under the same patents as the Willson and the Shawinigan Company. They all operate under the same patents.

Q. So they may all manufacture and sell the same product?—A. Exactly.

Q. And does Mr. Willson control the Shawinigan Company?—A. I don't know.

Q. Then when did you first learn that the prices were not reasonable, having regard to the cost?—A. With reference to the carbide?

Q. Yes.—A. Why, we have no data concerning that at all, as far as I know.

Q. Not even to the present time?—A. Not even to the present time. I have absolutely no knowledge as to the cost of production of carbide, and as the plant is a very expensive one, it is not possible for the government, even if it took advantage of the Patent Act—as I learned recently they are able to do—to go into the manufacture itself.

Q. Were you aware before that advantage might be taken of the Patent Act?—A. No, I was not.

Q. Probably you learned that during the sitting of the commission?—A. During the sitting of his lordship.

Q. Was that known in the department, to your knowledge?—A. As far as I know it does not appear to have been.

Q. I see.

Hon. Mr. CASSELS.—It has cost a lot of money to learn it.

Mr. WATSON.—Yes.

Q. Now, Mr. Fraser, you are quite aware that the broad suggestion is made that you may have obtained some personal interest, directly or indirectly, in connection with the transactions with these carbide companies ?—A. I have heard it stated.

Q. What, if anything, have you to say ?—A. I state it is absolutely incorrect. I have not profited, directly or indirectly, in connection with any transactions between the Department of Marine and Fisheries and contractors, or any contractor.

Q. Do you know if anyone has, connected with the department ?—A. I do not.

Q. What had you to do with the horn or diaphone fog signal ?—A. My connection with the Fog Signal Company came about the time of the division of the technical branch of the Marine Department. At that time the work which was to be done by the new branch was not clearly defined, and the minister was of the opinion, the then minister, was of the opinion that fog alarm renewals—not new plants erected and put up, but renewals of the existing plants were a necessary part of the work of the new branch, and in that connection certain fog signal plants were ordered with the consent of the minister from the Canadian Fog Signal Company and partially installed. It took some little time to do that. The work was in the commissioner of lights branch, I think, less than a year. It was found during the installation of those plants that the buildings were too small to hold the new material. It then became necessary to reconstruct them, and the matter being referred to Mr. Prefontaine, he then ruled again that the work should properly go to the construction branch, and it went back to Colonel Anderson.

Q. In which branch did it commence?—A. Under the chief engineer, Colonel Anderson.

Q. How long did it progress with him?—A. The exact dates I cannot give you.

Q. About a year or so apparently ?—A. Probably two years, perhaps two or three years, I am not exactly sure about that, I think so.

Q. Then while in his department, and at the time of its introduction did you have personally to do with it, or who had responsibility then ?—A. I presume he did, the chief engineer, Mr. B. H. Fraser, had charge of that work while it was introduced and up to its establishment as a successful aid to navigation.

Q. He was your superior officer in that department?—A. At that time, up to November, 1903.

Q. Up to 1903 ?—A. Yes, exactly.

Q. He says that you were guilty of professional misconduct, or breach of etiquette or ethics?—A. That is a matter of opinion. I had no option or choice in the matter so far as the division went.

Q. Then who first fixed the prices?—A. For diaphones?

Q. Yes?—A. Colonel Anderson.

Q. When did you first learn the prices of these?—A. The cost of the diaphone itself?

Q. The prices being paid?—A. You mean for the——

Q. By the department?—A. You mean for the sound producer, the diaphone itself?

Q. Yes?—A. When the first tenders were called for, I suppose about three years ago, and some time after the work left my branch.

Q. But before that, and before the division, they had been purchased in connection with the plant?—A. Yes, both together as a complete plant.

Q. Yes, complete. Of course the cost of the plant was well known by reason of prior purchases?—A. It no doubt could have been well known if the matter was taken up in detail and worked out.

Q. It would not take very much detail. You had been buying similar plant for years and years, had you not?—A. Not personally.

Q. The department had?—A. The department had.

Q. Then when did you first learn of the actual cost of the diaphone?—A. As soon as the first tender came in, as I say, a year or so after the work left my branch.

Q. Not until after that?—A. Not until after that.

Q. What had you to do with that then?—A. With which? Absolutely nothing at all.

Q. Were you called upon to make any reports or recommendations in regard to it?—A. As to the cost of the sound producer or diaphone itself?

Q. Yes?—A. It was absolutely out of my field at that time, I had no connection with it at all.

Q. Did you have any communication, any dealings with those people, the fog signal people?—A. I came in contact with the fog signal people in connection with the first orders.

Q. With the first orders?—A. Yes.

Q. Now, what inducements were held out by them to officials of the department, if any?—A. As far as I know, I do not know of any. I cannot speak of anybody else. So far as I am personally concerned, none at all, absolutely none.

Q. Now, there is a clear charge—we are going over old matter—referring to this report, and you are one of the chief officials having charge of expenditure of the department, you were?—A. That is correct.

Q. What was the amount of the annual expenditure in your branch?—A. In my branch it varied.

Q. On an average about how much?—A. About $600,000.

Q. $600,000?—A. Pardon me just one minute. Probably a million dollars. A great deal of that was expenditure really not controlled in any way by me. What I mean to say——

Q. That is upon your recommendation?—A. No, only part of it. Take, for example, the salaries of light-keepers which would amount to $300,000 a year; that was absolutely uncontrollable expenditure; the amount for maintenance of lights, which would be about $600,000 a year, that in the sense of expending would be uncontrollable expenditure, largely under the charge of the agents. That construction vote, half of which was under the commissioner of lights branch, which would run to $600,000 or $700,000 a year, that you might call controllable expenditure under that branch.

Q. And you had to do with that?—A. Yes.

Q. That was upon your recommendation?—A. Very largely.

Q. Was it possible for anyone else to check that accurately?—A. How do you mean, check accurately?

Q. What I want to know is, is it possible that anyone else should be in a position to share responsibility with the head of the branch, in a practical way?—A. Practically for his own portion of the expenditure—no, I think not. I think the head of each branch is practically responsible for the expenditure of money that comes under his branch.

Q. Do you mean necessarily so?—A. I think so.

Q. That is a matter of detail, of maintenance?—A. I do not understand your reference to the word 'maintenance.'

Q. Whether or not it is possible in the ordinary course of the performance of the duty of the chief official and deputy minister to share in the responsibility in those recommendations, and as a matter of detail?—A. Unquestionably the deputy minister is technically responsible for everything going on in his department, everything.

Q. I am leaving out technical responsibility. I refer to it in a practical way?—A. You mean actually?

Q. Yes?—A. That rests with the head of the branch. I do not see that the deputy minister can revise it at all.

Q. You do not see how he can?—A. No. He is bound to accept the recommendation of the proper officer.

Q. I mean practical everyday operation?—A. You are referring to expenditure.

Q. Yes. Then in connection with your branch you are prepared to assume responsibility?—A. Absolutely, unless an officer is overruled in any particular case I think the financial responsibility should rest with him.

Q. Then, you make your contracts subject to approval by the deputy and to confirmation by the——?—A. Minister.

Q. By the minister?—A. Certainly.

Q. Now, you have dealt for the most part with what firms?—A. Oh, I do not know that you can pick out any one firm and say: 'That is pre-eminently the firm that the branch of the department has dealt with.' It has dealt with a number.

Q. Your chief expenditure was with what firms?—A. I think the chief expenditure was with the International Marine Signal Company. I think the largest item was with that particular concern.

Q. Yes. That is what we heard about that. Now, it is said that buoys were ordered in advance of the demands?—A. That is not correct, it is a misstatement.

Q. Was that ever so?—A. No, not to my knowledge, it was never so.

Q. And it is said that buoys after being ordered were allowed to remain for an undue time undelivered?—A. No.

Q. And after delivery to remain idle?—A. Oh no. You have got to keep a reserve of buoys, a reserve of gas buoys for any service, and we have not kept as large a proportion of our buoys as a reserve as we should have kept. As far as buoys being paid for and lying here in Ottawa, I do not think that the period of time would extend beyond 30 days. Now, it is impossible to co-ordinate all the branches of your service and get everything to work smoothly like clockwork. What I mean to say is, if we want a number of buoys for a particular stretch we have to make provision to place those buoys, we have to arrange for boats, for mooring stones, chains and everything. There may be some delay in getting ready to do that part of the work. But, the suggestion that has been made, there is absolutely nothing in it at all.

Q. But we have a record here in the commissioners' report of 10 or 12 buoys lying idle at Prescott, and being sent from there to Halifax, and about. You know what I refer to?—A. No. Those buoys—if it is the particular part of the commissioners' report you refer to—those buoys never went to Prescott. The commissioners are wrong in their finding, in that they are mistaken. They refer to 12 buoys—am I correct?

Q. Yes?—A. Which were ordered to be shipped to Prescott, and then they raise a question as to where they were, they say they cannot find any trace of them. As a matter of fact they dealt with the general files of the department, and there were two additional supply files which they did not get, which showed where these buoys went. Prescott is the central depot for lighthouse apparatus and buoys, and if we have any spare supply it goes there. As we need it it is sent from Prescott to where required. Those 12 buoys, an order was sent for those 12 buoys, but before they had an opportunity to ship from Ottawa to that point, instructions were given to Prescott, as the central shipping point, to send 9 of those buoys to New Brunswick. In order to save expense the officer in charge at Prescott directed the manufacturer to ship the 9 buoys direct from Ottawa, and that was the disposition of them. The commissioners did not ask any questions, and did not go far enough to find out.

Q. Well, was information not sought from you?—A. By them?

Q. Yes?—A. No.

Q. Did you have any communications with them?—A. I suppose I talked with Mr. Fyshe for 25 minutes one day about lunch time in my office. He asked no specific questions. I gave him a general description of the work of the branch, described generally lighthouse construction, and that was all there was, no questions. I supplied him with plans of buoys, but he did not seek any information.

Q. He did not?—A. Absolutely not at all from me.

Q. Is it an increasing expenditure?—A. For gas buoys?

Q. Yes.—A. It unquestionably will be, it is bound to be.

Q. Why so?—A. Take the Province of British Columbia, it is only the last two or three years that anything has been done there. Trade is increasing, everything has to be in proportion. Probably there will be an expenditure of three-quarters of a million dollars in lighting the approaches to Prince Rupert, the new Grand Trunk Pacific port, as soon as ready to take freight for the trans-Pacific trade.

Q. Is there anything to take the place, that you know of, of the present supply ? —A. The present gas buoys ?

Q. Yes.—A. There is nothing I know of at the present time.

Q. Then what other supplies do you purchase for the most part ?—A. Oh, well —of course, now you mean at the present time, or in the past ?

Q. During the period of your commissionership—— ?—A. I suppose——

Q. You purchased supplies of what character ?—A. You distinguish supplies from apparatus ?

Q. No, I did not intend to, I should cover that. What are your chief purchases, apart from the buoys ?—A. Well, we purchase gas buoys. We did formerly, not now, fog signals, that is a matter I am not concerned with and outside lighthouse apparatus.

Q. Is it in connection with that you have been making purchases from firms such as Merwin, Brooks & Company, and others ?—A. The firm Merwin represents does not supply lighthouse lanterns, the only thing they supply to the department is gas lanterns used in connection formerly with the old Pintsch buoys, and latterly with the new Willson buoys.

Q. And what did you purchase from Brooks & Co. ?—A. I understand they are representatives for Barbier, Benard & Turenne. They supply us with lighthouse apparatus, that is large flashing lights and lanterns, and things like that.

Q. And have you been giving them practically all the orders in that line ?—A. Not at all. The firm of Merwin gets all the orders in the gas lantern line, nobody else makes them. I understand the patent device ran out some years ago, but nobody else manufactures it. I may say, if it is relevant, the prices which we paid Mr. Merwin's firm for standard gas lanterns is now the price which the United States government is paying and has paid for many years past. Up to a year or so ago the price was appreciably higher, and I obtained a reduction from $450 to $300 on those same gas lanterns, and we have in service about 300 of them.

Q. Yes ?—A. That is the only reference I wish to make to gas lanterns.

Q. It is said the purchases were excessive ?—A. Excessive in quantity ?

Q. Yes.—A. That is not correct.

Q. And the prices very excessive ?—A. You are speaking of one specific firm ?

Q. Yes, Merwin & Co.—A. Absolutely wrong.

Q. Who has fixed the prices ?—A. The prices are submitted to the department, and if correct, accepted by them.

Q. Of course the department means yourself in that respect ?—A. That is the recommending officer, yes.

Q. As recommending officer ?—A. Correct.

Q. Has that been done with or without contract ?—A. Well, I understand this morning that a letter is a contract. Is that correct ?

Q. It may be a contract by correspondence.—A. Generally by contract on correspondence in that case.

Q. But not by a formal written document ?—A. Not by a formal written document ? There has been no occasion.

Q. What has been the usual course ?—A. To make arrangements by correspondence.

Q. I see. That has been the usual course. There has been complaint about your individual transactions as an official with these companies; is not that so ?—A. I understand it is. I judge it in a general way from what evidence has been given here.

Q. Now, that relates, as I understand, to excessive prices that you have paid to these firms, and that you have dealt exclusively with them at these excessive prices ?— A. That statement is broad, and is not in its entirety correct. There is only one instance of what might be called excessive prices, nothing else.

Q. When was the one instance ?—A. That is a matter which was referred to in the Public Accounts Committee in 1906 with reference to a matter of certain machinery, and has reference to the purchase of certain machinery. That is the only instance in which there has been what might be called excessive prices.

Q. And in that case an excessive price was paid?—A. It was so shown.

Q. How do you explain that?—A. I explain that simply in this way; that when it became necessary to obtain this material I was directed by the then minister to get it from one person. When this invoice came in for that material it was laid before the minister. I was not able to tell him the exact percentage of increase in costs, but I explained to him it was very high, and he virtually gave me directions to pass the bills. I may say here I did not give this explanation when the matter was before the Public Accounts Committee, but I have no intention of taking the onus of responsibility in that matter any further.

Q. To whom are you referring?—A. The late Minister of Marine..

Hon. Mr. CASSELS.—What explanation did you give?—A. Before the Public Accounts Committee?

Q. Yes?—A. Nobody asked me.

Mr. GODFREY.—He did not give any.

Mr. WATSON.—Well, you assumed responsibility for it?—A. By direction virtually. Do not misunderstand me. It may not excuse me in this particular case, but that is the explanation. Now, you cannot find anything else in the accounts I have passed, so far as I know, of excessive prices.

Q. What was ordered at that time?—A. Certain standard machinery. I mean to say lathes, planers, and things like that.

Q. At what disbursement or expense, speaking roundly?—A. I think the total expenditure was $18,000.

Q. $18,000?—A. Yes.

Q. To what an amount was it an excessive payment?—A. I understand the percentage of profit works out roughly at 50 per cent to a middleman.

Q. On that transaction?—A. Yes.

Q. Had you knowledge of that at the time?—A. Not detailed knowledge; I have since. What I mean is I had not the detailed prices, but I knew generally speaking the prices were high.

Q. And you made the recommendation?—A. It was not a case I mean to say——

Q. Did you certify it on?—A. Wait a minute. A list of what was required was submitted, and instructions given to obtain it from this particular firm.

Q. Did you certify the accounts on?—A. Certainly, that is the point.

Q. Was that repeated, did that occur again?—A. No, it did not.

Q. Who was the middleman?—A. The firm of F. S. Brooks, I believe.

Q. Practically the same firm ?—A. As what ?

Q. As Merwin ?—A. I don't know.

Q. Did you not know ?—A. No, I did not.

Q. Eh ?—A. No, I did not know at the time.

Q. Your own personal relations with them have been very close, I understand ? —A. No, you are mistaken in that.

Q. Is that not so ?—A. That is not so.

Q. What do you mean by middlemen ?—A. Well, the evidence before the Public Accounts Committee showed that after those orders were sent to this particular firm they turned them over to somebody else to fill. Consequently they became middle men in the filling of the order for the department.

Q. That is, they went through the form of turning them over for the purpose of additional profit ?—A. Apparently that was so.

Q. How often have you known that sort of thing occur?—A. I think that is the only case I have knowledge of.

Q. You think, are you sure ?—A. To the best of my recollection and belief.

Q. Have you ever in any other contract with the department known of middlemen? Now just try and think ?—A. I am not able to recollect any at the present minute.

Q. You are not, eh ? What commissions have you been paid by the department, or allowed or included in the price ?—A. How do you mean, commissions ?

Q. Commissions on the purchases or sales, either way?—A. Do you mean the amount of profit allowed to the person that supplies ?

Q. No; his commission ?—A. Well, I don't understand your question.

Q. You don't eh ?—A. No.

Q. Have you ever yourself received a commission?—A. No, I have not.

Q. Do you know of anyone who has received a commission ?—A. No, I do not.

Q. Have you ever heard of any such thing ?—A. No, I have not, I don't know of any case at all.

Q. Is there such a thing as a discount in your branch ?—A. No, there is not.

Q. For cash ?—A. As far as I know, no.

Q. Has there ever been ?—A. Not to the best of my recollection.

Q. Why?—A. Because the prices are net, and if the lowest prices are quoted I should fancy that would be the end of it.

Q. Have you ever asked for discount ?—A. No. You can get just as low a price at net prices as at a higher price, with discount off. The discount may look a little better, but it may not be better in the end.

Q. We all know how it may be done, and may not be done. We want to find out how it was, as a matter of fact?—A. Well——

Q. Sometimes it depends upon the asking, does it not, whether a discount is allowed ?—A. I don't know.

Q. You don't. You never asked for discount, then?—A. I never did. I always expected to get net prices on the quotations. I never took up the question of discount.

Q. Is it not the fact that your taking it for granted that people dealing with the government, some people at all events, would endeavour to extract higher prices than from ordinary customary customers ?—A. I generally believe that is the case. Pardon me if I give you a case.

Q. That ought to lead you to take extra precautions ?—A. Would it not ?

Q. Is not that so ?—A. Yes, I suppose so.

Q. Did you take extra precautions ?—A. Yes, in many cases. I want to give an illustration. I believe it is greatly better for me—in the course of the purchase of those lanterns we obtained a reduction in price from $450 to $300—to get down and get the best net price from the people who supplied, rather than get the list price and accept a nominal discount. We are paying $300 there as the net price where we formerly paid $450 .

Q. Who else besides Merwin and Brooks have been large sellers ?—A. Chance Brothers, Birmingham.

Q. And who else?—A. Well, at the moment I do not recollect any other firm that has done a large business with this department.

Q. Some of those are incorporated companies?—A. I presume so.

Q. Do you know of any official having an interest in a company dealing with the department?—A. Any official o fthe Marine Department?

Q. Yes?—A. No.

Q. Have you ever heard of such?—A. No.

Q. Have you ever heard of any official having an interest in the Willson Company?—A. No, I never heard it suggested.

Q. Or in the Canadian Fog Signal Company?—A. Never.

Q. Or anyone connected with the administration, directly or indirectly?—A. I never heard it suggested.

Q. You have been living at Prescott?—A. No, I never lived there.

Q. I thought you had a place there?—A. No, never.

Q. Near Prescott?—A. Maitland, 6 or 7 miles further up.

Q. Has that been your usual place of residence?—A. Only a short time during my life, in the summer time.

Q. Have you received personal benefits in connection with your own property or use of it by reason of your position in the department?—A. I have received no personal benefit as far as I know.

Q. By the use of men or material of the department?—A. Absolutely not at all.

Q. Eh?—A. No, I have not.

Q. Do you know of anyone that has?—A. No, I do not.

Q. Do you know of any gains or benefits or advantages that anyone has received by the use of departmental or government material or property?—A. No, I do not.

Q. Eh?—A. No, I do not.

Q. Has any such thing ever come to your knowledge?—A. It has not come to my knowledge.

Q. Were you here when the Auditor General gave his evidence?—A. I was present during the time.

Q. My recollection is that in effect he said that he had reached the conclusion that your certificates of prices, that the prices were fair and just, were not to be relied upon?—A. I think it was a most unjust thing for him to say. He has passed a million dollars or more of my certificates since he reached that conclusion. He has nothing to base it on. As he said himself, except that matter of expenditure which came up in the Public Accounts Committee, there is absolutely nothing else.

Q. Have you ever discussed the matter with him, or he with you?—A. Never.

Q. Did he ever make any personal representations to you?—A. He never did.

Q. Any communications between you?—A. Absolutely none, with reference to that matter.

Q. With reference to any matter with regard to your certificates?—A. No, not that I know of.

Q. Have your certificates ever been turned down?—A. Absolutely never.

Q. Or questioned?—A. Never.

Q. Do you mean that?—A. I say so.

Q. You were here, you understand? I think my recollection is accurate of what he said?—A. That is correct, I agree with you in that.

Q. That is a somewhat serious position, Mr. Fraser?—A. Exactly.

Q. How do you account for it?—A. I do not think it is a fair one, and it is not, as I said before, reasonable. This matter the Auditor General referred to is within two years, 1906, within that time, and certainly I would judge a million dollars worth of the accounts of the Marine Department have passed through his hands in the shape of certificates he speaks about in his evidence.

Mr. WATSON.—That transaction with Merwin and Brooks we will have an opportunity of making some further inquiry into, my lord, at Montreal, and I do not wish to pursue it further at the present time, because I want to get production of the books first.

Q. The books are there at Montreal, so I will have to ask you at a later time to attend for further examination?—A. At your pleasure.

Q. Have you any books or documents outside of the department?—A. Absolutely none.

Q. You wer working in the department sometimes after you ceased active direction and control, were you not?—A. Correct, quite right.

Q. All in connection with individual matters?—A. No. This was in connection, it was going over this Civil Service Report with reference to getting such information as might be required.

Q. I did not ask you before, I did not call upon you before—have you any knowledge of destruction of papers, correspondence or documents?—A. I have no knowledge.

Q. Eh?—A. I have no knowledge, absolutely none.

Q. Has there been anything of that kind done that you know of at all?—A. I have no knowledge at all. As far as my own personal information goes, I know nothing.

Q. Did you hear anything of the kind outside of this commission?—A. No, the first I knew about it was when it came up before his lordship during the sittings.

Q. Is there any foundation for that?—A. As far as my knowledge goes, no.

Q. Had you to do in a way, co-operation at all events, with the construction of those piers in Lake St. Peter?—A. Not guilty.

Q. What do you mean by ' not guilty'?—A. I had nothing to do with it.

Q. I did not make any charge against you, Mr. Fraser..

Hon. Mr. CASSELS.—He means there might be a presumption of guilt in others, but his is a plea of not guilty.

Mr. WATSON.—Well, did you have anything to do directly or indirectly in connection with those?—A. Absolutely not at all, no connection whatever. It is a matter that came entirely under the other branch, a case of construction.

Q. A case of construction. You have nothing to do in the way of lighting or maintenance in connection with that then?—A. In connection with those piers? Oh yes. The branch supplied the necessary steel holders to hold the compressed gas, and also furnished lanterns, but they were erected and placed in position by the construction men; it was merely furnishing certain material or store allowances, and so forth.

Q. How many piers went to wreck?—A. My information is not exact. I have not seen them.

Q. Do you know?—A. No, I really don't. You have more information than I have about that.

Q. Now, then, I ask you specifically—I am not quite sure at this moment whether I did—in regard to this report saying: 'There would seem to be a lack of conscience in the department. In connection with the enormous expenditures which are deemed necessary the word 'discount' never appears.' What do you say to that?—A. I don't understand the reference at all.

Q. ' There would seem to be a lack of conscience,' that is on the part of officials in the work?—A. How do you interpret that expression, ' lack of conscience?'

Q. How would you interpret, I say?—A. I don't know. I don't understand what the commissioners meant by that reference.

Q. Lack of conscience?—A. No.

Q. Certainly, absence of good conduct, at all events it would carry that far?—A. Yes.

Q. And the absence of good conduct would no doubt carry to the extent of improper conduct or misconduct?—A. Yes. I do not understand anything about the reference. If that is your interpretation, I do not understand it.

Q. In your department?—A. No, I don't believe it.

Q. Or by anyone else?—A. No. As far as I know of nothing that would come under that.

Q. Do you know of any benefits or advantages obtained by any other officials in the department?—A. No, I do not.

Q. Not at all?—A. No, not at all.

Q. How would the suggestion arise of serving two masters, how might that be applied?—A. I don't know, I am sure.

Q. Let me have information you think might be applied?—A. I don't know.

Q. Supposing people were so disposed, what would be the opportunity of application of it?—A. Chance to apply it?

Q. Yes?—A. No opportunity has come within my purview since I have been in the department to do that. I have had no opportunity to serve two masters. No suggestion has ever been made to me to serve two masters. Perhaps that is the better way to put it.

Q. Have you any knowledge or information of any such thing?—A. Of anybody else having served two masters?

Q. Yes?—A. Absolutely none.

Q. I will resume with you at a later time, if you please.

By Mr. Godfrey:

Q. One or two questions, Mr. Fraser. You are through, Mr. Watson?

Mr. WATSON.—For the present.

By Mr. Godfrey:

Q. Before adopting the International buoy, what tests were made?—A. Buoys were given a service test, in fact a more severe test than a service test.

Q. Explain to his lordship what the test was and how long it lasted?—A. Three buoys were furnished by Mr. Willson for testing purposes, and taken to Prescott and placed in the river. That happened in August or September, 1904. They remained there until the close of navigation, and in addition to that they remained out in the ice all the winter, and the test was carried on during the spring, which in my opinion was sufficiently satisfactory to enable the department to take up and use the buoys.

Q. And were these tests satisfactory on the part of the buoy, did it stand the tests all right?—A. It stood the tests, certainly. Just one moment. Before a certain large order was given there was another test made by direction of the lighthouse board, and a buoy was placed for a period of thirty days in an unusual position in the Bay of Fundy near the Lurcher lightship. It is a rough place and the tide is very heavy. That buoy also successfully finished its test.

Q. How long has one of those new buoys stayed lighted?—A. The standard gas buoy has remained lighted for over one year, 12 months.

Q. And how long did the old buoys stay lighted?—A. It depended to a certain extent, but generally speaking four months was the limit.

Q. So one of the advantages of the new buoy is, you have only to re-charge it every year?—A. Only 12 months, but as a matter of fact we charge oftener than that, because they probably scrape and paint the buoys before the carbide is exhausted, and in that event we take the opportunity of filling.

Q. I understand there is a difference in the way of charging?—A. Yes.

Q. Explain that?—A. The old buoys were charged by means of gas made at a special gas works.

Hon. Mr. CASSELS.—We have had all that.

By Mr. Godfrey:

Q. Then the carbide is just placed in the new buoys?—A. The same as you put in coal.

By Hon. Mr. Cassels:

Q. It drops into the water?—A. The carbide?

Q. Yes?—A. Well there is a central tube, and the carbide is poured in the same as you pour coal.

Q. And the water drops on the carbide?—A. The water attacks it from below.

Q. That is what I mean?—A. Yes, correct.

By Mr. Godfrey:

Q. You had several accidents?—A. They were with the old Pintsch buoys using compressed acetylene gas.

Q. What did that cost the department?—A. The Kingston accident cost $40,000. We have had no claim for damages in respect of Parry Sound.

Q. How many men were killed in the Kingston accident?—A. Unfortunately four.

Q. Parry Sound?—A. One.

Q. Now, something was said by the Auditor General about prepayment of $128,000 to the International Marine Signal Company?—A. That is as an advance.

Q. Yes ?—A. I cannot find any record of it at all.

Q. Now, will you explain just to what it refers, it refers to something ?—A. Why, that refers, as far as I can find out at the present moment, to certain buoys which were ready and paid for, and which I think Mr. Watson referred to as being held here, not shipped out at once.

Q. How long did that period extend over that those buoys were left there after payment ?—A. 30 to 40 days.

Q. And during that period they were being shipped out one by one ?—A. To the best of my recollection, subject to correction.

Q. Now, you spoke about difficulties of installation. How many special vessels did you have to charter at times ?—A. For the buoy service and other services ?

Q. Yes.—A. Well, that is a difficult question to answer. Do you mean for the whole country ?

Q. I mean at different times you have to charter special vessels ?—A. For what purposes ?

Q. For the purpose of installing buoys if one of the Dominion ships cannot be got ?—A. Yes, we paid $188,000 for the last fiscal year for chartering boats.

Q. That is unavoidable ?—A. Until such time as the department can get in steamers.

Q. And is there any delay ?—A. As I said to Mr. Watson, you cannot always You have got to get what they have.

Q. And is there any delay ?—A. As I said to Mr. Watson, you connot always co-ordinate the work to make it run properly in that way.

Q. Then there is that $15,000 buoy spoken of. What really took place ?—A. It was designed to take the place of a lightship and has been very successful in that respect.

Q. And does that effect any saving to the country ?—A. A lightship costs $100,000; this buoy $15,000. The light of the buoy is better than the light of the lightship, but the whistle on the buoy is not as good as the signal on the lightship.

Q. How do they compare in maintenance ?—A. A lightship cost $15,000 a year to maintain.

Q. What is the cost for the buoy ?—A. $250 to $500 a year.

Q. So, practically for an initial expenditure of $15,000 you save the cost of the lightship and its heavy annual cost of maintenance ?—A. It is probably not an absolutely fair comparison. As I said, the light on the buoy is better than the light on the lightship, but the signal, which is very important, is not as good as the signal on the lightship.

Q. Now, were you asked by Mr. Fyshe or any of these commissioners, or given an opportunity to explain these things as given here to-day ?—A. As I stated before, no, no oportunity at all, no questions were asked.

Q. All these things put in here against you in the commissioners' report you were not asked to explain before it was published ?—A. Absolutely not at all.

Q. Now, is there anything else you want to say ?—A. No. It is a very little thing. The only point I wish to state is this. I see in the commissioners' report they regret—I think I am right—they regret they did not have an opportunity of visiting Sorel and other places. As a matter of fact Messrs. Fyshe and Bazin did visit Prescott. The report is incorrect in that little detail.

WILLIAM STUMBLES, sworn.

Mr. WATSON.—I want to ask this witness just a few questions and also Mr. Noble. Then I am in a position to say to your lordship that I have brought before your lordship practically all the officials of the department, so that they have a chance to answer the charges that are made indirectly or directly in the report of the Civil Service Commissioners.

By Mr. Watson:

Q. What is your branch, Mr. Stumbles ?—A. I have been what they call the contract clerk in the department, sir. And I have had to do a good deal with tenders for supplies and tenders for all lighthouses and the buoy service, &c., gas buoy service, they come to me after they have been opened.

Q. After they have been opened ?—A. That is within the last year or so.

Q. Well, in connection with that——?—A. And I prepare the annual report.

Q. Have you had to do with the making of contracts and fixing of prices?—A. Making them out and the agreements—you mean fixing prices?

Q. The fixing the prices. Have you had to do with the fixing of prices?—A. The tenders come to me, sir. I have nothing to do with fixing the prices, and I put that price in the contract.

Q. You put the price in the contract?—A. Yes.

Q. Yes. But you are not in the spending department?—A. No, sir.

Q. Then you got your information or directions from the branches?—A. From the branches.

Q. They report to the deputy what they require to expend and the purposes for which it is required?—A. Yes, sir.

Q. Then, do I understand that the matter of advertising for tenders is through you or through the branch?—A. Yes, sir.

Q. That is right?—A. That is right.

Q. Then the amount of the expenditure is fixed by the others?—A. Yes.

Q. Who fixes the quantum of the prices ?—A. When tenders come in the man who sends the tender in fixes the price.

Q. Oh yes; but then is that submitted back to the other branch?—A. No, sir.

Q. Why not?—A. It is sent to the deputy minister.

Q. Well, to the deputy minister, and through the deputy minister to the head of the other branch?—A. To the minister.

Q. Yes. Then I want to know is it your discretion that is used or the discretion of someone else?—A. In most cases my discretion.

Q. Your discretion?—A. In most cases.

Q. Why your discretion?—A. When it obtains another executive branch?—A. I was dealing with the general buoy service, as I always did. It was left to my discretion to make a recommendation and not accept the lowest tender.

Q. The price of the buoys?—A. The price of the buoys.

Q. That would not be in your discretion, you had no practical knowledge?—A. Yes.

Q. What practical knowledge?—A. A good deal of practical knowledge.

Q. You were not in the department, were you? You were not, for instance in Mr. Fraser's or Col. Anderson's department?—A. Well, no, but I did work in connection, I was under Mr. Fraser and the other chief engineer.

Q. Well, now, for the present in the making of those contracts and in the furnishing of goods or supplies have you any knowledge of any improper acts or conduct on the part of contractors or by officials?—A. No, sir.

Q. Eh?—A. No.

Q. Any such thing ever come to your knowledge?—A. No, sir.

Q. Do you know of any commissions being paid to middlemen?—A. No.

Q. Or to officials?—A. No.

Q. Have you ever heard of any such thing?—A. No.

Q. Eh?—A. Never.

Q. You never have?—A. No, never.

Q. Do you know of any benefits or gains that are derived by officials or any of the officials?—A. No, I do not.

Q. Have you ever heard of any such thing?—A. No.

Q. Do you know of any interest that has ever been possessed by any official in a matter of contract or with contractors or people dealing with the department?—A. No, sir.

Q. Then, what is meant in the report by lack of conscience, misconduct on the part of officials?—A. I don't know.

Q. Do you know to whom that could possibly apply?—A. No, I don't.

Q. Eh?—A. No, I cannot imagine.

Q. Have you any knowledge of any such thing?—A. I have no knowledge.

Q. Then Mr. Stumbles, a letter was received at the department directed to me and to Mr. Perron, as counsel, written by one R. Purdy, which concerns you and which I bring to your attention. ' May 30th, 1898, New Westminster, British Columbia. I see that you are appointed to investigate matters in the Marine Department, and as I had a grievance I wish you would look into it. In 1898, in August, one W. W. Stumbles, of the Marine Department, got moneys belonging to me from the then inspector, John McNab, and he never returned it to me, although he promised to do so at the time or later when out here. I cannot understand why I should be treated so. Hoping you will look into it and see I get it returned, yours truly, R Purdy.' Now, that evidently refers to something in connection with your official duties, and I therefore take the opportunity to call your attention to it. What have you to say about it?—A. Well, I was sent out to investigate matters there, and there was some irregularity in connection with talking license fes. I secured all the money that I could from a certain officer, and I deposited that money with the department, turned it into the department, sent it immediately to the department by draft. There was part of that money that was held by this officer, this inspector of officials.

Q. What is his name?—A. His name is McNab. Part of that money should have been paid to Mr. Purdy, and instead of paying it to Mr. Purdy I paid it into the department, and I told him that I could not get it back, but, I said, ' Since you are bothering me so much about the money I will try and pay you myself.' I never paid it.

Q. How much was it?—A. About $30, I think. I never got a dollar of money from him personally.

Q. Do you mean that was paid into the department?—A. Yes, sir.

Q. Have you a record of that?—A. Yes, sir. There is a report in the department.

Q. Do you mean his moneys are in the department and do not belong to the department?—A. He says so. I only had to take his statement for it.

Q. Because if there improperly, why not get it back from the department?—A. Simply I sent every dollar and left the department to settle that.

Q. But it was under your direction. Why not follow it up, if you got a man's money improperly or by mistake and pay it over to the department by mistake, why not follow it up?—A. I did.

Q. Why did you not get the money back?—A. I could not get it.

Q. Why not?—A. Simply because I was told the money had been deposited to the credit of the Receiver General before I came home, and they did not bother about it.

Q. The department would not keep other people's money?—A. The department kept that.

Q. To whom did you explain that, to the deputy minister?—A. I explained it—I don't know I ever explained it to the deputy minister, but I explained it to Mr. Cunningham, who was then accountant of the fisheries branch.

Q. I see. So the explanation is between you and Mr. Cunningham?—A. Yes.

Q. Was he your superior officer?—A. No, I am connected with the marine branch.

Q. Why did you not submit it to the deputy minister and have it straightened out?—A. I may have mentioned it.

Q. Do you recollect?—A. I do not remember. That is a good many years ago. You have sprung this thing on me. That was 8 years ago.

By Hon. Mr. Cassels:

Q. Were those fees to which he was entitled?—A. Yes. He was a constable on the river and he had assisted in seizing some boats that were fishing illegally, and those fees were paid into the inspector, and he told me that the inspector had not paid him.

-Q. He was entitled to a share of those fees?—A. Yes; that was the law, that he was entitled to receive on seizure half the fees.

Q. Yes. He got half and——?—A. And the department received the other half.

By Mr. Watson:

Q. Have there been any similar occurrences?—A. I took everything and sent it to the department and let the department settle the matter.

Q. I understand you to say you did not gain personally a cent?—A. Yes.

Q. That is the fact?—A. That is the fact.

Q. Then are there any other matters of a similar kind?—A. What do you mean, of a similar kind? In that locality?

Q. Or any other locality?—A. What?

Q. Do agents pay you moneys for the department?—A. No.

Q. Do you ever receive moneys outside as an officer of the department?—A. I did in several cases.

Q. In several cases?—A. Yes.

Q. In any case where it has not been accounted for?—A. Never.

Q. Eh?—A. No, I have always accounted for it. I received it from his office and accounted to the department for it.

Q. Then has there been any improper act or misconduct on the part of yourself or anyone else to your knowledge?—A. No, sir.

Q. I may have to refer to you again at a later time, Mr. Stumbles.

(Mr. Purdy's letter marked Exhibit 50.)

WILLIAM H. NOBLE, sworn.

By Mr. Watson:

Q. What is your office?—A. Assistant commissioner of lights.

Q. That is under Mr. Noble?—A. Mr. J. F. Fraser.

Q. Mr. J. F. Fraser, I mean to say. How long have you been in that position? —A. I have been in it since 1903. I have been in the department for 25 years.

Q. In the department 25 years?—A. And previous to that I was in the Scotch lights for about 20 years.

Q. Oh, yes, that is all right. You have a good experience. Now, just a word this evening, subject to what may occur afterwards. You are familiar with this report of the Civil Service Commissioners?—A. I had an opportunity of glancing over the report.

Q. Have you any knowledge of conduct on the part of officials of the department which would lead to a conclusion of lack of conscience on their part, misconduct on their part?—A. No.

Q. Eh?—A. No.

Q. Has anything of the kind ever come to your notice or your knowledge on the part of anyone?—A. There have been irregularities.

Q. Speak up, please. What have they been?—A. In the matter of certificates.

Q. In the matter of certificates?—A. Yes.

Q. By whom?—A. Well, I have been put under the position to say that if I would not continue to certify to accounts that I might send in my resignation.

Q. You have indeed?—A. Yes.

Q. Who put you in that position?—A. Mr. J. F. Fraser.

Q. Mr. J. F. Fraser?—A. He brought that information, he said, from the deputy minister.

Q. Why did you not tell me this before, so that I could have examined you before examining him?—A. I didn't consider it my place to bring up anything until I was told.

Q. It is your duty to. I tried to get all the information possible, my lord. Well, then, you will have to give particulars. When did this occur with Mr. J. F. Fraser?—A. About two years ago.

Q. About two years ago, and where?—A. At Prescott.

Q. And what was it? Just tell what occurred, please?—A. Well, I had to certify to a number of accounts as fair and just.

Q. Yes?—A. And the Auditor General had called Mr. Fraser's and my attention to the fact that it was not proper that the responsibility should be put on me to do so, that I should certify to the accounts of goods received and prices arranged by the department, and I procured a stamp to that effect, that goods received and prices arranged by the department. This did not satisfy Mr. Fraser; so, as he told me, he brought a message to me that the deputy minister was very indignant and if I continued to antagonize the department I could send in my resignation.

Q. He brought you a statement that the deputy minister was very indignant? —A. And sent that message to me by him.

Q. What was the message, again?—A. Tha he was very indignant with my continuing to put on a stamp, and that if I continued to antagonize—I think tha was the word—the department I could send in my resignation.

Q. What was the stamp?—A. The stamp was to this effect: ' Goods received—no, certified correct goods received or checked by the storekeeper;' But the stamp was ' Certified correct, prices arranged by the department.'

Q. Prices arranged by the department. That is you substituted that instead of the statement 'prices reasonable and just?'—A. Fair and just.

Q. 'Fair and just,' I see. That you objected to?—A. Yes, I did.

Q. And you substituted the other?—A. Yes, on the suggestion of the Auditor General.

Q. Yes. And how long did you use that stamp that way?—A. Well, for some time after that in Prescott, for quite a time after that. Of course, on receiving that information I challenged him to force, I defied him.

Q. You defied who?—A. I defied him and the deputy.

Q. Did you have a personal interview with the deputy?—A. No, I did not.

Q. Did you have any direct communication with the deputy.?—A. No.

Q. Either by letter or verbally?—A. No.

Q. Then how did you defy the deputy?—A. Through Mr. Fraser.

Q. I see. That was your statement. You defied him through Mr. Fraser. Then what else took place about that?—A. Well, I quietly attended to my business. I wanted them to show their hands to see what they meant to do, whether they wanted me to resign or not.

Q. Well then, what else?—A. Well, I felt I have been suffering persecution ever since.

Q. Eh?—A. I felt I have been suffering persecution ever since.

Q. Persecution at whose hands?—A. Both the deputy's hands and Mr. J. F. Fraser's hands.

Q. In what respects at the hands of Mr. J. F. Fraser?—A. Well, we didn't get along together. I didn't approve of the policy of the work that was being done, and I found that, practically speaking, he seemed to have little use for me.

Q. Little use for you?—A. Yes.

Q. And what at the hands of the deputy minister?—A. Well, the deputy minister ignored me altogether.

Q. Eh?—A. He seemed to ignore me altogether.

Q. Have you had personal interviews with him?—A. Well, I had. I told him about certain extravagance, I complained to him.

Q. Extravagance by whom?—A. Well, in the expenses of Prescott.

Q. Yes?—A. And I knew it was no use saying any more about it.

Q. What was the answer to you ?—A. Oh, he didn't seem to say much about it. I can't just remember what he said, but I did my part, I let him know what I thought about it.

Q. Then in what way did he give you to understand he had little use for you, using your own expression ?—A. Things that come up lately wherein I used to act for Mr. Fraser during his absence, and lately I have been superseded by a much younger man.

Q. Who?—A. By Mr. Macphail.

Q. What position has he ?—A. He is acting temporarily.

Q. For the commissioner of lights?—A. For the commissioner of lights.

Q. And you are still assistant commissioner ?—A. Yes.

Q. And have you been receiving advances and promotion ?—A. No.

Q. In salary or otherwise ?—A. No.

Q. Since when ?—A. Since three years ago.

Q. When did this conversation take place that you have spoken of between you and Mr. Fraser ?—A. About two years ago.

Q. That was in respect to what contracts or disbursements ?—A. Well, it was in respect to certifying the accounts from Merwin, and there were several other accounts.

Q. What other accounts ?—A. Brooks & Co. They are on file and certified and can be seen there.

Q. Chance ?—A. I don't remember much of Chance.

Q. Merwin & Brooks ? Anybody else ?—A. I can't remember.

Q. And in respect to those you thought the prices were not fair and reasonable? —A. Well, in some cases they might have been, but I didn't consider it a fair position to put me in in all matters, because it might certainly occur where the prices were not fair and just.

Q. Did you know in some cases they were excessive, not fair and reasonable ?— A. Yes.

Q. Did you report that ?—A. Well, of course I took the stand that I would not certify any more.

Q. To Mr. Fraser ?—A. Yes.

Q. Did you report that to anyone else ?—A. Well, the accountant, Mr. Owen. I had several conversations with him as to the prices and expenditure at Prescott, and he had an opportunity of bringing the matter up before the department.

Q. Did you report to him that excessive prices were being charged?—A. To Mr. Owen?

Q. Yes?—A. Virtually I did, when I spoke to him.

Q. Virtually, but not in fact. Did he understand?—A. He understood it thoroughly.

Q. So you reported it to Mr. J. F. Fraser and Mr. Owen. To anyone else?—A. Well, I spoke to the deputy about extravagance.

Q. What did you say to him?—A. Well, I couldn't say very much because I felt it was a delicate matter.

Q. Well, what did you say and when?—A. It is about over two years ago.

Q. And what did you speak to him about, what particular matter?—A. Well, it was upon expenses in general I spoke to him about. I spoke to him about the heavy expenses at Prescott depot.

Q. Yes, in a general way?—A. Yes.

Q. What did you say to him?—A. I said that the expenses were very high and that they had been challenged by the accountant, in a measure.

Q. Yes, anything else?—A. No.

Q. Nothing else but that, I see. Then how long did you use that specially prepared stamp?—A. For probably about six months.

Hon. Mr. CASSELS.—What was on that stamp exactly?

By Mr. Watson:

Q. What was on the stamp usually?—A. ' Certified correct, prices arranged by the department.'

Q. Yes. 'Prices arranged by the department' substituted for ' prices fair and reasonable '?—A. ' Fair and just.'

By Hon. Mr. Cassels:

Q. Certified correct, prices arranged——?—A. By the department.

Q. What is the difference between the two?—A. Well, it cleared me of any responsibility as to the prices being fair and just, my lord.

Q. Well, what did you understand to be the meaning of fair and just?—A. My lord, goods were received at Prescott, and it was not fair to me, seeing I had nothing to arrange about the price.

Q. I quite understand that you were quite absolved. In certifying the prices were fair and reasonable you would not know anything about the prices, but what difference does it make when certified ' fair and correct, prices arranged by the department,' would not that be the same thing?—A. Certified correct as to the goods having been received.

Q. I thought you added to that, ' fair and correct, prices arranged by the department '?—A. No, my lord. I said goods in the first instance, goods received, that is checked by the storekeepers, and then my certificate was ' received, certified correct and the prices arranged by the department.'

Q. Your certificate merely went to the reception of the goods?—A. The same as on several of the accounts here.

By Mr. Watson:

Q. But the stamp shows ' prices arranged by the department '?—A. Yes.

Q. You signed that, but you thought that relieved you of any personal responsibility?—A. Yes; and that was the Auditor General's suggestion that the goods should be certified in that manner.

Q. Well, did that take place with anyone else besides yourself?—A. Not that I am aware of.

Q. What was the reason for that, what was said by the Auditor General?—A. The Auditor General called Mr. Fraser, at least Mr. Fraser and I went over to the Auditor General's office with reference to certifying accounts, and there and then the Auditor General in conversation with him suggested this change in the stamp.

Q. That is, for Mr. Fraser as well as for you?—A. No, for me.

Q. For you?—A. Well, I only took it for myself then.

Q. Well, your are assistant commissioner, you were acting in conjunction along with the commissioner sharing responsibility?—A. In some respects.

Q. Making contracts sometimes?—A. No.

Q. Never making contracts?—A. No.

Q. Now then, you used that stamp for about six months?—A. Well, I used it for some time after that.

Q. Well, what after that?—A. Well, I have not been at Prescott. I was in charge of the Prescott depot there, that time, and I have not been in charge of the Prescott depot during the last 9 months.

Q. Did you continue using that stamp as long as you remained there?—A. Yes.

Q. And have you used regularly the stamp, ' prices fair and just '?—A. I might in cases where I knew I had responsibility for the original prices.

By Hon. Mr. Cassels:

Q. Who gave orders to send goods to Prescott?—A. They were through the department here in Ottawa, but we also got goods from outside by calling for quotations.

Q. Was that done in Ottawa?—A. Yes, the quotations were sent in to Ottawa.
Q. Who made the requisitions, where were they made at?—A. At Prescott, that is, for small supplies.
Q. And then sent to Ottawa?—A. Yes.
Q. And then the goods were received at Prescott?—A. Yes.
Q. You would know nothing about the prices, and that is why you declined to certify?—A. Well, the prices were arranged for before the requisition was sent in; we knew about that.
Q. But you did not know whether it was a fair price?—A. These, of course, yes; we knew because we called for quotations from several firms. But, my lord, I am referring more especially to goods bought, for instance, from abroad, from Brooks & Company; lighthouse apparatus, &c.
Q. You are just referring to cases that did not come under your notice in the way of prices?—A. Yes.

By Mr. Watson:

. Then, did you know of any misconduct on the part of Mr. Fraser?—A. No.
. Eh?—A. No.
. Do you know of any advantages or gains he received?—A. No.
Q. Any arrangement between him and the people with whom he was dealing? —A. No.
Q. Had you any reason to suspect any secret relationship or understanding?— A. No, I have no grounds for saying so.
Q. Or any advantages that he might obtain?—A. No.
Q. Eh?—A. No.
Q. Do you know of any benefits that he received for himself at Prescott or elsewhere from the department through the work of men in the department or material in the department?—A. Not material, he may have received some courtesies through the men, but not material.
Q. What do you mean by courtesies through the men?—A. Well, sometimes they would take him up to his cottage—a small matter.
Q. What do you mean?—A. By manning his launch to take him up to his cottage.
Q. Do you mean just carrying him up in his launch?—A. Yes
Q. Anything else but that?—A. No.
Q. Do you know of any benefits or advantages to any one else——?—A. No.
Q. Than Mr. Fraser?—A. No.
Q. In the department or outside the department?—A. No.
Q. By the use of men or material or otherwise belonging to the department?— A. No.
Q. You do not?—A. No.

By Hon. Mr. Cassels:

Q. What is the nature of this excessive cost at Prescott? You say you called the minister's attention to the fact that the expenses at Prescott were too heavy?— A. There were a great many unnecessary outlays.
Q. In what respect, what is the nature of them?—A. Well, as to buildings and——
Mr. GODFREY.—What?—A. Buildings.

By Hon. Mr. Cassels:

Q. Yes?—A. And wharfage.
Q. Yes. Explain what you mean by being too heavy. You say wharfage, what do you mean by that?—A. By the erection of docks and other elaborate work that went on there.
Q. You thought they were spending too much money, spending money needlessly? —A. Yes, my lord.
Q. The money was expended?—A. Yes, it was expended.

Q. It was a question of judgment whether it should be done or not?—A. Yes.

Q. Your judgment was they need not have spent so much?—A. Yes.

By Mr. Godfrey:

Q. You are a Scotchman, Mr. Noble?—A. Yes.

Hon. Mr. CASSELS.—He is what?

Mr. GODFREY.—Scotch.

Hon. Mr. CASSELS.—He is none the worse for that.

Mr. GODFREY.—That is quite true, my lord.

Q. And you have a Scotchman's idea about expenditure?—A. Yes, sir.

Hon. Mr. CASSELS.—None the worse for that, either.

Mr. GODFREY.—That is quite true, my lord.

Q. How old a man are you, Mr. Noble?—A. 64.

Q. And you are a little sensitive about things, are you not?—A. Well, probably I am constituted that way.

Q. And this grievance against Mr. Fraser has been sort of working on your mind during the last two or three years?—A. It is a grievance because I was being held responsible for a great deal of outlay, or responsible in a measure, which I considered extravagant.

Q. I see. Then you seem to hold Mr. Fraser responsible for the fact that Mr. Macphail has been placed at the head of the department in his absence?—A. No, I don't hold Mr. Fraser responsible for that.

Q. You made that as a statement? Whom do you hold responsible for that?—A. Well, if any man is responsible it would be more especially the deputy minister.

Q. Well, I am told it was the minister who appointed Mr. Macphail, this young man, at the head of the branch during Mr. Fraser's absence. Do you know anything to contradict that?—A. No.

Q. Apparently the deputy minister seems to think Mr. Macphail a better man to place there than you. That is a matter of judgment which you do not wish to discuss?—A. No.

Q. Now, you are responsible for some purchases at Prescott, are you not?—A. Yes.

Q. You are in charge there?—A. I was up to nine months ago.

Q. I mean during this period you had this trouble with Mr. Fraser, there were certain expenditures that you were entirely responsible for?—A. Some.

Q. Yes, some. And in that case it was your duty to certify that the prices were just and fair in accordance with the general regulations of the department?—A. Yes, these goods I incurred or arranged for, that I know something about, that I know particularly about.

Q. Yes, in that case it was your duty to use the regular form of certificate, that prices were just and fair?—A. Yes, in that case.

Q. Was it not in those matters Mr. Fraser told you you must use the regular certificate of the department?—A. No, it was the changed stamp.

Q. He tells me he had no quarrel with you in the changed stamp in matters you had no personal knowledge of, but the trouble was in regard to matters under your own personal direction?—A. No.

Q. You say you do not understand it that way?—A. No, by no means.

Q. But you used that changed stamp for everything, did you not?—A. No, not if I had arranged for the purchase of the articles myself and knew the prices were correct. In that case the ordinary stamp, 'fair and just,' went on. If the articles were what I hadn't made arrangements for or had no opportunity of knowing whether they were fair prices, or, properly speaking, correct prices, I used the changed stamp.

Q. Now, did you ever make complaint to the minister in regard to any of these matters?—A. No, I never had any opportunity.

Q. Well, the post is open to you, is it not, Mr. Noble? You could send in a report?—A. I could send in a report. I did not send any, but I wished particularly to speak to the minister and was always blocked.

Q. Answer the question. You could send in a written formal report to the minister complaining of these matters?—A. Yes.

Q. Did you or did you not?—A. No.

Q. Why did you not do it ?—A. I thought it was no use.

Q. You thought the minister would pay no attention to you ?—A. I felt sure there was too much pressure against me.

Q. You are representing yourself as a very honest official. Why did you not go to the minister with this report or send it in in writing and satisfy your conscience ? —A. I felt it would be putting my head against a stone wall.

Q. In any event, you did not do it ?—A. No.

Q. Do you mean to insinuate the minister would pay no attention?—A. I had——

Q. Answer the question. Do you mean to say here to-day that any minister in charge of that department would have paid no attention to any formal report made to him in regard to anything you knew in connection with the department ?—A. Probably he might have paid attention, but I would have no chance against the other two men, my superiors.

Q. Do you insinuate in effect that nobody expects you to do your duty ?—A. I beg your pardon.

Q. Would not the minister have accepted your report ?—A. I cannot say what he would have done.

Q. Would he not have investigated and given you an opportunity to say anything you like ?—A. I cannot say.

Q. Do you mean to insinuate he would not ?—A. I am not insinuating anything.

Q. Now you talk of extravagance. Give us any particular instance ?—A. The whole acetylene system has been most extravagant.

Q. We have heard all about that. You are now referring to the buoy system ?— A. Yes.

Q. You don't pretend to set up your knowledge against experts in regard to that? —A. I set my experience up against any man's in Canada.

Q. Any man in Canada ?—A. Yes, my experience.

Q. Now, you were talking about the department at Prescott, the wharfage and building and so on. We want to get particulars. Give us particulars of this extravagance ?—A. Well, for instance, we had a gasolene launch there that was no use.

Q. Just stick to the two things, buildings and wharfage, those are the two things you mentioned to his lordship.—A. Well, there is a large amount of money spent on dockage and building docks.

Q. Well, I want to know in what respect it is extravagant ?—A. Because unnecessary.

Q. How is it unnecesssary ?—A. There is nothing to warrant it.

Q. You are just making that broad statement without giving us any further particulars. I want to file a statement of full particulars in regard to it if you can give us any. Can you give us any more than what you have done?—A. I am merely saying to the best of my knowledge—and it is practical—that a great deal of money was spent on that which was of no use.

Q. Now, give us any particulars in which money was spent which was of no use? —A. I am stating the fact.

Q. You are simply stating a broad fact and are not able to give a statement with any further particulars. Is that what I am to understand ?—A. Well, I don't know what more particulars you want.

By Hon. Mr. Cassels:

Q. What did they spend it on ?—A. Building.

Q. What kind of building ?—A. Building dockage, docks or piers.

Q. On building for the piers ?—A. Yes. There has been large expenditure on that, and also this last year a large boat-house was built, and I don't know of any boat to put in the house.

Q. A large boat-house built and no boat in it, is that what you say ?—A. Yes. I don't know of any boat to put into it.

Q. Do you know of a boat being put in since ?—A. Well, it appears too much money to be spending for a small matter like that.

Q. How much was spent on the boat-house?—A. It must have cost about $2,000.

Q. How much ?—A. About $2,000.

Q. Was it a pleasure boat ?—A. Well, as I say, there is no boat to put in it, my lord.

Q. Well, go on, and give the particulars, then.

Mr. GODFREY.—Mr. Fraser will explain that. I do not think I will bother Mr. Noble. I will call Mr. Fraser.

J. F. FRASER, recalled.

By Mr. Godfrey :

Q. You have heard this statement, Mr. Fraser, with regard to this certificate and some complaint which Mr. Noble seems to have against you. Explain that to his lordship ?—A. The point, your lordship, is this : The certificate which was in use at Prescott for a long time was the ordinary one which is in use in the department, briefly, that the material has been received and the prices charged are fair and just. Mr. Noble for sometime preceding, as he says the past nine months, was in immediate charge of that place. The suggestion—I think he is correct in saying it came from the Auditor General—was that in case of material delivered there which did not originate from the depot that he should use the certificate, 'Certified correct, prices arranged by the department at Ottawa.' Now, that is an unsatisfactory certificate in many respects, and it involves when the accounts come in a further certification of same by some one at headquarters, an official who knows something of the contract or arrangement, and in consultation with the deputy minister it was agreed that Mr. Noble should revert to the old certificate.

By Hon. Mr. Cassels:

Q. How could he revert to the old certificate ?—A. Because there was not anything came in that he did not have knowledge whether the price was a reasonable price or not.

Q. Well, his certificate would simply certify the prices had been arranged in Ottawa by the department and the goods had been received. Why should he pledge himself that the prices were reasonable ?—A. Because it involved direct looking into the matter by him, which was moreover a protection to the department.

Q. Do you mean when goods came in he had the right to check the prices bargained for by the officials at Ottawa?—A. Yes.

By Mr. Watson:

Q. As part of his duty ?—A. Certainly.

By Hon. Mr. Cassels :

Q. That is, if goods came in the prices of which had been contracted for in Ottawa, it was his business, if those prices were too high, to so certify ?—A. Certainly. It was an extra check for the department on that matter. That is the reason the deputy minister and myself agreed—at least, I suggested and the deputy minister agreed, which is more correct—that the old style should be used.

Q. Well, did you tell him it was his duty to check the prices to see if he could certify as to their correctness ?—A. If he could not certify he would certainly make a report to the department. I have no particular recollection of that one thing, but, as I say, it was an extra protection to the department to change the stamp back.

Q. That is the explanation?—A. Certainly; and I would say this, if the matter had to be done over again I would take exactly the same grounds.

Q. Well, I think you would take a wrong stand.—A. Perhaps.

By Mr. Godfrey :

Q. You insisted upon his satisfying himself absolutely ?—A. Yes; and there was not anything came in there he did not have knowledge of.

By Hon. Mr. Cassels :

Q. Were the prices in Ottawa fixed after tenders or after any rates at Prescott, did they fix the prices based upon the prices they got at Prescott ?—A. In some cases it was done.

Q. But in these particular cases the prices were arranged in Ottawa ?—A. Well, I don't know what specific instances he refers to.

Q. In some instances ?—A. In some instances they were.

Q. And the contracts were made in Ottawa ?—A. The contracts were made in Ottawa.

Q. And the prices would be fixed by the proper officer in Ottawa ?—A. The prices would be fixed by the proper officer in Ottawa.

Mr. WATSON:—How could he change them afterwards ?

By Mr. Godfrey :

Q. Then he need not certify them if not just and fair in his opinion ?—A. The objection was to the stamp itself. He could have left out the stamp altogether and sent the accounts in.

Q. That is to say, in any case that he could not honestly certify to you did not require him or inform him he must certify ?—A. Never. Mr. Noble never certified an account.

By Mr. Watson:

Q. What about the threat that he would be dismissed if he did not ?—A. That he could send in his resignation?

Q. That is what he said you said to him?—A. I have no recollection of saying that to him.

Q. Will you contradict what he said you said?—A. To the best of my recollection and belief, yes, I will.

By Mr. Godfrey:

Q. But what you wanted him to do was to assume the responsibility of finding out whether the prices were just?—A. Yes.

Hon. Mr. CASSELS.—It seems to me that is an absurdity.

Mr. GODFREY.—Why so, my lord?

Hon. Mr. CASSELS.—For this reason: You have got your department in Ottawa, the superior officers are in Ottawa, the contracting power is in Ottawa, they know exactly what class of goods they are contracting for, they make contracts through their authorized agents. This contract is for delivery at Prescott, and he certifies the goods are there according to the invoice.

Mr. GODFREY.—But they were at the request first of Mr. Noble; that was done by him from Prescott.

Hon. Mr. CASSELS.—No, on request from Ottawa, and Ottawa makes the contracts, fixes the prices, the superior officers do all that.

Mr. GODFREY.—Of course, it is a question as to who had the best ability to certify as to those prices.

Hon. Mr. CASSELS.—If the Ottawa authorities wanted Mr. Noble's check on the value of the fixed prices they would have written him.

WITNESS.—The objection was, my lord, to having that form of certificate on the accounts at all. If Mr. Noble had any objection to putting the other certificates on the is absolutely nothing to prevent him under the instructions he was working under before to send in the accounts to Ottawa without a certificate.

Hon. Mr. CASSELS.—That certificate practically did certify to the Ottawa authorities that the goods were received, and the Ottawa authorities took the responsibility of fixing the prices.

Mr. GODFREY.—You considered Mr. Noble should have the responsibility as to the prices?

By Hon. Mr. Cassels:

Q. You thought there was nothing in it, that he was simply disobeying orders?—A. A matter of discipline.

Q. That is practically what it amounts to?—A. And Mr. Noble has been a fit subject for discipline several times.

Q. That is your opinion. But that is all it comes to.

By Mr. Godfrey:

Q. Now, we have heard something about a boathouse, we have had that as one detail of extravagance. What do you say that boathouse was to be used for?—A. For the purpose of housing certain gasolene launches that belonged to Prescott—recently, I believe, one has been transferred to Montreal—and also for the purpose of housing certain small boats of the hydrographic survey now working on the Upper St. Lawrence and berthed at Prescott. The expenditure I think proper and necessary. There is not any portion of the work for the water front which is not absolutely required to make the depot as it should be.

Q. And you say there is nothing in this charge?—A. Absolutely nothing at all.

By Hon. Mr. Cassels:

Q. It was settled on by a superior officer?—A. Settled on and concurred in by a previous minister, and Mr. Brodeur never took exception to it.

By Mr. Godfrey:

Q. I suppose that is not a matter in which you had any opportunity of dealing with it?—A. Certainly. The plans for the water front were laid out by me and approved by my superiors. It is not a matter a subordinate of mine can properly question.

Mr. WATSON.—My lord, there is a communication that I received from Mr. Matthew F. Walsh, and I observe that it follows upon a similar communication addressed to your lordship. Mr. Walsh is referred to in the report in an indirect way by initials, and in conjunction with that a reference is made to a shaky hand.

Hon. Mr. CASSELS.—Shaking hand?

Mr. WATSON.—Shaky handwriting, trembling handwriting. Wr. Walsh communicated with Mr. Courtney, and incloses a letter from Mr. Courtney in which he expresses regret to Mr. Walsh that his colleagues should have used such an expression. I think that is all there is to it.

Hon. Mr. CASSELS.—Oh, yes. What page is that on?

Mr. WATSON.—131, my lord. There is a reference there in a paragraph about two-thirds of the way down. 'I have obtained a nautical almanac which I will send the *Anticosti* first opportunity. Will you please furnish the other supplies asked for.' (Across the lower left corner of this letter was written in a very shaky hand: 'Will the deputy minister please cause a list of stationery to be made out.—M. F. W.')

Hon. Mr. CASSELS.—I think Mr. Courtney's apology will set you right with the public. I do not think you need worry about that.

Mr. WATSON.—Then, my lord, I call attention again to the fact that in regard to the officials in charge and those who have any responsibility in the department, and upon whom any onus might lie of discharging themselves from the charges made, they have all been called before the court with one exception, I think Mr. Cowie, who is out of town. Your lordship has heard what they have said, and subject to a few of them being recalled after other witnesses have been examined, that portion of the evidence is exhausted, so it may not be necessary to recall any of them, with four or five exceptions, and there will be no interference therefore, I think, with the further organization or operation of the department, my lord. The other witnesses, some of whom are in Montreal and some in Quebec and a few others here in Ottawa, will necessarily, I find, have to be examined at a subsequent sitting of your lordship's commission, and it is not practicable to continue the present sittings.

I undersand it was arranged from the commencement there should be no sittings in July or August during part of the legal vacation, that not being convenient either to your lordship or to counsel. We did not expect that your lordship would be at liberty during this month after the circuit which you had arranged for in your own Court of Exchequer. Having that in mind I made arrangements some weeks ago after the last sitting by which I am obliged to leave. I will be sailing on the 23rd of this month, that is, next Tuesday, and therefore I am not able to attend further during this month. I will be pleased to attend if your lordship will fix a sitting after the vacation as early as possible, perhaps the 2nd of September, when the matter might be continued and brought to a close.

Hon. Mr. CASSELS.—The difficulty about it is this, I quite realize it was extremely hard on counsel to have met here last Monday, because when I left for the east I fully expected I would be away very much longer, and so intimated to you and Mr. Perron, and I am glad you found it possible to get here, as we have done considerable work of importance during the last few days.

Now, for myself I may say when I accepted the commission I accepted it on the terms which are very well known. On the 15th of April I wrote a letter to the Minister of Marine and Fisheries which I propose to read :

'Referring to the few words that passed between us yesterday in reference to the commission relating to the Marine and Fisheries Department, I am as anxious to proceed as the government are.

'I hope to leave for Toronto and spend Easter with my family, and will while there consider carefully the scope of the commission and the duties to be performed, and if proper arrangements are made for the carrying on of the business of the court, I will immediately on my return take up the work.

'I apprehend the desire is to have the meetings proceeded with promptly and not prolonged for an indefinite period.

'In my letter to Sir Wilfrid Laurier of the 2nd of April I pointed out that the work of the court was first to be considered. Sir Wilfrid in reply stated, "That if necessary to make provision for the dispatch of business in the Court of Exchequer, this is a matter as to which we will deem ourselves bound to give immediate effect on such lines as you suggest." I wrote Sir Wilfrid on the 6th making certain suggestions.

'"Allow me to call your attention to my court engagements." (And I set out in detail the list of engagements.)

'Now, it is obvious that if the investigation is to be proceeded with promptly some arrangement must be made for the conduct of the business of the court.

'You must pardon me for troubling you, but I think it well to let you know my willingness to proceed promptly, and my reasons why I cannot, unless provision for the conduct of the business of the court is made on the lines suggested.'

Now, I got this answer on the 18th :

'I was very glad to receive your letter of the 15th inst., intimating your desire to expedite the inquiry into the affairs of the Department of Marine and Fisheries.

'You will, I know, appreciate the anxiety of those whose actions and motives appear to have been questioned by the Civil Service Commissioners to have the very earliest opportunity of making their defence.

'As you point out, there is the business of the Exchequer Court, for which you have already arranged dates, to be considered. In view of this I have ventured to mention the matter to the Minister of Justice, who said he would discuss it with you. I am therefore in hopes that the result will be that it may be convenient for you to begin the inquiry on your return to Ottawa after the Easter holidays.'

From that day to this I have had no intimation from the Department of Justice, and I had to proceed east to St. John and Halifax and up to Sydney. I got back sooner than I anticipated and immediately took up the work. Had I been relieved I would have taken it up about the 20th of April and by this time the whole thing would have been finished.

Now comes the next step. It is obvious that nothing is to be gained by sitting here two or three days; that must be done in Montreal and Quebec. The vacation comes along on the 1st of July. Personally I have a large amount of arrears of work which I will have to make up for during vacation. I have got to try and make myself more familiar with the work of the Exchequer Court, and I shall endeavour to read up the judgments of other judges, and of course a good deal of my vacation will be fully occupied. I say frankly I do not intend to give up my vacation. I do not think any man can perform the duties of the Exchequer Court unless he gets rest given by vacation. After vacation I may say that circuits are fixed in Winnipeg and right up to Vancouver. The first circuit will necessitate my leaving on the 12th of September.

Meanwhile, there are some eight or ten appeals, involving several millions of dollars, which will have to be heard and disposed of somewhere between the 1st of September and the 12th, unless I am relieved, as you intimated to me this morning that I probably would be. If so, then I can take up this matter on the 2nd of September and go right through with it; otherwise you see how I am placed.

Mr. WATSON.—Yes, my lord. I understand the 2nd of September is the earliest possible date in any event.

Hon. Mr. CASSELS.—It would be breaking in on the traditions of the bar to take it up before September; you could not expect it.

Mr. GODFREY.—There is something I wish to mention, my lord.

Hon. Mr. CASSELS.—What day is the 2nd of September?

Mr. WATSON.—Either Tuesday or Wednesday.

Hon. Mr. CASSELS.—When can you get back from England?

Mr. WATSON.—A little after the middle of August.

Hon. Mr. CASSELS.—Pending the meeting on the 2nd of September, I do not think there will be much loss of time. I think nothing will be lost and a great deal gained, because the way it occurs to me is this: As I pointed out, the only way of getting the facts in this case is to get the contracts, ascertain the contract prices, ascertain the ruling market rates, then if you find a difference between the contract prices paid by the government and the ruling market rates, whoever entered into that contract has to come forward and explain. Well, we had an instance the other day about this horn business which shows the absolute necessity of going into that class of knowledge if there is to be any result at all from this commission.

It seems to me it is almost essential that you and Mr. Perron should be furnished with an independent skilled accountant who will be able to investigate into these matters, and in that way try to get at the truth of the matter. Take, for instance, the Northey company; that has to be investigated. There is an enormous difference between what ought to have been paid and was paid. These books ought to be investigated. Take this Willson company. The enormous purchase of buoys may be perfectly right, it may be perfectly correct, but it is essential that somebody who is skilled in tracking through books should go through those books in order to see whether the cost as about to be given by Mr. Willson is correct or not. The reasonableness of the purchases must depend altogether on these facts, and so it will be with other purchases.

I leave that to your own discretion. I think the labour is too great for counsel to probe into these matters in the way you have been probing into them, and I think if there is to be a thorough investigation some course such as I suggest should be adopted.

Mr. WATSON.—Yes, my lord.

Mr. GODFREY.—There is a matter, my lord, I wish to refer to. At the time, immediately after the report of the Civil Service Commissioners, my client, Mr. Fraser, was suspended pending this investigation. That was on the 3rd of April, and the suspension was not of any very great importance, as everybody thought, as your lordship thought, you would be able to get on with this investigation without any very great delay. But here we are over the middle of June and, as your lordship has just announced, we are to adjourn to the 2nd of September. Now, I submit that up to the present there is nothing which marks Mr. Fraser's conduct as reprehensible in any way, and I think your lordship might very fairly put him in the same position as the other officials who are continued.

Hon. Mr. CASSELS.—The trouble about it is, I did not suspend him.

Mr. GODFREY.—I know. At the same time I think your lordship ought to intimate to the Minister of Marine that there is nothing to date against Mr. Fraser.

Hon. Mr. CASSELS.—We do not know to date what the reasons for his suspension were.

Mr. GODFREY.—But so far as this commission is concerned?

Hon. Mr. CASSELS.—My functions are not to reinstate or anything else. A man might be suspended on the grounds of this last witness, Mr. Noble.

Mr. GODFREY.—I do not take that suggestion seriously, my lord, for a moment.

Hon. Mr. CASSELS.—I do not know any of the grounds of Mr. Fraser's suspension.

Mr. WATSON.—He might be suspended for disobedience.

Mr. GODFREY.—So far as this commission is concerned, I think your lordship should state there is nothing to warrant his suspension.

Hon. Mr. CASSELS.—I will authorize you to say this—the minister will read the evidence : Up to the present time I have not made up my mind at all about Mr. Fraser.

Mr. GODFREY.—I would argue very strongly there is nothing against him. Your lordship can see the unfortunate position he is in. He is losing salary, he is put to considerable expense, and he is not to blame, and in the natural course this inquiry should have been all over six weeks ago.

Hon. Mr. CASSELS.—There may be all kinds of reasons other than what I have given. I have done my best to go on with the commission. I felt that these gentlemen were under a cloud of suspicion and I considered that the commission should be proceeded with as expeditiously as possible. I got an offer of assistance, I read you the letter, but nothing further has been done.

Mr. GODFREY.—I am not suggesting with regard to the commission ; I am stating about the hardship.

Hon. Mr. CASSELS.—Do you know Mr. Brodeur ?

Mr. GODFREY.—Yes.

Hon. Mr. CASSELS.—Why not go and see him ?

Mr. GODFREY.—Yes, my lord, I certainly will, but I should like to be able to tell him from your lordship that my client——

Hon. Mr. CASSELS.—I can only tell you that up to the present time nothing has been found against him, but I have not made up my mind one way or the other.

Mr. GODFREY.—I will state that.

Hon. Mr. CASSELS.—State it in my own language.

Mr. GODFREY.—I will ; and I will make some observations of my own at the same time.

Hon. Mr. CASSELS.—At Montreal on the 2nd of September at 11 o'clock in the morning.

Mr. WATSON.—Yes, my lord.

(Adjourned accordingly.)

Lightning Source UK Ltd.
Milton Keynes UK
UKHW011609160119
335572UK00012B/1266/P